Scientology in Popular Culture

Scientology in Popular Culture

Influences and Struggles for Legitimacy

Stephen A. Kent and Susan Raine, Editors

 PRAEGER™

An Imprint of ABC-CLIO, LLC

Santa Barbara, California • Denver, Colorado

Library of Congress Cataloging in Publication Control Number: 2017007967

ISBN: 978-1-4408-3249-9
EISBN: 978-1-4408-3250-5

21 20 19 18 17   1 2 3 4 5

This book is also available as an eBook.

Praeger
An Imprint of ABC-CLIO, LLC

ABC-CLIO, LLC
130 Cremona Drive, P.O. Box 1911
Santa Barbara, California 93116-1911
www.abc-clio.com

This book is printed on acid-free paper ∞

Manufactured in the United States of America

Contents

Introduction

Susan Raine

If one were to pose the question, *What is Scientology's relationship with popular culture?*, most likely many individuals would respond with an array of comments about Hollywood celebrities such as Tom Cruise, Kirstie Alley, Leah Remini, and John Travolta; or perhaps they might remark on Scientology founder L. Ron Hubbard's career as a science fiction writer. It is not surprising that this question might elicit such limited, albeit relevant, responses on the nature of the relationship between the two entities. Indeed, many popular culture products including movies, television shows, magazines, and news media tend to focus on Scientology celebrities and the more salacious connections between Hubbard's science fiction works and Scientology doctrine.

Over the last two-and-a-half years since this volume was first conceived, celebrity Scientologists have indeed figured largely in some prominent popular culture forms. Since their split in 2012, and up to the present day, Tom Cruise and Katie Holmes have been the subject of frequent media attention, especially in the tabloid and online press.[1] The year 2013 saw ongoing media coverage of assault accusations against John Travolta.[2] Moreover, journalists have subjected Travolta to persistent inquiries into the status of his marriage to fellow Scientologist, Kelly Preston, as well as speculations about his sexual orientation.[3] Early 2015 saw the release of HBO's documentary, *Going Clear: Scientology and the Prison of Belief*. Directed by Alex Gibney and based on Lawrence Wright's 2013 book, *Going Clear: Scientology, Hollywood, and the Prison of Belief*, the documentary details the history of Scientology and examines its relationship with a number of Hollywood elites. The critical position that the work takes initiated a prominent response from the group. Just prior to the film's release, Scientology took steps to undermine Gibney and the documentary's legitimacy with a full-page advertisement in the *New York*

Times, as well as through comments on social media and in other venues.[4] Scientology's prerelease reaction, however, served only to stimulate further popular interest in the documentary. Then, in late 2015, Leah Remini's memoir of her life in Scientology, *Troublemaker*, appeared in bookstores. The popular actor best known for her role in the comedy *King of Queens* discusses her experiences as a Scientologist, from her early days as a Hollywood unknown, to her high-profile status as a well-known actress, to her very public fall from grace within the movement.

Because Scientology's relationship with celebrity receives a fair amount of popular coverage, much of the general public in North America and elsewhere is aware of it, even if they don't care to familiarize themselves further. When popular media coverage of Scientology focuses on Hollywood and other areas of celebrity membership, the reporting is sometimes negative, but as Cusack (2009) points out, often through this pairing, "Scientology is rendered familiar, and even (despite some bad press) potentially desirable to many. . . ."[5] Consequently, popular journalism has the ability to "normalize otherwise unusual or fringe phenomena."[6] Some reporting on celebrity and Scientology is quizzical in nature, and some is relatively neutral. In other areas of coverage, however, extremely negative narratives dominate, and these deleterious outcomes often have been the consequence of Scientology's own actions and reactions.[7] Certainly, access to celebrity Scientologists, whether the news frames the narratives negatively or positively, at the very least appears to hold a level of popular fascination that has not yet waned.

The other relationship between popular culture and Scientology with which many people may be familiar is Hubbard's career as a science fiction writer. In this case, many individuals may have at least some knowledge of his early career as a "pulp" science fiction writer although they may be less acquainted with his wide array of other types of novels and stories, including westerns, detective dramas, and naval and aerial adventures. Hubbard's more recent science fiction works from the 1980s, *Battlefield Earth* and the *Mission Earth* series, likely are known to many people too—even if they have not read any of them. And certainly, John Travolta's ill-fated movie adaptation of *Battlefield Earth*[8] as well as *South Park*'s now infamous "Trapped in the Closet"[9] episode reignited the public's awareness of the science fiction connection. A number of popular culture products have rather crudely taken elements of Hubbard's science fiction inspired narratives and oversimplified the connections between them and Scientology's beliefs and practices. Therefore, a number of media venues, including television shows, movies, websites, and blogs, frame the science fiction influence to the consuming public in a manner that strips the relationship of its deeper context. Inevitably, one-dimensional stereotypes and perceptions emerge, devoid of more nuanced discussion.

Celebrity and science fiction are indeed a part of the Scientology–popular culture nexus, but they are not the only connections that exist. One of the goals of this volume is to broaden the parameters of the discussion of the relationship between popular culture and Scientology by addressing the complex and dialectical nature of the connection between the two. This process not only requires that we examine more deeply those explicit linkages between Scientology and popular culture with which most people are familiar, but also it requires that we consider a much broader array of popular culture settings. In order to achieve this end, we have invited our contributors to take a variety of unique and creative approaches to thinking through different forms of popular culture and the variety of outcomes resulting from their associations with and connections to Scientology. We wanted to produce a collection of essays that would address the multiple sites of popular culture that have influenced—and in return have been influenced by—Scientology. Sometimes these influences are quite explicit, but on other occasions they are not as obvious and require deeper analyses to illuminate the interrelationships. Moreover, important also is the recognition that some facets of Dianetics and Scientology are *themselves* popular culture products. For example, Hubbard's *Dianetics: The Modern Science of Mental Health* became a popular book in the emergent body of self-help literature when it was first published in 1950. Other lesser known examples exist: the Apollo Stars were Hubbard's hand-picked "house" band, comprising members of the movement's elite Sea Organization (Sea Org). While traveling in the Mediterranean, the group got some airplay on Portuguese radio and released the album *The Power of Source* (1974) for popular consumption.

The *geographical* focus of our volume is the United States although some chapters do mention Scientology's activities in the United Kingdom, Canada, and, as mentioned above, the Mediterranean, as well as other locales. This volume, then, seeks to address some of the absences evident in current understandings and research on the nature of the relationship between American popular culture, Hubbard, Dianetics, and Scientology. The remainder of this introductory chapter addresses several areas. First, it speaks to the issue of defining "popular culture" and reviews some of the types of popular culture that the contributors include in their work. Second, it provides a brief overview of Scientology and some of its struggles with establishing various forms of social, cultural, and political legitimacy. The popular media has reported on many of these confrontations and consequently it has even become an integral part of the battles themselves. Third, it takes a tentative look at what the future holds for Scientology and what the relationship between Scientology and popular culture might look like. Finally, this introduction provides a summary outline of each of the chapters in this book.

POPULAR CULTURE

As with other researchers tackling the relationship between popular culture and religion,[10] the ambiguous nature of "popular culture" confronts our work. As other scholars have noted, no single definition completely encapsulates all that popular culture is and does, especially because, "Popular culture, by its very nature, changes rapidly, especially in its particular examples."[11] Moreover, academics whose entire focus is popular culture often disagree as to what precisely constitutes "popular culture" versus "high culture" and "folk culture."[12] Some scholars insist, for example, that by definition, popular culture must reach a large audience, whereas other scholars do not agree that this is a necessary criterion.[13] Certainly, a common approach is to include some type of quantitative dimension when figuring out if something is a part of popular culture or not.

Another way of delineating popular culture is simply to clearly define "high culture" so that what remains is automatically a part of popular culture (and folk culture). Scholars often define high culture as an elite form of written culture that is deliberately designed for a more limited audience. Folk culture has a more limited audience too, but it is usually oral in nature, reaching local audiences only. Finally, popular culture frequently is understood as any form of culture that reaches the masses and is disseminated in numerous formats.[14] Of course, value judgments are embedded in this divisive approach. Moreover, cultural products may occupy different categories depending on the historical and cultural context,[15] and in postmodern societies, the very distinction between high and popular culture is questioned.[16]

I do not intend to contribute further to these and other scholarly debates on what precisely constitutes popular culture, but I do recognize the need to identify what popular culture means to the present volume. Many definitions and extended discussions of popular culture link the concepts of entertainment, media, technological developments, and diverse mass audiences across large geographical spaces. In these cases, "popular" is specifically determined by "patterns of consumption" or by the frequency with which the product is not just consumed but also *produced*.[17]

This volume incorporates popular culture forms that do indeed conform to these expectations, but it is worth noting that in some cases, we include discussions that speak to Hubbard's or Scientology's *attempts* to gain entry into popular culture domains. For example, the chapters on visual art and music illustrate Hubbard's efforts at wide dissemination and influence using each form, but his actual success and influence are limited. Moreover, as the volume as a whole indicates, the references to popular culture emerge in a variety of different ways. Within the chapters of this volume the authors incorporate a wide array of components and subcomponents of popular culture, including the following: fiction novels (pulp fiction, science fiction, adventure fiction, and fantasy fiction), nonfiction (biographies, memoirs, and journalistic accounts), television (movies, documentaries, newscasts, serial dramas, and comedies), movies (blockbusters and niche audience), documentaries (television and cinematic release), newspapers (local and national), and the Internet (websites, blogs, and newsgroups), as well as magazines (paper format and online), art (illustrations and paintings on book covers and in advertising), music (live and recorded), celebrity (culture of, endorsements, and musical contributions), and self-help (literature and culture of). The scope of our volume then, incorporates forms of popular culture that no longer dominate in the marketplace (e.g., pulp fiction) alongside those that do (e.g., websites) and that are based on both "traditional" and more recent technological advances (e.g., broadsheet newspapers and blogs).

SCIENTOLOGY: AN ABBREVIATED OVERVIEW

The "Church of Scientology" and even just "Scientology" are contested and multilayered conceptual categories. For those unfamiliar with the web of propositions as to what specifically Scientology *is*, we include a brief synopsis here. To begin, however, I provide a condensed overview of Scientology.[18] The many influences and struggles for legitimacy that Hubbard and Scientology faced (and continue to encounter) are integral to both discussions.

A prolific author of pulp fiction novels and stories, Hubbard published *Dianetics: The Modern Science of Mental Health* in 1950. The book became a best seller in the United States and inspired an array of "therapeutic" organizations that sought to apply the principles and techniques that Hubbard had devised, the principal one being the practice of auditing—Scientology's form of counseling. The book offered readers a "new science," one that purported to open up new avenues of knowledge into the human mind. Inspired by a number of influences, including psychoanalysis, occultism, philosophy, and indigenous spirituality,[19] Hubbard claimed that his "science" was as valid as any other, and he made many attempts to illustrate its legitimacy as such.[20]

With *Dianetics*, Hubbard claimed that the human mind is composed of two main parts—the "reactive mind," which inhibits full human potential because of the "engrams" or painful memory traces it contains, and the "analytical mind," which is entirely rational and precise in its workings. According to Hubbard, only through the process of Dianetic auditing could one address these ability-inhibiting engrams in order to reach one's full potential—the state of "Clear." Despite his optimism that *Dianetics* would revolutionize human understanding of the mind, Hubbard's thesis was largely derided by many—including the American medical profession.[21] Therefore, although he enjoyed popular support for his ideas in the emergent self-help milieu, his new proposals did not garner any lasting official or institutional recognition.

Hubbard's deliberate "creation" of Scientology as a religion is broadly acknowledged.[22] He presented his new philosophy in 1951 and distinguished it from Dianetics by focusing not only on the human mind but also on the human spirit—or, in Scientology parlance, the "thetan." *Dianetics* remained foundational to Scientology, and Hubbard proposed that together they would provide therapeutic and spiritual solutions. Hubbard defined Scientology as "an applied religious philosophy and technology resolving problems of the spirit, life and thought" that, semantically, derives from "the Latin, *scio* (knowing) and the Greek *logos* (study)." Thus, he proposed that Scientology is "the study of wisdom."[23] Elsewhere, he described Scientology as a "religious philosophy," the goal of which is to help an individual achieve "Spiritual Freedom" as an "Immortal Being."[24]

Dianetic auditing is Scientology's form of counseling and entails one individual, the trained "auditor," who uses an E-meter (or lie detector) to access the mental processes of the reactive mind of the person being audited—the "preclear"—and thus help eradicate their engrams. Hubbard developed multiple levels of training and auditing in Scientology, so that even after achieving the state of "Clear," Scientologists are then required to take higher levels of therapy and training to address their spiritual nature and well-being. This focus entails dealing with the problem of "body thetans," immortal entities that, according to Hubbard, constantly reincarnate and occupy humans. The end goal of Scientology auditing and training at the upper levels is to free Scientologists of their body thetans so that they can achieve great personal empowerment as Operating Thetans or "OTs" (and many levels of OT training exist).[25] Somewhat paradoxically then, although most body thetans jeopardize human well-being because their eternal galactic experiences suppress human potential, Scientologists believe that one suitable thetan will allow for the person to transform into an extraordinarily capable individual.

Both Hubbard and Scientology have been plagued by challenges to their legitimacy. For example, although Hubbard was a successful pulp fiction writer from the early 1930s through to 1950, his pulp novels and stories of that era were never part of high-culture literature, and over time, even in the pulp milieu his popularity began to wane. Contemporary critics hold his pulp works in low regard—but Scientology continues to promote Hubbard as one of the world's best fiction authors.[26] Likewise, the group continues to endorse Hubbard as the world's foremost philosopher, explorer, adventurer, naval officer, engineer, scientist, educator, and artist (among other things).[27] From Scientology's perspective, there are no legitimate challenges to these and other claims that it has made about Hubbard. Extensive research, however, indicates flaws in official narratives about Hubbard and Scientology, revealing Hubbard's inflated versions of his achievements and even outright lies.[28] Consequently, while he continues to occupy the highest status within Scientology, outside of the movement, his authority in these areas, including as a religious leader, is very much contested.

Many scholars, journalists, social institutions, and members of the general public all have pondered the legitimacy of Scientology's status as a religion. In the United States and elsewhere, alternative religions often are marginalized and their legitimacy contested, so it is not surprising that this is the case for Scientology. Perhaps where Scientology differs from other new or alternative religious movements is in its frequent, targeted, and often aggressive attempts to achieve legitimacy in various parts of the globe. The various strategies that the movement has employed to this end have been widely reported in various popular forums, thus contributing to a general suspicion of Scientology and its motivations.

In the United States, following a protracted battle with the Internal Revenue Service (IRS), the IRS reinstated Scientology's tax-exempt status in 1993,[29] thus recognizing it as a not-for-profit entity and, ostensibly, acknowledging it as a religion. This status was a consequence of a protracted series of battles for religious recognition. Early in the 1970s several U.S. government organizations had started to accrue information on various Scientology activities. By way of response, and as a means to manage its image, Scientology instituted *Operation Snow White*,[30] a criminal enterprise that saw the movement place Scientologists within the IRS and several other government institutions. One Scientologist, Gerald Wolfe, worked in a clerical job for the IRS in Washington, where he illegally photocopied and subsequently stole over 30,000 pages of government documentation on Scientology.[31]

When the FBI searched Scientology offices, the agency found extensive evidence of other illegal activities. By 1980, 11 leading members of Scientology—including Hubbard's wife, Mary Sue Hubbard—were convicted for organizing a conspiracy to steal government documents from the United States Attorney's office, the IRS, and the Justice Department and for electronically bugging a government meeting.[32] Following these events, Scientology conducted an aggressive, but this time legal, campaign against the IRS, and by 1993 the IRS acquiesced.[33] In this case, although Scientology had ensured a level of legal legitimacy, many entities and individuals outside of the movement questioned it still.

In other countries, Scientology has been accorded tax exemption or charitable status as a nonprofit concern—for example, in New Zealand, the United Kingdom, and South Africa. Some other nation states including Portugal and Australia have simply recognized Scientology as a religion or religious community. In other regions, Scientology has been denied tax exemption or has been denied specific acceptance as a legitimate religious entity—for example, in Ireland and Germany. France has granted Scientology tax-exempt status but identifies it also as a *secte*. As such, the French government considers Scientology to potentially be dangerous.[34]

The ongoing problems that Scientology has with how others perceive it, in conjunction with its own antagonistic behaviors, has meant that the much-sought-after "religion" label has remained out of its reach both at an official level in many locations and within the popular imagination. Moreover, even in countries where the movement has been accorded tax-exempt or religious status—including in the United States—the movement's legitimacy is still under scrutiny because of the marginal status of alternative religions and cults. In Scientology's case, its very "strangeness" contributes to its fringe status, but so too does the ever-growing popular knowledge of how exactly "the Church of Scientology" came about in the first place.

Perhaps complicating the movement's quest for religious legitimacy is Scientology's campaign against psychiatry and the way in which Hubbard tried to replace psychiatry, psychology, and other forms of counseling and therapy with Scientology.[35] Periodically, Scientology's antipsychiatry focus finds its way into public discourses. Full-page newspaper advertisements against the antidepressant drug Prozac, Tom Cruise criticizing Brooke Shields's use of antidepressants, and his tirade against Matt Lauer are just a few high-profile examples.[36] For many, this therapeutic focus and the group's aggressive anti-psychiatry campaigns may dilute the notion that Scientology is a religion. Certainly, Scientologists do not consider the therapeutic components of their beliefs and practices to negate their religious identities—indeed, for them, the two are inexorably intertwined.

Illustrating the multifaceted nature of Scientology further are the multitude of organizational subcomponents that it comprises. It incorporates a number of affiliated bodies, including the World Institute for Scientology Enterprises (WISE), a lucrative organization that offers Scientology training and management techniques to businesses; the Association for Better Living and Education (ABLE), which promotes Hubbard's learning techniques to schools and community foundations; Narconon, a drug rehabilitation program (according to Scientology); Criminon, a Scientology prisoner rehabilitation program; and Citizens Commission on Human Rights (CCHR), a group that claims to act as a watchdog to the psychiatric community. Many private citizens, companies and organizations may encounter these affiliates without realizing their status as Scientology entities. Each of these organizations, as well as others, has attempted to legitimate their respective social and political positions both in North America and elsewhere. Various forms of popular culture monitor these quests for acceptance and validation. Again, popular culture coverage often is critical, stymying Scientology's attempts at legitimacy in the popular realm.

In tackling the question of Scientology's religious validity, scholars of religion (and other academic fields) have taken different approaches to understanding the multifaceted nature of what Scientology is and what it does. Most scholars identify that although many component parts of Scientology operate according to pseudoscientific, business, or therapeutic principles, other facets of it are religious, at least to the extent that Scientologists themselves *perceive* Scientology as a religion (i.e., those who join Scientology identify it as a religion, because, to them, that is precisely what it is).

Substantial variety exists, however, in exactly how scholars define and discuss Scientology, with some being more critical than others.[37] In his article, "Scientology—Is This a Religion?," Stephen A. Kent identifies that although certain aspects of Scientology can be understood as "religious," one should remain cognizant of Hubbard's own initial position: that Dianetics and Scientology are "therapeutic" and "scientific" entities. Moreover, he proposes that other dimensions of the organization—including business enterprises, political ambitions, pseudomedical, and pseudopsychiatric practices—obfuscate many of its religious qualities.[38] Recently, David G. Bromley addressed the business, therapeutic, and religious dimensions of Scientology to define it as a "prophetic, contractual religion"—a corporate enterprise that responds to and satisfies capitalist impulses alongside salvational needs by obscuring the boundaries between therapy and religion. It achieves this outcome within the bounds of a corporate-client contract.[39] Finally, indicating the general difficulties in approaching Scientology's status, Hugh Urban states in the Introduction to his book, *The Church of Scientology: the History of a New Religion*, that his goal is to "trace the rather complex, tangled, and often torturous history of how this controversial movement came to *describe itself* and eventually *become recognized as* a 'religion' in the United States—at least in the eyes of the Internal Revenue Service and the State Department."[40]

As is evident from just a brief overview, understanding and defining Scientology is a complex undertaking. It defies easy categorization by confounding commonly held assumptions about the nature of "religion" from both layperson and academic perspectives.

THE FUTURE OF SCIENTOLOGY AND THE ROLE OF POPULAR CULTURE

Recent years have seen a number of high-profile defectors from Scientology—some have been vocal while others remain quiet. Some of those who have left were celebrity adherents—actor Jason Beghe, director

Paul Haggis, singer Lisa Marie Presley, and actor Leah Remini.[41] Others receive less public attention: they are former high-ranking members of the organization, including Mike Rinder and Mark "Marty" Rathbun.[42] As well, David Miscavige's niece, Jenna Miscavige Hill, who left in 2005, published a memoir of her experiences in 2013.[43] The more vocal of those who have left have revealed in great detail some of the many problems that they claimed to have witnessed or experienced firsthand within Scientology. Their memoirs, websites, interviews, blog posts, and other forms of communication contribute to an ever-growing collective of critical voices. Thus, despite the ways in which Scientology can use forms of popular culture to its benefit, detrimental narratives appear to dominate.

In mass-media-saturated societies it seems almost impossible that any individual considering joining Scientology would not have come across the various negative, or at least skeptical, accounts of it. Scientology, by its own actions—perhaps especially in the David Miscavige era,[44] has scared off many of its most dedicated, long-term, and high-ranking practitioners. How then can it recover from this apparent decline in conversion and leakage from within? The nature of Scientology's decline—if this is indeed what is happening, is unknowable in its details. The group may slowly wither; or perhaps, as former Scientologist, Mark Rathbun suggests, Scientology's future lies in a complete reorganization or "reformation."

One might ask to what extent and in what manner will existing and emergent forms of popular culture participate in either of these scenarios? Will the sharing of information pertaining to Scientology continue to proliferate across popular culture forms? Can Scientology utilize popular culture to reshape public perception in meaningful ways? Perhaps the general public will become bored and disinterested in the sensationalized details of celebrity Scientologists, or conversely, the public appetite for any and all Scientology information will continue to prosper, driven by salacious revelations. Worth considering also is the age of many celebrity Scientologists—the most prominent and influential including Tom Cruise, Kirstie Alley, Chick Corea, and John Travolta are all over 50 years old. Unless Scientology can attract more young, dynamic, and popular celebrities (such as actor Laura Prepon)—who are also willing to publicly voice their support of the movement—then Scientology may find that public interest—and in some cases, conversion—wanes based on a loss of celebrity attraction.

A core concept for Scientologists is "Keep Scientology Working," more commonly referred to simply as "KSW." Hubbard introduced the concept in 1965.[45] The rationale for doing so was to impart to committed, upper-level Scientologists the seriousness of Scientology's actions in terms of the cosmic destiny of the planet. Consequently, Scientologists are expected to know verbatim the 10 directives that he outlined in this policy letter. Taken together, they seek to ensure the proper and continued application of Scientology "standard tech" along with the eradication of anything counter to it.[46] Despite current and future challenges to various aspects of Scientology's legitimacy, dedicated Scientologists, will, with incredible drive, commitment, and even aggression, continue to try to ensure that Scientology survives.

Finally, Scientology's future survival and quest for legitimacy has taken on some unusual dimensions. In the late 1980s—and following the death of Hubbard in 1986—the movement began the process of transcribing all of Hubbard's works onto stainless steel plates and locating them in titanium capsules in underground vaults built into a mountainside in a property it owns in Trementina, New Mexico. These vaults are designed to withstand attacks and natural disasters.

The vaults are managed by the Church of Spiritual Technology (CST)—a Scientology affiliate that takes care of all Scientology's copyright materials. The CST ensures that all Hubbard materials are secure in Trementina for future generations. It guards Hubbard's works using a series of security measures, and the compound incorporates a network of underground tunnels for controlled access. The base is located in a remote desert area away from public scrutiny, but Scientology has its own private airstrip to ensure access to its coveted archives. (It has its own water supply also.)[47]

The CST has its own organizational symbol—two overlapping circles, each with a diamond shape within. Scientology has replicated these symbols on the ground near the airstrip. Visible only from an aerial perspective, the enormous symbols are akin to giant crop circles.[48] Former Scientologists have indicated that the symbols are a guide marker for Scientologists returning from other parts of the universe. Indeed, the *Daily Mail* newspaper in the United Kingdom, which took the first close-up photographs of the site, has dubbed the base the "space alien cathedral."[49] Moreover, some ex-Scientologists have stated that the idea for the bunkers came from Hubbard's *Battlefield Earth* book.[50]

Despite Scientology's claim to be the "fastest growing religion in the world,"[51] it seems the movement may be losing its vitality. Certainly, the long-term future of Scientology appears to be tenuous, with its legitimacy in a number of regards facing constant scrutiny and challenges. Furthermore, despite Scientology's financial buoyancy—its estimated worth runs into billions of dollars[52]—its membership likely is floundering. If the vaults containing Hubbard's works survive an unknowable human future, however, then he might just do what he had hoped all along. In a letter to his first wife, Hubbard asserted: "I have high hopes of smashing my name into history so violently that it will take a legendary form even if all the books are destroyed."[53]

THE CHAPTERS

We have organized the chapters in this volume to address specific relationships between Hubbard, Scientology (and Dianetics), and popular culture in American society. Consequently, the volume starts by examining the
relationship between L. Ron Hubbard, Scientology, and the literary genre of
science fiction (SF). As the authors of the first three chapters illustrate, science fiction did indeed occupy a significant position in Hubbard's life, but the
relationship between the literary genre and Scientology is far more complex
than most popular culture portrayals indicate.

In the opening chapter, "Colonizing *Terra Incognita*: L. Ron Hubbard,
Scientology, and the Quest for Empire," Susan Raine observes the ways in
which Hubbard incorporated key motifs from the science fiction genre to
shape some of Scientology's narratives and ideologies. Focusing on several
dominant themes from the early SF tradition—namely, colonialism, empire,
and masculinity—Raine discusses the myriad ways that these tropes entered
into Hubbard's ideologies and practices.

In addition, Raine's chapter examines Hubbard's quest for both North
American and global legitimacy and how these goals propelled him to pursue a number of strategies that would facilitate his plans for expansion. She
discusses how, at the same time, he claimed to have accessed an alternate
dimension where he alone had acquired knowledge about the true nature of
galactic history and the universe. From this revelation, Hubbard proposed
that he would explore and conquer the uncharted territory of the mind
(what Hubbard identified as *terra incognita*) in order to address all human
problems and limitations. Raine contextualizes these twin processes as Hubbard's attempts to explore and colonize both the material and immaterial
dimensions of human existence. She uses the aforementioned science fiction
themes that permeate Hubbard's work to move beyond the simple and commonly held assumption that Scientology merely mirrors the science fiction
works of Hubbard and other pulp-era writers. Her analysis provides the context needed to appreciate in greater detail the intricacies of the relationship
between Hubbard the science fiction writer and Hubbard the therapeutic and
religious guru.

Despite Hubbard's quite convoluted, and at times inconsistent, history of
"thetans," scholars of Scientology have discussed and analyzed many aspects
of them. In the second chapter, "Typewriter in the Sky: L. Ron Hubbard's Fiction and the Birth of the Thetan," Hugh Urban offers a unique perspective
on Hubbard's concept of thetan by examining it in relation to the role of the
author of fiction. Using Hubbard's 1940 story, *Typewriter in the Sky*, Urban
explores the way in which Hubbard cast the author of fiction as a "godlike

being" who is able to fashion and control plotlines, characters, and their environments in any manner he chooses. Urban juxtaposes this analysis with an examination of Hubbard's concept of the "thetan"—a spiritual entity that is endowed with "godlike power" and who is also able to control the environments of others. To explore the parallels between these two entities, Urban examines first the supernatural elements of Hubbard's early fiction works, paying particular attention to the extraordinary powers that his characters possessed. Urban observes how Hubbard continued this theme of superior men or "supermen" in Dianetics and Scientology. Through these works, Hubbard developed further the idea of the ability to achieve such greatness in the face of seemingly insurmountable challenges—all within a cosmic context. The thetan played a vital role in this superior materialization. Indeed, the Operating Thetan *is* the materialization.

Urban concludes by contextualizing Hubbard's work as part of a broader philosophic shift. Thus, Hubbard's identification of the creative force and power of both writers and thetans are core to Urban's proposal that Hubbard's ideas may provide a conceptual bridge between the ideal of the "godlike genius" of artists proposed by the New Romantic authors of the early 19th century and the developing idea of the transformative and empowering nature of self that emerged in the 1960s with the New Age Movement.

Hubbard's late SF works have met with a great deal of negative criticism, and more generally, the contemporary science fiction literary community (authors, scholars, and critics) does not hold Hubbard's SF work in high regard.[54] In chapter 3, Stefano Bigliardi took on the momentous task of reading *Battlefield Earth* as well as the entire *Mission Earth* series (comprising 10 books). The result is "Earth as Battlefield and Mission: Knowledge, Technology, and Power in L. R. Hubbard's Late Novels." Rather than concentrate solely on the literary style and competency of these works, Bigliardi's reading and analysis focuses on the numerous ways that Hubbard formulated concepts of "knowledge" (in its broadest sense), "technology" (both actual and fictional), and "power relationships" in the novels. In addition to providing summaries of each of the novels, he examines each of these areas in detail and analyzes them within the context of the worldview that Hubbard created in his novels. Moreover, Bigliardi prefaces his analyses by discussing Hubbard's thoughts on the SF genre. Thus, he provides us with some insight into how Hubbard conceived of his work and of the science fiction genre more broadly.

Bigliardi follows up by framing these motifs using four distinct but interconnected levels of analysis: first, whether the novels constitute "effectively entertaining narratives"; second, whether they accomplish Hubbard's goals of representing his own definitions of *pure science fiction* and *satire*; third, the degree to which they link with Scientology's doctrines and beliefs; and fourth, the worldview that they communicate. Consequently, Bigliardi offers the most thorough academic analysis and discussion of Hubbard's later science fiction works to date.

The volume then shifts its focus to the relationship between Hollywood, celebrities, movies, television, and Scientology. These industries are dominant entities in American culture; moreover, their influence is global. In chapter 4, "Scientology's Recruitment Policies Targeting Celebrities," Stephen A. Kent provides an analysis of Scientology's recruitment and use of celebrities. Kent uses resource mobilization theory, in combination with Scientology's own celebrity policies, to analyze how Scientology developed a series of strategies that it hoped would help frame Scientology in a positive way to the public. Kent reviews these policies, examining the way that Hubbard designed them to provide guidelines for the following: aiding Scientologists in the pursuit of celebrity converts; attracting celebrities to Scientology; keeping celebrities committed to Scientology; training celebrity Scientologists to promote Scientology to other celebrities and to public institutions (including libraries, schools, hospitals, and universities); and encouraging celebrity Scientologists to advocate for the group to government and other influential bodies. As Kent reveals, Hubbard understood well the influence of the emergent celebrity culture, and he hoped that his policies would help capitalize on it.

Kent follows this chapter with "Celebrities Keeping Scientology Working." Hence, in chapter 5 he identifies several areas of significance in this regard and offers the following categories:

1. Placing celebrities in public events in which Scientologists were unlikely to be challenged or questioned
2. Designing and producing a celebrity centre event, acting in Scientology films, etc.
3. Supporting scientology through media and/or public interaction
4. Celebrities defending Scientology's pseudomedicine
5. Lobbying Scientology's interests with businesses and governments
6. Celebrities' financial donations to Scientology
7. Celebrities used as motivators to other celebrities concerning additional courses-enrollment

Kent's comprehensive overview also offers a discussion of the relative costs and benefits of Scientology's celebrity strategy. Although celebrity membership can bring the positive associations to Scientology that Hubbard sought, celebrities can also bring negative attention to the group when they behave in unexpected ways—for example, Tom Cruise's comments during an interview with *Today* host Matt Lauer. This chapter provides a rich array of detailed information explaining precisely what celebrities do to contribute to Scientology's quest for public and political legitimacy.

The problem of celebrity defection is the subject of chapter 6, "Scientology's Celebrity Apostates." This chapter examines the reasons for celebrity and other artists' defections from Scientology. As Kent proposes, having spent a good deal of effort attracting and maintaining celebrity followers, any subsequent loss of them can be a blow to Scientology, especially when celebrity apostates discuss their experiences with the movement in negative terms. The media pays close attention to celebrities, so when they leave Scientology, various media outlets are ready and waiting to cover their stories. Moreover, as Kent discusses, celebrity defectors often concretize their thoughts in lasting ways (e.g., through memoirs).

After first providing an overview of celebrity defection from Scientology and the ways in which such departures occur, Kent provides four case studies for analysis, highlighting the experiences of a range of well-known artistic figures. They are as follows: author and prominent counterculture figure William Burroughs; actor Jason Beghe; director Paul Haggis; and actor Leah Remini. Kent finishes his discussion by drawing on the scholarly literature on defection to analyze the defection motifs evident in each case. This chapter concludes Kent's significant contribution to the literature on Scientology's relationship with celebrity adherents.

From the infamous *South Park* episode to movies such as *Bowfinger* and *Talladega Nights: The Ballad of Ricky Bobby,* many television shows, movies, and stand-up comedians have satirized Scientology and its beliefs and practices. In chapter 7, "Hollywood Bites," Tami M. Bereska identifies and analyzes a wide array of entertainment references to and representations of Scientology, outlining some of the principal reasons why the group continues to engender such satirical wrath in a variety of popular culture settings. To provide the appropriate context, Bereska begins by outlining the importance of studying entertainment media. Integral to her discussion is the recognition of the way in which many forms of media often deviantize alternative religions—hence making them easy targets for satire and criticism. Moreover, as she identifies, media representations have significant impact on public perceptions. Bereska also examines, however, the ways in which Scientology has actively fostered a critical environment, and thus popular representations of the movement serve also as warnings to the public about the actual and potential problems associated with Scientology.

This chapter analyzes constructions of Scientology in a range of media produced in both in Hollywood and elsewhere. Bereska reviews a fascinating variety of television and movie representations, discussing not only those that make fun of Scientology beliefs and practices—as well as its celebrity adherents—but also those that have dramatized the movement in film and serial form.

In chapter 8, "Must-See Television: Interviews with Scientologists," Bereska continues her analysis by examining a selection of television interviews with Scientologists. Over the years, several television news anchors and chat show hosts, including Ted Koppel, Oprah Winfrey, and Matt Lauer, have interviewed Scientologists such as current leader David Miscavige and celebrity members, including Tom Cruise. These interviews became compelling television spectacles, and their legacies moved beyond their initial televised formats. Many of the pre-Internet-era interviews have been reposted on the immensely popular video-sharing website, YouTube. More recent interviews also end up on YouTube or elsewhere in the online environment—often as a matter of course. The "viral" status of such content serves only to attract further viewers.

This chapter analyzes the interviews by exploring the development of television interview techniques and approaches. Consequently, Bereska contextualizes interviews with Scientologists in terms of the broader trajectory of television-interview strategies. Then, she explains how, in a fascinating counter to new interview formats and strategies, Scientology, too, developed new *interviewee* techniques and practices. For example, Bereska illustrates Scientology's transition, from having important Scientology administrators such as Heber Jentzsch attend interviews to the use high-profile and well-liked celebrities instead. This chapter explores these and many other strategic shifts as both television programs and Scientology engaged in adaptive practices to try to gain the upper hand during these captivating encounters.

While television, movies, and celebrity have dominated much of America's popular culture relationship with Scientology, another critical facet has been newspaper coverage of the group. In chapter 9, "Presentations of Scientology in Prominent North American News Series," Terra Manca examines coverage from six news series that appeared in several North American newspapers between 1974 and 2009 (five U.S. news series and one Canadian).

In her analysis of the six news series, Manca focuses on three key areas. First, she reviews how each series represented Scientology in its news reports. Second, she summarizes the content of these series in relation to events involving Scientology. Third, she proposes that contrary to some research, the journalistic accounts of Scientology do not constitute a "moral panic" over Scientology. Rather, Manca proposes that they addressed a number of controversies that had tangible and wide-reaching individual, social, and political implications. Thus, the news series served an important social function: they provided the public with information on Scientology regarding some of its controversial and oftentimes criminal practices. As Manca's account reveals, this public need for information became particularly critical for the residents of Clearwater, Florida—a city that experienced an abundance of problems connected to Scientology's establishment of its Flag Land Base there.

Newspapers have provided the public with a good deal of information (and, at times, misinformation) on Scientology, but no form of mass media has been more problematic for Scientology than the Internet. In this arena, Scientology, ex-members, critics, and the general public have become embroiled over issues surrounding freedom of information and censorship. In chapter 10, "Scientology's Relationship with the Internet: The Struggles of Contemporary Perception Management," Max Halupka addresses two key areas. First, Halupka examines a variety of situations where Scientology has "gone into battle" with the Internet over the issue of access to information on the movement. He therefore provides an important update to Jim Lippard and Jeff Jacobsen's earlier work[55] on Scientology's fraught relationship with the Internet. The chapter focuses on several key struggles for control that Scientology has endured in the online environment, including the Usenet news group alt.religion.scientology, content posted on Wikipedia, the activities of hacktivist group Anonymous, and the search engine Google.

Second, Halupka examines the evolution of Scientology's perception management strategies from its inception through to the postmodern era—an era that is characterized by the fluid dissemination of information in the online environment. He proposes that within this context, Scientology has had to alter—and "soften"—its strategies when dealing with intense scrutiny and criticism. As Halupka asserts, the movement must control how it is perceived by the public in order to bolster its position as a legitimate religion and in order to maintain its profit-centric model that maintains its operations.

Perhaps the most overlooked forms of popular culture with regard to Scientology are art and music. This volume concludes with two chapters that rectify these omissions. In chapter 11, "Remember the Whole Track? The Hidden Persuaders in Scientology Art," by George Shaw and Susan Raine, the authors examine Hubbard's reasons for ordering new artwork for the covers to more than 20 Dianetics and Scientology publications. This chapter is the first scholarly work to examine the artwork of Scientology, and, as the authors note, they can discuss only a segment of Scientology's vast array of visual media.

Because of his "wall of fire" breakthrough and his claims to new knowledge, Hubbard commissioned new book cover designs that incorporated important "whole track" and "space opera" imagery. Given the significance of these two concepts in Hubbard's theology, Shaw and Raine reveal how, in each case, Hubbard devised new cover images that were meant to act as powerful symbolic reminders of past events. Hubbard intended the artwork—executed by accomplished Canadian artist and Scientologist, Richard Gorman—to effect particular favorable responses to Scientology in those who viewed them.

The authors situate Hubbard's use of these artworks by discussing some of his strategic motivations and influences. For example, they discuss Hubbard's belief in the efficacy of the "subliminal" advertising techniques that marketers allegedly used in the 1960s. Hubbard embraced subliminal theories, proposing that his use of them would provide Scientology with an influential tool. Coupled with this approach, Hubbard used symbolism from the Christian tradition in his artwork in his attempt to appeal to the public. Drawing on the legitimacy of Christianity in many parts of the world, Hubbard hoped to establish greater acceptability for Scientology through association.

This chapter provides a history and explanation of Hubbard's ideas for the book covers. Furthermore, the authors engage in a detailed analysis of a selection of the whole track covers.

In chapter 12, "L. Ron Hubbard's Foray into the World of Music," Mark Evans concludes our volume with his analysis of Hubbard and Scientology's musical projects. As Evans identifies, on several occasions Hubbard worked with some accomplished musicians, and he produced music in several genres. His musical legacy, however, is weak. His soundtracks and other musical endeavors have been critically disparaged and have all but disappeared from public attention except as online curiosities.

This chapter critically addresses several of Hubbard's and Scientology's musical outputs, analyzing them both for their musical quality as well as for their impact—or lack thereof. In addition to producing his own music, Hubbard also, as one might expect, wrote about the origins and importance of music to the world. Evans's chapter, therefore, identifies the numerous ways that Hubbard himself and Scientology promoted him as an important educator in this regard. In the same way that he considered himself the definitive authority on the visual arts, Hubbard considered himself to understand music and the communicative abilities of it in a manner superior to all others.

In this analysis of the music of Scientology, Evans focuses also on what might be considered its two largest projects—the Apollo Stars, a band made up of Sea Org members, and *The Road to Freedom*, an album that the group released in 1986, the year of Hubbard's death. As Evans notes, the Apollo Stars actually achieved a brief period of commercial success in Europe. *The Road to Freedom*, despite its celebrity lineup that included Chick Corea and John Travolta, failed in the marketplace, in part, as Evans surmises, because of its heavy doctrinal content.

IN CLOSING

Despite the assortment of coverage included in this volume, we suspect that much more could be said about the nature of Scientology's relationship with popular culture (and, of course, some other scholars have published works already on this relationship). We hope, however, that research continues to flourish in this fascinating area. Certainly, Hubbard's words and ideas, Scientology's ongoing practices and policies, as well as a superabundance of popular culture products all provide wonderful opportunities for further scholarship.

NOTES

1. For example, see the following: Lucy Buckland and Zoe Shenton, "Inside Tom Cruise and Katie Holmes Split," *Mirror*, November 6, 2013, http://www.mirror.co .uk/3am/celebrity-news/tom-cruise-katie-holmes-split-2682014; Marlow Stern, "Tom, Katie, and Suri: A Scientology Story," *Daily Beast*, June 3, 2015, http://www .thedailybeast.com/articles/2015/03/06/tom-katie-and-suri-a-scientology-story.html; Stephanie Marcus, "Tom Cruise Admits Katie Holmes Divorced Him to Protect Suri from Scientology," *Huffington Post*, November 8, 2013, http://www.huffingtonpost .com/2013/11/08/tom-cruise-katie-holmes-protect-suri-scientology_n_4240715.html.

2. For example, see the following: "John Travolta Sexual Assaults Payout? Not So Fast," *Huffington Post*, February 4, 2013, http://www.huffingtonpost.com/2013/04/02 /john-travolta-sexual-assault-lawsuits_n_3001581.html; Camille Dodero, "Document Shows John Travolta's Insurer Paid at Least $84,000 Last Year over Sexual Assault Claims," *Gawker*, February 4, 2013, http://gawker.com/5993260/document -shows-john-travolta-paid-at-least-84000-last-year-over-sexual-assault-claims; Andrei Harmsworth, "John Travolta Made to Fight 'Gay' Sexual Assault Case in Court," *Metro*, February 5, 2013, http://metro.co.uk/2013/02/05/john-travolta-made -to-fight-gay-sexual-assault-case-in-court-3382283/.

3. For example, see the following: Star Staff, "Divorce Bombshell! John Travolta & Kelly Preston in $240 Million Split after Gay Allegations—Why She Reached Her Limit," *Star*, September 22, 2016, http://starmagazine.com/photos/john-travolta -divorce-rumors-kelly-preston/photo/213412/; National Enquirer, "John Travolta Gay Sex Scandal Explodes," *National Enquirer*, April 16, 2016, http://www.nationalenquirer .com/celebrity/john-travolta-gay-sex-scandal-explodes; Hugo Daniel, "Pilot Who Claims He Had Six-Year Gay Affair with John Travolta Hits Back at Star's Put-Down That His Lawsuit Is Motivated by Greed," *Daily Mail*, September 19, 2014, http://www .dailymail.co.uk/tvshowbiz/article-2761186/Pilot-claims-six-year-gay-affair-John -Travolta-hits-stars-claim-lawsuit-motivated-greed.html.

4. Michael Cipley, "Documentary Draws Ire from the Church of Scientology," *New York Times*, January 15, 2015, http://www.nytimes.com/2015/01/16 /business/media/documentary-draws-ire-from-the-church-of-scientology.html?_r=0; Joe Satran, "Scientologists Deny Campaign against 'Going Clear' for Oscar Win,"

Huffington Post, June 10, 2015, http://www.huffingtonpost.com/entry/scientology -going-clear-oscar_us_56156ee8e4b0fad1591a8177.

5. Carole M. Cusack, "Celebrity, the Popular Media, and Scientology: Making Familiar the Unfamiliar," in *Scientology*, ed. James R. Lewis (New York: Oxford University Press, 2009), 389. This outcome, is due to the "cult of celebrity" which has accorded celebrities in Western culture an extraordinarily high status. Many members of the general public venerate celebrities and their lifestyles and may even want to identify further with their favorite stars by engaging in some of the same practices and behaviors (389–390).

6. Ibid., 400.

7. See James Lewis, "Scientology vs. the Media," *Alternative Spirituality and Religion Review* 6, no. 1 (2015): 61–78.

8. Roger Christian, *Battlefield Earth*, Warner Bros. (2000).

9. Trey Parker, "Trapped in the Closet," *South Park*, Season 9, Episode 12. Comedy Central (November 16, 2005).

10. For example, Bruce David Forbes and Jeffrey H. Mahan, eds., *Religion and Popular Culture in America* (Oakland, CA: University of California Press, 2005); and Terry Ray Clarke, "Introduction: What Is Religion? What Is Popular Culture? How Are They Related?," in *Understanding Religion and Popular Culture*, ed. Terry Ray Clark and Dan W. Clanton Jr. (New York: Routledge, 2012), 1–12.

11. Bruce David Forbes and Jeffrey H. Mahan, *Religion and Popular Culture in America*, ix.

12. Ibid., 2–3.

13. Ibid., 3.

14. Ibid.

15. John Storey, *Cultural Theory and Popular Culture*, 5th ed. (London: Pearson, 2008), 5–6.

16. Ibid., 12.

17. Susie O'Brien and Imre Szeman, *Popular Culture: A User's Guide*, 2nd ed. (Toronto: Nelson Education, 2010).

18. For a full history of the development of Dianetics and Scientology, see Jon Atack, *A Piece of Blue Sky: Scientology, Dianetics and L. Ron Hubbard Exposed* (New York: Lyle Stuart, 1990); Janet Reitman, *Inside Scientology: The Story of America's Most Secretive Religion* (New York: Houghton Mifflin Harcourt, 2011); Hugh Urban, *The Church of Scientology: A History of a New Religion* (Princeton: Princeton University Press, 2011); and Roy Wallis, *The Road to Total Freedom: A Sociological Study of Scientology*, first published in 1976 (New York: Columbia University Press, 1977).

19. Hugh Urban, *The Church of Scientology*, 39–48; Harriet Whitehead, "Reasonably Fantastic: Some Perspectives on Scientology, Science Fiction and Occultism," in *Religious Movements in Contemporary America*, ed. Irving I. Zaretsky and Mark P. Leone, 547–587 (Princeton: Princeton University Press, 1974).

20. Stephen A. Kent and Terra Manca, "A War over Mental Health Professionalism: Scientology versus Psychiatry," *Mental Health, Religion & Culture* 17, no. 1 (2014): 1–23.

21. Ibid., 6–7.

22. For example, see Stephen A. Kent, "The Creation of 'Religious' Scientology," *Religious Studies and Theology* 18, no. 2 (1999); and Hugh Urban, *The Church of Scientology: A History of a New Religion*, 58–59.

23. L. Ron Hubbard, *Scientology: A History of Man*. First published in 1952 (Copenhagen: Scientology Publications Organization, 1980). At the beginning of most, if not all, of Hubbard's works he provides a definition of Dianetics and Scientology. These definitions are fairly standard although some do vary in specific content.

24. L. Ron Hubbard, *Mission into Time*. First published in 1968 (Los Angeles: The American Saint Hill Organization, 1973).

25. Hugh Urban, *The Church of Scientology: A History of a New Religion*, 69–82, for a summary of body thetans.

26. William Sims Bainbridge conducted research on the popularity of many early SF authors. Initially, Hubbard's stories were quite popular, earning "slightly more than average enthusiasm." Later on his work is rated as "passable." William Sims Bainbridge "Science and Religion: The Case of Scientology," in *The Future of New Religious Movements*, ed. D. G. Bromley and P. E. Hammond (Macon: Mercer University Press, 1987), 63. Eventually, however, Hubbard's popularity waned considerably— so much so that today, "the science fiction subculture does not remember Hubbard fondly." Ibid., 67. John P. Brennan identifies Hubbard's pulp works as lacking grammatically and in need of improved editing. Moreover, he concludes that Hubbard's work is quite conventional for the period, although he does recognize Hubbard's better publications. John P. Brennan, "Hubbard, L(aFayette) Ron(ald)." *St. James Guide to Science Fiction Writers* (Detroit: St. James Press, 1996), 458.

27. Dorthe Refslund Christensen, "Inventing L. Ron Hubbard: On the Construction and Maintenance of the Hagiographic Mythology of Scientology's Founder," in *Controversial New Religions*, ed. James R. Lewis and Jesper Aagaard Petersen, 227–258 (Oxford: Oxford University Press, 2005).

28. Ibid., 232; Russell Miller, *Bare-Faced Messiah: The True Story of L. Ron Hubbard* (New York: Henry Holt, 1987).

29. First granted in 1957, then revoked following an IRS audit a decade later.

30. For discussions, see Susan Raine, "Surveillance in New Religious Movements: Scientology as a Case Study," *Religious Studies and Theology* 28, no. 1 (2009): 82–84; Janet Reitman, *Inside Scientology*, 114–115; and Hugh Urban, *The Church of Scientology: A History of a New Religion*, 167–170.

31. United States District Court for the District of Columbia. "United States of America v. Mary Sue Hubbard et al. Stipulation of Evidence." Criminal No. 78-401 (October 25, 1979), 42, 58–59, 81–83, 88–89, 253ff.

32. Jim Mann, "Five Scientology Leaders Receive Prison Sentences," *Los Angeles Times* (December 7, 1979), 7; United States District Court for the District of Columbia. "United States of America v. Jane Kember, Morris Budlong a/k/a Mo Budlong. Sentencing Memorandum of the United States of America." Criminal No. 78-401 (2) & (3) (December 16, 1980).

33. The group and its many associated organizations filed repeated lawsuits against the IRS in order to obtain tax-exempt status. Moreover, individual Scientologists filed several thousand lawsuits against the IRS. They stated that they should be able to claim tax deductions for expenses associated with auditing and other Scientology training.

34. John Bingham, "Scientology Is a Religion, Rules Supreme Court," *Daily Telegraph*, December 11, 2013, http://www.telegraph.co.uk/news/religion/10510301/Scientology-is-a-religion-rules-Supreme-Court.html; Douglas Frantz, "Scientology's Puzzling Journey from Tax Rebel to Tax Exempt," *New York Times*, March 9, 1997, http://www.nytimes.com/1997/03/09/us/scientology-s-puzzling-journey-from-tax-rebel-to-tax-exempt.html; James Kirchick, "Scientology Is Not a Religion," *Tablet*, July 24, 2012, http://www.tabletmag.com/jewish-news-and-politics/105996/scientology-is-not-a-religion; National Assembly of France Report No. 2468, http://www.assemblee-nationale.fr/rap-enq/r2468.asp; News, South Africa, "SA Church of Scientology Gets Tax Exemption," http://www.iol.co.za/news/south-africa/sa-church-of-scientology-gets-tax-exemption-381415#.UJ1bpeQ3sxB; New Zealand Herald, "Scientology Gets Tax-Exempt Status," http://www.nzherald.co.nz/nz/news/article.cfm?c_id=1&objectid=3048935; "Portugal," *International Religious Freedom Report 2007*. U.S. Department of State, http://www.state.gov/j/drl/rls/irf/2007/90194.htm; and Janet Reitman, *Inside Scientology*, xiii.

35. Stephen A. Kent and Terra Manca, "A War over Mental Health Professionalism: Scientology versus Psychiatry."

36. Archives Today, "Tom Cruise's Heated Interview with Matt Lauer," June 2, 2014, https://www.youtube.com/watch?v=tFgF1JPNR5E.

37. For example, Gordon Melton, *The Church of Scientology* (Salt Lake City: Signature Books, 2000). Melton offers an uncritical look at Scientology, and as such, he does not question Scientology's status. Conversely, Benjamin Beit-Hallahmi takes an extremely critical position. Benjamin Beit-Hallahmi, "Scientology: Religion or Racket?," *Marburg Journal of Religion* 8, no. 1 (2003): 26–28, http://archiv.ub.unimarburg.de/ep/0004/article/view/3724.

38. Stephen A. Kent, "Scientology—Is This a Religion?" *Marburg Journal of Religion* 4, no. 1 (1999). In another article, Kent identifies also the way in which Hubbard incorporated specific ideas in his development of a "religious" Scientology. Stephen A. Kent, "The Creation of 'Religious' Scientology," *Religious Studies and Theology* 18, no. 2 (1999).

39. David G. Bromley, "Making Sense of Scientology: Prophetic Contractual Religion," in *Scientology*, ed. James R. Lewis (New York: Oxford University Press, 2009), 83–101.

40. Hugh Urban, *The Church of Scientology: A History of a New Religion*, 3.

41. Actor Jason Beghe and director Paul Haggis both appear in Alex Gibney's documentary, *Going Clear*. Beghe has given interviews, contributed to documentaries, attended anti-Scientology protests, and has even sat on a panel on Scientology organized by the German government.

Haggis left Scientology after 35 years when he could no longer tolerate Scientology's public support of Proposition 8 in California. The largely Mormon-funded proposition aimed at overturning the legality of gay marriage in the state. (Proposition 8 was successful. The decision was overturned, however, when the Ninth Circuit Court

of Appeals overturned it on the grounds that it was unconstitutional.) In his open letter to the former head of Scientology's Celebrity Centre International, Tommy Davis
(who is the son of actor and Scientologist, Anne Archer), Haggis questions Davis's
lack of action regarding Haggis's prior correspondence over Proposition 8. Moreover,
Haggis outlines his increasing sense of outrage and disbelief at Scientology's inconsistencies and lies, http://www.scientology-cult.com/declarations-of-independence/59-
paul-haggis/158-paul-haggis-resigns-from-church-of-scientology.html.

Lisa Marie Presley, singer, and daughter of Elvis Presley, has remained quiet
about her time in Scientology, although some of her song lyrics indicate her disillusionment with the movement. Tony Ortega, "Lisa Marie Presley Says 'So Long'
to Scientology," *Village Voice* May 13, 2012, http://www.villagevoice.com/news
/lisa-marie-presley-says-so-long-to-scientology-6674826.

Since leaving Scientology, actor Leah Remini, who became a Scientologist at age
nine when her mother joined up, has appeared in a prominent interview with Dan
Harris on ABC's 20/20 (aired October 30, 2015) and published her book, *Troublemaker* (published November 3, 2015). She is a vocal critic of Scientology and has
articulated her praise for Alex Gibney's documentary.

42. Mike Rinder was a senior member of Scientology and of its Sea Org. A long-
time member, since leaving the movement in 2007, Rinder has discussed the abusive culture of Scientology, especially since Miscavige took over following Hubbard's
death in 1986. He discusses Scientology and his time as a member on his blog, *Something Can Be Done About It*, http://www.mikerindersblog.org/.

Another long-time high-ranking member of Scientology, Mark Rathbun, left
in 2004. He too has discussed his experiences in the movement, especially those
pertaining to Miscavige's alleged violence and authoritarian rule. In addition, he
has discussed Scientology's purported manipulation of Tom Cruise. Rathbun discusses Scientology at his website, *Moving On Up a Little Higher*, https://markrathbun
.wordpress.com/.

43. Jenna Miscavige Hill with Lisa Pulitzer, *Beyond Belief: My Secret Life Inside
Scientology and My Harrowing Escape* (New York: William Morrow Paperbacks, 2013).

44. At the time of writing, the father of current Scientology leader David Miscavige has just published a revealing—and scathing—account of his son in his book
Ruthless. Ron Miscavige with Dan Koon, *Ruthless: Scientology, My Son David Miscavige
and Me* (New York: St. Martin's Press, 2016).

45. L. Ron Hubbard, "Keeping Scientology Working, Series 1," *Hubbard Communications Policy Letter*, February 7, 1965.

46. Ibid.

47. Chris White, "EXCLUSIVE: Pictured Up Close for the First Time, Scientology's 'Alien Space Cathedral and Spaceship Landing Pad' Built in the New Mexico
Desert for the 'Return of Followers after Armageddon on Earth,'" *Mail Online*, August
16, 2013, http://www.dailymail.co.uk/news/article-2395235/EXCLUSIVE-Pictured
-close-time-Scientologys-secret-alien-space-cathedral-landing-pad-New-Mexico
-desert-return-followers-Armageddon-Earth.html.; See also Tony Ortega's interview
with Jon Atack for a full discussion of the base: http://tonyortega.org/2013/08/31
/the-history-of-scientologys-weird-vaults-the-bizarre-battlefield-earth-connection/.

48. Ibid.

49. Chris White, "EXCLUSIVE: Pictured Up Close for the First Time."

50. http://tonyortega.org/2013/08/31/the-history-of-scientologys-weird-vaults-the-bizarre-battlefield-earth-connection/.

51. Janet Reitman, *Inside Scientology: The Story of America's Most Secretive Religion* (New York: Houghton Mifflin Harcourt, 2011), xii. Scholars have come to opposite conclusions on the issue of Scientology's growth or decline. For an argument that it is growing, see James R. Lewis, "The Growth of Scientology and the Stark Model of Religious 'Success,'" in *Scientology*, ed. James R. Lewis (Oxford: Oxford University Press, 2009), 117–140. For an argument that it is declining, see Stephen A. Kent, "The Decline of Scientology," in *Dialog in Konfrontation—und die Wahrheit wird sie frei machen: Eine Festschrift für Thomas Gandow*, ed. Christoph Polster and Ede Ingolf Christiansen (Jena, Germany: Jenaer Akademische Verlagsgesellschaft, 2011), 113–146.

52. Ibid.

53. My thanks go to Tony Ortega and Jon Atack. During an interview with Ortega at the *Underground Bunker*, Atack and Ortega refer to Hubbard's words (which he wrote in a letter to his first wife) about smashing his name into history even if—as Ortega emphasizes—his books all are destroyed. Atack and Ortega surmise that one way to overcome this problem would be to do what Scientology has indeed done—construct a facility that is largely impervious to attack or any other type of disaster. Their discussion inspired me to use Hubbard's words at the end of this paragraph. Tony Ortega, "The History of Scientology's Weird Vaults: The Bizarre *Battlefield Earth* Connection!" *The Underground Bunker*, http://tonyortega.org/2013/08/31/the-history-of-scientologys-weird-vaults-the-bizarre-battlefield-earth-connection/.

54. William Sims Bainbridge, "Science and Religion: The Case of Scientology," 67.

55. Jim Lippard and Jeff Jacobsen, "Scientology v. the Internet: Free Speech & Copyright Infringement on the Information Super-Highway," *Skeptic* 3, no. 3 (1995): 35.

BIBLIOGRAPHY

Archives Today. "Tom Cruise's Heated Interview with Matt Lauer."

Atack, Jon. *A Piece of Blue Sky: Scientology, Dianetics and L. Ron Hubbard Exposed.* New York: Lyle Stuart, 1990.

Bainbridge, William Sims. "Science and Religion: The Case of Scientology." In *The Future of New Religious Movements*, edited by David G. Bromley and Philip E. Hammond, 59–79. Macon: Mercer University Press, 1987.

Beit-Hallahmi, Benjamin. "Scientology: Religion or Racket?," *Marburg Journal of Religion* 8, no. 1 (2003): 26–28. http://archiv.ub.uni-marburg.de/ep/0004/article/view/3724.

Bingham, John. "Scientology Is a Religion, Rules Supreme Court." *Daily Telegraph*, December 11, 2013. http://www.telegraph.co.uk/news/religion/10510301/Scientology-is-a-religion-rules-Supreme-Court.html.

Brennan, John P. "Hubbard, L(aFayette) Ron(ald)." *St. James Guide to Science Fiction Writers*. Detroit: St. James Press, 1996.

Bromley, David G. "Making Sense of Scientology: Prophetic Contractual Religion." In *Scientology*, edited by James R. Lewis, 83–101. New York: Oxford University Press, 2009.

Buckland, Lucy, and Shenton Zoe. "Inside Tom Cruise and Katie Holmes Split." *Mirror*, November 6, 2013. http://www.mirror.co.uk/3am/celebrity-news/tom -cruise-katie-holmes-split-2682014.

Christensen, Dorthe Refslund. "Inventing L. Ron Hubbard: On the Construction and Maintenance of the Hagiographic Mythology of Scientology's Founder." In *Controversial New Religions*, edited by James R. Lewis and Jesper Aagaard Petersen, 227–258. Oxford: Oxford University Press, 2005.

Christian, Roger. *Battlefield Earth*. Warner Bros., 2000.

Cipley, Michael. "Documentary Draws Ire from the Church of Scientology." *New York Times*, January 15, 2015. http://www.nytimes.com/2015/01/16/business /media/documentary-draws-ire-from-the-church-of-scientology.html?_r=0.

Clarke, Terry Ray. "Introduction: What Is Religion? What Is Popular Culture? How Are They Related?" In *Understanding Religion and Popular Culture*, edited by Terry Ray Clark and Dan W. Clanton Jr., 1–12. New York: Routledge, 2012.

Cusack, Carole M. "Celebrity, the Popular Media, and Scientology: Making Familiar the Unfamiliar." In *Scientology*, edited by James R. Lewis, 389–409. New York: Oxford University Press, 2009.

Daniel, Hugo. "Pilot Who Claims He Had Six-Year Gay Affair with John Travolta Hits Back at Star's Put-Down That His Lawsuit Is Motivated by Greed." *Daily Mail*, September 19, 2014. http://www.dailymail.co.uk/tvshowbiz/article-2761186 /Pilot-claims-six-year-gay-affair-John-Travolta-hits-stars-claim-lawsuit-motivated -greed.html.

Dodero, Camille. "Document Shows John Travolta's Insurer Paid at Least $84,000 Last Year Over Sexual Assault Claims." *Gawker*, February 4, 2013. http:// gawker.com/5993260/document-shows-john-travolta-paid-at-least-84000-last -year-over-sexual-assault-claims.

Forbes, Bruce David and Jeffrey H. Mahan, eds. *Religion and Popular Culture in America*. Oakland, CA: University of California Press, 2005.

Frantz, Douglas. "Scientology's Puzzling Journey from Tax Rebel to Tax Exempt." *New York Times*, March 9, 1997.

Gibney, Alex. *Going Clear: Scientology and the Prison of Belief*. HBO Documentary Films, 2015.

Harmsworth, Andrei. "John Travolta Made to Fight 'Gay' Sexual Assault Case in Court." *Metro*, February 5, 2013. http://metro.co.uk/2013/02/05/john-travolta -made-to-fight-gay-sexual-assault-case-in-court-3382283/.

Hubbard, L. Ron. "Keeping Scientology Working, Series 1." *Hubbard Communications Policy Letter*, February 7, 1965.

Hubbard, L. Ron. *Mission into Time*. First published in 1968. Los Angeles: The American Saint Hill Organization, 1973.

Hubbard, L. Ron. *Scientology: A History of Man*. First published in 1952. Copenhagen: Scientology Publications Organization, 1980.

Huffington Post. "John Travolta Sexual Assaults Payout? Not So Fast," *The Huffington Post*, February 4, 2013. http://www.huffingtonpost.com/2013/04/02/john -travolta-sexual-assault-lawsuits_n_3001581.html.

IOL News, South Africa. "SA Church of Scientology Gets Tax Exemption." http:// www.iol.co.za/news/south-africa/sa-church-of-scientology-gets-tax-exemption -381415#.UJ1bpeQ3sxB.

Kent, Stephen A. "The Creation of 'Religious' Scientology." *Religious Studies and Theology* 18 (1999): 97–127.

Kent, Stephen A. "The Decline of Scientology." In *Dialog in Konfrontation—und die Wahrheit wird sie frei machen: Eine Festschrift für Thomas Gandow*, edited by Christoph Polster and Ede Ingolf Christiansen, 113–146. Jena, Germany: Jenaer Akademische Verlagsgesellschaft, 2011.

Kent, Stephen A. "Scientology—Is This a Religion?" *Marburg Journal of Religion* 4 (1999): 1–23. https://www.uni-marburg.de/fb03/ivk/mjr/pdfs/1999/articles/kent 1999.pdf.

Kent, Stephen A., and Terra A. Manca "A War over Mental Health Professionalism: Scientology versus Psychiatry." *Mental Health, Religion & Culture* 1 (2012): 1–23.

Kirchick, James. "Scientology Is Not a Religion." *Tablet*, July 24, 2012. http://www .tabletmag.com/jewish-news-and-politics/105996/scientology-is-not-a-religion.

Lewis, James R. "The Growth of Scientology and the Stark Model of Religious 'Success.'" In *Scientology*, edited by James R. Lewis, 117–140. (Oxford: Oxford University Press, 2009).

Lewis, James R. "Scientology vs. the Media." *Alternative Spirituality and Religion Review* 6, no. 1 (2015): 61–78.

Lippard, Jim, and Jeff Jacobsen. "Scientology v. the Internet: Free Speech & Copyright Infringement on the Information Super-Highway." *Skeptic* 3, no. 3 (1995): 35–41.

Mann, Jim. "Five Scientology Leaders Receive Prison Sentences." *Los Angeles Times*, December 7, 1979.

Marcus, Stephanie. "Tom Cruise Admits Katie Holmes Divorced Him to Protect Suri from Scientology." *Huffington Post*, November 8, 2013. http:// www.huffingtonpost.com/2013/11/08/tom-cruise-katie-holmes-protect-suri -scientology_n_4440715.html.

Melton, Gordon. *The Church of Scientology*. Salt Lake City: Signature Books, 2000.

Miller, Russell. *Bare-Faced Messiah: The True Story of L. Ron Hubbard*. New York: Henry Holt, 1987.

Miscavige, Ron, with Dan Koon. *Ruthless: Scientology, My Son David Miscavige, and Me*. New York: St. Martin's Press, 2016.

Miscavige Hill, Jenna, with Lisa Pulitzer. *Beyond Belief: My Secret Life Inside Scientology and My Harrowing Escape*. New York: William Morrow Paperbacks, 2013.

National Assembly of France Report No. 2468. http://www.assemblee-nationale.fr/rap -enq/r2468.asp.

National Enquirer. "John Travolta Gay Sex Scandal Explodes." *National Enquirer*, April 16, 2016. http://www.nationalenquirer.com/celebrity/john -travolta-gay-sex-scandal-explodes.

New Zealand Herald. "Scientology Gets Tax-Exempt Status." *New Zealand Herald*, December 27, 2002. http://www.nzherald.co.nz/nz/news/article.cfm?c_id=1 &objectid=3048935.

O'Brien, Susie, and Imre Szeman. *Popular Culture: A User's Guide*. Second edition. Toronto: Nelson Education, 2010.

Ortega, Tony. "The History of Scientology's Weird Vaults: The Bizarre *Battlefield Earth* Connection!" *The Underground Bunker*, n.d. http://tonyortega.org/2013/08/31/the -history-of-scientologys-weird-vaults-the-bizarre-battlefield-earth-connection/.

Ortega, Tony. "Lisa Marie Presley Says 'So Long' to Scientology," *Village Voice*, May 13, 2012. http://www.villagevoice.com/news/lisa-marie-presley-says-so-long-to -scientology-6674826.

Ortega, Tony. "Scientology Leader's Father Signs a Book Deal for 'If He Dies, He Dies.'" n.d. http://tonyortega.org/2015/06/30/scientology-leaders-father-signs-a -book-deal-for-if-he-dies-he-dies/.

Parker, Trey. "Trapped in the Closet." *South Park*, Season 9, Episode 12. Comedy Central. November 16, 2005.

Raine, Susan. "Surveillance in New Religious Movements: Scientology as a Case Study." *Religious Studies and Theology* 28 (2009): 63–94.

Rathbun, Mark. *Moving On Up a Little Higher*. https://markrathbun.wordpress.com/.

Reitman, Janet. *Inside Scientology: The Story of America's Most Secretive Religion*. New York: Houghton Mifflin Harcourt, 2011.

Remini, Leah. *Troublemaker*. New York: Ballantine Books, 2015.

Rinder, Mike. *Something Can Be Done About It*. http://www.mikerindersblog.org/.

Satran, Joe. "Scientologists Deny Campaign against 'Going Clear' for Oscar Win." *Huffington Post*, June 10, 2015. http://www.huffingtonpost.com/entry /scientology-going-clear-oscar_us_56156ee8e4b0fad1591a8177.

Star Staff. "Divorce Bombshell! John Travolta & Kelly Preston in $240 Million Split After Gay Allegations—Why She Reached Her Limit." *Star*, September 22, 2016. http://starmagazine.com/photos/john-travolta-divorce-rumors-kelly-preston /photo/213412/.

Stern, Marlow. "Tom, Katie, and Suri: A Scientology Story." *Daily Beast*, June 3, 2015. http://www.thedailybeast.com/articles/2015/03/06/tom-katie-and-suri-a -scientology-story.html.

Storey, John. *Cultural Theory and Popular Culture*. Fifth edition. London: Pearson, 2008.

United States District Court for the District of Columbia. "United States of America v. Jane Kember, Morris Budlong a/k/a Mo Budlong. Sentencing Memorandum of the United States of America." Criminal No. 78-401 (2) & (3). December 16, 1980.

United States District Court for the District of Columbia. "United States of America v. Mary Sue Hubbard et al. Stipulation of Evidence." Criminal No. 78-401. October 25, 1979.

Urban, Hugh. *The Church of Scientology: A History of a New Religion*. Princeton: Princeton University Press, 2011.

U.S. Department of State. "Portugal." *International Religious Freedom Report 2007*. http://www.state.gov/j/drl/rls/irf/2007/90194.htm.

Wallis, Roy. *The Road to Total Freedom: A Sociological Study of Scientology*. First published in 1976. New York: Columbia University Press, 1977.

White, Chris. "EXCLUSIVE: Pictured up close for the first time, Scientology's 'alien space cathedral and spaceship landing pad' built in the New Mexico desert for the 'return of followers after Armageddon on Earth.'" *Mail Online*, August 16, 2013. http://www.dailymail.co.uk/news/article-2395235/EXCLUSIVE-Pictured -close-time-Scientologys-secret-alien-space-cathedral-landing-pad-New -Mexico-desert-return-followers-Armageddon-Earth.html.

Whitehead, Harriet. "Reasonably Fantastic: Some Perspectives on Scientology, Science Fiction and Occultism." In *Religious Movements in Contemporary America*, edited by Irving I. Zaretsky and Mark P. Leone, 547–587. Princeton: Princeton University Press, 1974.

Wright, Lawrence. *Going Clear: Scientology, Hollywood, & Prison of Belief*. New York: Vintage Books, 2013.

1

Colonizing *Terra Incognita*: L. Ron Hubbard, Scientology, and the Quest for Empire

Susan Raine

INTRODUCTION

Charting and conquering the nefarious thetan colonization of the human citizens of planet Earth became one of the central goals of L. Ron Hubbard's early Scientology philosophy. Certainly, "clearing the planet," was, and remains, a vital directive for Scientologists. The process of planetary clearing involves removing engrams, and ultimately the intrusive thetan presence that causes them, thus releasing humans from the emotional and physical constraints imposed by these invasive entities.[1] In order for this process to occur at a global scale, however, the entire population of Earth would need to adopt Scientology practices. Somewhat ironically then, in order to free the population from an occupied state, a single moral philosophy must be adopted and practiced—rigorously so, in order for it to be successful.

As this chapter proposes, Scientology's proposition that a single worldview and set of associated practices should be adhered to, can be understood as a colonial aim. The territory under colonial consideration is that of the human mind. Indeed, Hubbard classified the mind as *terra incognita*— literally, "unexplored territory"[2]—claiming that only he had the ability to voyage into it. If he could realize this colonial goal, however, then the material world that the mind and body inhabit also would be part of the colonial reach and associated empire-building process. As this chapter illustrates, Hubbard developed a number of strategies for controlling both the immaterial and material dimensions of humanity.

This chapter builds upon my prior discussion of the parallels between Scientology and the literary genre of science fiction (SF). Previously, I argued that Scientology is, in part, a science fiction narrative—specifically one that is associated with the SF subgenre of *space opera*.[3] In that article, I presented the ways in which Hubbard had transformed early American SF influences and concepts into a religion, such that fictional narratives and ideas took shape as a new *science* and then as a *religious philosophy*. This process was a complex one, revealing Hubbard's propensity to blur the margins of realities, counterrealities, science fiction, and science fact. His cornucopia of ideas birthed the development of a Scientology reality, with Hubbard presenting his followers with an unconventional cultural space in which to reconfigure and reassess the human condition. This new space allowed him to mobilize a body of resistance against what would become a known enemy to Scientologists—thetans and their universes. This enemy (along with others that Hubbard would reveal) remains hidden to the rest of the global population—that is to say, to non-Scientologists, until they can become informed of them through conversion to Scientology.

The themes of colonialism, empire building, militarism, and male heroic agency are the ones to which I return. Each theme was present in the literary world of Hubbard's youth, and eventually each in turn was embraced by the pulp fiction genre to which he contributed. The linkages between the political goals of colonialism, late 19th-century and early 20th-century colonial and science fiction, and Hubbard's own personal adventures do much to illuminate Hubbard's proclivity for colonial discourse. A matrix of ideas and influences converged whereby Hubbard crafted himself as the head of the resistance against galactic colonizers—as manifest by thetan encroachment into the human world—while he developed also an expansionist agenda that situated Scientology *as* a colonial force. Hubbard had established a strategy to eradicate enemies (both Earthbound and cosmic) while launching a new world empire that he claimed would improve the conditions of all who subscribed to it.

READING COLONIALISM, MASCULINITY, AND RELIGION IN SCIENCE FICTION

Colonial Adventures on Earth and across the Cosmos

During the Victorian era, popular adventure stories incorporated the themes of European colonization and empire building, reflecting the specter of capitalism as a global force that uncovered "new" and "exotic" locales for its economic pursuits. The fictional adventurers and explorers mirrored the colonizers who came into contact with a myriad of hitherto previously "unknown" peoples.[4] The readers of such fantastic and exciting stories were, therefore, able to participate in the colonial process, consuming tales of conquest, glory, and exotic Others.

Nascent capitalist empires spurred such endeavors and shaped the rhetoric of them.[5] Critically, because the nations that became the target of colonial ambition were not Western, the colonial discourses of the time framed them as experiencing an "earlier stage of Western social development," thus projecting colonizing processes as a "natural" part of their progression.[6] The "progress" that colonization brings is clearly defined from a Eurocentric perspective—one that, for the colonizers, justifies the need to transform populations from their "savage," feral, and unenlightened states to the agendas of the "superior" white empire builders. The Social Darwinist narratives that dominated expansionist discourses of the time rationalized the need, and even the perceived *duty*, of colonizing forces to carry out their expansion plans.[7] These adventure stories persuaded their readers of the greatness of imperialism and adventure.

Such glorious pursuits became formative to science fiction: the scope of European expansion around the world eventually rendered most of Earth's population as "discovered," so in due course the authors of adventure tales turned to a new, mostly unexamined frontier to satisfy their lust for thrills: that of space.[8] Those nation states that have a history of colonization and empire building—for example, the United States, the United Kingdom, Germany, France, Soviet Russia, and Japan—also have generated most of the world's science fiction. This positive correlation exists in part because SF recapitulates colonial ambition and empire building through its fictional narratives.[9] The colonial conquests of the nation entered into new terrain as the SF genres that each country spawned reimagined the imperial agendas in SF scenarios—consequently, the conditions of actual imperialism become the "growing pains of the imaginary Empire" in SF.[10] The relationship between historical forms of colonialism and emergent SF is foundational to the genre,[11] so much so that "no informed reader can doubt that allusions to colonial history and situations are ubiquitous features of early science fiction motifs and plots."[12] By the turn of the 20th century, galactic empires had entered into pulp SF territory as author Robert W. Cole "imagined Victoria's glorious British Empire extending its dominion to the stars, so that ours should not be the only sun never to set upon it."[13]

Despite the real world limitations of physics, SF writers embraced the potential for human adventure at a galactic level, thus expanding the potential for human empire building beyond the confines of Earth.[14] Important contributors to the development of the SF genre including Isaac Asimov, E. E. Smith, and Edmund Hamilton all forefronted imperial ambition in their major works.[15] In particular, Asimov founded the future history narrative in imperial terms.[16] Themes of empire, colonization and federation dominated the pulp world of the era,[17] and, of course, Hubbard was a part of this emergent genre.[18] The works of these and later SF writers are not necessarily meant to be predictive in nature; instead the use of empire and colonialism in SF is an effective way to critique human abuses of power during Earthbound colonial enterprises.[19]

While imperial goals are linked to capitalist enterprise and therefore can be understood as economic policy, Csicsery-Ronay Jr. (2003) proposes that just as important is an understanding of the role of developing technologies in colonial nation states and the potential to implement, as SF narratives illustrate, "technoscientific regimes" at a global level.[20] The particular technologies, whether forms of weaponry, modes of transportation, or even medical advances, all facilitated imperial ambitions. Moreover, these new technologies provided the fuel for SF narratives that pushed the boundaries of scientific and technological advances further still.[21] By the early to mid-20th century, American SF stories incorporated and fantasized the potentials of actual new technologies: SF writers imagined nuclear power, for example, as a technology, that if realized, would bring about immense positive social progress. This optimism was quashed after the bombing of Hiroshima. Henceforth, the transformative potential of nuclear technologies took on a very different meaning.[22]

The imperial trajectory of Hubbard's homeland, the United States, was quite different from that of European nations. Because the United States revolted *against* British colonial rule early in its history, it self-identified as "anticolonial" preferring to consider itself a benefactor to those territories that it has since come to "administer."[23] American SF, however, is like other national bodies of SF literature, steeped in imperial and colonial tropes. Perhaps the margins of British colonialism in the new world and subsequent American expansion plans as codified in Manifest Destiny (as well as American "pursuits" in the Philippines, Guam, and elsewhere[24]) are blurred so that the *reality* of American colonialism is reenacted in SF while the anticolonial rhetoric is continued at the state level.

Masters of Their Universes

Who were the colonizers in American, European, and others' histories? Who reenacted these colonial histories in pulp adventure and SF novels? The masculine ideals for empire-building men found their way into the popular literature of colonizing nation states, such that the heroic adventures of heterosexual, white men came to dominate not only the political narratives of colonialism, but also colonial adventure fiction and science fiction. (Moreover, most religions have been, and remain, patriarchal in nature; science too has been largely a masculine endeavor until relatively recently—and in some fields, it still is.)

Woollacott (2006) examined British imperial ideal masculinity for young boys and men as crafted during the Victorian and Edwardian eras. Authors rewrote the male exploits of the British Empire in books for boys so that "imperial annexation, expansion, aggressive posturing, and outright warfare" were supported as the exemplar to a generation of British males.[25] Similarly, American pulp publications crafted a hypermasculinity, presenting to their readers a series of rugged, assertive, goal-oriented and successful adventuring men in pulp Westerns, colonial adventure stories, naval and military tales and more.[26] Amy Kaplan's analysis of late 19th-century American novels identifies that "Nationhood and manhood have long been intimately related in American history through the dynamic of territorial expansion."[27] The expansion of one's empire becomes a reflection of one's masculinity.[28]

Power, control, adventure, and conquest were specifically male pursuits—and they came to be reenacted through cultural products such as books, magazines, comics, and movies. Looking to SF stories, one can see that heroic male protagonists did not *necessarily* have to be physically assertive—indeed, often they were not. Instead, their heroism and superiority emerged from their intellectual and visionary abilities. Indeed, these were consistent themes, so that regardless of the specific details of the plot, we are left with the "recurring story of a young man and his initiation into the masculine mysteries of science."[29] A particular "superman" archetype emerged out of the SF literature: the scientist as superman is a man of knowledge, one who is able to control his environment by achieving mastery over all problems that he might encounter. SF stories projected the evolution of these men over time to become superior humans with advanced mental capabilities.[30] And, of course, technology is an integral part of this superman ideal: these men of science could invent all manner of ingenious technological advances.

Hence, the trope of the superiority of white men dominated much of the SF of the era—and in this regard the influence of Social Darwinism emerges once more. Indeed, as Bould and Vint (2011) note, the exploits of hetero-sexual, white men characterized the majority of science fiction from the early 20th century on.[31]

Pairing the masculine pursuit for adventure and conquest with the vision-ary man of science and ideal superman, we see a tapestry of ideas emerge in the literature that inspired Hubbard *and* to which he was a contributing author. (And, as Attebery [2006] remarks, Hubbard's fiction books and his Dianetics and Scientology proposals revolve around the same hypothesis: "that the mind's untapped powers could transform ordinary humans into psy-chic supermen."[32])

These narratives that packaged motifs of colonialism, adventure, sci-ence and technological advancement, and much more, positioned men as discoverers, conquerors, and heroes: the key progenitors and builders of all that was and would become important to the human condition.[33] One need only peruse the front covers of such popular literature to ascertain the importance of men to the storylines. Images of strong, dashing, adventurers, men of groundbreaking scientific research, and swashbuckling saviors of vulnerable populations, (not to mention passive and defenseless women) capture the essence of what readers would consume in the pages therein. Men, of course, were also the *authors* of the vast majority of SF stories. Girls and women were not considered intellectual enough—not scientific enough—to understand such masculine pleasures. Certainly, they could not write such work, and surely, they would not read it either. Carter (1977) identifies that this condescension helps to explain why "pulp science fiction for so many years was virtually an all-male ghetto."[34]

Locating Religion in the Colonial Process: Enlightening or Tyrannical?

Colonialism and religion are "intimately interrelated" for a number of reasons, not least because religion has often been used as a rationalization for colonization in the first place.[35] Most frequently, Christianity, both in Catholic and Protestant forms—has been associated with colonial expansion throughout history, although other religions including Islam and even Buddhism have prospered due to colonial projects.[36] Although sectarian and cultic religions have never had the political backing, social dominance, and, therefore, power to initiate or inspire imperial goals, they often do succeed in nation states and regions of the world where European and American colonization has taken place already. Consequently, in the shadow of official forms of Christianity, sectarian movements such as the Jehovah's Witnesses and the Latter-Day Saints (Mormons), are able to proselytize beyond their country of origin.

Some anthropologists have conceived of the religious conversion that takes place alongside imperial projects as a "colonization of consciousness." According to this model of conversion, the colonizers directly attempt to convert the subjects to their religious ideology, while at a much more profound level, a complete "reformation" from the preexisting culture takes place.[37] Suffice it is to say, this approach is highly critical of religion's relationship to colonization and assumes that the preexisting beliefs and culture are preferable to the new one.[38] Historians have reconsidered the work of religious (usually Christian) missionaries from seeing them first, as benevolent outreach workers, to later, realizing them as fervent ideologues willing to rationalize all manner of immoral practices for the colonial state. Often, however, the missionaries conformed to neither end of these conceptual extremities.[39]

Science fiction, too, typically treats religion with a great deal of suspicion, skepticism, and even hostility. As such, SF authors have incorporated religion into their story lines so that it appears as a superstitious, uncivilized practice—one that alien "Others," engage in. In such narratives, archaic superstitious beliefs are vanquished by rationalist-scientific thinking and discourses.[40] Religion is presented not only as "primitive" but also as "dangerous and misleading." Often, in such settings, religion is presented as so powerful that humans and alien populations alike are unable to reject and eliminate it from society.[41] This disdain has not resulted in religion's expulsion from the genre. On the contrary, SF, has "*always* been preoccupied with religion, even if only as its antagonist."[42] The very ubiquity of religious belief systems on Earth seems to ensure that SF writers *must* tackle it not only here as an earthly phenomenon, but also as one on other planets and in other cosmic dimensions. Put simply, SF cannot ignore religion.

Somewhat paradoxically, religion and SF actually have some common features, especially when one considers them from a functional standpoint.[43] Hence, although SF tends to be characterized by rationalist discourses one can see that science fiction functions, like religion, in the following ways: it proposes ideas and theories about the nature of humanity,[44] it offers deeply prophetic glimpses into our future,[45] and it regularly examines the nature of salvation.[46] Concerning the latter point, SF narratives frequently depict messiah-like figures who guide humans to a better future and society.[47] As Engler suggests, both religion and SF "explore[s] the links between short-term individual agency and long-term social and cosmic order."[48] Historically, human custom, as shaped by religion, has been to assess how our behaviors in this lifetime have bearing on a larger transcendent order.[49]

Pushing the comparison between SF and religion further, Adam Roberts concludes—while acknowledging that not all would agree with him—that, "at a basic level religion is in the business of extrapolating elaborate and fantastical narratives out of reality, making them not only internally consistent and credible (as far as possible) but also beguiling, offering people magic and meaning, consolation and a sense of wonder lacking from the mundane. SF is in exactly the same business."[50]

To understand how the aforementioned motifs coalesce to form a lens through which one can further view Hubbard and Scientology, I turn now to the core analyses of this chapter. Hubbard is a difficult individual to understand fully, and it is not my intention to provide a chronologic biography or psychological assessment of him here—others have done so already.[51] Rather, I discuss Hubbard, his influences, his ambitions, and his achievements, by paying particular attention to the facets of his life that might help us comprehend better the imperial and colonial themes evident in his life's works and the ways that they came together with his science fiction *as* reality.[52]

HUBBARD'S QUEST FOR IMPERIAL ADVENTURE

As a colonial force, Scientology does not conform to typical expectations of societal dominance, integration with political power, and so forth. Instead, Scientology's imperial desires were born from the explicit ambitions of its founder, L. Ron Hubbard, and the influences on his life: science fiction and adventure stories, his time in the U.S. Navy, and his exposure to different cultures and societies, to name just a few. How Hubbard viewed himself and others is important to comprehending the development of imperial and colonial motifs in his life and beliefs.[53]

By the time Hubbard was just a young man, he had indeed experienced a great deal of travel and adventure himself. (Throughout his life, he had been keen not only to explore at every opportunity but also to craft the *image* of explorer whenever possible.[54]) Hubbard's father was in the U.S. Navy, so consequently, Hubbard traveled with his family when his father was stationed in Guam. Hubbard claimed that he traveled extensively in Asia, although Miller (1987) found that his travels were less widespread than he had stated.[55] During World War II, Hubbard served with the U.S. Navy, but again Hubbard's version of his service is at odds with official documentation. Rather than being an accomplished war veteran and hero as he claimed, naval records show that he was given very little responsibility and that his superiors considered him quite incompetent.[56] Nonetheless, Hubbard self-identified as a consummate hero, explorer, and adventurer akin to the masculine ideals presented in pulp tales, which, by 1934, he was also writing.[57]

Hubbard came of age during a time of deep adventurous romanticism and idealism. The ideals of masculine adventure permeated Hubbard's vision of what an ideal life should look like. In the May 1935 edition of the magazine, *Thrilling Adventures*, Hubbard responded to a letter from a fan who had asked him for advice about traveling to China and Mexico. In his response, Hubbard sympathized with the questioner's quest for further adventure, saying, "The idea may sound nutty, but all adventure comes from loco thoughts. A sane man isn't apt to stumble into excitement, because, consciously or unconsciously, he is plotting twenty-four hours a day how to save himself the trouble of being annoyed."[58] It seems that Hubbard needed adventure; he needed to have the constant stimulation and excitement of planning and enacting his plans for exploration. Writing in his journal in 1943, he reflected: "The anatomy of adventure has been explored quite often. Young men are born with a will to it . . ." Hubbard lamented, however, that often men do not fulfil this will, succumbing, instead, to material comforts and marriage. In this lengthy journal entry, he mourns the loss of any real further space in the world left for adventure, identifying that all has been seen and done already. In perhaps a telling statement, he wrote, "I am restless still. I have no goal short of the planets and stars . . ."[59]

Although Hubbard continued to travel, it seems that he found new and more compelling adventures in the human mind. Combining the new technologies and concepts of SF stories with the thrill of adventure tales, Hubbard presented Dianetics to the world.[60] He wrote: "Dianetics is an adventure. It is an exploration into *terra incognita*, the human mind, that vast and hitherto unknown realm half an inch back of our foreheads."[61] He continued, "Your first voyage into your own *terra incognita* will be through the pages of this book." And so, for Scientologists, the term "*terra incognita*" became synonymous with "the human mind."[62] So too began Hubbard's plans to explore, document, and colonize this complex space. In this case, the *practice* of empire was auditing; the new technology of empire[63] was the E-meter (which was, according to Hubbard, "better known as a 'lie detector'"[64]). Hubbard's exploration into *terra incognita* would become a defining feature of Scientology because it provided the portal through which he could conquer enemy thetans.

Themes of colonial ambition emerged on many fronts in Hubbard's world. After determining the importance of *terra incognita*, he had to figure out ways to realize his ambitions. One such way was to establish institutional dominance within nation states—an ambitious goal by anyone's standards. An unusual piece of the "Hubbard puzzle" is important in this regard: Hubbard believed that he was the reincarnation of British business tycoon and imperialist Cecil Rhodes[65] after whom Rhodesia (now, Zimbabwe) was named. His belief that he was the reincarnation of Rhodes is significant: that he self-identified with one of the most ambitious British imperialists bolsters further the image of Hubbard as a man for whom expansionist plans knew no limitations. Having believed that he had been a successful colonizer in a past life, there was no reason for Hubbard to fear failure in his present one. Moreover, he often articulated his plans in bold terms, once stating, "We own quite a bit of property over the world. We will be acquiring more, as well as some countries."[66]

When his mission to establish institutional influence at the level of government, education, mental health, and so forth failed in Australia,[67] he went to Rhodesia, where, upon his arrival, he drafted and presented to Ian Smith's then government, a new constitution for the country. This constitution claimed to foster greater equality between black and white populations, although the details of it revealed that it would ensure the maintenance of white power. Despite his efforts to ingratiate himself with politicians, the business community, and the press, the government denied Hubbard temporary residence and forced him to leave the country.[68] Episodes such as this one might have quashed the goals and confidence of many individuals, and while Hubbard did have his demons, he always regrouped and continued with his plans for expanding Scientology across the globe. Similar attempts were made in Corfu and Morocco. Depending on the nation state in question, Scientology crafts its image in a manner that is most likely to be receptive to the host under consideration.[69] Moreover, Scientology has maintained the mandate of "Getting the technology of LRH [i.e., Scientology's founder L. Ron Hubbard] into new territories of the world."[70]

Hubbard's exposure to colonial ideas came from other areas of his life too, including from the science fiction culture of which he was a member. He was regular contributor to John Campbell's, *Astounding Science Fiction*,[71] the leading SF magazine during the Golden Age of the genre. Hubbard was part of a group of writers whose stories focused on themes of great technological and scientific progress—including those stories that proposed that such advancements would foster greater spiritual understanding and experiences.[72] The Othering of alien entities, the colonization of other planets, and the battling of evil aliens was standard fare in pulp SF. Certainly, the superiority of white men (especially scientists) was taken for granted in these narratives. According to SF writer, Isaac Asimov, Campbell came to prefer to publish the kind of SF stories that specifically depicted the superiority of the human species above all others. Indeed, Asimov reported that Campbell "did seem to take for granted, somehow, the stereotype of the Nordic white as the true representative of Man the Explorer, Man the Darer, Man the Victor."[73] No doubt, this sensibility aligned with Hubbard's (and probably with many other writers during the period). Not only did Hubbard identify the importance of exploration, but evidence exists that he considered *white* men as superior to others.[74] While such racism might appear at odds with Hubbard's claimed goals for equality and freedom for all in addition to his seemingly inclusive approach to other cultures (e.g., his discussion of the Blackfoot in North America[75]), one can discern a deeper sense of superiority in his narratives—one that mirrors the colonial claims of "civilizing" others for their "own benefit."[76] Hubbard's view of non-Scientologists, those uncolonized others, is enlightening also: he referred to them as "WOGS," which is a deeply offensive racial slur first used by British colonizers and that persists in racist discourses both in the United Kingdom and in Australia.[77]

COLONIZING *TERRA INCOGNITA* WITH THETANS AND OTHER COSMIC DEMONS

Hubbard's concept of the thetan evolved over time during the course of his various lectures and writings, and it came to occupy a prominent position in Scientology theology. Eventually, Hubbard proposed that the presence of body thetans posed the most significant threat to human well-being: by occupying our bodies and influencing our behaviors, they impede our abilities to become free from psychic and physical pains. Delving into *terra incognita* via auditing and other procedures became absolutely essential to their removal. Thus, the need to clear the planet and even the universe (the latter being one of the goals of the Sea Org) became imperative.

When Hubbard claimed to have broken the "the wall of fire" (the Xenu narrative also known as "Incident II") and survived, he stated that he acquired devastating knowledge through this bizarre experience—knowledge that Scientologists only receive upon completion of OT III. At this point, Scientologists are informed that 75 million years ago, Xenu, the ruler of a Galactic Confederacy of 178 billion people, 26 stars and 76 planets including Earth (or "Teegeeack" as it was then known), conducted atrocities in order to solve the confederacy's pressing overpopulation issues. Xenu seconded the excess population to Teegeeack (in planes that were like DC-8s). There, the confederacy placed the unfortunate populous inside volcanoes and then bombarded them with hydrogen bombs. The spirits of these individuals—or thetans—then were subjected to religious and technological implants for 36 days (priests and psychiatrists supervised these implants, known as the R6 implants). Then the thetans were sent on to either Hawaii or Los Palmas where they were clustered together. According to Hubbard, clusters of *body thetans* attach themselves to humans, causing many problems for them. The story of Xenu's conduct ends when he is captured six years later and imprisoned in a mountain where he remains still.[78]

Hubbard proposed that every person on Earth *is* a thetan, in that thetans reside *in* human bodies. Hubbard claimed that this bodily occupation could be compared to the concept of *spirit*. Thetans relocate from one human to another at the point of an individual's physical death,[79] and Hubbard identified them as being responsible for the core disposition and personality of persons.[80] Due to their infinite existences, thetans create a great deal of accumulated trauma for the individual currently under occupation. As such, the thetans' previous lives, memories, and implants generate anxiety, stress, and irrationality for the human in which they reside. In turn, these emotional and mental states obstruct individuals from achieving their full abilities and potentials.[81]

A recurring event on the *whole track* (Hubbard's term for the complete history of the universe—one that is trillions of years old[82]) is the forcible implantation (by a variety of alien entities at off-Earth locales) of false information (on a wide variety of topics including religion) in thetans while they are "between lives." Hubbard described implants as a way to "dispose of captured armies" as "a means to overwhelm the thetan" or to "'fit' a thetan to a colonization project," among many other objectives. Furthermore, implants are responsible for "all varieties of illness, apathy, degradation, neurosis and insanity."[83] Hubbard claimed that *all* people on Earth are implanted[84] and that implants have occurred over vast periods of time. The necessary task of converting all of Earth's inhabitants to Scientology remains vital.

Aside from the problem of thetans, Hubbard's version of the universe includes a number of other enemies also. One such cosmic entity was Arsclycus—an ancient and ever-expanding society "not built on a planet, it was just built in space." He claimed that people were brought to Arsclycus to work as slaves. Moreover, each time they perished, they arrived back yet again, sometimes for about 10,000 successive lifetimes. Eventually, due to the unsustainable nature of its expansion, Arsclycus blew up.[85] Another enemy, the Helatrobus regime, was guilty of implanting numerous implants that transpired around 52 and 38 trillion years ago.[86]

Perhaps the most prominent enemy is the malevolent Marcab Confederacy (of which the warlord, Xenu, is a part). It is composed of "various planets united into a very vast civilization which has come forward up through the last 200,000 years, and is formed out of the fragments of earlier civilizations."[87] The Marcabs are particularly important because of their alleged role in an upcoming violent takeover of Earth. In 1980, Hubbard decided to release a hitherto secret message to Scientologists who had achieved the level of OT VIII. In it, he outlined the Marcab Confederacy's plans to return to Earth in a "mass Marcabian landing." In this alarming disclosure, he warned that some of their enemies have arrived on Earth already, and are "in the general populace."[88]

According to Hubbard, this final conquest of Earth has been part of a much larger project—one that has seen the "enslavement of mankind" by the world's religions—a deliberative ploy by the Marcabs to make us entirely malleable. A series of implants, ones that "gives the subject population greater and greater susceptibility to the telepathic impingement and direction of the controllers" have contributed to this end. Hubbard claimed that most of this information is readily available in Revelation in the Bible, just embedded in the language of Christianity. As such, he claimed, "My mission could be said to fulfil the Biblical promise represented by this brief anti-Christ period. During this period there is a fleeting opportunity for the whole scenario to be effectively derailed." Hubbard goes on to identify that he would depart his present body soon and would return as a political figure so as to "postpone and then halt a series of events designed to make happy slaves of us all."[89]

The galaxy, however, is populated by yet other entities with colonial ambitions. Part of another galactic society, *invader forces*, are, according to Hubbard, an "electronics people" who evolved in a different manner from humans due to their home being a "heavy gravity planet." These forces have endeavored to exact imperial control over the entire MEST universe.[90] Only one of the five forces has yet to attempt an invasion, but Hubbard advised that they will try to do so several million years from now.[91] Each invader force is physically different and Hubbard describes a typical member of the *fifth invader force* as perceiving itself as a "very strange insect-like creature with unthinkably horrible hands."[92]

In addition to these galactic enemies with which most humans were unfamiliar, Hubbard revealed with his 1968 policy, "The War," a more recognizable enemy within the empire—psychiatrists.[93] According to Hubbard, psychiatrists (and other mental health professionals) are responsible for all that ails Western nations, including criminal behavior. Indeed, Hubbard identified that psychiatry was the "*sole* cause of humanity's decline."[94] Since the publication of Dianetics, Hubbard had taken it upon himself to replace psychiatry with Dianetics and then Scientology. While psychiatrists are recognizable citizens of contemporaneous planet Earth, Hubbard cast them also as part of his space opera mythology, claiming that they, along with priests, had been responsible for implanting thetans during Incident II. Consequently, both priests and psychiatrists "were the ultimate embodiment of evil."[95] Taking on such an apparently fierce enemy did not phase Hubbard. Used to the idea of forging new territories for himself and tackling combative enemies, Hubbard stated simply, "It is a tough war. All wars are tough. It isn't over."[96] Aside from psychiatrists, Hubbard identified other people, too, as enemies. For example, any person he a declared Suppressive Person (SP) became, de facto, an enemy of Scientology. Additionally, those individuals he identified as Potential Trouble Sources (PTSs) might eventually become foes of Hubbard and Scientology, if their behavior is not "corrected."[97]

Maintaining Hubbard's empire of the mind—one that opened the portal to galactic empires and enemies, required a number of surveillance strategies.[98] Scientology auditing is the most common form of colonial maintenance, eliciting as it does doctrinal conformity via surveillance measures including confessions.[99] One form of auditing is Security Checking,[100] a process that uses an E-Meter to detect violations to the Scientology code of conduct. According to Hubbard, they were "remedy[ing] the compulsion or obsession to commit acts which have to be withheld, i.e. we are remedying unreasonable action." He continued, "A **check** is made to see whether a person has any counter-intentions toward Scn or Scientology Churches."[101] Security Checks can incorporate an immense variety of questions, but some of them clearly point to the pressing problems of power, empire, colonization, and insurgency. The following is a sample of such questions: "Have you ever enslaved a population?"; "Have you ever implanted anyone?"; "Have you ever annihilated a population?"; "Have you ever destroyed a culture?"; "Have you ever bred bodies for degrading purposes?"; "Did you come to Earth for evil purposes?"; "Have you ever caused a planet to disappear?"; "Have you ever started a war?"; "Have you ever torn out someone's tongue?"; "Do you deserve to be free?"; and "Do you deserve to be enslaved?"[102]

Taken together, these ideas about colonizing forces and malevolent enemies foster in Scientologists an urgency around the need to create a globalized Scientology protectorate. The necessity of defending Earth from an array of terrible enemies becomes ever clearer for Scientologists as they advance up through the Scientology hierarchy.

HUBBARD'S COSMIC NAVY: THE SEA ORG

"The Sea Organization is the actual nexus that controls the Scientology empire."[103]

Both in early SF novels and in scientific and political discourses, sea and space offered the promise of resources and knowledge, if colonized. Melissa Lingen noted that "While sea travel is less common in science fiction than space travel, its assumptions and preoccupations have shaped the genre."[104] Consequently, "The language of sea travel has made its way into air and space throughout the history of science fiction."[105] Moreover, the parallels in language likely stem from the fact that "The tropes of sea voyages also provide familiarity in tales of space travel."[106]

If one understands Scientology as, in part, a space opera narrative—one that draws on the tropes of colonial adventure, then SF scholar John Rieder's definition of space opera is fruitful given my discussion here of the Sea Org. He defines space opera as:

> that group of narratives that revivifies the moribund adventure romance plots of nineteenth-century imperialist popular culture by imagining outer space as a larger version of the terrestrial ocean, treating space vehicles as if they were high tech sailing ships and the distance and differences between planets or solar systems as if they were merely the distances and differences between continents.[107]

While space travel might offer humans with potential colonies in the future, sea travel, has, historically, been the key vehicle for empire building on Earth. As an "old school" adventurer who also embraced the technologies of new sciences, Hubbard felt equally at home journeying the oceans as he did journeying the cosmos (if only in his mind). Moreover, it was while on a sea voyage that took him to Las Palmas in the Canary Islands that Hubbard claimed to have traveled through the "Wall of Fire," a seemingly intangible portal that allowed him to take the ultimate adventure into the mysteries of the human condition. This time-traveling experience transcended the impossibilities of actual science and allowed Hubbard to bolster his claims to being the sole purveyor of truth.

Hubbard designed the Sea Org as kind of space navy, melding SF space ideas with Earthbound naval ones. Moreover, the Sea Org comprises Scientology's "aristocracy"—those most dedicated to Scientology's missions both on Earth and across the universe with the goal of "clearing" both.[108] The Sea Org's motto, "We Come Back,"[109] indicates its members' constant reincarnation within the cosmos. Sea Org members must sign a billion-year contract that illustrates their commitment to "return life after life to fulfill 'Ron's purpose.'"[110] Moreover, as Jon Atack recalls, an apparently confidential Sea Org directive "claimed that governments of the world were on the verge of collapse. The Sea Org would survive and pick up the pieces."[111] Incorporating naval-style uniforms and ranks, and the trappings and etiquette of naval life, the Sea Org allowed Hubbard to present himself to his most dedicated followers as *commodore*. More critically, having clashed with national authorities in several nation states, the Sea Org offered Hubbard protection from national rule and summons. On international waters he felt safe to continue the expansion of his reach; consequently, Hubbard spent several years continuously at sea.

Hubbard's *A Mission into Time* recounts the first voyage of the newly formed Sea Org. The introduction of the book identifies that the work within is the result of "an exploration into time *and* space." His trip to the Mediterranean, the objective of which was to search for past lives through a "test whole track recall . . . combined all the know-how of a life's work on land and sea and with the mind and spirit."[112] Despite the mission, this short book does not actually reveal that much; rather it is a quite mundane account of visits to various ancient Mediterranean sites. More revealing is Jon Atack's account of some of the events that took place as Hubbard attempted to confirm his own discoveries of the true nature of human history.

Atack identifies that during the Sea Org's mission to the Mediterranean, Hubbard told the crew of a concealed "space station" in the northern part of the Greek island of Corsica. Allegedly, the space station stored "an immense Mothership and a fleet of smaller spacecraft" that would be accessible to Hubbard because their designers had "predicted Hubbard's palm print"—which was how the space station would be accessed. Sea Org members were excited by the prospect that Hubbard might leave Earth on the Mothership, perhaps in order to establish a "Space Org." Unfortunately for them, Hubbard aborted his galactic mission when he ran into trouble with Spanish port authorities.[113]

Despite obstacles and drawbacks, Hubbard always had several plans for furthering the Scientology empire and for dealing with enemies in it. Former

Scientologist, Jesse Prince, claims that Hubbard issued a series of unusual directives to Sea Org members. For example, those residing "in the Advanced Orgs [run by Sea Org members] in Edinburgh and Los Angeles, staff were ordered to wear all-white uniforms, with silver boots, to mimic the Galactic Patrol of seventy-five million years before." He also circulated a mandate called "Zones of Action" to all Sea Orgs that summarized his plans:

> Scientology was going to take over those areas controlled by Smersh (the evil organization fought by the fictional James Bond), rake in enormous amounts of cash, clean up psychotherapy, infiltrate and reorganize every minority group, and befriend the worst foes of the Western nations. Hubbard's stated intention was to undermine a supposed Fascist conspiracy to rule the world.[114]

The Sea Org was Hubbard's mobile center of operations—an administrative body from which he could run his empire and plan future conquests. It epitomized Hubbard's love of both sea and space motifs, offering as it did, a way for him to allegedly traverse the boundaries between the two realms. The Sea Org's time spent afloat came to an end by the mid-70s, but its mission continues from Scientology's Flag Land Base in Clearwater, Florida.[115]

A MAN OF GREAT IMPORTANCE

In the first edition of *Dianetics: The Modern Science of Mental Health*, Hubbard confidently announced that "The creation of dianetics is a milestone for Man comparable to his discovery of fire and superior to his inventions of the wheel and arch."[116] From this statement and countless others, Hubbard clearly believed in his own self-importance as the world's foremost thinker, inventor, and scientist.[117] Hubbard's evolution of self, had, at its core, an unwavering sense of superiority, and as one can see from his Scientology space opera narratives, he considered himself the savior of the universe: he alone could conquer our enemies, and, at the same time, build an empire that would maintain the security of Earth's inhabitants for millennia to come. Like the imperialists of history, as well as those in novels and pulp fiction, he appeared unstoppable. This allegedly time- and dimension-traveling figure, who claimed to have proven historians wrong,[118] presented himself as the means to human progress and prosperity.

Despite the difficulties involved in establishing the "facts" of Hubbard's life, what is evident, is that Hubbard *did* travel, he *did* indeed encounter an array of cultures and experiences at a young age, and, perhaps most significantly, he was in possession of a vivid and seemingly limitless imagination. As Hugh Urban comments,

> Perhaps the one truly unique feature of Hubbard's biography is that *he was himself a prolific author of science fiction and fantasy tales and thus had an unusually creative hand in the elaboration of his own narrative.* Indeed, he effectively fashioned the story of a hero—even a superhero. (emphasis in original)[119]

Hubbard fused the ideals of science fiction superhero with those of religious savior. As McKee remarks, "There are inherent messianic qualities in the SF concept of the superhero—an individual with exceptional abilities who sacrifices part of his or her life for the greater good."[120] The dual tropes of the archetypal SF superman and the imperial explorer and adventurer come together in Hubbard's self-identity. Hubbard's masculinity—his ideal view of himself blended the exemplars generated both in colonial fiction and in science fiction.

Hubbard's identity seems to have emerged out of the fantastic tales of his generation—tales that he would reenact as reality with himself as the "good guy" hero. At times, he did quite candidly reveal a darker side to his goals. For example, one of his affirmations, "All men shall be my slaves. All women shall succumb to my charms. All mankind shall grovel at my feet and not know why,"[121] offers a telling glimpse into his ambitions and his perceived capabilities. As the colonial hero of his SF space opera fantasy, Hubbard regarded himself as the only leader that the residents of Earth need follow. To achieve this end, it appears that he was willing to systematically set out and enforce his vision. At a time when the United States was claiming the title as the most powerful nation on Earth, Hubbard had declared himself its most important, its most enlightened, and its most knowledgeable man. His power derived from his claim to understand the reality of the human condition and his ability to offer solutions to it.

CONCLUSION

I began this chapter by reiterating my prior observation that many of Hubbard's key Scientology narratives are essentially retellings of human history and the human condition as a SF space opera chronicle. The purpose of this chapter has been to elaborate on Hubbard's incorporation of some of the fundamental elements of the early (and contemporary) SF tradition and their emergence out of real-world social and political conditions. Consequently,

I have looked at the connections between "real world" masculinity, religion, and empire, their subsequent usage in the SF genre, and their incorporation in both forms into Hubbard's ideologies.

By terraforming the human mind to be receptive to new claims about the nature of the universe, Hubbard laid the foundations for his own empire within *terra incognita*. The process of empire building took on multiple dimensions as Hubbard first prepared the *terra* with new knowledge and then proceeded to establish a large bureaucracy around this new information. This process began with Dianetics and continued through Scientology, and incorporated a wealth of ideas and plans gleaned from his entire life's experiences.

As with the goals of colonial nations, Scientology encourages the "civilizing" practice of its doctrines so that the uninitiated/uncolonized might be able to "improve" their state, all while the explicit goals of empire are conducted. Scientology's promises to make the world a better place were, and remain, compelling objectives for many committed Scientologists. The goal to expand Scientology around the globe makes sense in terms of helping humanity on Earth and in the cosmos beyond. Hubbard's SF—and other— narratives compel Scientologists to be agents of social change. Hence, Scientologists, like many protagonists in SF novels, are driven by the assumption that they bring about "progress" within their own and other cultures that they encounter. The imperial and colonial dimensions of SF space opera narratives find parallels in Hubbard's mythologies: thetans, invader forces, psychiatrists, psychologists, and Marcabs—all these entities are enemies in Hubbard's empire. A paradox lies in Hubbard's ideology: in vanquishing the enemies of other empires we must submit ourselves fully to the conditions of his.

While colonization of *terra incognita* necessitated a leap of faith into alternative dimensions, histories, and conceptions of self, the management of this new empire required a material bureaucratic structure—one that could navigate the problems generated by the tangible conditions of human reality. The operation of Hubbard's empire required a great deal of administrative work, and Hubbard established many Scientology Orgs around the globe so that he could spread Scientology's reach and at the same time, institute the appropriate maintenance and control over his territory. The Hubbard Communications Office (HCO), for example, provided a means for Hubbard to disseminate information and policy (via HCO Bulletins) to all Scientology groups around the world. The Guardian's Office (later renamed the Office of Special Affairs) was established in 1966 to defend Scientology "against its many real and imagined enemies."[122] According to Hubbard's wife, Mary-Sue Hubbard (who was the head of the Guardian's Office), the primary goal of it was "to sweep aside opposition sufficiently to create a vacuum into which Scientology can expand."[123] Under an intelligence gathering mandate, the

Guardian's Office became adept at acquiring information, often with the end goal of silencing its critics and dispensing with the competition.

Hubbard had always envisioned the implementation of a grand plan—a set of strategies that would realize both the immaterial and physical empires that he sought. This plan inhabits the very fabric of Scientology—often implicitly so. At times, however, Hubbard was very forthright in his approach to empire building. The systematic nature of Hubbard's plans are illustrated in the secret Guardian Order 060971 (seized by the FBI) in which Scientology's colonization goals are set out clearly. In this document, Hubbard identified "vital targets" that would require actions such as "Depopularizing the enemy to the point of obliteration" as well as "Taking over the control or allegiance of the heads or proprietors of all news media" and by "Taking over the control or allegiance of key political figures." Finally, by "Taking over the control or allegiance of those who monitor international finance,"[124] Scientology could secure its dominance at a global level. Evidently, Scientology's quest for a material bureaucratic empire, that could foster the continuance of his control of *terra incognita*, was thoroughly laid out over a series of evolving strategies. As Stephen Kent observes, "Not only does Scientology attempt to contain, if not eradicate, perceived enemies who might limit its international resource acquisitions and operations; it also endeavors to gain support and resources from persons and organizations among national and international elites."[125] Consequently, Scientology engages in multipronged attacks against a variety of influential and "elite" institutions and groups, including, as Kent (1999) illustrates, psychiatry, the Cult Awareness Network (CAN) and even Interpol.[126]

Perhaps one of Scientology's most "successful," but nonetheless tumultuous, imperial ambitions has been its presence in, or "occupation of"[127] the town of Clearwater in Florida. Scientology began acquiring properties in the town in 1975, beginning with the purchase of the stately (but rather rundown) Fort Harrison Hotel. In order to establish its new spiritual headquarters there, the Flag Land Base, Scientologists were ordered to "identify key media and political leaders and either win their allegiance or, if that failed, discredit them through a variety of covert tactics"[128] From the start, Scientology antagonized the local population: secrecy, surveillance tactics, attempts to ruin the then mayor Gabriel Cazares's reputation, harassment of locals, and the infiltration of Scientologists into key employment positions (including the Chamber of Commerce) all contributed to a great deal of anxiety and ill-feeling in the town.[129] The extent of Scientology's disruption in Clearwater has been immense and the strained relationship has continued unabated.

During his lifetime, Hubbard founded an empire of the mind that required a material superstructure to support it. It seems likely that Hubbard traversed the immaterial and material worlds of his empire through the portals of his own mind. Uninhibited by the strictures of our largely shared physical reality, like the protagonists of many a SF novel, Hubbard found alternative means to enter into concealed dimensions—ones where he could experience different realities that he would then share with his most dedicated followers. But this sharing of knowledge was not democratic. Rather, Hubbard fashioned an elaborate and costly system of dissemination for the ever-evolving ideology that he proposed. Hence, *the Bridge to Total Freedom* ensured that the costs of empire building could be sustained.

NOTES

1. Hubbard proposed that we have many body thetans and that extensive auditing (Scientology's form of therapy) is required in order to free us from them. According to Hubbard, although we need to eradicate the majority of these invasive thetans, we are possessed by one that is a "good fit" that will allow us to develop our true potentials—to become "Operating Thetans." For a succinct summary of thetans and Hubbard's approach to dealing with them, see Hugh Urban, *The Church of Scientology: A History of a New Religion* (Princeton: Princeton University Press, 2011), 69–82.

2. Hubbard popularized the concept of the human mind as *terra incognita* in Dianetics. He first published this idea, however, in a paper titled, "Terra Incognita: The Mind" published in *The Explorers Journal* XXVIII (Winter-Spring 1950). This short paper also is available online at http://www.carolineletkeman.org/sp/images/stories/hcob/terra-incognita.pdf.

3. Susan Raine, "Astounding History: L. Ron Hubbard's Scientology Space Opera," *Religion* 45, no. 1 (2015): 66–88. This article could be read as a "Part One" to the present chapter as it illustrates the parallels between Scientology and the space opera tradition in the SF genre. Moreover, it introduces some of the ideas that I elaborate upon here.

4. John Rieder, *Colonialism and the Emergence of Science Fiction* (Middletown, CT: Wesleyan University Press, 2008), 4.

5. Ibid., 27.

6. Ibid., 26.

7. Ibid., 30.

8. Ibid., 4.

9. Istvan Csicsery-Ronay Jr., "Science Fiction and Empire," *Science Fiction Studies* 30 (2003): 231.

10. Ibid., 232.

11. John Rieder, *Colonialism and the Emergence*, 2–3.

12. Ibid., 3. The SF tradition incorporates an abundance of influences including colonial adventure fiction, utopian and dystopian fiction, tales of future wars, apocalyptic fiction, science fantasy, and stories of science and invention. All have contributed to the emergence and development of the SF genre. See Mark Bould and Sherryl

Vint, eds., *The Routledge Concise History of Science Fiction* (Routledge, 2011) for full discussions of these and other influences to the early SF tradition. The melding of assorted spheres of literature (and their reflection of real world, social, cultural, and political dynamics) is critical to understanding the entirety of what SF is and does, but for the present discussion imperial and colonial themes are of most significance given their prominence in Hubbard's theological narratives.

13. *Encyclopedia of Science Fiction*, "Galactic Empires," http://www.sf-encyclopedia .com/entry/galactic_empires. The quote is taken from Cole's 1900 story, *The Struggle for Empire: A Story of the Year 2236*. See also Patricia Kerslake, "Galactic Empire," in *The Greenwood Encyclopedia of Science Fiction and Fantasy: Themes, Works, and Wonders. Vol. 1*, ed. Gary Westfahl (Westport, CT: Greenwood, 2005), 325.

14. Patricia Kerslake, "Galactic Empire," 325.

15. Ibid.

16. *Encyclopedia of Science Fiction*, "Galactic Empires."

17. Ibid.

18. See William Sims Bainbridge, "Science and Religion: The Case of Scientology," in *The Future of New Religious Movements*, ed. David G. Bromley and Philip E. Hammond (Macon, GA: Mercer University Press, 1987), 59–79; and Susan Raine, "Astounding History: L. Ron Hubbard's Scientology Space Opera," for discussions of Hubbard's contributions to the early pulp SF genre.

19. Patricia Kerslake, "Galactic Empire," 326.

20. See Istvan Csicsery-Ronay Jr., "Science Fiction and Empire."

21. Ibid., 233.

22. Albert I. Berger, "Towards a Science of the Nuclear Mind: Science Fiction Origins of Dianetics," *Science Fiction Studies* 16 (1989): 134; and Mark L. Brake and Neil Hook, *Different Engines: How Science Drives Fiction and Fiction Drives Science* (Macmillan, 2008), 106.

23. Hazel McFerson, "United States," in *Colonialism: An International Social, Cultural and Political Encyclopedia*, ed. E. Melvin (Santa Barbara, CA: ABC-CLIO, 2006), 604. Following the Revolutionary War against British rule, American colonialism emerged in the late 1700s and continued throughout the 1800s as territorial expansion consolidated the new United States. This process typically resulted in the oppression of indigenous peoples who inhabited these regions. Just as the American West was part of the colonial project of settlers to the new world, early interplanetary science fiction depicted new galactic worlds as the American West. In these tales, the indigenous peoples—"Indians" in colonial language—of North America were rewritten as the alien lifeforms on newly discovered/colonized planets. See Paul A. Carter, *The Creation of Tomorrow: Fifty Years of Magazine Science Fiction* (New York: Columbia University Press), 62.

24. Hazel McFerson, "United States," 604.

25. Angela Woollacott, *Gender and Empire* (Houndmills, U.K.: Palgrave Macmillan, 2006), 59.

26. See Amy Kaplan, "Romancing the Empire: The Embodiment of American Masculinity in the Popular Historical Novel of the 1890s," *American Literary History* 9 (1990): 659–690; Archer Jones, "The Pulps: A Mirror into Learning," *North*

American Review September (1969): 35–47; and C. Boatright Mody, "The Formula in Cowboy Fiction and Drama," *Western Folklore* 28 (1938): 136–145.

27. Amy Kaplan, "Romancing the Empire," 661.

28. As Catherine E. Manathunga notes, "Colonization was a primarily patriarchal venture invented and implemented by men for the benefit of their imperial societies in which women were perceived as only occupying the invisible space of the private domestic sphere." She identifies that women were, however, "both agents and victims, participants and recipients" of the colonizing process. See Catherine E. Manathunga, "Women," in *Colonialism: An International Social, Cultural, and Political Encyclopedia*, ed. E. Melvin (Santa Barbara, CA: ABC-CLIO, 2003), 630–631.

29. Brian Attebery, *Decoding Gender in Science Fiction* (Abingdon, U.K.: Routledge, 2002), 43.

30. Paul A. Carter, *The Creation of Tomorrow: Fifty Years of Magazine Science Fiction*, 145–146. Advanced superior mental abilities and powers were one signifier of the superman, but a physical version emerged also with Siegel and Shuster's *Superman*. But this character while physically powerful, also possessed mental powers and was immortal—even godlike.

31. Mark Bould and Sherryl Vint, eds., *The Routledge Concise History of Science Fiction* (Abingdon, U.K.: Routledge, 2011), 46.

32. Brian Attebery, *Decoding Gender in Science Fiction*, 40.

33. See Brian Attebery, *Decoding Gender in Science Fiction* for discussion of gender in SF.

34. Paul A. Carter, *The Creation of Tomorrow: Fifty Years of Magazine Science Fiction*, 170.

35. Lisa J. M. Piorier, "Religion," in *Colonialism: An International Social, Cultural, and Political Encyclopedia*, ed. E. Melvin (Santa Barbara, CA: ABC-CLIO, 2003), 496.

36. Ibid.

37. J. L. Comaroff and J. Comaroff, *Ethnography and the Historical Imagination* (Boulder, CO: Westview Press, 1992).

38. See Nathaniel Roberts, "Is Conversion A 'Colonization of Consciousness?'" *Anthropological Theory* 12 (2012).

39. See Edward E. Andrews, "Christian Missions and Colonial Empires Reconsidered: A Black Evangelist in West Africa 1766–1816," *Journal of Church and State* 51 (2010).

40. Farah Mendlesohn, "Religion and Science Fiction," in Edward James and Farah Mendlesohn, eds., *The Cambridge Companion to Science Fiction* (Cambridge: Cambridge University Press), 264–265.

41. Ibid., 269.

42. Peter Pels, "Amazing Stories: How Science Fiction Sacralizes the Secular," in *Deus in Machina: Religion, Technology, and the Things in Between*, ed. Jeremy Stolow (New York: Fordham University Press, 2013), 214.

43. See Steven Engler, "Science Fiction, Religion, and Social Change," in *The Influence of Imagination: Essays on Science Fiction and Fantasy as Agents of Social Change*, ed. Lee Easton and Randy Schroeder (Jefferson, NC: McFarland, 2008); and Gabriel McKee, *The Gospel According to Science Fiction* (Louisville, KY: John Knox Press, 2007).

44. Steven Engler, "Science Fiction, Religion, and Social Change," 108; and James A. Herrick, *Scientific Mythologies: How Science and Science Fiction Forge New Religious Beliefs* (Westmont, IL: IVP Academic, 2008), 23.

45. Gabriel McKee, *The Gospel According to Science Fiction*, xiv; and James A. Herrick, *Scientific Mythologies: How Science and Science Fiction Forge New Religious Beliefs*, 23.

46. James A. Herrick, *Scientific Mythologies: How Science and Science Fiction Forge New Religious Beliefs*, 23.

47. Gabriel McKee, *The Gospel According to Science Fiction*, xiv; and James A. Herrick, *Scientific Mythologies: How Science and Science Fiction Forge New Religious Beliefs*, 128.

48. Steven Engler, "Science Fiction, Religion, and Social Change," 109.

49. Ibid., 110.

50. Adam Roberts, "Does God Need a Starship? Science Fiction and Religion," in *Strange Divisions & Alien Territories: the Sub-genres of Science Fiction*, ed. Keith Brooke (Palgrave Macmillan, 2012), 112.

51. See, for example, Jon Atack, *A Piece of Blue Sky: Scientology, Dianetics and L. Ron Hubbard Exposed* (New York: Lyle Stuart, 1990); Jodi Lane Jodi and Stephen A. Kent, "Malignant Narcissism, L. Ron Hubbard, and Scientology's Policies of Narcissistic Rage," *Criminologie* 41 (2008): 117–155 (English translation); Russell Miller, *Bare-Faced Messiah: The True Story of L. Ron Hubbard* (New York: Henry Holt, 1987); Janet Reitman, *Inside Scientology: The Story of America's Most Secretive Religion* (Boston: Houghton Mifflin Harcourt, 2011); and Hugh Urban, *The Church of Scientology: A History of a New Religion* (Princeton: Princeton University Press, 2011).

52. Susan Raine, "Astounding History: L. Ron Hubbard's Scientology Space Opera."

53. Assessing the perceptions of others (especially after their death) is a tricky and perhaps a risky endeavor, but Hubbard left an immense amount of material for researchers to work with—although the sheer magnitude and *variety* of his work complicates analyses still further. Still, some of the persistent themes help in the ongoing project of comprehending who he was, how he viewed himself, and how he regarded others.

54. Hubbard described endless adventures that he had claimed to experience around the globe. In his stories, he often positioned himself as the learned and capable teacher to those peoples he encountered. See Russell Miller, *Bare-Faced Messiah: The True Story of L. Ron Hubbard*, 40–58. Further evidence of his drive to adventure was his membership with the Scouts (although he may have inflated his role as the youngest ever Eagle Scout) and his membership, later, as an adult, with the Explorers Club—an esteemed organization to which his application was accepted (but without due fact-checking processes that would have revealed fabrications in his resume). See Russell Miller, *Bare-Faced Messiah: The True Story of L. Ron Hubbard*, 84–85.

55. See Ibid.

56. Ibid., 97–99.

57. Hubbard had short stories published at George Washington University in 1932.

58. L. Ron Hubbard, *Thrilling Adventures* (May 1935), http://lrhpulps.weebly.com/thrilling-adventure.html.

59. L. Ron Hubbard, "14 Oct 1943," in *Ron, Letters and Journals: Early Years of Adventure* (L. Ron Hubbard Library, 1997), 9.

60. SF magazine, *Astounding Science Fiction*, first published Hubbard's essay on Dianetics in its May 1950 edition.

61. L. Ron Hubbard, *Dianetics: The Modern Science of Mental Health*, 1968 edition (Los Angeles: The Publications Organization World Wide), xxv.

62. Ibid.

63. Istvan Csicsery-Ronay Jr., "Science Fiction and Empire."

64. L. Ron Hubbard, "Security Checks," HCO Bulletin, in *The Technical Bulletins of Dianetics and Scientology. Vol. IV.* 1976 (Los Angeles: The American Saint Hill Organization, 1960). The E-meter was the creation of fellow SF writer, Volney Mathison. See Hugh Urban, *The Church of Scientology: A History of a New Religion*, 49.

65. Jon Atack, *A Piece of Blue Sky: Scientology, Dianetics and L. Ron Hubbard Exposed*, 166; and Russell Miller, *Bare-Faced Messiah: The True Story of L. Ron Hubbard*, 257.

66. L. Ron Hubbard as cited in Bent Corydon, *L. Ron Hubbard: Messiah or Madman?* (Fort Lee, NJ: Barricade Books, 1987), 71.

67. See Russell Miller, *Bare-Faced Messiah: The True Story of L. Ron Hubbard*, 249–255.

68. Jon Atack, *A Piece of Blue Sky: Scientology, Dianetics and L. Ron Hubbard Exposed*, 166; and Russell Miller, *Bare-Faced Messiah: The True Story of L. Ron Hubbard*, 258–259.

69. For a summary, see Stephen A. Kent, "The Globalization of Scientology: Influence, Control and Opposition in Transnational Markets," *Religion* 29 (1999): 154.

70. *International Management* 1987, 3 as cited in Stephen A. Kent, "The Globalization of Scientology: Influence, Control and Opposition in Transnational Markets," *Religion* 29 (1999): 148.

71. John Campbell was impressed by Hubbard's Dianetics thesis and was an active supporter of it for period of time. He and some other early Hubbard enthusiasts eventually lost interest in Hubbard's work. See Paul A. Carter, *The Creation of Tomorrow: Fifty Years of Magazine Science Fiction*, 158–159. For example, Campbell and SF author Van Vogt became disenchanted with Hubbard's ideas when he proposed that auditors examine the past lives of their clients. See Harriet Whitehead, "Reasonably Fantastic: Some Perspectives on Scientology, Science Fiction and Occultism," in *Religious Movements in Contemporary America*, ed. Irving I. Zaretsky and Mark P. Leone (Princeton: Princeton University Press, 1974), 579.

72. Albert I. Berger, "Towards a Science of the Nuclear Mind: Science Fiction Origins of Dianetics," 124–125.

73. Isaac Asimov, cited in Paul A. Carter, *The Creation of Tomorrow: Fifty Years of Magazine Science Fiction*, 77.

74. For example, see L. Ron Hubbard *Professional Auditor's Bulletin*, no. 119 (September 1, 1957), in which he states, "The South African native is probably the one impossible person to train in the entire world? He is probably impossible by any

human standard." In L. Ron Hubbard, *The Fundamentals of Thought* (Los Angeles: The American Saint Hill Organization, 1956/1972), 82. Hubbard stated, "Just as individuals can be seen, by observing nations, so we see the African tribesman, with his complete contempt for truth and his emphasis on brutality and savagery for others but not for himself, is a no-civilization. And we see at the other extreme, China, slavishly dedicated to ancient scholars, incapable of generating within herself sufficient rulers to continue, without bloodshed, a nation." Other similar comments exist in other works by Hubbard. Moreover, he allegedly stated in a 1928 personal journal: "A Chinaman cannot live up to a thing, he always drags it down. They smell of all the baths they didn't take. The trouble with China is, there are too many chinks here." See http://www.lermanet.com/barwell/hubbard-the-racist.txt.

75. Although Hubbard claimed that he became a "blood brother" of the Blackfoot native Americans at the age of four, Joel Sappell and Robert assert that the Blackfoot band to which Hubbard referred actually lived some 100 miles from where Hubbard lived and have never engaged in blood brother rituals. See Joel Sappell and Robert Welkos, "The Making of L. Ron Hubbard: Staking a Claim to Blood Brotherhood," *Los Angeles Times*, June 24, 1990, A38:5.

76. Hubbard lists Herbert Spencer—Social Darwinist and progenitor the concept of "survival of the fittest"—as an influence on his works. L. Ron Hubbard. *Scientology 8-8008*. 1967 edition (Los Angeles: The American Saint Hill Organization, 1953), viii.

77. Hubbard's official definition of a WOG is as follows: "1. **Worthy Oriental gentleman**. This means a common run-of-the-mill garden-variety humanoid. . . . 2. a **wog** is somebody who isn't even trying." L. Ron Hubbard, *Dianetics and Scientology Technical Dictionary* (Los Angeles: The Publications Organization, 1975), 471. "WOG." Regardless of which definition one uses, a dichotomy between superiority and inferiority is evident.

78. As cited, for example, in Jon Atack, *A Piece of Blue Sky: Scientology, Dianetics and L. Ron Hubbard Exposed*, 31–32; Stephen A. Kent, "The Creation of 'Religious' Scientology," *Religious Studies and Theology* 18 (1999): 103–104; and Mikael Rothstein, "'His Name was Xenu. He used renegades . . .': Aspects of Scientology's Founding Myth," in *Scientology*, ed. James Lewis (Oxford: Oxford University Press, 2009), 365–388.

79. L. Ron. Hubbard, *Have You Lived This Life Before?* 1977 edition (Los Angeles: The Publications Organization, 1950), 40–41, 44.

80. L. Ron Hubbard, *A History of Man*. 1980 edition (Los Angeles: Scientology Publications Organization, 1952), 54.

81. See L. Ron Hubbard, *A History of Man*. 1980 edition (Los Angeles: Scientology Publications Organization, 1952), for his thesis on this and other issues.

82. Ibid.

83. L. Ron Hubbard, "Routine 3: The Nature of Formation of the GPM," *Hubbard Communication Office Bulletin*, July 14, 1963a.

84. Ibid.

85. L. Ron Hubbard, "Opening: What Is to Be Done in Course," Recorded Lecture, *The Philadelphia Doctorate Course*, December 1, 1952a.

86. L. Ron Hubbard, "Routine 3: The Nature of Formation of the GPM," *Hubbard Communication Office Bulletin*.

87. L. Ron Hubbard, *Dianetics and Scientology Technical Dictionary* (Los Angeles: Publications Organization, 1975), 243.

88. L. Ron Hubbard, "OT VIII Series 1. Confidential Student Briefing," HCO Bulletin, May 5, 1980. Hubbard Communication Office, 1980.

89. Ibid.

90. Hubbard's concept of MEST refers to the *nature* of the universe—the totality of matter, energy, space, and time. Hubbard communicated in detail the many ways in which, according to him, the MEST universe shapes our perceptions of reality. For example, see L. Ron Hubbard, *Scientology 8-8008* (Los Angeles: The American Saint Hill Organization, 1953).

91. L. Ron Hubbard, *Dianetics and Scientology Technical Dictionary* (Los Angeles: Publications Organization, 1975), 216.

92. L. Ron Hubbard, *Scientology 8-8008*. Eighth edition (Los Angeles: The American Saint Hill Organization, 1967), 132.

93. L. Ron Hubbard, "The War," *Executive Directive from L. Ron Hubbard*. November 29, 1968.

94. Stephen A. Kent and Terra Manca, "A War over Mental Health Professionalism: Scientology Versus Psychiatry," *Mental Health, Religion & Culture* 17 (2012): 9.

95. Ibid.

96. L. Ron Hubbard, "The War," *Executive Directive from L. Ron Hubbard*.

97. Hubbard proposed that "A SUPPRESSIVE PERSON or GROUP is one that actively seeks to suppress or damage Scientology or a Scientologist by Suppressive Acts." See L. Ron Hubbard, *Introduction to Scientology Ethics*, 3rd ed. (Los Angeles: The American Saint Hill Organization, 1970), 48. A Potential Trouble Source (PTS) is someone who is swayed by a suppressive person. See Jon Atack, *A Piece of Blue Sky: Scientology, Dianetics and L. Ron Hubbard Exposed*, 155.

98. See Susan Raine, "Surveillance in New Religious Movements: Scientology as a Case Study," *Religious Studies and Theology* 28 (2009): 63–94. This article discusses the numerous ways that conformity is established and maintained through a variety of surveillance techniques.

99. Ibid.

100. Established in 1960, this process is also known as Sec Checking and Confessional Auditing. Although Hubbard officially declared the discontinuance of Security Checking in 1968—see L. Ron Hubbard, "Security Checks Abolished," 1968 HCO Policy Letter, in *The Organization Executive Course: An Encyclopaedia of Scientology Policy. HCO Division 1*. Second edition (Los Angeles: Publications Organization, 1976), 486—former members confirm to its continued use. See Jon Atack, *A Piece of Blue Sky: Scientology, Dianetics and L. Ron Hubbard Exposed*, 147–152; Bent Corydon, *L. Ron Hubbard, Messiah or Madman?*, 150; and Monica Pignotti "My Nine Lives in Scientology," 1989, retrieved November 10, 2003 from http://www-2.cscmu.edu/~dst/Library/Shelf/pignotti/

101. L. Ron Hubbard, *Dianetics and Scientology Technical Dictionary*. Emphasis in the original (Publications Organization, 1975), 376.

102. L. Ron Hubbard, "Sec Check Whole Track," HCO Bulletin, in *The Technical Bulletins of Dianetics and Scientology. Vol. IV* (Los Angeles: The American Saint Hill Organization, 1976). These questions come from the Whole Track Security Check, which Hubbard designed to probe into a person's alleged multiple incarnations on the whole track. This ended up being difficult, so eventually Hubbard applied the questions to the person's current lifetime only. See Jon Atack, *A Piece of Blue Sky: Scientology, Dianetics and L. Ron Hubbard Exposed*, 152.

103. Former high-ranking Scientologist and Sea Org member, Jesse Prince, described the Sea Org in this way in his affidavit in the following case: Estate Of Lisa McPherson, by and Through The Personal Representative, Dell Liebreich VS. Section "H" Church of Scientology Flag Service Organization, Inc.; Case No. 97-01235. In The Circuit Court Of The Thirteenth Judicial Circuit In And For Hillsborough County, State Of Florida General Civil Division. 1999. Affidavit available at http://www.cs.cmu.edu/~dst/NOTs/prince-affidavit.txt and http://www.xenu.net/archive/so/.

104. Melissa Lingen, "Sea Travel," in *The Greenwood Encyclopedia of Science Fiction and Fantasy: Themes, Works, and Wonders. Vol. 2*, ed. Gary Westfahl (Greenwood, 2005), 699.

105. Ibid.

106. Ibid., 698.

107. John Rieder, "Empire as Thought Experiment. Review of Patricia Kerslake, *Science Fiction and Empire* (2007)," *Extrapolation* 49 (2008): 324–328. My thanks to Steven Engler for directing me to this definition.

108. L. Ron Hubbard, *The Sea Org*. Pamphlet. 1980 edition (The Church of Scientology, 1967).

109. The Church of Scientology International, "The Sea Organization," http://www.bonafidescientology.org/Chapter/05/page09.htm.

110. Jon Atack, *A Piece of Blue Sky: Scientology, Dianetics and L. Ron Hubbard Exposed*, 20.

111. Ibid., 21.

112. L. Ron Hubbard, *Mission into Time* (Los Angeles: The American Saint Hill Organization, 1973), 22–23.

113. Jon Atack, *A Piece of Blue Sky: Scientology, Dianetics and L. Ron Hubbard Exposed*, 178–179.

114. Ibid., 192.

115. The Sea Org both at sea and on land has been plagued by accusations of human rights violations. See Stephen A. Kent, "Scientology—Is This a Religion?" *Marburg Journal of Religion* 4 (1999): 1–23; and Stephen A. Kent, "Brainwashing Programs in the Family/the Children of God and Scientology," in *Misunderstanding Cults: Searching for Objectivity in a Controversial Field*, ed. Benjamin Zablocki and Thomas Robbins (University of Toronto Press, 2001), 349–378.

116. L. Ron Hubbard, *Dianetics: the Modern Science of Mental Health* (Hermitage House, 1950), ix.

117. The importance of men of science is imbedded in the early science fiction culture of which Hubbard was a part. It is integral to Hubbard's rhetoric, given that he considered his work to be scientific. Being scientific was very important to him as science was developing greater levels of respect over the course of the 20th century. Furthermore, the early American SF tradition extolled the virtues of scientists, framing them as exceptional individuals who offered impressive and transformative new ideas and technologies. See Albert I. Berger, "Towards a Science of the Nuclear Mind: Science Fiction Origins of Dianetics," 133. Moreover, one can see the melding of science and adventure in "science adventurism"—a concept that surely Hubbard would have felt comfortable with. See William Sims Bainbridge, "The Cultural Context of Scientology" in James R. Lewis, *Scientology* (Oxford: Oxford University Press), 39.

118. L. Ron Hubbard, *Mission into Time*, 31–33.

119. Hugh Urban, *The Church of Scientology: A History of a New Religion*, 32–33.

120. Gabriel McKee, *The Gospel According to Science Fiction*, 143.

121. Bent Corydon, *L. Ron Hubbard, Messiah or Madman?*, 58.

122. Hugh Urban, *The Church of Scientology: A History of a New Religion*, 110.

123. Mary-Sue Hubbard, "Primary Function," *Guardian Order* of October 10, 1974 http://www.xenu.net/archive/go/go1366/go1366.htm.

124. Guardian Order 060971 (seized by the FBI), http://www.xenu.net/archive/judge_quotes.html.

125. Stephen A. Kent, "The Globalization of Scientology: Influence, Control and Opposition in Transnational Markets," *Religion* 29 (1999): 153.

126. Ibid.

127. Janet Reitman, *Inside Scientology*.

128. Ibid., 194.

129. Ibid., 192–195.

BIBLIOGRAPHY

Atack, Jon. *A Piece of Blue Sky: Scientology, Dianetics and L. Ron Hubbard Exposed.* New York: Lyle Stuart, 1990.

Attebery, Brian. "The Magazine Era: 1926–1960." In *The Cambridge Companion to Science Fiction*, edited by Edward James and Farah Mendlesohn, 32–47. Cambridge: Cambridge University Press, 2003.

Bainbridge, William Sims. "The Cultural Context of Scientology." In *Scientology*, edited by James R. Lewis, 35–51. Oxford: Oxford University Press, 2009.

Bainbridge, William Sims. "Science and Religion: The Case of Scientology." In *The Future of New Religious Movements*, edited by David G. Bromley and Philip E. Hammond, 59–79. Macon, GA: Mercer University Press, 1987.

Berger, Albert I. "Towards a Science of the Nuclear Mind: Science Fiction Origins of Dianetics." *Science Fiction Studies* 16 (1989): 123–144.

Boatright, Mody C. "The Formula in Cowboy Fiction and Drama." *Western Folklore* 28 (1969): 136–145.

Bould, Mark, and Sherryl Vint. *The Routledge Concise History of Science Fiction*. London: Routledge, 2011.

Brake, Mark L., and Neil Hook. *Different Engines: How Science Drives Fiction and Fiction Drives Science*. New York: Macmillan, 2008.

Carter, Paul. *The Creation of Tomorrow: Fifty Years of Magazine Science Fiction*. New York: Columbia University Press, 1977.

Christensen, Dorthe Refslund. "Inventing L. Ron Hubbard: On the Construction and Maintenance of the Hagiographic Mythology of Scientology's Founder." In *Controversial New Religions*, edited by James R. Lewis and Jesper Aagaard Petersen, 227–258. Oxford: Oxford University Press, 2005.

Church of Scientology International, The. "The Sea Organization." Accessed November 26, 2015. http://www.bonafidescientology.org/Chapter/05/page09 .htm.

Comaroff, J. L., and J. Comaroff. *Ethnography and the Historical Imagination*. Boulder, CO: Westview Press, 1992.

Corydon, Bent. *L. Ron Hubbard, Messiah or Madman?* 1996 edition. New Jersey: Barricade Books, 1987.

Csicsery-Ronay, Istvan, Jr. "Science Fiction and Empire." *Science Fiction Studies* 30 (2003): 231–245.

del Ray, Lester. *The World of Science Fiction: The History of a Subculture*. New York: Ballantine Books, 1979.

Engler, Steven. "Science Fiction, Religion, and Social Change." In *The Influence of Imagination: Essays on Science Fiction and Fantasy as Agents of Social Change*, edited by Lee Easton and Randy Schroeder, 108–117. Jefferson, NC: McFarland, 2008.

Gruenschloss, Andreas. "Scientology, A 'New Age' Religion?" In *Scientology*, edited by James R. Lewis, 225–243. Oxford: Oxford University Press, 2009.

Herrick, James A. *Scientific Mythologies: How Science and Science Fiction Forge New Religious Beliefs*. Westmont, IL IVP Academic, 2008.

Hubbard, L. Ron. "Chart of Attitude: Rising Scale Processing." December 11, 1952. *The Philadelphia Doctorate Course*. Recorded Lecture, 2004.

Hubbard, L. Ron. *Dianetics: The Modern Science of Mental Health*. Hermitage House, 1950.

Hubbard, L. Ron. *Dianetics and Scientology Technical Dictionary*. Los Angeles: The Publications Organization, 1975.

Hubbard, L. Ron. *Have You Lived This Life Before?* First published 1950. Los Angeles: The Publications Organization, 1977.

Hubbard, L. Ron. *A History of Man*. First published 1952. Copenhagen: Scientology Publications Organization, 1980.

Hubbard, L. Ron. *Introduction to Scientology Ethics*, 3d ed. Los Angeles: The American Saint Hill Organization, 1970.

Hubbard, L. Ron. "Long Form Step III: Differentiation on Theta Clearing." *The Philadelphia Doctorate Course*. January 19, 1953. Recorded Lecture. Los Angeles: Bridge Publications, 2004.

Hubbard, L. Ron. *Mission into Time*. Los Angeles: The American Saint Hill Organization, 1973.

Hubbard, L. Ron. "Opening: What Is to Be Done in Course." December 1, 1952. *The Philadelphia Doctorate Course*. Recorded Lecture. Los Angeles: Bridge Publications, 2004.

Hubbard, L. Ron. "Port Orchard, Washington. January 1, 1938." *Ron the Philosopher*. Accessed November 2013. http://www.ronthephilosopher.org/phlspher/page08.htm.

Hubbard, L. Ron. "Routine 3: The Nature of Formation of the GPM." *Hubbard Communication Office Bulletin*. July 14, 1963.

Hubbard, L. Ron. "Routine 3RN Line Plots." *Hubbard Communication Office Bulletin*. July 14, 1963.

Hubbard, L. Ron. "R3N Corrections." *Hubbard Communication Office Bulletin*. July 24, 1963.

Hubbard, L. Ron. *Scientology 8-8008*, 8th ed. First published 1953. Los Angeles: The American Saint Hill Organization, 1967.

Hubbard, L. Ron. "Sec Check Whole Track." HCO Bulletin, 1961. In *The Technical Bulletins of Dianetics and Scientology. Vol. IV*. Los Angeles: The American Saint Hill Organization, 1976.

Hubbard, L. Ron. "Security Checks." HCO Bulletin, 1960. In *The Technical Bulletins of Dianetics and Scientology. Vol. IV*. Los Angeles: The American Saint Hill Organization, 1976.

Hubbard, L. Ron. "Security Checks Abolished." HCO Policy Letter, 1968. In *The Organization Executive Course: An Encyclopaedia of Scientology Policy*. HCO Division 1, 2d ed. Los Angeles: Publications Organization, 1976.

Hubbard, L. Ron. "Terra Incognita: The Mind." *The Explorers Journal* XXVIII (Winter-Spring 1950): Accessed August 14, 2015. http://www.carolineletkeman.org/sp/images/stories/hcob/terra-incognita.pdf.

Jones, Archer. "The Pulps: A Mirror into Yearning." *North American Review* (1938): 35–47.

Kent, Stephen A. "Brainwashing Programs in the Family/the Children of God and Scientology." In *Misunderstanding Cults: Searching for Objectivity in a Controversial Field*, edited by Benjamin Zablocki and Thomas Robbins, 349–378. Toronto: University of Toronto Press, 2001.

Kent, Stephen A. "The Creation of 'Religious' Scientology." *Religious Studies and Theology* 18 (1999): 97–127.

Kent, Stephen A. *From Slogans to Mantras: Social Protest and Religious Conversion in the Late Vietnam Era*. Syracuse: Syracuse University Press, 2001.

Kent, Stephen A. "The Globalization of Scientology: Influence, Control and Opposition in Transnational Markets." *Religion* 29 (1999): 147–169.

Kent, Stephen A. "Scientology—Is This a Religion?" *Marburg Journal of Religion* 4 (1999): 1–23.

Kent, Stephen A., and Terra A. Manca. "A War over Mental Health Professionalism: Scientology Versus Psychiatry." *Mental Health, Religion and Culture* 1 (2012): 1–23.

Lane, Jodi, and Stephen A. Kent. "Malignant Narcissism, L. Ron Hubbard, and Scientology's Policies of Narcissistic Rage." English translation. *Criminologie* 41 (2008): 117–155.

Lewis, James R., ed. *Scientology*. Oxford: Oxford University Press, 2009.

Manathunga, Catherine E. "Women." In *Colonialism: An International Social, Cultural, and Political Encyclopedia*, edited by Melvin E. Page, 630–631. Santa Barbara: ABC-CLIO, 2003.

McFerson, Hazel. "United States." In *Colonialism: An International Social, Cultural, and Political Encyclopedia*, edited by Melvin E. Page, 604–608. Santa Barbara, CA: ABC-CLIO, 2003.

McKee, Gabriel. *The Gospel According to Science Fiction*. Louisville: Westminster John Knox Press, 2007.

Mendlesohn, Farah. "Religion and Science Fiction." In *The Cambridge Companion to Science Fiction*, edited by Edward James and Farah Mendlesohn, 264–275. Cambridge: Cambridge University Press, 2003.

Miller, Russell. *Bare-Faced Messiah: The True Story of L. Ron Hubbard*. New York: Henry Holt, 1987.

Page, Melvin E., ed. *Colonialism: An International Social, Cultural, and Political Encyclopedia*. Santa Barbara: ABC-CLIO, 2003.

Pels, Peter. "Amazing Stories: How Science Fiction Sacralizes the Secular." In *Deus in Machina: Religion, Technology, and the Things in Between*, edited by Jeremy Stolow, 213–237. New York: Fordham University Press, 2013.

Pignotti, Monica. "My Nine Lives in Scientology." Accessed November 10, 2003. http://www-2.cscmu.edu/~dst/Library/Shelf/pignotti/.

Poirier, Lisa J. M. "Religion." In *Colonialism: An International Social, Cultural, and Political Encyclopedia*, edited by Melvin E. Page, 496–497. Santa Barbara: ABC-CLIO, 2003.

Raine, Susan. "Astounding History: L. Ron Hubbard's Scientology Space Opera." *Religion* 45 (2015): 66–88.

Raine, Susan. "Surveillance in New Religious Movements: Scientology as a Case Study." *Religious Studies and Theology* 28 (2009): 63–94.

Reitman, Janet. *Inside Scientology: The Story of America's Most Secretive Religion*. New York: Houghton Mifflin Harcourt, 2011.

Rieder, John. "Empire as Thought Experiment. Review of Patricia Kerslake, Science Fiction and Empire (2007)." *Extrapolation* 49 (2008): 324–328.

Rieder, John. "Science Fiction, Colonialism, and the Plot of Invasion." *Extrapolation* 46 (2005): 373–394.

Roberts, Adam. "Does God Need a Starship? Science Fiction and Religion." In *Strange Divisions & Alien Territories: The Sub-genres of Science Fiction*, edited by Keith Brooke. New York: Palgrave Macmillan, 2012.

Roberts, Nathaniel. "Is Conversion A 'Colonization of Consciousness?'" *Anthropological Theory* 12 (2012): 271–294.

Rothstein, Mikael. "'His Name was Xenu. He used renegades . . .': Aspects of Scientology's Founding Myth." In *Scientology*, edited by James Lewis, 365–388. Oxford: Oxford University Press, 2009.

Seed, David. "The Course of Empire: A Survey of the Imperial Theme in Early Anglophone Science Fiction." *Science Fiction Studies* 37 (2010): 230–252.

Stowlow, Jeremy, ed. *Deus in Machina: Religion, Technology, and the Things in Between*. New York: Fordham University Press, 2013.

Urban, Hugh. *The Church of Scientology: A History of a New Religion*. Princeton: Princeton University Press, 2011.

Wallis, Roy. *The Road to Total Freedom: A Sociological Study of Scientology*. New York: Columbia University Press, 1977.

Westfahl, Gary. "Beyond Logic and Literacy: The Strange Case of Space Opera." *Extrapolation* 35 (1994): 176–185.

Westfahl, Gary, ed. *The Greenwood Encyclopedia of Science Fiction and Fantasy: Themes, Works, and Wonders. Vol. 1*. Westport, CT: Greenwood Press, 2005.

Westfahl, Gary, ed. *The Greenwood Encyclopedia of Science Fiction and Fantasy: Themes, Works, and Wonders. Vol. 2*. Westport, CT: Greenwood Press, 2005.

Westfahl, Gary. *The Mechanics of Wonder: The Creation of the Idea of Science Fiction*. Liverpool: Liverpool University Press, 1998.

Westfahl, Gary. "Space Opera." In *The Cambridge Companion to Science Fiction*, edited by Edward James and Farah Mendlesohn, 197–208. Cambridge: Cambridge University Press, 2003.

Whitehead, Harriet. "Reasonably Fantastic: Some Perspectives on Scientology, Science Fiction and Occultism." In *Religious Movements in Contemporary America*, edited by Irving I. Zaretsky and Mark P. Leone, 547–587. Princeton: Princeton University Press, 1974.

Williamson, Jack. *Wonder's Child: My Life in Science Fiction*. New York: Blue Jay Books, 1985.

Woolacott, Angela. *Gender and Empire*. Houndmills, U.K.: Palgrave Macmillan, 2006.

2

Typewriter in the Sky: L. Ron Hubbard's Fiction and the Birth of the Thetan

Hugh B. Urban

The way you feel about stories sometimes. It's—well, sort of divine, somehow. Here we are able to make and break characters and tangle up their lives and all . . . When I go knocking out the wordage and really get interested in my characters it almost makes me feel like—a god or something.

—L. Ron Hubbard, *Typewriter in the Sky* (1940)[1]

Highest potentiality of theta is evidently the creation and management of universes . . . Let's take a writer sitting at his desk, and he's pounding a typewriter, and so what's he doing? Inventing time and space and energy and matter and so on.

—L. Ron Hubbard, *Secrets of the MEST Universe* (1952)[2]

If most non-Scientologists know anything about L. Ron Hubbard, they probably know that he first made his career as an author of science fiction, fantasy, and adventure tales before founding the Church of Scientology. Indeed, Hubbard was one of the most—if not *the* most—prolific authors during the "golden age" of sci-fi in the decade before World War II, and it has been widely noted that many of his fictional themes were carried over into his early lectures on Scientology.[3] In an infamous episode that savagely mocked Scientology, the American TV satire *South Park* highlighted this link between Hubbard's science fiction and the religion of Scientology. "Wasn't L. Ron Hubbard a science-fiction writer?" asks the father of the central character, Stan. To this the representative of Scientology responds, "Yes. But he was also a prophet who knew the secret truth about the nature of life." Stan—who has been identified by the church as the reincarnation of Hubbard—then concludes, "This is just too much."[4]

For many journalists and critics, Hubbard's career as a science fiction writer has been an easy excuse to dismiss Scientology as a mere concoction of this writer's already active imagination—as yet another "space opera" fantasy to complement his vast body of space opera stories and novels. As the *Los Angeles Times* put it in 1990, "to the uninitiated, Hubbard's theology would resemble pure science fiction, complete with galactic battles, interplanetary civilizations and tyrants who roam the universe."[5]

In this chapter, however, I will offer a rather different reading of Hubbard's fiction and its significance for the early Church of Scientology. Hubbard's fiction, I will suggest, was not merely a source of imaginative inspiration for his elaborate Scientology cosmology (though it may also have been that).[6] Rather, at a more profound level, Hubbard's understanding of fiction and his concept of the author were integral to his later formulation of Scientology's metaphysics—and specifically, to his conception of the spiritual being or thetan, which has potentially unlimited and godlike power. As we see as early as stories such as *Typewriter in the Sky* (1940), Hubbard compared the author of fiction to a godlike being who can create myriad new universes out of his imagination, manipulating them at will. Conversely, in his Scientology writings of the 1950s, Hubbard also explicitly compared the power of the spiritual self or thetan to that of a *writer*, who can create, inhabit, manipulate, and destroy entire universes at will, as a matter of its own "self-determination."[7]

To conclude, I will place Hubbard and his work in a broader historical context. The idea of the author as a divinely creative being did not, of course, originate entirely with Hubbard but had several historical antecedents. Perhaps most notably, it begins to appear in German and English Romantic literature with the ideal of the author as a genius, a figure with "godlike" and "superhuman powers," who creates worlds *ex nihilo* through his imagination.[8] It also had antecedents in 19th-century spiritual movements such as New Thought and the idea of the mind as a divine power that transcends and can transform the material world.[9] And finally, there were also clear antecedents in South Asian traditions such as Hinduism, from which Hubbard explicitly borrowed. Hubbard's concept of the thetan is clearly indebted to the Hindu concept of the *atman* or spiritual self, which is ultimately identical with *brahman* or Ultimate Reality; and he would eventually claim for the liberated thetan all the supernatural abilities likewise claimed for an enlightened *yogi*.[10] An ingenious and eclectic spiritual *bricoleur*,[11] Hubbard wove all of these various influences together in his concept of the thetan as "author of its own universe." Yet Hubbard arguably gave this idea its most radical modern formulation and in this sense really anticipated much of the New Age movement that emerged in the 1960s and 1970s. As J. Gordon Melton notes, "No single idea so permeated the New Age movement as the notion that we create our own reality."[12] Hubbard's writings—both fictional and religious—should be recognized as one of the key influences in that complex mélange of spiritual ideas.

Finally, this deeper understanding of the links between Hubbard's fiction and his Scientology writings, I will suggest, offers a useful alternative to the common questions that most readers ask: "Did Hubbard just make this Scientology stuff up (in the same way that he imagined his creative works of science fiction)?" Or "did he really believe any of this?" If we take seriously Hubbard's central idea that the individual can create new realities, the answer to these two questions is "yes" and "yes."

SPACE OPERA AND SOLDIERS OF LIGHT: SUPERNATURAL THEMES IN HUBBARD'S EARLY FICTION

Hubbard began publishing short stories in 1934 and quickly established himself as a phenomenally prolific author, producing a staggering number of works over the next two decades. Indeed, he wrote so much and so rapidly that he was forced to publish his works under a wide array of pseudonyms, donning titles such as Winchester Remington Colt, Kurt von Rachen, René Lafayette, Joe Blitz, Legionnaire 148, and many, many others.[13]

Supernatural themes run throughout Hubbard's early fiction, often revealing direct and indirect continuities with his later writings on Dianetics and Scientology. As we see in early tales in magazines such as *Unknown*, his stories often attribute exceptional powers to the mind, such as "the power to heal or kill by thought alone."[14] As he asked in his 1940 novel, *Fear*,

> [A]re we now "blind" to extramaterial agencies? And might we not, at any given moment, experience a sudden rebirth of that sense and, as vividly as a lightning flash, see those things which jealously menace our existences? If we could but see, for even so brief a period, the supernatural, would we then begin to understand the complexities which beset man? . . . Are there not men in this world today who have converse with the supernatural, but who cannot demonstrate or explain and be believed because of the lack in others of that peculiar sense?[15]

Some of the most interesting of Hubbard's early science fiction—and perhaps the most relevant for his later Church of Scientology—appears in his series of tales about a character named "Ole Doc Methuselah." Published in *Astounding Science Fiction* from 1947 to 1950 under the pseudonym René Lafayette, these tales center on a boldly adventurous space hero and physician who is a member of the "the most elite organization of the cosmos" called the Soldiers of Light. Composed of 600 selfless heroes who have dedicated themselves to the "ultimate preservation of mankind," the Soldiers of Light take as their emblem the symbol of two crossed rods. On his spaceship "the Hound of Heaven," Ole Doc embarks on an "unending journey through the trackless galaxy," enjoying a series of "astonishing adventures on many worlds."[16]

It is not difficult to see in the Ole Doc Methuselah stories the seeds of many aspects of the Church of Scientology, which would be founded just a few years later. Like the Soldiers of Light, who work under the symbol of the crossed rods to fight disease and save humankind, the Church of Scientology would work under the symbol of the eight-pointed cross to fight both physical and spiritual disease. Like this elite group of Soldiers of Light, Hubbard's naval order, the Sea Org, would later serve as the elite inner core of his church, sworn by billion-year contracts to save the entire planet. And like Ole Doc himself, who endlessly roams the galaxy in his spaceship, having adventures on many worlds, Hubbard would also spend years roaming the earth's oceans on his ship, exploring ever-new spiritual universes. As we will see below, the ultimate goal of Scientology's advanced training is the state of Operating Thetan, in which the spiritual self or thetan is liberated from the bonds of the physical body and is free to travel to any corner of the universe.[17]

However, perhaps the most striking element in Hubbard's early fiction that reappears in his later Scientology writings is his emphasis on the unlimited, even godlike power of the writer himself. For the writer has the all-creative power to generate entire universes out of his imagination, to populate them, and to destroy them. The clearest example of the divine power of the author appears in *Typewriter in the Sky*, which was first published as a two-part serial in *Unknown Fantasy Fiction* in 1940. Here the pulp fiction author, Horace Hackett, has the power not just to create universes out of his imagination but also to insert his actual human friends into the stories, where they suffer the fate of his fictional characters. Thus, his friend Mike de Wolf finds himself unwittingly playing the part of a character in a swashbuckling tale set on the high seas of the Caribbean in the 17th century. At the end of the book, Mike returns to his hometown of New York, but as he looks up to the sky, he catches a fleeting glimpse of a divine typist in the clouds against the moon: "Up there—God? In a dirty bathrobe?"[18] And so, he is left wondering if he might be yet another character in someone else's story. As the author, Horace

Hackett himself reflects at one point in the novel, the power of the writer is a truly "godlike" ability to fashion worlds and control people's lives:

> The way you feel about stories sometimes. It's—well, sort of divine, somehow. Here we are able to make and break characters and tangle up their lives and all, and sometimes the characters get so big for us that they sort of write themselves. . . .
>
> When I go knocking out the wordage and really get interested in my characters it almost makes me feel like—a god or something . . .
>
> It's a great business . . . Nothing like being a writer.[19]

Indeed, Hackett as an author is said to wield the very same power over his imaginary universe as the traditional God does over this material world. Thus, when a Catholic priest in the story invokes the name of God, the character Mike cannot help thinking about the "true identity of this priest's god and vividly imagining Horace Hackett."[20] As we will see below, this godlike power to create and manipulate new universes would later be described as the ultimate goal of Scientology itself—the goal of a liberated spirit or "Operating Thetan," which is not only free of the limitations of the physical universe but also free to create its own universe.

"HOMO NOVIS, HERE WE COME": THE BIRTH OF DIANETICS

Beginning in the early 1950s, Hubbard turned his energies from science fiction to a new science of the mind called Dianetics. The transition between Hubbard's science fiction writings and his work on Dianetics was, in many ways, a fairly smooth one. Dianetics itself first appeared in the May 1950 issue of *Astounding Science Fiction*, a popular magazine to which Hubbard was a regular contributor. The cover of this issue featured an apelike, alien creature with yellow cat eyes, whom readers would learn is the Duke of Kraakahaym from the Empire of Skontar.[21] As George Pendle notes, Dianetics was not presented as science fiction, but it did appeal to the same sorts of readers of this and similar magazines: "its language was clearly tailored to the science fiction fan. Like the Charles Atlas bodybuilding advertisements that also ran in the pulp pages, Dianetics promised to transform the reader's 'normal brain' into an 'optimum brain' and thus help man continue his process of evolution toward a higher organism."[22]

From the very outset, Hubbard claimed that his new science of Dianetics would lead to a vastly superior state of human existence and well-being. In an issue of *Marvel Science Stories* published in 1951, he presented Dianetics as the path to a new kind of human, a Homo superior or Homo novis, far surpassing the ordinary abilities, health, and intellect of mere Homo sapiens.[23] As he put it in a lecture the following year entitled A *History of Man*, the Homo novis is "about a skyscraper higher than Homo sapiens. . . . Compared to a Homo sapiens, Homo novis is very high and godlike."[24] As fellow science fiction writer, Jack Williamson put it, Dianetics offered nothing less than "the promise to liberate the superman trapped inside us."[25]

It is worth noting, however, that Hubbard was not the first science fiction writer to offer these speculations about a future new state of humanity. In fact, the very same ideal of a "Homo novis" or "superman" had been expressed by fellow science fiction writer Robert Heinlein just a couple of years before in a story entitled "Gulf," which was also published in *Astounding Science Fiction* in 1949. Here the "superman or New Man, Homo novis" refers to a secret society of geniuses who would have the ability to protect humanity, banding together and remaining genetically separate in order to create a new species of benevolent rulers:

> Supermen are superthinkers; anything else is a side issue . . . New Man will beat out homo sap in homo sap's own specialty—rational thought, the ability to recognize data, store them, integrate them, evaluate correctly the result.[26]
>
> There have been New Men all through history; I doubt if most of them suspected that their difference entitled them to be called a different breed.[27]

In addition to Heinlein, there is also very likely some influence from the German philosopher Friedrich Nietzsche in Hubbard's concept of the Homo novis. Although Hubbard only referred to Nietzsche briefly and rather dismissively in his published work, [28] his concept of the new man or "superman" clearly has much in common with Nietzsche's *Ubermensch* ("overman"), which was well known by this time through English translations of Nietzsche's writings during the early 20th century.[29] As we will see below, Nietzsche's influence can probably be seen in the later, more developed ideas of Scientology of the 1950s as well.

Hubbard, however, took the idea of a new man much further than either Heinlein or Nietzsche had probably imagined. Already by 1952, Hubbard was claiming that a truly "self-determined being" would be far beyond even the Homo novis imagined in his publications of just a few years before: "Compared to a truly self-determined being, Homo novis is an ant ready to die under anybody's misstep."[30] As we will see below, he would soon claim that his new religion of Scientology could unleash the ultimate power of the spiritual self, a power capable of creating and destroying entire universes.

SCIENTOLOGY AND THE BIRTH OF THE THETAN

Dianetics was briefly very successful as a cultural fad, selling thousands of copies, spreading like wildfire across the United States and England, and spawning a wide array of small Dianetics clubs. Yet already by 1951, the Dianetics movement had run into financial trouble and then went bankrupt by 1952. Out of the ashes of Dianetics, however, Hubbard created a new and even more ambitious movement—indeed, a "church" and self-identified religion—called Scientology in December 1953. Despite its new name and self-consciously religious trappings, Hubbard's early Scientology movement continued many of the science fiction themes already present in Dianetics. If anything, it took them much further, and we can see even more explicit continuities between Hubbard's science fiction and Scientology.

The most infamous and controversial portion of Hubbard's space opera narrative is contained in the confidential upper levels of Scientology training that describe the mysterious figure of Xenu (or Xemu), the ruler of a Galactic Confederacy who lived 75 million years ago. This is the narrative that was viciously satirized in an episode of the animated television satire *South Park* in 2005. However, the Xenu story was itself a relatively late innovation, revealed in the late 1960s as part of Hubbard's advanced Operating Thetan (OT) materials. In fact, the Xenu story is just one small part of a far more elaborate set of space opera narratives that began in the earliest Scientology lectures of the 1950s.[31] As Susan Raine concludes, one could say that "Hubbard designed Scientology as a space opera, transforming fiction into reality as a means to set out his elaborate ideas in a real-world setting."[32]

One of the most important innovations in the shift from Dianetics to Scientology in the 1950s was Hubbard's concept of theta—his general term for spirit or spiritual reality—and the thetan—his term for the individual spiritual entity, which is our true identity as an immortal being. Beginning in 1951, Hubbard claimed that he had scientifically identified and isolated the spiritual self, the thetan, which is at once separable from the physical body and possessed of unlimited powers.[33] In Hubbard's early Scientology cosmology, the thetan is a godlike entity of infinite potential, originally able to create, maintain, and control its own universe. As David Bromley explains, "At one time thetans were godlike, celestial entities, possessed their distinctive individuality and created and controlled their 'Home Universes.'"[34]

For reasons that are not entirely clear, however, the once all-powerful thetan has become enmeshed in this present universe of matter, energy, space, and time (MEST), which Hubbard describes as a "trap," a "prison," and an "illusion."[35] As Hubbard explained in lectures from the early 1950s, the universe that we call "reality" is in fact a *collective fiction* and the result of a process of *mutual agreement*, created and maintained by our own continual acceptance that it should be considered real: "What is commonly believed to be truth is agreement upon natural law . . . [T]he MEST universe . . . is itself an agreed-upon illusion."[36]

> There is no question here of whether space, energy or objects are *real*. Things are as real as one is certain of their reality. Reality is, here on Earth, "agreement as to what is." This does not prevent barriers or time from being formidably *real*. It does not mean, either, that space, energy or time are not illusions. It is as one knows it is. For one makes, by a process of continuous automatic duplication, all that one perceives.[37]

This idea of this universe as a kind of illusion or fiction has much in common with a number of earlier philosophical and religious ideas. More than one author has noted the similarities of this image of the godlike thetan trapped in matter to early Christian Gnostic cosmology, and Hubbard himself would sometimes describe Scientology as a "gnostic religion."[38] Perhaps even more clearly, however, Hubbard's idea of reality as a sort of "mutual agreement" and collective fiction has clear antecedents in the work of Friedrich Nietzsche, which, as we saw above, probably also influenced his idea of the "new man" or Homo novis. Hubbard's idea of reality as mutual agreement is particularly reminiscent of Nietzsche's famous definition of truth as a "mobile army of metaphors . . . a sum of human relations . . . Truths are illusions about which one has forgotten that this is what they are." [39] Hubbard's notion of reality as agreement also recalls the Nietzschean idea of perspectivism, or the idea that "The world . . . is *interpretable*. It has no meaning behind it but countless meanings."[40] Finally, we should note that this idea of "reality as mutual agreement" also bears a striking resemblance to the idea of the "social construction of reality," which would soon become widely popularized by sociologists such as Peter Berger and Thomas Luckmann in the late 1960s.[41] Indeed, one could argue that Hubbard foreshadowed many of Berger and Luckmann's ideas by a decade or more.

Whatever its philosophical origins, however, Hubbard's space opera cosmology describes the thetan entering into the MEST universe beginning roughly 60 trillion years ago. This vast period of time is called the "Whole Track" or the entire "Time Track" of our past lives in this universe. During that vast span of time, we have each lived countless lives in various forms—sometimes as humans, sometimes as aliens, sometimes as animals, sometimes as beings with the power to destroy entire worlds:

So you've been in and out of bodies, you've been thought people, you've been this, you've been that. You've been sheep, goats, spacemen, space officers. You've been governors, kings, princes, ditch-diggers, slaves, glaziers, carpenters, bricklayers, amusement park barkers, operators. You have turned planets into parks and parks into cinders. You. At one time on the track, have had weapons in your hands of sufficient magnitude to just say "Boom!" and the whole planet goes up . . . You talk about drama.[42]

In other works, such as *Have You Lived Before This Life* (1958), Hubbard records the past life memories of various individuals uncovered through Scientology auditing. Many of these include remarkable adventures on other worlds, often occurring tens of thousands or even trillions of years in the past, such as inhabiting a "Space Command post on Earth" 17,543 years ago, or being interrogated by Martian automatons, or swimming as a Manta Ray under the sea of another world, or flying a saucer over an ocean on a distant planet.[43]

It is not difficult to see the parallels between these Scientology narratives and Hubbard's own science fiction. Indeed, these accounts of the thetan's adventures on various worlds in distant galaxies sounds very much like the tales of Ole Doc Methuselah and his voyages to distant realms. In fact, Hubbard himself was fairly explicit about the links between science fiction and his own elaborate description of the history of the universe. The author of science fiction is in fact partially remembering the *history* of the universe, but he is mistakenly projecting it *forward* in time: "The science fiction writer's memory is faulty, and he gets himself all restimulated and so forth and doesn't remember straight. Some of them remember quite well, but then they reverse the time . . . and put it all into the future."[44]

Ultimately, in Hubbard's early lectures, the goal of Scientology is to realize and unleash the unlimited power of the thetan. The thetan is, after all, originally a being of infinite potential; the goal of auditing is therefore to release it from its entrapment in MEST and so reawaken its tremendous power to shape and reshape reality. Both Hubbard's early lectures and various testimonials from Scientologists claim an array of powers for the liberated thetan. These include not just optimal psychological and physical health, but also paranormal abilities such as the power to see through walls, telepathy, and "remote viewing" or seeing events from distances outside the body. Scientology publications such as *Advance!* and *Source* include numerous success stories from individuals who acquire powers both miraculous and mundane. Some recount being able to prevent rain from falling, while others claim to be able to shut off a neighbor's noisy sprinkler system and fix broken appliances.[45] "I love it," wrote one enthusiastic Scientologist, "like Superman!"[46]

One of the most often reported powers of the liberated thetan is "exteriorization" or the ability to travel outside the physical body. Beginning by first moving just a few feet in back of the head, the thetan eventually learns to travel at great distances beyond the body, not just around the earth, but also to the Moon, the Sun, Mars, and other planets. Like Ole Doc Methuselah, the thetan ultimately embarks on a "Grand Tour" of the universe, sliding down plumes on the Sun and going inside black holes: "So you say, 'Find a plume and slide down on it on to the face of the Sun' . . . You could have him find Mars. 'Be outside Mars and move down the surface.' But he's immediately going to discover the force field of Mars . . . It's not science fiction."[47]

At the highest stages, the thetan can not only travel at will around the known universe, it ultimately has the ability to "create its own universe."[48] As he developed Scientology in the 1950s, Hubbard described different stats of the thetan, such as "Cleared Theta Clear" and finally "Operating Thetan" (OT). Thus, someone who has achieved Cleared Theta Clear is "a person who is able to create his own universe or, living in the MEST universe, is able to create illusions perceived by others at will, to handle MEST universe objects without mechanical means and to have and feel no need of bodies or even the MEST universe."[49] And any world that the Clear Theta Clear chooses to create will in fact be far better, richer, and in fact *"more real"* than the so-called real world—that is, "sharper and brighter than the MEST universe itself."[50]

One who has achieved the state of Operating Thetan, meanwhile, can essentially do *anything* it pleases. The state of OT is one in which the thetan is not just liberated but empowered to do anything it chooses, create anything, or go anywhere: "He would be able to be anywhere as a fine point or everywhere as a generalized area . . . [H]e could be anything at will."[51] The liberated thetan could even freely create a personal paradise, populating it with heavenly beings and infinite pleasures at will: "You make forty mock-ups and they dance back and forth, put blue veils on them, and put them in a sky with clouds, and you have a Mohammedan heaven."[52]

Therefore, the thetan who realizes his power to create and destroy universes would in effect be "beyond God"—that is, beyond whichever so-called god happened to create this particular MEST universe. Indeed, Hubbard suggests that the thetan has been deceived into worshiping such a god by mainstream religion and so has forgotten its own power to create universes: "What passed for God for the MEST universe is not the goddest God there is by an awful long way . . . [W]hoever made that MEST universe was a usurper of one's own universe. And this has been sold to the individual, and it has sold the individual out of its ability to make and control universes."[53] In effect, as Hubbard's former staff member Cyril Voster, recalls, "[Hubbard] was saying that you and everyone else with the use of Scientology . . . could become a god. And we were all, if you like, fallen gods."[54] Indeed, an advertisement for Operating Thetan in *Source* magazine promises that one can even become "mightier than Apollo," a "powerful and causative being," with mastery "in the sea, sky, and earth," and "a truly godlike power."[55]

The acquisition of superpowers remains a central goal of Scientology practice to this day. Beginning in 1998, the church began construction of a massive complex called the Super Power Building in Clearwater, Florida, designed to offer the confidential Scientology training known as the "Super Power Rundown." According to Hubbard, this Super Power training is "a super fantastic, but confidential series of rundowns that can be done on anybody . . . that puts the person into fantastic shape unleashing Super Power of a thetan. This means that it puts Scientologists into a new realm of ability enabling them to create a new world."[56]

Here we see that the full power of the thetan is ultimately the same as that of the *writer*, as Hubbard understands it—namely, the power to create, manipulate, and destroy one's own universe. Hubbard himself made this connection between the divine power of the thetan and the divine power of the author quite explicit in several lectures from the early 1950s, such as this one from 1952. Just as the writer has the ability to create worlds through his imagination, so too, the thetan has the divine ability to create and manipulate entire new universes. Again, this is a matter of first learning to "*disagree*" with the existing MEST reality and then developing the ability to create an alternative reality of unlimited possibilities:

> Highest of thetan is evidently the creation and management of universes. The way you create and manage a universe is you invent some space and then you have to invent some time . . . And that's very simple to do . . . there's actually no limitations upon the creation of this . . .
>
> Let's take a writer sitting at his desk, and he's pounding a typewriter, and so what's he doing? Inventing time and space, and energy and matter and so on. Only trouble is, he takes it out and he compares it to the real universe and the real universe says, "I'm real because I can kick your shins in, but that cliff you just invented in that story, it isn't even vaguely going to hurt anybody." And the fellow has been beaten down like this for an awful long space of time, so he doesn't bother to fix up his cliffs so that if you kick them they kick back. This doesn't say he can't . . .
>
> Now, this universe, of course, doesn't occupy all the space there is and it doesn't occupy all the time there is. You could compose another

universe and it wouldn't go at right angles to this universe, because this universe, if you knew the truth of it, isn't here . . . This universe really isn't here; it's an illusion.[57]

In this telling passage, the godlike power of the thetan is described as simply an *extension* of the godlike, world-creating power of the author. The only difference between the two is that the latter has not yet realized that he is, in fact, creating new universes that are as real as, if not *more* real than, MEST universe itself.

CONCLUSIONS: THE LEGACY OF HUBBARD'S WORK IN THE NEW AGE AND BEYOND

To conclude, I would like to briefly discuss the legacy of Hubbard's fiction more broadly in New Age and alternative spirituality since the 1960s. Again, this ideal of the author as a divine being creating worlds from his imagination is not entirely original to Hubbard. We can see aspects of this ideal already in 19th-century English and German Romantic literature, particularly in the "cult of the genius," or the ideal of the artist as a figure with "godlike powers," able to generate new worlds out of his creative imagination. As Darrin McMahon notes in his history of genius, the Romantics embraced the ideal of "the genius's enchanted lineage, celebrating it openly with references to the prophets and protectors, the saviors and apostles, the angels and genii who had formerly watched over human beings. That the genius was their heir—a modern hero in possession of superhuman powers—was made explicit."[58] As Percy Bysshe Shelley famously put it in 1821, truly great writers possess a mysterious "power of communicating and receiving intense and impassioned conceptions"; they generate a kind of "electric life, which burns within their words. They measure the circumference and sound the depths of human nature with a comprehensive and penetrating spirit . . . Poets are the hierophants of an unapprehended inspiration."[59] We should note that Nietzsche was another great 19th-century advocate of the "religion of genius," though he also acknowledged that the genius might be perceived by others as an evil individual, despite his greatness: "He would manipulate falsehood, force, the most ruthless self-interest as his instruments so skillfully he could only be called an evil, demonic being, even though his ultimate goals would be 'great and good.'"[60]

A second clear antecedent of Hubbard's notion of the divine power of the mind is the New Thought movement, which also emerged in the 19th century and had a tremendous influence on most later forms of New Age and alternative spirituality. As the International New Thought Alliance put it in a statement of 1916, its core principles rest upon the idea of the "Divinity of Man and his Infinite Possibilities through the creative power of constructive thinking." For New Thought advocates such as Phineas P. Quimby, all human ills such as disability and disease are in fact a result of incorrect *thinking*, and therefore the ability to heal the body and transform material reality itself lies through the divine power of Mind.[61]

Yet despite these many eclectic influences, Hubbard articulated what is arguably the boldest and most radical formulation of the idea that we can in fact create our own realities. In Hubbard's thetan, the romantic ideal of the author as divine genius is combined with the ideal of the divine power of mind and the supernatural powers of the spirit, culminating in the goal of imagining and creating one's own universe. This is an idea that would later become a central tenant of the broader New Age movement of the 1960s and 1970s.

Just a decade after Hubbard, key channelers such as Jane Roberts would begin to articulate this same idea of the divine, creative power of the human mind. As Roberts put it, speaking with the voice of her channeled entity, "Seth": "In reality you project your own energy out to form the physical world. Therefore, to change your world, it is yourself you must change. You must change what you project."[62] While Hubbard had used the metaphor of a typewriter to describe the divine, creative power of the individual, Roberts used the metaphor of radio and television, suggesting that we "change the channels" of our consciousness in order to "tune in" to new and better realities.[63] A few years later, in the 1970s, other hugely influential channelers such as JZ Knight and her channeled entity Ramtha would express the very same idea, proclaiming that God lies within every human being and that we all have the divine power to create, recreate and transform our own realities: "Instead of being a reactive person, to be a master of the reality, even our house, even our family, our workplace, our greater place of enjoyment. That instead of reacting in the old ways, that we absolutely cultivate the ability to create new realities."[64]

In this sense, Hubbard might be seen as key link between older 19th-century currents such as New Thought and the New Age movement that flourished just a few decades after the birth of Scientology. Wedding the Romantic ideal of the author as a being of "godlike, superhuman powers" with the New Thought ideal of transformative power of mind, Hubbard gave the ideal of "creating new realities" one of its earliest and most radical formulations.

Finally, this idea of the author as creator of new realities also helps resolve the question that my students always ask about Scientology: Did he just make it all up? Or did he really believe any of this stuff about space opera, past lives on other planets, and the superhuman power of the thetan? Based on

Hubbard's own fiction and his early writings on Scientology, the answer to *both* of these questions is clearly the affirmative. That is, Hubbard believed in the power of the individual thetan—like the power of a science fiction writer—to create new realities. And these new realities would in fact be *more real* than the so-called "real" universe itself, which for Hubbard is actually an illusion and a product of mutual agreement. As Hubbard himself put it in one particularly telling moment during his *Philadelphia Doctorate Course* lectures of 1952,

> Now all this, of course—I'm just kidding you mostly. I don't believe that you've been in the universe seventy-six trillion years . . . I don't believe any of these things and I don't want to be agreed with about them . . . All I'm asking is that we take a look at this information, and then go through a series of class-assigned exercises . . . In other words, let's see if we can't disagree with this universe, just a little bit.[65]

In this sense, Hubbard's religion of Scientology and all its elaborate space opera cosmology might best be understood as an imaginative attempt to *disagree with the universe*—that is, to create an alternative world in which the ultimate potential of the thetan (or writer) might be liberated. Indeed, Scientology is perhaps best understood as a religion of the *author*, a religion based on a profound faith in the ability of the individual to *write his own story*, to imagine his own universe, and to become all powerful within that universe.

Of course, the story of L. Hubbard and the Church of Scientology is also a story of intense controversy, scandal, and criticism. Not only has Scientology been frequently dismissed as science fiction nonsense, but its leadership has long been accused of fraud, abuse, and criminal activities. In the eyes of many critics, Hubbard was not simply imagining alternative universes and new realities; he was also *imposing* his version of reality onto his followers, often in ways that were manipulative, damaging, and destructive. To cite just a few of countless possible examples, Nancy Many was a former high-ranking Scientologist and head of the church's Celebrity Centre in Hollywood. After leaving the church, she concluded that Hubbard was less a religious leader than a delusional charlatan who fabricated a pseudo-religion in pursuit of his own wealth and power: "The man was mercurial . . . Now I feel that he was a sociopath. I think L. Ron Hubbard created a criminal, human-trafficking, human-rights abusing money tree."[66] Similarly, Hubbard's former medical officer, Jim Dincalci, listed Hubbard's traits as "paranoid personality. Delusions of grandeur. Pathological lying." Others, such as psychiatry professor Stephen Wiseman, have diagnosed Hubbard as a "malignant narcissist" characterized by "aggressive grandiosity."[67] In the eyes of his many critics, Hubbard was manipulating his followers in the fabricated reality of Scientology in the same way that the writer Horace Hackett had manipulated his characters in the fabricated narratives of *Typewriter in the Sky.*

Herein, perhaps, lies the core of Scientology's intensely controversial history. Praised by some as the ultimate means to free the unlimited potential of the human spirit and derided by others as a dangerous cult of greed promising false hopes and delusional dreams, Scientology embodies both the grandest aspirations and the darkest fears of the human imagination itself.

NOTES

1. Hubbard, *Typewriter in the Sky* (Los Angeles: Galaxy Press, 2013), 57.

2. Hubbard, *Secrets of the MEST Universe* (Los Angeles: Bridge Publications, 1990), 54.

3. See Harriet Whitehead, "Reasonably Fantastic: Some Perspectives on Scientology, Science Fiction, and Occultism," in *Religious Movements in Contemporary America,* ed. I. I. Zaretsky and M. P. Leone (Princeton: Princeton University Press, 1974); Hugh B. Urban, *The Church of Scientology: A History of a New Religion* (Princeton: Princeton University Press, 2011), 33–39; Susan Raine, "Astounding History: L. Ron Hubbard's Scientology Space Opera," *Religion* 45, no. 1 (2015): 66–88.

4. "Trapped in the Closet," *South Park,* November 16, 2005.

5. Joel Sappell and Robert W. Welkos, "Defining the Theology," *Los Angeles Times,* June 24, 1990, http://www.latimes.com/local/la-scientologyidea062490-story .html#page=1.

6. See Raine, "Astounding History."

7. Hubbard, *Fear and Typewriter in the Sky,* 57; Hubbard, *Secrets of the MEST Universe,* 54. See Urban, *Church of Scientology,* 36–37, 79–82.

8. See Darrin McMahon, *Divine Fury: A History of Genius* (New York: Basic Books, 2013), 115.

9. On New Thought, see William James's classic work, *The Varieties of Religious Experience: A Study in Human Nature* (New York: Penguin, 1982), 71ff.; and more recent works such as Courtney Bender, *The New Metaphysicals: Spirituality and the American Imagination* (Chicago: University of Chicago Press, 2010).

10. When Hubbard first began to present Scientology as a "religion" he first compared it explicitly to Hinduism and Buddhism. See Hubbard, *The Phoenix Lectures: Freeing the Human Spirit* (Los Angeles: Golden Era Productions, 2007), 34. See also Stephen Kent, "Scientology's Relationship with Eastern Religions," *Journal of Contemporary Religion* 11, no. 1 (1996): 30; Urban, *Church of Scientology,* chapter 2.

11. On Hubbard as spiritual *bricoleur,* see Urban, *Church of Scientology,* chapter 1.

12. J. Gordon Melton, *Finding Enlightenment: Ramtha's School of Ancient Wisdom* (Hillsboro, OR: Beyond Words Publishing, 1998), 64. See Wouter J. Hanegraaff, *New Age Religion and Western Culture: Esotericism in the Mirror of Secular Thought* (Albany, NY: SUNY Press, 1996), 207; Hugh B. Urban, "The Medium is the Message

in the Spacious Present: Channeling, Television and the New Age," in *Handbook of Spiritualism and Channeling*, ed. Cathy Gutierrez (Leiden: Brill), 319–339.

13. See Urban, *Church of Scientology*, chapter 1; Raine, "Astounding History."

14. Pendle, *Strange Angel: The Otherworldly Life of John Whiteside Parsons* (Orlando: Harcourt, 2005), 253.

15. Hubbard, *Fear* (Los Angeles: Galaxy Press, 1992), 71.

16. Hubbard, *Ole Doc Methuselah* (Los Angeles: Bridge Publications, 1992), xv. See also Hubbard, *To the Stars* (Los Angeles: Galaxy Press, 2004), 210.

17. See Urban, *Church of Scientology*, chapter 1.

18. Hubbard, *Typewriter*, 192.

19. Hubbard, *Typewriter*, 57.

20. Hubbard, *Typewriter*, 103.

21. Hubbard, "Dianetics: The Evolution of a Science," *Astounding Science Fiction* 45, no. 3 (May 1950): 43–87.

22. Pendle, *Strange Angel: The Otherworldly Life of John Whiteside Parsons* (Orlando: Harcourt, 2005), 272.

23. Hubbard, "The Dianetics Question: Homo Superior, Here We Come," *Marvel Science Stories* (May 1951): 111–113.

24. Hubbard, *A History of Man* (Los Angeles: Bridge Publications, 2007), 62–63.

25. Williamson, *Wonder's Child: My Life in Science Fiction* (New York: Bluejay Books, 1984), 186.

26. Heinlein, *Assignment in Eternity* (Riverdale, NY: Baen Publishing, 1953), 58.

27. Heinlein, *Assignment*, 61.

28. See Hubbard, *Technical Bulletins of Dianetics and Scientology*, vol. 1 (Los Angeles: Scientology Publications, 1976), 294.

29. It is really worth comparing Hubbard's description of the Homo novis and superman to Nietzsche's famous formulation. See Walter Kaufmann, trans., *The Portable Nietzsche* (New York: Penguin, 1977), 124: "I teach you the overman. Man is something that shall be overcome . . . What is the ape to man? A laughing stock or a painful embarrassment. And man shall be just that for the overman: a laughingstock or a painful embarrassment."

30. Hubbard, *History of Man*, 62–63.

31. See Hubbard, *A Series of Lectures on the Whole Track* (Los Angeles: Bridge Publications, 1990); Hubbard, *Technique 88: Incidents on the Track Before Earth* (Los Angeles: Golden Era Productions, 2007); among numerous other works.

32. Raine, "Astounding History," 18; see Urban, *Church of Scientology*, 73–77.

33. See Hubbard, "The Parts of Man" (1956), in *The Technical Bulletins of Dianetics and Scientology*, vol. 2 (Los Angeles: Bridge Publications, 1976), 428; Hubbard, *What Is Scientology?* (Los Angeles: Bridge Publications, 1992), 209; Hubbard, *Dianetics and Scientology Technical Dictionary* (Los Angeles: Publication Organizations, 1975), 431.

34. Bromley, "Making Sense of Scientology: Prophetic, Contractual Religion," in James R. Lewis, ed., *Scientology* (New York: Oxford University Press, 2009), 91.

35. It is worth comparing Nietzsche and Hubbard here. As Nietzsche famously put it, "In the great whirlpool of forces man stands with the conceit that this whirlpool

is rational and has a rational aim: an error!" (*Portable Nietzsche*, 50). Compare this with Hubbard's *History of Man*, 62–63: "This universe is a rough universe. It is a terrible and deadly universe. Only the strong survive it, only the ruthless can own it . . . Fighting this battle for survival, and fight it he must, a being in the MEST universe cannot seem to afford decency or charity or ethics. He cannot afford any weakness, any mercy. The moment he does, he is lost—for he is surrounded by chilled, coarse rock and molten energy which, no matter the state of aberration of his social surroundings, will engulf him instantly that he ceases to obey the very least laws of MEST. This is a universe of force. It is not a universe of reason."

36. Hubbard, *Secrets of the MEST Universe*, 73. See Hubbard, *Scientology 8-8008* (Los Angeles: Church of Scientology of California, 1976), 61.

37. Hubbard, *The Creation of Human Ability* (Los Angeles: Bridge Publications, 2007), 349.

38. See Urban, *Church of Scientology*, 70; Mary Farrell Bednarowski, *New Religions and the Theological Imagination in America* (Bloomington: Indiana University Press, 1989), 34–35.

39. Nietzsche, "On Truth and Lie in an Extra-Moral Sense," in *The Portable Nietzsche*, 46–47: "What, then, is truth? A mobile army of metaphors, metonyms, and anthropomorphisms—in short, a sum of human relations . . . which after long use seem firm, canonical, and obligatory to a people; truths are illusions about which one has forgotten that this is what they are."

40. Nietzsche, *The Will to Power* (New York: Vintage, 1968), 261: "The world . . . is *interpretable*. It has no meaning behind it but countless meanings—'Perspectivism.'"

41. See Peter L. Berger and Thomas Luckmann, *The Social Construction of Reality: A Treatise in the Sociology of Knowledge* (New York: Anchor, 1967), 19–20: "The world of everyday life is not only taken for granted as reality by ordinary members of society . . . It is a world that originates in their thoughts and actions and is maintained by these."

42. Hubbard, *Technique 88*, 341.

43. Hubbard, *Have You Lived Before This Life? A Scientific Survey* (London: Hubbard Association of Scientologists, 1958), 108.

44. Hubbard, *A Series of Lectures*, tape 5.

45. "OT Adventures," *Source* 50 (1985): 13; "OT Phenomena," *Advance!* 33 (1975): 8. See also Urban, "The Occult Roots of Scientology? L. Ron Hubbard, Aleister Crowley and the Origins of a Controversial New Religion," *Nova Religio* 15, no. 3 (2012): 91–116.

46. "OT Phenomena Success," *Advance!* 17 (1973): 14–17; "Success Beyond Man's Wildest Dreams," *Advance!* 7 (1969): 3.

47. Hubbard, *Phoenix Lectures*, 471; see Urban, *The Church*, 77–79; Urban, "The Occult Roots."

48. Hubbard, *Philadelphia*, xi. See Hubbard, *Secrets of the MEST Universe*, 13.

49. Hubbard, *Scientology 8-8008*, 175.

50. Hubbard, *Scientology 8-8008*, 272. See Hubbard, *Secrets of the MEST Universe*, 93–94: "The most real universe is, of course, one's own illusory universe and should

be completely rehabilitated before one attempts to perceive or handle the MEST universe."

51. Hubbard, *Phoenix*, 373. See Hubbard, *Secrets of the MEST*, 61: "The biggest foe of the MEST universe is the person who can invent a universe, because you can invent a universe good enough and big enough that it'd eat this one up, if you concentrated on it hard enough."

52. Hubbard, *Philadelphia*, 6.

53. Hubbard, *Philadelphia*, 14.

54. Vosper, interview in Channel 4 Television, "Secret Lives: L. Ron Hubbard" (1997).

55. "Mightier than Apollo," *Source* (June/July 1979): 13. See Hubbard, *Secrets of the MEST Universe*, 85: "what it is is the only really easy solution a thetan ever had here on Earth: to be Diana, Artemis, or something of the sort, go around and spread legends about oneself, and so on. Actually interfere with, or fool around with, MEST bodies, and it's . . . You see, it's no joke, no joke."

56. Hubbard, *Dianetics and Scientology Technical Dictionary* (Los Angeles: Publication Organizations, 1975), 413.

57. Hubbard, *Secrets of the MEST Universe*, 54; see also Urban, "The Occult Roots."

58. McMahon, *Divine Fury*, 115.

59. Shelley, *A Defense of Poetry and Other Essays* (1840; CreateSpace, 2014), 37.

60. Nietzsche, *Human, All Too Human*, quoted in McMahon, *Divine Fury*, 196. As Nietzsche put it elsewhere, "My religion . . . lies in working for the production of genius" (McMahon, *Divine Fury*, 195).

61. "New Thought Religious Movement," *Encyclopedia Britannica*, 2015, http://www.britannica.com/event/New-Thought.

62. Jane Roberts, *The Seth Material* (Englewood Cliffs, NJ: Prentice Hall, 1970), 3.

63. See Roberts, *Seth Material*, 66, 252, 271; Urban, "Medium is the Message."

64. Knight, interviewed on *CNN Larry King Live*, August 2, 2008. See also Ramtha, *A Beginner's Guide to Creating Reality* (JZ Publishing, 2004).

65. Hubbard, *Philadelphia*, 4.

66. Many, interviewed in Hugh B. Urban, *New Age, Neopagan and New Religious Movements* (Berkeley: University of California Press, 2015), 145–146. The literature by ex-Scientologists and critics is obviously vast. See, for example, Nancy Many, *My Billion Year Contract: Memoir of a Former Scientologist* (CNM Publishing, 2009); Marc Headley, *Blown for Good: Behind the Iron Curtain of Scientology* (BFG Books, Inc., 2009); Janet Reitman, *Inside Scientology: The Story of America's Most Secretive Religion* (Mariner Books, 2013). For a discussion of these issues, see Urban, *The Church of Scientology*, chapter 4 and conclusion.

67. Lawrence Wright, *Going Clear: Scientology, Hollywood and the Prison of Belief* (New York: Vintage, 2013), 62. See also Stephen Kent, *Brainwashing in Scientology's Rehabilitation Project Force* (Hamburg: Interior Ministry, 2000); Susan Raine, "Surveillance in a New Religious Movement: Scientology as a Test Case," *Religious Studies and Theology* 28, no. 1 (2009): 63–94.

BIBLIOGRAPHY

Bednarowski, Mary Farrell. *New Religions and the Theological Imagination in America.* Bloomington: Indiana University Press, 1989.

Bender, Courtney. *The New Metaphysicals: Spirituality and the American Imagination.* Chicago: University of Chicago Press, 2010.

Berger, Peter L., and Thomas Luckmann. *The Social Construction of Reality: A Treatise in the Sociology of Knowledge.* New York: Anchor, 1967.

Bromley, David. "Making Sense of Scientology: Prophetic, Contractual Religion." In *Scientology*, edited by James R. Lewis. New York: Oxford University Press, 2009.

Hanegraaff, Wouter J. *New Age Religion and Western Culture: Esotericism in the Mirror of Secular Thought.* Albany: State University of New York Press, 1996.

Headley, Marc. *Blown for Good: Behind the Iron Curtain of Scientology.* BFG Books, 2009.

Heinlein, Robert A. *Assignment in Eternity.* Riverdale, NY: Baen Publishing, 1953.

Hubbard, L. Ron. *The Creation of Human Ability.* Los Angeles: Bridge Publications, 2007.

Hubbard, L. Ron. "Dianetics: The Evolution of a Science." *Astounding Science Fiction* 45, no. 3 (May 1950): 43–87.

Hubbard, L. Ron. *Dianetics and Scientology Technical Dictionary.* Los Angeles: Publication Organizations, 1975.

Hubbard, L. Ron. "The Dianetics Question: Homo Superior, Here We Come." *Marvel Science Stories* (May 1951): 111–113.

Hubbard, L. Ron. *Fear.* Los Angeles: Galaxy Press, 1992.

Hubbard, L. Ron. *Have You Lived Before This Life? A Scientific Survey.* London: Hubbard Association of Scientologists, 1958.

Hubbard, L. Ron. *A History of Man.* Los Angeles: Bridge Publications, 2007.

Hubbard, L. Ron. *Ole Doc Methuselah.* Los Angeles: Bridge Publications, 1992.

Hubbard, L. Ron. *The Philadelphia Doctorate Course.* Los Angeles: Golden Era Production, 2001.

Hubbard, L. Ron. *The Phoenix Lectures: Freeing the Human Spirit.* Los Angeles: Golden Era Productions, 2007.

Hubbard, L. Ron. *Scientology 8-8008.* Los Angeles: Church of Scientology of California, 1976.

Hubbard, L. Ron. *Secrets of the MEST Universe.* Los Angeles: Bridge Publications, 1990.

Hubbard, L. Ron. *A Series of Lectures on the Whole Track.* Los Angeles: Bridge Publications, 1990.

Hubbard, L. Ron. *The Technical Bulletins of Dianetics and Scientology*, volume 2. Los Angeles: Bridge Publications, 1976.

Hubbard, L. Ron. *Technique 88: Incidents on the Track Before Earth.* Los Angeles: Golden Era Productions, 2007.

Hubbard, L. Ron. *To the Stars.* Hollywood, CA: Galaxy Press, 2004.

Hubbard, L. Ron. *Typewriter in the Sky.* Los Angeles: Galaxy Press, 2013.

Hubbard, L. Ron. *What Is Scientology?* Los Angeles: Bridge Publications, 1992.

James, William. *The Varieties of Religious Experience: A Study in Human Nature.* New York: Penguin, 1982.

Kaufmann, Walter, trans. *The Portable Nietzsche*. New York: Penguin, 1977.

Kent, Stephen. *Brainwashing in Scientology's Rehabilitation Project Force*. Hamburg: Interior Ministry, 2000.

Kent, Stephen. "Scientology's Relationship with Eastern Religions." *Journal of Contemporary Religion* 11, no. 1 (1996) 21–36.

Many, Nancy. *My Billion Year Contract: A Memoir of a Former Scientologist*. CNM Publishing, 2009.

McMahon, Darrin. *Divine Fury: A History of Genius*. New York: Basic Books, 2013.

Melton, J. Gordon. *Finding Enlightenment: Ramtha's School of Ancient Wisdom*. Hillsboro, OR: Beyond Words Publishing, 1998.

Nietzsche, Friedrich. *The Will to Power*. New York: Vintage, 1968.

Pendle, George. *Strange Angel: The Otherworldly Life of John Whiteside Parsons*. Orlando, FL: Harcourt, 2005.

Quimby, Phineas P. *The Complete Writings*, edited by E. Seale. Marina Del Rey, CA: DeVross, 1988.

Raine, Susan. "Astounding History: L. Ron Hubbard's Scientology Space Opera." *Religion* 45, no. 1 (2015): 66–88.

Raine, Susan. "Surveillance in a New Religious Movement: Scientology as a Test Case." *Religious Studies and Theology* 28, no. 1 (2009): 63–94.

Ramtha. *A Beginner's Guide to Creating Reality*. JZ Publishing, 2004.

Reitman, Janet. *Inside Scientology: The Story of America's Most Secretive Religion*. Mariner Books, 2013.

Roberts, Jane. *The Seth Material*. Englewood Cliffs, NJ: Prentice Hall, 1970.

Shelley, Percy Bysshe. *A Defense of Poetry and Other Essays*. CreateSpace, 2014. First published 1840.

Urban, Hugh B. *The Church of Scientology: A History of a New Religion*. Princeton: Princeton University Press, 2011.

Urban, Hugh B. "The Medium is the Message in the Spacious Present: Channeling, Television and the New Age." In *Handbook of Spiritualism and Channeling*, edited by Cathy Gutierrez, 319–339. Leiden: Brill, 2015.

Urban, Hugh B. *New Age, Neopagan and New Religious Movements: Alternative Spirituality in Contemporary America*. Berkeley: University of California Press, 2015.

Urban, Hugh B. "The Occult Roots of Scientology? L. Ron Hubbard, Aleister Crowley and the Origins of a Controversial New Religion." *Nova Religio* 15, no. 3 (2012): 91–116.

Whitehead, Harriet. "Reasonably Fantastic: Some Perspectives on Scientology, Science Fiction, and Occultism." In *Religious Movements in Contemporary America*, edited by I. I. Zaretsky and M. P. Leone. Princeton: Princeton University Press, 1974.

Williamson, Jack. *Wonder's Child: My Life in Science Fiction*. New York: Bluejay Books, 1984.

Wright, Lawrence. *Going Clear: Scientology, Hollywood, and the Prison of Belief*. New York: Vintage, 2013.

3

Earth as Battlefield and Mission: Knowledge, Technology, and Power in L. R. Hubbard's Late Novels

Stefano Bigliardi

> Blito-P3 is the only place anyone has ever heard of where a butter gum and a criminal can rise by normal social processes to a point of absolute planetary control.
>
> —*Mission Earth: The Invaders Plan*, 580

INTRODUCTION

In August 1982, Lafayette Ron Hubbard (1911–1986) published, with St. Martin's Press of New York, the novel *Battlefield Earth: A Saga of the Year 3000*. Scientology's publishing companies, Bridge Publications and Galaxy Press, also published it later.[1] In October 1985, three months before Hubbard's death, the first book of his *Mission Earth* series appeared. The series is a novel in 10 volumes, and its publication was completed in September 1987.[2] The initial publisher, Bridge Publications, employed the term "dekalogy" to characterize such a series. Most likely, Hubbard fashioned this word himself. *Mission Earth* comprises the following volumes: *The Invaders Plan* (October 1985); *Black Genesis: Fortress of Evil* (March 1986); *The Enemy Within* (May 1986); *An Alien Affair* (August 1986); *Fortune of Fear* (October 1986); *Death Quest* (January 1987); *Voyage of Vengeance* (May 1987); *Disaster* (June 1987); *Villainy Victorious* (September 1987); and *The Doomed Planet* (September 1987).[3] The massive novels (*Battlefield Earth* counts in hardcover edition more than 750 pages, *Mission Earth* over 3,992) marked Hubbard's return to science-fiction writing since his golden days as a prolific pulp-fiction writer in the 1940s.

Both novels, according to their publishers, were met enthusiastically both by critics and the public, and indeed they did top best-seller lists in the United States. However, their critical reception, if one doesn't only take into account critics quoted in the volumes' editions as well as on their covers, was rather mixed and in some cases tended to blatantly ridicule the books both as to their narrative substance and writing technique.[4] Finally, there are serious reasons to think that the sales of both novels were inflated by prompting Scientologists to repeatedly purchase copies of the books.[5] In 2000, *Battlefield Earth* was adapted into a movie by director Roger Christian starring, among others, Scientologist John Travolta; it performed poorly at the box office and met with destructive criticism as one of the worst movies of all time.[6] Among the first scholars who engaged in an extensive recognition and analysis of Hubbard's output was Marco Frenschkowski, who after a brief review of the novels stated:

> [They have] so far received almost no attention, which perhaps they do deserve a bit more. They also have some quite interesting characters, especially when read with a deconstructionist approach. These 11 later novels by Hubbard are not Scientology propaganda literature, but have some topics in common, especially the very strong opposition against 20th century psychology and psychiatry, which is seen as a major source of evil. All open allusions to Scientology are strictly avoided. They are not as successful in their use of suspense and humour as Hubbard's early tales, but have to say perhaps more about the complex personality of their author.[7]

These pages take up Frenschkowski's invitation to critically reconsider Hubbard's late novels.[8] However, this is not *primarily* a detailed analysis of such novels from a narrative/stylistic viewpoint, an assessment of their literary worth, or a comparison of their content with Scientology's doctrines, even though I will touch upon all of these aspects. Furthermore, due to the extent and complexity of the works, some characters, subplots, and secondary themes will be necessarily left unexplored. Moreover, I do not venture at all into a reconstruction of *Battlefield Earth* and *Mission Earth*'s critical reception and controversy thereon. Rather, I read them with a particular focus on the way in which *knowledge* (broadly conceived so to include *natural science*) and *technology* (whether *real* or *fictional*) are conceptualized in their narratives and how they are related to the *power relationships* among characters. Finally, I link such aspects to the worldview expressed in the books. The results of my analysis can therefore be used by experts in science fiction, in Hubbard's biography and literature, and in Scientology's doctrines to complement their own observations.

DEDICATIONS AND INTRODUCTIONS

Battlefield Earth (*BE*) opens with a dedication: "This brand-new novel is dedicated to Robert A. Heinlein, A. E. van Vogt, John W. Campbell, Jr., and all the merry crew of science fiction and fantasy writers of the thirties and forties—The Golden Age—who made science fiction and fantasy the respected and popular literary genres they have become today." The expression "merry crew" is further made explicit in a note that actually occupies the whole page and that lists 80 authors, with the specification that "they are all worth rereading, every one" (*BE* xi). The list includes some well-known names such as Isaac Asimov, Robert Bloch, Ray Bradbury, Edgar Rice Burroughs, Karel Capek, Arthur C. Clarke, Aldous Huxley, H. P. Lovecraft, George Orwell, and H. G. Wells.

In the introduction, Hubbard states that the book was born in a period in which he had little to do and wanted to amuse himself by going back to what had been his professional occupation between 1930 and 1950, although as he explains, at that time he used it "to finance more serious researches" (*BE* xiii). He then expands on the activities and ideas of John W. Campbell Jr. (1910–1971), the editor of *Astounding Science Fiction* for which Hubbard started writing in 1938 (*BE* xiii). According to Hubbard, "Campbell played no small part in driving this society into the space age" (*BE* xv). Hubbard, who embraces Campbell's views, emphasizes that science fiction is neither sheer speculation on already existing science nor pure prophecy; rather, it plays an inspiring role for the scientists who read it: "It is the herald of possibility. It is the plea that someone should work on the future. . . . It is the dream that precedes the dawn when the inventor or the scientist awakens and goes to his books or his lab saying, 'I wonder whether I could make that dream come true in the world of real science'" (*BE* xvi). Hubbard insists that science fiction in the Golden Age had "a mission" (*BE* xix) and how it was avidly read by scientists; he even recalls an episode in which, while visiting "a major university's science department" he was recognized and congratulated by "professors and deans." He also states that "for a while, before and after World War II, [he] was in rather steady association with the new era of scientists, the boys who built the bomb, who were beginning to get the feeling of rockets" (*BE* xix).

In his introduction, Hubbard tries as well to keep science fiction distinct from fantasy. Both are based on imagination, on the representation of what is fictional; yet science fiction should elaborate on "the material universe and sciences; these can include economics, sociology, medicine, and suchlike, all of which have a material base" (*BE* xvii). In Hubbard's words, fantasy is easier to write: "science fiction, to be credible, has to be based on some degree of plausibility; fantasy gives no limits at all. . . . In fantasy, a guy has no sword in his hand; bang, there's a magic sword in his hand" (*BE* xviii–xix). According to Hubbard, "fantasy" was composed of ingredients that, at the time in which he is writing, have "vanished from the stage," such as "spiritualism, mythology, magic, divination, the supernatural" (*BE* xvii–xviii). However, he points out that materialistic science, whose success has eclipsed them, often "runs into (and sometimes adopts) such things as the Egyptian myths that man came from mud"; this doesn't mean, he specifies, that he necessarily believes in those ingredients of fantasy: "I am only saying"—he writes—"that there is another realm besides dedicated—and even simple-minded- materialism" (*BE* xviii). In the concluding paragraphs of the introduction, Hubbard states that *Battlefield Earth* is "pure science fiction": "to show that science fiction is not science fiction because of a particular kind of plot, [*Battlefield Earth*] contains practically every type of story there is—detective, spy, adventure, western, love, air war. . . . All except fantasy—there is none of it." He also adds that, since the term "science" also refers to economics, sociology, and medicine, "they are in here, too" (*BE* xx). As to Dianetics and Scientology, he states: "Some . . . may wonder that I did not include my own serious subjects in this book. It was with no thought of dismissal of them. It was just that I put on my professional writer's hat. I also did not want to give anybody the idea I was doing a press relations job for my other serious work" (*BE* xxi).

Mission Earth: The Invaders Plan (*IP*) is dedicated "To YOU, the millions of science fiction fans and general public who welcomed me back to the world of fiction so warmly, and to the critics and media who so pleasantly applauded the novel 'Battlefield Earth.' It's great working for you!" (*IP* i, Hubbard's capitalization). Also, this novel opens with an introduction signed by the author[9] entitled "Science Fiction and Satire." The text, semiacademic in character, recalls the history of satire as a literary genre dating back to Greek and Roman times. He points out how it was often intertwined with science fiction, when the description of the future on Earth or of an alien civilization was used to criticize present society. Referring to the narrative contained in the introduction to *Battlefield Earth*, the author specifies that when he was invited by Campbell to write science fiction he decided to expand on "people and the human potential" rather than on machine developments (*IP* vii). Satire is precisely the aspect of science fiction that he has decided to explore in *Mission Earth*, and he emphasizes that it is different from mere comedy: "Comedy . . . relies on the audience seeing a misplaced or unjustified emotion" (*IP* vii) whereas "satire is achieved by a caricature [and] . . . it is essentially concerned with exposing some flaw or excess" (*IP* viii). Hubbard emphasizes as well that "Satire . . . require[s] a discernment. One must be able to recognize what the joke is about" (*IP* ix). It is not written for the targets of satire itself, but "for others so that, like the fable, they can see that 'the emperor has no clothes'" (*IP* ix).

PLOT OVERVIEWS

Battlefield Earth (BE) takes place in the year 3000. Human beings are reduced to approximately 35,000 units scattered in isolated tribes on Earth after their planet has been colonized 1000 years earlier by an alien race, the Psychlos, who were attracted there by a Pioneer satellite. Psychlos have wolf-like amber eyes, and their faces are similar to human ones, but their eyebrows, eyelids, nose, and lips are made of bone; they are hairy and are nine feet tall; they are not made of cells but of viruses, and on Earth they need a special breathe-gas. Pitiless and rapacious in its constant search for precious minerals, the Psychlos empire also predates other civilizations in the universe.

The book's action begins in the Rocky Mountains, where Jonnie Goodboy Tyler, a human from a local tribe, decides to leave his village and explore the surroundings despite legends about the "demons" that chase and kill human beings. In the ruins of Denver, he is soon captured by Terl, the Psychlos chief of security. Terl is an ordinary example of his race. Prior to capturing Jonnie, Terl developed an interest in terrestrial history, discovering that the Rocky Mountains can be mined for gold. Moreover, he discovered that his company plans on extending his term on Earth, a location that he hates. Terl needs humans to perform the excavations since the gold lode is surrounded by radiation due to unused nuclear mines. Radiation is already affecting the humans, but it would prove fatal to the Psychlos, whose "breathe-gas" simply explodes when exposed to radioactivity. Terl ensures Jonnie's collaboration by capturing his friends Chrissie (who is to become Jonnie's wife) and her sister Pattie. Terl's plan is to teleport the gold in coffins used to ship dead Psychlos back to their planet. Meanwhile, Jonnie gains knowledge about Psychlos civilization (in particular, he learns their language with the help of discs) as well as Earth's past history.

While devising his own plans to leave the planet and get rich, Terl discovers that his superior, Numph, has organized a scam to steal money and minerals, and so Terl eventually kills him. Under the pretext of recruiting mining personnel, Jonnie travels to Scotland with Terl where he gathers a group of locals who start collaborating with him to set up a revolt. Terl does not understand English, and he is used to inspecting the mining site through a drone. However, Jonnie has recruited some body doubles that give the Psychlos the impression that he is at the mining site, while in fact he is exploring Earth and making new contacts and allies. Jonnie and the Scots manage to ship nuclear bombs to attack the Psychlos who are therefore destroyed; subsequently, they turn into a sun. Jonnie then manages to reorganize Earth under a confederation, in order to counter his rival, Brown Staffor, who would like to take possession of Earth. The newly established confederation opposes an alien race, the Tolneps, that aims at invading Earth, as well as the Galactic bank that similarly wants to take possession of the planet and sell it due to the Psychlos' unpaid debts. Meanwhile, more is discovered about the Psychlos: their mathematical system, how their teleportation works, and that they actually were subjugated by their upper class and manipulated through the insertion of devices implanted in their brains that deprived them of empathy (and prevented females from learning mathematics). Removing the device cures the few surviving Psychlos. Teleportation technology is extended to all the planets of the Confederation. Once Earth is settled and the major problems are solved, Jonnie voluntarily disappears together with his family.

In *Mission Earth: The Invaders Plan* (IP), the first of the ME series, the authorities of the planet Voltar plan an invasion of Earth (Blito-P3 in their language). Upon realizing that the terrestrials are ruining their own planet through pollution, they decide to send the Fleet Engineer Jettero Heller to save it 100 years prior to the scheduled conquest. This interferes with the plans of Lombar Hisst, chief of the Coordinated Information Apparatus, a governmental organization composed of former convicts, who intends to usurp Voltar's empire (an imperial confederacy that comprises 120 planets and is ruled by the emperor through a Grand Council).

Hisst is already using the Earth for the production of drugs that he uses to enslave Voltar's aristocracy. Hisst appoints the inept secret agent Soltan Gris to stop Heller. (In fact, the story is told from Gris's viewpoint as if it was a written confession to Voltarian authorities.) Heller is helped by the Comtess Krak, a trainer, who eventually becomes his lover. With great subterfuge, Heller implanted a device in his head that allows Gris to see and hear through his eyes and ears. The spaceship carrying Heller and Gris leaves Voltar and heads back to Earth.

The second novel in the series, *Black Genesis: Fortress of Evil* (BG) finds Heller and Gris in a Voltarian base on Earth, located in Afyon, Turkey. Gris, who in Turkey uses the pseudonym Sultan Bey, finds out that he is controlled by Hisst through a spy and threatened with death in case of failure. Gris provides Heller with a fake identity that is actually meant to attract attention to him while sending him on a pretext to the United States. Heller's new identity is Delbert John Rockecenter Jr., the son of the richest man on Earth—a man whose corporation controls the whole planet through the oil industry. However, Heller, who on Earth looks like an extremely handsome teenager, familiarizes himself with terrestrial society, avoids Gris's traps, and allies himself with the Corleone family, which manages a brothel in New York where he happens to sojourn. Heller also enrolls in a college called Empire University to study nuclear engineering. He is strongly opposed there by Miss Simmons, a secretary and a teacher, who hates all those who are interested in nuclear applications. Eventually, Heller saves her from a rape attempt.

The third novel in Hubbard's dekalogy, *The Enemy Within* (EW), begins with Heller implementing his plans by putting together a group of volunteers from the university campus, including the finance genius, Izzy Epstein. Meanwhile, the Rockecenter Corporation has become aware of his intentions and tries to destroy his reputation through a media campaign orchestrated by the expert J. Walter Madison. Gris purchases a Turkish concubine named Utanc who, rather than pleasing him, begins manipulating him to obtain money and expensive commodities.

The series continues with *An Alien Affair* (AA). Heller successfully faces Gris's repeated attempts at having him murdered as well as those set up by the Narcotici mob, the Corleone family's archenemies. The reader is also given several insights into the Rockecenter's manipulative techniques that include the usage of drugs, psychology, psychiatry, and rock and roll music. Meanwhile, Gris has his penis medically enlarged and begins lusting after the book's female characters.

In *Fortune of Fear* (FF), Comtess Krak arrives at the base in Afyon and soon heads to the United States in order to join Heller. However, Gris manages to have a device implanted in her similar to Heller's. In this novel, Heller, using a Voltarian device that allows him to see into the future, leaves the casinos of Atlantic City broke and even finally wins ownership of the *whole* city. Gris comes into possession of an enormous amount of gold and engages in the systematic rape of female characters—including two lesbians who are thus "cured" of their homosexuality. Similarly, Comtess Krak manages to win Miss Simmons's affection for Heller by implanting in her the false memory of a rape that cures her from her hatred of men.

Death Quest (DQ) is the sixth book in the series. In it, Gris hires a necrophiliac professional killer to kill Countess Krak, but the man ends up chasing Gris himself and gets killed in his turn. Gris also begins to interact with a teenage nymphomaniac called Teenie Whopper. In *Voyage of Vengeance* (VO), the seventh novel, Gris begins a cruise around the Mediterranean together with Teenie. He manages to have Countess Krak imprisoned, while Heller believes she has died in the crash of her airplane—a crash that Gris caused when he used his spaceship to intercept her flight from the United States to Turkey.

Book number eight, *Disaster* (D), relates how Heller frees Countess Krak. Relieved, Heller overtly starts opposing the Rockecenter Corporation. As part of his plan, he makes the whole oil supply on Earth radioactive and therefore useless; he releases spores into the air that clean it; and he provides the planet with a new energy source—a black hole orbiting around the planet. The process is not completely devoid of accidents: Heller sets out to drop ice he has collected on Saturn onto the North Pole in order to stabilize the terrestrial orbit. Attacked by an enemy spaceship, he drops the load and the Soviet Union is wiped out. Heller becomes aware of Gris's devious plans (as discussed in the previous novel), and he is taken back to Voltar to be judged for his crimes (this event justifies the form of the narrative up to this volume). At this point, the narrator changes: it is no longer Gris, but instead, a Voltarian investigative journalist, Monte Pennwell. The time frame is 100 years after the events reported so far. Pennwell has been uncovering Gris and Heller's vicissitudes together along with the Voltarian plans to conquer Earth.

In *Villainy Victorious* (VV), J. Walter Madison and Teenie Whopper travel to Voltar and start disrupting its society through terrestrial techniques: PR, narcotics, and the diffusion of sexual deviance. Teenie in particular turns the male children of the Voltarian aristocracy into lustful "catamites."

The Doomed Planet (DP) is the final novel of Hubbard's *Mission Earth* series. In it, Voltar is finally reconquered by Heller, who reveals how Hisst had subjugated its emperor through the usage of drugs. Order is restored in the empire, and a massive cover-up is implemented in order to eliminate any signs of past devastation. Earth is erased from the charts, and its existence is systematically denied (as is the case with the Voltarian Censor's statements that introduce each volume). Monte Pennwell himself (actually a lazy character who only acts out of ambition) fails in his attempt to reveal the story, the cover-up, as well as at prompting his fellow Voltarians into implementing the invasion, and he is sent into exile. However, his books on his family's initiative are published on Earth with Heller's approval.

KNOWLEDGE

Both in *Battlefield Earth* and in *Mission Earth*, knowledge, broadly defined, plays a pivotal role. The possession, by the characters, of a specific *skill* or *piece of information*, lack thereof, or access thereto, defines their respective roles and shapes their decisions or actions. Knowledge takes some basic, intertwined forms.[10]

Knowledge is, first of all, *linguistic*. Jonnie Goodboy Tyler starts understanding Psychlos civilization after acquiring their language through the discs recorded by another civilization that had, in turn, been conquered by them: "Life became a long parade of discs, stacks of discs . . . Jonnie kept on, kept on cramming years of education into weeks and months. There was so MUCH to know! He had to know it ALL!" (*BE* 73–74, Hubbard's emphasis).[11] Terl is prevented from understanding human plans because he does not speak English, and eventually he manages to lure terrestrials by using terms that stand for feelings unknown to Psychlos (cf. *BE* 458 and 474). Some major problems to the unification of the terrestrials are represented by linguistic differences: eventually Psychlo is adopted, and upon understanding that it is made up of "words and technical developments stolen from other people in the universe," it is called "Techno" (see *BE* 448–449, 848). In *Mission Earth* Gris is appointed for the mission because of his knowledge of Italian and Turkish (*IP* 18). Heller has to acquire terrestrial languages (including different accents, cf. *IP* 120 ff.). The Voltar robotranslator has a hard time rendering all terms in human language (and it replaces each vulgar term with a "bleep" [cf. *IP*, 6–9]), and *Battlefield Earth* is analogously, although incidentally, presented as a translation (BE, 1).

Second, *knowledge* is about the characters' respective plans and intentions. Terl devises a plot to escape Earth and get rich and has to keep it hidden from his superiors. Jonnie has a plan for insurrection that needs to be carried out without the Psychlos' knowledge. Later on, Terl tries to make an alliance with Jonnie's archenemy, and once more he plays several tricks (such as learning and using terms for feelings that he actually does not feel) in order to keep his intentions secret. The whole story of *Mission Earth* is about keeping several secrets—that is, keeping specific pieces of knowledge hidden: mainly, Gris's identity and plans from Heller, and Heller's identity and plans from the terrestrials. Conversely, the success of Heller's mission relies on his capacity to prove wrong the information diffused by black PR. According to Hubbard's device, the books themselves are a revelation. In reading them, Gris and Pennwell uncover Voltar's plans concerning Earth, but at the same time, Voltarian authorities constantly deny the truth of that very message.

Finally, knowledge is *practical know-how* strictly intertwined with *scientific knowledge*. *Battlefield Earth* begins when Terl gets to know the details of human history, including the existence of gold mines (in a conversation reported in the opening pages, he states that he "dug up" books "out of curiosity" [BE 2]). Jonnie's plans rely on the awareness that the Psychlos' breathe-gas explodes when exposed to radioactivity. After the defeat of the Psychlos, the humans engage in a long struggle to understand Psychlos mathematics, how teleportation works, and how the devices in their brains can be deactivated. Similarly, in *Mission Earth*, what marks the greatest difference between Voltar and Earth is the latter's lack of understanding of the mechanism of faster-than-light travel, as well as the principles allowing the construction of devices that can replace polluting technology or contain the damage already caused by it.

In both *Battlefield Earth* and *Mission Earth* entire civilizations (the Psychlos, the terrestrials, and later the Voltarians) are held in subjugation by social groups who keep and diffuse what Hubbard defines as a false and manipulative form of knowledge: psychology and psychiatry that lead people into a wrong (i.e., materialistic) understanding of themselves.

Psychology and psychiatry are constantly attacked and ridiculed throughout all of *Mission Earth*. It all starts when Gris begins learning about Earth as part of his training prior to the mission: "One can choose his own technical subjects for reading so I chose a subject they call, down there, 'psychology.' It is a government monopoly but it is taught in their universities. They claim everybody is evil. They say sentient beings are animals and have no soul. . . . This last is unique to Earth and is not believed on any other planet anywhere" (*IP* 302–303). Psychology and psychiatry are actually represented as the main ideological weapon employed by the Rockecenter Corporation[12] to keep Earth under its control, and they are associated with drug consumption and homosexuality as practices encouraged by psychologists and psychiatrists: "Many a psychiatrist and a psychologist augmented his income by making LSD in his kitchen and spreading it around" (*VV* 273); "'there is no cure except to have sex with a handsome young man.' It was the standard psychiatric remedy" (*VV* 284).[13]

Psychology is attacked in *Battlefield Earth* as well, albeit more incidentally. For instance, once the humans have discovered the influence of electrical impulses over Psychlo corpses, we read what one character surmises: "Nothing new in this. . . . Some man-scientist did this maybe thirteen hundred years ago and thought he'd found the secret of all thought and made up a cult about it called 'psychology'" (*BE* 550). Even more importantly, it is discovered that the Psychlos themselves were manipulated and corrupted by a group called "catrists." A Psychlo called Soth recalls:

> There was this group of carnival performers—you know, mountebanks, frauds. *They* were the original Psychlos. They used to hypnotize people on the stage and make them do funny things to get the audience to laugh at them . . . they were in charge of the schools and of the medical centers. . . . [Psychlos] means "brain," according to some old dictionaries. Another form of the word means "property of." Everyone became the property of the Psychlos.

Anyway, members of this mob of cutthroats began calling themselves "catrists." That means "mental doctors." So the people became "Psychlos" or "brains" and the "catrist" or "mental doctor" was the real, hidden government. They taught all the children. They inspected every citizen. They suppressed religion. They told people how to think. (*BE* 1026, emphasis by Hubbard)

A role similar to psychology and psychiatry is played by black PR. Actually presented as intertwined with psychology and psychiatry themselves, black PR is the expertise that allows the manipulation of the public's general perception and opinion of specific characters. We read for instance: "They had done such a marvelous job on the media that now, today, a psychiatrist could commit murder several times a day, including Sunday, and could do anything, even exhibit himself in front of children, and the media . . . would praise him to the skies and say how scientific and necessary it all was" (*VV* 266). This theme is dominant throughout all of *Mission Earth*, but polemical remarks against PR are present in *Battlefield Earth* as well, in which, for instance, a Psychlo asks: "You ever notice that the public relations department always puts their fairy tales so far back nobody can ever check them?" (*BE* 4). Journalism is similarly attacked in both novels, first and foremost as a tool of PR but also through the representation of grotesque journalists. In *Mission Earth*, as we have seen, Monte Pennwell plays an important role. In *Battlefield Earth*, mention is made of a similarly ambitious and mischievous journalist, Roof Arsebogger (cf. *BE* 761–762).

The only opinion-maker who is presented as a positive figure is that of a Scottish historian, MacDermott, who is included in Jonnie's team. While introducing him, Hubbard states a rare, positive remark about institutionalized education (otherwise mocked, for instance with the representation of the Empire University in *Mission Earth*):

A scholarly old fellow showed up who lamented the fact that no one would be writing the history that would become legend. It turned out that he was the dean of literature of a sort of underground university that had been eking along for centuries, and on the argument that he had two capable replacements for himself and—due to his age and poor heath—was expendable anyway, he could not be left behind. (*BE* 206)

Later on it is narrated that MacDermott, with a young aide, digs up information from old books and discovers the location of large uranium deposits (*BE* 270). Overall, the Scots are described as highly literate (*BE* 204).

TECHNOLOGY

Reference to technology is pervasive in both novels. Technology mainly comes in four forms common to the two novels. Some devices imagined and described by Hubbard are related to *learning*. Such is the case with the discs that allow Jonnie to learn Psychlo, and similar devices are used by Voltarians to learn terrestrial languages. Other devices are related to *transportation*: the most notable cases are, of course, Psychlos teleportation and the spaceships of Voltar, equipped with a "Will-be Was" engine. ("The feared time drives that allow Jettero Heller to cover the 22 1/2-light-year distance between Blito-P3 (Earth) and Voltar in a little over three days" [D 11]). It is even described in detail through the words of Heller:

> Now, in the center of a Will-be Was there is an ordinary warp-drive engine just to give power and influence space. There is a sensor, not unlike this time-sight, but very big. It reads where time predetermines a mass to be. Then the engine makes a synthetic mass that time incorrectly reads to be half as big as a planet. The ordinary power plant thrusts this apparent mass against time itself. According to the time pattern, that mass, apparently HUGE, should not be there. Time rejects it. You get a thrust from the rejection. But, of course, the thrust is far too great as the mass is only synthetic. This causes the engine base to be literally hurled through space. (BG 34)

Third, *weaponry* is a key form of technology. The most notable case is that of nuclear bombs in *Battlefield Earth*, but weapons play an important role throughout all of the *Mission Earth* series as well. Finally, technology linked to *control* and *manipulation* exists. Such is the case in *Battlefield Earth* with the drones Terl uses to observe the mining site, as well as the "picto-recorders" used both by Psychlos and humans. Moreover, the devices implanted in the Psychlos brains also represent a form of technological control. In *Mission Earth*, the "Bugging Gear" played a major role. Gris used this technology to observe Heller and Krak's actions (this plot line also allowed Hubbard to justify location shifts without changing the narrator). Equally important are the "hypnohelmets" that implant false memories: the "blueflash" is used to produce unconsciousness in the population of an area where a Voltarian spaceship is about to land, and the "Control Star" is a device disguised as a star-shaped medallion that Gris could use to paralyze his adversaries. On Voltar, "homeview"—a device that is strongly reminiscent of television—is used for manipulation (IP 162; VV 58).[14]

Two kinds of technology that are mentioned only in *Mission Earth* are "cellology" and Heller's inventions on Earth. Cellology allows Voltarians radical modifications of bodies to bring about sudden healing and bodily enhancement, or, more frequently, to produce freaks—this allows Hubbard to expand on the description of horrible monsters (see for instance *IP* 92–93 and *VO* 316). Finally, Heller's devices and findings allow him to avoid or wipe out the damage produced by pollution (cf. for instance *EW* 231 and 358).

POWER

"Terl knew leverage when he saw it. As a veteran security officer, he depended on leverage at every turn. And advantage. And blackmail. A method of forcing compliance" (*BE* 83–84). "Leverage, leverage, all was leverage" (*BE* 101). Early on in *Battlefield Earth*, Terl realizes that "leverage" plays a fundamental role in his relationships both with his fellow Psychlos and with terrestrials. "Leverage" and, more generally, the capacity to keep other characters in check, is pervasive throughout *Battlefield Earth* and *Mission Earth*. Rather than symbols of specific ideals, the characters are "placeholders" defined by power roles (analogously to the pieces in a game of checkers, defined by their moves and positions). Such power roles shift—and shifts are usually produced by the possession of a certain kind of technology, which in turn is usually dependent on access to some relevant piece of information—that is, dependent on knowledge, as broadly conceived.

One can identify some notable examples. In *Battlefield Earth*, it is critical for Terl to gain power over Numph and to understand that he has devised a major fraud. Similarly, it is important for Jonnie to gain power over Terl, to speak a language Terl does not understand, to understand that Psychlos breathe-gas cannot be exposed to radiation, and to understand how ancient nuclear devices work. Finally, it is crucial for Jonnie and for the terrestrials to master Psychlos teleportation technology, which in turn requires understanding Psychlo mathematics (notably, Hubbard describes both Psychlo teleportation consoles and mathematics as intentionally devised to confuse and mislead external observers [cf. *BE* 727–728]).

All of *Mission Earth* is about shifting power roles related to the characters' awareness of other characters' intentions and roles. Such awareness is usually gained (or manipulated) through devices like the "Bugging Gear" or the "hypnohelmets" and through the use of techniques such as black PR. The power of the Rockecenter foundation over Earth endures as long as Heller's alternative devices are not available, and, more generally, the most relevant difference between Voltar and the Earth consists in the former's more advanced level of technological development. (There is even a passage in which the terrestrials are mocked by a Voltarian since their science excludes faster-than-light travel.)

A theme strictly related to power is money. We have already touched upon Jonnie's successful defense against intergalactic bankers (who are also physically represented as sharks). Money plays an important part in *Mission Earth* as well, especially, but not exclusively, from the viewpoint of Gris, who is constantly looking for ways to make money (analogously to Terl in *Battlefield Earth*) and who is constantly threatened with bankruptcy.

INTERPRETATION

Battlefield Earth and *Mission Earth* can be examined and interpreted according to four different but interrelated levels. We can ask whether they are effectively entertaining narratives, whether they fulfill Hubbard's own goals (being *pure science-fiction* as he defines it, and *satire*), to what extent they are connected to Scientology's doctrines, and finally, which worldview they represent and convey.

As to the literary aspect, Frenschkowski writes:

> When reading Hubbard's fiction myself, I had expected him to be third-rate hack writer as he is mostly seen by his critics. He is not. Before founding Dianetics he was a good, competent second rate writer in many fields writing not for self-fulfillment but for a living. In this regard he is much overrated by Scientologists but also much underrated by critics who read him only with the glasses of antipathy against Scientology.[15]

Regarding specifically *Mission Earth*, he states that the 10 volumes "are disappointing: [They do not] entertain. Many of the scenes (especially some sexual encounters) are incredibly grotesque, not in a pornographic sense, but they are violently aggressive about modern American ideals."[16]

All in all I agree with Frenschkowsi's evaluation. *Battlefield Earth* makes for a fairly entertaining if somewhat timeworn narrative with some convoluted passages, especially those dealing with Jonnie confronting the Galactic Bank. *Mission Earth* is exceedingly long, convoluted, and slow paced. Thirty years after its first publication, the impact of obscene passages is attenuated. Moreover, the narrative devices that are supposed to be amusing, such as the substitution of each vulgar word with "bleep,"[17] the puns carried by names like those of Countess Krak and the concubine Utanc,[18] the homosexual Gaylov (D 103), the credit card Squeeza (FF 45),[19] the numerous offensive observations about nationalities,[20] women,[21] and homosexuals,[22] and the remarks about psychology and psychiatry are shallow and repetitive.

Hubbard is not completely self-consistent, and he does not live up to the expectations he himself creates with his introductory statements to both novels. Concerning science fiction, the introduction to *Battlefield Earth* is ambiguous in the first place. On the one hand, Hubbard states that this genre has to be based on science as it is broadly conceived. Undoubtedly, in this respect he did write a science fiction novel that contains a number of scientific-sounding theories used to describe alien devices. On the other hand, he characterizes science fiction as having an inspirational role toward scientists, and he boasts having been (together with other authors) widely acknowledged by them in the "golden years." It is hard to see how *Battlefield Earth* and *Mission Earth* can provide scientists with inspiration for any technological developments since all the devices mentioned, as we have seen, basically amplify possibilities already within human reach.

Furthermore, Hubbard is ambiguous in the introduction itself since he also adds that he is dissatisfied with science's materialistic developments. One might suppose that his novel contains an indication of a doctrine that constitutes an alternative to it. It is true that *Battlefield Earth* contains repeated criticisms of psychology and psychiatry. However, the criticisms are negative and destructive, and Hubbard does not indicate any alternative way—be it Scientology's theology or any other nonmaterialistic teaching.

Similar observations hold for *Mission Earth*, that, in addition, are presented as satire. As we have seen, for satire to be enjoyed, presupposes, according to the introduction signed by Hubbard, that one understands what its target is: "discernment." This does happen in *Mission Earth*—but simply in too repetitive, too simplistic, and nonuniform ways. *Repetitive* because Hubbard makes similar statements about psychology, psychiatry, and PR over and over again. *Simplistic* because most of the puns that "conceal" a reference to real people and institutions are obvious (e.g., "Rockecenter," "Coordinated Information Apparatus").[23] *Nonuniform* because other references are direct (i.e., not even mediated by a pseudonym or a pun); for instance, Hubbard talks explicitly about the APA (*VV* 265), CIA (*DP* 140), *Coca-Cola* (*FF* 87), FBI (*BG* 185, 191), Internal Revenue Service (*BG* 335), Interpol (*VO* 169), KGB (*BG* 41; *DP* 139), SS (*DP* 140), *The Beatles* (*VV* 83), *Star Trek* (defined as "garbage," *VO* 139), De Sade (*FF* 275), Dumas (*VO* 212), Euclid (*BG* 364), Freud (*AA* 273; *VO* 183; *VV* 96, 281), Garibaldi (*VO* 230), Goebbels (*DQ* 95), Hakluyt (*AA* 78), Hitler (*DQ* 96), J. Edgar Hoover (*BG* 192; *AA* 250), Howard Hughes (*DQ* 203), Jesus Christ (*VO* 145), J. F. Kennedy (*DQ* 114), Keynes (*DP* 41), Lincoln (*DQ* 115), Marx (*DP* 41), Newton (*BG* 364), Martin Luther King Jr. (*DQ* 114), Shakespeare (*VV* 110), Tchaikovskij (*EW* 62), and Wagner (*AA* 168).[24]

I have already partially answered the question regarding the two novels' relevance to Scientology. As Frenschkowski states, they are not Scientology propaganda. Hubbard does not touch upon the doctrine regarding individual souls (or *thetans* in Scientology jargon) and the incidents that affected them according to the theory and version of human history that are central to Scientology's beliefs and practices (Hubbard 1952). However, reference to Scientology-related themes such as the aforementioned criticism of psychiatry and psychology is pervasive enough to contradict Hubbard's own statement in the introduction to *Battlefield Earth* when he writes that such work is unrelated to his "serious" one. In at least one passage of *Mission Earth* Heller seems to echo Hubbard's own theory of matter, space, time, and energy (*BG* 32), but again, a few paragraphs are not enough to describe the "dekalogy" overall as a vessel for Scientology's teachings.[25] It is perhaps safer to state that Hubbard did set out to write something with only his "hat as a professional writer" on, and that by doing so, he basically wanted to entertain (himself as well as the readers), but any time he had to mention elements of the vision of the world entertained by his characters, he recurred to fragments of his Scientological teaching.

If we cannot only explain the vision of the world behind *Battlefield Earth* and *Mission Earth* in terms of Scientology, which *Weltanschauung* do they express and convey? I think that the key to answering this question is precisely the examination of knowledge, technology, and power as they are intertwined in the narratives. To begin with, it should be noted how no sharp opposition between worlds or visions can really be identified in the two novels. It is true that Jonnie Goodboy Tyler represents a "knight-in-shining-armour" character who is turned into a religious figure for all terrestrials replacing old myths and eventually, as in some messianic narratives, even disappears after completing his mission (cf. *BE* 449 and 1050). However, there is no clear opposition between *good* and *evil* (nor between *extraterrestrial* and *terrestrial*) if one looks at the narrative as a whole and in depth. The Psychlos are initially described as cruel sociopaths ("Greed, profit and corruption were understood to be the nature of every individual. There were no decencies or virtues" [*BE* 967]), but we discover that they have not always been like that—their degeneration being due to a proliferation of psychiatry and psychology analogous to the one that Hubbard/Scientology identified and condemned on actual Earth. It is to be observed, moreover, that the few surviving Psychlos are cured and hence normalized. The terrestrials reconquer the Earth and defeat their invaders by means of an atomic devastation that, although unintentional (Jonnie is not aware of the chain reaction he is unleashing), is not any better than the intergalactic genocides attributed to the Psychlos themselves. The Earth is restored, but it is rather a "corrected version" of the one that had been destroyed millennia earlier than an ideal new society—it includes the usage of money ("The notes had one denomination: one Earth credit. . . . The woodblock bill was very nicely printed. It said Earth planetary bank. . . . it had, squarely in the center of it, in a big oval, a portrait of *Jonnie Goodboy Tyler!*" [BE 523–524, emphasis by Hubbard]), and Jonnie triumphs over bankers[26] and diplomats[27] by beating them at their own game.

The absence of a clear contraposition or alternative is even more marked in *Mission Earth*. Jettero Heller is supposedly a totally positive character analogous to Jonnie Goodboy Tyler, but he does not refrain from massive usage of violence, and he is as fond of sex and money as Gris is (albeit Hubbard does not indulge in details, he reports on Heller's frequent sexual intercourse with the Countess, and Heller, as we have recalled, conquers Atlantic City through his casino gains). Intrigue, lies, and manipulation are connected to each and every character, not only to the villains.

Finally, and more importantly, there is no such thing as a place or a society described as totally alternative or positive. Not the Earth, dominated by the Rockecenter Corporation: true, in the end the terrestrials get rid of environmental problems as well as of evil powers, but Hubbard does not inform us about any further reorganization nor of the long-term effects of such liberation. Actually, as alluded to in several points of the novel, Earth has been colonized by a mythological hero called Prince Caucalsia, who fled from his home planet Manco (the same one as Heller and Krak) during an event called the "Great Rebellion."

As for politics, democracy and communism are both ridiculed through the words of a minor character called Vantagio (belonging to the Corleone mob): "so that's what the 'democratic process' is: the politicians give the people things the politicians don't own in order to get elected. . . . [Communism] is where the people are forbidden to own anything so that the commissars can grab it all for themselves" (*EW* 180).

In one passage of the last novel the strong analogies between Earth and Voltar are described by filtering them through Heller's thoughts:

Seeing it [Earth] made him feel a bit bitter. It was such a nice planet: too bad they had made so little usage of the heritage Prince Caucalsia had given them—that made so many things similar culturally between Voltar and Earth. Too bad they valued it so little. It was a shame they had been so corrupted by their own primitives they had permitted themselves to go so far astray. The clutter of *isms* and hates could all be solved if they just realized that only a handful of men were using them for personal exploitation. Their political creeds were just nonsense and lies manufactured for the benefit of the few, while pretending that they answered the demands of the many. And the way culture was fixated on logistics as a single concentration excluded it from attainment of the real and valuable things in life. A can of soup was equated on their communication lines—measured by volume of minutes—far, far more important than a man's soul. (*DP* 214–215, emphasis by Hubbard)

Later on, Heller, explaining why the terrestrials will never develop space travel, states:

Only two things motivate their [i.e., the terrestrials'] thinking: one is commerce, the other is war. . . . But actually there is another factor which defeats them at every turn and that is an oddity in leadership. Even a casual study of their history shows that they only worship and obey leaders who kill: *Caesar, Napoleon, Bismarck, Hitler, Eisenhower* are just a few names. They revere scientists the same way: The biggest known names basically made it possible to build the biggest weapons. Einstein, for instance. It's a pretty primitive attitude. I doubt they could attain space travel before such ills as bad leadership, *socialism*, inflation and other things ate them up internally. (*DP* 219–220, emphasis by Hubbard)

A minor character, Captain Roke, adds at this point: "It's a clutter of primitive and modern, but the think they use in utilizing the modern is primitive. They'll blow up culturally before they ever get to a stage of real space travel" (*DP* 220).

However, on closer inspection, not even Voltar is represented as a totally alternative or positive place. It is indeed a planet that is described as vulnerable to "terrestrial evils" such as black PR (articulated, according to Hubbard, in "Confidence, Coverage, Controversy" [cf. *AA* 154]), psychology, psychiatry, and narcotics, and that escapes a usurpation attempt. Divorce does not exist on it, and bigamy is punished with death (*DP* 31); but from the very beginning it has a plan to conquer Earth (and the universe), and it hosts an institution such as the Coordinated Information Apparatus (not to mention that on Voltar a discipline such as the aforementioned "cellology" that yields freaks was developed).[28] It is remarkable that harmony in the end is restored on Voltar but at the price of a huge cover-up, which logically entails lying and manipulating on a massive scale.[29]

Any narrative that does not only intend to criticize actual society but also indicate an alternative way of living or thinking usually does so by introducing a hero or a world that incarnates such ideals. Such a hero or such a world can be finally defeated (not all science fiction novels and movies end on a happy note), and this conveys a pessimistic viewpoint, but the alternative is expressed anyway. In this kind of novel there is usually a form of *knowledge* that is represented as alternative (or that represents the alternative). Such knowledge can be a *doctrine* or a *way of life* (e.g., that of the Jedi in *Star Wars*) or some kind of *awareness* that motivates subversive action (e.g., knowing the real nature of Soylent Green in the movie with the same name[30]). There seems to be nothing of the sort in Hubbard's late novels. As we have seen, knowledge is usually functional to technology, and both are always functional to power relationships. Power relationships are the only elements that, strong/alternative moral values being absent, really push the action forward and define the characters.

As we have seen, Hubbard does make some (vague) statements against materialism in the introduction to *Battlefield Earth*, but in the end he does not express any articulated, alternative take on life and reality in the two novels (cf. also *EW* 230 and *VO* 16). He is very explicit and violent about what he is *against* (psychiatry and psychology), but any time they are defeated, there is only a new power relationship that replaces an old one. The *constructive* part, be it theoretical or political, is constantly weak, inconsistent, or even absent. Everything in *Battlefield Earth* and in *Mission Earth* literally stays on Earth. Earth is, as stated in the titles, with perhaps involuntary but revealing sincerity, *the* battlefield and *the* mission. Earth was (or can be) destroyed by unearthly beings (who are actually very much analogous to the inhabitants of Earth)—Earth is saved. That psychology and psychiatry as well as black PR and pollution are expelled from the saved Earth does not really matter, because Hubbard does *not* expand on how the saved or restored Earth looks after such liberation and why it can be considered better than the reality we know.[31] Hubbard's imagination seems to become feeble in this case: he conceives of spectacular destruction scenes, but he is not as efficacious in depicting peaceful, day-after landscapes.[32] Dystopia prevails over utopia, and both are very much like actual Earth. For instance, the planets saved, respectively by Jonnie and Heller, are still highly hierarchical systems. It is a "revised reality" and not a completely alternative one.[33]

Scientology as a body of doctrines, if not as an institutionalized religion, is defined as a "way to total freedom," and it supposedly teaches a spirituality alternative to materialism. In this sense it is optimistic, alternative, and constructive. Hubbard's late novels seemingly convey a vision of the world that is pessimistic, destructive, and replete with resentment.

NOTES

1. I did not always have the original editions at my disposal. Page numbers refer to the editions reported in the bibliography. The original publication year, if different from that of the edition I perused, is indicated in square brackets in the bibliography. For brevity's sake, although this chapter conforms to CMS bibliographic standards,

both *Battlefield Earth* and the single volumes constituting *Mission Earth* are referred to through abbreviations indicated in square brackets in the bibliography.

2. Robert Vaughn Young (1938–2003), who worked inside Scientology in different high-level positions and who claimed to have ghosted two interviews and other texts for Hubbard, also states that he was involved in the production of *Mission Earth*. He relates:

> When Hubbard's manuscript of "Mission Earth" (or "ME" as we called it) came in to Author Services, Inc. (ASI), it arrived as one volume, typed on legal-sized paper and on a manual. It came in a banker's box with each chapter in a separate file folder. And not ordinary file folders. I don't know where they got them but they were heavy, thick and dark red. . . . The manuscript came with instructions. Hubbard said it should be cut up into three or maybe ten sections and for us to decide and suggest. Well, ten volumes make more money than three do so naturally we said ten. Great, he said, and more instructions followed.

Vaughn Young also reports that he was responsible for deciding the exact points into which the volumes had to be cut, for inventing all titles (except *Villainy Victorious*— that was Hubbard's choice), for editing the manuscripts, for authoring the introduction about satire, and for writing the texts opening all the volumes after the first one. These were, namely, the "Censor's Disclaimer," the "Translator's Preface," and the initial section in which the narrator resumes the events previously told as a narrative device to avoid any confusion experienced by readers who purchased any volume subsequent to the first one. The insertion of maps showing where the action was taking place, according to Vaughn Young, was Hubbard's idea (Robert Vaughn Young, "Hubbard's 'Mission Earth'—the Rest of the Story," 2000. http://www.holysmoke .org/rvy/rvy2.htm). Cover images both for *Battlefield Earth* and for *Mission Earth* were created by the illustrator Gerry Grace.

3. The official Web page for the novel lists *BE* lists translations in Bulgarian, Chinese, Czech, Dutch, Estonian, German, French (France and Canada), Hebrew, Hungarian, Italian, Japanese, Korean, Lithuanian, Polish, Portuguese (Portugal and Brazil), Russian, Serbo-Croatian, Spanish (Castilian and Latin American), Russian, and Swedish. Hubbard also composed a soundtrack to the book entitled *Space Jazz* (Hubbard, 1982). According to the Church of Scientology International (private communication via e-mail), as of June 2015, *Mission Earth* has been translated into Brazilian, Bulgarian, Chinese, Czech, French, German, Hebrew, Hungarian, Indonesian, Italian, Japanese, Lithuanian, Portuguese, Russian, Spanish (Castilian), and Thai.

4. Mike McIntyre reports, for instance, about ME: "The *New York Times* gave up after the first volume, dismissing it as 'a paralyzingly slow-moving adventure enlivened by interludes of kinky sex, sendups of effeminate homosexuals and a disregard of conventional grammar so global as to suggest a satire on the possibility of communication through language.'" Mike McIntyre, "Hubbard Hot-Author Status Called Illusion," *San Diego Union*, April 15, 1990, http://www.ex-cult.org/Groups/Scientology /sandiego.txt.

5. See McIntyre, "Hubbard Hot-Author Status Called Illusion"; Vaughn Young, "Hubbard's 'Mission Earth'; Robert W. Welkos and Joel Sappel, "Costly Strategy Continues to Turn Out Bestsellers," *Los Angeles Times*, June 28, 1990, http://www.latimes.com/local/la-scientology062890-story.html#page=2. According to McIntyre's source it was precisely the promise of extensive sales that proved convincing to St. Martin's Press: Hubbard wanted to prove his worth as a writer by publishing with a publisher not related to Scientology.

6. See Duncan Campbell, "Does John Travolta's Battlefield Earth Contain Subliminal Messages Recruiting Scientologists? Amid a Flurry of Bizarre Claims and Counterclaims, Only One Thing Is Certain: It Is One of the Worst Movies Ever Made," *Guardian*, May 31, 2000, http://www.theguardian.com/culture/2000/may/31/artsfeatures3; Thomas C. Tobin, "Battlefield of Dreams," *St. Petersburg Times*, May 12, 1990. http://www.sptimes.com/News/051200/news_pf/Floridian/Battlefield_of_dreams.shtml; Internet Movie Database, *Battlefield Earth*.

7. Marco Frenschkowski, "L. Ron Hubbard and Scientology: An Annotated Bibliographical Survey of Primary and Selected Secondary Literature," *Marburg Journal of Religion* 4, no. 1 (1999): 7.

8. Critical or scholarly essays analyzing *Battlefield Earth* and *Mission Earth* are virtually nonexistent. An exception seems to be Adam Possamai and Alphia Possamai-Inesedy, "*Battlefield Earth* and Scientology: A Cultural/Religious Industry à la Frankfurt School?," in *Handbook of New Religions and Cultural Production*, ed. Carole M. Cusack and Alex Norman, 583–600, Leiden: Brill, 2012. However, this essay does not engage in depth with the novel. Given that the present monograph's focus is on Scientology and popular culture, I have chosen to peruse, quote at length, and give full credit to bloggers and other authors publishing on the web, although sometimes under pseudonyms, whenever their pieces seemed well informed and argued and expressed some interesting insight.

9. Vaughn Young claims its authorship and states that it was read, approved, and slightly modified by Hubbard. See note 2.

10. In order not to clutter the text, in this paragraph as well as in the following ones, I directly quote the novels when quotations and passages are highly relevant to a specific topic or when they are unique instances of the concept or object I am touching upon. With the sole exception of the caricature of psychology and psychiatry, the pervasiveness of which I want to demonstrate, I do *not* venture to list all the mentions of an element, be it conceptual or material, which is repeatedly mentioned in the narrative (for instance, all the times a "hypnohelmet" is used in *Mission Earth*).

11. Jonnie learns a good deal of information about the Earth through "old-fashioned" books as well. One of the most efficacious passages of the novel is the one in which he discovers the books: "Queer, thick rectangles stood on those shelves. Rows of them. . . . What a strange object! It was a box that wasn't a box. The covers slid sideways away from each other, enclosing a packet of thin, remarkably thin slices that had black marks on them, lots of little, tiny black marks all in orderly rows. What a strange object! How complicated!" (*BE* 40).

12. The Rockecenter foundation that Hubbard writes of is most definitely a parody of the Rockefeller family in the United States. They are one of the wealthiest and

most powerful families having made a fortune through oil, finance, etc. Their dynasty started in the early 20th century and would have been at its apex by the time Hubbard was writing these books.

13. This is only a selection. Similar remarks and passages pepper all of *Mission Earth*. See, for instance: *IP* 306, 542; *BG* 146, 177; *EW* 137–138, 195–196; *FF* 177; *DQ* 127; *VO* 372; *VV* 266; *DP* 144–145, 291.

14. For a detailed catalogue of Voltarian manipulation devices, see *FF* 20. A machine that artificially elicits feelings is described in *VO* 20.

15. Frenschkowski, "L. Ron Hubbard and Scientology," 6.

16. Frenschkowski, "L. Ron Hubbard and Scientology," 6.

17. In fact the novel is interspersed with words such as "bleeptch," "bleepard," and "bleepulation" that betray which original term has been substituted.

18. Partially in Hubbard's defense, we might mention that the Turkish word *utanç* does exist (and means "shame" or "pudicity"); however, the malicious intention in the name's choice seems blatant.

19. Further cheap puns include mention of the Massachusetts Institute of Wrectology (*AA* 92), the National Association of Mental Stealth (*DQ* 195), a graduation *Magna Cum Loud* (*DP* 266), a character called Dolores Pubiano de Cópula (*DQ* 240), and the *Slime* magazine (*VV* 281).

20. A major role is played by the mafia, and Gris makes racist remarks about the Italians over and over again (see, for instance, *BG* 294, 320; *AA* 47, 138; *FF* 146; *VO* 220, 222, 226, 227). Yet the Turks (*EW* 160) and the French (*VO* 208) are also mocked. Also, Hubbard's caricaturized accents can be seen as an expression of racism (besides being one of his favorite stylistic devices). Outrageous remarks are also made about Islam ("Mohammedan religion," *BG* 308).

21. Gris constantly makes misogynous remarks (see, for instance, *IP* 205, 227, 441; *BG* 82; *FF* 258; *DQ* 11; *VV* 286); however, besides the specific character's ideas, it is the representation of women through female characters, including "positive" ones, that betrays a deep-seated hatred and disdain for women.

22. What's more, Gris's homophobic remarks are quite frequent (see, for instance, *BG* 316; *EW* 176; *AA* 224; *FF* 34; *D* 137–138) but overall Hubbard's representation of homosexuals, most notably through the two lesbians "cured" by Gris and the evil "catamites," is deeply homophobic. Besides, the "diffusion of homosexuality" is explicitly presented as a corrupting and manipulating tactic implemented by the Rockecenter Corporation and even as a cure recommended by psychiatrists (cf. *VV* 284).

23. Regarding the overall efficaciousness of Hubbard's narrative, the blogger Adam Whitehead states:

> On the surface this is a fairly random but not entirely valueless story.
> Old-school, yes, but with some potential for exploring themes about
> nuclear self-destruction, the problem of dwindling energy supplies and
> the corruption of power, whilst having the main villain as the central
> POV character for 75% of its length is an unusual and potentially
> fascinating move. Hubbard, of course, doesn't actually fulfill any of

this potential. Instead, the series mounts a sustained, shock-and-awe assault on the reader's intelligence, taste and suspension of disbelief that is awesome to behold (though thoroughly unpleasant to experience). With *Battlefield Earth*, by virtue of its far-future setting, Hubbard was unable to really do much in the way of satire or commentary on modern American values." (Whitehead 2011)

Concerning the repetitiveness of Hubbard's satirical message, Modemac, discussing *An Alien Affair*, writes:

> [Hubbard is] hoping for comparisons to Voltaire (note the resemblance to the name "Voltar"), Huxley, or Swift. But unfortunately for Hubbard, his satire is far too blatant and obvious: by now, the theme of the series has been spelled out (Earth is under control by evil psychiatric demons), and the story is beating us over the head with it, again and again and again." (Modemac 2013e)

24. Furthermore, some of the most blatant references are to adversaries of Hubbard himself. For instance, a blog contributor who writes under the nickname "Danger Mouse" in the *Ex Scientologist Message Board* points out:

> Hubbard takes satirical aim at several organizations that had caused him trouble, such as Time-Life (here renamed Slime-Tripe). One of Hubbard's critics once derided him as "just another Whiz Kid." Here Heller watches with amusement as Slime-Tripe's publicity campaign popularizes his double, also known as the Whiz Kid, who makes an ass of himself in the media while Heller is busy trying to save the world. Hubbard is obviously making the point that he barely recognized the person he was described to be in the press. . . . Those who smear Heller for trying to save the earth happen to correspond to those who Hubbard felt were trying to smear him: 60 Minutes, Carl Sagan, Bob Woodward, Time-Life, Clearwater Sun, St. Petersburg Times, Los Angeles Times, Portland Times, etc. . . . [R]eporter Betty Orsini of the St. Petersburg Times . . . won a Pulitzer for her articles uncovering Scientology's purchase of the Fort Harrison Hotel in Clearwater. Heller refers to her as "Betty Horseheinie."

The same anonymous contributor observes that Heller's travel in the United States "[retraces] some of the route of Hubbard's road trip from Florida to New York and then back to DC, with Mike & Kima Douglas in January 1976"; that "Heller flees, eludes the Coast Guard and finds refuge on a luxury yacht in international waters, just as Hubbard himself did in the late 1960s and early 1970s"; and, finally, that Gris's travels "[retrace] L. Ron Hubbard's sea voyages with his Sea Org from September 1967 to August 1975) visiting the Bahamas, Morocco, France, Italy, Greece, and eventually back to Turkey." "Danger Mouse" [blogger's nickname], 2013. "Hubbard's 'Magnum Opus'—Mission Earth." *Ex Scientologist Message Board*, January 18, 2013 (8:13 a.m.), http://www.forum.exscn.net/showthread .php?30098-Hubbard-s-quot-Magnum-Opus-quot-Mission-Earth.

25. In this I differ from the bloggers whose insights are quoted in this chapter and who generally tend to present the novels at stake as "packaged Scientology doctrine," identifying it almost exclusively with the criticism of psychology and psychiatry. I should also add that the narrative of the intergalactic bank in *Battlefield Earth* does have some points analogous to that of Xenu (see Mikael Rothstein, "'His name was Xenu. He used renegades . . .': Aspects of Scientology's Founding Myth," in *Scientology*, ed. James A. Lewis, 365–387, Oxford and New York: Oxford University Press, 2009) and that a tax revolt on a planet is incidentally mentioned in *Mission Earth* (*IP* 37).

26. Lord Voraz, exponent of the alien race that wants to expropriate Earth because of Psychlos debts, sums up his principles as follows: "Money is everything and all things and talent are for sale. And that's the heart and soul of banking, the very cornerstone of business. A first principle" (*BE* 944). He and his race are described as shark-like in appearance (*BE* 898).

27. At some point Jonnie gets a crash-course in diplomacy that encompasses the following principles: "All diplomacy is a matter of compromise . . . There is a middle ground between the two opposite poles of impossible demands . . . which will become the eventual treaty or agreement. . . Always work for the most advantageous position you can get" (*BE* 830).

28. As to its religion, Hubbard refers incidentally to Voltar's Gods and priests (cf. *IP* 183) but he never develops this point.

29. I substantially agree here with the blogger Modemac (Eric Walker) when he states:

> Now that we've returned to Voltar after leaving it at the end of the first book, it's worth mentioning one of Hubbard's biggest failings in this series: despite the epic, interminable length of this "dekalogy," the story is surprisingly small in scope. By using a science fiction approach to look at Earth from an "alien" point of view, Hubbard uses the planet Voltar (and its 120-planet empire, of which we only see one other planet named Calabar in one small chapter of this book) to show us an innocent, uncorrupted society—presumably what our own society would be if it had not been corrupted by evil drugs and evil psychiatrists. Yet, there's nothing truly "alien" about this society, other than the fact that it has advanced technology. So when Earth's evils are introduced into Voltar by Hisst (drugs), Teenie (sex), and Madison (media PR), the innocent Voltarians have no defenses and are completely corrupted. (Modemac 2013j)

30. A 1973 science fiction movie by Richard Fleischer based on the 1966 novel *Make Room! Make Room!* by Harry Harrison, which revolves around the mysterious composition of a synthetic food on which humanity relies upon in a dystopian 2022.

31. This point is well described by Modemac when he states:

As a capstone to the series, *The Doomed Planet* spells out everything that needs to be done to save the world: namely, consolidate all the nations and peoples of the world into one single, benevolent corporation that works for the good of Mankind. We know this single corporation is good because "Mankind is basically good" (Hubbard's words, as quoted ad infinitum by Scientologists) and Mankind will never succumb to temptation as long as the evil demons of psychology and psychiatry are kept under lock and key, hidden far away from prying eyes by well-meaning censors. Of course, once the world is freed from the prison of psychology and psychiatry (referred to as "the psychs" within Scientology), then the evils of drugs and perverted sex will vanish. No one will have any need for them anymore, once the world is free! (Modemac 2013k)

32. In *Battlefield Earth*, even taxation is reintroduced (cf. *BE* 1039), and, as we have already observed, Psychlos language is adopted, albeit with another name.

33. This interpretation resonates with a possible reading of *Mission Earth*'s main characters as reflecting Hubbard's self-perception. An anonymous blogger writing under the nickname "Purple Rain" in the post started by the afore-mentioned "Danger Mouse" states:

I always read the Mission Earth books as Heller = Hubbard, but now I think they were both Hubbard. Heller was the "ideal" self and Gris was the self he was struggling with. And I do kind of believe it was a struggle—like he really wanted to be a Heller and often even believed he was (certainly enough to convince others). But Gris was the monster inside. ("Purple Rain" [blogger's nickname], January 19, 2013 (12:14 a.m.) comment on "Danger Mouse" [blogger's nickname]. 2013. "Hubbard's 'Magnum Opus'—Mission Earth." *Ex Scientologist Message Board*, January 18, 2013 (8:13 a.m.): http://www.forum.exscn.net/showthread .php?30098-Hubbard-s-quot-Magnum-Opus-quot-Mission-Earth).

Analogously, Modemac writes:

The most interesting thing about the Mission Earth series is the way it gives us an insight into Hubbard's mind, both by showing us the type of selfless, heroic person Hubbard wanted to be (Jettero Heller), and by revealing the psyche of the greedy, cowardly, criminally insane person he really was (Soltan Gris). The fact that he could spend eight whole books telling the story from the point of view of a sadistic, self-centered criminal shows us who Hubbard really identified with. (Modemac 2013a)

Something that the bloggers do not seem to take into account is that Hubbard ends up overlapping with another character of *Mission Earth* described as a loser: Monte Pennwell.

BIBLIOGRAPHY

Campbell, Duncan. "Does John Travolta's Battlefield Earth Contain Subliminal Messages Recruiting Scientologists? Amid a Flurry of Bizarre Claims and Counterclaims, Only One Thing Is Certain: It Is One of the Worst Movies Ever Made." *Guardian*, May 31, 2000. http://www.theguardian.com/culture/2000/may/31/artsfeatures3.

Danger Mouse [blogger's nickname]. "Hubbard's 'Magnum Opus'—Mission Earth." *Ex Scientologist Message Board*, January 18, 2013. http://www.forum.exscn.net/showthread.php?30098-Hubbard-s-quot-Magnum-Opus- quot-Mission-Earth.

Frenschkowski, Marco. "L. Ron Hubbard and Scientology: An Annotated Bibliographical Survey of Primary and Selected Secondary Literature." *Marburg Journal of Religion* 4, no. 1 (1999): 1–24.

Hubbard, Lafayette Ron. *Battlefield Earth* [novel]. Official Web page, 2014. http://battlefieldearth.com/.

Hubbard, Lafayette Ron. *Battlefield Earth: A Saga of the Year 3000.* Los Angeles: Galaxy Press, 2005 (1982). [BE]

Hubbard, Lafayette Ron. *Mission Earth: An Alien Affair.* Hollywood: Galaxy Press, 1986. [AA]

Hubbard, Lafayette Ron. *Mission Earth: Black Genesis: Fortress of Evil.* Los Angeles: Bridge Publications, 1986. [BG]

Hubbard, Lafayette Ron. *Mission Earth: Death Quest.* Los Angeles: Bridge Publications, 1986. [DQ]

Hubbard, Lafayette Ron. *Mission Earth: Disaster.* Redhill, U.K.: New Era Publications, 1987. [D]

Hubbard, Lafayette Ron. *Mission Earth: The Doomed Planet.* Hollywood: Galaxy Press, 1987. [DP]

Hubbard, Lafayette Ron. *Mission Earth: The Enemy Within.* Los Angeles: Bridge Publications, 1986. [EW]

Hubbard, Lafayette Ron. *Mission Earth: Fortune of Fear.* Los Angeles: Bridge Publications, 1986. [FF]

Hubbard, Lafayette Ron. *Mission Earth: The Invaders Plan.* Hollywood: Galaxy Press, 2003 (1985). [IP]

Hubbard, Lafayette Ron. *Mission Earth: Villainy Victorious.* Los Angeles: Bridge Publications, 1987. [VV]

Hubbard, Lafayette Ron. *Mission Earth: Voyage of Vengeance.* Los Angeles: Bridge Publications, 1987. [VO]

Hubbard, Lafayette Ron. *Scientology: A History of Man. A List and Description of the Principal Incidents to Be Found in a Human Being.* Copenhagen: New Era Publications, 2007 (1952).

Hubbard, Lafayette Ron. *Space Jazz.* Applause Records. Golden Era Musicians, 1982.

Internet Movie Database. *Battlefield Earth.* http://www.imdb.com/title/tt0185183/.

McIntyre, Mike. "Hubbard Hot-Author Status Called Illusion." *San Diego Union*, April 15, 1990. http://www.ex-cult.org/Groups/Scientology/sandiego.txt.

Modemac (blogger nickname of Eric Walker). Mission Earth. http://www.modemac.com/cgi-bin/wiki.pl/Mission_Earth.

Modemac. Mission Earth—An Alien Affair. http://www.modemac.com/cgi-bin/wiki
.pl/Mission_Earth_-_An_Alien_Affair.

Modemac. Mission Earth—Villainy Victorious. http://www.modemac.com/cgi-bin
/wiki.pl/Mission_Earth_-_Villainy_Victorious.

Possamai, Adam, and Alphia Possamai-Inesedy. "*Battlefield Earth* and Scientology: A
Cultural/Religious Industry à la Frankfurt School?" In *Handbook of New Religions and Cultural Production*, edited by Carole M. Cusack and Alex Norman,
583–600. Leiden: Brill, 2012.

Rothstein, Mikael. "'His name was Xenu. He used renegades . . .': Aspects of Scientology's Founding Myth." In *Scientology*, edited by James A. Lewis, 365–387.
Oxford and New York: Oxford University Press, 2009.

Tobin, Thomas C. "Battlefield of Dreams." *St. Petersburg Times*, May 12, 1990. http://
www.sptimes.com/News/051200/news_pf/Floridian/Battlefield_of_dreams
.shtml.

Vaughn Young, Robert. "Hubbard's 'Mission Earth'—The Rest of the Story." 2000.
http://www.holysmoke.org/rvy/rvy2.htm.

Welkos, Robert W., and Joel Sappel. "Costly Strategy Continues to Turn Out Bestsellers." *Los Angeles Times*, June 28, 1990. http://www.latimes.com/local/la
-scientology062890-story.html#page=2.

Whitehead, Adam. 2011. "Staring into the Abyss: My Brush with L. Ron Hubbard's
MISSION EARTH." http://thewertzone.blogspot.mx/2011/01/staring-into-abyss
-my-brush-with-l-ron.html.

4

Scientology's Recruitment Policies Targeting Celebrities

Stephen A. Kent

INTRODUCTION

Four years after L. Ron Hubbard noted the influence that celebrities had on the consumer patterns of the general public, he developed his insights into a policy aimed at using celebrity star power to promote Dianetics and Scientology throughout society. That policy became the foundation for a Scientology marketing program that has operated for nearly 45 years and has involved some of the West's highest-profile celebrity personalities from the entertainment and sports industries. The Scientology organization specifically recruits celebrities and provides some of them with career-enhancing connections with other Scientologists in "the business" (as people in Los Angeles refer to Hollywood's entertainment-related enterprises). For celebrities who undergo intensive training in Scientology's beliefs, practices, and public relations positions, Scientology grants them a special status within the organization and actively uses them as deployable agents to proselytize to others in society.

Scientology's relationship with its celebrity members has many facets, and this chapter will tackle only one of them. It examines the actual Scientology policies and procedures that Hubbard and others formulated, applied, and modified regarding celebrity recruitment and deployment. Setting aside for the moment discussing what the exact nature of Scientology is—a sect? a cult? a new religion? a marginal medical group?—it remains the most aggressive of post–World War II ideological groups to actively seek large numbers of celebrities as members. It seems fortuitous for Hubbard that the evolution and development of Dianetics into Scientology occurred in the early 1950s, which was the same period that early television was growing in the United

States. Having spent time in the Hollywood area before and soon after World War II,[1] he already was somewhat familiar with the cultural influence that movie stars had. With the increase in television shows and expanding hours of programming, Hubbard saw a new group of stars emerge in a new medium, and he wanted their voices and that medium on his side. In, for example, the 1955 list of celebrities that Hubbard wanted to recruit (and which I discuss below), a dozen or so of them were television personalities.

Worth mentioning is that an analysis of celebrities becoming involved in causes is far more complicated when discussing Scientologists versus non-member celebrities. Nonmember celebrities, who are by far the most typical of stars in "the business," in some part make decisions about involvement in social movements "through a rationalized celebrity industry" composed of "tightly linked subindustries" including "public relations, entertainment law, management, and talent agencies, tied to each other and to news media and entertainment production companies."[2] Agents and public relations people in this rationalized celebrity industry assess whether involvement in a particular social movement might harm celebrities' public images, and they advise the celebrities accordingly. Celebrity elites, however, operating on behalf of Scientology have an additional level of control and direction over the organization's high-profile members, and it may be that decisions about celebrities' involvements in issues and social movements reflect others' assessments about what is best for the public image, first and foremost, of Scientology.

Because I have access to so many primary sources on Scientology celebrities, I present Scientology's celebrity deployment in a manner that stays as close to the original information as possible. In order to do so, I have loosely framed this chapter with the concept of elites as an important facet of resource mobilization theory,[3] which first appeared in the 1960s and which I and other scholars have used to interpret organizations in the 1970s and beyond.[4] According to resource mobilization theory, celebrity members of organizations are elites because they have access to significant "resource pools"[5] (wealth, media contacts, political influence, discretionary time, etc.),[6] which those organizations may be able to utilize for their own corporate ends. Moreover, many of Scientology's celebrities are *international cultural elites* because of their relationships with various global media, which gives these celebrities opportunities to attempt to influence societies and/or cultures, especially involving styles, tastes, and entertainment.[7] The primary and secondary documents that I utilized in this chapter are on file in the archival collection that I oversee on alternative religions, housed within the University of Alberta Library system.

DIANETICS AND SCIENTOLOGY POLICIES ABOUT CELEBRITIES

By 1951—only a year after Hubbard launched his best-selling book on Dianetics—he wrote about the impact of celebrities on popular culture. In retrospect, he likely was beginning to ponder how he could use their persuasive power to market what he felt were his own contributions to the mental health field:

Ideas, and not battle[s], mark the forward progress of mankind. Individuals, and not masses, form the culture of the race. On a lesser scale actors and other artists work continually to give tomorrow a new form. Hollywood makes a picture which strikes the public fancy, and tomorrow we have girls made up like a star walking along the streets of the small towns of America. A Hollywood interior decorator dresses a set which takes the eye of the American audience, and tomorrow that set is seen as the apartments of Miami Beach and other resorts. A culture is as rich and capable of surviving as it has imaginative artists, skilled men of science, a high ethic level, workable government, land and natural resources, in about that order of importance.[8]

At some point in the next few years, Hubbard realized that Hollywood stars and other celebrities could take the ideas of Dianetics (and eventually Scientology) and inspire the public with them. After all, he already believed that "a culture is only as great as its dreams, and its dreams are dreamed by artists."[9] If only he could get celebrities to incorporate the propagation of Dianetics into their dreams, then surely public opinion would follow quickly.

Four years later in a Scientology magazine/newsletter named *Ability*, Hubbard translated his observations about celebrities into a policy. He wanted celebrity figures to convert to Scientology, and he elicited the help of his followers to recruit them. He began the policy by highlighting celebrities' potential importance and probable value to the Scientology cause:

If we are to do anything about society at large, we must do something about its communication lines.

One of the parts of this plan is Project Celebrity.

There are many to whom America and the world listens. On the backs of these are carried most of the enthusiasms on which society runs. It is vital, on our Third Dynamic [i.e., society, town, and nation], to put such persons into wonderful condition.

It is obvious what would happen to America if we helped its leaders to help others. Project Celebrity is a part of that program. It is obvious what would happen to Scientology if prime communicators benefitting from it would mention it now and again.[10]

In Hubbard's mind, the road ahead was clear for Scientology and celebrities. They first would take Scientology courses, then speak about their benefits while doing interviews for the media. Essential for the attainment of this project was the involvement of celebrities, many of whose already successful careers (Hubbard believed) would rise to even greater heights.

Contemporaneous Scientologists received Hubbard's directive to systematically seek celebrities to recruit, using one's own money and other resources along with certain encouragements provided by the Hubbard Association of Scientologists International (HASI) and the Hubbard Dianetics Research Foundation (HDRF). The policy provided a list of 63 celebrities (57 men and 6 women) whom Hubbard wanted his followers to recruit, and it read like a "who's who" of prominent persons of the period. They were from diverse segments within the celebrity world: news broadcasters/reporters Walter Winchell, Edward R. Murrow, and Lowell Thomas; entertainers Ed Sullivan, Milton Berle, Groucho Marx, Bing Crosby, Bob Hope, and Red Skelton; actors James Stewart and Charles Laughton; authors Ernest Hemingway and Dorothy Killgallen; pianist Liberace; and others who were widely known in the period, including perhaps one of the most influential figures in Hollywood, Walt Disney.[11]

Apparently this pressure at least to identify prominent celebrities and other opinion leaders went on for decades. Former Scientology member of 15 years, Lisa Halverson, reported in 1993:

When I was a student with the Celebrity Centre . . . , sometimes uniformed personnel would come into the course room and ask us to write down names of what they call in Scientology "opinion leaders," heavy hitters of some sort in whatever sphere of activity [it] might be—in business, politics, and arts and entertainment.[12]

Hubbard specifically hoped that some of his followers would take up his call to recruit people who were on the list.

To a contemporary ear some 60 years later, Hubbard's instructions about pursuing celebrities sound uncomfortably like stalking, and before the year was out Hubbard himself even used the word to describe the program:

Herein you find a list of celebrities. If you want one of these, write us at once, giving the ONE celebrity you have selected. We will then allocate this person to you as your game.

Having been awarded one of these celebrities, it will be up to you to learn what you can about your quarry and then put yourself at every hand across his or her path, and not permitting discouragements or "no's" or clerks or secretaries to intervene, in the days or weeks or months, to bring your celebrity into a formal auditing session and deliver an amount of good auditing necessary to (1) make him much more effective, and (2) make him aware of the benefits of Scientology on the Third Dynamic.

Finance, your pay, your expenses on this hunt are up to you.[13]

Shortly thereafter, Hubbard added, "these celebrities are well guarded, well barricaded, over-worked, aloof quarry. If you bring one of them home you will get a small plaque as your reward."[14]

No indication exists that Hubbard ever had to issue any small plaques as a result of this campaign, but it is worth noting that the famous movie director, Cecil B. DeMille, was on the list, and his nephew and adopted son, Richard DeMille (1922–2009), was an early Hubbard convert and close assistant.[15] In any case, decades later Scientologist and Celebrity Centre attendee, Diana Canova, remembered, "There was always pressure to get other celebrities in."[16]

In the subsequent issue of *Ability*, Hubbard continued his discussion of the new Project Celebrity program. He provided anonymity for anyone pursuing a celebrity, stating, "*Ability* assures all hunters that reports, names, progress, and all other material concerning Project Celebrity will not be published anywhere."[17] Hubbard also assured his followers that celebrities needed auditing and were aware of their need: "You can find in almost every press release from one of these people that they are not only in need of auditing, THEY ARE KEENLY AWARE of the need for auditing."[18] Later in the same issue, readers learned that in Phoenix, Arizona, Project Celebrity now had as its chairman a Doctor in Scientology, Richard F. Steeves [*sic*], whom Hubbard indicated cryptically, "has very considerable past experience with the stalking, approach, bagging, and trophying of people in many facets of life."[19]

Two *Bulletins* Hubbard issued in June 1960 presented his grand vision for global Scientology dissemination throughout all layers of society. Even though he did not mention celebrities *per se* in either one, both had obvious implications for them and their role as disseminators of the ideology. On June 10, Hubbard released, "What We Expect of a Scientologist," which was a statement of sufficient importance that he reissued it in 1980. In it he argued, "a professional Scientologist is one who expertly uses Scientology on any area or level of the society."[20] One need not be a trained, full-time auditor to be a professional Scientologist; one need only

get trained as a pro [public relations officer] and go out and up in the world of action and of life. Hit for the key spots by whatever means. . . . Make a good sound living at it, drive a good car, but get your job done, handle and better the people you meet and bring about a better earth. . . . [I]nvade every activity there is on a high level of success and make our influence felt on the comm [i.e., communication] lines of the world.[21]

In a June 23 *Bulletin*, Hubbard floated the idea to his members about identifying various zones in society in which Scientologists could concentrate their dissemination work, insisting that "Improvement is the common denominator of all our ideas, and of course each one has a zone of interest where he or she feels improvement is most needed or where he or she would be most comfortable in doing the work of improvement."[22]

Hubbard never formally implemented this "special zone plan" (as he called it) but revealed his belief that people had particular areas in society where they could be most effective in disseminating Scientology. Elsewhere he made it clear that celebrities' effectiveness should be on the level of public communication, and—after the establishment of the Celebrity Centre—he determined that it was "responsible for ensuring that celebrities expand in their area of power."[23]

On January 1, 1963, Hubbard spun a new angle concerning the recruitment of celebrities. He informed his followers, "Rapid dissemination can be attained . . . , by the rehabilitation of celebrities who are just beyond or just approaching their prime. This includes any person *well* known to the public and well liked but who has passed his or her prime, or any rising figure."[24] This same wording became part of a *Hubbard Communications Policy Letter* of May 23, 1976, which in turn the organization revised in January 1991.[25] He also reiterated part of this policy in October 1969, writing, "Celebrity Centres should work to rehabilitate old or faded artists. With a small processing staff, they can do wonders for artists."[26] Almost the same wording opened a *Hubbard Communications Office Policy Letter*, dated November 6, 1980.[27] Whether Scientologists could target celebrities according to their career trajectories would be difficult, yet in some cases by no means impossible, but the logic behind obtaining them at one of these two career periods was insightful. For Scientologists (including Hubbard), celebrity involvement with Scientology would help their careers. Consequently, celebrities whose careers were expanding would continue to do so, and they might attribute their continued success to their Scientology involvement. Likewise, celebrities whose careers were slipping also might attribute a change in fortune to their participation in Scientology and its programs. For social psychologists, it matters little whether Scientology involvement actually helps celebrities at any career stage; it matters a great deal that people attribute either their continuous success or their renewed success to their involvement. As actor Anne Archer stated in a Scientology commercial that encouraged celebrities to get additional auditing at the Celebrity Centre, "After my first auditing, I got my first big picture."[28]

The *Flag Order* that Hubbard issued on May 3, 1969, suggested that Scientology was having some success recruiting celebrities but that problems were occurring around overly enthusiastic Scientologists using their involvement in public announcements without their permission:

> No org or Scientologist is to use the name of a celebrity as being a Scientologist or to use such a name to promote or disseminate, without the express written permission of said celebrity.
>
> Protect their rights. What they say packs weight; therefore many want to be really sure before endorsing anything. If we rush them, push them, [or] use their names without permission, we only cause ARC breaks and a withdrawal.[29]

I am not aware of any incidents involving celebrities around this period, but the fact that Hubbard reissued this *Flag Order* in late June 1988 suggests that, periodically, Scientologists used celebrities' names in endorsements without their permission. Previously, for example, persons working with Scientology's (supposed) drug rehabilitation program, Narconon, experienced bad press in 1981 when they used celebrities' names in endorsements without their permission.[30] Even after, however, this 1988 *Flag Order* circulated within Scientology, the organization found itself in a dispute with race car driver, Mario Andretti, over seven Dianetics logos he found across the front of the Porsche that he soon was to drive in a Tampa, Florida, race. In late November, he demanded successfully that the logos were to be removed, because "it's not something I believe in, so I don't want to make it appear like I'm endorsing it."[31]

Scientology facilities specifically devoted to celebrities first appeared in 1969, the idea of deeply committed and beloved Scientologist, Yvonne Jentzsch (1927–1978).[32] In writing, she presented the idea of celebrity facilities to Hubbard, who approved the idea and brought in his daughter, Diana Hubbard, to oversee the project. She and Jentzsch worked on key aspects of the project, which had the name "The Booking Office," a term that referred to earlier theater days in which celebrities bought tickets to specific reserved seats for performances. Jentzsch was the person to first call these facilities "Celebrity Centres" (with the British spelling).[33] Based in Los Angeles, Jentzsch facilitated the establishment of celebrity centers in San Francisco, Las Vegas, Phoenix, New York, and within a few years, San Diego.[34] In 1969

Scientology rented space for the Celebrity Centre and other projects in a formerly elegant Los Angeles chateau named Fifield Manor, with Celebrity Centre opening its doors on July 18, 1969.[35] Scientology bought the building in 1973 and began restorations, then moved in on November 29, 1975.[36] It became Scientology's flagship celebrity facility, named the Celebrity Centre International.[37]

A Church of Scientology International public relations magazine described this beautifully restored Hollywood landmark and grounds:

> Originally named the *Chateau Elysee*, this historical building was designed and constructed as a 17th century French-Normandy chateau between 1927 and 1929 for the wife of film pioneer Thomas H. Ince. . . .
>
> The building is recognized as a Historical Landmark for Hollywood and the state of California, and recent renovations were done with close attention to authentic detail.
>
> During the Golden Age of Hollywood, the *Manor Hotel* was a home-away-from-home for many celebrities and prominent citizens. Now, more than 70 years after its original construction, it is the home of Celebrity Centre International.[38]

By any measure, the renovations were extensive and beautifully finished. A description of the sheer size and diversity of the renovations gives some idea about the extensiveness of the project:

> The first-floor houses classrooms, where believers take class in communication, marriage, etc. Up to 40 people a day, from celebs and CEOs to struggling guitarists and children, study there.
>
> There's a screening room for movies and Scientology films, and a small theater. And a roped-off office for Hubbard, the late science fiction writer and *Dianetics* author who is Scientology's core. He has an office in every Celebrity Centre.[39]

To avoid any confusion, Scientologists maintain these offices for when Hubbard's thetan (or spirit-like entity) assumes another body and returns to continue his earthly mission.

Other parts of the building also are worth noting. "The bottom, windowless floor of the main building houses the Purification Rooms," where Scientologists go through their program's controversial drug and radiation purging program involving running, vitamins, and sauna.[40] Scattered throughout the seven-story building are 77 apartments where some of the stars stay when they are in town.[41] Clearly the renovations were in-depth, completely gutting the building's insides—so it might be important to know who actually did them.

John Richardson's long article about celebrities referred to the "1 million man-hours of labor" behind the renovation but fails to inform who the laborers were.[42] The U.S. newspaper, *USA Today*, published an article on celebrities in 1994, which claimed that "most of the antique furnishings have been refinished by a Scientology-run warehouse of Scientology-believing carpenters."[43] Of course, Scientology does not have, nor has it ever had, a warehouse of believing carpenters. What it did have, and by all indications still does have, is a forced labor contingent of members, some of whom are entering the Sea Organization; others of whom are Sea Organization members who have run afoul of leadership. The forced labor contingent of members is called the Estates Project Force (EPF), and is composed of aspirants to the Sea Org whose so-called training routines involve such activities as drywalling, cleaning, painting, sanding, etc.[44] More complicated and often dangerous repairs are assigned to Sea Org members serving in its Rehabilitation Project Force (RPF). Their assignments ranged from flooring, electrical and mechanical work, major carpentry jobs, and so forth, receiving pay that was at least a fraction of what regular tradespeople would receive. (For these and other reasons, former Scientologist Amy Scobee, who was on the RPF for five-and-a-half years, defined it as "a controlled slave labor camp to which is assigned anyone arbitrarily deemed a liability for actions or thoughts] considered to be in opposition to the group."[45])

Former RPF member, Steve Hall, gave a brief description of what he remembered life to have been like when like working on the Celebrity Centre's Manor Hotel:

> I did painting at first and later was switched over to carpentry. Everything you do, you're given a deadline. "When are you getting this door painted? Thirty-five minutes." If you weren't done on time you had to do 20 pushups. You get 10 minutes a day for personal time. Ten minutes! It's basically like a chain gang. You're not allowed to speak to anybody unless they speak to you.[46]

Use of RPF labor is especially controversial, since the program uses forced labor and other techniques that led to charges that it is either a slave labor or brainwashing facility, which in either case grossly violates human rights.[47] Consequently, involvement of EPF and RPF staffers shed light on one of the major criticisms of the organization's treatment of celebrities: celebrity pampering is made possible by (what critics see as) exploitation of ordinary members.

The policy foundation for pampering celebrities appeared during the same period that Scientology was developing the Celebrity Centre for them. A 1973 *Sea Organization Flag Order* made a clear distinction between them and regular members:

> Celebrities are very special people and have a very distinct line of dissemination. They have Comm. [communication] lines that others do not have and many medias to get their dissemination through.
>
> Because of their value as disseminators it is unwise to make them staff members working full time as any other sea Org member does in an organization, rather they should be allowed to be the Celebrity they are, utilizing their talent, to get them more and more into the public eye. If these celebrities want to join the Sea Org they may be awarded the status of HONORARY SEA ORG Members. . . .
>
> This award is given after an exam given by Celebrity Center Qual [Qualifications] Division on Scientology basics, a certificate is issued to the Celebrity Honorary Sea Org Member. . . .
>
> Celebrities are Valuable, treat them that way; they can help put more people on the bridge by use of their abilities and their media, those that become Honorary SO [Sea Organization] Members have shown their dedication and are Welcomed.[48]

Celebrities were not to receive a Sea Org salary, but, as Honorary Sea Org Members, they were Field Staff Members, which entitled them to either 10 percent or 15 percent commissions on the costs of all Scientology courses or training that any of their recruits took.[49]

Evolving around the same period was Scientology officials' understanding of the role that the Celebrity Centre itself was to in the overall organization. One of Hubbard's daughters, Diana Hubbard Horwich, presented a definition of the Celebrity Centre in 1974 in which she stated that the exact purpose of Celebrity Centre is:

> TO HELP LRH [L. Ron Hubbard] SELL AND DELIVER HIGH STANDARD DIANETICS AND SCIENTOLOGY SERVICES TO CELEBRITIES AND THUS CONVERT EARTH'S TOP STRATA OF BEINGS INTO SCIENTOLOGISTS.[50]

Then in 1980, a *Hubbard Communications Office Policy Letter* reissued an earlier *Policy Letter* from October 28, 1973, which stated that "The PURPOSE of Celebrity Centre is: TO FORWARD THE EXPANSION AND POPULARIZATION OF SCIENTOLOGY THROUGH THE ARTS, WHILE

REMAINING SOLVENT AND USING HIGHEST QUALITY TECH."[51]
Around this same period, Hubbard's definition of a celebrity appeared in a
1976 *Policy Letter* (revised in 1991), and that same year Hubbard included it
in the group's management dictionary. A celebrity is:

ANY PERSON IMPORTANT IN HIS FIELD OR AN OPINION
LEADER OR HIS ENTOURAGE, BUSINESS ASSOCIATES, FAM-
ILY OR FRIENDS WITH PARTICULAR ATTENTION TO THE
ARTS, SPORTS, AND MANAGEMENT AND GOVERNMENT.[52]

In an extensively planned program dated in the next year (May 31, 1977),
the director of the Celebrity Centre International, Yvonne Jentzsch, coau-
thored a systematic policy to train celebrities in ways to facilitate their ability
to disseminate Scientology to target groups around the world.

CELEBRITIES AND SCIENTOLOGY'S PUBLIC RELATIONS ORGANIZATION

Jentzsch was popular within the Scientology organization and by all
accounts worked herself tirelessly on behalf of Celebrity Centre International
until her untimely death from a brain tumor. The program that she developed
with Sea Org Chief, Harriet Foster, laid out the purpose, policy, courses, programs, projects, and ideal outcomes of a public relations organization that
depended heavily upon the role of celebrities. Its goal was "broad public recognition, acceptance and acknowledgement of LRH [i.e., L. Ron Hubbard],
Dianetics and Scientology effectively caused with perfect PR [i.e., public rela-
tions] towards the attainment of a new civilization."[53]

The purpose of the public relations organization was to capitalize on
"opinion leaders'" abilities to disseminate Scientology Technology to various
public bodies and organizations. Success in this regard would lead to societal
enhancement and the fostering of "a favorable operating climate, so Scientology organizations can expand, prosper and be viable," with the rest of society
following suit.[54] Notice that the ultimate purpose of the public relations programs was to get all of society to follow Hubbard's policies as disseminated by
opinion leaders.

The plans for this public relations program made clear the role that celebrities were to play:

The celebrities will go into cultural and art groups, sporting bodies,
clubs, associations, etc. and all their specific publics. Scientology celebrities and Scientologists will have excellent preparatory work done and

programs and projects with targets; this will enable more and more of the society to use LRH's Tech, getting it in a standard organized manner, that will vastly improve society now, and introduce a new way of life for the public. The PRO Org will also utilize the Success stories and well publicize the good works achieved, by the use of LRH's Technology; it will use all the media in liaison with the GO [i.e., Guardian's Office] and every form of communication line possible to mold opinions so that Dianetics and Scientology become the thing to do. It will help to remove barriers to honest production . . . , and to ensure LRH's materials are interpreted by the public and used; it will keep LRH and Management informed and advise if policy is needed so it can set, and connect up continuously the publics to LRH, Scientology and Dianetics.[55]

In order to implement these plans, this *Executive Directive* offered 23 suggestions for programs.

Some of the proposed programs involved procedures within Scientology—routing new celebrities into Scientology courses; establishing a training unit (called a Hatting Unit) that can train celebrities on how they can apply Hubbard's technology to specific issues; etc. Others outlined assignments that celebrities were to undertake. Scientology policy-makers proposed that celebrities could be proactive and influential in a number of public venues including the following: a variety of public offices, assorted community groups, fan clubs, campaigns and movements extolling the virtues of Scientology Technology, and in the press. Some opportunities for celebrity activism and endorsement targeted the arts community specifically. As such, celebrities were to promote Scientology and Hubbard's works at arts festivals, theatres, art workshops, seminars, and other appropriate venues. Finally, celebrities also should endorse Scientology amongst professionals—doctors, lawyers and so forth, as well as in hospitals, universities and other similar institutions. The goal was always to further LRH Tech.[56]

Under Jentzsch's direction, Hubbard approved the overall public relations organization but failed to give her a working budget, forcing her to scrounge for money to implement programs.[57] Funding issues aside, however, the overall package provides deep insight into how Scientology officials want to utilize celebrities in efforts to promote Hubbard and his technology.

Contents of a secret ("not for distribution") public relations office course (first used in 1969, reissued in 1975) provided insight into questions that Scientology staff anticipated reporters and others might ask public relations personnel in interviews.[58] The three-page bulletin provided response scenarios to: (1) "answering non-loaded questions," (2) providing "no answer," (3) "non sequitur events" (in this case, answers to questions about issues that have nothing apparently to do with Scientology), (4) "handling a suppressive [i.e., hostile] T.V. interviewer," and four ways to handle a suppressive person [i.e., someone attempting to harm Scientology]. The four ways to handle a suppressive person were particularly interesting,[59] since sometimes members of the public can observe Scientology spokespeople attempting to use them against hostile media interviewers. In response to such a hostile person and his or her question, Scientology public relations personnel first can try to overwhelm the interviewer "by such things as shouting, banging, pointing, swearing," until the interviewer "is caved in" (i.e., collapses in defeat).[60] Next, the Scientologist can try "being knowingly covertly hostile" by "using the word as a rapier and plunges it at the reporter, so the reporter introverts and drops the question."[61] Next, a public relations official learns when to use "stalling for time,"[62] and finally, when and how to use "verbal karate"— taking a reporter's comment and turning it back on him or her, "either by a snide remark, question or comment, or by physical overwhelm."[63] It is likely that BBC reporter, John Sweeney, was on the receiving end of some of these (and related) techniques when he was preparing a story about Scientology in 2007.[64]

A more extensive public relations course for celebrities began in June 1977, which laid out the need that both stars and Scientology itself had for it:

> INFORMATION: Celebrities are continuously on TV, doing radio shows and press interviews, etc. Many want to talk about LRH [L. Ron Hubbard], Dianetics and Scientology but have had no hatting [training], and rather than make a mistake, they do not bring these subjects up and so lose opportunities to help others know more about LRH, Dianetics and Scientology. Celebrities are very willing to use the media but need hatting. Hence this checksheet so these celebrity resources can be used as part of Scientology expansion.
>
> In doing this checksheet celebrities will have expertise in using LRH's tech to further their own careers. . . .[65]

These study materials, therefore, were the kind of instructions that Scientologists might be able to use when in interviews with persons who were either uninformed or antagonistic to the group. They provided opportunities to study Dianetics, Scientology, and Hubbard in sufficient depth that one could get through many media interviews. They did not provide, however, opportunities to study (with an eye toward refuting) criticisms that opponents have toward Scientology's positions on psychiatric treatment, drug treatment, religious freedom, specific biographical claims about Hubbard himself, and church/state separation, which sometimes cause Scientologists problems in public debates. In essence, Scientology's public relations and media training may protect the image of the organization and its founder among the members but leaves them vulnerable to well-informed and closely scrutinizing critics, debaters, and examiners.

In order to assist Public Relations Officers in their dissemination efforts, in 1979 (then reissued in 1982) Hubbard established a publication that he named HOTLINE as their official newsletter. The publication's purpose:

> is to feed PROs information they can use which will get word of mouth and which will help them build an image. It gives information and releases they can get into newspapers, magazines and periodicals.[66]

The HOTLINE editor is supposed to identify an area of concern to society, then find out the answers to the following questions:

A. How does LRH fit into this?
B. What has LRH done with regard to it?
C. What has LRH produced to resolve it or aid it?
D. What LRH works are the authorities neglecting concerning this?
E. What quotable statement has LRH made about it?
F. what opinion leaders or groups has he befriended or worked with, to bring about a betterment of conditions on this subject?
G. What official recognition or indisputable public recognition has LRH received for work in this sphere?

Each issue of the newsletter was to utilize these questions in order to build its motif. [67] Hubbard was very clear, however, that even though a celebrity who went through and applied this training was informed on key aspects of Scientology and his own biography:

> An Honorary LRH PRO is NOT a spokesman for the Church of Scientology and does not attempt to represent the Church or answer questions which concern Church affairs. These he [sic] promptly refers to the Guardian's Office. He IS authorized to get published LRH quotes and articles, or news releases concerning LRH and to answer questions concerning L. Ron Hubbard and his activities, using the information provided him [sic] in his Honorary LRH Personal PRO Press Pack and HOTLINE.[68]

In short, HOTLINE and PRO training credentialed Scientology celebrities to further the positive image of the organization and its founder to the public but not to answer questions about the operations of the organization itself. On a related matter, an October 1980 *Policy Letter* clarified aspects of the related publication *Celebrity* magazine. It was to feature names of celebrities, emphasizing how Scientology training and auditing can advance their careers.[69]

By 1988, the Church of Scientology International distributed a three-page application form for persons who wanted to receive training to be an Honorary LRH Personal Public Relations Officer. The cover sheet stated, "If you are interested in participating in an active program of helping make Ron the most acclaimed and widely read author of all time, through TV and radio, news articles, public speaking, dissemination, events, etc. fill in this application form."[70] Aside from the information that one would expect an application form to request, (name, address phone number, job experience, etc.), it also asked questions like, "Are you here to obtain news stories or generally disrupt the organization?," "Are you a flagrant criminal or wanted?," and "Are you related to or connected to intelligence agencies either by past history or immediate familial connections?"[71] Obviously the group was concerned about spies and plants from governmental agencies or the media.

CONCLUSION

A history of Scientology's celebrity policies reflects Hubbard's realized dream of society's opinion makers proselytizing about the organization and its founder in all areas or zones of society where they have influence. Researchers, however, need in-depth accounts about when and why some early celebrities began calling themselves Scientologists if we are to assess the efficacy of these policies. Moreover, the establishment of the Celebrity Centre may have been an enormous boost in celebrity recruitment efforts, but we need more research in order to be certain. Given the fleeting nature of radio and television interviews, it probably will be impossible to acquire copies about celebrity interviews prior to receiving public relations office training, but if we did then perhaps we could assess how that training helped Scientology leaders shape the organizational messages that they wanted to convey. We have no idea how many celebrities there have been and whether they entered the organization through opportunities provided by Hubbard's policies. Obviously the study of Scientology's celebrities is in its infancy, but even now researchers can see how systematic and persistent have been Scientology's efforts to bring them in, then deploy them in the cause of "keeping Scientology working."

NOTES

1. See Russell Miller, *Bare-Faced Messiah: The True Story of L. Ron Hubbard* (Toronto: Key Porter Books, 1987), 69, 135.

2. David S. Meyer and Joshua Gamson, "The Challenge of Cultural Elites: Celebrities and Social Movements," *Sociological Inquiry* 65, no. 2 (May 1995): 184.

3. Ibid., 183.

4. For example, Stephen A. Kent, "Hollywood's Celebrity Lobbyists and the Clinton Administration's American Foreign Policy Toward German Scientology," *Journal of Religion and Popular Culture* 1, no. 1 (Spring 2002).

5. John D. McCarthy and Mayer N. Zald, "Resource Mobilization and Social Movements: A Partial Theory," *American Journal of Sociology* 82, no. 6 (May 1977): 1221.

6. Ibid., 1224.

7. This definition is a revision of one that I provided earlier for cultural elites in Stephen A. Kent, "Hollywood Celebrity Lobbyists and the Clinton Administration's American Foreign Policy Toward German Scientology," *Journal of Religion and Popular Culture* 1, no. 1 (Spring 2002): n.1.

8. L. Ron Hubbard, *Science of Survival: Simplified, Faster Dianetic Techniques* (Wichita, KS: The Hubbard Dianetic Foundation, 1951), Book One, 98.

9. Ibid., Book Two, 239.

10. L. Ron Hubbard, "Project Celebrity," *Ability* Minor II, Hubbard Communications Office, 1955, 2.

11. Ibid.

12. Lisa Halverson, quoted in John H. Richardson, "Catch a Rising Star," *Premiere*, September 1993, 92.

13. Ibid. (capitalization in original).

14. Ibid.

15. DeMille was not recruited; he joined Scientology in late 1950 or early 1951 after reading the Dianetics article in *Astounding Science Fiction* (Miller, *Bare-Faced Messiah*, 174). Presumably DeMille read "Dianetics: The Evolution of a Science," which appeared in *Astounding Science Fiction* in May 1950. He became Hubbard's assistant and was still with the organization in some capacity through mid-February 1954 (*Los Angeles Times*, "Former Dancer Divorced from Richard DeMille," February 20, 1954, 2).

16. Diana Canova, quoted in Richardson, "Catch a Rising Star," 91.

17. L. Ron Hubbard, "Project Celebrity," *Ability* Minor III, Hubbard Communications Office, 1955, 9.

18. L. Ron Hubbard, "Celebrity Chairman Appointed," *Ability* Minor III, Hubbard Communications Office, 1955, 11.

19. Ibid. (capitals in original). Richard F. (Dick) Steves was a prominent Scientologist in the movement. Surviving correspondence places him in California, probably from early December 1953 through at least mid-November 1955 (Florian DeDonato to Mr. Richard F. Steves, November 1, 1955 [received November 14, 1955]), then as

Secretary to Washington, D.C.'s Academy of Scientology in late October 1957 (Dick Steves to J. B. Farber, October 28, 1957).

20. L. Ron Hubbard, "What We Expect of a Scientologist," *Hubbard Communications Office Policy Letter*, June 10, 1960; reissued as *Hubbard Communications Office Bulletin*, October 26, 1980, 1.

21. Ibid., 2–3.

22. L. Ron Hubbard, "Special Zone Plan," *Hubbard Communication Office Bulletin*, June 23, AD 10 [1960], in L. Ron Hubbard, *The Technical Bulletins of Dianetics and Scientology Volume 4, 1960–1961* (Copenhagen: Scientology Publications, 1976), 112.

23. L. Ron Hubbard, *Modern Management Technology Defined* (Copenhagen: New Era Publications 1976), 68.

24. L. Ron Hubbard, "Objective Three: Celebrities," *Hubbard Communication Office Policy Letter*, January 1, AD 13 (1963, italics in original).

25. L. Ron Hubbard (Revision assisted by LRH Technical Research and Compilation), "Celebrities," *Hubbard Communications Office Policy Letter*, May 23, 1976, revised January 10, 1991.

26. L. Ron Hubbard, "The Rehabilitation of Artists," *Hubbard Communications Office Policy Letter*, October 5, 1969.

27. L. Ron Hubbard (Compiled and Issued by Celebrity Centre Advices Project I/C), "The Rehabilitation of Artists," *Hubbard Communications Office Policy Letter*, November 6, 1980.

28. See the large advertisement in Church of Scientology Celebrity Centre International, *Celebrity* Issue 246 (1991): 18.

29. L. Ron Hubbard (Assisted by CO OTL LA, Revision Assisted by LRH Technical Research and Compilations), "Celebrities," *Sea Organization Flag Order* 1975R, ED13R INT, May 3, 1969, revised June 25, 1988. ARC stands for affinity, reality, and communication, which Hubbard asserted were the key elements to understanding. An ARC break involves a problem with the relationship among these concepts. See L. Ron Hubbard, *Dianetics and Scientology Technical Dictionary* (Los Angeles: Publications Organization, 1975), 21.

30. David McCrindell, "Bizarre Brainwashing Cult Cons Top Stars into Backing Its Drug Program," *National Enquirer*, April 21, 1981. The celebrities who complained about the unauthorized use of their names were Henry Winkler, Hal Linden, Phyllis Diller, Rob Reiner, and Lou Ferrigno.

31. Andretti, quoted in Thomas C. Tobin and Joe Wilson, "Andretti Orders Dianetics Logo Taken Off His Car," *St. Petersburg Times*, November 27, 1988, http://www.scientology-lies.com/press/st-petersburg-times/1988-11-27/andretti-orders -dianetics-logo-taken-off-his-car.html.

32. See several articles in Church of Scientology Celebrity Centre, *Celebrity* [no number], 1984.

33. Howard Dickman, "Yvonne Gillham Jentzsch," *Scientoliopedia*, http://scientolipedia.org/info/Yvonne_Gillham_Jentzsch#Scientology.27s_Celebrity _Centres_.281969_to_1977.29, Section "7 Scientology's Celebrity Centres (1969 to 1977)," last modified August 14, 2015.

34. Ibid.

35. Advanced Organizations of Los Angeles, "Celebrity Centre," *Advance* 6/I, 1969, 8.

36. *Los Angeles Times*, "Scientologists Will Move into Larger Quarters," November 29, 1975, Part 1, 31. See also Church of Scientology Celebrity Centre International, "Diana Starts the New Celebrity Centre in Motion," *Celebrity* 18 Minor (1976): 5.

37. CSI, "What is Celebrity Centre?" *The Church of Scientology Celebrity Centre International: The Oasis of Creative Freedom* [Public Relations Magazine], 1993, 8.

38. Ibid., 9.

39. Karen Thomas, "Celebrities Find Haven and a Stage," *USA Today*, November 30, 1994, D2.

40. Ibid.

41. Ibid.; see also, Church of Scientology Celebrity Centre International, "Come Stay at the Manor Hotel," *Celebrity* (1987): 15.

42. Richardson, "Catch a Rising Star," 91.

43. Thomas, "Celebrities Find Haven and a Stage," D2.

44. See Stephen A. Kent, *Brainwashing in Scientology's Rehabilitation Project Force (RPF)* (Hamburg: Interior Ministry, 2000), 19.

45. Amy Scobee, *Scientology Abuse at the Top* (Puyallup, WA: Scobee Publishing, 2010), 7, n.2.

46. Hall, quoted in Jim Edwards, "This Man Alleges He Was Held for Months in a Scientology 'Reform' Prison," *Business Insider*, July 22, 2012, http://www.businessinsider.com/this-man-alleges-he-was-held-for-months-in-a-scientology-reform-prison-2012-7.

47. Ibid. For additional evidence that "the RPF furnished only a portion of the labor for Celebrity Centre and worked alongside professional contractors," see Dana Goodyear, "Chateau Scientology," *New Yorker*, January 14, 2008, 41.

48. Kim Dunleavy (for the Board of Directors of the Churches of Scientology), "Celebrities and the Sea Organization," *Sea Organization Flag Order 3323*, May 9, 1973 (capitalization in original).

49. Ibid.; see also the definition of "Field Staff Member" in Hubbard, *Modern Management Technology Defined*, 201.

50. D. H. Horwich, "Celebrity Centre Purpose," *Flag Order #3484*, August 1, 1974.

51. L. Ron Hubbard (Compiled and Issued by Donna Matteson), "Celebrity Centre Purpose," *Hubbard Communications Office Policy Letter*, November 12, 1980, reissue of L. Ron Hubbard, "Celebrity Centre Purpose," *Hubbard Communications Office Policy Letter*, October 28, 1973.

52. L. Ron Hubbard (Revision assisted by LRH Technical Research and Compilations), "Celebrities," 1976, revised 1991 (capitals in original); Hubbard, *Modern Management Technology Defined*, 67.

53. Yvonne Jentzsch and Harriet Foster, "Commanding Officer, Public Relations Organization, Administrative Scale," *Executive Directive SO ED 932 INT*, May 31, 1977, 1.

54. Ibid.

55. Ibid., 2.

56. Ibid., 3.

57. Skip Press, "Death By Devotion: Tragic Tale of Scientology Celebrity Brainchild Yvonne Jentzsch," *TMR*, August 4, 2011, www.themortonreport.com/discoveries/stranger/death-by-devotion/.

58. Sheila Gaiman (from the Hat Write-Up of David Gaiman), "Reporter TRs [Training Routines]," *Board Technical Bulletin*, June 21, 1975 (cancels *HCO Bulletin* of December 10, 1969, 3 pp.).

59. Ibid., 2–3.

60. Ibid., 2.

61. Ibid.

62. Ibid., 2–3.

63. Ibid., 3.

64. John Sweeney, *The Church of Fear: Inside the Weird World of Scientology* (London: Silvertail Books, 2013), 259, 280–281.

65. Yvonne Jentzsch for Sue Anderson, "Celebrity Media Handling Checksheet," *Sea Organization Executive Directive 930 Int, Pilot Only*, June 24, 1977, 1 (capitalization and underlining in original).

66. L. Ron Hubbard (Assisted by LRH Personal PRO), "'HOTLINE,' Policy of," *Hubbard Communications Office Policy Letter*, September 25, 1979 (reissued October 31, 1982), 470, in L. Ron Hubbard, *The Management Series* Volume 2 (Copenhagen: New Era Publications, 1983).

67. Ibid., 471.

68. Ibid., 472.

69. L. Ron Hubbard (Compiled and Issued by Donna Matteson), "Celebrity Centre Magazine, *Celebrity*," *Hubbard Communications Office Policy Letter*, October 15, 1980, 1 p.

70. CSI, *Honorary LRH Personal Public Relations Officer Application Form*, 1988 (Cover Sheet).

71. Ibid., Form.

BIBLIOGRAPHY

Advanced Organizations of Los Angeles. "Celebrity Centre." *Advance* 6/I. 1969.

Church of Scientology Celebrity Centre. *Celebrity* [no number]. 1984.

Church of Scientology Celebrity Centre International. *Celebrity* Issue 246 (1991): 18.

Church of Scientology Celebrity Centre International. "Come Stay at the Manor Hotel." *Celebrity* Issue 205 (1987): 15.

CSI. *Honorary LRH Personal Public Relations Officer Application Form*. 1988.

CSI. "What Is Celebrity Centre?" The Church of Scientology Celebrity Centre, Church of Scientology International: The Oasis of Creative Freedom [Public Relations Magazine]. 1993.

Dunleavy, Kima, for the Board of Directors of the Churches of Scientology. "Celebrities and the Sea Organization." *Sea Organization Flag Order 3323*. May 9, 1973.

Edwards, Jim. "This Man Alleges He Was Held for Months in a Scientology 'Reform' Prison." *Business Insider*. July 22, 2012. http://www.businessinsider.com/this -man-alleges-he-was-held-for-months-in-a-scientology-reform-prison-2012-7.

Gaiman, Sheila (from the Hat Write-Up of David Gaiman). "Reporter TRs [Training Routines]." *Board Technical Bulletin*. June 21, 1975. Cancels *HCO Bulletin* of December 10, 1969.

Goodyear, Dana. "Chateau Scientology." *New Yorker*. January 14, 2008. http://www .newyorker.com/magazine/2008/01/14/chateau-scientology.

Horwich, D. H. "Celebrity Centre Purpose." *Flag Order* 3484. August 1, 1974.

Hubbard, L. Ron. *Dianetics and Scientology Technical Dictionary*. Los Angeles: Publications Organization, 1975.

Hubbard, L. Ron. *Modern Management Technology Defined*. Copenhagen: New Era Publications, 1976.

Hubbard, L. Ron. "Objective Three: Celebrities." *Hubbard Communication Office Policy Letter*. January 1, AD 13 [1963]. In L. Ron Hubbard, *The Organization Executive Course*, Public Division Volume 7 (Los Angeles: Bridge Publications, 1974), 509.

Hubbard, L. Ron. "Project Celebrity." *Ability* Minor II Hubbard Communications Office, 1955.

Hubbard, L. Ron. "Project Celebrity Chairman Appointed." *Ability* Minor III Hubbard Communications Office, 1955.

Hubbard, L. Ron. "The Rehabilitation of Artists." *Hubbard Communications Office Policy Letter*. October 5, 1969.

Hubbard, L. Ron. *Science of Survival: Simplified, Faster Dianetic Techniques*. Wichita, KS: The Hubbard Dianetic Foundation, 1951.

Hubbard, L. Ron. "Special Zone Plan." *Hubbard Communication Office Bulletin*. June 23, AD 10 [1960]. In L. Ron Hubbard, *The Technical Bulletins of Dianetics and Scientology*, Volume 4, 1960–1961 (Copenhagen: Scientology Publications, 1976), 111–115.

Hubbard, L. Ron. "What We Expect of a Scientologist." *Hubbard Communications Office Policy Letter*, June 10, 1960. In L. Ron Hubbard, *The Organization Executive Course*, Public Division Volume 6 (Los Angeles: Bridge Publications, 1991), 828–830.

Hubbard, L. Ron (Assisted by CO OTL LA, and revision assisted by LRH Technical Research and Compilations). "Celebrities." *Sea Organization Flag Order* 1975R, ED 13R INT. Revised June 25, 1988.

Hubbard, L. Ron (Assisted by LRH Personal PRO). "'HOTLINE,' Policy of." *Hubbard Communications Office Policy Letter* of September 25, 1979, reissued October 31, 1982. In L. Ron Hubbard, *The Management Series* Volume 2 (Copenhagen: New Era Publications, 1983).

Hubbard, L. Ron (Compiled and Issued by Celebrity Centre Advices Project I/C). "The Rehabilitation of Artists." *Hubbard Communications Office Policy Letter*. November 6, 1980. In L. Ron Hubbard, *The Organization Executive Course*, Public Division Volume 6 (Los Angeles: Bridge Publications, 1991), 135.

Hubbard, L. Ron (Compiled and Issued by Donna Matteson). "Celebrity Centre Magazine. *Celebrity*." *Hubbard Communications Office Policy Letter*. October 15, 1980.

Hubbard, L. Ron. "1980." In L. Ron Hubbard, *The Organization Executive Course*, Public Division Volume 6 (Los Angeles: Bridge Publications, 1991), 13.

Hubbard, L. Ron (Revision assisted by LRH Technical Research and Compilation). "Celebrities." *Hubbard Communications Office Policy Letter.* May 23, 1976, revised January 10, 1991. In L. Ron Hubbard, *The Organization Executive Course*, Public Division Volume 6, revision assisted by LRH Technical Research and Compilations (Los Angeles: Bridge Publications, 1991), 139.

Jentzsch, Yvonne, and Harriet Foster. "Commanding Officer, Public Relations Organization, Administrative Scale." *Executive Directive SO ED 932 IN.* May 31, 1977, 6 pp.

Jentzsch, Yvonne, for Sue Anderson. "Celebrity Media Handling Checksheet." *Sea Organization Executive Directive 930 Int, Pilot Only.* June 24, 1977 [capitalization and underlining in original].

Kent, Stephen A. *Brainwashing in Scientology's Rehabilitation Project Force (RPF).* Hamburg: Interior Ministry, 2000. https://skent.ualberta.ca/contributions/scientology/brainwashing-in-scientologys-rehabilitation-project-force-rpf/.

Kent, Stephen A. "Hollywood's Celebrity Lobbyists and the Clinton Administration's American Foreign Policy toward German Scientology." *Journal of Religion and Popular Culture* 1, no. 1 (Spring 2002). https://skent.ualberta.ca/wp-content/uploads/2015/07/Scientologys-Celebrity-Lobbyists.pdf.

Los Angeles Times. "Scientologists Will Move into Larger Quarters." *Los Angeles Times.* November 29, 1975.

McCarthy, John D., and Mayer N. Zald. "Resource Mobilization and Social Movements: A Partial Theory." *American Journal of Sociology* 82, no. 6 (May 1977): 1212–1239.

McCrindell, David. "Bizarre Brainwashing Cult Cons Top Stars into Backing Its Drug Program." *National Enquirer.* April 21, 1981.

Meyer, David S., and Joshua Gamson. "The Challenge of Cultural Elites: Celebrities and Social Movements." *Sociological Inquiry* 65, no. 2 (May 1995): 181–206.

Miller, Russell. *Bare-Faced Messiah: The True Story of L. Ron Hubbard.* London: Key Porter Books, 1987.

Press, Skip. "Death by Devotion: Tragic Tale of Scientology Celebrity Centre Brainchild Yvonne Jentzsch." *TMR.* August 4, 2011. http://www.themortonreport.com/discoveries/stranger/death-by-devotion/.

Richardson, John H. "Catch a Rising Star." *Premiere.* September 1993. http://www.spaink.net/cos/essays/richardson_rising.html.

Scobee, Amy. *Scientology Abuse at the Top.* Puyallup, WA: Scobee Publishing, 2010.

Sweeney, John. *The Church of Fear: Inside the Weird World of Scientology.* London: Silvertail Books, 2013.

Thomas, Karen. "Celebrities Find Haven and a Stage." *USA Today.* November 30, 1994.

Tobin, Thomas C., and Joe Wilson. "Andretti Orders Dianetics Logo Taken Off His Car." *St. Petersburg Times*, November 27, 1988. http://www.scientology-lies.com/press/st-petersburg-times/1988-11-27/andretti-orders-dianetics-logo-taken-off-his-car.html.

5

Celebrities Keeping Scientology Working

Stephen A. Kent

L. Ron Hubbard was prescient with his realization about the impact that stars and celebrities had upon ordinary people in mass culture. People imitated and emulated them, often modeling aspects of their own lives according to what actors did on stage or how they lived their lives off-camera. Statements that he made about the celebrities in the entertainment industry fostered among some of them an inflated feeling of self-importance, portraying them as artists who shaped the development of civilization. The artists who absorbed this inflated view of their contributions did so as they socialized into the subcultural world that Hubbard created, in which they equated civilizational advance with furthering Scientology's influence. Serving Scientology, therefore, was a means by which they felt that they were contributing to society's advancement, and if by doing so, they caught the eye of a producer looking to fill a part in a film, then ever so much the better.

This chapter examines the way that Scientology utilizes celebrities in the organization's overall effort to "keep Scientology working." I kept in mind the overall description of elites that appears in resource mobilization theory, since these celebrities have the flexible time, resources, and media connections that allows them to open areas nationally or internationally in which they can proselytize. More importantly, however, might be the significance of having celebrity status itself, because that status carries with it forms of unique, valuable assets that its possessors can use to influence others in society. My analysis, therefore, focuses on how Scientology celebrities attempt to translate the power and elite status that they have acquired as stars into other forms of influence—such as economic, which involves money and wealth—or sociopolitical, which involves social and political institutional structures.

Celebrity Magazine (eventually just calling itself *Celebrity*) provides glimpses into the kinds of donations in time, talent, and wealth that converts made to and for the organization. The research collection that I oversee for the University of Alberta Library contains approximately 215 issues from 1972 through 2007, and a research assistant of mine, Alexis Brown, went through each of them, identifying instances of celebrities engaged in some sort of service activity designed to enhance Scientology's or L. Ron Hubbard's images or fortunes. Subsequently, I went through the larger list and narrowed down the examples into categories, which provide the basis for much of the analysis in this chapter. I also supplemented these individual incidents with primary and secondary material I had on file.

The story that emerges is one of impressive commitment on the part of talented members to further the successes of the organization to which they belong, often suggesting sacrifices of considerable time, wealth, and talent. On a theoretical level, however, we see an organization mobilizing people in the entertainment industry in ways that probably are unprecedented in modern life. The following subheadings illustrate the nature of Scientology's deployment of its elite celebrities.

PLACING CELEBRITIES IN PUBLIC EVENTS IN WHICH SCIENTOLOGISTS WERE UNLIKELY TO BE CHALLENGED OR QUESTIONED

One context in which celebrities disseminated Scientology involved public events, where the content of the occurrence had nothing to do with Scientology *per se* (to use the language of Scientology, it is "other-intentioned"), but opportunities existed to place Scientology in the minds of audiences or participants. Opportunities of this nature are legion, and Scientologists took advantage of them. For example, a 2004 *Celebrity* magazine reported on Lynsey Bartilson's (b. 1983) participation in (what it called) the annual Christmas Parade, along with "two hundred Scientology Volunteer Ministers. The parade was attended by over a hundred thousand people, and viewed by even more on television."[1] These activities and others got Scientology and its programs into the public eye, brought some attention to the Scientologists themselves, but posed little likelihood that the members would have been quizzed or challenged about the organization or its practices. Nevertheless, Bartilson had been an Honorary Public Relations Officer since at least 2001.[2] Participating in public events[3] such as riding on floats and waving to crowds are ways that Scientologists placed their group's name or brand into the public arena with very few risks of receiving critical questions from others.

Significant dissemination of the Scientology brand or name took place through music. In 1986, 26 celebrities contributed to the taping and production of an album of songs that Hubbard wrote. Hubbard himself had inspired the record's creation:

I am composing a special album of ten Scientology songs. In doing these I discovered that it is potentially a very heavy dissemination tool. The songs actually would tell public persons what Scientology was all about. I have been trying for thirty-four years to develop a dissemination tool for the general public. If a musical dissemination tool existed, Scientologists could play it for their friends while enjoying it themselves. Thus, we have here what could be a very valuable dissemination tool. [4]

Entitled *The Road to Freedom*, among the Scientology participants on the album were actors John Travolta (b. 1954), Karen Black (1939–2013), and Lee Purcell (b. 1947); among the vocalists, award-winning Nicki Hopkins (1944–1994) on piano and Chick Corea on keyboard and percussion accompaniment. Amid great fanfare, the album's launch took place in singer-turned-politician and Scientology entrepreneur Sonny Bono's (1935–1998) Los Angeles restaurant.[5] Not long after its release, a Celebrity Centre magazine claimed that "tens of thousands of copies have been sold."[6]

Chick Corea used music as a dissemination tool in another way—at his concerts, he gave away Scientology publications to the audience. In Spanish and Portuguese performances, Corea claimed to have distributed 5,000 copies of Hubbard's *The Way to Happiness*. Separate from any concerts, several Scientologists (including businessman Bryan Zwan,[7] Nancy Cartwright, and Isaac Hayes) made substantial book donations.[8] Viewed together, these and other book distributions (including ones made by musician Isaac Hayes) must have amounted to (conservatively) hundreds of thousands of dollars in expenses to the sponsoring celebrities.

Hubbard had written about the importance of books as a dissemination tool as far back as 1959.[9] Consequently, the Public Relations Office projects to place books in libraries and other places are a direct response to one of Hubbard's many missives.[10] In order to make it easy for Scientologists to disseminate books, the LRH Personal PRO Continental Offices established library delivery services on every continent.[11]

Thus far, all of the examples involved dissemination activities that celebrities undertook without having to interact directly with potentially critical media. Another activity, however, that some celebrities performed in attempts to bring public attention to their group while avoiding press scrutiny involved acknowledging or thanking Scientology or Hubbard when receiving prestigious awards. John Travolta, for example, thanked Hubbard in 1990 when he won a People's Choice Award,[12] then again in 1996, when he received a "Golden Globe Award.[13] Especially if televised, Hollywood awards ceremonies reach millions of people, and Scientologists who offer gratitude to Hubbard or the organization do so in contexts where they have only a very short few moments in which to make remarks without any press question follow-ups (at least at that time).

What unites all of these activities is that they were attempts at attention-seeking. Scholars realize that:

> *Attention* is a key resource for social movements. Attention is the means through which a social movement can introduce and fight for its preferred framing, convince broader publics of its cause, recruit new members, attempt to neutralize opposition framing, access solidarity, and mobilize its own adherents.[14]

Despite some limitations, members of social movements typically dedicate time and effort to attention-attracting activities. In a world with so much going on, people forget—indeed they have to forget—a great deal that passes before them. Scientologists, however, do not want their group to be forgotten. They want people to remember it—and eventually join.

DESIGNING AND PRODUCING A CELEBRITY CENTRE EVENT, ACTING IN SCIENTOLOGY FILMS, ETC.

A second activity that three celebrities undertook for Scientology involved participation in another event involving awards recognition and entertainment but that the Celebrity Centre itself sponsored. In 1988, Celebrity Centre International celebrated its 19th anniversary, and Scientology celebrities oversaw the production. Paul Haggis (b. 1953), who shared two Emmys that year for his work on the television show, *Thirtysomething*,[15] directed the event; multiple–Emmy award winner for animation, Jeffrey Scott (b. 1952),[16] was the writer; and Public Relations Officer Patrick Gualtieri (1945–2015) produced the evening. The three of them had tightly scripted the busy event, from the arrival of 2,500 guests at 6:30 p.m. to the celebration's closing at 10:10 p.m. John Travolta, along with the husband-and-wife team of Chick Corea and Gayle Moran (b. 1948[?]), received Celebrity Centre International Dissemination awards. Hubbard quotes about the importance of celebrities were interspersed throughout the evening.[17] The entire affair was a dazzling display of talent, packaged by Scientology celebrities themselves to rival any other glittering event in Hollywood. Designing, then implementing the affair, was a tremendous service to Scientology.

Of lesser service, but service nonetheless, involves celebrities who perform in various training films or public relations films produced by Golden Era Studios. Well known for his role in Scientology "documercials" (i.e., documentary commercials), veteran stage and screen actor, Michael Fairman (b. 1934), performed in numerous productions, including one on *Dianetics*. Five or six of his performances were under the direction of a Scientology director, Mitchell Brisker,[18] and he "loved working at Golden Era Productions, which is the most wonderful place I've ever worked."[19] Researchers, however, simply do not know if actors such as Fairman were paid for their performances, just as we do not know for certain whether Haggis, Scott, and Gualtieri received compensation for their troubles.

SUPPORTING SCIENTOLOGY THROUGH MEDIA AND/OR PUBLIC INTERACTION

Celebrities reach out to the public about Scientology in a diverse number of ways. including presentations to elementary schools, community groups, and universities, in addition to lengthy radio and television interviews.[20] Outreach and recruitment through acting classes has been an especially fruitful endeavor, especially because many members and potential recruits are, or aspire to be, actors. Each month the Celebrity Centre International offers classes related to the profession.[21] One well-known Hollywood acting trainer, especially known for weaving Scientology techniques with acting skills, was Milton Katselas (1933–2008).

The relationship between Katselas and Scientology goes back to 1958 in New York City, when Scientologist Airic Leonardson introduced Scientology to him. At the time, however, Katselas was (to use his words) "flying high" after two Broadway successes, so he felt no need to look into it.[22] Half a decade, later, however, Katselas was having unspecified "difficulties,"[23] so he met again with Leonardson, who put him in touch with a Scientology auditor. Reflecting back upon his auditing, Katselas indicated that he "discovered a lot through Scientology," especially since the mental-image pictures that he generated in auditing reminded him of pictures that he created in painting.[24] Katselas's name appeared in Scientology documents in May 1971, when Hubbard was on his ship, the *Apollo*, and moored at Casablanca, Morocco. In Hubbard's *Orders of the Day* for May 5, 1971, he informed his crew about correspondence he was having with the successful screenwriter:

The top Broadway hit man, Milton Katselas, through Celebrity Centre sent me a screen play that deals with some Scientology materials.

I received it as he requested, [and] went over it. As an old screen writer I found some ways to polish it and telexed him that I would.

He has just telexed back very thrilled. In one week he did Grade VI, went Clear, was taken on at Columbia Pictures to direct his Broadway hit and got my assurance I'd help work on the new screen play. To quote "All in One Week. Wow."[25]

Tentatively, the film script was titled *To Be Continued*, and it had something to do with the subject of reincarnation, which likely would have interested Hubbard.[26] However, it never appears to have gone into production.

In 1972, Katselas visited the *Apollo* in order to meet with Hubbard about the script as well as to receive some auditing.[27] He spent around two weeks at Flag (as the *Apollo* was called then)

meeting and talking with [Hubbard], usually late at night until dawn on the material. So he really had the hat [i.e., the role] called writer, and I was holding the hat called director/writer. We had just a marvelous time talking about many, many things, and also spending very specific time on this project, which is one I still have to make some day. . . . Ron was extremely helpful in relation to the script, and all those notes and things we now have compiled. . . .

I saw him two or three times after that, within a period of about two years, I guess. Each time we had a wonderful rapport and a feeling with each other, with a lot of jokes, and a lot of laughs.[28]

All the while, Katselas took Scientology courses, eventually reaching OT V.

Katselas could have climbed even higher in Scientology courses, but he claimed to have gotten what he wanted and stopped. This refusal to continue on Scientology's "bridge to total freedom," along with his decisions (at least in his later life) not to go to Scientology events and parties or to run his acting school as an official World in Scientology Enterprises (WISE) business, landed him in the middle of a dispute with Honorary Public Relations Officer and Scientologist Jenna Elfman (b. 1971), who doubted his commitment.[29] (He had joined WISE in 1994[30] but apparently had let his membership and involvement lapse.) As a result of this dispute, about a hundred students left his classes.[31]

Surprisingly, at the time of her criticism (June 2004)[32] of Katselas, Elfman (known now especially for her television work in *Dharma and Greg*) was in an acting program that Katselas owned. In 1978, Katselas founded and taught at the Beverly Hills Playhouse, which in Hollywood became the most acclaimed acting school in the city. He did not teach Scientology at his workshops, not directly at least, but Scientology and Hubbard permeated the atmosphere and writings related to the instruction. According to author Janet Reitman, Katselas's acting classes were "an unofficial feeder to Celebrity

Centre, particularly during the 1990s and early 2000s, when roughly one-fifth of the school's approximately five hundred students were studying Scientology."[33] In the years leading up to his death, the executive director of his school and some former faculty members were Scientologists.[34] As with Scientology, the language that he used was peppered with Hubbard's terms—roller coasters, suppressive people, potential trouble sources, etc.[35] He made students purchase an acting manual that he wrote, and it, too, was spiced with L. Ron Hubbard quotes.[36]

Occasionally some aspiring actors like Giovanni Ribisi (b. 1974)[37] or Jenna Elfman[38] became active in Scientology and then took Katselas's acting lessons, but very commonly, actors discovered Scientology through (or at least while enrolled in) Katselas's program. (Some celebrities, such as Nancy Cartwright[39] and Priscilla Presley,[40] also were students of Katselas, but I cannot determine if their training with him occurred before or after their initial Scientology contact.) The celebrities who entered Scientology after involvement with Katselas include movie actress Anne Archer (b. 1947)[41] and her Emmy Award-winning husband, Terry Jastrow (b. 1948),[42] actor (and eventual defector) Jason Beghe (b. 1960),[43] television actor Catherine Bell (b. 1968),[44] television and film star (and eventual defector) Cathy Lee Crosby (b. 1944),[45] actress Kelly Preston (b. 1962),[46] and character actor Jeffrey Tambor (b. 1944).[47] According to Lawrence Wright, for each of his students who took Scientology courses, Katselas received a 10 percent commission.[48] The connection between the Beverly Hills Playhouse and Scientology severed with Katselas's death in 2008.[49]

Despite Katselas's use of many Scientology terms, he never became a public advocate for Scientology's social reform programs. Other Scientologists, however, did. Examples are numerous. Jeff Pomerantz (b. 1943), for example, was an LRH PRO [Public Relations Officer] and Honorary Sea Org member, and also was the National Chairman of the Celebrity Committee for the Way to Happiness Foundation.[50] In 1989, Honorary LRH Public Relations Officer Michael Fairman did an hour-long national radio interview in which he promoted Dianetics.[51] Voice-actor Nancy Cartwright was the spokesperson for Applied Scholastics, and once a month she worked with reading-challenged children.[52] Actress Anne Archer, too, was an International Spokesperson for Applied Scholastics.[53] Singer Amanda Ambrose (1925–2007) was an OT VIII Scientology celebrity and was the first president of Applied Scholastics, and she performed at the Narconon Chilocco facility in Oklahoma.[54] Kirstie Alley (b. 1951) was the International Spokesperson for Narconon and traveled to Florence, Italy, to open a Celebrity Centre.[55]

Occasionally, a serious issue occurred that Scientology officials felt warranted public protest. One such incident occurred in 1985, when a Portland,

Oregon, court ruled that Scientology had defrauded former Scientologist Julie Christofferson Titchbourne. "On May 18, 1985, after two days of deliberation, the jury awarded $39 million in damages: $20 million against Hubbard, $7.5 million against the Church of Scientology of California, and $1.5 million against the Church of Scientology Mission of Davis."[56] In response, Scientology leaders organized what came to be called "The Battle of Portland." Throughout the remaining days of May and into June, Scientologists (including John Travolta, Karen Black, Edgar Winter [b. 1946], Chick Corea, and Nicki Hopkins) marched, rallied, and protested against the decision, claiming that their religion was under attack.[57] Travolta's attendance and press conference at the protest was significant because it put to rest suspicions that he may have been drifting away from involvement with the group.[58] For reasons that had nothing to do with the protests, the judge declared a mistrial in late June 1985, and Scientology reached a confidential, out-of-court settlement with Titchbourne in 1986.[59]

Later in the 1990s, other Scientologists led rallies in Germany against what Scientology called "antireligious discrimination" reminiscent of what Jews experienced in the early days of Nazism. In 1991, for example, Dutch singer Andrik Schapers, "united 2,500 Scientologists for a Religious Crusade in Europe where they together presented a document which was officially accepted by the Legal Affairs and Human Rights Committee of the Council of Europe."[60]

As tensions grew between Germany and the United States, more Scientology-sponsored protests and marches occurred in Germany, some led by U.S. celebrities Isaac Hayes, Chick Corea, and Anne Archer.[61] Leading Scientologists in the International Association of Scientologists (IAS) took note of Archer's involvement at a Frankfurt event, and they included it among the reasons why she won a 1997 IAS Freedom Medal.[62] She and her husband, Jeff Jastrow, were IAS Lifetime Members, meaning that they had paid $5,000 (U.S.) for the privilege.[63]

A noteworthy effort on the part of a PRO took place in 1997, when BBC television Channel 4 was preparing an investigative biography on Hubbard himself. Apparently phoning from the United States, John Travolta called Channel 4's controller, "imploring him not to allow the showing of a documentary on the life of L. Ron Hubbard. . . ."[64] Channel 4 officials had no intention to pull the piece, however, so the documentary ran anyway. Several years earlier, in 1993, the IAS had given Travolta an IAS Freedom Medal Award, indicating, "[t]he press coverage John creates with his activities is unsurpassed: to date there have been more than 54,000 column inches of favorable press for LRH, Dianetics and Scientology. John even promoted the use of basic Dianetics principles during the delivery of his newly born son."[65]

Examples abound, therefore, of celebrities publicly supporting Scientology programs and issues. Only rarely in these public events do the celebrities encounter difficulties, probably because they can speak generally about the topics or groups they represent without having to go into deep and complicated analyses of them. On at least one memorable issue and on one memorable occasion, however, Scientologists encountered problems when publicly attempting to defend aspects of the organization's pseudoscience. The issue involved the medical condition of Jett Travolta (1992–2009), who had a seizure and died as a result.

CELEBRITIES DEFENDING SCIENTOLOGY'S PSEUDOMEDICINE

Scientologists have become disadvantaged regarding medical knowledge because Scientology embraces various forms of antimedical pseudoscience.[66] Put simply, when Scientologists speak about medical issues, they do not know what they are talking about. Consequently, even when Scientologists Kelly Preston and Tom Cruise, for example, tried to explain personal or family-related medical issues, their explanations simply were wrong.

While her disabled son, Jett (1992–2009), was still alive, Kelly Preston lectured on the damages possibly caused by an infant's early exposure to an array of chemicals and drugs, including antibiotics, carpet-cleaning chemicals, and yard pesticides. Jett had been exposed to some of these products, and Preston insisted that they likely caused a condition named Kawasaki syndrome that she claimed afflicted him. As a detoxicant for people, Preston endorsed the Purification Rundown on the *Montel Williams* show, and a Scientology magazine carried this account to Scientologists.[67] Nine months after Jett's tragic death, John Travolta admitted that his son had autism, which led critics to wonder "whether Jett may have gone without appropriate treatment for years because of the church's teaching."[68] Reporter Kim Masters stated what seemed like the most accurate conclusion: "[I]t does not appear that Jett received the early intervention recommended for autistic children. But perhaps he was, at some point, given medication" but then removed from it.[69] The obvious implication was that Jett's celebrity Scientology parents were blinded to the possible value of regular medical treatment, since involvement with psychologists, psychiatrists, and psychiatric medication to treat seizures and related autistic conditions were inimical to Scientology's antipsychiatric stance.

The media occasion that drew additional negative attention to Scientology's mental health positions occurred in 2005, when NBC television interviewer Matt Lauer agitated Tom Cruise over the topics of psychiatry, postpartum depressants, and behavior modification drugs prescribed to children. In the televised interview on June 24, 2005, Cruise indicated that he always had been opposed to psychiatry; opposed prescribing Ritalin and Adderall for hyperactivity in children; opposed the use of electroshock in psychiatric treatment; and opposed actor Brooke Shields's advocacy of women benefitting from antidepressants after childbirth. In a haughty tone, Cruise called Lauer "glib" and pronounced that he, not Lauer, understood the history of psychiatry. At times Cruise finger-pointed and interrupted Lauer and at least once lashed out at him verbally.[70] Not surprisingly, shortly after the interview, Cruise's publicist called Lauer, asking him not to run the interview segment in which the antidepressant debate took place. Lauer refused.[71]

Responses to the Lauer/Cruise interview were intense.[72] While Cruise's position received some support,[73] opposition to his rejection of psychiatric drug intervention for depression and childhood hyperactivity elicited a storm of protest, beginning with the actor who had written about her own positive experience with the antidepressant, Paxil, for her postpartum depression, and which Cruise had criticized. In an opinion page for the *New York Times* a week after the interview, Brooke Shields responded to what she called Cruise's "ridiculous rant." Shields wrote about feeling "completely overwhelmed" by the birth of her child, not knowing what to do with this "stranger" whom she dreaded, and could not stand hearing the infant girl cry. At moments, she even was suicidal. After, however, her doctor diagnosed that she was suffering from postpartum depression, a prescription for the antidepressant Paxil, along with weekly therapy sessions, saved her and her family.

Having recently published a book about her postpartum experiences,[74] Shields indicated that "comments like those made by Tom Cruise are a disservice to mothers everywhere. To suggest that I was wrong to take drugs to deal with my depression, and that instead I should have taken vitamins and exercised shows an utter lack of understanding about postpartum depression and childbirth in general."[75]

Mental health organizations also rose to the challenge, and quickly. On the same day that the interview aired, the American Psychiatric Association, the National Alliance for the Mentally Ill, and the National Mental Health Association issued a joint statement, which concluded with a specific criticism of the Scientology actor: "It is irresponsible for Mr. Cruise to use his movie publicity tour to promote his own ideological views and deter people with mental illness from getting the care they need."[76] In addition, the executive director of the *Journal of Clinical Investigation* wrote a devastating editorial article entitled "Tom Cruise Is Dangerous and Irresponsible."[77] Nearly 15 months (September 1, 2006) after his interview with Matt Lauer, Tom Cruise apologized to Brooke Shields for his comments about her postpartum illness, and Shields accepted.[78] (Shields and her husband even attended the Katie Holmes/Tom Cruise wedding in November of that year.)[79]

Fallout from the interview, however, still continued into 2007, when Brooke Shields presented her postpartum depression story at the American Psychiatric Association meeting. In appreciation, attendees at the session rose in a standing ovation.[80]

Cruise's comments to Matt Lauer were not the first ones to get him in trouble over making medically related claims that fly in the face of science. In 2003, Cruise claimed that L. Ron Hubbard's Study Technology[81] cured his dyslexia. Directors, however, of both the executive directors of the National Dyslexic Association[82] and the International Dyslexia Association[83] responded critically to his claim. Curiously, after years of claiming that he had dyslexia in his youth, he denied it in 1992,[84] only to bring it up again in 2009.[85]

Cruise's unauthorized biographer, Andrew Morton, offered an explanation about Cruise's alleged dyslexic cure:

> Perhaps more accurately, the actor's reading trajectory conforms to scientific research that has discovered that while dyslexia cannot be cured, it can be dealt with if caught at a sufficiently early age and a program of remedial education put into effect. This is precisely what he received at his elementary school.[86]

Morton identified that Cruise's compassionate and caring mother and his committed and observant school teachers likely contributed to his coping and learning strategies. Critically, Morton proposed that Cruise had reconceptualized his experiences so that Scientology became the sole reason for his success.[87] In short, Morton was arguing that, like many converts to groups with strong ideologies, Cruise altered his autobiography to fit his particular group's belief system.

British sociologist of celebrity, Chris Rojek, offered a broader explanation of Cruise's unappealing and excessive behavior:

> Superstardom gives many celebrities the confidence and license to behave as if their word is the universal law. This can result in an outspokenness and inflexibility about private and public issues, which many see as strident and insensitive. In some cases, media criticism produces defensive obstinacy so that the word of the celebrity comes across as belligerent, intemperate and mule-headed.[88]

In Cruise's case, "he was also more assertive, less deferential and more conscious of his status as a Scientologist and superstar."[89] While these observations may be true in a general sense about Cruise, they do not mention that, to the extent that he saw himself espousing universal law, the law was not of his own making. He was espousing the beliefs of L. Ron Hubbard and Scientology. Rojek at least mentioned Cruise's Scientology involvement, but its influence may have been far greater on him than Rojek suggested.

The most prominent, pseudoscientific Scientology program that many celebrities have supported is the organization's controversial drug treatment program, Narconon. Celebrities have done so at least since the early 1970s, and the types of support that they have provided divides into six categories. First are the *personal testimonies* or *testimonials*[90]—celebrities' statements endorsing Narconon because they took the program and they believe that it got them off of drugs. Three celebrities exemplify this category: television and movie stars Kirstie Alley, Juliette Lewis (b. 1973), and Nicki Hopkins. Alley's account about her involvement appeared in her December 1997 cover story in *Biography* magazine, although some dispute exists about whether she actually spent time in a Narconon program.[91] Born in and having grown up in Kansas, Alley spoke about dropping out of college, having a string of boyfriends, becoming an interior decorator, and developing a cocaine habit. Her desire to become involved with Scientology required her to become "drug free," which she claimed to have accomplished through L. Ron Hubbard's technology. So impressed with it (and guilty over the persons she initiated into drug use), she eventually became the spokesperson for Narconon.[92] Her visit to the Newkirk, Oklahoma, Narconon facility in November 1990 received media attention, almost certainly because of her celebrity status.[93]

During the early years of her career, Alley was a prominent and popular female actor on television and in the movies, appearing as a Vulcan in *Star Trek II: The Wrath of Khan*, and then later as the female bar owner in the popular sitcom, *Cheers*, for which she won an Emmy. These achievements and talk show appearances helped make her a likeable, household name (a likeability that diminished later as she displayed temper tantrums and poor judgment regarding her weight gain),[94] and she had overcome personal hardship.

In many instances, members of the public engage in "para-social relationships" with media personalities, which in practice are "unilateral relationships . . . that affect us in ways that resemble any other relationships with a person." Viewers "'know' such a [celebrity] persona in somewhat the same way they know their chosen friends; through direct observation and interpretation of his [or her] appearance, his [or her] gestures and voice, [and] his [or her] conversation and conduct in a variety of situations."[95] It is plausible, therefore, that Alley was able to "sway" some people with addiction issues to enroll in Narconon or at least convince their parents to send them to one. For many media consumers, following Alley's advice would have seemed to them like taking guidance from a friend. Other celebrities of somewhat lesser public status (such as Juliette Lewis[96] and Nicki Hopkins[97]) have advocated for Narconon, and their messages may have reached audiences outside of the organization.

A second way that some Scientology celebrities have contributed to Narconon is through *public discussions* of the program. This level of involvement is different from telling one's story to a magazine or newspaper reporter to the extent that discussions (such as talk show appearances) may be live, can extend for a half hour or more, and likely will involve direct and possibly pointed questions about Narconon and its techniques. In early 1990, for example, Alley and a Scientology toxicologist/author, Michael Wisner, both appeared on the *Phil Donahue Show*, "talking about the effects of toxins in our environment and the solution for such effects: the Purification Rundown,"[98] which is one of the courses on the Narconon program. (Celebrity Scientologists simply may do the Purification Rundown because they have covered the other aspects of Narconon within their usual Scientology courses.) Alley lacked the expertise to appear alone on a program about toxins, so Wisner probably handled the more scientific questions, although (whenever possible) with answers within Scientology's ideology.

A third way that Scientology celebrities support Narconon is through what I call *status endorsements*.[99] They may never have gone through Narconon, but they endorse it anyway, hoping that the influence of their status will propel some people to sign up. For example, the program received a significant endorsement from the football player-turned-Scientologist, John Brodie, who played quarterback with the San Francisco 49ers for 17 consecutive seasons, beginning in 1957 and retiring in 1973. He was the National Football League's Most Valuable Player in 1970.[100] In the late 1960s, Brodie was facing a quarterback's nightmare—he was having trouble with his throwing arm. After medications failed to correct it, Scientology auditing (he believed) restored his football-passing ability.[101]

Brodie's perceived experience of healing through what he called "spiritual consultation" sufficiently moved him that he decided to retire from football after the 1973 session and devote himself to Scientology and Narconon.[102] Prior to retiring, however, Brodie organized an exhibition football game for San Francisco youth charity fund, and in January 1974 San Francisco mayor Joseph Alioto gave Brodie a $1,000 check for Narconon from that fund, which had come from that exhibition game.[103] Brodie remained with Scientology until around 1982, when he left over the way in which "some Scientology henchmen were overly aggressive with some of his friends"[104] who "were harassed or expelled following a power struggle with the organization's leadership."[105]

A fourth way that some Scientology celebrities support Narconon is through *individual donations*. For example, the Austrian artist, Gottfried Helnwien (b. 1948), donated "a great deal of art," over $150,000 worth, to the Chilocco New Life Center in Oklahoma.[106] Arguably, Tom Cruise's fundraising efforts for a Long Island Narconon facility for 9/11 first responders also fit this pattern, to the extent that he helped raise $1.2 million for it.[107]

Collective donations are a fifth way that some Scientology celebrities, often along with select friends and contacts, engage in charitable acts on behalf of Narconon. The charity football game that John Brodie organized in 1973 is one example of such an action, but there are others. John Travolta, for example, turned his 1999 launch of a movie into a Narconon fundraiser.[108] Beyond individual endorsements, Scientology has organized celebrity support for Narconon for at least 35 years, beginning after "a Celebrity Campaign against PCP and other harmful drugs" in August 1979 evolved into the Friends of Narconon.[109] Friends of Narconon still has a presence on the Internet at the end of 2016 (as Friends of Narconon International), with its president (Robert Hernandez) offering antidrug briefings and Narconon-related antidrug information.[110]

Another long-standing celebrity fundraising group for Narconon calls itself the "Drug Free Heroes." In the mid-1980s, "[t]hrough guest appearances, media interviews, lectures, charity softball games, and other events, the drug-free heroes represent the Narconon drug education and prevention program and promote getting high on goals, not drugs."[111] In 1990 (and probably at other times), Narconon International also sponsored a charity softball game for Narconon.[112] A group calling itself the Narconon All-Stars still participates in sporting events and other promotional activities,[113] and the drug Free Heroes group has an annual awards gala.[114]

In late 1980 or early 1981, then Scientologist Cathy Lee Crosby teamed up with a friend, Robert Evans, who was the former head of Paramount Pictures, to begin a program entitled, "Get High on Yourself." She convinced numerous celebrities, only a few of whom were Scientologists, to sing the jingle associated with the campaign. Scientology was not directly involved with the program, but the organization surreptitiously provided each celebrity with a Scientology assistant. The campaign's goal, after all, "was a public relations cornerstone of Narconon."[115]

Unexpectedly, however, in 1981, some of the stars whose names appeared on a list of 170 or more Friends of Narconon that Crosby had given a congressional committee, and some who participated in charity sports events, objected to having their names endorsing the Scientology antidrug program. Celebrities including Henry Winkler, Hal Linden, Phyllis Diller, Rob Reiner, and Lou Ferrigno wanted their names removed from Friends of Narconon lists, with most of them expressing displeasure at having their names used in endorsements for a Scientology program.[116] Subsequently, Hubbard revised and printed an existing policy that prohibited using celebrities' names without their permission: "No org or Scientologist is to use the name of a celebrity as being a Scientologist or to use such a name to promote or disseminate without the express written permission of said celebrity."[117]

Hubbard apparently realized that using celebrities' names in unauthorized manners could cause grave difficulties for any Scientology activity, but he also felt the need to have his own name mentioned in relation to the Narconon program. On November 24, 1980, Hubbard typed a note to an unspecified person or persons, indicating that he had received some Narconon publicity about a charity game, but felt that his name also should appear in it:

> Some Narconon publicity—it had to do with a charity game—came my way.
>
> I noticed that my name was not mentioned in it.
>
> It is understandable that NN [i.e., Narconon] would not use the name Scn [i.e., Scientology]. That would connect it with the church and church and state must be kept separate.
>
> However, in order to make a bridge back over into Scn, it would seem necessary to use my name in NN publicity.
>
> In times of attack it is especially necessary to keep the name up in lights.
>
> With the Purif RD [i.e., Purification Rundown] and other onslaughts into the drug arena, some effort should be made to connect my name with it.[118]

Citing his recent publication of a nonreligious "book of morals" and a science fiction novel, Hubbard indicated that he was "pushing in the direction of the non-Church sector" and wanted his name in that sector exposed to the public.[119]

LOBBYING SCIENTOLOGY'S INTERESTS WITH BUSINESSES AND GOVERNMENTS

The most difficult and riskiest of Scientology's deployments of celebrities involves sending them before business or governmental investigative committees that are examining issues relevant to Scientology's ideology or existence. Larger bodies (such as federal governments) may have assigned these committees with providing information and recommendations needed to create or amend policies or laws, so any failures on Scientology's part to represent its positions favorably may have dire consequences.

As both the complexities increase regarding the issues that the celebrity spokespersons have to address, and as the expertise increases of examining committee members, the likelihood also increases of celebrity testimonies failing. Celebrities may be skilled at reading prepared statements and (after Public Relations Office training) explaining Scientology itself, but they usually lack specific training (in areas such as international politics or medicine) about which committee members likely will ask probing questions. A differing possibility that also might be true, however, is that statements presented by celebrities may escape close scrutiny simply because committee members are dazzled by the mere presence of stars, and they do not want to appear rude or challenging by probing into their statements. It is exceedingly difficult to know precisely what effect celebrities' statements have on committees, but they seem to have significant impact as morale boosters to Scientology members, who read about these presentations in either Scientology publications or the popular press.

Scientology's celebrity lobbying likely takes place on four levels: local, regional (including state or province), national, and international. Scientologists other than celebrities likely do much of this lobbying, as would be the case with people acting on behalf of front groups such as the Citizens Commission on Human Rights. Most of the available material, however, highlights lobbying efforts by celebrities on the national level of the U.S. government, although occasionally we get glimpses of their involvement in local or regional presentations and campaigns.

Federally, Scientology's lobbying efforts have been extensive, with celebrities gaining access to numerous committee hearings, meetings with influential politicians, and access to people in the White House. Facilitating these contacts has been a succession of public relations firms, hired to represent Scientology's interests and facilitate high-level governmental meetings. Conversely, much community lobbying took place that did not involve celebrities. As these community activities continued throughout the 1990s, Scientology took a step on the local level that it already had done on a federal level—it hired high-profile lawyer, Ed Armstrong, and his firm (Johnson, Blakely, Pope Bokor Ruppel & Burns) to represent its interests. One of Armstrong's successful events was the gala, 75th anniversary of the Fort Harrison Hotel, an event attended by judges, civic leaders, and politicians. Then in 2003, Scientology hired former political consultant, Mary Repper, as an additional, well-connected local figure to aid Scientology with its image issues. Repper then "used Scientology's celebrities to form bonds. She hosted dinner parties with Tom Cruise and an array of elected officials including Tampa Mayor Pam Iorio. And she arranged for John Travolta to visit Tampa's Italian Club."[120]

Scientology's increasingly normalized status with Floridians may have been a factor in the decision to have Kirstie Alley and Kelly Preston testify before the state's House Education Council in April 2005. (Both Alley and Preston—the latter though her husband, John Travolta—owned houses in the state.)[121] They testified about the alleged dangers of psychiatric treatment and prescription drugs for children, with Alley's testimony barely intelligible because she cried heavily as she spoke. Even before they testified, however, the council had stripped the bill of a section that the Scientologists would have endorsed heartily, "that before a school could refer a child for mental health treatment, it would have to tell parents there are no medical tests to diagnose mental illness. It also would have required schools to tell parents a mental disorder diagnosis will go on a student's permanent record." The council chairman, Dennis Baxley, had a son who was a psychiatrist, and he objected to the manner in which the Scientologists' discredited the profession by ignoring the "wonderful things" that psychiatrists also do for people.[122] On the same day, the two celebrities also testified about a similar bill before the Senate Education Committee.[123] A version of the House bill passed, only to have Governor Jeb Bush veto it.[124]

Bills to restrict the mental health access of children also had surfaced around this period in Utah, New Hampshire, and Arizona—almost certainly the work of the Citizens Commission on Human Rights (CCHR).[125] In Arizona, CCHR drafted much of a legislative bill designed to increase regulation of drug trials involving tranquilizers and other mind-altering drugs; in fact, the group was behind some two dozen bills regarding drug regulation, often in relation to children.[126] Legislative member and medical doctor, Robert Cannell (D-Yuma), was frustrated that a group that had "spokesmen that are movie actors not scientists" [127] was so influential, even to the point of Scientology spending thousands of dollars on Hollywood trips for his colleagues, where they had "attended celebrity-studded award ceremonies, an anniversary gala at the Celebrity Centre church and the grand opening of [CCHR's] museum, *Psychiatry: An Industry of Death.* Legislators met John Travolta and other high-profile guests and learned more about the church's campaigns and programs."[128] Whatever stigma the Scientology organization may have had in previous periods, many Arizona legislators overcame any feelings of contamination by traveling, dining, and celebrating with some of the group's celebrity elites.

The aurora of celebrity, however, did not always dazzle state legislators—in May 2011, Nancy Cartwright appeared before the Illinois House Elementary and Secondary Education Committee in support of a bill endorsing a children's program based upon Scientology that was under consideration for use in the schools. At least a few legislators, however, were concerned about church/state boundary issues, and the author of the particular bill agreed to rewrite it so as to eliminate any references to the Scientology program.[129] Clearly, Scientology celebrity status did not always open doors to receptive state legislators.

On the U.S. federal level, Scientology's access to the corridors of power has been uneven but at times impressive. A relatively early congressional presentation took place in late September 1980, when Scientology celebrity Cathy Lee Crosby (b. 1944) testified before the U.S. House of Representatives Select Committee on Narcotic Abuse Control about what to do concerning the problem of drugs among youth.[130] As a Narconon spokesperson, she used her presentation to plug Narconon and the Purification Rundown. Scientology's promotional newspaper to members, *The Auditor*, reported on her testimony.[131]

In 1996 and 1997, Scientology's Religious Technology Center paid almost $725,000 to a District of Columbia lobbying firm, Federal Legislative Associates, and its managing partner, David H. Miller, to represent the organization's interests on Capitol Hill.[132] Miller admitted that Scientology's star power aided his lobbying efforts because "members such as actors [Anne] Archer and [John] Travolta and musicians [Chick] Corea and Isaac Hayes are willing to speak up for their beliefs."[133] The fact that Miller mentioned these Scientology celebrities by name adds weight to the likelihood that he was involved in arranging for Honorary Public Relations Officers Travolta, Corea, and Hayes to appear before the Commission on Security and Cooperation in Europe (CSCE) on September 18, 1997. The CSCE was a governmental body that "monitors compliance with the Helsinki Accords and advances comprehensive security through promotion of human rights, democracy, and economic, environmental and military cooperation in the OSCE region."[134] On this date, the commission heard three presentations about how U.S. Scientologists believed that the Germans were discriminating against their organization.[135] Corea's presentation likely had particular significance, since the Baden-Württemberg government in 1993 had refused to invite him to play in a state-sponsored concert, fearing that he would use the opportunity to proselytize.[136]

The three celebrities were successful in conveying Scientology's description of the alleged discrimination, but they unable to explain why Germany had taken an anti-Scientology stance. For example, when a member of the commission asked Corea why Germany was exhibiting such animosity toward Scientology, all he could utter for as answer was, "We're dealing within incredible, weird, wild emotions."[137] In order to have offered an insightful explanation, Corea or the other celebrities would have had to repeat to the committee critical and potentially negative issues about Scientology itself (at least as the Germans saw it). The negative issues about Scientology that German officials held were no secret at the time of the CSCE hearing, and many of the issues received mention in the large study of *New Religious and Ideological Communities and Psychogroups in the Federal Republic of Germany*,[138] published in the year after the CSCE hearing.[139]

Celebrity Scientologists' public relations training only had prepared Travolta, Hayes, and Corea to say positive things (what Scientologists call *theta*) about L. Ron Hubbard and Scientology. Saying negative things (*entheta*) about the group, even in the context of summarizing an opponent's position, would have placed the person giving testimony perilously close to committing a "suppressive act"—something that Scientology policy identified as harming the group and therefore was punishable by the organization itself. As far back as 1965, Hubbard included among a list of suppressive acts, "testifying hostilely before state or public inquiries into Scientology to suppress it."[140] Consequently, if Scientology witnesses testifying before the CSCE or any other official body were to have engaged in an open dialogue about any Scientology-related issue, then they likely would have faced punishment within their own organization.

The years 1997 and 1998 saw Scientologists gain access to Washington's corridors of power, and we do not know (likely aside from the CSCE presentation) what role if any a Scientology lobbyist played in making arrangements. The background for the access began in April 1997 during Philadelphia's hosting of a conference on volunteerism, attended both by John Travolta and President Bill Clinton. The two met after Travolta had made a presentation about Hubbard-inspired educational materials. The president praised him for his contribution, then indicated that he would love to help him with Scientology's troubles in Germany.[141] Following up on his statement, Clinton appointed his national security advisor, Sandy Berger, with the assignment of monitoring the Germany/Scientology situation.[142] Then when Travolta and Corea were in Washington in September 1997 (presumably for their CSCE presentations), a White House staff member arranged a meeting between the two Scientologists and Berger—something akin to what a senator would receive.[143] Taken together, the meetings between sympathetic U.S. government officials and propagandizing Scientologists probably contributed to the U.S. State Department's criticisms of Germany's religious freedom record, beginning in its 1993 *Human Rights Report on Germany* and continuing in subsequent reports and similar federally sponsored religious freedom reports, White House daily press briefings, and so on, through 2009.[144] The Germans, however, did not change their positions toward Scientology because of the U.S. criticisms; if anything, these criticisms diminished the stature of U.S. politicians in informed German politicians' eyes.[145]

Additional celebrity lobbying has gone on over the years, such as Isaac Hayes's 1993 meeting "with the Black Congressional Caucus about the application of LRH study technology and appeared on national television to give his personal story of how Scientology has expanded his career."[146] Two years later he won the IAS's Freedom Medal and "spoke to two thousand attendees in Cincinnati at the National Conference of Representatives of HUD (Housing and Urban Development) about the World Literacy Crusade and L. Ron Hubbard's study technology."[147] Anne Archer also lobbied for a Scientology educational program, Applied Scholastics, on Capitol Hill in August 1993.[148] A decade later, in 2003, Juliette Lewis went to Capitol Hill, lobbying for a Scientology-endorsed project "to stop educational authorities from requiring 'problem' schoolchildren to take mood-altering medication."[149] I do not have any specifics about these meetings and lobbying efforts, including who arranged them and what impact they may have had. Scientologist Greg Mitchell was Scientology's Washington lobbyist from 2003 at least into 2015 (costing the organization over $1 million during that period),[150] but his only use of a celebrity that I know of was in 2006. On December 11 of that year, Mitchell, along with Scientologist and actor Jenna Elfman, threw a party "at the restored townhouse near Dupont Circle where Hubbard got his start and held the first Scientology wedding."[151] Alas, I have no information about who dropped by that evening.

As late as 2003 (during the George W. Bush administration), Scientologists were still welcomed in meetings with White House officials. On June 13 of that year, Tom Cruise had a private engagement with Deputy Secretary of State Richard Armitage. Scientologist Tom Davis, head of the Hollywood Celebrity Centre, and Kurt Weiland, an Austrian Scientologist who was director of external affairs for the organization's Office of Special Affairs, also were present. Armitage listened to their concerns "about the treatment of Scientologists in some foreign countries, particularly Germany."[152] Cruise reminded Armitage that he already had discussed issues of religious intolerance with the U.S. ambassadors in Germany, France, and Spain. The day after this meeting Cruise met another official—Vice President Dick Chaney's chief of staff, Scooter Libby.[153] Celebrity Scientologists, therefore, were not limited to federal government access merely during the Clinton administration.

CELEBRITIES' FINANCIAL DONATIONS TO SCIENTOLOGY

A number of Scientology celebrities are very rich, and the organization does its best to ensure that some of that wealth ends up in its coffers. A website dedicated to revealing celebrities' financial worth places Jenna Elfman at $16 million,[154] Kirstie Alley at $30 million,[155] Nancy Cartwright at $60 million (and receiving $300,000 per episode of *The Simpsons,* on which she provides the voice for the character, Bart),[156] John Travolta at $170 million,[157] and Tom Cruise at $470 million.[158] Even factoring the lavish lifestyles that many celebrity stars live, they still can have significant discretionary funds that they can disperse as they please. For Scientology celebrities, some of their discretionary funds are likely to go to the organization and its projects.

One set of figures involving Scientology celebrity donations appeared in the United Kingdom's *Guardian* newspaper in early 2008. Reporter David McNamee stated that Kirstie Alley donated $5 million to the Church of Scientology, which was the same amount that Tom Cruise had donated over a five-year period. John Travolta had given $1 million, and Priscilla Presley (with an estimated net worth of $100 million) donated $50,000.[159] Travolta's million-dollar donation was to the IAS and had taken place in the summer of 2007. Before the year was out, the IAS received an additional $1.5 million from him.[160] Also in 2007, Nancy Cartwright donated $10 million.[161] Evidence from a 2005 IAS magazine indicates that up until that time, Tom Cruise had donated $2.5 million to the IAS, and Leah Remini had donated at least $1 million.[162]

Remini confirmed this million-dollar figure after she left the group, adding that she had "donated millions of dollars to my church to help set an example."[163] She recalled that Scientology's quest for money was "relentless," and every time she left the Celebrity Centre, a fundraiser from the IAS was waiting for her, asking for more donations.[164] After Paul Haggis also left the organization, he, too, provided insight into the amount of his Scientology contributions. He spent an estimated $100,000 on various Scientology initiatives (not including courses), $250,000 to the IAS, and $10,000 (divided with his wife) toward a new building in Nashville. As journalist/writer Lawrence Wright surmised, "[t]he demands for money—'regging' it's called in Scientology, because the calls come from the Registrar's Office—never stopped. Paul gave them money just to keep them from calling."[165] It appears that both Haggis and Remini had similar experiences with Scientology fundraisers.

Hubbard's statements in the 1950s about the importance of celebrities mentioned their value in relation to their media contacts; he may not have realized that they also would have enormous discretionary funds at their disposal. Media contacts and enormous discretionary funds have proven to be two significant reasons that Scientologists have treated celebrity constituent adherents (i.e., persons who believe and provide resources) specially. After Hubbard's death in 1986, the organization continued paying special attention to celebrities, as indicated by former member Amy Scobee's reflections about improvements she made to the Celebrity Centre after October 1991. Among other achievements, she upgraded the appearance and training of both the Celebrity Centre and the Manor Hotel staff; she hired professionals in the restaurant business who got the restaurant upgraded to four stars; and she restored the career counseling service within Celebrity Centre International.[166] With some pride, Scobee indicated that, under her guidance, Celebrity Centre International "had become a place where celebrities could be serviced and bring in their friends to introduce them to Scientology."[167] While overseeing these upgrades, Scobee also learned the extent to which Scientology catered to Tom Cruise.

Cruise was not the first celebrity to receive Scientology's special attention. As far back as early July, 1978, Hubbard rewarded John Travolta for his "major contributions in the dissemination of Dianetics and Scientology" by giving him a $1,500 service award for his newest Scientology course.[168] Over the ensuing years he also has proven to be a major financial contributor.[169]

Scientology's involvement with Cruise goes far beyond an offer of a financial break for additional courses. Scobee indicated that "David Miscavige had several of us catering to Tom, behind the scenes."[170] Scientology staff performed numerous unspecified services for his household; Scientologists installed the audiovisual system in his private theatre; and a Scientologist handled his investments. [171] Likewise, when Cruise visited the Scientology facility in Hemet, California, his good friend (and head of Scientology), David Miscavige, "was seeing to Cruise's every need, assigning a special staff to prepare his meals, do his laundry and handle a variety of other tasks, some of which required around-the-clock work."[172] This level of attention to Cruise's needs was the norm: for his late December 1990 marriage to Nicole Kidman (b. 1967), Miscavige "arranged for two Scientology chefs and other Sea Org disciples to cater and care for the newlyweds and their guests."[173]

CELEBRITIES USED AS MOTIVATORS TO OTHER CELEBRITIES CONCERNING ADDITIONAL COURSES-ENROLLMENT

Successful Scientology celebrities can be quite rich, but far more are at various stages of having careers and degrees of wealth. Some people who define themselves as actors or entertainers are attempting to break into the industry, while others have had a few small opportunities but are waiting for a big break. What Scientology has done in this irregular market is portray itself as a means to success, with its courses and auditing removing personal blocks and providing insights and skills that dramatically improve aspiring entertainers' abilities to audition and then perform.

However much the Celebrity Centre aspires to assist its attendees, it operates within the wider Scientology organization that has as a financial goal, "MAKE MONEY, MAKE MORE MONEY, MAKE OTHER PEOPLE

PRODUCE SO AS TO MAKE MONEY."[174] Consequently, it uses its magazine, *Celebrity*, as an attempt to make people who have "produced" (i.e., have succeeded in the entertainment industry) serve as inspiration to the newer celebrity aspirants. Almost every issue contains a multipage interview about a celebrity who also usually is on the cover. The article mentions some of the professional successes that the celebrity artist has had and also lists the Scientology courses that he or she has taken or is enrolled in.

For example, Jenna Elfman is on the cover of *Celebrity* Major Issue 298 in 1996. The lead-in to the interview listed her professional accomplishments in commercials and television shows and then began with the question, "How did you get into Scientology?" Very quickly Elfman entered into an extended description about the personal benefits (involving clarity of mind and perception) that she claimed she experienced after the Purification Rundown. She mentioned her coursework on a course for Clears called the New Hubbard Solo Auditor Course Part One, and then described her attainment of Clear as "*Incredible!* I have certainty." She concluded her interview by saying, "The reactive mind can be gotten rid of with Dianetics and Scientology and then you won't have to worry about pushing it away, ever again. The effort comes off and you can just move forward as yourself![175]

No figures exist about how much money celebrities spend on Scientology courses, and no indications exist if people are inspired to take courses by articles in *Celebrity*. Former member Paul Haggis estimated that he had spent $100,000 on courses and auditing,[176] but we do not know how variable this figure would be for others. Suffice it to say, however, that aspiring celebrities experience constant pressure to "move up the Bridge," and the *Celebrity* interviews are designed to facilitate the process.

CONCLUSION

This chapter identifies the numerous ways that, in the immediate past, Scientology celebrities have engaged in a variety of activities that have capitalized upon their celebrity status. Consequently, they have been able to present Scientology either informally or formally in a variety of public venues. Scientology's use of celebrity continues in the present day and likely will remain critical in the future as the movement tries to remain attractive to new converts and influential in political and other institutions. The media influence of some celebrities only was local; others had media impact on a regional level. Increasing the range of their exposure, an additional level of celebrities have exposure and media influence on a national level, while a smaller number of elite celebrities had international influence according to the global media attention that they received and/or commanded. In the

1990s, U.S. government committees that dealt with international issues had hearings about various European countries' critical responses to some U.S.-based sects. Elite celebrity Scientologists had at least some influence in this regard. Discussion in Germany about possible boycotts of movies and concerts featuring Scientology members gave Scientologists particular interest in the government's hearings. Scientology celebrities, therefore, claimed "*standing*, that is, *recognizable* legitimate interest in the outcome of a political question or movement."[177]

Scientology celebrity elites also had some political sway in other areas. U.S. congressman from California's 44th District, the late Sonny Bono, was one such figure of influence. Bono was a member of the Judiciary Committee, and he "became instrumental in convincing the Clinton administration's Office of the United States Trade Representative to lobby Sweden to stop allowing public access to Scientology's scriptures."[178] He supported a Scientology lawsuit which demanded that Netcom On-Line Communications Series take down Scientology's scriptures,[179] and after his death, Congress passed a bill that revised copyright law and named it in his honor because of his work on the issue.[180] No evidence exists, however, about Bono attempting to arrange political meetings with Scientology lobbyists. Other facilitators, like lobbyists, were more likely to have done so.

Some of Scientology's access to the government probably did not depend on the actions of lobbyists. Researchers know nothing about any level of planning that went into positioning John Travolta at the April 1997 President's Summit for America's Future on volunteerism,[181] but the meeting of the president and the actor certainly reflected the confluence of "all of the contacts, acquaintances and constituents"[182] that the two of them had. Scientology's extensive contacts with the Clinton administration occurred after that Clinton/Travolta meeting, and the complexity of arranging for Scientologists to meet White House officials and testify before the Commission on Security and Cooperation in Europe are the kinds of activities that Scientology's paid lobbyist was likely to do. This was a high-profile relationship between Scientology and government, and it is illustrative of the reach that elite celebrity influence can have.

Social movement theorists realize that "politicians are not immune from the lure of celebrity contact."[183] As a consequence of the nature of their professions, celebrities tend not to be embedded with institutional policymakers, but they

> have high "status honor" because of the "style of life" that many of them lead, the cultural impact that they have, and the social "distance and exclusiveness" that they keep. . . . Frequently because of these attributes,

celebrities gain entry into political settings as politicians defer to their status, enhance their own images by associating with cultural icons, and often benefit from their campaign-contribution generosity.[184]

The relationship between celebrities and politicians often is reciprocal. Thus, the celebrity-lobbyist is not the only party in the equation to benefit from the association. Politicians sometimes defer to celebrities' status because they possess a level of charismatic authority to which they themselves aspire, and they feel a kind of "charisma through association" by being near them.[185] The extensive photograph-snapping and autograph seeking that occurred among the politicians and their staff bears out this interpretation.[186]

At bottom, Scientology celebrities' meetings with, and presentations to, government officials were attempts to turn the status of celebrity into political power, thus removing the likelihood of European (especially German) boycotts of films starring Scientologists. Potentially tens of millions of dollars may have been at stake if even the German boycott attempts had been successful. Moreover, Scientologists' contributions to campaigns indicated the tangible economic advantage of aligning with Scientology. Three months before New York Republican Congressman Benjamin Gilman (1922–2016) cosponsored an ultimately unsuccessful bill in 1999 that was critical of Germany's protection of religious freedom, his campaign coffer received 10 donations from Scientologists totaling $7,400, all on the same day (July 2, 1998).[187]

The big question remains, therefore, whether Scientology's celebrity lobbying efforts to Congress were successful. The answer varies, depending up what one uses as a measure. Ultimately, U.S. pressure on Germany to relax its opposition against Scientology had no effect other than to rile up the Germans about U.S. interference in domestic German affairs. Moreover, congressional members who developed their understanding of Germany's anti-Scientology actions never received a clear or accurate rendition of the reasons, because Scientologists are prohibited from stating negative things about the organization. Simply examining the impact, however, that Scientology's lobbying efforts had in formulating the U.S. government's criticisms of Germany's Scientology stance, the lobbying efforts were a resounding success.

This conclusion is based upon a speech made by Congressman Gilman shortly before he retired but after he had stepped down from chairing the International Relations Committee. In 2002, he was an honored guest at a Celebrity Centre Gala. To an audience of some 1,200 Scientologists, Gilman

explained how human rights violations are not always obvious and well known, and in fact a much more subtle oppression exists for hundreds of minority religions in countries that are otherwise known for their strong democratic values—such as Germany, France and Spain. On behalf of all religions, Scientologists took it upon themselves to educate members of Congress on the more subtle but real violations of human rights that take place.

Gilman went on to thank Scientologists for addressing these violations and for "visiting Capital [sic] Hill, the State Department and the White House to fight for human rights, in addition to attending human rights conferences and staging demonstrations and human rights marches and marathons."[188] From Gilman's comments, it appears that many congressional members and senators received their educations about alleged French and German human rights violations against Scientology and other controversial groups from the Scientology lobbying effort.

If indeed Scientology's federal lobbying efforts were successful (on the measure of governmental impact), why then have Scientology's medically related comments about Narconon and pharmaceuticals been received so poorly, even though a few of their concerns proved to have some merit? The answer lies in what passes for expertise within the political field versus the medical field, along with understanding how one gained entry into each one. People entered politics through elections, which means that new people entered the profession after every election cycle. Citizens voted them into office. Professional boundaries, therefore, were fluid. Aspects of Scientologists' training, moreover, involved the belief that it was a persecuted religion, which was exactly in line with the issues of religious freedom that several U.S. governmental committees and personnel were examining. Medical boundaries, in contrast, were rigid, and one gained entry into the profession only after years of education in certified institutions, followed by apprenticeships and formal examinations. After decades of struggle, the medical profession gained "absolute control of bodily ills,"[189] which eventually expanded to include mental ills.[190] Persons, therefore, who passed through the various professional tests were protective about their field of expertise and react loudly when someone lacking professional credentials makes factually incorrect public comments. In this case, aspects of Scientology's training involved nonscientific claims about the causes and cures of numerous illnesses and conditions, and these nonscientific claims clashed with the established medical community considered to be acceptable science. If this brief set of observations is correct, then it seems unlikely that Scientology or its spokespersons ever will receive scientific acceptance.

It may take future defections from highly placed Scientologists or celebrities before we can answer questions about how particular celebrities become assigned to what causes; whether the organization, through the Celebrity

Centre, pays any celebrities for doing commercial work for it; and how lobbying activities became coordinated on Capitol Hill. We also do not know how many Scientology celebrities there are at any given time and what the numbers of recruits versus defectors there are. Importantly, we do not have a good idea about the finances associated with the Celebrity Centre's operation, especially in relation to the larger organization. The answers to these and other questions are important, since the extensiveness of Scientology's use of celebrities remains unrivaled in the modern world.

NOTES

1. Church of Scientology Celebrity Centre International, "Livewire; Celebrity Scientologists in Action: Hollywood Christmas Parade," *Celebrity* 354 (2004): 15; see also Church of Scientology Celebrity Centre International, "Livewire; Celebrity Scientologists in Action: Lynsey Bartilson," *Celebrity* 344 (2003): 16. For Scientology musicians Chick Corea (b. 1941) and Stanley Clarke (b. 1951, who eventually left the group) riding in a Santa Claus Lane parade in 1997, see Church of Scientology Celebrity Centre International, "Celebrity Livewire," *Celebrity* Minor Issue 28 (1977): 16.

2. CSI, "Honorary PROs in Action: Honorary PROs are Cheering Up the World! Jenna Elfman, Marisol Nichols and Lynsey Bartilson Promote *The Joy of Creating*," *Good News*, 2001, 4.

3. For an example of a Formula One race car driver placing a *Dianetics* logo on the side of his car, see Church of Scientology Celebrity Centre International, "Celebrity Livewire," *Celebrity* 229 (1989): 13. For examples of Scientology groups involved in beach clean-up projects, see Church of Scientology Celebrity Centre International, "Celebrity Centre News and Events: Celebrity Centre's Adopted Beach Gets Spring Cleaned," *Celebrity* 313 (1998): 8; and Church of Scientology Celebrity Centre International, "Celebrity Centre News and Events: CC International Surf Club Awarded 'Adopt a Beach Volunteers of the Year,'" *Celebrity* 330 (2001): 9.

4. L. Ron Hubbard, quoted in Rose Goss, "The Joy of Creating *The Road to Total Freedom*," *Celebrity* Church of Scientology Celebrity Centre International Special Edition (1986): 7.

5. Ibid., 9. For insights into Bono's involvement with Scientology, see various comments in Ann Louise Bardach, "Proud Mary," *George*, August 1999, 76ff.

6. Church of Scientology Celebrity Centre International, "Celebrity Centre Network News," *Celebrity* Special Edition (1986): 21.

7. Physicist Bryan Zwan holds a doctorate in physics, and in the late 1990s he went public with a company that developed a fiber-optic diagnostic device. Calling the company Digital Lightwave, Zwan was its CEO until he resigned in 1997 amid allegations of fraud and mismanagement. He sold company stocks, however, at the right time, acquiring a net worth of an estimated $600 million and placing him among one of the 400 richest Americans in 2001. Part of alleged mismanagement involved

massive amounts of donations to Scientology, along with running the organization according to Hubbard's business model. He returned as CEO and saw the stock value of shares skyrocket, then crash, leading to the demise of the company. Deborah O'Neil and Jeff Harrington, "The CEO and His Church," *St. Petersburg Times*, June 2, 2002, http://www.sptimes.com/2002/06/02/news_pf/TampaBay/The_CEO_and_his_churc .shtml. By 2010 he was back in the business of speculative financing, having created and was managing Forge, which financed a Merrill Lynch-created collateralized debt obligation company called Forge 1. Companies like Forge 1 were involved with buying, and then repacking and selling (as speculative investments), these and related risky ventures. Their financial recklessness contributed to the housing collapse in the mid- to late 2000s. Robert Trigaux, "Deeper Look at How Wall Street's Self-Dealing Led to Housing Bubble Cites Role of Clearwater Financier," *Tampa Bay Times*, August 30, 2010, http://www.tampabay.com/blogs/venturebiz/content/deeper-look-how-wall -streets-self-dealing-led-housing-bubble-cites-role-clearwater-financier.

8. Church of Scientology Celebrity Centre International, "Celebrity Centre News," *Celebrity* 275 (1994): 7, 11. Cartwright (b. 1957) is the voice behind *The Simpsons'* television cartoon character, Bart, and actor and musician Hayes (1942– 2008) was an Honorary PRO (Public Relations Officer). CSI, "Honorary PROs on the Move," *Hotline* 3, no. 7 (1998): 6.

9. L. Ron Hubbard, "Dissemination Tips," *Hubbard Communication Office Bulletin* (September 15, 1959): 101, quoted in L. Ron Hubbard, *The Organization Executive Course* 6 (Los Angeles: Publications Organization, 1974), 101–103.

10. CSI, "Connecting the World to Source Through Libraries," *Hotline* VII, no. 2 (1996): 2.

11. Ibid.

12. Church of Scientology Celebrity Centre International, "Celebrity Interview of the Month: Actor John Travolta," *Celebrity* 236 (1990): 12.

13. Church of Scientology Celebrity Centre International, "Celebrity Livewire," *Celebrity* 290 (1996): 14, 15. See also Church of Scientology Celebrity Centre International, "Celebrity Livewire," *Celebrity* 292 (1996): 16.

14. Zeynep Tufekci, "'Not This One': Social Movements, the Attention Economy, and Activism," *American Behavioral Scientist* 57, no. 7 (2013): 849 (italics in original).

15. "Paul Haggis, Awards," IMDb, 1990–2016, http://www.imdb.com/name/nm 0353673/awards.

16. For Jeffrey Scott's Emmy (and other) Awards, see Jeffrey Scott, "Angle on Awards," 2000–2010, http://www.jeffreyscott.tv/KudosAwards.htm.

17. Church of Scientology Celebrity Centre International, "Celebrity Livewire," *Celebrity* 222 (1988): 18–19, 21; Celebrity Centre International, "19th Anniversay [*sic*] Celebration, Final Draft" (September 24, 1988).

18. Kristi Wachter, "Mitchell Brisker—Scientology Service Completions," February 15, 2016, http://www.truthaboutscientology.com/stats/by-name/m/mitchell -brisker.html.

19. Church of Scientology Celebrity Centre International, "Michael Fairman," *Celebrity* Minor Issue 265 (1993): 11.

20. Church of Scientology Celebrity Centre International, "Celebrity Centre News," *Celebrity* 276 (1994): 9.

21. Church of Scientology Celebrity Centre International, *Events in March 1998 at Celebrity Centre International* (1998): n.p.

22. Church of Scientology Celebrity Centre International, "Milton Katselas," *Celebrity* 12th Anniversary Special Edition (1981): 10; Church of Scientology Celebrity Centre International, "Milton Katselas," *Celebrity* Major Issue 13 (1975): 14.

23. Ibid. Katselas did not specify in these interviews what he was having difficulties about, but elsewhere he indicated that he had a problem with methamphetamine in the mid- to late 1960s but kicked the habit. Randye Hoder, "The Star of His Own Show," *Buzz*, March 1998, http://home.snafu.de/tilman/prolinks/9803_2.txt.

24. Church of Scientology Celebrity Centre International, "Milton Katselas," *Celebrity* 12th Anniversary Special Edition (1981): 10.

25. L. Ron Hubbard, "Orders of the Day," no. 122 (May 5, 1971): 2 (capitals in original). Katselas "was nominated for a Tony award for the Broadway production of *Butterflies Are Free* in 1969, and also directed the 1972 movie version starring Goldie Hawn, Edward Albert, and Eileen Heckart, who won an academy award for her role." Hoder, "Star of His Own Show,"

26. Church of Scientology Celebrity Centre International, "Milton Katselas," *Celebrity* 29 (1978): 17.

27. I cannot determine where the two met. For the first nine months of 1972, the *Apollo* traveled between Portugal and Morocco, and spent time in each country's ports. A picture of Katselas in his 1975 interview has him standing in front of a ship—the *Apollo* name on the side of the ship and over his right shoulder—so I suspect that he was standing on a dock. See Church of Scientology Celebrity Centre International, "Milton Katselas," *Celebrity* Major Issue 13 (1975): 16.

28. Church of Scientology Celebrity Centre International, "Milton Katselas," *Celebrity* 29 (1978): 17.

29. Oppenheimer, "The Actualizer." For Elfman as an Honorary PRO, see CSI, "Honorary PROs in Action," 4.

30. WISE International, "WISE Welcomes New Members," *Prosperity* 34 (1994): 24.

31. Ibid., 259.

32. Lawrence Wright, *Going Clear: Scientology, Hollywood, & the Prison of Belief* (New York: Alfred A. Knopf, 2013), 258–259.

33. Janet Reitman, *Inside Scientology: The Story of America's Most Secretive Religion* (New York: Houghton Mifflin Harcourt, 2011), 266.

34. Ibid.

35. Ibid.

36. Milton Katselas, "Milton Katselas Acting Class," n.d., 6, 12, 13, 77, 121.

37. Oppenheimer, "The Actualizer."

38. Church of Scientology Celebrity Centre International, "Jenna Elfman," *Celebrity* 330 (2001): 11.

39. Church of Scientology Celebrity Centre International, "Nancy Cartwright," *Celebrity* Minor Issue 237 (1990): 13. For a book about her work on *The Simpsons*

television show, see Nancy Cartwright, *My Life as a 10-Year-Old Boy* (New York: Hyperion, 2000). At the end of the book, she listed some organizations for which she volunteered, and they included "the following organizations that utilize the research of the humanitarian L. Ron Hubbard: Narconon—a Drug rehab program; The Way to Happiness—a guide to happy living; and the World Literacy Crusade—assisting those who have trouble learning." Ibid., 270.

40. Church of Scientology Celebrity Centre International, "Priscilla Presley," *Celebrity* Minor Issue 253 (1992): 15.

41. Wright, *Going Clear*, 332–335.

42. Church of Scientology Celebrity Centre International, "Terry Jastrow," *Celebrity* Minor Issue 245 (1991): 9.

43. Church of Scientology Celebrity Centre International, "Jason Beghe: Actor/ Clear, Hubbard Basic Art Course Graduate," *Celebrity* Minor Issue 285 (1995): 14.

44. Church of Scientology Celebrity Centre International, "Catherine Bell," *Celebrity* 326 (2000): 10.

45. Church of Scientology Celebrity Centre, "Cathy Lee Crosby," *Celebrity* Minor Issue 30 (1978): 11.

46. Church of Scientology Celebrity Centre International, "Kelly Preston," *Celebrity* 344 (2003): 12.

47. Oppenheimer, "The Actualizer."

48. Wright, *Going Clear*, 163.

49. Ibid., 259.

50. Church of Scientology Celebrity Centre International, "A Special Interview with Actor Jeff Pomerantz," *Celebrity* (1984): 11.

51. Church of Scientology Celebrity Centre International, "Celebrity Livewire." *Celebrity* Major Issue 232 (1989): 12.

52. Church of Scientology Celebrity Centre International, "Celebrity Interview of the Month: Nancy Cartwright," *Celebrity* Major Issue 259 (1992): 9.

53. Church of Scientology Celebrity Centre International, "Scientology Artists in the Spotlight of the World," *Celebrity* Special Issue 296 (1996): 14.

54. Church of Scientology Celebrity Centre International, "Celebrity Livewire," *Celebrity* Major Issue 274 (1994): 15.

55. Church of Scientology Celebrity Centre International, "Scientology Artists in the Spotlight of the World," *Celebrity* Special Issue 296 (1996): 12.

56. Jon Atack, *A Piece of Blue Sky: Scientology, Dianetics, and L. Ron Hubbard Exposed* (New York: Lyle Stuart, 1990), 348.

57. Dianna Waggoner, "Scientology's Stars Rally Against a $39 Mil Award," *People*, June 10, 1985, 59–60; Wright, *Going Clear*, 180–181.

58. Wright, *Going Clear*, 181.

59. Atack, *Piece of Blue Sky*, 357.

60. Church of Scientology Celebrity Centre International, "Celebrity Livewire," *Celebrity* 244 (1991): 10. Note that the article misspelled his last name with two letter 'p's.

61. Jörg Schindler, "The Freedom of Thought of the 'Crusaders,'" *Frankfurter Rundschau,* July 27, 1997 (English translation).

62. IASA, "1997 IAS Freedom Medal Winner: Anne Archer—Exemplifying the Quality of Courage," *Impact* 75 (1997): 33.

63. International Association of Scientologists, "General Membership News," 2003–2016; http://www.iasmembership.org/member/rules.html. See the advertisement in IASA, Ibid., 2.

64. Chris Blackhurst, "Travolta Begs Channel 4 Not to Attack Scientology," *Independent,* November 8, 1997.

65. International Association of Scientologists, "The IAS Freedom Medal Awards," *Impact* 22 (1993): 7–8.

66. Stephen A. Kent and Terra Manca, "A War over Mental Health Professionalism: Scientology Versus Psychiatry," *Mental Health, Religion & Culture* 17 no. 1 (2014): 1–23, doi:10.1080/13674676.2012. 737552; Terra Manca, "Alternative Therapy, Dianetics, and Scientology," *Marburg Journal of Religion* 15 (2010): 1–20.

67. Church of Scientology Celebrity Centre International, "Kelly Preston," *Celebrity* 344 (2003): 14; see also Rick Ross, "Montel Williams, a Shill for Scientology?," *Cult News from Rick Ross,* March 12, 2003, http://www.cultnews.com/archives/000031.html.

68. Kim Masters, "Travolta's Scientology Turning Point?," *Daily Beast,* September 27, 2009, http://www.thedailybeast.com/articles/2009/09/27/travoltas-scientology-turning-point.html.

69. Ibid.

70. "Tom Cruise's Heated Interview with Matt Lauer," YouTube video, 13:55, posted by "Today," June 2, 2014, https://www.youtube.com/watch?v=tFgF1JPNR5E; Andrew Morton, *Tom Cruise: An Unauthorized Biography* (New York: St. Martin's Press, 2008), 280–287.

71. Jade Watkins, "Matt Lauer Admits to 'Cold War Period' with Tom Cruise After THAT 'Glib' Jibe and Reveals Actor Wanted Rant Removed from Air," *Daily Mail,* June 21, 2013, http://www.dailymail.co.uk/tvshowbiz/article-2345978/Matt-Lauer-admits-cold-war-period-Tom-Cruise-called-glib-infamous-interview-reveals-actor-wanted-rant-removed-air.html.

72. Worth noting was the editorial in the *Chicago Tribune,* which said, "If vitamins and exercise alone can explain why Tom Cruise is so, um, knowledgeable and well-grounded, pass the Prozac." MSNBC reporter, Paige Newman, concluded, "It will take more than Cruise's power of positive thinking to bring back the nice guy with the megawatt smile. Now, he's the zealot who jumps on Oprah's couch like a love-crazed monkey and lectures America about our nasty pharmaceutical habits." Perhaps the most surprising reaction came from the socialist-controlled municipal Assembly of Paris, which approved a motion "never to welcome the actor Tom Cruise, spokesman for Scientology and self-declared militant for this organization." See also Iain Johnstone, *Tom Cruise: All the World's a Stage* (London: Hodder & Stoughton 2006), 50.

73. Psychology Debunked, "War of the Worlds: Tom Cruise vs. Psychiatry," July 17, 2005, http://www.psychologydebunked.com/email0507_War%20of%20the%20 Worlds.htm.

74. Brooke Shields, *Down Came the Rain* (New York: Hyperion), 2005.

75. Brooke Shields, "War of Words," *New York Times*, July 1, 2005, http://www .nytimes.com/2005/07/01/opinion/war-of-words.html.

76. National Alliance on Mental Illness, "The Mental Health Community Responds to Cruise's *Today Show* Interview," June 24, 2005, https://www.nami.org/Press-Media /Press-Releases/2005/The-Mental-Health-Community-Responds-to-Tom-Cruise.

77. Ushma S. Neill, "Tom Cruise Is Dangerous and Irresponsible," *Journal of Clinical Investigation* 115, no. (August 2005): 1964, http://wwwjei.org.

78. *People*, "Brooke Shields: Tom Cruise Apologized," September 2, 2006, http:// www.people.com/people/article/0,,1531255,00.html.

79. Leah Remini and Rebecca Paley, *Troublemaker: Surviving Hollywood and Scientology* (New York: Ballantine Books, 2015), 136.

80. WilmzBrewxs, "Brooke Shields, John Nash, and the national APA meeting," *AskDrJones*, June 9, 2007, http://askdrjones.com/index.php/brooke-shields-john -nash-and-the-national-apa-meeting/.

81. Study Technology (or Study Tech) claims to identify three barriers to learning then offers solutions to each. The first barrier is that ideas or items presented to readers lack mass, so the solution is either to show the read the actual item that is in the text or have the reader use various small objects (erasers paper clips, bottle caps, etc.) to build mock-ups of the ideas or items. The second barrier is that the new material is on too steep a gradient for the readers, with the solution being to reduce the difficulty of the material's level. The third barrier involves readers going past words in the text that they do not understand. The solution is for readers always to look up in a dictionary these unknown or misunderstood words. L. Ron Hubbard, [Based on the Works of], *The Scientology Handbook* (Los Angeles: Bridge Publications, 1994), 5–17.

82. Phillip Pasho quoted in Carol Forsloff, "Tom Cruise Again Asserts Scientology Cured His Dyslexia," *Digital Journal*, March 6, 2009, http://www.digitaljournal .com/article/268639.

83. J. Thomas Viall, quoted in Ibid.

84. "Top Gun Tom Under Fire!," *National Enquirer*, August 7, 2003, http://www .nationalenquirer.com/celebrity/top-gun-tom-under-fire/.

85. Forsloff, "Tom Cruise Again Asserts Scientology Cured His Dyslexia."

86. Cruise, quoted in Morton, *Tom Cruise*, 249.

87. Ibid.

88. Chris Rojek, *Fame Attack: The Inflation of Celebrity and Its Consequences* (London: Bloomsbury Academic, 2012), 149.

89. Ibid.,150.

90. See Puja Khatri, "Celebrity Endorsement: A Strategic Promotion Perspective," *Indian Media Studies Journal* 1, no. 1 (July–December 2006): 27.

91. For those doubts, see Janet Reitman, *Inside Scientology: The Story of America's Most Secretive Religion* (New York: Houghton Mifflin Harcourt, 2011), 268.

92. Janet Cawley, "Bold, Beautiful, and No Bull: Straight Talk from the Never-Boring Kirstie Alley," *Biography*, December 1997, 33; see Lawrence Grobel, "Cheers to Kirstie Alley," *TV Guide*, April 9, 1994, 19. Sources differ, however, about exactly what year Alley did the drug treatment program. Cawley said that Alley arrived in Los Angeles in 1981, but a short biography piece on Alley in Torrance, California's newspaper, *Daily Breeze*, specifically stated that she did the Los Angeles Narconon program in 1979. Alley herself gave the 1979 date in an interview that UPI published in 1990. See *Daily Breeze*, "Alley Finds Wonderful Life Without Drugs," *Daily Breeze* (Torrance, California). November 28, 1990, A2; Vernon Scott, "'Narconon Saved My Life'—Kirstie Alley," *UPI*, May 3, 1990.

93. Ibid.

94. See, for example, Tony Brenna, Lesley Abravanel, and Neil Blincow, "Kirstie: 'I Don't Want Fat Sex!'" *Star*, November 29, 2004, 48–49. The cover of the magazine has a hefty Alley apparently giving the photographer two middle fingers; one of the three pictures inside the article itself is of Alley eating French fries; and a second, full-page photograph is of Alley wearing brownish-red-tinted glasses covering fierce eyes with an angry look on her face and a wide open mouth (as she probably was yelling).

95. David Giles, *Illusions of Immortality: A Psychology of Fame and Celebrity* (London: Macmillan Press, 2004), 62.

96. Juliette Lewis, quoted in Kira Cochrane, "I'm a Man-Loving Feminist," *Guardian*, September 17, 2008, available on-line.

97. Church of Scientology Celebrity Centre, "Nicki Hopkins," *Celebrity* (1981): 9; Church of Scientology Celebrity Center International, "Celebrity Interview of the Month: Nicki Hopkins," *Celebrity* Major Issue 226 (1989): 11.

98. Church of Scientology Celebrity Centre International, "Celebrity Livewire," *Celebrity* Minor Issue 235 (1990): 12.

99. See Khatri, "Celebrity Endorsement," 27.

100. Daniel Brown, "Hall of Fame Push for John Brodie," *San Jose Mercury News* (July 30, 2015), http://www.mercurynews.com/2015/07/30/hall-of-fame-push-for-john-brodie/.

101. Bette Orsini, "Celebrities Testify for Scientology," *St. Petersburg Times*, March 20, 1976, 1B.

102. Bob Oates, "John Brodie: Passer to Preacher," *Los Angeles Times*, November 16, 1973, Part III, 10, 1.

103. *Chronicle Sporting Green*, "Brodie Receives Narconon Check," January 10, 1974.

104. A. J. Daulerio, "Whither the Scientologist Athlete?," *Deadspin*, June 7, 2009, available on-line.

105. Jacob Davidson, "Stars Who Quit Scientology." *Time*, July 11, 2013, available on-line.

106. Church of Scientology Celebrity Centre International, "Celebrity Livewire," *Celebrity* Minor Issue 235 (1990): 12.

107. *New York Daily News*, "An Air of Intrigue," July 1, 2004.

108. *Narconon Newsletter for Narconon International*, "John Travolta Benefit for Narconon International," 11/2 (1999): 1.

109. "The Friends of Narconon" (no pl. or d.), 1p. [unpublished stencil].

110. See http://www.friendsofnarconon.org/index.php, accessed November 27, 2016.

111. Social Coordination International, "Celebs Star in Drug-Free Hero Campaign," *Inroads* 5 (1986): 3.

112. "Narconon Celebrity All-Stars vs. Hollywood Pro-Stunt Team," North Hollywood High School (May 19, 1990), 8pp., Program.

113. Narconon, "Celebrity Support for Narconon Drug Prevention," accessed July 19, 2015, http://www.narconon.org/about-narconon/celebrity-support.html #top.

114. Drug Free Heroes, "8th Annual Drug-Free Heroes Awards Gala," accessed September 13, 2015.

115. Reitman, *Inside Scientology*, 258–259.

116. David McCrindell, "Bizarre Brainwashing Cult Cons Top Stars into Backing Its Drug Program," *National Enquirer*, April 21, 1981, 48.

117. L. Ron Hubbard (Assisted by CO OTL LA), "Celebrities," *Sea Organization Flag Order* 1975R (May 3, 1969, Revised June 25, 1988).

118. R. [L. Ron Hubbard], "NN Credit," November 24, 1980, 1.

119. Ibid.

120. Robert Farley, "Striving for Mainstream, Building New Connections," *Tampa Bay Times*, July 19, 2004, http://www.sptimes.com/2004/07/19/Tampabay/Striving_for_mainstre.shtml.

121. Thomas C. Tobin, "Kirstie Alley Buys Presley Mansion," *St. Petersburg Times*, May 17, 2000, http://www.sptimes.com/News/051700/NorthPinellas/Kirstie_Alley_buys_Pr.shtml; CelebrityDetective.com, "John Travolta's Home Ocala, Florida Pictures, Facts," n.d., http://www.celebritydetective.com/Celebrity_Homes_John-Travolta-house.html.

122. Alisa Ulferts, "Panel Waters Down Limits on Student Mental Services," *Tampabay.com*, April 20, 2005, http://www.sptimes.com/2005/04/20/news_pf/State/Panel_waters_down_lim.shtml.

123. Ibid.

124. Leslie Larson, "Jeb Bush Has Had a Few Run-Ins with Scientology," *Business Insider*, March 31, 2015, http://www.businessinsider.com/jeb-bush-has-had-a-few-run-ins-with-scientology-2015-3.

125. See Katharine Mieszkowski, "Scientology's War on Psychiatry," *Salon*, July 1, 2005, http://www.salon.com/2005/07/01/sci_psy/.

126. Amanda J. Crawford, "Scientology Group Finds Support in Legislature; Tinseltown Trips Linked to Anti-psychiatry Push," *Arizona Republic*, March 11, 2006, http://culteducation.com/group/1284-scientology/25671-scientology-group-finds-support-in-legislature.html.

127. Ibid.

128. Ibid.

129. Joseph L. Conn, "'Bart Simpson' Voice Nancy Cartwright Lobbies for Scientology in Schools," *AUSCS Sun*, May 15, 2011, http://www.opposingviews.com/i/bart-simpson-voice-nancy-cartwright-lobbies-for-scientology-in-schools.

130. *Hearing on the Federal Drug Strategy: Prospects For the 1980's, Before the U.S. House of Representatives, Select Comm. on Narcotics Abuse and Control*, 96th Cong. (September 23, 1980). http://babel.hathitrust.org/cgi/pt?id=pst.000020611927;view =1up;seq=5.

131. Church of Scientology of California American Saint Hill Organization, "Actress Talks to House of Representatives about Purification Rundown." *Auditor World Wide* 168 (1980): 4.

132. David Dahl, "Scientology's Influence Grows in Washington," *St. Petersburg Times Online*, March 29, 1998, http://www.sptimes.com/Worldandnation/32998 /Scientology_s_influen.html.

133. Ibid.

134. Commission on Security and Cooperation in Europe, https://www.csce.gov /about-csce/our-structure?FuseAction=AboutCommission.WorkOfCommission," n.d.

135. Commission on Security and Cooperation in Europe, "Religious Intolerance in Europe Today," Hearing, September 18, 1997, http://home.snafu.de/tilman/krasel /germany/csce2.html #coreal.

136. Sheila McGregor, "Blog: Anti Dianetics: Scientology and the German State," October 4, 2010, https://antidianetics.wordpress.com/2010/10/04/scientology -and-the-german-state/.

137. Commission on Security and Cooperation in Europe, "Religious Intolerance."

138. Enquete Commission, *New Religious and Ideological Communities and Psychogroups in the Federal Republic of Germany*, translated by Wolfgang Fehlberg and Monica Ulloa-Fehlberg (Bonn: Deutscher Bundestag Referat Öffentlichkeitsarbeit, 1998), 344–349.

139. These issues included Scientology's use of "defamatory pieces of writing— often produced abroad—. . . to make personal attacks on its critics and to demean them" (Ibid., 241). Some of these "critics and ex-members have been persecuted with 'psychoterror'" (Ibid., 347). German officials noted the pressure that individual Scientologists were under pressure to buy "scientifically worthless" E-meters at grossly inflated prices (Ibid., 262). A federal Labor Court had ruled that Scientology was not a religious community (Ibid., 271), and other information indicated that the organization has "a decidedly commercial orientation" (Ibid., 348). German officials were concerned "that the organization reacts extremely aggressively to public criticism in many cases," and "that the organization is pursuing unconstitutional aspirations" (Ibid., 347, see 349). German authorities had received information that "the Scientology Organization was running institutions that resembled penal camps (Rehabilitation Project Force), in which members were abused and detained against their will. According to these reports, the Scientology Organization systematically violates human rights" (Ibid.).

140. L. Ron Hubbard, "Ethics, Suppressive Acts, Suppression of Scientology and Scientologists, The Fair Game Law," *Hubbard Communications Office Policy Letter* (March 1, 1965): 553. Quoted in L. Ron Hubbard, *The Organization Executive Course*, HCO Division 1 (Copenhagen: Scientology Publications Organization, 1970), 552–557.

141. Josh Young, "Bill Clinton's Grand Seduction," *George*, March 1998, 106ff.

142. Ibid.

143. Ibid.

144. Stephen A. Kent, "Hollywood's Celebrity Lobbyists and the Clinton Administration's American Foreign Policy toward German scientology," *Journal of Religion and Popular Culture* 1 no. 1 (Spring 2002), doi:10.31.38/jrpc.1.1.002; see the excellent, in-depth website by Tilman Hausherr, "Clearwatergate: US Politics and Scientology," accessed February 26, 2016, http://home.snafu.de/tilman/politics.html.

145. I draw this conclusion from several talks with members of the Enquete Commission, plus one incident that I witnessed during the Commission members' visit in late February 1998. I was one of the people who met with these members, and my meeting came immediately after they met with a U.S. official. Apparently Enquete Commission member, Ursula Caberta, had asked the official about Scientology's Rehabilitation Project Force operating in the United States, which Germans (and others) considered to be a significant human right abuse. The U.S. official had no idea what the question was about—he had no idea what the RPF was. The incident simply reinforced how uniformed German officials thought their U.S. counterparts were. For German officials' perspective on Scientology's lobbying efforts against their country with U.S. politicians in this period, see Enquete Commission, *New Religions and Ideological Communities*, 229.

146. Church of Scientology Celebrity Centre International, "Celebrity Centre News," *Celebrity* 272 (1993): 6.

147. Church of Scientology Celebrity Centre International, "Celebrity Livewire," *Celebrity* 287 (1995): 12.

148. Merrie Morris, "Merrie-Go-Round," *Washington Times*, August 3, 1993, E1; Lois Romano, "The Reliable Source," *Washington Post*, August 3, 1993, E3.

149. Lloyd Grove, "The Reliable Source: Juliette Lewis's Prescription for Reform," *Washington Post*, March 5, 2003, C3.

150. Hunter Walker, "Meet Scientology's Lobbyist Who Works the Halls of Congress for the Church," *Business Insider*, April 8, 2015, http://www.businessinsider.com/church-of-scientology-washington-lobbyist-2015-4.

151. "'Tis the Season for a Scientology Party," *Wall Street Journal*, December 11, 2006.

152. Morton, *Tom Cruise*, 242–243.

153. Ibid.

154. "Jenna Elfman Net Worth," accessed February 27, 2016, http://www.celebrity networth.com/richest-celebrities/actors/jenna-elfman-net-worth/. I offer the information from this website with some caution, since it does not say how it arrived at the figures of movie stars' wealth or on what date the calculations were made. (The information, however, appears to be relatively current.) Nevertheless, I see nothing in the figures that would lead me to challenge or question their basic accuracy.

155. "Kirstie Alley Net Worth," accessed February 27, 2016, http://www.celebrity networth.com/richest-celebrities/actors/kirstie-alley-net-worth/.

156. "Nancy Cartwright Net Worth," accessed February 27, 2016, http://www .celebritynetworth.com/richest-celebrities/actors/nancy-cartwright-net-worth/.

The British paper, the *Times*, placed her income per show at an estimated $400,000. Chris Ayres, "Simpson's Producers 'Have a Cow' as Bart Lends His Voice to Scientologists," *Times* (U.K.), January 30, 2009, http://www.thetimes.co.uk/tto/arts/tv-radio /article2446537.ece.

157. "John Travolta Net Worth," accessed February 27, 2016, http://www.celebrity networth.com/richest-celebrities/actors/john-travolta-net-worth/.

158. "Tom Cruise Net Worth," accessed February 27, 2016, http://www.celebrity networth.com/richest-celebrities/actors/tom-cruise-net-worth/.

159. David McNamee, "How Can Springfield's Voice of Reason Be a Scientologist?," *Guardian*, February 6, 2008, http://www.theguardian.com/culture/tvandradioblog/2008 /feb/06/howcanspringfields voiceof; "Priscilla Presley Net Worth," accessed February 28, 2016, http://www.celebritynetworth.com/richest-celebrities/actors/priscilla-presley -net-worth/.

160. "John Travolta Donates an Additional $1.5 Million to Fight Scientology's Critics," last modified March 3, 2008, http://www.forum.exscn.net/archive/index .php/t-4749.html.

161. McNamee, "How Can Springfield's Voice." Ayres, "Simpsons Producers."

162. Tony Ortega, "When Tom Cruise Was One of Scientology's Biggest Donors: A Look Back," *The Underground Bunker*, 2015, http://tonyortega.org/2015/06 /07/when-tom-cruise-was-one-of-scientologys-biggest-donors-a-look-back/; Remini, *Troublemaker*, 124.

163. Remini, *Troublemaker*, 121.

164. Ibid., 123–124.

165. Wright, *Going Clear*, 216.

166. Scobee, *Abuse at the Top*, 71–74.

167. Ibid., 75.

168. L. Ron Hubbard, "John Travolta," *The Church of Scientology Celebrity Centre Good Newsletter* #15 (1978) (capitalization in original).

169. One biography of Travolta indicated that, "inspired by Hubbardism, he gave to charities promoting drug rehabilitation, the rain forest, the clean-up of radioactive food in Russia, cancer, Aids research and programmes for the learning-disabled." Nigel Andrews, *Travolta: The Life* (London: Bloomsbury, 1998), 274. Unfortunately, the author did not name the charities.

170. Scobee, *Abuse at the Top*, 70.

171. Ibid., 200.

172. Claire Hoffman and Kim Christensen, "Tom Cruise and Scientology," *Los Angeles Times*, December 18, 2005, http://www.latimes.com/news/la-fi-scientology 18dec18-storyhtml.

173. Morton, *Tom Cruise*, 151.

174. L. Ron Hubbard, "Income Flows and Pools: Principles of Money and Management," *Hubbard Communications Office Policy Letter*, March 9, 1972, in L. Ron Hubbard, *The Management Series 1970–1974*. 1974, updated reprint. (Los Angeles: Church of Scientology of California, 1975), 384.

175. Church of Scientology Celebrity Centre International, "Celebrity Interview of the Month: Actress Jenna Elfman," *Celebrity* Minor Issue 298 (1996): 8, 10.

176. Wright, *Going Clear*, 216.
177. David S. Meyer and Joshua Gamson, "The Challenge of Cultural Elites: Celebrities and Social Movements," *Sociological Inquiry* 65, no. 2 (May 1995): 189 (italics in original).
178. Ann Louise Bardach, "Proud Mary," *George*, August 1999, 91.
179. Ibid.
180. Sonny Bono Copyright Term Extension Act, S. 505, 105th Cong. (January 27, 1998), http://www.copyright.gov/legislation/s505.pdf.
181. Kent, "Hollywood's Celebrity Lobbyists."
182. Christian Lahusen, *The Rhetoric of Moral Protest: Public Campaigns, Celebrity Endorsement, and Political Mobilization* (Berlin: Walter de Gruyter, 1996), 118.
183. Meyer and Gamson, "The Challenge of Cultural Elites," 186.
184. Kent, "Hollywood's Celebrity-Lobbyists"; see H. H. Gerth, *Max Weber: Essays in Sociology*, ed. C. Wright Mills (New York: Oxford University Press, 1946), 186–187, 190–191.
185. Kent, "Hollywood's Celebrity Lobbyists."
186. Ibid.
187. Ibid.; Stephen A. Kent, "The French and German versus American Debate Over 'New Religions,' Scientology, and Human Rights," *Marburg Journal of Religion* 6, no. 1 (January 2001): 11.
188. Benjamin Gilman, quoted in Church of Scientology Celebrity Centre International, "Celebrity Centre's 33rd Annual Anniversary Gala," *Celebrity* 342 (2002): 14.
189. Andrew Abbott, *The System of Professions* (Chicago: University of Chicago Press, 1988), 21.
190. Ibid., 21–23.

BIBLIOGRAPHY

Abbott, Andrew. *The System of Professions*. Chicago: University of Chicago Press, 1988.
"Alley Finds Wonderful Life Without Drugs." *Daily Breeze* (Torrance, California). November 28, 1990.
Andrews, Nigel. *Travolta: The Life*. London: Bloomsbury, 1998.
Atack, Jon. *A Piece of Blue Sky: Scientology, Dianetics and L. Ron Hubbard Exposed*. New York: Lyle Stuart, 1990.
Ayres, Chris. "Simpson's Producers 'Have a Cow' as Bart Lends His Voice to Scientologists." *Times* (U.K.). January 30, 2009. http://www.thetimes.co.uk/tto/arts/tv-radio/article2446537.ece.
Bardach, Ann Louise. "Proud Mary." *George*. August 1999.
Benjamin Gilman. Quoted in Church of Scientology Celebrity Centre International. "Celebrity Centre's 33rd Annual Anniversary Gala." *Celebrity* 342 (2002): 14.
Blackhurst, Chris. "Travolta Begs Channel 4 Not to Attack Scientology." *Independent*. November 8, 1997.
Breitbart, Andrew, and Mark Ebner. *Hollywood Interrupted: Insanity Chic in Babylon—The Case against Celebrity*. Hoboken, New Jersey: John Wiley & Sons, 2004.

Brenna, Tony, Lesley Abravanel, and Neil Blincow. "Kirstie: 'I Don't Want Fat Sex!'" *Star*. November 29, 2004.

Brown, Daniel. "Hall of Fame Push for John Brodie." *San Jose Mercury News*. July 30, 2015. http://www.mercurynews.com/2015/07/30/hall-of-fame-push-for-john-brodie/

Butterflies Are Free. Directed by Milton Katselas. Booth Theatre, New York, NY, October 21, 1969–July 2, 1972.

Butterflies Are Free. Directed by Milton Katselas. San Francisco, CA: Frankovich Productions, 1972.

Cartwright, Nancy. *My Life as a 10-Year-Old Boy*. New York: Hyperion, 2000.

Cawley, Janet. "Bold, Beautiful, and No Bull: Straight Talk from the Never-Boring Kirstie Alley." *Biography*. December 1997.

Celebrity Centre International. "19th Anniversay [sic] Celebration, Final Draft." September 24, 1988.

CelebrityDetective.com. "John Travolta's Home Ocala, Florida Pictures, Facts." n.d. http://www.celebritydetective.com/Celebrity_Homes_John-Travolta-house .html.

Chicago Tribune. "Cruise Control, Please." July 1, 2005. http://articles.chicagotribune com/2005-07-01/news/0507010295_1_cruise-control-postpartum-tactician.

Chronicle Sporting Green. "Brodie Receives Narconon Check." January 10, 1974.

Church of Scientology Celebrity Centre. "Cathy Lee Crosby." *Celebrity* Minor Issue 30 (1978): 10–11.

Church of Scientology Celebrity Centre. "Nicki Hopkins." *Celebrity* (1981): 8–9.

Church of Scientology Celebrity Centre International. "Catherine Bell." *Celebrity* 326 (2000): 10–13.

Church of Scientology Celebrity Centre International. "Celebrity Centre Network News." *Celebrity* Special Edition (1986): 21.

Church of Scientology Celebrity Centre International. "Celebrity Centre News." *Celebrity* 272 (1993): 6–7, 11.

Church of Scientology Celebrity Centre International. "Celebrity Centre News." *Celebrity* 275 (1994): 6–7, 11.

Church of Scientology Celebrity Centre International. "Celebrity Centre News." *Celebrity* 276 (1994): 6–9.

Church of Scientology Celebrity Centre International. "Celebrity Centre News and Events: CC International Surf Club Awarded 'Adopt a Beach Volunteers of the Year.'" *Celebrity* 330 (2001): 8–9.

Church of Scientology Celebrity Centre International. "Celebrity Centre News and Events: Celebrity Centre's Adopted Beach Gets Spring Cleaned." *Celebrity* 313 (1998): 6–9.

Church of Scientology Celebrity Centre International. "Celebrity Centre's 33rd Annual Anniversary Gala." *Celebrity* 342 (2002): 12–17.

Church of Scientology Celebrity Centre International. "Celebrity Interview of the Month: Actor John Travolta." *Celebrity* 236 (1990): 8–9, 12.

Church of Scientology Celebrity Centre International. "Celebrity Interview of the Month: Actress Jenna Elfman." *Celebrity* Minor Issue 298 (1996): 8–10.

Church of Scientology Celebrity Centre International. "Celebrity Interview of the Month: Nancy Cartwright." *Celebrity* Major Issue 259 (1992): 8–9, 12.

Church of Scientology Celebrity Centre International. "Celebrity Interview of the Month: Nicki Hopkins." *Celebrity* Major Issue 226 (1989): 10–13.

Church of Scientology Celebrity Centre International. "Celebrity Livewire." *Celebrity* Minor Issue 28 (1977): 16.

Church of Scientology Celebrity Centre International. "Celebrity Livewire." *Celebrity* 222 (1988): 18–19, 21.

Church of Scientology Celebrity Centre International. "Celebrity Livewire." *Celebrity* 229 (1989): 12–14.

Church of Scientology Celebrity Centre International. "Celebrity Livewire." *Celebrity* Major Issue 232 (1989): 12–14.

Church of Scientology Celebrity Centre International. "Celebrity Livewire." *Celebrity* Minor Issue 235 (1990): 12–13.

Church of Scientology Celebrity Centre International. "Celebrity Livewire." *Celebrity* 244 (1991): 10–11.

Church of Scientology Celebrity Centre International. "Celebrity Livewire." *Celebrity* Major Issue 274 (1994): 14–15.

Church of Scientology Celebrity Centre International. "Celebrity Livewire." *Celebrity* 287 (1995): 12–15.

Church of Scientology Celebrity Centre International. "Celebrity Livewire." *Celebrity* 290 (1996): 14–15.

Church of Scientology Celebrity Centre International. "Celebrity Livewire." *Celebrity* 292 (1996): 16–17.

Church of Scientology Celebrity Centre International. *Events in March 1998 at Celebrity Centre International,* 1998.

Church of Scientology Celebrity Centre International. "Jason Beghe: Actor/Clear, Hubbard Basic Art Course Graduate." *Celebrity* Minor Issue 285 (1995): 14–15.

Church of Scientology Celebrity Centre International. "Jenna Elfman." *Celebrity* 330 (2001): 10–13.

Church of Scientology Celebrity Centre International. "Kelly Preston." *Celebrity* 344 (2003): 12–15.

Church of Scientology Celebrity Centre International. "Livewire; Celebrity Scientologists in Action: Hollywood Christmas Parade." *Celebrity* 354 (2004): 14–15.

Church of Scientology Celebrity Centre International. "Livewire; Celebrity Scientologists in Action: Lynsey Bartilson." *Celebrity* 344 (2003): 16–17.

Church of Scientology Celebrity Centre International. "Michael Fairman." *Celebrity* Minor Issue 265 (1993): 8–11.

Church of Scientology Celebrity Centre International. "Milton Katselas." *Celebrity* 29 (1978): 14–15, 17.

Church of Scientology Celebrity Centre International. "Milton Katselas." *Celebrity* 12th Anniversary Special Edition (1981): 10–11.

Church of Scientology Celebrity Centre International. "Milton Katselas." *Celebrity* Major Issue 13 (1975): 14–17.

Church of Scientology Celebrity Centre International. "Nancy Cartwright." *Celebrity* Minor Issue 237 (1990): 12–13, 16.

Church of Scientology Celebrity Centre International. "Priscilla Presley." *Celebrity Minor* Issue 253 (1992): 10–11, 15–16.

Church of Scientology Celebrity Centre International. "Scientology Artists in the Spotlight of the World." *Celebrity* Special Issue 296 (1996): 12–15.

Church of Scientology Celebrity Centre International. "A Special Interview with Actor Jeff Pomerantz." *Celebrity* (1984): 10–11.

Church of Scientology Celebrity Centre International. "Terry Jastrow." *Celebrity Minor* Issue 245 (1991): 8–9, 13.

Church of Scientology of California American Saint Hill Organization. "Actress Talks to House of Representatives About Purification Rundown." *Auditor World Wide* 168 (1980): 4.

Commission on Security and Cooperation in Europe. n.d. http://csce.gov/index.cfm?FuseAction=AboutCommission.WorkOfCommission.

Commission on Security and Cooperation in Europe. "Religious Intolerance in Europe Today." Hearing, September 18, 1997. http://home.snafu.de/tilman/krasel/germany/csce2.html#corea1.

Conn, Joseph L. "'Bart Simpson' Voice Nancy Cartwright Lobbies for Scientology in Schools." *AUSCS Sun.* May 15, 2011. http://www.opposingviews.com/i/bart-simpson-voice-nancy-cartwright-lobbies-for-scientology-in-schools.

Crawford, Amanda J. "Scientology Group Finds Support in Legislature; Tinseltown Trips Linked to Anti-psychiatry Push." *Arizona Republic.* March 11, 2006. http://culteducation.com/group/1284-scientology/25671-scientology-group-finds-support-in-legislature.html.

CSI. "Connecting the World to Source Through Libraries." *Hotline* VII, no. 2 (1996): 2–3.

CSI. "Honorary PROs in Action." 4.

CSI. "Honorary PROs in Action: Honorary PROs Are Cheering up the World! Jenna Elfman, Marisol Nichols and Lynsey Bartilson Promote *The Joy of Creating*." *Good News.* 2001.

CSI. "Honorary PROs on the Move." *Hotline* 3, no. 7 (1998): 6.

Dahl, David. "Scientology's Influence Grows in Washington." *St. Petersburg Times Online.* March 29, 1998. http://www.sptimes.com/Worldandnation/32998/Scientology_s_influen.html.

Daulerio, A. J. "Whither the Scientologist Athlete?" *Deadspin.* June 7, 2009.

Davidson, Jacob. "Stars Who Quit Scientology." *Time.* July 11, 2013.

Drug Free Heroes. "8th Annual Drug-Free Heroes Awards Gala." Accessed September 13, 2015.

Enquete Commission. *New Religious and Ideological Communities and Psychogroups in the Federal Republic of Germany.* Translated by Wolfgang Fehlberg and Monica Ulloa-Fehlberg. Bonn: Deutscher Bundestag Referat Öffentlichkeitsarbeit, 1998.

Farley, Robert. "Striving for Mainstream, Building New Connections." *Tampabay.* July 19, 2004. http://www.sptimes.com/2004/07/19/Tampabay/Striving_for_mainstre.shtml.

Forsloff, Carol. "Tom Cruise Again Asserts Scientology Cured His Dyslexia." *Digital Journal.* March 6, 2009. http://www.digitaljournal.com/article/268639.

Friends of Narconon. Accessed November 27, 2016. http://www.friendsofnarconon
.org.

"The Friends of Narconon" [unpublished stencil]. In H. H. *Max Weber: Essays in Sociology*, edited by C. Wright Mills. New York: Oxford University Press, 1946.

Giles, David. *Illusions of Immortality: A Psychology of Fame and Celebrity*. London: Macmillan Press, 2000.

Goss, Rose. "The Joy of Creating *The Road to Total Freedom*." *Celebrity* Church of Scientology Celebrity Centre International Special Edition (1986): 4–14.

Grobel, Lawrence. "Cheers to Kirstie Alley." *TV Guide*. April 9, 1994.

Grove, Lloyd. "The Reliable Source: Juliette Lewis's Prescription for Reform." *Washington Post*. March 5, 2003, C3.

Hausherr, Tilman. "Clearwatergate: US Politics and Scientology." Accessed February 26, 2016. http://home.snafu.de/tilman/politics.html.

Hoder, Randye. "The Star of His Own Show." *Buzz*. March 1998. http://home.snafu
.de/tilman/prolinks/9803_2.txt.

Hoffman, Claire, and Kim Christensen. "Tom Cruise and Scientology." *Los Angeles Times*. December 18, 2005. http://www.latimes.com/news/la-fi-scientology
18dec18-story.html.

Hubbard, L. Ron (assisted by CO OTL LA). "Celebrities." *Sea Organization Flag Order* 1975R (May 3, 1969, revised June 25, 1988).

Hubbard, L. Ron [Based on the Works of]. *The Scientology Handbook*. Los Angeles: Bridge Publications, 1994.

Hubbard, L. Ron. "Dissemination Tips." *Hubbard Communication Office Bulletin* (September 15, 1959): 101. Quoted in L. Ron Hubbard, *The Organization Executive Course* 6. Los Angeles: Publications Organization, 1974.

Hubbard, L. Ron. "Ethics, Suppressive Acts, Suppression of Scientology and Scientologists, Fair Game Law." *Hubbard Communications Office Policy Letter* (March 1, 1965): 553.

Hubbard, L. Ron. "Income Flows and Pools: Principles of Money and Management." *Hubbard Communications Office Policy Letter* (March 9, 1972). In L. Ron Hubbard. *The Management Series 1970–1974*, 384. 1974, updated reprint. Los Angeles: Church of Scientology of California, 1975.

Hubbard, L. Ron. "John Travolta." *The Church of Scientology Celebrity Centre Good Newsletter* #15 (1978).

Hubbard, L. Ron. "Orders of the Day." Vol. No. 122 (May 5, 1971).

IASA. "1997 IAS Freedom Medal Winner: Anne Archer—Exemplifying the Quality of Courage." *Impact* 75 (1997): 33.

International Association of Scientologists. "General Membership News." 2003–2016. http://www.iasmembership.org/member/rules.html.

International Association of Scientologists. "The IAS Freedom Medal Awards." *Impact* 22 (1993): 6–8.

"Jenna Elfman Net Worth." Accessed February 27, 2016. http://www.celebritynet
worth.com/richest-celebrities/actors/jenna-elfman-net-worth/.

Johnstone, Iain. *Tom Cruise: All the World's a Stage*. London: Hodder & Stoughton, 2006.

"John Travolta Benefit for Narconon International." *Narconon Newsletter for Narconon International* 11/2 (1999): 1.

"John Travolta Donates An Additional $1.5 Million to Fight Scientology's Critics." Accessed March 3, 2008. http://www.forum.exscn.net/archive/index.php/t-4749 .html.

"John Travolta Net Worth." Accessed February 27, 2016. http://www.celebritynet worth.com/richest-celebrities/actors/john-travolta-net-worth/.

Katselas, Milton. "Milton Katselas Acting Class." n.p. or d.

Kent, Stephen A., and Terra Manca. "A War over Mental Health Professionalism: Scientology Versus Psychiatry." *Mental Health, Religion & Culture* 17, no. 1 (2014): 1–23. doi:10.1080/13674676.2012.737552.

Kent, Stephen A. "The French and German versus American Debate Over 'New Religions,' Scientology, and Human Rights." *Marburg Journal of Religion* 6, no. 1 (January 2001): 1–63.

Kent, Stephen A. "Hollywood's Celebrity Lobbyists and the Clinton Administration's American Foreign Policy Toward German Scientology." *Journal of Religion and Popular Culture* 1, no. 1 (Spring 2002). https://skent.ualberta.ca/wp-content /uploads/2015/07/Scientologys-Celebrity-Lobbyists.pdf.

Khatri, Puja. "Celebrity Endorsement: A Strategic Promotion Perspective." *Indian Media Studies Journal* 1, no. 1 (July–December 2006): 27–37.

"Kirstie Alley Net Worth." Accessed February 27, 2016. http://www.celebritynet worth.com/richest-celebrities/actors/kirstie-alley-net-worth/.

Lahusen, Christian. *The Rhetoric of Moral Protest: Public Campaigns, Celebrity Endorsement, and Political Mobilization.* Berlin: Walter de Gruyter, 1996.

Larson, Leslie. "Jeb Bush Has Had a Few Run-Ins with Scientology." *Business Insider.* March 31, 2015. http://www.businessinsider.com/jeb-bush-has-had-a-few-run -ins-with-scientology-2015-3.

Lewis, Juliette quoted in Kira Cochrane, "I'm a Man-Loving Feminist." *Guardian.* September 17, 2008.

Manca, Terra. "Alternative Therapy, Dianetics, and Scientology." *Marburg Journal of Religion* 15 (2010): 1–20.

Masters, Kim. "Travolta's Scientology Turning Point?" *Daily Beast.* September 27, 2009. http://www.thedailybeast.com/articles/2009/09/27/travoltas-scientology -turning-point.html.

McCrindell, David. "Bizarre Brainwashing Cult Cons Top Stars into Backing Its Drug Program." *National Enquirer.* April 21, 1981.

McGregor, Sheila. "Blog: Anti Dianetics: Scientology and the German State." Last modified October 4, 2010. https://antidianetics.wordpress.com/2010/10/04 /scientology-and-the-german-state/.

McNamee, David. "How Can Springfield's Voice of Reason Be a Scientologist?" *Guardian.* February 6, 2008. http://www.theguardian.com/culture/tvandradio blog/2008/feb/06/howcanspringfieldsvoiceof.

Meyer, David S., and Joshua Gamson. "The Challenge of Cultural Elites: Celebrities and Social Movements." *Sociological Inquiry* 65 no. 2 (May 1995): 181–206.

Mieszkowski, Katharine. "Scientology's War on Psychiatry." *Salon.* July 1, 2005. http://www.salon.com/2005/07/01/sci_psy/.

Morris, Merrie. "Merrie-Go-Round." *Washington Times.* August 3, 1993, E1.

Morton, Andrew. *Tom Cruise: An Unauthorized Biography.* New York: St. Martin's Press, 2008.

"Nancy Cartwright Net Worth." Accessed February 27, 2016. http://www.celebrity networth.com/richest-celebrities/actors/nancy-cartwright-net-worth/.

"Narconon—A Drug Rehab Program." 2016. http://www.narconon.org.

"Narconon Celebrity All-Stars vs. Hollywood Pro-Stunt Team." North Hollywood High School (May 19, 1990). Program.

Narconon. "Celebrity Support for Narconon Drug Prevention." Accessed July 19, 2015. http://www.narconon.org/about-narconon/celebrity-support.html#top.

National Alliance on Mental Illness. "The Mental Health Community Responds to Cruise's *Today Show* Interview." June 24, 2005. https://www.nami.org /Press-Media/Press-Releases/2005/The-Mental-Health-Community-Responds -to-Tom-Cruise.

National Enquirer. "Top Gun Tom Under Fire!" August 7, 2003. http://www.national enquirer.com/celebrity/top-gun-tom-under-fire/.

Neill, Ushma S. "Tom Cruise Is Dangerous and Irresponsible." *Journal of Clinical Investigation* 115, no. 8 (August 2005): 1964–1965. http://www.jci.org.

New York Daily News. "An Air of Intrigue." July 1, 2004.

Newman, Paige. "Give Me Back the Old Tom Cruise." *Today*. June 2, 2005. http:// www.today.com/popculture/give-me-back-old-tom-cruise-wbna8077790.

Oates, Bob. "John Brodie: Passer to Preacher." *Los Angeles Times*. November 16, 1973, Part III.

O'Neil, Deborah, and Jeff Harrington. "The CEO and His Church." *St. Petersburg Times*. June 2, 2002. http://www.sptimes.com/2002/06/02/news_pf/TampaBay /The_CEO_and_his_churc.shtml.

Oppenheimer, Mark. "The Actualizer." *New York Times Magazine*. July 15, 2007. http://www.nytimes.com/2007/07/15/magazine/15Katselas-t.html.

Orsini, Bette. "Celebrities Testify for Scientology." *St. Petersburg Times*. March 20, 1976.

Ortega, Tony. "When Tom Cruise Was One of Scientology's Biggest Donors: A Look Back." *The Underground Bunker*. 2015. http://tonyortega.org/2015/06/07 /when-tom-cruise-was-one-of-scientologys-biggest-donors-a-look-back/.

"Paul Haggis, Awards." IMDb. 1990–2016. http://www.imdb.com/name/nm0353673 /awards.

People. "Brooke Shields: Tom Cruise Apologized." September 2, 2006. http://www .people.com/people/article/0,,1531255,00.html.

"Priscilla Presley Net Worth." Accessed February 28, 2016. http://www.celebritynet worth.com/richest-celebrities/actors/priscilla-presley-net-worth/.

Psychology Debunked. "War of the Worlds: Tom Cruise vs. Psychiatry." July 17, 2005. http://www.psychologydebunked.com/email0507_War%20of%20the%20Worlds .html.

Reitman, Janet. *Inside Scientology: The Story of America's Most Secretive Religion*. New York: Houghton Mifflin Harcourt, 2011.

Remini, Leah, and Rebecca Paley. *Troublemaker: Surviving Hollywood and Scientology*. New York: Ballantine Books, 2015.

R. [L. Ron Hubbard]. "NN Credit." November 24, 1980.

Rojek, Chris. *Fame Attack: The Inflation of Celebrity and its Consequences*. London: Bloomsbury Academic, 2012.

Romano, Lois. "The Reliable Source." *Washington Post*. August 3, 1993, E3.

Ross, Rick. "Montel Williams, a Shill for Scientology?" *Cult News from Rick Ross.* March 12, 2003. http://www.cultnews.com/archives/000031.html.

Schindler, Jörg. "The Freedom of Thought of the 'Crusaders.'" *Frankfurter Rundschau.* July 27, 1997.

Scobee, Amy. *Scientology Abuse at the Top.* Puyallup, Washington: Scobee Publishing, 2010.

Scott, Jeffrey. "Angle on Awards." Kudos & Awards—Emmy-Winning Animation Screenwriter Jeffrey Scott. 2000–2010. http://www.jeffreyscott.tv/Kudos Awards.htm.

Scott, Vernon. "'Narconon Saved My Life'—Kirstie Alley." *UPI.* May 3, 1990.

Shields, Brooke. *Down Came the Rain.* New York: Hyperion, 2005.

Shields, Brooke. "War of Words." *New York Times.* July 1, 2005. http://www.nytimes .com/2005/07/01/opinion/war-of-words.html.

Social Coordination International. "Celebs Star in Drug-Free Hero Campaign." *Inroads* 5 (1986): 3.

Sonny Bono Copyright Term Extension Act, S. 505. 105th Cong. (January 27, 1998). http://www.copyright.gov/legislation/s505.pdf.

"'Tis the Season for a Scientology Party." *Wall Street Journal.* December 11, 2006.

Tobin, Thomas C. "Kirstie Alley Buys Presley Mansion." *St. Petersburg Times.* May 17, 2000. http://www.sptimes.com/News/051700/NorthPinellas/Kirstie_Alley _buys_Pr.shtml.

"Tom Cruise Net Worth." Accessed February 27, 2016. http://www.celebritynet worth.com/richest-celebrities/actors/tom-cruise-net-worth/.

"Tom Cruise's Heated Interview with Matt Lauer." YouTube video, 13:55. Posted by "Today," June 2, 2014. https://www.youtube.com/watch?v=tFgF1JPNR5E.

Trigaux, Robert. "Deeper Look at How Wall Street's Self-Dealing Led to Housing Bubble Cites Role of Clearwater Financier." *Tampa Bay Times.* August 30, 2010. http://www.tampabay.com/blogs/venturebiz/content/deeper-look-how-wall -streets-self-dealing-led-housing-bubble-cites-role-clearwater-financier.

Tufekci, Zeynep. "'Not This One': Social Movements, the Attention Economy, and Activism," *American Behavioral Scientist* 57, no. 7 (2013): 848–870.

Ulferts, Alisa. "Panel Waters Down Limits on Student Mental Services." *Tampabay. com.* April 20, 2005. http://www.sptimes.com/2005/04/20/news_pf/State/Panel _waters_down_lim.shtml.

U.S. House of Representatives. *Hearing on the Federal Drug Strategy: Prospects For the 1980's, Before the U.S. House of Representatives, Select Comm. on Narcotics Abuse and Control,* 96th Cong. (September 23, 1980). http://babel.hathitrust .org/cgi/pt?id=pst.000020611927;view=1up;seq=5.

Wachter, Kristi. "Mitchell Brisker—Scientology Service Completions." February 15, 2016. http://www.truthaboutscientology.com/stats/by-name/m/mitchellbrisker .html.

Waggoner, Dianna. "Scientology's Stars Rally against a $39 Mil Award." *People.* June 10, 1985.

Walker, Hunter. "Meet Scientology's Lobbyist Who Works the Halls of Congress for the Church." *Business Insider.* April 8, 2015. http://www.businessinsider.com /church-of-scientology-washington-lobbyist-2015-4.

Walls, Jeannette. "Tom Cruise Won't Always Have Paris." *Today*. Last modified July 13, 2005. http://www.today.com/id/8545431/ns/today-entertainment/t /tom-cruise-wont-always-have-paris/#.WFcy5yhOTdk.

Watkins, Jade. "Matt Lauer Admits to 'Cold War Period' with Tom Cruise after THAT 'Glib' Jibe and Reveals Actor Wanted Rant Removed from Air." *Daily Mail*. June 21, 2013. http://www.dailymail.co.uk/tvshowbiz/article-2345978/Matt -Lauer-admits-cold-war-period-Tom-Cruise-called-glib-infamous-interview -reveals-actor-wanted-rant-removed-air.html.

"The Way to Happiness—A Guide to Happy Living." 1995–2016. http://www.the waytohappiness.org.

WilmzBrewxs. "Brooke Shields, John Nash, and the National APA Meeting." *Ask-DrJones*. June 9, 2007. http://askdrjones.com/index.php/brooke-shields-john -nash-and-the-national-apa-meeting/.

WISE International. "WISE Welcomes New Members." *Prosperity* 34 (1994): 24.

"World Literacy Crusade—Assisting Those Who Have Trouble Learning." 1996–2016. http://www.applied scholastics.org.

Wright, Lawrence. *Going Clear: Scientology, Hollywood, & the Prison of Belief*. New York: Alfred A. Knopf, 2013.

Young, Josh. "Bill Clinton's Grand Seduction." *George*. March 1998.

6

Scientology's Celebrity Apostates

Stephen A. Kent

INTRODUCTION

Having spent so much time and energy recruiting, and then pampering, celebrities, along with pestering them for additional contributions, the last thing that Scientology officials want to happen is for celebrities to leave (and even worse, to leave and criticize). Departures, however, occur from all groups, so inevitably they occur regarding Scientology celebrities. The members who depart are variously called defectors, former or ex-members, apostates, or people who have deconverted. Conservatively, dozens of celebrities have followed this general pattern by having exited Scientology. For example, anti-Scientology activist, Tilman Hausherr, began the online list of Scientologists and former Scientologists in 1997, and his updated list has 138 celebrities with documented Scientology involvement (in varying degrees), which includes 35 documented cases of celebrity apostates. The Scientology involvement of an additional number of people (over 125) is less certain.[1]

Although the process of deconversion has received less scholarly attention than has conversion, still the literature on the topic is extensive and far too vast to summarize here. What is possible, however, is to use categories that appeared in a reference article on deconversion that appeared in print in 2015.[2] It provided a fairly comprehensive review of deconversion literature, and many aspects that it identified within scholarly literature have relevance for conceptualizing the four Scientology deconversions that I discuss in this chapter. I supplement this reference article with Heinz Streib's impressive publication on deconversion, published in 2014, which provides additional insight into the phenomenon of renouncing previously held beliefs.[3]

The definition of deconversion that Ashley Samaha and I used fits well into a discussion of deconversion among Scientology's celebrities, partly because it avoids the question of whether Scientology is a religion or some other social entity or entities. We defined deconversion as "a multidimensional process involving 'loss of specific religious experiences; intellectual doubt, denial, or disagreement with specific beliefs; moral criticism; emotional suffering; and disaffiliation from [one's previous] community.'"[4] This definition works well when discussing deconversion from Scientology, since it is sufficiently broad in scope to allow us to avoid the question, "is Scientology a religion?" The deconversion experiences that it identifies occur in any number of groups that involve community associations involving supernatural (i.e., religious) or secular beliefs.

A review of accounts from both mainstream and sectarian religions indicates that deconversion likely occurs for reasons of intellectual doubt, weakened social bonds, or moral doubt about beliefs and/or practices.[5] Following Stuart Wright's work on departing sectarian groups, a number of factors begin the deconversion process. First, reduction of social isolation occurs in relation to the outside, wider society. Second, two-person intimacy may challenge the group's demand to be the primary focus of attachment and attention. Third, people are less likely to allow intense scrutiny of one's personal life and thoughts outside of emergency or crises situations (such as millenialist expectations). Fourth, defections and deconversions increase the more that people feel their organizations are not meeting their affective, socioemotional needs. Finally, deconversions increase in the face of questions concerning leaders' moral lapses.[6]

I will return to these deconversion characteristics in the conclusion of this chapter, and I will examine the deconversion accounts of four ex-Scientologists—William Burroughs, Jason Beghe, Paul Haggis, and Leah Remini—about whom extensive evidence exists concerning their very public departures from Scientology.[7] Most departures from that organization, however, are not nearly so public with so much information available to analyze, so the earlier part of this chapter is a summary of various deconversion accounts or events that I will leave to others to analyze.

QUIET OR PRAISEWORTHY DEPARTURES

Examples exist of celebrities who tried Scientology for a while, took some courses, but then gradually drifted away to something else. Critic and social commentator, Aldous Huxley (1894–1963), for instance, tried using Dianetics to recall his past, especially in relation to his father, but achieved little success. He commented privately in correspondence about his failure with Dianetics, then offered some observations about L. Ron Hubbard. He never made these comments publicly, however, and simply moved along to another personal development system.[8] Actor Patrick Swayze (1952–2009) tried Scientology among other belief systems, trying to make sense out of his father's death. It is not clear if Swayze found what he was looking for, but if he did, then it was not in Scientology, since he left it not long after he tried it.[9] In 2007, actor Jeffrey Tambor (b. 1944) announced, "I have nothing against it, but I am no longer a Scientologist."[10] Scientology may attempt to win back celebrities such as these, but as long as they do not criticize the organization, the celebrities probably will not have any aggressive or intrusive actions taken against themselves.

Comedian Jerry Seinfeld (b. 1954) used a different departure strategy: he praised what Scientology courses taught him about communication:

> I last really studied, oh, it's almost 30 years ago. But what I did do, I really liked, in terms of it's very . . . it was interesting. Believe it or not . . . it's extremely intellectual and clinical in its approach to problem-solving, which really appealed to me. . . . In my early years of stand-up, it was very helpful. I took a couple of courses. One of them was in communication, and I learned some things about communication that really got my act going.
>
> It was just things about understanding the communications cycle . . . Even the volume at which I'm speaking now is the right volume for where you're sitting. I'm almost performing, in a way.
>
> You would just understand that there's this kind of voice, and then there's this kind of voice, and then there's this kind of voice. I wasn't a natural performer at all, so I learned. I was always a pretty good writer in the beginning, but I really had to learn how to perform. Just a little thing like that, understanding that really helped me on stage to understand how you have to invade the space of the audience a little bit. I learned that early on. It was a very helpful thing to learn. You have to invade them just a little bit. Not too much, because then it's obnoxious. But you can't be short of them either, or you won't control them.
>
> They have a lot of very good technology. That's what really appealed to me about it. It's not faith-based. It's all technology. And I'm obsessed with technology.[11]

While Scientology officials may not have liked his conclusion that their ideology was "not faith-based," Seinfeld's comments about what he gained were positive, even if he did not give a reason for his departure.

SOME CRITICAL CELEBRITY APOSTATES

Negative comments about Scientology, however, by apostate Scientology celebrities were common. Among the more unique departure statements came from songwriter and singer Lisa Marie Presley (b. 1968). She buried her departure notice in music lyrics on an album, *Storm and Grace*, in May 2012. In her song, "You Ain't Seen Nothin' Yet," she used some terms about herself that have negative meanings inside of the organization, clearly implying that now she was out of it. In the song, she identified herself as "suppressive," which is a term that Scientology uses to designate perceived opponents, and then she indicated, "Well, you ain't seen nothin' yet."[12] The lyrics imply that Presley had Scientology handlers who controlled all aspects of her life. As she figured out that they were limiting what she saw and heard, the handlers' response to her growing independence was that she was becoming evil and a Suppressive Person—an enemy to the Church. Her misbehaving, however, against Scientology's constraints only has just begun.[13] A cryptic denunciation may have been safer for her, since anything that might have her declared as a Suppressive Person would cost her all contact with her mother, who is still a member. Her departure received widespread coverage on the Internet, but it seems not to have caused major damage to the organization. (A recent report, however, indicates that she now is working behind the scenes to discredit David Miscavige, so any assessment of the damage that her departure has caused may be premature.)[14]

A FEW LOUDLY CRITICAL CELEBRITY APOSTATES

William S. Burroughs

Another critical apostate whose impact is difficult to gauge with certainty is that of the American writer, drug user, and counterculture figure, William S. Burroughs (1914–1997), although Scientology's reaction to his apostasy suggests that organizational leaders worried about damage that it might have caused. Known among the Beat generation for his dramatic and disturbing portrayals of the drug culture, Burroughs counted among his friends such Beat elites as Allen Ginsberg, Neal Cassady, and Jack Kerouac. While in Tangiers, Morocco, in the autumn of 1959, Burroughs first learned basic Dianetics and Scientology principles from a friend and probably read *Dianetics* during this time.[15] He did not begin auditing, however, until September 1967, when he was not far from Scientology's British headquarters at Saint Hill, East Grinstead.[16] He found auditing to be a powerful procedure, immensely more effective in recalling a traumatic childhood incident than psychoanalysis.[17] Wanting more Scientology, he began taking courses, first in London, then (in January 1968) at Saint Hill Manor.[18] On May 30, 1968, Scientology opened an Advanced Org in Edinburgh, Scotland, and Burroughs (who had been to the city before and liked it) transferred to the new facility. Remarkably, he went Clear on June 15, 1968, after eighty hours of auditing.[19] Undoubtedly because of his notoriety, this achievement was an important occasion for Scientologists, who ran nearly a full-page report about "the internationally famous American author," who was "Clear 1163," in one of its magazines distributed to members.[20] About the state he had achieved, Burroughs enthused, "It feels marvelous! Things you've had all your life, things you think nothing can be done about—suddenly they're not there any more!"[21]

What Burroughs failed to reveal, however, in his enthusiastic Clear exclamations was that he had developed concerns about Scientology's founder, L. Ron Hubbard, even though the two never met. He took note, for example, of the fact that so many Scientology women sexually idolized him in their dreams. Burroughs felt that Hubbard was not discouraging such fantasies because he was building an authoritarian personality cult around himself. He also reacted against Hubbard's view of persons who were outside Scientology, which he called WOGS (a derogatory, colonialist term meaning "Worthy Oriental Gentleman").[22]

Before taking various courses, Burroughs had to undergo routine security (or sec) checks, which Scientology leaders believed would uncover any negative attitudes or actions in people's lives that might hurt the organization.[23] Burroughs hated these checks, thinking that they smacked of authoritarian, thought-police intrusions. We only know the name of one of the sec checks that he underwent (and I will return to it in a moment), but a basic one had existed since 1961 and was called "The Only Valid Security Check." While hooked up to an E-Meter acting in the capacity of a crude lie detector, a person answered 174 questions on everything from criminal behavior to sexual practices. Given Burroughs's lifestyle as a drug-using, pro-Communist, misogynist, homosexual who accidentally killed his wife,[24] it is impossible to imagine how he ever would have gotten through it. Questions included ones like: "Have you ever been a drug addict?"; "Have you ever practised Homosexuality?"; and "Do you feel Communism has some good points?" These and other lifestyle questions were ones that Burroughs would have found intrusive, just as he would have felt toward the "thought crimes" questions like, "Have you ever had any unkind thoughts about L. Ron Hubbard?" and a parallel question about Hubbard's wife, Mary Sue Hubbard.[25] (Keep in mind that Burroughs used to use pictures of Hubbard as targets when he practiced shooting his air pistol.[26]) Scientologists working with Burroughs thought he harbored unkind thoughts toward Hubbard, so they required him to undergo the Johannesburg (or Jo'burg) Security Check, which took him three weeks and eighty hours of auditing to complete.[27] (The fact that Burroughs passed these security checks speaks volumes about how inaccurate they were.) He went Clear but, shortly thereafter, Burroughs left formal Scientology training, never to take classes or courses on it again. His disdain for sec checks were major factors in his decision to leave Scientology, even though he remained impressed with auditing.

Even before Burroughs began courses in 1967, he had been writing columns about the group and its practices for the men's magazine, *Mayfair*. Over the years, much that he wrote about Scientology was positive, even at times being more complimentary to the group and its techniques in print than he was in private correspondence. In any case, after he departed the formal organization, Burroughs continued writing for *Mayfair*, and some of his articles included his reports about experimenting with some of the Scientology techniques he had learned while he was a formal student. From, however, the viewpoint of Scientology's leaders, Burroughs was practicing Scientology outside of the group's control and altering the technology through his experiments. He was using some Scientology concepts and techniques with people who were not taking appropriate Scientology courses inside an authorized Scientology facility. These actions caught up with him on January 27, 1969, when Scientology issued a *Hubbard Communications Office Ethic Order* placing him in a condition of Treason, barring him from all Scientology facilities and preventing him from taking further courses.[28] Even still, some of his writings about Scientology later that year remained complimentary, especially about the E-Meter.[29]

The content and tone of those writings turned in a decidedly critical direction in late 1969, when Burroughs realized "that his work was responsible for introducing young people to what he could now see was a cult."[30] His essay to them came out in January 1970, first in an underground paper, then in *Mayfair*, and finally (in March) in the *Los Angeles Free Press*. In 1972, Burroughs republished the essay, this time bundling it with five other writings critical of the organization.[31]

The first two paragraphs of the essay provide much insight into Burroughs's criticisms of Scientology. He addressed his essay directly to youth in the counterculture:

> In view of the fact that my article and statements on Scientology may have influenced young people to associate themselves with the so called Church of Scientology, I feel an obligation to make my present view on the subject quite clear.
>
> Some of the techniques are highly valuable and warrant further study and experimentation. The E Meter is a useful device . . . (many variations of this instrument are possible). On the other hand I am in flat disagreement with the organizational policy. Organizational policy can only impede the advancement of knowledge. There is a basic incompatibility between any organization and freedom of thought. . . .

It is precisely organizational necessities that have prevented Scientology from obtaining the serious consideration merited by the importance of Mr. Hubbard's discoveries. Scientologists are not prepared to accept intelligent and sometimes critical evaluation. They demand unquestioning acceptance.[32]

Burroughs was objecting to the fact that the organization controlled the release of Hubbard's knowledge by requiring that people acquire it only by enrolling in (often expensive) courses presented by the organization itself, then passing through an intrusive, peculiar, and expensive sec check. He believed that Scientologists should welcome opportunities for researchers and other non-Scientology bodies to investigate the scientific examination of the techniques.

Burroughs's own morally libertarian, pro-Communist views were obvious in the next set of criticisms, specifically against Hubbard, whom he had never liked:

Mr. Hubbard's overtly fascist utterances (China is the real threat to world peace, Scientology is protecting the home, the church, the family, decent morals . . . positively no wife swapping. It's a dirty Communist trick . . . national boundaries, the concepts if RIGHT and WRONG against evil free thinking psychiatrist[s]) can hardly recommend him to the militant students. Certainly it is time for the Scientologists to come out in plain English on one side or the other, if they expect the trust and support of young people. Which side are you on Hubbard, which side are you on?[33]

While Burroughs did not try answering the question for him, obviously he would have located Hubbard with society's conservative Establishment, since he was creating a cult of personality around himself instead of leading a movement advocating fundamental structural and social change.[34]

Three prominent Scientologists responded to Burroughs, including Hubbard himself. All three responses were surprisingly subdued, almost completely avoiding any personal attacks against the apostate writer himself. The first response came at the end of March 1970 from Gordon Mustain, who was the Deputy Guardian for Public Relations, U.S. Churches of Scientology. He went about responding systematically:

Your objections to Scientology appear to be twofold; first, that it is administered via an organization; and secondly, that what you consider to be Mr. Hubbard's political viewpoint differs considerably from your own.[35]

Mustain then proceeded with a fairly systematic response, a substantial portion of which was a sustained attack against psychiatry.

Mustain defended the dissemination of Scientology through an organization by arguing for its necessity. Axioms, he indicated, formed the bases of Scientology philosophy, and the group's technology provided the means through which the philosophy disseminated. Mustain's implication was that organizational policy facilitated the systematic application of the technology. Burroughs had called for the free dissemination of Scientology's insights to young people,[36] but Mustain replied that he himself had once been a hippy desiring the expansion of consciousness but saw the hippies' failure to attain that expansion because of their use of drugs, especially hallucinogens. His hippie phase "ended in frustration and disillusionment."[37] Scientology, however, succeeded where the counterculture failed:

> But I found Scientology a workable way of getting my head straight and helping others get theirs straight, and I found a group of people working towards the same goals (freedom, peace, spiritual awareness, tolerance, and elimination of double think) that I had been working towards for years.[38]

In essence, Mustain had turned around Burroughs's fantasized hope that free-thinking hippies could receive and develop Scientology without the confines of Scientology's organizational structures and their restrictions.

On a different topic, Burroughs had raised the issue about why Scientology was so vehemently opposed to psychiatry, and Mustain offered a fairly typical array of reputed facts and anecdotes against the profession. They included alleged examples of inappropriate psychiatric hospitalization, high psychiatric deaths, and harmful psychiatric treatments.[39] The second Scientologist to reply to Burroughs, Hubbard's wife Mary Sue Hubbard (1931–2002, married to LRH 1952–1986), extended Scientology's criticism of the psychiatric profession. Concisely, she summarized what she thought the difference were between psychiatry and Scientology:

> Scientology wants protections for the individual against easy seizure; established psychiatry want easy seizure without due process of law. Scientology wants an end to treatments which are harmful ant not effective; established psychiatry says it can not do without them. The intention of Scientology is to bring about reforms in psychiatry, but the intention of psychiatry is completely to suppress Scientology as evidenced.[40]

As portrayed by Mary Sue Hubbard, therefore, Scientology was a group defending individual rights, but the Establishment had refused to take from it even its generous offers of help and improvement regarding a host of social and personal issues.[41] Indeed, because of the way that the Establishment (including the press) treated Scientology, Mary Sue Hubbard concluded that "at the moment we are the niggers of the press."[42] Hubbard, who was on his ship, the *Apollo*, at the time this article appeared, informed his shipmates that "MSH has just had a hard hitting article by her published in the British *Mayfair*."[43]

A careful read, however, of L. Ron Hubbard's response to Burroughs, in the context of developments during that period within Scientology itself, brings forth a different perspective on the group, one whose intent focused upon psychiatry's elimination:

> The psychiatric efforts to get rid of a dangerous competitor [i.e., Scientology] is having the effect of forcing the Scientologist to handle government influences and reorganize to take over the entire field of mental healing. The Scientologist never would have dreamed of this. For years he acted with full regard for spheres of influence. He turned away both the physically ill and the insane.[44]

In contrast, therefore, to Mary Sue Hubbard's statement that Scientology was a psychiatric reformist movement, LRH indicated that Scientology was a take-all competitor, with the assumption that a victorious Scientology would replace psychiatry with its own techniques.

Hubbard's offering turns out to be the more accurate of the two interpretations. On November 29, 1968, which was prior to his response to Burroughs, Hubbard had issued an Executive Directive entitled, "The War," in which he outlined his vision of the national and international effort by psychiatry to destroy Scientology. Now Scientology, Hubbard proclaimed, was fighting back. Moreover, "[o]ur error was in failing to take over total control of all mental healing in the West. Well, we'll do that too."[45] Then again in December 2, 1969, an unidentified author, which had to be Hubbard himself, composed (on legal-length paper) a five-page document "[w]ritten for the Guardian and her offices." Mary Sue Hubbard was the person who ran the Guardian Office, and only Hubbard was above her. Under the subtitle, "The War," the document announced:

> Our war has been forced to become "to take over absolutely the field of mental healing on this planet in all forms."
> That was not the original purpose. The original purpose was to clear Earth. The battles suffered developed the data that we had an enemy who would have to be gotten out of the way and this meant we were at war.[46]

Hubbard alluded to this war in his response to Burroughs, although he greatly turned down its intensity. Mary Sue Hubbard also knew of this war but veered away from even alluding to it in her response to Burroughs. Burroughs likely had no idea of the ferocity of Hubbard's antipathy to psychiatry and therefore did not appreciate how deep and pervasive the organization's hostility to psychiatry was.

The three Scientologists made other claims about Scientology in an attempt to refute Burroughs while not alienating him further. (After all, he had said that much of the technology, such as auditing, worked.) Hubbard claimed, for example, that Scientology had abolished the security checks that Burroughs hated so much,[47] when in fact they remained in the repertoire of Scientology technology. By 1975 they would reappear as "confessionals,"[48] then again in 1978 as "confessionals" and "Integrity processing."[49] Beyond, however, individual statements with which one might quarrel, what remains striking about all three of the Scientology responses is how respectful they were toward Burroughs. Mustain ended his response with an invitation: "This is the other side of the coin. When you've looked it over, if you wish to pursue it further, write. I'd be interested in seeing your comments." Mary Sue Hubbard ended her essay with a comment about the center based around his revolutionary ideas that Burroughs had hoped to establish:[50]

> Maybe, Mr. Burroughs, you are a catalyst for just such a centre as you envision. Certainly the benefit to mankind of such researches into man's inner awareness would be greater than the doubtful good of man's current space programmes and much less costly.[51]

Admittedly this statement was not effusive, but it did provide some faint praise to one of Burroughs's dreams.

The tone of L. Ron Hubbard's response to Burroughs also was polite, almost to the point of being deferential. This politeness was surprising in light of what Hubbard had written a decade earlier about how to respond to critics:

> If attacked on some vulnerable point by anyone or anything or any organization, ALWAYS FIND OR MANUFACTURE ENOUGH THREAT AGAINST THEM TO CAUSE THEM TO SUE FOR PEACE. Peace is brought with an advantage, so make the advantage and then settle. Don't ever defend. Always attack. Don't ever do nothing. Unexpected attacks in the rear of the enemy's front ranks work best.[52]

In short, Hubbard told his followers to attack a Scientology attacker sufficiently hard to make them desist with their criticisms.

In light of this policy, one might expect that Burroughs's critical essay about Hubbard and his creation, containing references to "Hubbard's overtly fascist utterances"[53] and "his grandiose claims"[54] might have evoked Hubbard's ire. Instead, near the beginning of his response, Hubbard announced, "I am hardly likely to attack a man for whom I have great respect. He is perfectly entitled to his views as to express them."[55] He then ended his essay by concluding:

> As a famous celebrity, a pal of mine for years, once said, "If only people would criticize more and honestly and to the point! I feel when they don't they are not my friends."
>
> So I count William Burroughs as a friend of mine. Whatever he writes he is trying to make things right, just like the Scientologists.[56]

Rather than criticize Burroughs or attack his character, Hubbard seems to have praised him! The note about his response, however, that Hubbard sent to his *Apollo* shipmates had a somewhat different tone:

> *Mayfair* magazine UK published an article by me as a "World Exclusive." It may effectively handle a lot of things. It ended off the William Burroughs thing. It said why we're attacked and attacks hard. It appeared on the stands just before Parliament adjourned. Captain AOUK [Advanced Organization, United Kingdom] said it acted like an S & D [search and discovery of Suppressive Persons] on the crew there.[57]

Despite what Hubbard implied, the exchange was not quite over.

Whether this praise reflected Hubbard's professional esteem for another writer we do not know, but it had a positive effect on Burroughs. He had the last word in the debate, and he used it to support Hubbard's critical positions on the mass media and generally to agree with him about the poor quality of most psychiatrists. He implied, however, the current problems were a greater fault than what psychiatrists have claimed; the entire Establishment was unworkable. He did not offer any more directed criticisms of Scientology.[58] Although for years afterward, aspects of Scientology appeared in Burroughs's writings, "[i]n the final years, Burroughs appeared to think a great deal about Scientology, although he had absolutely nothing positive to say."[59]

It is impossible to gauge how much influence Burroughs had on potential young converts, either initially as a catalyst to conversion, then later
as a dissuader to the same generation. His writings in a men's magazine
would have reached a very small (and probably disinterested) audience but
so would the three Scientology rebuttals to Burroughs and his criticisms.
The entire debate took place before the advent of the Internet, although
much of it now is retrievable through persistent searching. He was a prominent writer, so people recognized his name, but his literature was sufficiently
avant-garde that his work was an acquired taste. After Burroughs, no other
high-profile celebrity defections from Scientology took place until the new
century, but thus far the departures of three of them have been loud and
consequential.

Jason Beghe

By the close of the first decade of this second millennium, the Internet had
become a major media vehicle for the dissemination of accounts about loud
and critical Scientology celebrity defections. Hollywood actor Jason Beghe
was the first to fully exploit it. Like so many others, Beghe joined Scientology
through Milton Katselas's acting class. He read a critical newspaper article
about what Scientologists were like, but it did not resonate with the respect he
had for his acting teacher, whom he had heard was a Scientologist. He asked
two Scientologists in his class, Bodhi Elfman and Mary Thompson, about Scientology, and Mary gave him a copy of *What Is Scientology?* Impressed by what
he read, he mentioned this impression to Elfman, who then took him over to
the Celebrity Centre. Almost immediately he signed up for the two courses,
and within his first 13 months had taken over 14 courses and services.[60]

Beghe continued his rapid rise through the courses, auditing himself
through OT III in 1997 and attesting to OT V in 2003.[61] He also had gone
Clear in 1995, which he described:

> Here's what it's like to be Clear. Say you're born with a big heavy bag
> and you have been carrying it around on your back for your entire life.
>
> Because you are born with it, you don't know anything is wrong—it's
> just part of life. You think it is normal to have this big, heavy thing
> that's like a 50 lb. back-pack with you all the time.
>
> Now you get into Scientology and all of a sudden you start to lighten
> the load. The more you go up The Bridge, the more weight you take out
> of the bag. When you finally go clear, it's hard to imagine how you have
> lived with that huge weight on your back all that time.[62]

If one were to speculate about what was in Beghe's personal, heavy back-pack that he carried around for years and believed it was normal, then one might offer that it had to do with anger. When asked, for example, about whether any similarities existed between himself and a police character that he played on television, Beghe answered, "I have a bad temper and I'm rash."[63] Likewise, in a letter sent by a Church of Scientology International official (Karen Pouw) to Andy Greene, who was the associate editor of *Rolling Stone* magazine (in an attempt to convince the magazine not to use Beghe as a source), Pouw stated, "for background, Jason Beghe first came to us for help with his anger management issues in 1994. . . . When he left the Church, he blamed it for his inability to control his lifelong hair-trigger temper."[64] It seems that Scientology courses did not alleviate his anger problem, since he pleaded *nolo contende* [no contest] to a criminal misdemeanor assault charge involving a process server (Javier Hernandez) whom he struck. Beghe's version of the incident was that he "touched him because he refused to leave my property. I used remarkable restraint, frankly."[65] The lawsuit, however, described the incident differently:

> Beghe became enraged, and ran down the driveway after Mr. Hernandez. Beghe reached him and struck Mr. Hernandez in the back of his head with his hand or fist, knocking Mr. Hernandez' [sic] phone out of his hand onto the ground. Beghe repeatedly punched Mr. Hernandez in the back including "kidney punches" and on the back of his head as he tried to escape.[66]

Initially demanding $1 million, the case settled with Beghe paying Hernandez $16,500 and $2,500 to Hernandez's girlfriend who was with him on the day of the assault.[67]

Several (but not necessarily contradictory) accounts exist about how and why Beghe turned against Scientology. Putting together these accounts, it seems that his initial experience with Scientology was positive and represented by the quotes that he gave in *Celebrity* magazine articles about him. His doubts about Scientology may have begun before taking a series of courses called L11 and L12 in 1996. In order to take them, Beghe underwent the False Purpose Rundown, which is similar to a security check in that it probes into one's life looking for incidents holding oneself back from advancement but that one had not recalled previously. Beghe claimed that for weeks (at $1,000 an hour) he was grilled in sessions lasting up to six hours, looking of incidents that he was withholding. There were none showing up, which drove disbelieving auditors to dig even more. Finally his auditors allowed him to take the two L courses, the first of which was supposed to empower the person by removing one's "implant to harm."[68]

Consequently, both Beghe and other Scientologists were perplexed when, in 1999, he was in a life-threatening car accident—something that should not have happened at his level of advancement. Scientologists set out to find the accident's cause and eventually concluded that it was because Beghe had a homosexual friend.[69] This quest to find someone associated with Beghe who was harming ("suppressing") the reputedly empowering effects of Scientology's powers may explain why Beghe completed two PTS/SP [Potential Trouble Source/Suppressive Person] courses, one in 2000 and the other in 2002.[70] In any case, his doubts about Scientology likely began with this explanation.[71] By now, his Scientology training was going badly, taking him three to five years to attain OT V when it only should have taken him three to five weeks.[72]

He married in 2000 a woman who also was in Scientology and who delivered their first child in a silent birth.[73] Upon learning that he was going to be a father, Beghe took an inventory of his life and "'realized that Scientology wasn't me."[74] He and his wife both left, but it took him about a year to disconnect from the organization. He was out by about August 2007.[75] Looking back on the Scientology courses and the promises attached to them, he realized that "it's all magical thinking."[76] The more courses and auditing he took, the more harm he believed they did, partly because they were brainwashing him to think like Hubbard.[77]

Details and dates around his departure and subsequent public criticisms are somewhat jumbled. Probably among Beghe's earliest attempts to get assistance with his departure took place when he contacted Andreas Heldal-Lund (b. 1964), a Norwegian man who ran the critical anti-Scientology website, Operation Clambake (xenu.net). Apparently Heldal-Lund put Beghe in touch with Scientology critic and videographer, Mark Bunker, who taped over two hours of an interview with Beghe three months after he had left, which Bunker posted on the Internet in early June 2008. In addition, Beghe was in touch with a local Los Angeles former Scientologist, Tory Christman (b. 1947), who in turn put him in touch with anti-Scientology Internet reporter, Tony Ortega (b. 1963), who subsequently posted articles about him. Beghe's basic allegation against Scientology is that auditing made him (and, he was sure, others) worse, not better. In essence, Beghe had concluded that none of Scientology's most basic services worked—they were simply part of a fraud. Neither Clears nor OTs gained any special powers. Homosexuals were not degraded beings, but he felt that too many Scientologists believed they were. Moreover, freeing himself from Scientology meant that the constant demand for money also stopped, as did the need to undergo irritating security tests before taking upper-level material. In late summer 2008, Beghe traveled to Germany and spoke to Hamburg officials and others about his experiences and concerns, claiming that private investigators followed him throughout the trip.[78]

Paul Haggis

According to author Lawrence Wright, Beghe answered an audition call in the summer of 2009 for a film that Paul Haggis (b. 1953) was casting. Beghe informed Haggis about his departure from Scientology (expecting that Haggis would reject him as a suppressive person), but Haggis insisted that he alone made casting decisions. Beghe told Haggis about his denunciation of Scientology on the Internet, and subsequently Haggis watched it, then contacted Beghe for a meeting because he, too, had some questions about Scientology policies, practices, and beliefs. In the meeting, Beghe shared with Haggis that in the late 1990s, he was having emotional problems, which Scientology courses and auditing only made worse. He felt that these courses and auditing installed Hubbard's "ways of looking at things," making one into "You the Scientologist" at the expense of you the person.[79] Beghe especially disturbed Haggis when he told the director what had happened to him after leaving: "he claimed that none of his Scientology friends would talk to him, his son had been kicked out of school, [and] he was being followed by private investigators and threatened with lawsuits."[80]

By the time Beghe and Haggis met in 2011, Haggis had been a Scientologist for around 36 years, having first become involved in 1975 while he still was living in Ontario, Canada. He visited Los Angeles in 1976, during which time he took sufficient courses to go Clear, moved back to Ontario in 1977 for a brief period, then returned (with his wife at the time) to Los Angeles.[81] By the early 1980s he had progressed up the Bridge to OT VII where he remained, [82] although subsequently he did the Purification Rundown some time prior to 1986. When interviewed in *Celebrity* magazine in 1986, he heaped praise on the Purification Rundown, indicating:

> I found I could think a lot more clearly. Getting rid of all those residual toxins and medicines and drugs really had an effect. . . . But the big benefit was mental rather than physical. I really did feel more alert and more aware and more at ease—I wasn't running in six directions to get something done, or bouncing off walls when something went wrong. I was able to calmly hold a position, look at a problem and then go about handling it.[83]

In turn, he recommended the rundown to a highly emotional colleague who was on several prescriptions, and with her doctor's permission she stopped her medications and began the purification program. Haggis reported that, upon her completion, "if you met her today you wouldn't know she was the same person. She's lucid and stable and funnier than ever. If she hadn't done the program, I doubt she'd be working right now. . . ."[84]

Interestingly, Haggis did not reveal in his *Celebrity* interview that he was never able to read much of Hubbard's foundational book, *Dianetics*, having found it "impenetrable" after about the first 30 pages.[85] Equally serious was his reaction to the OT III story. As reported by Lawrence Wright:

> Carrying an empty, locked, briefcase, Haggis went to the Advanced Organization building in Los Angeles where the [OT] material was held. A supervisor then handed him a folder, which Haggis put on a briefcase. He entered a study room, where he finally got to examine the secret document—a couple of pages, in Hubbard's bold scrawl. After a few minutes, he returned to the supervisor.
>
> "I don't understand," Haggis said.
>
> "Do you know the words?" the supervisor asked.
>
> "I know the words, I just don't understand."
>
> "Go back and read it again."
>
> Haggis did so. In a moment, he returned. "Is this a metaphor?" he asked the supervisor.
>
> "No," the supervisor responded. "It is what it is. Do the actions that are required."
>
> Maybe it's an insanity test, Haggis thought—if you believe it, you're automatically kicked out. "I sat with that for a while," he says. But when he read it again he decided, "This is madness."[86]

Even though Haggis had a visceral reaction against this seminal Scientology document, he overlooked it. We do not know if Haggis shared these problems when he met with Beghe, whose own issues with Scientology included auditing and courses that, he concluded, simply did not work.

This meeting between Beghe and Haggis took place six or seven months after Haggis's troubles with Scientology had begun. In November 2008, California passed an antigay marriage vote (Proposition 8), and one of Haggis's two gay daughters informed him that Scientology's Church of San Diego had endorsed it publically. Incensed at what he saw as an egregious stand against human rights, Haggis shot off an e-mail to Scientology spokesperson Tommy Davis (b. 1972), demanding that the organization make a public declaration supporting gay rights. On a number of grounds, Davis refused, saying that the lone Scientologist who had made the endorsement had been disciplined, and, anyway, the endorsement had attracted almost no public attention. In the last e-mail on this issue that Haggis sent to Davis in February 2009, Haggis insisted that the issue was "not a P.R. issue, it is a moral issue" about which Scientology shamed itself.[87] Beghe, of course, held similar views, objecting to his Scientology assistant's attempt to blame his car accident on his association with a gay friend.

The issues that Haggis harbored grew exponentially after—for the first time in his life—he began searching the Internet (after e-mail communication with Davis broke down) for Scientology information. Among the issues troubling Haggis was his discovery that Scientology spokesperson, Tommy Davis, had lied to a reporter about a policy known as disconnection. Disconnection required members to cease communication with—to disconnect from—people whom Scientology leaders deemed to be threats to "keeping Scientology working" by their engagement in actions such as criticizing, doubting, or opposing the organization and/or its leaders.[88] Davis denied the policy's existence; less than a year earlier (2007), however, Haggis's wife had to disconnect from her parents for the second time.[89]

More distressing Internet discoveries followed. Haggis found a lengthy investigative report on alleged violence within the Sea Org., much of it reputedly committed by the chairman of the board and current Scientology head, David Miscavige (b. 1960). Based upon accounts by formerly high-ranking executives—Marty Rathbun, Mike Rinder, Tom De Vocht, and Amy Scobee—reporters Joe Childs and Thomas C. Tobin of the *Tampa Bay Times* uncovered a culture of violence infusing the Sea Org and originating from the very top. "Physical violence permeated Scientology's international management team. Miscavige set the tone, routinely attacking his lieutenants. Rinder says the leader attacked him some 50 times."[90] More distressing was his discovery (probably from Jenna Miscavige Hill's Ex-Scientology Kids website) that some very young teens and preteen children had signed billion year contracts as they worked in the Sea Org. He unloaded on Wright that "'They were ten years old, twelve years old, signing billion-year contracts—and their parents went along with this? . . . Scrubbing pots, manual labor—that so deeply touched me. My God, it horrified me!' The stories of the Sea Org children reminded Haggis of the child slaves in Haiti."[91] Wright concluded his discussion of Haggis's reaction to children signing billion year contracts by saying, "in what seemed like a very unguarded comment, he said, 'I would gladly bring down the church for this one thing.'"[92]

On August 19, 2009, roughly six months after the conclusion of Haggis's e-mails to Davis about getting Scientology to make a firm statement defending homosexuality, Haggis wrote to him again, this time to resign from the organization. His cited four reasons for doing so. The first reason was his disapproval of Scientology's unwillingness to issue a statement that would have supported homosexuality as being a key element of human rights. The second reason related to Davis's denial of a policy on disconnection. Third, he stated that the violent atmosphere within the Sea Org indicated "serious, indefensible human and civil rights violations." Fourth, he was outraged that Scientology most certainly used material from one of the critic's supposedly confidential confessional files as part of the organization's attempt to discredit her through character assassination. At the end of the letter, Haggis concluded that he "could no longer be a part of this group," and resigned from it.[93]

A few days after sending the letter, Haggis found a group of Scientologists on his front lawn, intending to talk him into reconsidering his resignation. Celebrities in the group included Anne Archer and her producer/husband, Terry Jastrow, Emmy-winning composer Mark Isham, Earthlink founder Sky Dayton, and several people he did not know.[94] Haggis listened to their arguments but was not swayed from his decision. He did agree, however, not to distribute his letter further.[95] Ex-Scientology official Marty Rathbun, however, already had a copy, and two months later he asked Haggis if he could publish it on his blog. Haggis did not try to prevent him from doing so. Subsequently Rathbun's blog site received 51,000 hits in one afternoon, and reporters were attempting to reach Haggis from around the world. One reporter who did reach him was *New Yorker* writer and author Lawrence Wright, who subsequently presented a two-part article in the magazine in February 2011. That magazine article became the basis for a book, *Going Clear*, in 2013, and the book in turn provided the impetus for Alex Gibney's 2015 investigative report, *Going Clear: Scientology and the Prison of Belief*.[96] Jason Beghe and especially Paul Haggis played prominent roles in the documentary.

Leah Remini

Almost all that we know about actor Leah Remini's involvement in, and break with, Scientology comes from her 2015 autobiography, *Troublemaker: Surviving Hollywood and Scientology*. Although the book is skimpy on dates of events, it nevertheless provides an interesting story of a celebrity who increasingly grew to be at odds with Scientology's two most powerful figures, David Miscavige and Tom Cruise, and the organizational behaviors and policies that reinforced their statuses. Once having broken with the organization, Remini's displeasure with it both broadened and deepened, to the point that she reached a near total rejection of it as a group offering anything of value.

In the beginning, however, her feelings about Scientology were very different. With a verbally, emotionally, and psychologically abusive father leaving Remini's mother when Leah was still a child (around 11 years old[97]), her mother joined Scientology in New York City, hoping to make a better life for herself.[98] Soon Leah and her sister were making the trip to the New York org from their New Jersey home and began taking courses—the Training Routines, the Success Through Communications course, and Scientology Life Improvement courses.[99] While taking these courses, Remini recorded the first of several observations she would make about Scientologist children—that children as young as seven years old were auditing.[100]

As still a child herself—one suspects that she was in very early teens—being a Scientologist meant a great deal to Remini, a girl who previously felt that she had never fit in with her peers.[101] For a poor child who never felt like she fit in, participation in Scientology gave Remini a sense of specialness—she said superiority—that probably goes a long way toward explaining why, over the years, she witnessed and experienced aspects of the organization that disturbed her but that she put out of her mind. It was far easier for her to concentrate on what she felt worked for her life than to explore issues that might have shattered that comfort.

Again, Remini frustrates by not giving dates, but sometime during her late adolescence and early teens, she, her sister, and her mother moved to the large Scientology facility in Clearwater, Florida, where she and her mother both signed Sea Org's billion year contracts.[102] She then entered the Estates Project Force, which she described as something like a boot camp for Sea Org. It involved doing hard labor for 12 hours a day—projects "like pulling up tree roots with bare hands, working heavy machinery on the grounds of [Scientology property], or cleaning bathrooms and hotel rooms."[103] In addition, for two-and-a-half hours a day, they studied Sea Org policies and procedures. [104] During Remini's training at the Fort Harrison Hotel, a Sea Org official caught her sitting in a public area where paying guests were, and for this infraction a senior Sea Org member took her out into the harbor and threw her overboard.[105] The sheer inappropriateness of this action, especially against a young teen, never seemed to strike the minds of any of the parties involved or Remini's family, partly because the Sea Org member justified his action by citing an L. Ron Hubbard policy.[106]

Something involving children that did bother the young Remini when she saw it was the condition of the children's nursery:

> The first time I went to the nursery I was devastated by what I found. The person in charge was a kid like me, just some random teenage Sea Org member on post, who was hardly qualified to be taking care

of children. [Remini's younger sister] Shannon was crying and soaked with urine in her crib. Before changing her and returning to my post, I vowed I wouldn't let her grow up this way. The neglect was overwhelming. I would immediately demand that the person on post clean up and change the babies.[107]

Remini told her mother about the conditions, and the mother tried but failed to use appropriate organizational structures to get conditions approved. In Remini's autobiography, the conditions of the children's nursery were the first issues involving Scientology that "really weighed on me. Though I was buying into the program, it raised a question inside me. While I didn't care so much about me, I wondered if we were doing right by this baby."[108] The family's dilemma, however, was that they had nowhere else to go.[109]

Out of the Estates Project Force and into the Sea Org, Remini worked 14-hour days, staying awake by smoking cigarettes and drinking coffee but rarely attending the eighth grade (probably meaning that she was between 12 and 14 years old).[110] Not long into her Sea Org career, however, someone wrote up Remini for having engaged in premarital sex with a boy. (Her boyfriend had lightly touched her breasts over her clothes.) For this transgression of Scientology policy about sex, Remini was facing assignment to the Rehabilitation Project Force (RPF). She had a good idea what the RPF was, since often she had seen people on it working around the Fort Harrison:

In 110-degree Florida heat and humidity, these men, women, and even children were forced to wear all black from head to toe as they did heavy MEST work (MEST is an acronym for matter, energy, space, and time) like cleaning grease traps in the kitchen or scrubbing dumpsters. And that wasn't all they had to do for their "spiritual rehabilitation." They also had to run everywhere they went—to the bathroom, to the galley, anywhere. They had virtually no liberties. As long as they were in the RPF they worked pretty much seven days a week, 365 days a year, and that's not including all the time spent doing security checks for their transgressions.[111]

Remini's mother, however, refused to allow her daughter to enter the RPF and instead initiated an administrative procedure that led to her two daughters being dismissed from the Sea Org. Knowing that now they should move out of Clearwater but without any place to go, they headed to another locale where the Scientology subculture was strong—Los Angeles.[112]

Sleeping at first on the floor of the apartment of her mother's friend, Remini and the rest of her family launched their new lives. Already behind in school for a year, Remini convinced her mother to let her drop out of school.

She began working a series of low-paying jobs to pay off a freeloader's debt from the courses she had received for free while a Sea Org member.

She found, and soon began to run with, unsupervised children and teens of Sea Org parents. About these children and teens:

> [I]n Scientology, minors are considered spiritual beings and not children in need of protection and guidance. You are the only person responsible for the condition of your life, regardless of your age. The Sea Org members believed that their kids could make up their own minds. As a result, these kids could no longer live with their parents, most of whom had berthing in [Scientology's sleeping facilities].[113]

Somehow, amid what at times must have felt like chaos, Remini (who had no acting training) began auditioning for acting parts in television and movies. She landed her first small part in 1988.[114] In the fall of 1988, auditions were held for a show about models called *Living Dolls*. Remini wanted to be hired as a character, so to prepare for the audition she underwent exercises that were directly out of Scientology's Success Through Communication course and the Tone Scale. She got selected and acted on the show for a year until it wrapped up in December 1989.[115]

Into the early 1990s, Remini continued to win parts on television shows, and at some point in this period she began taking Scientology courses and auditing again. (Presumably she paid off her freeloader's debt.) Reflecting back on any gains she believed at the time to have acquired, Remini interpreted:

> What I didn't realize at the time was that all the understanding I gained through auditing only related back to my life in the church and helped me be a Scientologist. My "gains" in Scientology were not related to the real world. I was so entrenched in the church that it had become my everything. I couldn't question that.[116]

This interpretation—that Scientology did not help Remini in the real world—was certainly *not* what came across in a *Celebrity* magazine cover article in 1995. She informed readers:

> I really can't imagine what I would be like without Scientology tech in my life. It has helped me in my career, it has helped me in my life. I've noticed that when I stay on lines and actively move on The Bridge, and I am doing so because I want to go free, it just so happens that my career flourishes as does my life in general.[117]

Within about two years of providing these comments to *Celebrity* magazine, she landed a starring character on the television show, *The King of Queens*.[118] Issues in her private life were straightening out, too, in this period: in 1996 she met Angelo Pagán, whom she would marry (in a pared-down Scientology wedding) in 2002.[119] In 2004, she gave birth to her only child but did not follow Scientology's strict "silent birth" procedures.[120]

Remini's growing success merited her a second cover story interview in *Celebrity* magazine in 2002. She spoke about how her mother taught her to do the first Training Routine, TR-0, which allowed her to improve her relationship with her older sister. Moreover, because she said that she was not "raised with any real moral values," she received values from Hubbard's *The Way to Happiness*.[121] Receiving auditing on the Grades and attesting to Clear allowed Remini (she said) to get beyond the anxiety of auditions and her constant self-criticisms even before reading for a part. She indicated. "I felt a real sense of peace when I achieved the state of Clear."[122] When asked how, "as a successful actress with an incredibly busy schedule," she managed still to fit in time for Scientology courses, Remini's reply did not really answer the question but instead affirmed it: "I have never felt better then when I am on course or getting auditing."[123] Later in the interview, she mentioned the 9/11 attacks against the United States and offered, "Can you imagine what this place would be like if we were all Clear? . . . LRH gave us a huge gift. Let's give back." In this spirit, she thanked her "supervisor and auditors for not giving up on me and for treating me with love and kindness. The same with the church itself."[124] This interpretation—that Scientology personnel treated her with love and kindness—would diminish over the next few years as she increasingly had run-ins with the church over issues that she felt were inconsequential and banal.

Remini's answers to questions in both of her *Celebrity* interviews suggest that she understood the roles that she played in and for the organization. Years later, in her autobiography, she would write:

> As a celebrity Scientologist, you are expected to be an example not only to the outside world but also to other Scientologists. Moving up the Bridge is important in setting an example for the group. And so is donating money. A lot of money.[125]

With a significant, steady income from her on successful television series, Remini's status within Scientology rose, and she began being invited to social events comprising the rich, inner circle of celebrities. As her status rose, so did the demands on her for donations. She estimated that she donated millions dollars before she left.[126] Problems quickly arose, however, around her donations when she demanded proof about how Scientologists used them or planned to use them. For example, she gave $50,000 to a charity that Kirstie Alley was running to help the New Orleans survivors, but she became angry when no one gave her pictures of volunteers distributing bottled water as she had been told they were going to. Likewise, she withdrew a tentative offer to make a $100,000 donation for a community southwest of downtown Los Angeles when she learned that the charity plan involved distributing turkeys along with *The Way to Happiness* book. (She had expected that her donation would have gone toward something practical, like a kids' center, to watch children while their parents worked.)[127] She did make, however, a million-dollar donation to the International Association of Scientologists, which apparently elevated her to the status of someone who could associate with Tom Cruise.[128] Things did not always go well for her, however, at his dinner parties. During one party, in which Cruise "was manhandling Katie, dipping her in a forceful way and then making out with her," a slightly upset Remini quipped to the couple, "you guys might want to get a room. . . ." She never imagined how much trouble she would get in for saying it. At another event in Cruise's house, she witnessed what she considered to be an angry and unwarranted outburst toward his staff. On a third occasion, she was among guests whom Cruise manipulated into playing hide-and-seek with him in his 7,000-square-foot house. She concluded that Cruise might have been arrested emotionally at the age when he experienced his first major box-office success (in his case, which was when he was 21).[129]

She and her husband received an invitation to what some observers were calling the wedding of the century—Tom Cruise and Katie Holmes—to be held in Rome in November 2006. Cruise asked Remini to invite actor and performer Jennifer Lopez and husband Marc Anthony to the wedding, and Lopez accepted for them both, even though they barely knew Cruise. Remini was surprised to see Brooke Shields there, but at some point realized that Cruise had invited many of them simply for public relations reasons regarding Scientology itself.[130]

This revelation was only the first of many that Remini had about Scientology, which sent her on a personal (and ultimately futile) mission to reform the organization.

What she observed she did not like. She saw Sea Org members drinking; she saw high-ranking Scientologists Tommy Davis and Jessica Feshbach together, without their respective spouses, physically interacting as if they were a couple. Most disturbing to her was that David Miscavige was there without his wife and appeared instead to be with his assistant, Laurisse Stuckenbrock. (When Remini asked Tommy Davis about her whereabouts, Davis snarled, "You don't have the rank to be asking about Shelly Miscavige."[131]) She thought that high-ranking Norman Starkey was manhandling and dancing inappropriately with Brooke Shields. Overall, Remini thought that the involvement of upper-level Sea Org members in the Cruise/Holmes wedding was not in accordance with Scientology policy and that Sea Org members behaved badly at it. She planned to return home and write Knowledge Reports about what she had witnessed, which would catalyze the organization to get itself back on policy and ethics.[132]

Upon returning to the United States, Remini quickly left for Clearwater in order to proceed up to OT VII. Before beginning the course, however, she was hit with a pile of Knowledge Reports about her behavior at the wedding! Remini concluded, however, that "[a]ll my crimes were on the spectrum of things that you have immature fights about in your teenage years."[133] These reports, however, were sufficiently serious that she had to go through security checks, in which:

> My auditor went at me for hours, days, weeks, and then months. It was relentless—absolutely relentless—as we went around and around on the same questions:
>
> > *What have you done to Tom?*
> > *Do you have evil intentions toward Tom?*
> > *Do you have sexual intentions toward Tom?*
> > *What have you done to Katie?*
> > *Do you have evil intentions toward Katie?*
> > *What have you done to David Miscavige?*
> > *Do you have evil intention toward David Miscavige?*

It was understood that the only reason I was saying those things about such high-level Scientologists was because I myself was guilty of such crimes.[134]

Persons whom Scientology security checks have to pay for the experience, and Remini had to put out an undisclosed amount of money to cover her ordeal.

Arguably, it got worse for her, since she next had to undergo a Truth Rundown. In this procedure, an auditor examines all relevant documents in order to determine what negative deeds or words a member has said or claimed to have seen about Scientology or its leadership and then pushes the person to identify what he or she did to cause those negative perceptions or deeds. In other words, the Truth Rundown attempted to get complainants to blame themselves for anything negative they believed that they knew or saw. She broke, and the process worked. "After weeks and weeks of twelve hours a day in auditing, they broke me and I retracted almost everything, I admitted that I caused a problem at the wedding." The entire trip cost her $300,000, spent on what she called "auditing to get reprogrammed."[135]

In 2007, Tommy Davis and Mike Rinder invited Remini to join Anne Archer, Kirstie Alley, and Juliette Lewis in discussing and defending Scientology with BBC reporter John Sweeney. Someone from the Office of Special Affairs (OSA) drilled them in the technique of dead agenting, which involved "shutting down any criticism of the church by disproving the veracity of the source of information," often with *ad hominem* attacks.[136] Remini also knew of the Fair Game Policy, in which an enemy of Scientology "may be deprived of property or injured by any means by any Scientologist without any discipline of the Scientologist. May be tricked, sued, or lied to or destroyed."[137] Apparently some combination of dead agenting and fair game had broken down Sweeney, and Mike Rinder and Tommy Davis were laughing about it. She protested to them, insisting, "What you're doing is wrong. He's in your house. You should treat him with respect. I don't think we're doing ourselves any favors." She refused to sign release papers that would have allowed one or both parties to use her interview publicly.[138]

When Cruise and Holmes announced their divorce in 2012, Remini felt vindicated about Starkey—whom she felt had been inappropriate with Brooke Shields—after she learned that he flew back from Italy in disgrace. Jessica Feshbach and Tommy Davis took extended leaves from the Sea Org and got married. No one, however, still was able to answer her question about where David Miscavige's wife, Shelly, was. Remini received a $300,000 credit to her account for what she had gone through (security checks, the Truth Rundown, etc.) in Clearwater.[139] David Miscavige himself assured her that she was fine but being kept out of sight because suppressive persons constantly were trying to subpoena her. Uncertain as to whether Miscavige was telling the truth, Remini reached out to some Suppressive Persons who only recently had defected from the organization.[140] Defector Mike Rinder told her that Scientology's management "was continually subjected to, and inflicted physical beatings on, other Sea Org members" and that they were backed by LRH policy in doing so.[141] Rinder and former captain of the Flag Service Organization, Debbie Cook, informed her about the Hole, which was a double-wide trailer on property that Scientology owns in Southern California where disfavored upper-level Sea Org members were held, humiliated, and punished.[142] Her conversation with Debbie Cook motivated her, for the first time in her life, to search the Internet for information about Scientology. What see discovered made her cry and then ask, "How could I have been blind to the stories that the rest of the world knew?" She then answered her own question: "The reason for their blind faith lies in their core belief that they alone have the answers to eradicate the ills of humanity. You run back to the safety of the group that shares your mentality, and in this way your world becomes very insular."[143]

Remini made the mistake of not following her own insights by trying to tell some Scientology friends about the information she was acquiring and the sources from which she was acquiring it. They refused to examine anything and probably are the persons who wrote Knowledge Reports about her to the organization.[144] Remini's Scientology handlers learned about these reports and confronted her, but she held her ground and counterattacked regarding Scientology's disconnection policy. She demanded to know why all Scientologists have to separate or disconnect from Suppressive Persons, but Tom Cruise was still allowed to see ex-wives and Suppressive Persons Nicole Kidman and Katie Holmes? Seemingly, she had come to believe that the finessing of Tom Cruise's needs at the expense of other Scientologists was hypocritical. When Miscavige attempted to salvage Remini, she laid into him about the number of individuals and families forced into debt in order to continue courses on The Bridge.[145] When a Scientology handler told Remini that LRH policy told her to disconnect from her stepfather because he was a suppressive person, she instead "decided to sever ties with Scientology permanently."[146]

CONCLUSION: SCIENTOLOGY CELEBRITY DECONVERSIONS AND THE SOCIAL SCIENCES

Three of the four conversions examined here are what social scientists call declarative departures.[147] Individuals announce their reasons for leaving a group, often by presenting information to the media or the public about what life was like on the inside or what they *remember or are willing to tell*. In other words, they declare the reasons for their departure, possibly in a manner that paints themselves in positive light. The reason or reasons for the exiting are obvious from the accounts, almost always involving physical, emotional, and/or sexual abuses; leadership struggles; financial malfeasance; or doctrinal heterodoxy. Consequently, defectors' accounts often portray the defecting members as having little other choice except to leave. A similar way to view these departures is to look at them as "heretical exits," in which involve disaffiliating and terminating from a group are appropriating a previously heretical belief system (i.e., secularism) to explain one's previous involvement.[148]

While it is possible that these accounts are biased intentionally, unintentional bias also may creep in as one tries to settle scores while leaving. Memory, too, is imprecise, and one necessarily recalls incidents in the past through the lens of more recent times. Declarative departures almost always intend to damage the reputation of the remaining groups and enhance the image of the apostates. Certainly ex-members can, and sometimes do, lie, and they may give unambiguous interpretations to issues and events that, in reality, call for nuance and shades of gray.

My own experience, however, with apostates' departure accounts is that most of them are more-or-less accurate and involve honest reporting. In addition to people's basic sense of integrity, critical apostates know that their former groups may examine their criticisms carefully and pounce on any inaccuracies. Often, accounts or other forms of documentation will support defectors' claims, giving them increased reliability.

In this chapter, three of the former members' accounts are declarative. William Burroughs published his critical reasons for leaving Scientology in a newspaper, magazine, and eventually a book; Jason Beghe put his departure account on the Internet; and Leah Remini wrote a book about her involvement in, then departure from, Scientology. Paul Haggis's departure account, however, is more difficult to categorize. Stuart Wright identified "overt departures" as ones categorized by quiet departures that occur after negotiations fail to resolve issues with organizational leaders.[149] Consequently, the leaders know about the deconversion, but the departing former member does not draw attention to it among outside parties. Haggis's deconversion shared characteristics with overt departures, but eventually he declared his reasons for leaving to the press. He had conducted an extensive e-mail correspondence with Scientology spokesperson Tommy Davis before he undertook the private fact-finding venture that eventually culminated in his departure, and he announced that departure in a final e-mail to Davis himself. Several days later, to a group of Scientologists on his front lawn who were trying to reconvert him, he agreed that he would not disseminate his e-mailed resignation any further. However, another vocal ex-member, Marty Rathbun, already had a copy, and when Rathbun asked Haggis two months later if he could post his resignation e-mail on his blog, Haggis did not stop him, and it quickly went viral. Consequently, Haggis's deconversion contained elements of both overt and declarative departures, but certainly after his statement went public, he participated in media events that were critical of his former group.

As separate factors, intellectualism/intellectual doubts and psychological stress have correlated with deconversion from some mainstream religions,[150] but variations of both may help explain Beghe's deconversion. Gradually, he came to the conclusion that the courses did not work, to the extent that they did not bequeath special powers to Scientologists who reached various levels. After he was an OT, he had a nearly fatal car accident, which neither he nor his Scientology handlers thought was possible. One of his handlers, however, asserted that Beghe must have been in the presence of a Suppressive Person (causing some sort of magical power loss), which likely was a particular gay friend. Beghe did not accept the explanation,[151] and he noticed that the continuing auditing courses were making him feel worse, not better and more empowered. Eventually he realized that the course claims and the auditing claims were magical, and he rejected them (and felt better being outside of Scientology's confines and concepts).

In addition to issues about *how* people deconverted, *why* they did so also are important to know. *Moral doubts* were central to Haggis's decision to both start questioning Scientology and then to leave. A moral doubt that he first had raised 10 months earlier with spokesperson Davis involved Scientology's position on gay rights. The name of the Church of Scientology of San Diego had appeared on an advertisement against gay marriages (California's Proposition 8), and Haggis was outraged. He demanded that Tommy Davis make a public statement saying that Scientology supported gay rights, but Davis refused, saying that the San Diego org's opposition had not attracted much notice, so it was better to leave it alone. When Haggis wrote his severance letter to Davis in August 2009, the first reason that he gave for his decision to leave was Davis's refusal to support gay rights.

Gay rights, however, was not the only issue that drove Haggis to resign from Scientology. While searching the Internet for information, Haggis found Scientology's responses to several high-level executives, and he realized that some of the material that current officials used to defend the organization came from the defectors' supposedly confidential confessional or auditing files. Specifically about one defector, Haggis charged, "You took Amy Scobee's most intimate admissions about her sexual life and passed them onto the press and then smeared them all over the pages [of] your newsletter!" [152] He expressed his moral outrage at the use of this confidential information by stating, "that kind of character assassination is unconscionable."[153]

Moral doubt about the lifestyles of either other members or leaders can motivate defection, as persons perceive others as hypocrites—people who say one thing but live another.[154] Hypocrisy is what Remini claimed to have seen during and around the Cruise/Holmes wedding. Any number of other issues could have initiated doubts about Scientology leading to defection: the "overwhelming" neglect that she has witnessed regarding Sea Org children in a nursery;[155] the operation of the Rehabilitation Project Force, which even included children;[156] Hubbard's prohibitions on thinking critically;[157] constant demands for financial contributions;[158] and so on. None of these issues drove her to defect or even to question seriously her involvement in Scientology. What finally drove her to leave was the extent to which Scientology's elites allowed themselves allegedly to commit adultery, drunkenness, sexual harassment in the context of inappropriate dancing, secrecy about a missing person, unacceptable resource misallocations (at least in her mind) toward Tom Cruise's lifestyle, obligatory social disconnections from Scientology-critical family and friends, and constant reports against one another for alleged Scientology violations.[159] Subsequent to leaving Scientology, Remini was a contestant on the television show, *Dancing with the Stars*. She devised the idea of using her departure from Scientology as the basis for a dance routine, which she and her partner choreographed and performed. In it, she was a puppet to the puppetmaster, and the puppetmaster was what she called the "Church of Hypocrisy."[160]

William Burroughs's sense of Scientology hypocrisy was of an entirely different nature from either Haggis's or Remini's. In an era when youth were challenging what they considered to be unjust authority, Burroughs felt that Hubbard was creating a cult around himself—one that allowed no intelligent or critical questioning and that supported an array of conservative social and sexual values. To be sure, these were moral concerns, but they (except perhaps for one concerning authoritarianism) were rooted deeply in the cultural politics of the era. Burroughs's abounding disdain for sec checks, however, certainly had parallels in complaint by two of the three other celebrities, and we will return to them shortly.

Weakened social bonds frequently appear as another factor in deconversion and they do, too, in Scientology apostate accounts, albeit in a way that is somewhat unique in existing academic literature. The general assumption in scholarship is that when individuals' support networks of family and/or friends depart from or disintegrate within groups, the remaining individuals are more likely to leave than when those networks were strong.[161] Regarding Scientology, however, some members defected because they rejected Scientology policy that required them to disconnect from persons whom the organization determines is a Suppressive Person. Often, such persons were family or friends, as was the case with Haggis's in-laws, with whom their daughter—his wife—broke off contact because of their Suppressive Persons designation. Haggis proclaimed that he found such disconnection orders "morally reprehensible."[162] Jason Beghe told Haggis about being disconnected from Scientology friends after he left.[163] In Remini's case, the final incident was when her handler told her that LRH (presumably through policy) was telling her to disconnect from her stepfather. In response, Remini exploded:

> I'm not going to have a church tell me who I can and cannot talk to. That day is done. Where does it stop? What if my mother was an SP? Should I disconnect from my mother? Do you think I'd disconnect from anyone after the way you and the church have treated me?[164]

True to policy, almost all of Remini's Scientology friends disconnected from her.[165]

The important variant to the contribution that weakened social bonds had to defecting Scientologists Haggis and Remini is that, after their doubts initially appeared, they broke form official policy and turned to the Internet. They went to sources who were outside the social bonds of Scientology for information. What they found (in terms of critical material) stunned them. After reading online Davis's rebuttals to critics, Haggis confessed that "I was left feeling outraged, and frankly, more than a little stupid."[166] After spending time on the Internet, a humbled Remini asked, "How could I have been blinded to the stories that the rest of the world knew?"[167] In these cases, doubting Scientologists loosened bonds with their group and reached into the forbidden world of Internet criticism. Inspired by the Internet, both doubters then spoke with Suppressive Persons, which meant further diminishing the social bonds with current members. They deliberately weakened social bonds in ways that allowed forbidden information and social contacts from the outside to reach them.

Beginning in late November 2016, Remini presented an eight-part television series on the A&E network in which she interviewed many people who claimed (like her) to have been victimized. After a Church of Scientology official attempted to block the shows by writing caustic letters to network officials about Remini, she responded with a legal demand for $1.5 million in compensation and damages, which Scientology, in response, refused to pay.[168]

UNIQUE CONTRIBUTORS TO SCIENTOLOGY CELEBRITY DECONVERSIONS: RELENTLESS DONATION PRESSURE AND DISDAIN OF SECURITY CHECKS

At least two activities that deconverting Scientologists mentioned as activities they had disliked in the group were the constant requests and demands for financial contributions and the obligation to undergo security checks. In and of themselves, neither of these activities was enough to make deconversion necessary, but both were ancillary reasons why people left. Both of these activities have parallels in some other high-demand groups, so it is likely that they play similar roles in deconversions in other contexts. Beghe, for example, complained that some auditors for upper-level courses cost $1,000 an hour, and he had to use them for weeks.[169] Haggis reported that he spent $100,000 on courses in addition to about the same amount to various Scientology causes, plus $250,000 to the International Association of Scientologists. "The demands for money—'regging,' it's called in Scientology, because the calls come from the Registrar's Office—never stopped. Paul gave them money just to keep them from calling."[170] Remini, who donated millions of dollars to Scientology, said that she did so out of a "combination of coercion and responsibility. When I heard from the church the causes my money was being put toward, I believed them," she indicated. Nevertheless, "[t]he church is relentless when it comes to fundraising and solicitation. The plea is always a variation on the same refrain: 'You've got to step up, because if you do it, people who are not contributing will start to. So you need to do this to save the planet.'"[171] In one instance, her business manager, who was a Scientologist, advised her against donating to a Scientology request because she did not have the money. The organization pulled in the business manager and put him through a sec check.[172]

When Remini went to Clearwater after the Cruise/Holmes wedding to do additional courses, instead she spent $300,000 "on auditing to get reprogrammed."[173] Much of that money went toward paying for sec checks, in which her "auditor went at me for hours, days, weeks, then months. It was relentless—absolutely relentless as we went around and around on the same questions."[174] Despite the money that she paid, she never got to take the courses she had traveled to Clearwater to complete. In contrast, Burroughs's complains about sec checks were that they were demeaning and insulting—a waste of time. While Burroughs was at Saint Hill, so many people were getting sec checked that a Scientologist had to deliver his in a broom closet. Sec checks, he felt, were one way that Hubbard was developing a cult a personality, and it sickened Burroughs.[175] In his 1970 critical publication on Scientology, Burroughs mistakenly stated that the organization had discontinued sec checks, but he was correct in identifying the continuing practice associated with sec checks—the assignment of "conditions" to members as indications of their relationship to the operation of Scientology. Negative conditions included the labels, "Nonexistence," "Liability," "Treason," and "Doubt" for people who had committed offenses against the organization, and people labeled as Liabilities had to wear grey rags around their arms.[176] He retorted, "Does Mr. Hubbard seriously expect mature scientists, artists, and professional men who have distinguished themselves in their respective fields to submit to this prep school nonsense?"[177]

Looking back on the four deconversion accounts summarized in the chapter, intellectual doubt and psychological strain, along with moral doubts about leaders and other members, can be factors in Scientology celebrity deconversions as they are with other groups. Issues around social isolation are complicated, because some of the celebrity defectors had to build some social distance between themselves and other Scientologists in order to undertake efforts to acquire critical information from the Internet and Suppressive Persons. For them, the issue was not that internal social bonds had weakened; it was that they had to loosen them in order to acquire (what for them was) new information. Almost all of the defectors disliked security checks and the constant demand for donations, and these last two contributing factors may not have entered the academic literature on deconversion even though they likely also apply to some other high-demand subcultures.

At some point in the future there likely will be more declaratory celebrity deconversions or heretical exits, which will provide additional material for analysis. As I was completing an earlier draft of this article, author Tony Ortega revealed that Lisa Marie Presley was behind the distribution to various media of police reports and interviews indicating that David Miscavige had hired private detectives to follow his estranged father. As she hoped, the media she targeted produced stories about it. Ortega ended his piece cryptically, indicating, "our sources tell us she has more planned."[178] Perhaps additional celebrities will be exiting the organization fairly soon.

NOTES

1. Tilman Hausherr, "Celebrities in Scientology FAQ," January 25, 1997, revised June 21, 2015, lists 70 Scientology celebrities, 21 Scientology celebrity rumored dabblers, and 21 former Scientologists. Andy Cush, "A Comprehensive Updated List of Every Celebrity Linked to Scientology," April 2, 2015. Another is in a source that most serious academics avoid—Wikipedia—which lists 59 current Scientology celebrities, 26 former members, and 13 deceased members (Wikipedia, "List of Scientologists," accessed February 28, 2016, https://en.wikipedia.org/wiki/List_of_Scientologists).

2. Stephen Kent and Ashley Samaha, "Deconversion," *Vocabulary for the Study of Religion*, Volume 1, A–E, ed. Robert A. Segal and Kocku von Stuckrad (Leiden: E. J. Brill, 2015), 387–392.

3. Heinz Streib, "Deconversion," *The Oxford Handbook of Religious Conversion*, ed. Lewis Rambo and Charles Farhadian (Oxford: Oxford University Press, 2014).

4. Kent and Samaha, "Deconversion," 387, quoted in Heinz Streib and Barbara Keller, "The Varieties of Deconversion Experiences: Contours of a Concept in Respect to Empirical Research," *Archiv für Religionspsychologie/Archive for the Psychology of Religion* 26, no. 1 (2005): 191.

5. Ibid., 388–389.

6. Ibid., 389; based upon Stuart Wright, *Leaving Cults: The Dynamics of Defection* (Washington: Society for the Scientific Study of Religion, 1987), 25, 31, 38, 44, 46.

7. The definition of apostates that sociologist David Bromley offered is worth mentioning here: "The apostate role is thus defined as one that occurs in a highly polarized situation in which an organization member undertakes a total change of loyalties by allying with one or more elements of an oppositional coalition without the consent of the organization." David G. Bromley, "The Social Construction of Contested Exit Roles: Defectors, Whistleblowers, and Apostates," in David G. Bromley, ed., *The Politics of Religious Apostasy: The Role of Apostates in the Transformation of Religious Movements* (Westport: Praeger, 1998), 36.

8. David King Dunaway, *Huxley in Hollywood* (New York: Harper and Row, 1989), 278.

9. Michelle Leach, "Little Known Brushes with the Religion," *SheKnows Canada*, July 12, 2012, http://www.sheknows.com/entertainment/articles/965647/4-stars-who-flirted-with-scientology.

10. Cush, "A Comprehensive Updated List."

11. Jerry Seinfeld, "Interview with Jerry Seinfeld," *Parade*, September 18, 2007, http://parade.com/50123/parade/interview-with-jerry-seinfeld/.

12. Lisa Marie Presley, "You Ain't Seen Nothin' Yet," *Storm and Grace*, Universal Republic, May 15, 2012.

13. Tony Ortega, "Is Lisa Marie Presley Telling Off Scientology in a Song?," *Village Voice*, April 12, 2012, http://www.villagevoice.com/news/is-lisa-marie-presley-telling-off-scientology-in-a-song-6726607.

14. Tony Ortega, "How Lisa Marie Presley Became Scientology Leader David Miscavige's Worst Nightmare," *Underground Bunker*, April 21, 2016, http://tonyortega.org/2016/04/21/how-lisa-marie-presley-became-scientology-leader-david-miscaviges-worst-nightmare/.

15. David S. Wills, *Scientologist! William S. Burroughs and the "Weird Cult"* (United Kingdom: Beatdom Books, 2013), 57, 59.

16. Ibid., 107.

17. Ted Morgan, *Literary Outlaw: The Life and Times of William S. Burroughs* (New York: Henry Holt, 1988), 440–441.

18. Wills, *Scientologist!*, 107, 109, 119.

19. Ibid., 128–129.

20. *Advance Magazine*, "William Burroughs: Clear 1163," Issue 2 Volume 1, 1968, 5.

21. Burroughs quoted in Ibid.

22. Morgan, *Literary Outlaw*, 441.

23. For an academic discussion of security checks, see Susan Raine, "Surveillance in New Religious Movements: Scientology as a Case Study," *Religious Studies and Theology* (2009): 73–75.

24. Ibid., 194–196.

25. L. Ron Hubbard, "The Only Valid Security Check," *Hubbard Communications Office Policy Letter*, May 22, 1961, in L. Ron Hubbard, *The Technical Bulletins of Dianetics and Scientology* Volume IV, 1960–1961 (Copenhagen: Scientology Publications, 1976), 275–281 (capitalization in original).

26. Morgan, *Literary Outlaw*, 442.

27. Ibid.

28. Wills, *Scientologist!*, 144–145.

29. Ibid., 147–149.

30. Ibid., 152.

31. William Burroughs, *Ali's Smile, Naked Scientology*, 5th ed., 2000 (Bonn: Expanded Media Editions, 1972).

32. William Burroughs, "Burroughs on Scientology," *Los Angeles Free Press*, March 6, 1970, 33.

33. Ibid.

34. Wills, _Scientologist!_, 125.

35. Gordon Mustain, "Organization Electrodes: Open Letter to William Burroughs," _Los Angeles Free Press_, March 27–April 2, 1970, 29.

36. Burroughs, "Burroughs on Scientology," 41.

37. Mustain, "Organized Electrodes," 36.

38. Ibid. For a larger analysis about counterculture youth and anti–Vietnam War protestors converting to groups like Scientology, see Stephen A. Kent, _From Slogans to Mantras: Social Protest and Religious Conversion in the Late Vietnam War Era_ (Syracuse: Syracuse University Press, 2001).

39. Ibid.

40. Mary Sue Hubbard, "Mr. Burroughs, You're Wrong about My Husband," _Mayfair_, June 1970, 53.

41. Ibid.

42. Ibid.

43. L. Ron Hubbard, "Orders of the Day," Vol. III, No. 96, April 6, 1970, 2.

44. L. Ron Hubbard, "A Reply to William Burroughs," _Mayfair_, August 1970, 6 (article reprint).

45. L. Ron Hubbard, "The War," _Executive Directive from L. Ron Hubbard_, November 29, 1968, 2.

46. [L. Ron Hubbard], "Confidential: Intelligence Actions; Covert Intelligence; Data Collection," CS-G [_Church of Scientology-Guardian_], Dec[ember] 2, 1969, 5.

47. Hubbard, "A Reply to William Burroughs," 4.

48. In mid-1975, for example, the "Johannesburg Security Check" that Burroughs hated reappeared as the "Johannesburg Confessional." L. Ron Hubbard, "Johannesburg Confessional List—Revised," _Hubbard Communications Office Policy Letter_, May 20, 1975, in L. Ron Hubbard, _The Technical Bulletins of Dianetics and Scientology_, Volume VIII, 1975 (Copenhagen: Scientology Publications, 1976), 419–422.

49. L. Ron Hubbard, "Confessional Procedure," _Hubbard Communications Office Bulletin_, November 30, 1978, in L. Ron Hubbard, _The Technical Bulletins of Dianetics and Scientology_, Volume XII, 1978–1979 (Copenhagen: Scientology Publications, 1976), 245.

50. Wills, _Scientologist!_, 105.

51. Mary Sue Hubbard, "Mr. Burroughs, You're Wrong about My Husband," 53.

52. L. Ron Hubbard, "Department of Govt Affairs," _Hubbard Communications Office Policy Letter_, August 15, 1960, in _The Organization Executive Course_, Executive Division 7 (Los Angeles: Church of Scientology of California, 1974), 484 (capitals in original).

53. Burroughs, "Burroughs on Scientology," 33.

54. Ibid., 41.

55. Hubbard, "A Reply to William Burroughs," 3.

56. Ibid., 6.

57. L. Ron Hubbard, "Orders of the Day," Vol. III, No. 156, June 5, 1970.

58. William Burroughs, ". . . And a Final Word from William Burroughs," *Mayfair*, August 1970, 6.

59. Wills, *Scientologist!*, 206.

60. Church of Scientology Celebrity Centre International, "Jason Beghe: Actor/ Clear, Hubbard Basic Art Course Graduate," *Celebrity* Minor Issue 285 (1995): 14.

61. Church of Scientology Celebrity Centre International, "Jason Beghe," *Celebrity* Major Issue 303 (1997): 13; Kristi Wachter, "Jason Beghe and Scientology," *Scientology Lies*, accessed March 13, 2016, http://www.scientology-lies.com/faq/celebrities /jason-beghe.html.

62. Church of Scientology Celebrity Centre International, "Jason Beghe: Actor/ Clear," 15.

63. Beghe, quoted in Scott Widener, "Jason Beghe Turned a Tough Break into a Tough Role as 'Chicago P.D.'s' Rogue Officer Hank Voight," *New York Daily News*, April 23, 2014, http://www.nydailynews.com/entertainment/tv-movies/jason-beghe -tough-break-led-memorable-voice-article-1.1765027.

64. Karin Pouw to Andy Greene, *Church of Scientology International*, March 18, 2015, 1.

65. Beghe, quoted in Tony Ortega, "Jason Beghe's Letter to Scientology Attorneys: Yes, I'll Settle Your $1 Million Lawsuit for $19K," *Village Voice*, August 17, 2012, http://www.villagevoice.com/news/jason-beghes-letter-to-scientology-attorneys-yes -ill-settle-your-1-million-lawsuit-for-19k-6681723.

66. Ibid.

67. Ibid.

68. Operation Clambake, "The L Rundown," accessed March 17, 2016, http:// www.xenu.net/archive/L-Rundowns/.

69. Tony Ortega, "Scientology's First Celebrity Defector Reveals Church Secrets," *Village Voice*, April 15, 2008, http://www.villagevoice.com/news/scientologys-first -celebrity-defector-reveals-church-secrets-6391153; Tony Ortega, "Scientology's 'Super Power Rundown:' What Is It, Anyway?," *Village Voice*, January 11, 2012, http://www .villagevoice.com/news/scientologys-super-power-rundown-what-is-it-anyway-6700611.

70. Wachter, "Jason Beghe and Scientology."

71. Alex Henderson, "10 People Who Turned against Scientology and Revealed Its Bizarre Secrets," *AlterNet*, July 1, 2015, http://www.alternet.org/10 -people-who-turned-against-scientology-and-revealed-its-bizarre-secrets.

72. Ortega, "Scientology's First Celebrity."

73. Roger Friedman, "Actor Jason Beghe: Scientology Is 'Brainwashing,'" *Fox News*, April 16, 2008, http://www.foxnews.com/story/2008/04/16/actor-jason-beghe -scientology-is-brainwashing.html.

74. Hubmesh, "Actor Jason Beghe, Age 55, Talks about How He Decided to Leave the Scientology Church When His Wife Got Pregnant with the First of Their Children," February 2, 2016, http://hubmesh.com/actor-jason-beghe-age-55-talks-about -how-he-decided-to-leave-the-scientology-church-when-his-wife-got-pregnant -with-the-first-of-their-children.html.

75. Ortega, "Scientology's First Celebrity Defector."

76. Beghe, quoted in Ortega, "Scientology's Super Power Rundown."

77. PageSix.com, "Ex-Scientologist Rips Church," April 16, 2008, http://pagesix .com/2008/04/16/ex-scientologist-rips-church/; Ortega, "Scientology's First Celebrity Defector."

78. Tony Ortega, "Jason Beghe Is Still Denouncing Scientology—This Time in Germany," *Village Voice*, September 16, 2008.

79. Beghe, quoted in Lawrence Wright, *Going Clear: Scientology, Hollywood, & the Prison of Belief*, 320–321. (New York: Alfred A. Knopf, 2013).

80. Ibid., 321.

81. Lawrence Wright, "The Apostate: Paul Haggis vs. the Church of Scientology," *New Yorker*, February 14 & 21, 2011, 6, 5, http://www.newyorker.com/magazine /2011/02/14/the-apostate-lawrence-wright.

82. Ibid., 28.

83. Church of Scientology Celebrity Centre International, "Celebrity Interview of the Month, Executive Producer Paul Haggis," *Celebrity* (1986): 7, 11.

84. Ibid., 22.

85. Wright, "The Apostate," 6.

86. Ibid., 8. For a discussion of the security around the O.T. story, see Susan Raine, "Surveillance in New Religious Movements," 86.

87. Wright, "The Apostate," 14.

88. Hubbard's official policy on disconnection stated, "The term 'disconnection' is defined as a self-determined decision made by an individual that he is not going to be connected to another. It is a severing of a communication line." Several paragraphs later he added, "A Scientologist can become PTS [i.e., a potential trouble source] by reason of being connected to someone that is antagonistic to Scientology or its tenets. In order to resolve the PTS condition, he either HANDLES the other person's antagonism . . . , or, as a last resort when all attempts to handle have failed, he disconnects from the person." L. Ron Hubbard, "PTSness and Disconnection," *Hubbard Communications Office Bulletin*, September 10, 1983, in L. Ron Hubbard, *The Organization Executive Course*, HCO Division, Volume 1 (Los Angeles: Bridge Publications, 1991), 1041–1044 (capitals in original).

89. Wright, "The Apostate," 14–15.

90. Joe Childs and Thomas C. Tobin, "Scientology: The Truth Rundown, Part 1 of 3 in a Special Report on the Church of Scientology," *Tampa Bay Times*, June 21, 2009, 1, http://www.tampabay.com/specials/2009/reports/project/part1.shtml.

91. Wright, "The Apostate," 19. Haggis specifically mentioned the Exscientologykids.com website, created by David Miscavige's niece, Jenna Miscavige Hill. Wright ("The Apostate," 19) mentioned that she joined the Sea Org at 14, but her subsequent autobiography has her signing the billion year Sea Org contract at seven. See Jenna Miscavige Hill and Lisa Pulitzer, *Beyond Belief: My Secret Life Inside Scientology and My Harrowing Escape* (New York: William Morrow, 2013), 7–9.

92. Haggis, quoted in Ibid., 19.

93. Paul Haggis to Tommy Davis, August 19. 2009, in "Paul Haggis Resigns from Church of Scientology," October 23, 2009, http://www.scientology-cult.com

/declarations-of-independence/59-paul-haggis/158-paul-haggis-resigns-from-church
-of-scientology.html.

94. In Alex Gibney, *Going Clear: Scientology and the Prison of Belief*, GC Productions, 2015, at around 1.44.00, Haggis indicated that the number of people on his lawn were ten.

95. The account in Gibney varies slightly from the account in Wright's initial article. Wright indicated that Haggis agreed not to disseminate the latter further (Wright, "The Apostate," 19.) In Gibney, *Going Clear*, Haggis indicated that he had sent copies of the letter to 25 other Scientologists and also to Marty Rathbun. He gave the impression that he did not agree to remain quiet about his discoveries.

96. Gibney, *Going Clear*.

97. Church of Scientology Celebrity Centre International, "Celebrity Interview with Leah Remini," 2002, 19.

98. Remini and Paley, *Troublemaker*, 6–11.

99. Ibid., 13.

100. Ibid., 15.

101. Ibid., 17.

102. Ibid., 24.

103. Ibid., 25.

104. Ibid.

105. Ibid., 27.

106. Ibid., 28. For Hubbard's practice of overboarding Sea Org members as punishment, see Russell Miller, *Bare-Faced Messiah: The True Story of L. Ron Hubbard* (New York: Henry Holt, 1987), 288, 292, 294, 295.

107. Remini and Paley, *Troublemaker*, 30.

108. Ibid.

109. Ibid., 31.

110. Ibid., 33.

111. Ibid., 37.

112. Ibid., 38–39.

113. Ibid., 45–46.

114. Ibid., 46–57.

115. Ibid., 57–67.

116. Ibid., 75.

117. Church of Scientology Celebrity Centre International, "Celebrity Interview of the Month: Leah Remini," *Celebrity* Major Issue 288 (1995): 12.

118. Remini and Paley, *Troublemaker*, 88–94.

119. Ibid., 79, 96–99.

120. Ibid., 101–103.

121. Church of Scientology Celebrity Centre International, "Celebrity Interview of the Month: Leah Remini," *Celebrity* Issue 342 (2002): 19.

122. Ibid., 20–21.

123. Ibid., 21.

124. Ibid.

125. Remini and Paley, *Troublemaker*, 121.

126. Ibid.
127. Ibid., 122–123.
128. Ibid., 124–125.
129. Ibid., 125–128.
130. Ibid., 136–137.
131. Ibid., 142.
132. Ibid., 137–148.
133. Ibid., 150. One action, for example, that got Remini in trouble was asking the wedding coordinator if she and her husband could sit next to Jennifer Lopez and her husband. What Remini did not realize until later was that, by changing tables, she was unable to promote Scientology to nonmembers who were sitting at her original location, and thereby she had committed a transgression. Ibid., 144.
134. Ibid., 151–152.
135. Ibid., 154–155.
136. Ibid., 157–158.
137. Ibid., 159.
138. Remini in Ibid., 159–160.
139. Ibid., 172–174, 178.
140. Ibid., 179.
141. Ibid., 180.
142. Ibid., 180–182.
143. Ibid., 182.
144. Ibid., 182–184.
145. Ibid., 184–188.
146. Ibid., 194.
147. Ibid., 390; based upon Wright, *Leaving Cults*, 72–73.
148. See Streib, "Deconversion," 272.
149. Wright, *Leaving Cults*, 69–72.
150. Kent and Samaha, "Deconversion," 388. For intellectualism and deconversion, see David Caplovitz and Fred Sherrow, *The Religious Drop-Outs: Apostasy among College Graduates* (Beverly Hills: Sage, 1977), 182; Streib, "Deconversion," 272. For psychological stress and deconversion, see Robert Wuthnow and Charles Y. Glock, "Religious Loyalty, Defection, and Experimentation Among College Youth," *Journal for the Scientific Study of Religion* 12, no. 2 (1973): 173–175; and Streib, "Deconversion," 272 (on emotional suffering).
151. Ortega, "Scientology's First Celebrity Defector," 4.
152. Paul Haggis to Tommy Davis, August 19, 2009, in "Paul Haggis Resigns from Church of Scientology."
153. Ibid.
154. Kent and Samaha, "Deconversion," 389; see Streib, "Deconversion," 272 (on moral criticism).
155. Remini and Paley, *Troublemaker*, 30.
156. Ibid., 37.
157. Ibid., 73.

158. Ibid., 121, 124.
159. Ibid., 134–155.
160. Ibid., 219.
161. Kent and Samaha, "Deconversion," 389.
162. Paul Haggis to Tommy Davis, August 19, 2009, in "Paul Haggis Resigns from Church of Scientology."
163. Wright, *Going Clear*, 321.
164. Remini and Paley, *Troublemaker*, 194.
165. Ibid., 214–217.
166. Paul Haggis to Tommy Davis, August 19, 2009, in "Paul Haggis Resigns from Church of Scientology."
167. Remini and Paley, *Troublemaker*, 182.
168. Tony Ortega, "Leah Remini Demands $1.5 Million from Scientology for Interfering with her A&E Series," *The Underground Bunker*, November 22, 2016, http://tonyortega.org/2016/11/22/leah-remini-demands-1-5-million-from-scientology -for-interfering-with-her-ae-series/.
169. Ortega, "Scientology's First Celebrity Defector."
170. Wright, *Going Clear*, 216.
171. Remini and Paley, *Troublemaker*, 121.
172. Ibid., 204.
173. Ibid., 155.
174. Ibid., 151.
175. Wills, *Scientologist!*, 125.
176. Ibid., 14–15. Burroughs was not specific about what condition required people to wear the gray rag, but Hubbard's biographer, Russell Miller, specified that it was people labeled "Liability." See Miller, *Bare-Faced Messiah*, 251–252.
177. Burroughs, *Naked Scientology*, 15.
178. Tony Ortega, "How Lisa Marie Presley."

BIBLIOGRAPHY

Advance Magazine. "William Burroughs: Clear 1163." Issue 2, Vol. 1. Edinburgh, Scotland: Publications Organization World Wide, 1968.

Bromley, David G. "The Social Construction of Contested Exit Roles: Defectors, Whistleblowers, and Apostates." In *The Politics of Religious Apostasy: The Role of Apostates in the Transformation of Religious Movements*, edited by David G. Bromley. Westport: Praeger, 1998.

Burroughs, William. *Ali's Smile, Naked Scientology*. 5th Edition, 2000. Bonn: Expanded Media Editions, 1972.

Burroughs, William. ". . . And a Final Word from William Burroughs." *Mayfair.* August 1970.

Burroughs, William. "Burroughs on Scientology." *Los Angeles Free Press.* March 6, 1970.

Caplovitz, David, and Fred Sherrow. *The Religious Drop-Outs: Apostasy among College Graduates.* Beverly Hills: Sage, 1977.

Childs, Joe, and Thomas C. Tobin. "Scientology: The Truth Rundown. Part 1 of 3 in a Special Report on the Church of Scientology." *Tampa Bay Times.* June 21, 2009. http://www.tampabay.com/specials/2009/reports/project/part1.shtml.

Church of Scientology Celebrity Centre International. "Celebrity Interview of the Month: Executive Producer Paul Haggis." *Celebrity* (1986): 6–7, 11–12.

Church of Scientology Celebrity Centre International. "Celebrity Interview of the Month: Leah Remini." *Celebrity* Major Issue 288 (1995): 10–12.

Church of Scientology Celebrity Centre International. "Celebrity Interview of the Month: Leah Remini." *Celebrity* 342 (2002): 18–21.

Church of Scientology Celebrity Centre International. "Jason Beghe." *Celebrity* Major Issue 303 (1997): 12–14.

Church of Scientology Celebrity Centre International. "Jason Beghe: Actor/Clear, Hubbard Basic Art Course Graduate." *Celebrity* Minor Issue 285 (1995): 14–15.

Cush, Andy. "A Comprehensive Updated List of Every Celebrity Linked to Scientology." *Gawker.* April 2, 2015. http://gawker.com/a-comprehensive-updated -list-of-every-celebrity-linked-1694554276.

Dunaway, David King. *Huxley in Hollywood.* New York: Harper and Row, 1989.

Friedman, Roger. "Actor Jason Beghe: Scientology Is 'Brainwashing.'" *Fox News.* April 16, 2008. http://www.foxnews.com/story/2008/04/16/actor-jason-beghe -scientology-is-brainwashing.html.

Haggis, Paul, to Tommy Davis. August 19, 2009. In "Paul Haggis Resigns from Church of Scientology." October 23, 2009. http://www.scientology-cult.com /declarations-of-independence/59-paul-haggis/158-paul-haggis-resigns-from -church-of-scientology.html.

Hausherr, Tilman. "Celebrities in Scientology FAQ." January 25, 1997. Revised June 21, 2015. http://home.snafu.de/tilman/faq-you/celeb.txt.

Henderson, Alex. "10 People Who Turned against Scientology and Revealed Its Bizarre Secrets." *AlterNet.* July 1, 2015. http://www.alternet.org/10-people-who -turned-against-scientology-and-revealed-its-bizarre-secrets.

Hill, Jenna Miscavige, and Lisa Pulitzer. *Beyond Belief: My Secret Life Inside Scientology and My Harrowing Escape.* New York: William Morrow, 2013.

Hubbard, L. Ron. "Confessional Procedure." *Hubbard Communications Office Bulletin.* November 30, 1978. In L. Ron Hubbard, *The Technical Bulletins of Dianetics and Scientology,* Volume XII, 1978–1979, 245–250. Copenhagen: Scientology Publications, 1976.

Hubbard, L. Ron. "Department of Govt Affairs." *Hubbard Communications Office Policy Letter.* August 15, 1960. In L. Ron Hubbard, *The Organization Executive Course,* Executive Division 7, 483–485. Los Angeles: Church of Scientology of California, 1974.

Hubbard, L. Ron. *Letter.* May 20, 1975. In L. Ron Hubbard, *The Technical Bulletins of Dianetics and Scientology,* Volume VIII, 1975, 419–422. Copenhagen: Scientology Publications, 1976.

Hubbard, L. Ron. "The Only Valid Security Check." *Hubbard Communications Office Policy Letter.* May 22, 1961. In L. Ron Hubbard, *The Technical Bulletins of Dianetics and Scientology,* Volume IV, 1960–1961. Copenhagen: Scientology Publications, 1976.

Hubbard, L. Ron. "Orders of the Day." vol. III, no. 96. April 6, 1970.

Hubbard, L. Ron. "Orders of the Day." Vol. III, No. 156. June 5, 1970.

Hubbard, L. Ron. "PTSness and Disconnection." *Hubbard Communications Office Bulletin*, September 10, 1983. In L. Ron Hubbard, *The Organization Executive Course*, HCO Division Volume 1, 1041–1044. Los Angeles: Bridge Publications, 1991.

Hubbard, L. Ron. "A Reply to William Burroughs." *Mayfair*. August 1970 (article reprint).

Hubbard, L. Ron. "The War." *Executive Directive from L. Ron Hubbard*. November 29, 1968. In [Hubbard, L. Ron], "Confidential: Intelligence Actions; Covert Intelligence; Data Collection," CS-G [*Church of Scientology-Guardian*], Dec[ember] 2, 1969.

Hubbard, Mary Sue. "Mr. Burroughs, You're Wrong about My Husband." *Mayfair*. June 1970.

Hubmesh. "Actor Jason Beghe, Age 55, Talks About How He Decided to Leave the Scientology Church When His Wife Got Pregnant with the First of Their Children." February 2, 2016. http://hubmesh.com/actor-jason-beghe-age-55-talks-about-how-he-decided-to-leave-the-scientology-church-when-his-wife-got-pregnant-with-the-first-of-their-children.html.

Kent, Stephen A. *From Slogans to Mantras: Social Protest and Religious Conversion in the Late Vietnam War Era*. Syracuse: Syracuse University Press, 2001.

Kent, Stephen A., and Ashley Samaha. "Deconversion." In *Vocabulary for the Study of Religion*. Volume 1, A–E., edited by Robert A. Segal and Kocku von Stuckrad. Leiden: E. J. Brill, 2015.

Leach, Michelle. "Little Known Brushes with the Religion." *SheKnows Canada*. July 12, 2012. http://www.sheknows.com/entertainment/articles/965647/4-stars-who-flirted-with-scientology.

Miller, Russell. *Bare-Faced Messiah: The True Story of L. Ron Hubbard*. London: Key Porter Books, 1987.

Morgan, Ted. *Literary Outlaw: The Life and Times of William S. Burroughs*. New York: Henry Holt, 1988.

Mustain, Gordon. "Organization Electrodes: Open Letter to William Burroughs." *Los Angeles Free Press*. March 27–April 2, 1970.

Operation Clambake. "The L Rundown." Accessed March 17, 2016. http://www.xenu.net/archive/L-Rundowns/.

Ortega, Tony. "How Lisa Marie Presley Became Scientology Leader David Miscavige's Worst Nightmare." *Underground Bunker*. April 21, 2016. http://tonyortega.org/2016/04/21/how-lisa-marie-presley-became-scientology-leader-david-miscaviges-worst-nightmare/.

Ortega, Tony. "Is Lisa Marie Presley Telling Off Scientology in a Song?" *Village Voice*. April 12, 2012. http://www.villagevoice.com/news/is-lisa-marie-presley-telling-off-scientology-in-a-song-6726607.

Ortega, Tony. "Jason Beghe Is Still Denouncing Scientology—This Time in Germany." *Village Voice*. September 16, 2008. http://www.villagevoice.com/news/jason-beghe-is-still-denouncing-scientology-this-time-in-germany-6677638.

Ortega, Tony. "Jason Beghe's Letter to Scientology Attorneys: Yes, I'll Settle Your $1 Million Lawsuit for $19K." *Village Voice*. August 17, 2012. http://www.villagevoice.com/news/jason-beghes-letter-to-scientology-attorneys-yes-ill-settle-your-1-million-lawsuit-for-19k-6681723.

Ortega, Tony. "Leah Remini Demands $1.5 Million from Scientology for Interfering with Her A&E Series." *The Underground Bunker.* November 22, 2016.

Ortega, Tony. "Scientology's First Celebrity Defector Reveals Church Secrets." *Village Voice.* April 15, 2008. http://www.villagevoice.com/news/scientologys-first-celebrity-defector-reveals-church-secrets-6391153.

Ortega, Tony. "Scientology's 'Super Power Rundown:' What Is It, Anyway?" *Village Voice.* January 11, 2012. http://www.villagevoice.com/news/scientologys-super-power-rundown-what-is-it-anyway-6700611.

PageSix.com. "Ex-Scientologist Rips Church." April 16, 2008. http://pagesix.com/2008/04/16/ex-scientologist-rips-church/.

Pouw, Karin, to Andy Greene. *Church of Scientology International.* March 18, 2015. http://assets.rollingstone.com/pdf/Church_of_Scientology_letter.pdf.

Presley, Lisa Marie. "You Ain't Seen Nothin' Yet." *Storm and Grace.* Universal Republic. May 15, 2012. http://www.azlyrics.com/lyrics/lisamariepresley/youaintseennothinyet.html.

Raine, Susan. "Surveillance in New Religious Movements: Scientology as a Case Study." *Religious Studies and Theology* (2009): 63–94.

Seinfeld, Jerry. "Interview with Jerry Seinfeld." *Parade.* September 18, 2007. http://parade.com/50123/parade/interview-with-jerry-seinfeld/.

Streib, Heinz. "Deconversion." *The Oxford Handbook of Religious Conversion.* Edited by Lewis Rambo and Charles Farhadian. Oxford: Oxford University Press, 2014.

Wachter, Kristi. "Jason Beghe and Scientology." *Scientology Lies.* Accessed March 13, 2016. http://www.scientology-lies.com/faq/celebrities/jason-beghe.html.

Widener, Scott. "Jason Beghe Turned a Tough Break into a Tough Role as 'Chicago P.D.'s' Rogue Officer Hank Voight." *New York Daily News.* April 23, 2014. http://www.nydailynews.com/entertainment/tv-movies/jason-beghe-tough-break-led-memorable-voice-article-1.1765027.

Wikipedia. "List of Scientologists." https://en.wikipedia.org/wiki/List_of_Scientologists. Accessed February 28, 2016.

Wills, David S. *Scientologist! William S. Burroughs and the "Weird Cult."* United Kingdom: Beatdom Books, 2013.

Wright, Lawrence. "The Apostate: Paul Haggis vs. the Church of Scientology." *New Yorker.* February 14 & 21, 2011. http://www.newyorker.com/magazine/2011/02/14/the-apostate-lawrence-wright.

Wright, Lawrence. *Going Clear: Scientology, Hollywood, & the Prison of Belief.* New York: Alfred A. Knopf, 2013.

Wright, Stuart. *Leaving Cults: The Dynamics of Defection.* Washington: Society for the Scientific Study of Religion, 1987.

Wuthnow, Robert, and Charles Y. Glock. "Religious Loyalty, Defection, and Experimentation among College Youth." *Journal for the Scientific Study of Religion* 12, no. 2 (1973): 157–180.

7

Hollywood Bites

Tami M. Bereska

The Church of Scientology has a long history with the media. Both fictional and nonfictional forms of media include many references to, and representations of, Scientology. Some can be thought of as emerging from Scientology. For example, the film *Battlefield Earth* is based on L. Ron Hubbard's science fiction novel of the same name, and the plot of *Phenomenon* reflects aspects of the Scientology belief system (such as the extraordinary intelligence and memories of devout practitioners); both movies star celebrity Scientologist John Travolta.[1] In other cases media representations are explicitly or implicitly directed toward Scientology, and can be thought of as a form of critique; the Church of Scientology has demonstrated various negative responses to these particular types of references and representations. This chapter analyzes those critical mediated constructions of Scientology in a range of dramatic and comedic forms of media produced in Hollywood and elsewhere. To contextualize that analysis, the chapter first outlines the importance and value of studying entertainment media. Going beyond mere innocuous diversion, these forms of media play a key role in the construction of deviance and normality in society and have measurable effects on audience perceptions and actions. Representations of Scientology are then analyzed within the context of the overarching frames that existing research has found to be active in portrayals of new religious movements (NRMs). Particular frames govern the Scientology narrative, a narrative that is, at its core, a story of fraudulent leaders, meaningless doctrine, and well-orchestrated money-making scams. That narrative constructs Scientology as a deviant Other in need of social control. Indeed, this narrative *is* a form of social control that reinforces, reproduces, and maintains the Othering of Scientology in society.

THE MEDIA IN MODERN LIFE

The media is important. To even state this may seem unnecessary to many people. Of course it is important. The media surrounds us—newspapers, music, film, television, magazines, comics, books, radio, websites, smartphone applications, and more. As time progresses, it has an ever-increasing presence in our professional and personal lives. In 2014–2015, per capita use of only a limited range of forms of media (television, radio, magazines, newspapers, and the Internet) among U.S. and Canadian adults totaled more than 60 hours per week and has been steadily increasing.[2] But the importance of the media extends beyond the micro level of individual use, permeating larger social structures and processes. The "social order is increasingly mediated, [in that] social action is shaped and informed by media technologies and the logics that orient behavior and perceptions."[3]

The centrality of the media at both the micro- and macrolevels has led media scholar Jackson Katz to claim that it is "the single greatest pedagogical force of our time."[4] Activist Malcolm X (1925–1965) drew attention to the nature of that force, highlighting structures and processes of power: "The media's the most powerful entity on earth. They have the power to make the innocent guilty and to make the guilty innocent, and that's power."[5] Although some might dismiss those specific statements as hyperbole, there is little doubt that the media plays an important part in shaping public debates, identifying social problems, and defining boundaries (between good and bad, right and wrong, "us" and "them").[6]

The media constructs symbolic identity markers that define membership in particular communities, compiles representations or portrayals of those communities, and through a process of Othering, sets apart certain communities as problems that are in need of social control.[7] This process of Othering lies at the core of the media's relationship with NRMs, and especially the Church of Scientology.

MEDIATED CONSTRUCTIONS OF RELIGIOUS "OTHERS": NEWS AND ENTERTAINMENT MEDIA

Research on the relationship between the media and religion has tended to focus on print media, particularly the news.[8] The centrality of the "problem frame" in the narratives that compose the news (whether in print or broadcast form) means that negative images of NRMs are pervasive.[9] According to James R. Lewis, NRMs become folk devils, and journalists become the moral entrepreneurs who problematize NRMs (and especially their leaders), thereby constructing moral panics about these groups.[10] As this paper progresses we will see that some NRMs are more likely than others to be problematized. Furthermore, the notion of moral panics points to *exaggerated* concerns over particular groups. In fact, with some NRMs (such as Scientology) those concerns may not be exaggerated but perhaps reflective of real threats to social or public harm.[11]

Lewis points out that negative images of NRMs are integrated into entertainment media as well. David Feltmate concurs and goes a step further by arguing that the images contained in entertainment media may play an even larger role than the news in the Othering of NRMs: "While the nightly news runs in cycles, and NRM controversies come and go, programmes such as *The Simpsons, South Park*, and *Family Guy* maintain this spectrum of NRM's relevance through innocuous repetition."[12] But perhaps it would be more accurate to say "*seemingly* innocuous repetition," because research suggests that the negative images of NRMs in entertainment media are far from insignificant. Fiction may be intended to entertain, but it contains implicit arguments as well, and where NRMs are concerned, those implicit arguments take on a moral tone. [13]

Social psychologists and media scholars find that the arguments contained within works of fiction do influence people's attitudes, through a process of "narrative persuasion."[14] The Extended Elaboration Likelihood Model outlines two components to this process. The first is narrative transportation or absorption, wherein the audience becomes caught up in the storyline of the novel, movie, or television episode. The second component is involvement with the characters, in that the audience identifies with, and in a sense *becomes*, the main characters; if the characters are well known or well liked, involvement is of a greater magnitude. These two components of narrative persuasion limit counterarguing, thereby reducing resistance to the implicit moral arguments contained in a work of fiction.

Numerous studies have revealed narrative persuasion at work across a wide range of topic areas. For example, Melanie Colette Green and Timothy C. Brock found that reading a short story ("Murder at the Mall") caused research participants to perceive shopping malls as unsafe spaces and increased their negative attitudes toward people with mental disorders.[15] Similarly, Juan-José Iguarta and Isabel Barrios found that filmgoers expressed disapproval of the Catholic organization Opus Dei after seeing it portrayed negatively in the film *Camino*.[16] The effects of narrative persuasion extend beyond mere attitudes, affecting social action as well. For example, research conducted in more than a dozen countries around the world and, using multiple methodologies, has clearly demonstrated that images of smoking in movies are just as influential, and perhaps even more influential, than tobacco advertising and marketing. There is a strong dose-response effect, in that (controlling for other variables) the more images of tobacco use in movies that youth are exposed to, the more positive their attitudes toward smoking, the more likely they are to express an intention to smoke, and the greater the likelihood of smoking initiation.[17]

As the efficacy of narrative persuasion has been increasingly documented, research on fictional portrayals contained in novels, television programs, and movies has grown. Joseph Laycock points out that although entertainment media have been analyzed by scholars in a wide variety of fields (such as gender studies and ethnic studies), "new religious studies has been slow to consider" the importance of analyzing fictional media representations.[18] Recently, a growing number of scholars of NRMs have begun to enter this realm. Television has been the focus of the bulk of this research and has identified several frames that structure the ways NRMs are represented.

NEW RELIGIOUS MOVEMENTS ON FICTIONAL TELEVISION

Lynn S. Neal refers to television as "the central storyteller in and of American life."[19] Included in that storytelling are stories of NRMs and, more specifically, NRMs as unacceptable Others. Neal's analysis of five fictional television episodes from 1998 to 2008 reveals an ongoing "cult narrative" based on a limited set of frames that present cults as "fiscal and sexual scams" steered by fraudulent and sexually depraved leaders, who use brainwashing to achieve their personal (and sometimes violent) goals.[20] Laycock's analysis of the evolving portrayals of cults over the last half century highlights representations of the leaders as well, as "either con artists or suicidal maniacs."[21]

Neal draws attention to specific visual and verbal cues (or what many scholars may refer to as *frames*) that serve to distinguish between the cultic Other and mainstream society. These frames draw attention to five key symbolic identity markers: clothing that is distinct from that of mainstream characters on the show; settings in isolated locations (such as farms or deserts); communal living; delusional beliefs; and visibility of the group's "oddness" (such as group chanting in public venues). The cult narrative deviantizes the NRMs being portrayed and serves as a mechanism of social control that "uphold[s] dominant religious and cultural norms, while marginalizing supposedly strange or deviant religious groups."[22]

Although Neal finds the majority of television episodes between 1958 and 2008 that have focused on NRMs have been dramas, comedies also marginalize certain religious groups through satire, "the use of wit, especially irony, sarcasm, and ridicule, to criticize faults."[23] In fact, satire may be an especially effective tool in the Othering process. It serves as a complement to the process of narrative persuasion described earlier, in that the positive mood evoked by humor prevents high-effort, critical thinking and thereby further limits counterarguing. According to Terry Ray Clark, satire is an "educational tool" that "contributes to the maintenance of a free and open society" by using humor to "create a more reflective, more critical thinking, and therefore wiser audience."[24] Of course, a critically thinking audience can be a threatening force to some, especially those being satirized. Thus, sociologist Peter L. Berger refers to satire as "the deliberate use of the comic for the purposes of attack"—an intentional and subversive weapon of destruction.[25] The use of this weapon against religious belief systems and their affiliated groups goes back centuries, "critiquing what some consider potentially dangerous, excessive, or just plain silly beliefs and practices."[26] Any religious beliefs or practices can be subject to satirization—Christianity, Judaism, and Eastern religions have all been satirized at various times and in various places.[27] However, those that teeter on the periphery of the mainstream, such as NRMs, are especially subject to satirization.

Although NRMs as a whole tend to be marginalized in satire, the nature of their Otherness varies. Feltmate proposes that when looking at religious satire in adult animated sitcoms, there are four different categories of NRMs[28]: First are those that are constructed as Others by virtue of remaining outside of the mainstream but yet are otherwise *accepted*. For instance, Wicca features prominently in several episodes of *The Simpsons*, and in large part, its "feminist politics and creative spirituality" are portrayed positively.[29] Second are NRMs that are *annoying*. Some of their beliefs and practices are presented as unusual, but the groups are shown to be relatively harmless. For example, *The Simpsons* satirizes the door-knocking of Mormons and Jehovah's Witnesses but does not denigrate the groups. Third are NRMs that are theologically *misguided*, and their members portrayed as "wilfully stupid"[30] Some of these groups may be misguided but harmless, while others are misguided and untrustworthy. For instance, while *South Park* portrays Mormons as the former, Scientology is portrayed as the latter because of its corrupt leaders who "lie, cheat, and steal."[31] Finally, some NRMs are *dangerous* because of brainwashing (such as The Movementarians in *The Simpsons*) or mass violence/suicide (such as the Heaven's Helpers Youth Cult) in *Family Guy*.

Taken together, the works of Neal and Feltmate outline a range of frames that are used to structure fictional television's representations of NRMs and that construct those religious groups as unacceptable Others who are distinct from mainstream society. Some groups are portrayed as more unacceptable than others. In particular, some NRMs may engage in actions that are not only perceived to be but are also a very real threat. Scientology is an organization that has a long and well-documented history of deliberate antagonism against mainstream social institutions and private citizens, including harassment campaigns against journalists, jurists, judges, and scholars.[32] These campaigns are institutionalized in the organization's policies, such as its 1960 "Special Zone Plan," which outlines the infiltration of government agencies (such as law enforcement and the FBI) and civil society groups (such as the news media).[33] Its history with the justice system is what scholar Benjamin Beit-Hallahmi refers to as "extraordinary:" "not just hundreds of cases of litigational and official inquiries, but scores of convictions for such crimes as burglary [e.g., of the offices of the IRS and the Justice Department]; forgery; obstruction of justice, and fraud."[34] Thus, rather than being a passive victim of negative media attention, the organization's actions in fact foster a negative media climate.

MEDIATED CONSTRUCTIONS OF SCIENTOLOGY

Public concerns about Scientology have waxed and waned over the decades, but Lewis argues that attention to Scientology "has become white hot in the second decade of the twenty-first century."[35] Because these concerns are frequently played out within the media, it becomes particularly important to analyze the frames that govern representations of Scientology in entertainment media.

Entertainment media contains innumerable references to, and representations of, Scientology. In some cases explicit references to Scientology (or to prominent celebrity Scientologists) are made. Examples include the movies *Airplane, The Bridge, Until Nothing Remains, Superhero Movie, Talladega Nights: The Ballad of Ricky Bobby,* and the television shows *Seinfeld* and *South Park*.[36] Explicit references are potentially dangerous to the creators of these forms of media, in that the Church of Scientology has a long history of litigious behavior in response to media references about their organization.[37] Consequently, some media creators make implicit references to Scientology instead. A quasi-fictionalized religious group may lie at the center of a television episode or film, but the similarities to Scientology are clear to informed observers: Eventualism (*Schizopolis*), MindHead (*Bowfinger*), Church of Scientific Spiritualism (*The Profit*), Church of Scienetics (*The L.A. Complex*), and The Cause (*The Master*).[38]

REFERENCES TO SCIENTOLOGY

A number of pieces of entertainment media include passing references to Scientology and/or celebrity Scientologists. For example, in one scene in the movie *Airplane*, Scientology is just one of several NRMs collecting donations from passersby in an airport; a pilot is forced to physically repel these fundraising assaults by pushing, punching, and throwing the individuals involved.

One of the most well-known references is in a classic episode of the television sitcom *Seinfeld* ("The Parking Garage"). As the main characters Jerry, George, Elaine, and Kramer are wandering around a shopping mall's parkade searching for their car, a woman who they had previously met in the mall drives by. She stops and gives them a ride through the parkade to aid their search. However, soon the car screeches to a halt, and she throws the four of them out of the car. Clearly, George has said something to offend her. He exclaims, "I'm sorry! I don't even know L. Ron Hubbard!" Jerry follows up by saying, "Boy, those Scientologists sure can be sensitive," a clear reference to the Church of Scientology's reactions to media portrayals.[39]

One of the fan-favorite scenes in the Will Ferrell movie *Talladega Nights: The Ballad of Ricky Bobby* includes a satirical reference to celebrity Scientologist Tom Cruise. As race car driver Ricky Bobby is running away from a nonexistent racetrack fire, wearing nothing but his underwear, he prays for his life. His prayer is to those he believes might be able to help him, including Jesus, Allah, "Jewish God," Oprah Winfrey, and Tom Cruise. In this joke, Tom Cruise is satirized as a godlike figure, and it is also a reference to several highly publicized instances of Cruise rescuing people from harm (such as car accidents) in the 1990s.[40] When actor Will Ferrell was asked in interviews about whether he was concerned that he might be persecuted by the Church of Scientology for this reference, he jokingly replied that, indeed, he was so concerned he became a Scientologist just to be on the safe side. Ironically, two years after the film was released, a Church of Scientology video featuring Tom Cruise was leaked on YouTube. In this video he talks about how, as a Scientologist, one cannot just pass by the scene of accidents without stopping because, "You know you're the only one who can really help."[41]

A passing reference to Scientology that audiences never had the chance to see was in the 1991 film *Delirious*, starring John Candy. In the rough cut of the movie, one of the female characters tells her brother that John Candy's character has a "strange power" over her. In response, her brother asks, "Do you think he's a Scientologist?" Upon hearing of that reference, the Church of Scientology undertook a well-orchestrated campaign that included the threat of lawsuits and, allegedly, the director's house being broken into and vandalized. The final edit of the film did not include that scene.[42]

In some cases, there is more than just a passing reference to Scientology or Scientologists. Skits that satirize or parody Scientology can be several minutes in length. For example, Tom Cruise has been the subject of several comedic skits. A Church of Scientology video that features Tom Cruise has been parodied in the film *Superhero Movie*, by talk-show host Craig Ferguson on *The Late Late Show with Craig Ferguson*, and by actor Jerry O'Connell on his *Funny or Die* channel. In an interview more than seven years after filming the parody, Jerry O'Connell stated that he still does everything he can to avoid encountering Tom Cruise: "I don't think there'll be a confrontation, but why poke *that* bear?"[43] (emphasis added).

The Church of Scientology's 1990 music video ("We Stand Tall") was also the subject of a skit, on a 2015 episode of *Saturday Night Live*. The skit satirizes several aspects of Scientology (although it refers to the group as the Church of Neurotology), but of particular note is its references to the dark side of the church. Several individuals featured in the music video are singled out as having left the group since the video was made, some going on to become vocal critics. Others are featured as victims of oppressive practices, such as "missing," "sued to death," and "living in a hole." Some are reflective of those oppressive practices; for example, one singer is described as someone who blackmails gay celebrities.[44]

Several movies and television shows go beyond brief references to Scientology. Instead, Scientology (or a fictional Scientology-like group) lies at the center of a plotline. On television, the animated comedy *The Simpsons* features an episode ("The Joy of Sect") that has the Simpsons family join a religious group known as the Movementarians, a group that is a pastiche of several real NRMs, including Scientology. The leader of the Movementarians looks like L. Ron Hubbard, members must agree to live in military-style housing for 100,000 years (a reference to the one billion year contract that members of Scientology's Sea Org must sign), and the group responds to criticism with a team of lawyers (similar to the Church of Scientology's litigious nature) and by purchasing local news stations (a reference to the church's efforts to control its representation in the media).[45]

In an episode of *South Park* ("Trapped in the Closet") not only does one of the characters decide to join the Church of Scientology, but his e-meter reading reveals he is the reincarnation of L. Ron Hubbard. One year later, a scheduled rerun of this episode was preempted by Viacom, Comedy Central's parent company. Viacom is also the parent company of Paramount Pictures, which was set to release the movie *Mission Impossible III*, starring Tom Cruise; reportedly, Cruise refused to promote the movie if the *South Park* episode was broadcast.[46]

In a multiepisode story arc, the Canadian serial drama *The L.A. Complex* features a character who is a successful young actor recruited by his sister to join a Scientology-like group (the Church of Scienetics). A large mansion comprises its headquarters, personality tests are given to prospective members to identify how significant their problems are, and a series of programs are provided to overcome those problems.[47]

The German television movie *Until Nothing Remains* tells the story of a young couple and their son joining the Church of Scientology. Over time, the husband becomes disillusioned and leaves but his wife and son remain. The film is loosely based on the story of a German man, Heiner von Rönn. In real life, the Church of Scientology opposed the broadcast of this film and as a result of their legal efforts, was able to broadcast a 40-minute rebuttal on the television network the following day.[48]

Plots based on Scientology are found in feature films as well. The dramatic film *The Bridge* paints a negative picture of Scientology. One of the characters is prevented by the church from seeing his daughter, who lives at the Flag Land Base, the spiritual headquarters of the Church of Scientology. His daughter later mysteriously dies of a fall from one of the buildings on the base (a reference to a number of suspicious deaths that have actually occurred at Flag Land Base, the most publicized of which was Lisa McPherson's unusual death in 1995).[49] The character's death galvanizes protests against the church, which contribute to a member's decision to leave, even though she has already achieved a state of Clear.[50]

The Master tells the story of Lancaster Dodd, founder of a group known as "The Cause," and a young World War II veteran who is drawn into (and yet also disillusioned by) the movement. Although some of the people involved in the film have denied that it is based on Scientology, innumerable similarities between the film and the early years of Scientology have been noted. Not only does the actor who plays Lancaster Dodd (Philip Seymour Hoffman) look remarkably like L. Ron Hubbard, but a former member of the Sea Org outlines 22 detailed similarities between The Cause and Scientology. These similarities range from the aspects of the doctrine (e.g., one's current life is affected by harmful past memories) to characteristics of the leaders: spending time sailing on a four-masted schooner early in life, writing science fiction novels, and referring to dissenters as "squirrels."[51]

Schizopolis is a comedic art film about a man who becomes the speechwriter for the leader of a quasi-religious self-help group known as Eventualism. He—and the others who work in the headquarters—are harassed and abused by their supervisors, much like allegations by ex-employees of the Church of Scientology. The reference to Scientology is also evident in the cover of the book *Eventualism*, which features an erupting volcano—similar to the cover of the book *Dianetics*.[52]

In the comedy *Bowfinger*, a movie studio executive agrees to distribute a financially bereft filmmaker's movie only if it stars the action star of the day (Kit Ramsey), who is a member of the celebrity-courting religious group MindHead. The filmmaker cannot afford the actor's salary, so covertly films him, without the actor's knowledge. The other (paid) actors in the movie walk up to Kit Ramsey and say their lines from the science fiction script. As Kit does not realize a movie is being filmed, he interprets the dialogue on the basis of MindHead's belief system and thereby believes that an alien invasion is actually occurring.

The Profit satirizes Scientology in telling the story of L. Conrad Powers, the leader of the Church of Scientific Spiritualism. This group has an extra-terrestrial doctrine, courts celebrities as members, has clashes with the IRS, infiltrates the FBI, and uses a "Mind Meter" as a tool for personal and spiritual development. A lawsuit by the Church of Scientology resulted in a court order that prohibited the release of this film in the United States.

REPRESENTATIONS OF SCIENTOLOGY

References to Scientology have been made on television and in feature films, using both drama and comedy, and in periods ranging from a few seconds (for a passing remark) to more than an hour (for multiepisode television arcs and feature films). The nature of these references fit within, and expand upon, the overarching frames of NRMs previously identified in research.[53]

THE SCIENTOLOGY NARRATIVE

Much like the "cult narrative" described in previous research, at the core of the Scientology narrative lies fraudulent leaders and money-making scams. The consequences of the scam are clearly portrayed in the German television movie *Until Nothing Remains*, where a couple is manipulated into joining the Church of Scientology. When the husband finally leaves the church, he has lost everything—not only his wife and son but also the family inheritance, which his wife has given to the church.[54]

The multiepisode story arc about the Church of Scienetics on the serial television drama *The L.A. Complex* reveals a complex, carefully planned scam.[55] It begins when one of the characters (Connor) is visited by a young woman (Charlotte) who tells him she is his long-lost sister, who he hasn't seen since his mother abandoned him with his abusive father many years earlier. Charlotte conveys how similar she and Connor are, from the scars on their arms due to self-mutilation to a history of using medication to treat a mental illness. However, Charlotte points out that, unlike Connor, she has overcome those problems—she was saved by Scienetics.

Connor agrees to accompany her to the Scienetics headquarters, where he is introduced to a beautiful, blonde woman (Roxanne) who will be his "channel" (i.e., his Scienetics liaison). He receives a tour of the facility and grounds and takes a (free) personality test that reveals an exceptional level of intelligence but also an exceptional level of anxiety. Roxanne tells him that Scienetics can help him discard his negative psychological characteristics and thereby enhance his intelligence even further. At first, Connor is hesitant and wants to talk to his sister, but Roxanne tells him that she is currently in a program session; he must wait. While the two of them wait, she brings up details of his abuse and abandonment as a child, which causes Connor tremendous emotional pain. Now when she tells him that Scienetics can help with that pain, he is ready to sign up. The initial "detoxification" package (much like Scientology's introductory Purification Rundown program) will cost somewhere between $5,000 and $10,000—a pittance for a "rich and famous actor" like him, and after all, "nothing is expensive when your life is at stake."

At a later point, one of Connor's friends warns him about the group, telling him to investigate it on the Internet before giving them any more money. Connor is concerned about the information he finds online, including his discovery that Charlotte will receive a finder's fee—10 percent of the money that he paid for his initial package. He returns to the headquarters and demands to see someone. Once again, he is told he must wait. Coincidentally (or not so coincidentally), while he waits in the lobby, a legendary actor whom he idolizes emerges from one of the session rooms, introduces himself, and gives an awestruck Connor his phone number so they can get to know each other better. Connor's concerns disappear, and he begins a journey deeper into the Church of Scienetics.

On the television show *South Park*, young Stan is also manipulated into joining Scientology. The episode begins with his friends telling him that nothing fun is free. Soon, Stan walks past a Scientology office at a local strip mall; the people working there tell him they can give him a personality test that is both fun *and* free. The test reveals that Stan is "miserable and totally depressed," something that he exclaims he never even realized. It turns out that the personality test was free, but the program to cure his misery and depression costs $250. When his e-meter reading reveals him as the reincarnation of L. Ron Hubbard, the leader of the Church of Scientology (David Miscavige) directs Stan to compile his every thought in a book that will become the new theological foundation for the church. When Stan states that the book should be free of charge to everyone, the leader protests, arguing that the two of them can make $3 million with it. He tells Stan, "That's how a scam works!" The episode closes with Stan telling the crowd of worshipping Scientologists outside his door that church is just a "big fat global scam" and subsequently being threatened with lawsuits.

Meaningless doctrine lies at the heart of the scam. For example, in *The Master* leader Lancaster Dodd's son tells a new member of The Cause that his father is just making the whole thing up as he goes along, a sentiment also echoed in *South Park*. Through satire, the film *Schizopolis* is able to reflect the lack of meaning in a powerful way. In one scene, the leader of Eventualism

(T. Azimuth Schwitters) directs his speechwriter to write a very important speech. His instructions sound ridiculous: "It should lay out a new course of action, but one that can change direction at any moment." "It should be lengthy enough to seem substantial, yet concise enough to feel breezy." "The general thrust should be embedded in one's mind forever, but specific words should be forgotten the moment they are heard."[56]

Not only are scams perpetrated by the leaders, but the leaders themselves are inherently fraudulent. For instance, in the movie *The Profit*, the man who would later found the Church of Scientific Spiritualism (L. Conrad Powers) is shown to be a con artist early in life. He is paid $20,000 to sell a sailboat, but instead he runs away with the $20,000 and steals the sailboat. His Church of Scientific Spiritualism would later go on to be investigated by the IRS and would infiltrate the FBI.

In both dramatic and comedic television and film, the Scientology narrative is a story of con artist leaders who espouse meaningless doctrine and create complex, carefully planned scams to build a mass of devoted, unquestioning followers and bilk them out of their money. In some cases, the Church of Scientology (or its quasi-fictional counterpart) is portrayed as what Feltmate would call a "misguided and untrustworthy" religious movement.[57] Members lose their money and, in some cases, their self-respect. However, in other instances, the church is portrayed in a way that goes beyond being "untrustworthy." A man loses not only his money but also his family upon leaving Scientology in *Until Nothing Remains*.[58] Former members end up "missing" or "living in a hole" or in "Neurotology prison" in the parody of the "We Stand Tall" music video on *Saturday Night Live*.[59] A devoted Scientologist loses her life in *The Bridge*—an event that viewers are led to believe was caused by the church.[60] In these instances, Scientology enters the realm of what Feltmate would refer to as a "dangerous" religious movement.[61]

Stories of Scientology as misguided and untrustworthy, or as dangerous, are composed of specific frames: distinctive clothing, isolation, collectivities, foolish beliefs or behaviors, and visibility. These frames are based on, and in some cases extensions of, those identified in Neal's research on five fictional television episodes that focused on cults.[62]

The "Distinctive Clothing" Frame

Distinctive clothing draws boundaries between insiders and outsiders.[63] In several cases, elite members or employees wear militaristic uniforms (e.g., *Bowfinger*, *South Park*, *The Profit*)—a reference to the uniforms worn in different branches of Scientology, such as Sea Org. Although the people working in the Church of Scienetics' headquarters on *The L.A. Complex* do not wear uniforms, their formal-looking office attire (such as one might see in a high-profile law office) sets them apart from the casual clothing worn by the other characters on the show. Clothing may be distinctive in other ways as well. For example, people entering the MindHead compound (*Bowfinger*) are greeted by the unusual site of everyone wearing white pyramids on their heads. The uniforms worn by Scientology employees on *South Park* are gray and drab, standing in stark contrast to the colorful clothes worn by other characters on the show; Stan's appointment as the reincarnation of L. Ron Hubbard is marked by him emerging from his home looking like a Greek god, wearing a white toga and a wreath of golden leaves on his head.[64] The various parodies of Church of Scientology's video featuring Tom Cruise copy his black turtleneck sweater.[65] In all of these cases, distinctive clothing helps construct Scientology as the Other.

The "Isolation" Frame

Neal finds that on fictional television shows, cults are frequently located in isolated geographical settings, such as farms and deserts. However, the Scientology narrative in television and film reflects a variety of forms of isolation. Sometimes it is geographical isolation. For example, L. Ron Hubbard (*South Park*) and Lancaster Dodd (*The Master*) have spent periods of time living on sailboats.[66] But physical isolation can take other forms as well. MindHead (*Bowfinger*) and the Church of Scienetics (*The L.A. Complex*) are located in urban areas, but the buildings are set in the center of large compounds. The separation of the Scienetics' building from the outside world is further highlighted by the spa-like music playing in the background, a noticeable contrast to the pop, rock, and hip hop music that otherwise serves as the soundtrack to the show.[67] In *Schizopolis*, the main offices of Eventualism are not physically isolated, but the employees sometimes are—as virtual slaves to their jobs, trapped in their office tower.[68]

Isolation can also be social, rather than physical, where members are separated from family or friends. In *The Bridge*, a father is prevented from visiting his daughter on the Church of Scientology's Flag Land Base, despite his best efforts. Upon her death, his ex-wife (who is still a member) won't even allow him to attend the funeral.[69] Social isolation may be self-directed, in that members choose to distance themselves from nonmembers. In *South Park*, Stan's friends are critical of his decision to join Scientology. In response, he tells them that if they can't accept Scientology, they are no longer his friends.[70]

Even the distinct nomenclature used in Scientology can be thought of as a form of isolation, in that (at least prior to information being leaked on the Internet) only fellow Scientologists could understand terms like "fair game," "clear," or "SP." The Church of Scientology video featuring Tom Cruise is filled with this special language, referring to "KSW" (Keeping Scientology Working), "SP" (Suppressive Person), and "PTS" (Potential Trouble Source). The parodies of this video satirize the nomenclature. For example, Jerry O'Connell's parody refers to "PYT" ("Pretty Young Thing," a Michael Jackson song), "WAYATW" (why are you acting this way), and "KFC" (the fried chicken restaurant).[71] The Scientology-like groups in television shows and films also have distinct nomenclatures. For example, when Connor (*The L.A. Complex*) is confused by the terminology of Scienetics (such as "channel"), he is reassured that he will become familiar with it as he goes along.[72] Whether it is through geographical, physical, social, or discursive isolation, entertainment media locates Scientology "somewhere else"—somewhere other than where the rest of us are located.

The "Collectivity" Frame

Another of the visual cues that Neal finds characterizes cults on television is communal living. Communal living is sometimes seen in representations of Scientology in television and film as well, where some members are shown living in close proximity, such as on a compound or in a housing complex (e.g., *The Bridge*; *Until Nothing Remains*; *The Profit*). But other representations of collectivity are also part of the Scientology narrative. Members and employees do not necessarily live together (or even in close proximity) but gather together for particular periods of time in certain physical spaces. Employees gather in the organization's headquarters or offices, as do members who are undergoing treatment (*The Master*; *The L.A. Complex*; *Schizopolis*; *The Bridge*; *Until Nothing Remains*; *The Profit*; *Bowfinger*). Sometimes they gather in public spaces. For instance, a large, worshipping crowd gathers outside of Stan's home on *South Park* when he is identified as the reincarnation of L. Ron Hubbard. Even *Saturday Night Live*'s parody of Scientology's music video features a large group of perhaps hundreds of members of the Church of Neurotology singing together.[73] Entertainment media tell us that where we find one Scientologist, we will likely find many. In this sense, Scientology may be thought of as not just a singular Other but rather a group of countless Others.

The "Foolish Beliefs or Behaviors" Frame

Neal identifies delusional beliefs as one of the cues that characterizes cults on television, highlighting unrealistic beliefs and members' blind devotion.[74] While those characteristics are evident in a number of ways in representations of Scientology or Scientology-like groups in television and film, the Scientology narrative goes even a step further. The beliefs are portrayed as not just unrealistic but as foolish or ridiculous, and they frequently serve as a source of humor. On the animated comedy *South Park*, when the story of Xenu is being told, a message flashes on the screen: "This is what Scientologists actually believe." Similarly, the intergalactic beliefs of MindHead (*Bowfinger*) and the Church of Scientific Spiritualism (*The Profit*) are the subject of numerous jokes in those satirical feature films.[75]

The foolish nature of the beliefs leads some people to question their involvement with the group. In an episode of *The L.A. Complex*, one of Connor's friends laughs out loud when he learns that Connor is studying Scienetics. He refers to the Scienetics as "crazy" and based on "ballistic federations," "ghouls in volcanoes," and the "evil lord Nee-Zu." When Connor's online search reveals that those strange ideas are actually a part of Scienetics, it leads him to question his involvement with the group.[76] Similarly, in *The Bridge* a group of protesters asks a member of Scientology if she knows about the ridiculous story of Xenu; hearing that story is one of the factors that leads her to leave Scientology.[77]

Not only does the Scientology narrative portray the belief system as foolish or ridiculous but sometimes also the behaviors of its members (especially its celebrity members). For example, Tom Cruise and John Travolta are parodied in *South Park*, locking themselves in a closet and refusing to come out.[78] In *Bowfinger*, members of MindHead wear silly-looking paper pyramids on their heads when they are on the organization's compound. Furthermore, celebrity member Kit Ramsey is frequently made to look like a buffoon, such as when he panics because he thinks aliens are invading Earth.[79] Parodies of the Church of Scientology video featuring Tom Cruise portray him not just as someone with ridiculous beliefs but as a person who fits a stereotypical image of mental illness. All three parodies include maniacal laughter, bulging eyes, and bizarre gestures. Craig Ferguson's parody consists primarily of strange noises instead of words. Jerry O'Connell starts speaking nonsense about rabbits eating apples, followed by the arrival of elephants. In *Superhero Movie*, the Tom Cruise character proclaims that he can eat planets and can fly. At a later point, he seems to either be asleep or in a trance, only to suddenly awaken and exclaim, "There was a farmer had a dog and Bingo was his name-o!"[80] Scientology is, at the very least, a foolish and ridiculous Other—and according to some representations, the beliefs and the people involved may be just plain "crazy."

The "Visibility" Frame

Just as Neal finds that the "oddness" of cults is made highly visible in fictional television shows (such as through group chanting), so too is Scientology's otherness.[81] One of the ways visibility is enhanced is through highlighting celebrity. In some cases, real celebrities such as Tom Cruise, John Travolta, or rapper R.

Kelly are portrayed (e.g., *South Park*, *Superhero Movie*). In other instances, fictional celebrities appear as members or as being courted by the organization: Kit Ramsey in *Bowfinger*, a Tom Cruise-esque actor in *The Profit*, "rich and famous" Connor in *The L.A. Complex*. Distinctive clothing, special terminology, and foolish behaviors also provide visibility. When Scientology, or a fictional Scientology-like group, is the butt of a joke in a satirical television show or film, the group becomes more visible. Parody in itself enhances visibility by turning people into larger-than-life caricatures. Viewers come to understand that Scientology is the Other because they can *see* its otherness in so many ways.

The Scientology narrative contained in entertainment media is, at its core, a story of fraudulent leaders, meaningless doctrine, and well-orchestrated money-making scams. In that narrative, distinctive clothing, isolation, collectivity, foolish beliefs and behaviors, and visibility frame Scientology, constructing it as a deviant Other in need of social control. Indeed, this narrative *is* a form of social control that reinforces, reproduces, and maintains the Othering of Scientology in society, outside of the realm of entertainment media.

CONCLUSION

When NRMs are portrayed in entertainment media, the lines between fiction and nonfiction are blurred in that mediated representations draw upon a larger cultural stock of knowledge about NRMs.[82] When those representations are of an actual (or presumed) religious group rather than a purely fictionalized one, those boundaries become blurred even further. This is clearly the case with representations of Scientology. When a television show or movie makes explicit references to Scientology, what is fact and what is fiction becomes somewhat ambiguous. For example, a fictional character mysteriously dies on the Flag Land Base, but that fictional death points to several mysterious deaths that have actually occurred on the compound.[83] Even when entertainment media portray a fictionalized group (such as the Church of Scienetics) in order to avoid persecution by the Church of Scientology, the references to Scientology are clear: Scientology's e-meters become "mind-meters"; groups clash with the IRS or infiltrate the FBI; leaders look remarkably like L. Ron Hubbard; groups court celebrities as members; intergalactic ideas inform the doctrine; covers of books look like the cover of *Dianetics*; Jerry O'Connell's promotional video for the Writers' Guild of America is an obvious parody of the Scientology video featuring Tom Cruise, down to the clothing worn.[84]

The cultural stock of knowledge about NRMs serves as the lens through which movies and television shows are interpreted.[85] That stock of knowledge about Scientology is what enables the audience to laugh at the satirization of Scientology in *South Park*, *Bowfinger*, *The Profit*, *Schizopolis*, and the parodies of Tom Cruise. It makes them recoil in concern, offense, or outrage in dramatic media like *The L.A. Complex*, *The Bridge*, *The Master*, and *Until Nothing Remains*.[86] But then, these fictionalized portrayals subsequently contribute to that larger cultural stock of knowledge. They "offer a particular interpretation" of those real characteristics and events that the organization has been involved in and "also provide viewers with a way to interpret present or future . . . events."[87] The suspicious death of a Scientology member in *The Bridge* overlaps with audience interpretations of actual deaths that have occurred.[88] Parodies of Tom Cruise become part of the lens through which people interpret his failed marriages in the past or interviews on talk shows or news programs in the future.[89]

The lines between fiction and nonfiction become blurred even further in that the news media has increasingly placed a premium on the importance of grabbing the audience's attention through entertainment—in a manner commonly referred to as "newstainment."[90] The public's views, news media, and entertainment media form a nexus in which each reinforces the others. Representations of Scientology in entertainment media reinforce news stories about the group and vice versa. Entertainment and news media narratives reinforce the public's views of Scientology and vice versa. And then when the Church of Scientology responds to media representations in a coercive or litigious manner—practices institutionalized in the organization's policies— those actions further reinforce media narratives and the public's views. All combine to reinforce, maintain, and build the cultural stock of knowledge about Scientology. And in the digital age, the cultural stock of knowledge is located online—the news stories, the television episodes, the films (even those that were prohibited from release in certain parts of the world), the interviews with past and present members, the documents, the doctrine. The Internet has become, in the words of Lewis, Scientology's "Waterloo."[91] The cultural stock of knowledge about Scientology is readily accessible to more people than ever before—novelists, journalists, filmmakers, screenwriters, stand-up comedians, and members of the public. It is one in which Scientology is constructed as a fraudulent, foolish, untrustworthy, and potentially dangerous Other—constructed not only by news and entertainment media but by the organizations own actions as well.

NOTES

1. Corey Mandell and J. D. Shapiro, *Battlefield Earth*, streaming film, directed by Roger Christian (Burbank, CA: Warner Bros., 2000), http://itunes.ca; Gerald Di Pego, *Phenomenon*, streaming film, directed by Jon Turteltaub (Burbank, CA: Touchstone Pictures, 1996), http://itunes.ca.

208

Scientology in Popular Culture

2. Statista, "Average Time Spent with Major Media per Day in the United States as of October 2015 (in minutes)," accessed January 10, 2016, http://www.statistia .com/statistics/276683/media-use-in-the-us/; Interactive Advertising Bureau (IAB) of Canada, *2014 CMUST (Canadian Media Usage Trends)* (Toronto, ON: IAB, 2014); Interactive Advertising Bureau (IAB) of Canada, *2010 Canadian Media Usage Trends Study* (Toronto, ON: IAB, 2011).

3. David L. Altheide, "Media Logic, Social Control, and Fear," *Communications Theory* 23 (2013): 225, doi:10.1111/comt.12017.

4. Jackson Katz and Jeremy Earp, *Tough Guise: Violence, Media and the Crisis in Masculinity*, DVD, directed by Sut Jhally (Northampton, MA: Media Education Foundation, 1999).

5. Linn Washington, Jr., "Probing the President: The Media's Paralysis of Analysis? Race, the Press and the White House," in *Redefining Black Power: Reflections on the State of Black America*, ed. Joanne Griffith (San Francisco, CA: City Lights Books, 2013), 115.

6. Tami M. Bereska, *Deviance, Conformity, and Social Control in Canada*, 4th edition (Toronto, ON: Pearson Education Canada, 2014), 96.

7. Chris Greer and Yvonne Jewkes, "Extremes of Otherness: Media Images of Social Exclusion," *Social Justice* 32, no. 1 (2005): 20, http://www.socialjusticejournal .org/archive/99_32_1/99_03Greer.pdf.

8. Lynn S. Neal, "'They're Freaks!' The Cult Stereotype in Fictional Television Shows, 1958–2008," *Nova Religio: Journal of Alternative and Emergent Religions* 14, no. 3 (2011): 83, doi:10.1525/nr.2011.14.3.8; David Feltmate, "New Religious Movements in Adult Animated Sitcoms—A Spectrum of Portrayals," *Religion Compass* 5/7 (2011): 350, doi:10.1111/j.1749-8171.2011.00287.x; Joseph Laycock, "Where Do They Get These Ideas? Changing Ideas of Cults in the Mirror of Popular Culture," *Journal of the American Academy of Religion* 81, no. 1 (2013): 81, doi:10.1093/jaarel /lfs091.

9. Altheide, "Media Logic," 232.

10. James R. Lewis, "Scientology vs. the Media," *Alternative Spirituality and Religion Review* 6, no. 1 (2015): 73, doi:10.5840/asrr201572010. For a discussion of moral entrepreneurs, see Howard S. Becker, *Outsiders: Studies in the Sociology of Deviance* (New York: The Free Press, 1963). For a discussion of folk devils and moral panics, see Stanley Cohen, *Folk Devils and Moral Panics: The Creation of the Mods and Rockers* (Oxford, UK: Blackwell, 1972).

11. Benjamin Beit-Hallahmi, "Scientology: Religion or Racket?," *Marburg Journal of Religion*, 8, no. 1 (2003): 26–28, http://archiv.ub.uni-marburg.de/ep/0004/article/ view/3724; Douglas Franz, "Distrust in Clearwater—A Special Report. Death of a Scientologist Heightens Suspicions in a Florida Town," *New York Times*, December 1, 1997, http://www.nytimes.com/1997/12/01/us/distrust-clearwater-special-report-death -scientologist-heightens-suspicions.html?pagewanted=all.

12. Feltmate, "New Religious Movements," 350.

13. Juan-José Iguarta and Isabel Barrios, "Changing Real World Beliefs with Controversial Movies: Processes and Mechanisms of Narrative Persuasion," *Journal of Communication*, 62 (2012): 514, doi:10.1111/j.1460-2466.2012.01640.x.

14. Iguarta and Barrios, "Changing Real World Beliefs," 514; Melanie C. Green and Timothy C. Brock, "The Role of Transportation in the Persuasiveness of Public Narratives," *Journal of Personality and Social Psychology*, 79, no. 5 (2000): 702–704, doi:10.1037//0022-3514.79.5.701.

15. Green and Brock, "The Role of Transportation," 705.

16. Iguarta and Barrios, "Changing Real World Beliefs," 523.

17. World Health Organization, *Smoke-Free Movies: From Evidence to Action* (Geneva, CH: WHO, 2011), 2–7.

18. Laycock, "Where Do They Get," 81.

19. Neal, "'They're Freaks!,'" 84.

20. The five television episodes were as follows: "The Joy of Sect" (*The Simpsons*), "The Cult" (*Everybody Loves Raymond*), "Charisma" (*Law and Order: Special Victims Unit*), "Shooting Stars" (*CSI*), and "Minimal Loss" (*Criminal Minds*); Neal, "'They're Freaks!,'" 95.

21. Laycock, "Where Do They Get," 97.

22. Neal, "'They're Freaks!,'" 83.

23. *Encarta Dictionary: English (North America)*, Microsoft Word, s.v. "satire."

24. Terry Ray Clark, "Saved by Satire? Learning to Value Popular Culture's Critique of Sacred Traditions," in *Understanding Religion and Popular Culture: Theories, Themes, Products and Practices*, ed. Terry Ray Clark and Dan W. Clanton (New York, NY: Routledge, 2012), 13–17.

25. Peter L. Berger, *Redeeming Laughter: The Comic Dimension of Human Experience* (Berlin: Walter de Gruyter, 1997), 167.

26. Clark, "Saved by Satire," 16.

27. Ibid., 14–24.

28. Feltmate, "New Religious Movements," 343–350.

29. Ibid., 343–344.

30. Ibid., 348–349.

31. Ibid.

32. Beit-Hallahmi, "Scientology," 26–29; The Walrus, "Scientology Attacks! Going to War with L. Ron Hubbard's Disciples," *Walrus*, April 2015, http://thewalrus.ca/scientology-attacks/.

33. Roy Wallis, "Road to Total Freedom," cited in Beit-Hallahmi, "Scientology," 29.

34. Beit-Hallahmi, "Scientology," 27.

35. Lewis, "Scientology vs. the Media," 73.

36. Jim Abrahams, David Zucker, and Jerry Zucker, *Airplane*, streaming film, directed by Jim Abrahams, David Zucker, and Jerry Zucker (Hollywood, CA: Paramount Pictures, 1980), http://itunes.ca; Brett Hanover, "The Bridge," YouTube video, directed by Brett Hanover (Memphis, TN: Brett Hanover, 2006), posted by Conspiracy Cult, October 5, 2011, https://www.youtube.com/watch?v=s-DkG6kKASc; Niki Stein, "Until Nothing Remains," YouTube video, directed by Niki Stein (Potsdam, DE: teamWorx Television and Film, 2010), posted by Enturbulator General, June 11, 2015, https://www.youtube.com/watch?v=wpfjb8zG-WI; Craig Mazin, *Superhero Movie*, streaming film, directed by Craig Mazin (New York, NY: Dimension Films, 2008), http://itunes.ca; Will Ferrell and Adam McKay, *Talladega Nights: The Ballad*

of Ricky Bobby, streaming film, directed by Adam McKay (Culver City, CA: Columbia Tri Star Pictures, 2006), http://itunes.ca; Larry David and Jerry Seinfeld, *Seinfeld*, "The Parking Garage," DVD, directed by Tom Cherones (1991; Culver City, CA: Sony Pictures Home Entertainment, 2013); Trey Parker, Matt Stone, and Brian Graden, *South Park*, "Trapped in the Closet," streaming television episode, directed by Trey Parker (New York, NY: Braniff/Parker-Stone Studios, 2005), http://itunes.ca.

37. Beit-Hallahmi, "Scientology," 26.

38. Steven Soderbergh, "Schizopolis," YouTube video, directed by Steven Soderbergh (Helena, MT: 406 Productions, 1996), posted by Jake Maringoni, May 12, 2015, https://www.youtube.com/results?search_query=schizopolis+full+movie; Steve Martin, *Bowfinger*, streaming film, directed by Frank Oz (Orlando, FL: Universal Pictures, 1999), http://itunes.ca; Peter N. Alexander, "The Profit," YouTube video, directed by Peter N. Alexander (Tampa, FL: Courage Productions, 2001), posted by Wilfried Handl, March 19, 2015, https://www.youtube.com/watch?v=D67OvQyGMF8; Lara Azzopardi, Martin Gero, and Kate Hewlett, *The L.A. Complex*, "Make It Right," streaming film, directed by Peter Wellington (Toronto, ON: Epitome Pictures, 2012), http://itunes.ca; Lara Azzopardi, Martin Gero, and Kate Hewlett, *The L.A. Complex*, "Now or Never," streaming film, directed by Peter Wellington (Toronto, ON: Epitome Pictures, 2012), http://itunes.ca; Paul Thomas Anderson, *The Master*, streaming film, directed by Paul Thomas Anderson (New York, NY: Weinstein Company, 2012), http://netflix.ca.

39. David and Seinfeld, *Seinfeld*, "The Parking Garage."

40. Ferrell and McKay, *Talladega Nights*; Beverly Jenkins, "10 Celebrities Who Are Real-Life Heroes," *Oddee*, September 6, 2011, http://www.oddee.com/item_97886.aspx.

41. "Tom Cruise Scientology Rant," YouTube video, posted by nickmills2007, January 20, 2008, https://www.youtube.com/watch?v=4O2_rZIgrQI.

42. Lawrence J. Cohen and Fred Freeman, *Delirious*, streaming film, directed by Tom Mankiewicz (Beverly Hills, CA: MGM, 1991), http://itunes.ca; Reed Tucker, "Hey, Tom, Your Crack Is Showing," *New York Post*, September 16, 2012, http://nypost.com/2012/09/16/hey-tom-your-crack-is-showing/.

43. Mazin, *Superhero Movie*; The Late Late Show with Craig Ferguson, "Tom Cruise's Scientology Video from the Late Late Show," YouTube video, posted by Anonymoose861, January 26, 2008, https://www.youtube.com/watch?v=u87eQw6MTls; Jerry Minor and Jerry O'Connell, "Jerry O'Connell in the Parody Video Tom Cruise WANTS You to See," *Funny or Die*, published January 21, 2008, http://www.funnyordie.com/videos/3f716ffebe/jerry-oconnell-in-the-parody-video-tom-cruise-wants-you-to-see-from-jerry-minor-and-jerry-oconnell?_cc=__d___&_ccid=ymiv3q.o051mc; Todd Van Luling, "Jerry O'Connell Is Still Hiding from Tom Cruise and Scientology," *Huffington Post*, October 29, 2015, http://www.huffingtonpost.com/entry/tom-cruise-hiding-scientology_563250ffe4b0c66bae5b6d0d.

44. Church of Scientology, "We Stand Tall," YouTube video, posted by SoUpstat, June 19, 2011, https://www.youtube.com/watch?v=XyNh1j3dsp8; What's Trending Now, "SNL's 'Neurotology' Scientology Parody," YouTube video, 2:46, posted by What's Trending, April 6, 2015, https://www.youtube.com/watch?v=Fp3Jrz_Gxj8.

45. Matt Groening et al., *The Simpsons*, "The Joy of Sect," streaming film, directed by Steven Dean Moore (Los Angeles, CA: Gracie Films, 1998), http://netflix.ca.

46. Parker, Stone, and Graden, *South Park*, "Trapped in the Closet"; *Huffington Post*, "Church of Scientology Investigated 'South Park' Creators Matt Stone, Trey Parker: Report," *Huffington Post*, January 17, 2013, http://www.huffingtonpost .com/2011/10/24/church-of-scientology-investigate-south-park_n_1027538.html.

47. Azzopardi, Gero, and Hewlett, *The L.A. Complex*, "Make It Right"; Azzopardi, Gero, and Hewlett, *The L.A. Complex*, "Now or Never."

48. Stein, "Until Nothing Remains"; Michael Fröhlingsdorf, "Scientology Against ARD," *Spiegal Online Culture*, March 25, 2010, http://translate.google.com /translate?u=http%3A//www.spiegel.de/kultur/tv/scientology-gegen-ard-geschichten -die-vorne-und-hinten-nicht-stimmen-a-685577.html&hl=en&langpair=auto | en& tbb=1&ie=ISO-8859-1.

49. Franz, "Distrust in Clearwater"; "Deaths at Flag," last modified July 11, 2006, http://www.xenu-directory.net/mirrors/www.whyaretheydead.net/.

50. Hanover, "The Bridge"; Janet Reitman, *Inside Scientology: The Story of America's Most Secretive Religion* (Boston, MA: Houghton Mifflin Harcourt, 2011), 232–233.

51. Anderson, *The Master*; Marc Headley, "Is 'The Master' Based on Scientology and L. Ron Hubbard?," *The Daily Beast*, July 19, 2012, http://www.thedailybeast.com /articles/2012/07/19/is-the-master-based-on-scientology-and-l-ron-hubbard.html.

52. Soderbergh, "Schizopolis"; Marc Headley, *Blown for Good: Behind the Iron Curtain of Scientology* (Madison, WI: BFG Publishing, 2009); L. Ron Hubbard, *Dianetics* (Los Angeles, CA: Bridge Publications, 2007).

53. Neal, "'They're Freaks!,'" 88; Feltmate, "New Religious Movements," 349; Laycock, "Where Do They Get," 97.

54. Hanover, "The Bridge."

55. Azzopardi, Gero, and Hewlett, *The L.A. Complex*, "Make It Right."

56. Soderbergh, "Schizopolis."

57. Feltmate, "New Religious Movements," 346–347.

58. Stein, "Until Nothing Remains."

59. What's Trending Now, "SNL's 'Neurotology' Scientology Parody," https:// www.youtube.com/watch?v=Fp3Jrz_Gxj8.

60. Hanover, "The Bridge."

61. Feltmate, "New Religious Movements," 348–349.

62. Neal, "'They're Freaks!,'" 88.

63. Ibid.

64. Martin, *Bowfinger*; Parker, Stone, and Graden, *South Park*, "Trapped in the Closet"; Alexander, "The Profit."

65. "Tom Cruise Scientology Rant," https://www.youtube.com/watch?v=4O2 _rZIgrQI; The Late Late Show with Craig Ferguson, "Tom Cruise's Scientology Video," https://www.youtube.com/watch?v=u87eQw6MTls; Minor and O'Connell, "Jerry O'Connell in," http://www.funnyordie.com/videos/3f716ffebe/jerry-oconnell-in-the -parody-video-tom-cruise-wants-you-to-see-from-jerry-minor-and-jerry-oconnell? _cc=__d___&_ccid=ymiv3q.o051mc; Mazin, *Superhero Movie*.

66. Parker, Stone, and Graden, *South Park*, "Trapped in the Closet"; Anderson, *The Master*.

67. Martin, *Bowfinger*; Azzopardi, Gero, and Hewlett, *The L.A. Complex*, "Make It Right."

68. Soderbergh, "Schizopolis."

69. Hanover, "The Bridge."

70. Parker, Stone, and Graden, *South Park*, "Trapped in the Closet."

71. "Tom Cruise Scientology Rant," https://www.youtube.com/watch?v=4O2_rZIgrQI; Minor and O'Connell, "Jerry O'Connell in," http://www.funnyordie.com/videos/3f716ffebe/jerry-oconnell-in-the-parody-video-tom-cruise-wants-you-to-see-from-jerry-minor-and-jerry-oconnell?_cc=__d___&_ccid=ymiv3q.o051mc;

72. Azzopardi, Gero, and Hewlett, *The L.A. Complex*, "Make It Right."

73. Hanover, "The Bridge"; Stein, "Until Nothing Remains"; Ferrell and McKay, *Talladega Nights: The Ballad of Ricky Bobby*; Parker, Stone, and Graden, *South Park*, "Trapped in the Closet"; Soderbergh, "Schizopolis"; Martin, *Bowfinger*; Alexander, "The Profit"; Azzopardi, Gero, and Hewlett, *The L.A. Complex*, "Make It Right"; Anderson, *The Master*.

74. Neal, "'They're Freaks!,'" 91–92.

75. Parker, Stone, and Graden, *South Park*, "Trapped in the Closet"; Martin, *Bowfinger*; Alexander, "The Profit."

76. Azzopardi, Gero, and Hewlett, *The L.A. Complex*, "Make It Right."

77. Hanover, "The Bridge."

78. Parker, Stone, and Graden, *South Park*, "Trapped in the Closet."

79. Martin, *Bowfinger*.

80. The Late Late Show with Craig Ferguson, "Tom Cruise's Scientology Video," https://www.youtube.com/watch?v=u87eQw6MTls; Minor and O'Connell, "Jerry O'Connell In," http://www.funnyordie.com/videos/3f716ffebe/jerry-oconnell-in-the-parody-video-tom-cruise-wants-you-to-see-from-jerry-minor-and-jerry-oconnell?_cc=__d__&_ccid=ymiv3q.o051mc; Mazin, *Superhero Movie*.

81. Neal, "'They're Freaks!,'" 92–93.

82. Feltmate, "It's Funny Because," 227; Neal, "'They're Freaks!,'" 94–95; Jonathan Gray, "Watching *The Simpsons*," quoted in David Feltmate, "It's Funny Because It's True? *The Simpsons*, Satire, and the Significance of Religious Humor in Popular Culture," *Journal of the Academy of Religion*, 81, no. 1, 227.

83. Hanover, "The Bridge."

84. Azzopardi, Gero, and Hewlett, *The L.A. Complex*, "Make It Right"; Alexander, "The Profit"; Anderson, *The Master*; Minor and O'Connell, "Jerry O'Connell in," http://www.funnyordie.com/videos/3f716ffebe/jerry-oconnell-in-the-parody-video-tom-cruise-wants-you-to-see-from-jerry-minor-and-jerry-oconnell?_cc=__d__&_ccid=ymiv3q.o051mc.

85. Gray, "Watching *The Simpsons*," quoted in Feltmate, "It's Funny Because," 227; Neal, "'They're Freaks!,'" 85.

86. Parker, Stone, and Graden, *South Park*, "Trapped in the Closet"; Martin, *Bowfinger*; Alexander, "The Profit"; Soderbergh, "Schizopolis"; The Late Late Show

with Craig Ferguson, "Tom Cruise's Scientology Video," https://www.youtube.com
/watch?v=u87eQw6MTls; Minor and O'Connell, "Jerry O'Connell in," http://www
.funnyordie.com/videos/3f716ffebe/jerry-oconnell-in-the-parody-video-tom-cruise
-wants-you-to-see-from-jerry-minor-and-jerry-oconnell?_cc=__d___&_ccid=
ymiv3q.o051mc; Mazin, *Superhero Movie*; Azzopardi, Gero, and Hewlett, *The L.A.
Complex*, "Make It Right"; Hanover, "The Bridge"; Anderson, *The Master*; Stein,
"Until Nothing Remains."

87. Neal, "'They're Freaks!,'" 92–93.

88. Hanover, "The Bridge."

89. Note that a chapter focusing on news program interviews with prominent
Scientologists appears elsewhere in this volume.

90. Laycock, "Where Do They Get," 82; *Urban Dictionary*, s.v. "newstainment,"
accessed December 16, 2015, http://www.urbandictionary.com/define.php?term=
Newstainment.

91. Lewis, "Scientology vs. the Media," 61.

BIBLIOGRAPHY

Abrahams, Jim, David Zucker, and Jerry Zucker. *Airplane*, streaming film. Directed by
    Jim Abrahams, David Zucker, and Jerry Zucker. Hollywood, CA: Paramount
    Pictures, 1980. http://itunes.ca.
Alexander, Peter N. "The Profit." YouTube video. Directed by Peter N. Alexander.
    Tampa, FL: Courage Productions, 2001. Posted by Wilfried Handl, March 19,
    2015. https://www.youtube.com/watch?v=D67OvQyGMF8.
Altheide, David L. "Media Logic, Social Control, and Fear." *Communications Theory*,
    23 (2013): 223–238. doi:10.1111/comt.12017.
Anderson, Paul Thomas. *The Master*, streaming film. Directed by Paul Thomas
    Anderson. New York, NY: Weinstein Company, 2012. http://netflix.ca.
Azzopardi, Lara, Martin Gero, and Kate Hewlett. "Make It Right." *The L.A. Com-
    plex*, streaming television episode. Directed by Peter Wellington. Toronto, ON:
    Epitome Pictures, 2012. http://itunes.ca.
Azzopardi, Lara, Martin Gero, and Kate Hewlett. "Now or Never." *The L.A. Com-
    plex*, streaming television episode. Directed by Peter Wellington. Toronto, ON:
    Epitome Pictures, 2012. http://itunes.ca.
Becker, Howard. *Outsiders: Studies in the Sociology of Deviance*. New York, NY: The
    Free Press, 1963.
Beit-Hallahmi, Benjamin. "Scientology: Religion or Racket?," *Marburg Journal of
    Religion* 8, no. 1 (2003): 1–56. http://archiv.ub.uni-marburg.de/ep/0004/article
    /view/3724.
Bereska, Tami M. *Deviance, Conformity, and Social Control in Canada* (4th edition).
    Toronto, ON: Pearson Education Canada, 2014.
Berger, Peter L. *Redeeming Laughter: The Comic Dimension of Human Experience*. Ber-
    lin: Walter de Gruyter, 1997.
Church of Scientology. "We Stand Tall." YouTube video. Posted by SoUpstat, June
    19, 2011. https://www.youtube.com/watch?v=XyNh1j3dsp8.

Clark, Terry Ray. "Saved by Satire? Learning to Value Popular Culture's Critique of Sacred Traditions." In *Understanding Religion and Popular Culture: Theories, Themes, Products and Practices*, edited by Terry Ray Clark and Dan W. Clanton, 13–27. New York, NY: Routledge, 2012.

Cohen, Lawrence J., and Fred Freeman. *Delirious*, streaming film. Directed by Tom Mankiewicz. Beverly Hills, CA: MGM, 1991. http://itunes.ca.

Cohen, Stanley. *Folk Devils and Moral Panics: The Creation of the Mods and Rockers*. Oxford, UK: Blackwell, 1972.

David, Larry, and Jerry Seinfeld. "The Parking Garage." *Seinfeld*, DVD. Directed by Tom Cherones. 1991. Culver City, CA: Sony Pictures Home Entertainment, 2013.

Di Pego, Gerald. *Phenomenon*, streaming film. Directed by Jon Turteltaub. Burbank, CA: Touchstone Pictures, 1996. http://itunes.ca.

Feltmate, David. "It's Funny Because It's True? *The Simpsons*, Satire, and the Significance of Religious Humor in Popular Culture." *Journal of the Academy of Religion*, 81, no. 1 (2013): 222–245. doi:10.1093/jaarel/lfs100.

Feltmate, David. "New Religious Movements in Adult Animated Sitcoms—A Spectrum of Portrayals." *Religion Compass*, 5/7 (2011): 343–354. doi:10.1111/j.1749-8171.2011.00287.x.

Ferrell, Will, and Adam McKay. *Talladega Nights: The Ballad of Ricky Bobby*, streaming film. Directed by Adam McKay. Culver City, CA: Columbia Tri Star Pictures, 2006. http://itunes.ca.

Franz, Douglas. "Distrust in Clearwater—A Special Report: Death of a Scientologist Heightens Suspicions in a Florida Town." *New York Times*. December 1, 1997. http://www.nytimes.com/1997/12/01/us/distrust-clearwater-special-report-death-scientologist-heightens-suspicions.html?pagewanted=all.

Fröhlingsdorf, Michael. "Scientology Against ARD." Spiegal Online Culture. March 25, 2010. http://translate.google.com/translate?u=http%3A//www.spiegel.de/kultur/tv/scientology-gegen-ard-geschichten-die-vorne-und-hinten-nicht-stimmen-a-685577.html&hl=en&langpair=auto | en&tbb=1&ie=ISO-8859-1.

Green, Melanie C., and Timothy C. Brock. "The Role of Transportation in the Persuasiveness of Public Narratives." *Journal of Personality and Social Psychology* 79, no. 5 (2000): 701–721. doi:10.1037//0022-3514.79.5.701.

Greer, Chris, and Yvonne Jewkes. "Extremes of Otherness: Media Images of Social Exclusion." *Social Justice* 32, no. 1 (2005): 20–31. http://www.socialjusticejournal.org/archive/99_32_1/99_03Greer.pdf.

Groening, Matt, James L. Brooks, Sam Simon, and Steve O'Donnell. "The Joy of Sect." *The Simpsons*, streaming television episode. Directed by Steven Dean Moore. Los Angeles, CA: Gracie Films, 1998. http://netflix.ca.

Hanover, Brett. "The Bridge." YouTube video. Directed by Brett Hanover. Memphis, TN: Brett Hanover, 2006. Posted by Conspiracy Cult, October 5, 2011. https://www.youtube.com/watch?v=s-DkG6kKASc.

Headley, Marc. *Blown for Good: Behind the Iron Curtain of Scientology*. Madison, WI: BFG Publishing, 2009.

Headley, Marc. "Is 'The Master' Based on Scientology and L. Ron Hubbard?" *Daily Beast*. July 19, 2012. http://www.thedailybeast.com/articles/2012/07/19/is-the -master-based-on-scientology-and-l-ron-hubbard.html.

Hubbard, L. Ron. *Dianetics*. Los Angeles, CA: Bridge Publications, 2007.

Huffington Post. "Church of Scientology Investigated 'South Park' Creators Matt Stone, Trey Parker: Report." *Huffington Post*. January 17, 2013. http://www .huffingtonpost.com/2011/10/24/church-of-scientology-investigate-south -park_n_1027538.html.

Iguarta, Juan-José, and Isabel Barrios. "Changing Real World Beliefs with Contro- versial Movies: Processes and Mechanisms of Narrative Persuasion." *Journal of Communication* 62 (2012): 514–531. doi:10.1111/j.1460-2466.2012.01640.x.

Interactive Advertising Bureau (IAB) of Canada. *2010 Canadian Media Usage Trends Study*. Toronto, ON: IAB, 2011.

Interactive Advertising Bureau (IAB) of Canada. *2014 CMUST (Canadian Media Usage Trends)*. Toronto, ON: IAB, 2014.

Jenkins, Beverly. "10 Celebrities Who Are Real-Life Heroes." *Oddee*. September 6, 2011. http://www.oddee.com/item_97886.aspx.

Katz, Jackson, and Jeremy Earp. *Tough Guise: Violence, Media and the Crisis in Mas- culinity*, DVD. Directed by Sut Jhally. Northampton, MA: Media Education Foundation, 1999.

Late Late Show with Craig Ferguson, The. "Tom Cruise's Scientology Video from the Late Late Show." YouTube video. Posted by Anonymoose861, January 26, 2008. https://www.youtube.com/watch?v=u87eQw6MTls.

Laycock, Joseph. "Where Do They Get These Ideas? Changing Ideas of Cults in the Mirror of Popular Culture." *Journal of the American Academy of Religion* 81, no. 1 (2013): 80–106. doi:10.1093/jaarel/lfs091.

Lewis, James R. "Scientology vs. the Media." *Alternative Spirituality and Religion Review* 6, no. 1 (2015): 61–78. doi:10.5840/asrr201572010.

Mandell, Corey, and J. D. Shapiro. *Battlefield Earth*, streaming film. Directed by Roger Christian. Burbank, CA: Warner Bros, 2000. http://itunes.ca.

Martin, Steve. *Bowfinger*, streaming film. Directed by Frank Oz. Orlando, FL: Univer- sal Pictures, 1999. http://itunes.ca.

Mazin, Craig. *Superhero Movie*, streaming film. Directed by Craig Mazin. New York, NY: Dimension Films, 2008. http://itunes.ca.

Neal, Lynn S. "'They're Freaks!' The Cult Stereotype in Fictional Television Shows, 1958–2008." *Nova Religio: Journal of Alternative and Emergent Religions* 14, no. 3 (2011): 81–107. doi:10.1525/nr.2011.14.3.81.

O'Connell, Jerry, and Jerry Minor. "Jerry O'Connell in the Parody Video Tom Cruise WANTS You to See." *Funny or Die*. Published January 21, 2008. http://www .funnyordie.com/videos/3f716ffebe/jerry-oconnell-in-the-parody-video-tom -cruise-wants-you-to-see-from-jerry-minor-and-jerry-oconnell?_cc=__d___& _ccid=ymiv3q.o051mc.

Parker, Trey, Matt Stone, and Brian Graden. "Trapped in the Closet." *South Park*, streaming television episode. Directed by Trey Parker. New York, NY: Braniff/ Parker-Stone Studios, 2005. http://itunes.ca.

Reitman, Janet. *Inside Scientology: The Story of America's Most Secretive Religion.* Boston, MA: Houghton Mifflin Harcourt, 2011.

Soderbergh, Steven. "Schizopolis." YouTube video. Directed by Steven Soderbergh. Helena, MT: 406 Productions, 1996. Posted by Jake Maringoni, May 12, 2015.

Statista. "Average Time Spent with Major Media per Day in the United States as of October 2015 (in minutes)." Accessed January 10, 2016. http://www.statista .com/statistics/276683/media-use-in-the-us/.

Stein, Niki. "Until Nothing Remains." YouTube video. Directed by Niki Stein. Potsdam, DE: teamWorx Television and Film, 2010. Posted by Enturbulator General, June 11, 2015. https://www.youtube.com/watch?v=wpfjb8zG-WI.

"Tom Cruise Scientology Rant." YouTube video. Posted by nickmills2007, January 20, 2008. https://www.youtube.com/watch?v=4O2_rZIgrQI.

Tucker, Reed. "Hey, Tom, Your Crack Is Showing." *New York Post.* September 16, 2012. http://nypost.com/2012/09/16/hey-tom-your-crack-is-showing/.

Van Luling, Todd. "Jerry O'Connell Is Still Hiding from Tom Cruise and Scientology." *Huffington Post.* October 29, 2015. http://www.huffingtonpost.com/entry /tom-cruise-hiding-scientology_563250ffe4b0c66bae5b6d0d.

Walrus. "Scientology Attacks! Going to War with L. Ron Hubbard's Disciples." *Walrus.* April 2015. http://thewalrus.ca/scientology-attacks/.

Washington, Linn, Jr. "Probing the President: The Media's Paralysis of Analysis? Race, the Press, and the White House." In *Redefining Black Power: Reflections on the State of Black America,* edited by Joanne Griffith, 115–140. San Francisco, CA: City Lights Books, 2013.

What's Trending Now. "SNL's 'Neurotology' Scientology Parody." YouTube video. Posted by What's Trending, April 6, 2015. https://www.youtube.com/watch?v= Fp3Jrz_Gxj8.

World Health Organization. *Smoke-Free Movies: From Evidence to Action.* Geneva, CH: WHO, 2011.

8

Must-See Television: Interviews with Scientologists

Tami M. Bereska

Scientology has a long, fraught history with the media. It has been satirized and criticized in entertainment media and analyzed and exposed by news (and "newstainment") media.[1] The Church of Scientology's reactions to this media coverage—through litigation, harassment campaigns, and even criminal activities—have only served to magnify the media's attention to the organization.[2] In its relationship to Scientology, the media becomes a "contested arena" where the religious mainstream and religious fringe—the acceptable and the unacceptable—are constructed and debated.[3] Nowhere is this more evident than in television interviews. News anchors and talk show hosts including Ted Koppel, Oprah Winfrey, and Matt Lauer have interviewed Scientologists such as current leader David Miscavige and celebrity members including Tom Cruise, John Travolta, and Kirstie Alley. These interviews became compelling television spectacles and have gone viral online on YouTube. This chapter analyzes the interviews and how they have evolved over time.

THE INTERVIEW ENVIRONMENT

The television interview environment is complex, whether considering daytime talk shows like the iconic *The Oprah Winfrey Show*, entertainment industry programs like *Access Hollywood*, "tabloid" shows like *Inside Edition* or *A Current Affair*, or news programs such as *60 Minutes*. Talk show hosts and entertainment industry reporters are in a position where they must maintain a friendly and hospitable environment for their celebrity guests (or risk having that celebrity boycott the program in the future) and at the same time bring important information forward for their viewers. Producers of tabloid television need to address current issues that are often very serious in nature and yet package them in the sensationalistic and easy-to-digest way that their audience expects.

Television journalists on news programs are in an especially challenging position. Traditionally the news has been expected to be objective and unbiased. However, significant shifts occurred in the news industry beginning in the 1980s. As news media companies merged and ownership became more concentrated, the news developed into less of a public service and more of a corporate endeavor. The growing profit motive underlying news programs created a shift in its framing of information and events, with greater reliance on human interest and shock-exposé.[4]

As the boundaries between news and entertainment programming have diminished, the role of television journalists has shifted as well. They must strike a balance by appearing neutral and impartial (in order to maintain credibility) and yet assume the nonneutral roles required for the human interest and shock-exposé news frames.[5] Interviews embedded within the human interest frame focus on "the shaping of personal experience and the expression of emotion."[6] The interviewer must empathize with the interviewee and ask the particular types of questions that will elicit a similar emotion in the audience. Interviews that are embedded within the shock-exposé frame represent "'doing accountability' through questioning public figures."[7] In this case, interviewers play the role of devil's advocate, acting in an adversarial way in order to expose the truth.[8] Interviewers make use of a variety of techniques to strike this balance. For example, common techniques include drawing upon a third party's comments as the source for more adversarial questions, or beginning the interviews with the more traditional question-answer sequence and then gradually transitioning to more adversarial questions that challenge the interviewee's most recent responses.[9] Ian Hutchby refers to this new television environment as "hybrid" programming, combining traditional news broadcast techniques with confrontation and argument as "infotainment."[10] In the 21st century, the interviewer on a news program is no longer an impartial journalist but rather "advocate," "inquisitor," or "arbiter of truth."[11]

When it comes to stories that focus on religion, interviewers become "'heresiographers,' identifying false or inauthentic religion, thus symbolically establishing boundaries between a mainstream religious center and a suspect periphery."[12] Some religious groups are more likely than others to be the subject of hybrid programming (and especially tabloid television), and Bernard Doherty suggests that Scientology is especially well suited for that environment. It is an environment that is "generally designed to expose celebrity scandals, dishonest tradespeople, philandering politicians, welfare cheats and sinister cults. Scientology, with its enduring reputation of slick production values, celebrity endorsements, media courting and confrontational approach to critics, has fashioned itself into a ready-made *cause-célèbre*. . . ."[13]

NEW RELIGIOUS MOVEMENTS AND THE NEWS

Scholarly attention to the nonfictional television coverage of new religious movements (NRMs) is lacking, with most analyses focusing on print media.[14] For instance, Sean McCloud provides a comprehensive overview of shifts in the way NRMs have been portrayed in American news magazines. Between 1950 and 1965, two frames governed stories about NRMs. Many were portrayed as exotic—"weird, wonderful, colorful, mysterious—yet mostly harmless."[15] Stories described their esoteric practices and featured photographs of members with placid facial expressions and wearing unusual clothing. In this context, controversial practices or negative events were frequently glossed over. On the other hand, the Cold War had an effect on representations of some NRMs; in zealotry lay the potential for actions that could be un-American. Groups such as the Nation of Islam were portrayed as "zealous, emotional, dogmatic, . . . potentially subversive" and vulnerable to Communist influence or infiltration.[16]

In the late 1960s and early 1970s, the youth counterculture was at the center of media attention. Consequently, magazine stories about NRMs focused on those that were attracting the white, middle-class youth who were part of the counterculture. This was an era when the recognition and valuation of social diversity was on the rise, so journalists exercised some caution in order to acknowledge people's religious freedoms. Nonetheless, some stories indicated that there might be an emerging cause for concern, drawing upon interviews with parents who were worried about their young adult children who had been drawn away by various religious groups.[17] In 1969, this concern was highlighted when followers of leader Charles Manson murdered actress Sharon Tate and four others at his behest.[18]

It was in 1973 that news magazines began to emphasize the "cult menace."[19] Stories focused on brainwashing, exploitation, fraud, and psychological instability. The 1978 mass suicide by more than 900 members of the People's Temple Agricultural Project, under leader Jim Jones, reinforced the magnitude of the menace. "The zealous exotics of the Cold War mass movements had transformed into dangerous, brainwashing criminals."[20]

The "cult menace" continues to dominate the framing of NRMs in both print- and television-based news stories. According to some scholars, this frame is perceived as a form of bias that pervades the news. Thus, Joseph Laycock draws attention to "news media bias" and "stereotypes" that emerge when isolated incidents are portrayed as being just the "tip of the iceberg," and thereby indicative of larger problems with the group.[21] James R. Lewis outlines the role that journalists play in constructing NRMs as "folk devils," leading to moral panics (i.e., exaggerated and sensationalized concerns).[22] Doherty points to the absence of "fair and balanced" coverage of NRMs and outlines four factors that contribute to biased news stories: journalists' limited knowledge about the group, the growing economic and time constraints in the news industry, the sources used in news stories (such as concerned families or disgruntled, former members), and a lack of consistency and follow-up after the initial story.[23]

In part, these negative portrayals of NRMs are a product of the changing landscape of the news industry previously outlined—the shift to hybrid programming and infotainment. However, it is also important to exercise caution when making accusations of bias as the term, by definition, entails "distortion" or an "unfair" dislike.[24] In fact, not all negative portrayals of NRMs in the news media are necessarily distorted or unfair. New religious movements are diverse in belief and practice. The actions of some groups are such that they foster a negative media climate. Some groups constitute a very real threat of individual or social harm. Benjamin Beit-Hallahmi claims that this is the case with the Church of Scientology.[25]

THE CHURCH OF SCIENTOLOGY IN NEWS INTERVIEWS

Journalists began writing about Scientology not long after its founding. For instance, between 1960 and 1964 the Australian tabloid newspaper *Truth* ran a series of stories on the Hubbard Association of Scientologists International (HASI), the original corporation that managed all Scientology organizations. The effect of these news stories was considerable, leading to a government inquiry (the *Anderson Report*) that resulted in Scientology being banned in three Australian states.[26] A historical review by Barend van Driel and James T. Richardson finds that media attention to Scientology increased considerably in the 1970s, although there were some other groups that garnered greater attention (such as the Unification Church).[27] According to some scholars, in the 21st century Scientology is "the dominant target of journalistic coverage."[28]

The media's attention to Scientology waxes and wanes, although it has mounted over the years. It is in this context that television interviews with Scientologists take place. Arising from the human interest and shock exposé frames of the news and infotainment media, interviews typically escalate in the face of events involving the Church of Scientology or celebrity Scientologists; the interviews then largely focus on these most recent events.

Looking more closely at the interviews and their aftermath, we see interviewers increasingly acting as inquisitors or public advocates over the years. We see the Scientologists being interviewed resisting their interrogation by trying to shift their positioning in the conversation from defensive to offensive, a reflection of the instructions in one of L. Ron Hubbard's policy letters—"Don't ever defend. Always attack."[29] Finally, we see the Church of Scientology's various methods of managing their impressions in the fall-out from negative media coverage.

In the late 1970s, a series of incidents shone the media spotlight on the Church of Scientology. In a plan called Operation Goldmine, the organization initiated their attempts to take over the town of Clearwater, Florida, as a site for their spiritual headquarters—Flag Land Base. Using a false front company (United Churches of Florida), Scientology began purchasing property in the town. This discovery, along with others (such as a vicious attack campaign against the town's mayor and infiltration of the local newspaper) led to a series of articles in the *St. Petersburg Times*, culminating in a special report that received a Pulitzer Prize.[30]

In 1980, *60 Minutes* television journalist Mike Wallace prepared an investigative report on the events of Clearwater, broadcast several times during that year.[31] His report addresses the events in Clearwater as well as a number of other recent incidents involving the Church of Scientology. He interviews a number of people affected by the organization: Gabe Cazares (former mayor of Clearwater) and his wife about the harassment they were subjected to; *St. Petersburg Times* editor Eugene Patterson about the newspaper's offices being burglarized and journalists slandered; and author Paulette Cooper, who was framed for bomb threats by the Church of Scientology (after they stole her personal letterhead) and then mentally tortured in an well-orchestrated campaign dubbed "Operation Freakout."[32] Assistant U.S. Attorney for the District of Columbia Raymond Banoun is also present to outline the list of crimes for which nine members of the organization (including L. Ron Hubbard's wife) had recently been convicted: "Burglaries [of government offices], conspiracy to steal documents, conspiracy to forge government credentials, conspiracy to buy and wiretap government meetings, conspiracy to obstruct justice by lying to a grand jury, destroying evidence, submitting false evidence to a grand jury, harboring a fugitive, and kidnapping a witness."

Reverend Kenneth Whitman (President of the Church of Scientology in the United States) and David Gaiman (worldwide head of public relations for the organization) are the central Scientologists interviewed. They initially acknowledge these events "as a crisis point" for the organization, claiming that a handful of members acted in violation of the church's value system. Then they quickly turn the tables by arguing that the offenders believed they were merely protecting their religion against attack. Mike Wallace confronts them with church documents that suggest these events were not a result of a few members going rogue but rather reflective of the organization's policies. Whitman and Gaiman momentarily go on the defensive, claiming that the documents are being taken out of context. However, three church members who Wallace was permitted to speak to seemed very much unaware of details surrounding these events and instead emphasized the organization as a victim: "In the name of survival of a religion? If these people are trying to knock the religion down, what do you do? Sit back?" Indeed, these members state they actively avoid negative information about the organization: "I don't even read it. . . . Because it doesn't interest me. Let the people who have to handle it handle it."

As the decade progressed, a number of high-ranking members began to leave the Church of Scientology.[33] This gave the news media a new way to present stories on the organization. Ex-Scientologists were also sources of information that could be used in both human interest and shock-exposé stories—their own experiences as Scientologists as well as secret information documenting how fraud, lying, and abuse were institutionalized within the organization. For example, a 1983 episode of the ABC news program *20/20* featured four former Scientologists, including L. Ron Hubbard's son (L. Ron Hubbard Jr.).[34] In the interview, L. Ron Hubbard Jr. states that Scientology was a money-making scam from the time of its founding. Former member Andrea Schwartz illustrates the nature of the scam when describing her work in selling members various Scientology programs: "I would outline a program that closely matched his savings account or matched what he could buy, you know, by getting a loan or whatever." She and her husband Ford Schwartz go on to discuss the various times and ways that they helped hide the organization's money from the government.

Scientology's representative on this program is Reverend Heber Jentzsch. As correspondent John Stossel confronts him with various wrongdoings, Jentzsch uses the same technique used in the earlier *60 Minutes* story to shift responsibility away from the organization: "You're bound to have a few people who do not agree to the moral principles of the church." When L. Ron Hubbard Jr. points to the church as the organizing force behind these wrongdoings, Jentzsch targets Hubbard Jr., pointing out that "he admits he lied about the church"—referring to a time when Hubbard Jr. signed an affidavit to that effect. Hubbard Jr. argues that he did so under duress, while the organization was threatening his family.

As the news media industry was evolving at this time, so too was Scientology, as it maneuvered its way through this changing media environment. In interviews, their members become more aggressive, a clearer reflection of organizational policies for dealing with critics.[35] In a 1985 story on *60 Minutes*, the organization is on the offensive from the very beginning, insisting that they have their own cameras at the interview, a lawyer for interviewee Reverend Heber Jentzsch, and more than 100 Scientology observers. Jentzsch quickly goes on the attack, with Mike Wallace himself as his target. In response to Wallace's question about what Jentzsch means when he says that Scientology is "the only road to total freedom," Jentzsch insults Wallace's intelligence: "Oh what—there's some word there you don't understand?" In a voiceover, Wallace states that "in the course of reporting this story, it became apparent to us that Reverend Jentzsch is persuaded that 60 Minutes itself is somehow involved with others in a plot to destroy Scientology." His observation is supported when Jentzsch makes overt statements to that effect, such as when he criticizes Wallace's interviews with ex-Scientologists: "We say when Pearl Harbor happened, you'd be the first guy going over there to represent the Japanese 'cause he probably bruised his knee when he killed all of those Americans."

Media attention to Scientology continued into the 1990s. In May 1991, *Time* magazine published a scathing exposé on Scientology that documented its various misdeeds during the previous decade, including fraud, the deceptive use of several front agencies, and "infiltrating, burglarizing, and wiretapping more than 1000 private and government agencies."[36] In response, the Church of Scientology launched a smear campaign against journalist Richard Behar, a lawsuit against Behar and the magazine, and a 12-week national media campaign to discredit the magazine by drawing attention to a 1938 issue that named Adolf Hitler "Man of the Year."[37]

A few weeks after the article was published, Reverend Heber Jentzsch, two former Scientologists, and the president of the International Coalition for Religious freedom were interviewed on *Larry King Live*.[38] Referring to the *Time* magazine article, Jentzsch paints Scientology as the victim of "a rather despicable attack." As former member Lisa Halverson speaks of her experience with (and exit from) the organization, Jentzsch repeatedly interrupts in a barrage of attacks on others. He targets the (original) Cult Awareness Network: "[Lisa's] talking from the fact that she has been deprogrammed by people who are members of the Cult Awareness Network"; "They've held people against their will"; "Their founder was . . . a three-time convicted criminal"; "The Cult Awareness Network rapes people. . . ." He targets Larry King when King refers to the numerous criminal convictions of Scientologists: "Larry, do you read when somebody gets arrested that he's a Jew?" When Jerry Whitfield, a former member who provides consulting services to people leaving Scientology, is being interviewed, Jentzsch interrupts: "Ask Jerry how much he gets [paid] for deprogramming."

This episode of *Larry King Live* is particularly interesting in the way it illustrates the shift toward the sensationalism of tabloid television. Even the shock-exposé frame of hybrid programming is disregarded in favor of confrontation itself. All four guests—two ex-Scientologists, the president of the International Coalition for Religious Freedom, and Reverend Jentzsch— are collectively seated on stage with Larry King, enhancing the confrontational atmosphere. Although King begins with a series of information-based questions directed at each guest, as the show progresses he serves less as an interviewer and more as a facilitator of the confrontation. He allows the altercations between guests to escalate, intervening only periodically when it seems he wants the conversation to continue along a particular track. Even when a new opportunity to interrogate Jentzsch about the organization presents itself—an opportunity that would be invaluable as part of an exposé— King ignores it for the sake of pursuing more confrontation. A former member of Scientology (one who was explicitly referred to on the show) phones in and tells Larry that the International Coalition of Religious Freedom is not a neutral observer but rather is affiliated with the Church of Scientology itself. In fact, this caller points out that he was on *Larry King Live* the previous year (with a guest host while King was on vacation) speaking to that very fact. King pays no heed to that information and instead instructs the caller to "Give me one salient fact about Scientology that they do that Heber [Jentzsch] can respond to. . . that's evil."

The *Time* article and Scientology's response to it led to one especially well-known interview on the ABC news program *Nightline*. This would be leader David Miscavige's first television interview.[39] Although he reportedly spent several months rehearsing for the interview, it did not go well from the perspective of the Church of Scientology.[40] Miscavige did utilize the same techniques as Scientologists before him who had been interviewed over the years. In response to Ted Koppel's statement that people are reluctant to speak out against the organization out of fear of harassment, Miscavige paints Scientology as the victim: "The person getting harassed is myself and the church." He alleges that people, including journalist Richard Behar of *Time*, had conspired to kidnap Scientologists.

At various points during the interview, he also tries to take control of the direction of the conversation by attacking others. When asked for his view on the *Nightline* report on Scientology that had immediately preceded the interview, he claims that "Every single detractor on there is part of a religious hate group called the Cult Awareness Network and their sister group the American Family Foundation. . . . [To Scientology, those groups are] the same as the KKK would be to blacks." He refers to the *Time* article as having been written "at the behest of Eli Lilly," a psycho-pharmaceutical manufacturer.[41]

However, Miscavige is outmaneuvered by Koppel and repeatedly put on the defensive. He stumbles when trying to explain how Scientology would be of benefit to Koppel. When Miscavige says that Scientology could help Koppel improve his communication skills, Koppel replies that his communication skills seem to have served him well thus far in his career. Miscavige tries another angle, pointing out that Scientology can help people who are already at a "higher level" in life become even better; Koppel retorts, "you're interested in folks who've got money." Miscavige begins to argue that the organization's funds are used in support of various social causes and humanitarian efforts but then seems to remember that he should be attacking rather than defending. He suddenly refers back to the report that preceded the interview, pointing out that one of the former members featured in the report "is a girl who was kicked out for trying to bring criminals into the church." Despite Miscavige's efforts to regain control of the interview, Koppel turns the tables on him once again. Through the remainder of the interview, as claims and counterclaims are volleyed back and forth, Koppel is able to maintain the upper hand. It seems to become a *fait accompli* when, on the spot, Koppel extends this live interview for an additional half hour. Because there were no commercial breaks taken during this time, Miscavige had no choice but to continue. Miscavige's first live television interview would be his last, and Koppel would go on to win an Emmy Award for the show. It seems that the time had come when television journalists had caught on to Scientologists' interview strategies and found ways to beat them at their own game.

Following the *Nightline* interview with David Miscavige, the Church of Scientology largely retreated from televised interviews until the late 1990s. In 1998, the A&E network's show *Investigative Reports* broadcast the episode "Inside Scientology." [42] It was not live but rather a documentary that, in part, featured life inside the organization. It was made with the full support of the Church of Scientology and included interviews with Miscavige and a number of current members. The most prominent were celebrity Scientologists such as Tom Cruise, Jenna Elfman, Isaac Hayes, and John Travolta. With this documentary, the organization seemed to shift to a television media strategy where the leaders faded into the background and high-profile celebrities became Scientology's public face.

CELEBRITY SCIENTOLOGISTS AND "ENTERTAINMENT NEWS" INTERVIEWS

In the 21st century, Scientology became entwined with the media in new and different ways. Explicit and implicit references to, and portrayals of, the organization began to appear in fictional entertainment media in the 1990s, such as in the television series *Seinfeld* and movies *Schizopolis* and *Bowfinger*.[43] With the movie *The Profit* in 2001, these representations of Scientology in fictional entertainment media continued into the 21st century.[44] The mounting number of negative representations in fictional media, along with the growing presence of the Internet in people's lives, has made it ever more challenging for the Church of Scientology to manage its impression in the public mind. Beginning in the late 1990s, the Internet started to become an arena in which secret Scientology documents, practices, and dogma were widely shared by former members, despite the organization's litigious efforts.[45] The Internet also became a hub where various media-related events involving Scientology (such as news stories, television episodes, films, and video clips) were shared, commented upon, and stored. The celebrity faces of Scientology have featured prominently in the Internet environment.

Significant shifts in celebrity reporting occurred in the early 21st century.[46] For decades, celebrity gossip could be found in print media such as *National Enquirer*, *US*, and *People*. Those magazines also had a presence online early on. However, the magazines' websites were primarily a means of soliciting subscribers for their print versions; the websites did not have any celebrity gossip that was not available in the current week's print issue. In 2005, this changed with the first celebrity-reporting bloggers, as well as the emergence of the video-sharing site YouTube (which removed many technical barriers to uploading and viewing video content). These websites featured breaking celebrity news provided by various sources, including the public.[47] Actions or statements by celebrities could be reported globally within a matter of minutes, rather than being delayed until the next week's edition of a celebrity gossip print magazine. Much in the way that the evolution of the news industry impacted the nature of the news interview environment, the evolution of the online environment fundamentally altered the nature of celebrity. This had bold implications for the celebrity faces of Scientology that the organization was relying on for its public relations.

Celebrities' publicists face a difficult task. Their clients are interviewed in a variety of contexts: one-on-one planned interviews on television programs; press junkets for promoting their new movies or television shows (wherein a long line of reporters each has the opportunity to spend a few minutes with the actors); on the red carpet at premiere events and award shows; and even in passing when encountered by the paparazzi. The primary task of publicists is to maintain a positive image for their clients. That can be especially challenging when their client is one of the public faces for Scientology. However, it is not only taxing for publicists but also for the Church of Scientology, which is trying to manage its impressions with these celebrities. A careless statement in an interview can potentially harm an actor's career as well as contribute to negative views of Scientology. The nature of these implications is well illustrated by using actor Tom Cruise as a case study.

When publicist Pat Kingsley first started working with Cruise in the 1990s, she carefully controlled his public image. As more celebrities revealed their membership in the Church of Scientology, the entertainment news media became more interested in the organization and started to ask them more questions about it during interviews. For Kingsley, this practice was a potential danger zone. During press junkets, she made journalists sign contracts in which they agreed they would not sell any of Cruise's quotes to the tabloids. Television programs were forced to destroy all tapes of interviews with Cruise once the episodes aired. Because Kingsley was also the publicist for several other sought-after stars, the industry complied with her demands.[48] However, as more information about Scientology was being shared on the Internet and the list of people leaving the organization grew, the press was growing increasingly critical of Scientology. On the 2003 press junket for his movie *The Last Samurai*, Cruise wanted to promote Scientology. Kingsley disagreed, and some months later Cruise let her go, instead hiring his sister and a crew of Scientologists as his publicity team.[49]

Soon it would not be Cruise's comments about Scientology that threatened his career and the organization but rather his actions during an interview when asked about his personal life—and the way those actions took on a life of their own in the new online environment. In May 2005, a few weeks after meeting Katie Holmes (whom he would subsequently marry) Cruise appeared on *The Oprah Winfrey Show*, an event that has been well-documented in many places.[50] Rather than the serious and reserved actor he had been in previous interviews, in this instance he was joyful and exuberant over having fallen in love. He knelt down on his knees, slapped the stage, and stood on the couch. Before the day was over, the interview was one of the main topics of discussion online, and even the television news was showing video clips from the interview. As the story was shared in a variety of online settings, it began to change, becoming more dramatic and sensationalistic. Suddenly, Cruise was not just "standing" on the couch but "jumping" on it. The context of that behavior became invisible. Oprah had thanked him for his support at a recent event she had hosted where, in honoring two African American leaders, he stood on his chair and cheered. In fact, she said that she "loved his enthusiasm" in that act. That was when Cruise stood on the couch. In response to the audience's cheers and prodding, he stood on it again a few moments later. "All told, Cruise on the couch—the key image of what the gossip blogs deemed his meltdown—is less than three seconds of airtime."[51] And in a digital age, the video clips, memes, stories, and comments related to that event are still available, more than a decade later.

Oprah Winfrey's interview with Tom Cruise was only one of several events in 2005 that marred Cruise's image and cast Scientology in a negative light. One month later, Cruise is interviewed by Matt Lauer on *The Today Show*.[52] As soon as Matt Lauer brings up Scientology by referring to reports that Katie Holmes was "opening herself up" to Scientology, Cruise turns to the now-familiar attack strategy that became evident in interviews with the organization's representatives in previous decades. His first response is, "You know, Scientology is something you don't understand." When Lauer brings up Cruise's recent criticism of actress Brooke Shields's use of antidepressants, Cruise continues to target Lauer: "Do you know what Adderall is?"; "Do you know that Ritalin is a street drug?"; "Matt, I'm asking you a question"; "you're glib." Cruise goes on to criticize Lauer's lack of knowledge about psychopharmaceuticals, in contrast to himself, who has done the research and who "doesn't talk about things I don't understand." Despite Cruise using the attack strategy, Lauer is able to place him on the defensive at several points during the interview. In the end, Cruise appears in a negative light and once again, the Internet is abuzz with the event.

In November of that same year, Scientology is satirized in an episode of the television show *South Park*. In an event known as "Closetgate," in March 2006 allegations surface that the show's rebroadcast was preempted because Cruise threatened to pull out of promotions for the new *Mission Impossible* movie; Viacom was the parent company of both the television station on which *South Park* was broadcast and the movie's production company.[53] Cruise's infamous interviews in 2005, followed by these other media-related events, appeared to threaten his career. A 2006 *USA Today/Gallup Poll* found that 51 percent of respondents now had a negative image of Cruise, and his "Q Score" (a marketing measure of reputation with the public) had declined by 40 percent in just a little over one year.[54] The head of Viacom ended the company's relationship with him because of his "creative suicide" over the previous several months.[55] His image had changed in the eyes of the public, and "Hollywood was convinced he was poison, a religious fanatic, and possibly unhinged."[56] The image of Scientology had been tarnished as well. In managing the impressions of both himself and the organization, Cruise would not only become "increasingly silent about Scientology over the [next] ten years" but also enter a stage of "near total media silence."[57]

One exception was another interview with Oprah Winfrey in 2008, in Cruise's home in Telluride, Colorado. In this interview, Oprah asks him about Scientology—whether he feels it is unfairly criticized. His responses are measured, and an overt attack strategy is absent. Instead, the framing of his answers is more positive. People are "interested" in Scientology rather than critical. Scientology becomes the victim, in that the only problem is "sometimes people misinterpret," and as a solution "I think the best thing is for people to read about it themselves."[58] However, the public's view of Scientology was increasingly negative. Online comments on the show's website accused Cruise of being "fake" and were critical of Winfrey herself for not pushing him harder on a number of issues.[59]

Other celebrity Scientologists have come forward in interviews to discuss the organization. For instance, musician Beck addresses Scientology in a 2012 interview on MTV.[60] He begins his statements with Scientology as the victim by referring to the "intolerance" it faces, which is "insidious." Then he transitions to a more positive frame by addressing the positive aspects of Scientology. He says that "the good it's done speaks for itself" and goes on to list the organization's humanitarian work in education, drug treatment, and within prisons. The interviewer then shifts the topic to Beck's work on his new album.

Over the last several years, John Travolta appears to have become the *de facto* celebrity spokesperson for Scientology. In his interviews, his efforts to establish a human interest media frame (and preempt a shock-exposé frame) are evident. In 2010, he appeared on *Good Morning America* to talk about his new movie but also his recent trip to postearthquake Haiti, where he and his wife delivered supplies and physicians using his personal airplane.[61] He emphasizes positive aspects of Scientology and carefully balances mention of the organization within a larger context. For instance, in describing the challenges of ensuring that the emergency supplies were actually delivered to physicians in Haiti, he credits "the military and my volunteer ministers" for helping to save hundreds of lives. When he is asked how his family is coping following the death of his son, he states that "our church has helped us tremendously" and even has a special program for people who are grieving. But then he quickly emphasizes how helpful all of the letters, cards, and e-mails from supporting fans have also been. The interviewer then shifts the topic to Travolta's new movie.

Following the release of the documentary film *Going Clear* in 2015, Travolta again addressed Scientology in a number of interviews.[62] He appeared on *Good Morning America* in April of that year.[63] Amid the controversy generated by the documentary, Travolta initially comes across as critical to detractors, telling them "to take the time and read a book" and then directing them to specific books published by the organization. Then he shifts the conversation to the role of Scientology in his own life. He states that "my family has done well with it," "I've saved lives with it," and "I've save my own life with it" (once again referring to the death of his son several years earlier). The interviewer then moves to a new line of questioning that focuses on Travolta's new acting projects.

That same month, the newspaper *Tampa Bay Times* features an audio interview with John Travolta on its website.[64] In a statement reminiscent of interviews with members of Scientology in past decades, wherein they indicated that they avoided anything negative written about the organization, Travolta says that he will not be seeing the film. He initially focuses attention on the documentary, referring to the criticism of Scientology within the movie as the product "of people who are disgruntled." Then he turns to the positive and personal aspects of Scientology, reiterating many of his comments on *Good Morning America*, once again mentioning how his family has benefitted from it and how it has saved his life on multiple occasions.

The dual tasks of managing their own impressions as well as the impressions of Scientology have led some celebrity Scientologists to emphasize the positive and the personal in interviews. However, a 2013 radio show interview with Kirstie Alley features the actress referring to recent Scientology defector Leah Remini as "a bigot" and "my enemy."[65] The attack strategy that was evident in interviews with representatives of Scientology several decades ago maintains a presence.

CONCLUSION

According to some scholars, "the media serves as the central battleground in the struggles over moral codes" in society, the arena in which what is good or bad, right or wrong, moral or immoral is debated. [66] Nowhere is this more apparent than in television interviews. In television interviews with Scientologists, we see a negotiation of moral boundaries—a complex weaving of claims and counterclaims—that has been labeled the "deviance dance."[67] In the interviews themselves, Scientology is deviantized by the interviewer, fellow guests on the program, or members of the audience, and the Scientologists being interviewed quickly respond in ways to resist a negative label.

In earlier interviews, television news journalists would ask representatives of the Church of Scientology questions about recent events or controversies. It quickly became evident that the organization's primary means of resisting a negative label was to deviantize others. The attack strategy outlined in L. Ron Hubbard's policy letters, which justified legal action and harassment campaigns against critics, was also evident in the television interview environment. Rather than responding directly to questions posed by the interviewers, the interviewees would frequently attempt to shift the conversation to the deviance of others: ex-Scientologists had been forced to leave the organization because of horrible things they had done; critics were unintelligent, incompetent, or uninformed; the interview was part of a larger plot to discredit Scientology. As the news media industry evolved from neutral observer and reporter of facts to hybrid programming and tabloid television characterized by the shock-exposé frame, Scientology's attack strategy became more pronounced. In fact, it was sometimes even elicited by tabloid television interviewers themselves.

Over time, television journalists became familiar with this strategy and developed strategies of their own to counteract it. Representatives of Scientology were increasingly being put on the defensive in television interviews. Soon they appeared to retreat from those interviews, instead leaning more heavily on celebrity Scientologists to be the public faces of the organization. However, as the celebrity gossip industry changed with the expansion of the Internet, there were times when the actions and statements of celebrity Scientologists harmed the organization's image (as well as the celebrity's image) more than helped.

In recent years, a new television strategy appears to have emerged for Scientology, one that serves to manage the public's impression of the celebrity and of the organization. Using this strategy to elicit a human interest media frame, celebrities try to emphasize positive work done by the organization as well as the ways that their own personal lives have benefited from Scientology. However, when the organization is facing negative publicity, even the celebrity interviewees sometimes momentarily slip back into the attack strategy before once again highlighting the positive and the personal.

But lest we think that the organization itself has retreated from public commentary, we have only to look its response to actress Leah Remini after she left the organization. In 2015, she was interviewed on the show *20/20*. Representatives of the Church of Scientology did not appear on the program, but they did send a written rebuttal to ABC News in which they target Remini rather than respond to her accusations: "she treated everyone around her in a degrading, bullying manner"; "she was on the verge of being expelled [from Scientology]"; "she is joined at the hip with this collection of deadbeats, admitted liars, self-admitted perjurers, wife beaters, and worse."[68] One year later, when the A&E network announced that Remini would be hosting an eight-part docuseries about the Church of Scientology, the organization's spokesperson sent a letter to the network in an attempt to block the program. In this letter, they attack Remini as a "has-been actress" and "spoiled, entitled diva" responsible for inspiring "inflamed acts of religious hate" against the organization.[69] In response to the actions of Remini, the Church of Scientology once again portrays itself as the victim of unsolicited harassment at the hands of a horrible person who has an axe to grind. Given its history with the media, the organization's response is to be expected. However, more surprising is Remini's counterattack, a legal demand for $1.5 million in compensation for "reputational, emotional, and economic injuries."[70] Just as Ted

Koppel used the Church of Scientology's own media strategy to outmaneuver David Miscavige in an Emmy Award–winning interview, Remini has used another of the organization's well-known techniques in her counterattack— litigation. Remini's show (*Leah Remini: Scientology and the Aftermath*) would go on to considerable success, becoming the network's top-rated new show.[71] The Church of Scientology appears to no longer be the leader in the "deviance dance" between the organization and its critics.

NOTES

1. For a discussion of the satirization and criticism of Scientology in entertainment media, see "Hollywood Bites" in this volume.

2. Benjamin Beit-Hallahmi, "Scientology: Religion or Racket?," *Marburg Journal of Religion* 8, no. 1 (2003): 26–28, http://archiv.ub.uni-marburg.de/ep/0004/article /view/3724; The Walrus, "Scientology Attacks! Going to War with L. Ron Hubbard's Disciples," *Walrus*, April, 2015, http://thewalrus.ca/scientology-attacks/.

3. Sean McCloud, "From Exotics to Brainwashers: Portraying New Religions in Mass Media," *Religion Compass* 1, no. 1 (2007): 225, doi:10.1111/j.1749-8171.2006.00001.x.

4. Ibid., 224.

5. Steven Clayman and John Heritage, *The News Interview: Journalists and Public Figures on the Air* (Cambridge, UK: Cambridge University Press, 2002).

6. Martin Montgomery, "Rituals of Personal Experience in Television News Interviews," *Discourse and Communication* 4, no. 2 (2010): 185–186, doi:10.1177 /1750481310364322.

7. Ibid.

8. Clayman and Heritage, *The News Interview.*

9. Ibid.; Ian Hutchby, "Non-Neutrality and Argument in the Hybrid Political Interview," *Discourse Studies* 13, no. 3 (2011): 352, doi:10.1177/1461445611400665.

10. Hutchby, "Non-Neutrality and Argument," 350.

11. Ibid., 349.

12. McCloud, "From Exotics to Brainwashers," 223.

13. Bernard Doherty, "Sensational Scientology! The Church of Scientology and Australian Tabloid Television," *Nova Religio: The Journal of Alternative and Emergent Religions* 17, no. 3 (2014): 42, doi:10.1525/nr.2014.17.3.38.

14. Ibid., 41.

15. McCloud, "From Exotics to Brainwashers," 217.

16. Ibid.

17. Ibid., 218.

18. "Manson Family Murders Fast Facts," last modified August 24, 2015, http:// www.cnn.com/2013/09/30/us/manson-family-murders-fast-facts/.

19. McCloud, "From Exotics to Brainwashers," 219.

20. Ibid., 222; Jennifer Latson, "The Jonestown Massacre, Remembered," *Time*, November 18, 2014, http://time.com/3583781/jonestown-massacre/.

21. Joseph Laycock, "Where Do They Get These Ideas? Changing Ideas of Cults in the Mirror of Popular Culture," *Journal of the American Academy of Religion* 81, no. 1 (2013): 81–83, doi:10.1093/jaarel/lfs091.

22. James R. Lewis, "Scientology vs. the Media," *Alternative Spirituality and Religion Review* 6, no. 1 (2015): 73, doi:10.5840/asrr201572010. For a discussion of folk devils and moral panics, see Stanley Cohen, *Folk Devils and Moral Panics: The Creation of the Mods and Rockers* (Oxford, UK: Blackwell, 1972).

23. Doherty, "Sensational Scientology," 46–48.

24. *Encarta Dictionary: English (North America)*, s.v. "bias."

25. Beit-Hallahmi, "Scientology: Religion or Racket," 26–28.

26. Doherty, "Sensational Scientology," 38–39.

27. Barend van Driel and James T. Richardson, "Print Media Coverage of New Religious Movements: A Longitudinal Study," *Journal of Communication* 38, no. 3 (1988): 37–61, doi:10.1111/j.1460-2466.1988.tb02059.x.

28. Lewis, "Scientology vs. the Media," 62.

29. L. Ron Hubbard, "HCO Policy Letter of 15 August 1960," http://www.gerry armstrong.org/50grand/cult/fbi/pl-dept-govt-affairs.html.

30. Douglas Franz, "Religion's Search for a Home Base," *New York Times*, December 1, 1997, http://www.nytimes.com/1997/12/01/us/religion-s-search-for-a-home -base.html; Lawrence Wright, *Going Clear: Scientology, Hollywood, & the Prison of Belief* (New York, NY: Alfred A. Knopf, 2013), 131–132; "The Truth Rundown," accessed November 19, 2015, http://www.tampabay.com/specials/2009/reports/project/archive -stories.shtml; Charles Stafford, "Scientology: An In-Depth Profile of a New Force in Clearwater," *St. Petersburg Times*, January 9, 1980, http://www.sptimes.com/2006 /webspecials06/scientology/Scientology_Special_Report.pdf.

31. In different iterations, this *60 Minutes* report has been variously titled "The Clearwater Conspiracy" and "Scientology." It can be viewed on YouTube: Knowledge is Power, "Scientology Clearwater Conspiracy Operation Freakout Part 1," YouTube video, 6:38, posted January 2008, https://www.youtube.com/watch?v= nD8LOmQtwyg; Knowledge is Power, "Scientology Clearwater Conspiracy Operation Freakout Part 2," YouTube video, 8:33, posted January 2008, https://www.you tube.com/watch?v=Ql1M4ZHtNxA.

32. To learn more about Paulette Cooper and the FBI raids of Scientology offices that confirmed she was a target in Operation Freakout, see Paulette Cooper, "The Scandal Behind 'The Scandal of Scientology,'" accessed October 9, 2015, http://www .paulettecooper.com/scandal.htm.

33. For a discussion of celebrity defections in particular, see "Project Celebrity" in this volume.

34. Gordon Freedman and John Stossel, "In the Name of Religion," *20/20*, transcript (New York, NY: ABC News, 1983).

35. Hubbard, "HCO Policy Letter of 15 August 1960"; L. Ron Hubbard, "HCO Policy Letter of 25. February 1966," http://www.suppressiveperson.org/sp/archives/3236.

36. Richard Behar, "The Thriving Cult of Greed and Power," *Time*, May 6, 1991, https://www.cs.cmu.edu/~dst/Fishman/time-behar.html.

37. Wright, *Going Clear*, 224.

38. Tamara Haddad and Larry King, "The Church of Scientology: Religion or Business," *Larry King Live*, transcript (Washington, DC: CNN, 1991).

39. Alex Rodriguez, "Scientology Leader David Miscavige on ABC News Nightline FULL," YouTube video, 55:50, posted May 2015, https://www.youtube.com /watch?v=exzmE3vW_Tw.

40. Wright, *Going Clear*, 219.

41. For more on Scientology's war with psychiatry, see elsewhere in this volume.

42. Heidi Ewing, "Inside Scientology," *A&E Investigative Reports* (New York, NY: Tobin Pictures, 1998).

43. Larry David and Jerry Seinfeld, *Seinfeld*, "The Parking Garage," DVD, directed by Tom Cherones (1991; Culver City, CA: Sony Pictures Home Entertainment, 2013); Steven Soderbergh, "Schizopolis," YouTube video, directed by Steven Soderbergh (Helena, MT: 406 Productions, 1996), posted by Jake Maringoni, May 12, 2015, https://www.youtube.com/results?search_query=schizopolis+full+movie; Steve Martin, *Bowfinger*, streaming film, directed by Frank Oz (Orlando, FL: Universal Pictures, 1999), http://itunes.ca.

44. Peter N. Alexander, "The Profit," YouTube video, directed by Peter N. Alexander (Tampa, FL: Courage Productions, 2001), posted by Wilfried Handl, March 19, 2015, https://www.youtube.com/watch?v=D67OvQyGMF8; For an analysis of representations of Scientology in fictional television and film, see "Hollywood Bites" in this volume.

45. Lewis, "Scientology vs. the Media," 67.

46. Amy Nicholson, "How YouTube and Internet Journalism Destroyed Tom Cruise, Our Last Real Movie Star," *L.A. Weekly*, May 20, 2014, http://www.laweekly .com/news/how-youtube-and-internet-journalism-destroyed-tom-cruise-our-last-real -movie-star-4656549.

47. Ibid.

48. Ibid.

49. Ibid; Edward Zwick, *The Last Samurai*, streaming film, directed by Edward Zwick (Burbank, CA: Warner Bros., 2003).

50. For instance, see Wright, *Going Clear*, 291.

51. Nicholson, "How YouTube and Internet Journalism."

52. Today, "Tom Cruise's Heated Interview with Matt Lauer," YouTube video, 13:56, posted June 2014, https://www.youtube.com/watch?v=tFgF1JPNR5E.

53. Trey Parker, Matt Stone, and Brian Graden, *South Park*, "Trapped in the Closet," streaming television episode, directed by Trey Parker (New York, NY: Braniff/Parker-Stone Studios, 2005), http://itunes.ca; Huffington Post, "Church of Scientology Investigated 'South Park' Creators Matt Stone, Trey Parker: Report," *Huffington Post*, January 17, 2013, http://www.huffingtonpost.com/2011/10/24/church-of-scientology -investigate-south-park_n_1027538.html; Jason Guerrasio, "Here Are the 2 Topics Press Aren't Allowed to Ask Tom Cruise About While He Promotes the New 'Mission Impossible,'" *Business Insider*, July 30, 2015, http://www.businessinsider.com /mission-impossible-press-not-allowed-to-ask-tom-cruise-scientology-and-dating -questions-2015-7.

54. Donna Peberdy, "From Wimps to Wild Men: Bipolar Masculinity and the Paradoxical Performances of Tom Cruise," *Men and Masculinities* 13, no. 2: 246.

55. Melissa Marr, "Sumner Redstone Gives Tom Cruise His Walking Papers," *Wall Street Journal*, August 23, 2006, http://www.wsj.com/articles/SB115628557000642662.

56. Nicholson, "How YouTube and Internet Journalism."

57. Guerrasio, "Here Are the 2 Topics"; Nicholson, "How YouTube and Internet Journalism."

58. Homeadverts.com, "Oprah and Tom Cruise in Telluride, Colorado," You-Tube video, 42:37, posted January 14, 2015, https://www.youtube.com/watch?v=0z2-9clujCQ.

59. Peberdy, "From Wimps to Wild Men," 251.

60. Alex Rodriguez, "Beck Talks Scientology, Fatherhood and Staying Young," YouTube video, 4:04, posted March 14, 2014, https://www.youtube.com/watch?v=ToFsrOJrdCY.

61. Proximodiz' Scientology News, "ABC, 2 Feb. 2010: Good Morning America! With John Travolta about the Scientology Volunteer Ministers," YouTube video, 6:09, posted February 3, 2010, https://www.youtube.com/watch?v=hBBlug887NI.

62. Alex Gibney and Lawrence Wright, *Going Clear: Scientology and the Prison of Belief*, streaming film, directed by Alex Gibney (New York, NY: HBO Documentary Films, 2015).

63. Alex Rodriguez, "John Travolta on Scientology 2015," YouTube video, 1:32, posted April 20, 2015, https://www.youtube.com/watch?v=PKwdi_0Gk6w.

64. Steve Persall, "John Travolta Happy with Scientology, Won't See 'Going Clear,'" *Tampa Bay Times*, http://www.tampabay.com/things-to-do/movies/john-travolta-says-hes-happy-with-scientology-wont-see-going-clear/2224359.

65. Rick's Vids, "Kirstie Alley Goes After Leah Remini for Attacking Scientology," YouTube video, 2:00, https://www.youtube.com/watch?v=60BVRMForJc.

66. Tami M. Bereska, *Deviance, Conformity, and Social Control in Canada*, 4th edition (Toronto, ON: Pearson Education Canada, 2014), 21.

67. Ibid., 24.

68. ABC News, "Church of Scientology International's October 30, 2015 Statement to ABC News Regarding '20/20' Leah Remini Interview," accessed July 17, 2015, http://abcnews.go.com/2020/church-scientology-internationals-october-30-2015-statement-abc/story?id=34849323.

69. Tony Ortega, "EXCLUSIVE: See the Letter Scientology Sent to Scare A&E Out of Airing Leah Remini's Series," *The Underground Bunker*, November 19, 2016, http://tonyortega.org/2016/11/19/exclusive-see-the-letter-scientology-sent-to-scare-ae-out-of-airing-leah-reminis-series/.

70. Tony Ortega, "Leah Remini Demands $1.5 Million from Scientology for Interfering with Her A&E Series," *The Underground Bunker*, November 22, 2016, http://tonyortega.org/2016/11/22/leah-remini-demands-1-5-million-from-scientology-for-interfering-with-her-ae-series/.

71. Elizabeth Wagmeister, "How Leah Remini's New Show Has Jolted Scientology," *Variety*, December 20, 2016, http://variety.com/2016/tv/news/leah-remini-scientology-video-tom-cruise-john-travolta-1201945532/.

BIBLIOGRAPHY

ABC News. "Church of Scientology International's October 30, 2015 Statement to ABC News Regarding '20/20' Leah Remini Interview." Accessed July 17, 2015. http://abcnews.go.com/2020/church-scientology-internationals-october -30-2015-statement-abc/story?id=34849323.

Alexander, Peter N. "The Profit." YouTube video. Directed by Peter N. Alexander. Tampa, FL: Courage Productions, 2001. Posted by Wilfried Handl, March 19, 2015. https://www.youtube.com/watch?v=D67OvQyGMF8.

Behar, Richard. "The Thriving Cult of Greed and Power." *Time*. May 6, 1991. https:// www.cs.cmu.edu/~dst/Fishman/time-behar.html.

Beit-Hallahmi, Benjamin. "Scientology: Religion or Racket?" *Marburg Journal of Religion* 8, no. 1 (2003): 1–56. http://archiv.ub.uni-marburg.de/ep/0004/article /view/3724.

Bereska, Tami M. *Deviance, Conformity, and Social Control in Canada* (4th edition). Toronto, ON: Pearson Education Canada, 2014.

Clayman, Steven, and John Heritage. *The News Interview: Journalists and Public Figures on the Air*. Cambridge, UK: Cambridge University Press, 2002.

Cohen, Stanley. *Folk Devils and Moral Panics: The Creation of the Mods and Rockers*. Oxford, UK: Blackwell, 1972.

Cooper, Paulette. "The Scandal Behind 'The Scandal of Scientology.'" Accessed October 9, 2015. http://www.paulettecooper.com/scandal.htm.

David, Larry, and Jerry Seinfeld. "The Parking Garage." *Seinfeld*, DVD. Directed by Tom Cherones. 1991. Culver City, CA: Sony Pictures Home Entertainment, 2013.

Doherty, Bernard. "Sensational Scientology! The Church of Scientology and Australian Tabloid Television." *Nova Religio: The Journal of Alternative and Emergent Religions* 17, no. 3 (2014): 38–63. doi:10.1525/nr.2014.17.3.38.

Ewing, Heidi. "Inside Scientology." *A&E Investigative Reports*. New York: Tobin Pictures, 1998.

Franz, Douglas. "Religion's Search for a Home Base." *New York Times*, December 1, 1997. http://www.nytimes.com/1997/12/01/us/religion-s-search-for-a-home -base.html.

Freedman, Gordon, and John Stossel. "In the Name of Religion." *20/20*. Transcript. New York: ABC News, 1983.

Gibney, Alex, and Lawrence Wright. *Going Clear: Scientology and the Prison of Belief*, streaming film. Directed by Alex Gibney. New York: HBO Documentary Films, 2015.

Guerrasio, Jason. "Here Are the 2 Things Press Aren't Allowed to Ask Tom Cruise about While He Promotes the New 'Mission Impossible.'" *Business Insider*. July 30, 2015. http://www.businessinsider.com/mission-impossible-press-not -allowed-to-ask-tom-cruise-scientology-and-dating-questions-2015-7.

Haddad, Tamara, and Larry King. "The Church of Scientology: Religion or Business?" *Larry King Live*. Transcript. Washington, DC: CNN, 1991.

Homeadverts.com. "Oprah and Tom Cruise in Telluride, Colorado." YouTube video, 42:37. https://www.youtube.com/watch?v=0z2-9clujCQ.

Hubbard, L. Ron. "HCO Policy Letter of 15 August 1960." http://www.gerryarmstrong.org/50grand/cult/fbi/pl-dept-govt-affairs.html.

Hubbard, L. Ron. "HCO Policy Letter of 25 February 1966." http://www.suppressiveperson.org/sp/archives/3236.

Huffington Post. "Church of Scientology Investigated 'South Park' Creators Matt Stone, Trey Parker: Report." *Huffington Post*. January 17, 2013. http://www.huffingtonpost.com/2011/10/24/church-of-scientology-investigate-south-park_n_1027538.html.

Hutchby, Ian. "Non-Neutrality and Argument in the Hybrid Political Interview." *Discourse Studies* 13, no. 3 (2011): 349–365. doi:10.1177/1461445611400665.

Knowledge Is Power. "Scientology Clearwater Conspiracy Operation Freakout Part 1." YouTube video, 6:38. Posted January 2008. https://www.youtube.com/watch?v=nD8LOmQtwyg.

Knowledge Is Power. "Scientology Clearwater Conspiracy Operation Freakout Part 2." YouTube video, 8:33. Posted January 2008. https://www.youtube.com/watch?v=Ql1M4ZHtNxA.

Latson, Jennifer. "The Jonestown Massacre, Remembered." *Time*, November 18, 2014. http://time.com/3583781/jonestown-massacre/.

Laycock, Joseph. "Where Do They Get These Ideas? Changing Ideas of Cults in the Mirror of Popular Culture." *Journal of the American Academy of Religion* 81, no. 1 (2013): 80–106. doi:10.1093/jaarel/lfs091.

Lewis, James R. "Scientology vs. the Media." *Alternative Spirituality and Religion Review* 6, no. 1 (2015): 61–78. doi:10.5840/asrr201572010.

"Manson Family Murders Fast Facts." Last modified August 24, 2015. http://www.cnn.com/2013/09/30/us/manson-family-murders-fast-facts/.

Maraynes, Allan. "Scientology Update." *60 Minutes*. Transcript. New York: CBS News, 1985.

Marr, Melissa. "Sumner Redstone Gives Tom Cruise His Walking Papers." *Wall Street Journal*. August 23, 2006. http://www.wsj.com/articles/SB115628557000642662.

Martin, Steve. *Bowfinger*, streaming film. Directed by Frank Oz. Orlando, FL: Universal Pictures, 1999. http://itunes.ca.

McCloud, Sean. "From Exotics to Brainwashers: Portraying New Religions in Mass Media." *Religion Compass* 1, no. 1 (2007): 214–228. doi:10.1111/j.1749-8171.2006.00001.x.

Montgomery, Martin. "Rituals of Personal Experience in Television News Interviews," *Discourse and Communication* 4, no. 2 (2010), doi:10.1177/1750481310364322.

Nicholson, Amy. "How YouTube and Internet Journalism Destroyed Tom Cruise, Our Last Real Movie Star." *L.A. Weekly*. May 20, 2014. http://www.laweekly.com/news/how-youtube-and-internet-journalism-destroyed-tom-cruise-our-last-real-movie-star-4656549.

Ortega, Tony. "EXCLUSIVE: See the Letter Scientology Sent to Scare A&E Out of Airing Leah Remini's Series." *The Underground Bunker*. November 19, 2016. http://tonyortega.org/2016/11/19/exclusive-see-the-letter-scientology-sent-to-scare-ae-out-of-airing-leah-reminis-series/.

Ortega, Tony. "Leah Remini Demands $1.5 Million from Scientology for Interfering with Her A&E Series." *The Underground Bunker*. November 22, 2016.

http://tonyortega.org/2016/11/22/leah-remini-demands-1-5-million-from
-scientology-for-interfering-with-her-ae-series/.

Parker, Trey, Matt Stone, and Brian Graden. "Trapped in the Closet." *South Park*,
streaming television episode. Directed by Trey Parker. New York: Braniff/
Parker-Stone Studios, 2005. http://itunes.ca.

Peberdy, Donna. "From Wimps to Wild Men: Bipolar Masculinity and the Paradoxical
Performances of Tom Cruise." *Men and Masculinities* 13, no. 2 (2010): 231–254.

Persall, Steve. "John Travolta Happy with Scientology, Won't See 'Going Clear.'"
Tampa Bay Times. http://www.tampabay.com/things-to-do/movies/john-travolta
-says-hes-happy-with-scientology-wont-see-going-clear/2224359.

Proximodiz' Scientology News. "ABC, 2 Feb 2010: Good Morning America! With
John Travolta about the Scientology Volunteer Ministers." YouTube video, 6:09.
Posted February 3, 2010. https://www.youtube.com/watch?v=hBBlug887NI.

Rick's Vids. "Kirstie Alley Goes After Leah Remini for Attacking Scientology." You-
Tube video, 2:00. https://www.youtube.com/watch?v=60BVRMForJc.

Rodriguez, Alex. "Beck Talks Scientology, Fatherhood and Staying Young." You-
Tube video, 4:04. Posted March 14, 2014. https://www.youtube.com/watch?v=
ToFsrOJrdCY.

Rodriguez, Alex. "John Travolta on Scientology 2015." YouTube video, 1:32. Posted
April 20, 2015. https://www.youtube.com/watch?v=PKwdi_0Gk6w.

Rodriguez, Alex. "Scientology Leader David Miscavige on ABC News Nightline
FULL." YouTube video, 55:50. Posted May 2015. https://www.youtube.com
/watch?v=exzmE3vW_Tw.

Soderbergh, Steven. "Schizopolis." YouTube video. Directed by Steven Soderbergh.
Helena, MT: 406 Productions, 1996. Posted by Jake Maringoni, May 12, 2015.
https://www.youtube.com/results?search_query=schizopolis+full+movie.

Stafford, Charles. "Scientology: An In-Depth Profile of a New Force in Clearwater." *St.
Petersburg Times*, January 9, 1980. http://www.sptimes.com/2006/webspecials06
/scientology/Scientology_Special_Report.pdf.

Tampa Bay Times. "The Truth Rundown." Accessed November 19, 2015. http://www
.tampabay.com/specials/2009/reports/project/archive-stories.shtml.

Today. "Tom Cruise's Heated Interview with Matt Lauer." YouTube video, 13:55.
Posted June 2014. https://www.youtube.com/watch?v=tFgF1JPNR5E.

Van Driel, Barend, and James T. Richardson. "Print Media Coverage of New Religious Movements: A Longitudinal Study." *Journal of Communication* 38, no. 3
(1988): 37–61. doi:10.1111/j.1460-2466.1988.tb02059.x.

Wagmeister, E. "How Leah Remini's New Show Has Jolted Scientology." *Variety*.
December 20, 2016. http://variety.com/2016/tv/news/leah-remini-scientology
-video-tom-cruise-john-travolta-1201945532/.

Walrus. "Scientology Attacks! Going to War with L. Ron Hubbard's Disciples." *Walrus*. April 2015. http://thewalrus.ca/scientology-attacks/.

Wright, Lawrence. *Going Clear: Scientology, Hollywood, & the Prison of Belief*. New
York: Alfred A. Knopf, 2013.

Zwick, Edward. *The Last Samurai*, streaming film. Directed by Edward Zwick. Burbank, CA: Warner Bros., 2003.

9

Presentations of Scientology in Prominent North American News Series

Terra Manca

INTRODUCTION

Journalistic interest into founder L. Ron Hubbard's (1911–1986) claims preceded the creation of Scientology. Indeed, "Not long after its founder L. Ron Hubbard published his bestselling self-help book *Dianetics* in 1950, the movement became the subject of often withering critiques by a wide range of journalists. And for the next sixty years it was the focus of exposés in various publications."[1] Journalistic and academic accounts suggest that such exposés motivated Scientology to engage various easily sensationalized efforts to manage public relations. For example, one news series quoted Scientology spokesperson Nancy Reitze's denial that Scientology was taking over Clearwater, Florida. They cited her statement that that newspaper's stories risked victimizing Scientology to the point of creating another "Nazi Germany."[2] Other areas of journalistic interest have ranged from the actions and denials of Scientologists involved in covert and illegal operations, inaccurate representations of Hubbard's life and credentials, celebrity scandals, as well as an assortment of other oftentimes peculiar ideas and activities.

In this chapter, I review some of the coverage from six news series that appeared in several North American newspapers between 1974 and 2009. These series emerged during a lengthy period of publicized concerns about "cults," during which the nature of journalism changed. I focus on three areas for each of these series: First, I review how each series represented Scientology in its reports. Second, I summarize the content of these series in relation to events involving Scientology. Third, I argue that contrary to some research, the journalistic accounts of Scientology do not constitute mere "moral panic." Rather, they addressed a number of controversies that had tangible and wide-reaching social implications.

Many journalistic accounts *have* been very sensational and very critical of new religious movements (NRMs). Some scholars have voiced concern about media representations of Scientology and other NRMs.[3] Media accounts are influenced by commercial interests, often resulting in reports that reinforce stereotypes that reflect the sponsors' and readership's values.[4] This reinforcement frequently involves sensationalism or representations of controversies that *can* perpetuate "moral panics." By definition, a moral panic is "A condition, episode, person or group of persons [which] emerges to become defined as a threat to societal values and interests; its nature is presented in a stylized and stereotypical fashion by the mass media."[5]

Some academics have noted a cyclical relationship between sensationalism and such moral panics about Scientology. For example, both Roy Wallis (1975) and James R. Lewis (2015) asserted that Scientology's interactions with the media exemplify the "deviance-amplification model" of moral panic—eventually resulting in far-reaching, international moral panics about the group.[6] According to this model, the moral gatekeeping that occurs in journalistic reports about Scientology amplified Scientology's deviant— and sometimes criminal—activities. Scientology typically responded to media reports with surveillance, harassment, and litigation. The media, in turn, answered with increasingly negative stories about Scientology, which Scientology retaliated against, thereby providing more activities for journalists to cover.[7]

Some definitions of moral panic are applicable to the relationship between Scientology and the press. Other interpretations of moral panic, however, emphasize that concerns arising from moral panics are irrational in ways that inadequately explain Scientology's activities. For example, contrary to some explanations of the moral panic, Scientology's involvement in the city of Clearwater was anything but "fleeting." Indeed, in this case, journalistic reporting of Scientology's actions in this city were quite necessary rather than "fundamentally inappropriate." And, much of the "fear and concern" about Scientology's activities was more than just "a product of the human imagination."[8] In short, the alleged moral panics about Scientology lacked the irrationality and disproportionality that moral panic implies. Rather, very real and pressing concerns have continued to plague Clearwater since Scientology established its base there. As this chapter demonstrates, this is the case with other concerns about Scientology also.

Often, rational evidence has backed the panics surrounding Scientology. Wallis (1975) acknowledged this when he detailed the escalation of controversies surrounding Scientology in relation to its media representations.[9]

The secretive nature of Scientology has allowed it to gain immense power in a number of domains. The journalists who wrote the series in this chapter worked very hard to expose the problematic nature of this power.[10] Some studies—including Lewis's (2015) article—overlook various controversies, such as the death of Lisa McPherson or Scientology's aforementioned take-over of Clearwater, Florida. In such cases, news reports on Scientology often have emerged from *necessity*.

In providing necessary news reports, however, the press aligned with defi-nitions of moral panics in that it reflected and tried to enforce the normative values of mainstream society.[11] Furthermore, the publication of Scientology's illicit activities coincided with increasingly deviant actions against journal-ists. Journalists who wrote about Scientology experienced personal costs in the form of harassment and litigation. Numerous news accounts of Scientol-ogy have been particularly influential and informative.[12] The news series that I discuss in this chapter address an array of important issues, often long before academia and government agencies.

Although I propose that many journalistic accounts have been neces-sary to highlight a variety of concerns about Scientology, journalism is not exempt from criticism. One journalist from the news series I examine stated: "most journalists still aspire to be first and best on breaking news and sig-nificant, previously untold, developments. It is a deeply ingrained matter of professional pride, as well as a way to achieve recognition in journalism and to advance in one's career."[13] At times, he admitted, criticism of journalism is appropriate—for example, when journalists compete with similar stories.[14] Moreover, journalists' efforts are influenced by trying to find the core of the story amid pressing deadlines, chaotic events, obscure information, as well as their efforts to navigate "public relations professionals, partisan sources, and other 'spin doctors.'"[15] Of course, one could ask other questions about journalistic coverage of religion, such as why proportionately fewer news sto-ries expose controversies involving mainstream religions such as Christian-ity. Nevertheless, in the case of Scientology, it seems that the only means to avoid sensationalism entirely would be to cease reporting on it—or to report only stories that Scientology approves.[16]

SCIENTOLOGY IN NORTH AMERICAN NEWSPAPERS

In 1948, Scientology's founder, L. Ron Hubbard began work a new sci-ence of the human mind, which he called "Dianetics" ("meaning 'through' (*dia*) the 'mind' (*nous*)").[17] Hubbard gained widespread recognition for his lay-psychotherapy claims when many people read *Dianetics* in the May 1950 edition of the *Astounding Science Fiction* magazine. He expanded his thesis further, publishing *Dianetics: The Modern Science of Mental Health* later in 1950. Selling over 150,000 copies,[18] the book made best-seller lists in *Time*, the *New York Times Book Review*, *Look*, and other magazines.[19] With these initial successes, Hubbard found some supportive mainstream scientists and medical practitioners in the early 1950s.[20] For instance, Dr. Joseph Winter, who wrote the introduction of the first edition of *Dianetics*, attested to its ability to heal all ailments.[21] Hubbard initially provided media interviews and allowed the publicity surrounding Dianetics and Scientology to grow.

Despite some initial support, Hubbard experienced early criticisms of various aspects of Dianetics. For instance, critical book reviews[22] coincided with the emergent media interest in NRMs that began in the late 1950s.[23] Some reviews chided Hubbard's grandiose claims about curing diseases. These claims had implications for Dianetics' legal standing because they left Hubbard's practitioners vulnerable to accusations about practicing medicine without a license. By integrating Dianetics into a supposedly *religious* institution—namely, Scientology—Hubbard minimized accusations of medical malpractice from government organizations, healthcare professionals, and the mass media.[24]

Even so, numerous journalists criticized Scientology after Hubbard founded it in 1953. Hubbard developed policies to manage such criticism before the end of that decade.[25] In a widely quoted document from 1955, Hubbard explained:

> We are not interested in sensationalism, personalities, or the complexities of Scientological [*sic*] methodology being dispensed by the general public. As a subdivision of this, we do not want Scientology to be reported in the press, anywhere else than on the religious page of newspapers. . . . Therefore we should be very alert to sue for slander at the slightest chance so as to discourage the public presses from mentioning Scientology.[26]

Furthermore, in Hubbard's (1959) *Manual of Justice* he stated, "People attack Scientology; I never forget it, always even the score."[27] In 1965, Hubbard wrote and first announced his "fair game" policy to counter the group's critics and the media.[28] These policy letters accompanied increasingly negative media and government attention. Lewis (2015) and Wallis (1975) found that Scientology was concerned with regulating media portrayals to the extent that its members pursued actions against journalists—actions that fueled future negative media representations and then further measures against journalists.

By the 1960s, Scientology's actions had influenced how the media covered NRMs.[29] Scientology tried to "manage" critics and journalists via aggressive behaviors, covert operations, and litigation, such that, "Since the 1960s, Scientology has been an important player in determining how new religions are covered in the media."[30] Despite these hostile measures, news coverage continued to proliferate throughout the 1970s up to the 1990s. In the early 1970s, "NRMs were not yet seen by the media as a social problem."[31] At that time, media coverage about NRMs appeared less openly negative than later coverage, even though NRM controversies have existed throughout history.[32] Then, after the 1978 Jonestown massacre in Guyana and various controversies involving the Unification Church, news media labeled a variety of movements, including Scientology, with the word "cult."[33] Some academics argued that this labeling generated a moral panic that only receded in the 1990s.[34]

Over recent decades, it appears that Scientology has lost much of its influence over journalistic publications—in large part because information is increasingly accessible online.[35] This loss became prevalent in the 1980s as the rise of the Internet limited Scientology's ability to mediate public knowledge about the organization.[36] By the 1990s, widespread public Internet access intensified Scientology's concerns about accessibility to its doctrines, beliefs, and practices. These changes in availability of information influenced interactions between Scientologists and journalists who published critical accounts of Scientology.[37] During the course of changing media representations of NRMs, six newspaper series in particular gained attention because of their relevant, timely, and detailed coverage of Scientology's activities.

Below, I introduce each news series and describe *how* they represented Scientology. Then, I describe *what* topics they addressed by detailing some common narratives that I found among them. Finally, I explain *why* these stories related to concerns about media sensationalism and moral panic.

OVERVIEW OF SIX NEWS SERIES (1974–2009)

1974, St. Louis Post-Dispatch

In 1974, the *St. Louis Post-Dispatch* reported to St. Louis residents that Scientology had been expanding its influence in Missouri since 1969.[38] The authors of this series reported on Scientology's high financial costs to its adherents and the group's harassment of its critics and former members. It reported also on the elusive Sea Organization and on Scientology's denial of all illicit activities.[39] The authors referred to Scientology as a "paramilitary structure" and cited leaders from other religions to reinforce Scientology's difference from them. They described Scientology training as "vocational" and cited professionals who had labeled Dianetics "quackery."[40]

The series referred to documents from Scientology's conflict with the Food and Drug Administration (FDA) and used personal accounts from former Scientologists to describe Scientology's operations. In 1974, however, journalists had fewer resources than those who wrote news series following the Federal Bureau of Investigation (FBI) release of documents about Scientology in 1978. Hence, although this series provided an important early discussion, it is not as revealing as its many successors.

1979, *Clearwater Sun*

Five years later, the *Clearwater Sun* published a series in November 1979 that focused on the release of FBI documents the previous year. The authors explained why the documents were relevant to Clearwater and how the city had responded to Scientology's growing presence and influence there. This series also reviewed Scientology's formation, its secretive nature, and its institutional goals. Journalist Richard Lieby (1979) personalized the series with stories from city officials and residents who had firsthand experience with Scientology.[41]

Although very informative and much needed in the community, some of the coverage in this series was quite sensational. For example, the *Clearwater Sun* used a commonly cited quote from one of Hubbard's dictionaries, *Modern Management Technology Defined*, to demonstrate that Hubbard approved of bending the truth. This quote read, "truth is what is true for you."[42] Moreover, some of the stories and opinion pieces that justified *why* journalists were investigating Scientology employed moralistic language. For instance, one opinion piece boldly privileged mainstream religions by stating, "We wish the Scientology students would seriously consider an alternative: any of the dozens of churches and temples that Clearwater boasts. Their teachings go back a lot farther than L. Ron Hubbard's dianetic dreamings, and there's absolutely no charge."[43] This quote legitimized mainstream religious traditions based on the length of their existence, thus deviantizing Scientology in part at least because of its very "newness."

Similarly, editor, Ron Stuart, wrote an opinion piece about Scientology's hostile responses to the media prior to the release of FBI documents in 1978.[44] Stuart stated that he felt his "conscience was just as clear as if it had just received the best audit possible from an E-meter."[45] This statement poked unnecessary fun at Scientology's belief system. Then, at the end of the piece, the author concluded, "This newspaper doesn't forget, forgive or turn its back on the past history (or future plotting) of the Scientologists in Clearwater."[46] Despite some biased statements, however, the *Clearwater Sun* provided Clearwater residents with many much needed details about Scientology's activities in their community. Moreover, most of the articles in this series relied purely on the sensational nature of Scientology's activities to entice readers and thereby avoided further sensationalism in their reporting.

1979, *St. Petersburg Times*

In the same year, the *St. Petersburg Times*—located less than 25 miles from Clearwater—published a series on Scientology and its influence on the local area. This series resembled the *Clearwater Sun's* (1979) in that it offered readers the information they needed to contextualize and understand Scientology's intrusion in their community.[47] The *St. Petersburg Times* authors provided immaculately organized and richly detailed narratives about Scientology. They identified that despite Scientology's aggressive tactics and retaliations, the newspaper dutifully informed the public of the movement's activities in the area. Furthermore, they reported on Scientology's legal problems, the secrecy around the movement, Scientology's history and development as an organization, and why it appealed to new members.

The authors occasionally relied on sensational language. Correspondent Charles Stafford (1979) began his analysis by stating that when "old-time religion celebrates the birth of a child," Scientology "came sneaking into town: a religion with beliefs and practices so alien to the teaching of Jesus that are preached in Clearwater's Christian churches, so different from the law of the prophets that is taught in the city's synagogues."[48] Stafford (1979) then demonstrated Scientology's deviance from three Judeo-Christian commandments in order to introduce some of the group's most controversial activities. Thus, he employed the heading, "Thou shalt not steal," to examine Scientology's theft of Internal Revenue Service (IRS) documents. With the caption, "Thou shalt love thy neighbor and thyself," he introduced his overview of Project Normandy—a Scientology operation that distinguished its friends from its enemies in Clearwater. Finally, Stafford's heading, "Thou shalt not bear false witness against thy neighbor," explained a Scientology scheme to get reporter Mark Sableman fired from the *Clearwater Sun*.[49] Despite some use of moralistic language, the *St. Petersburg Times* provided extensive evidence about Scientology's contentious activities that were relevant to the local readership.

1980, *The Globe and Mail*

John Marshall wrote the 1980 series on Scientology for *The Globe and Mail* in Canada. He reviewed the activities and occurrences that the first three series investigated and then he detailed similar events and actions in the Canadian context.[50] Marshall situated his account of Scientology's activities with reference to Scientology's reaction to a previous series he had written in which he had reviewed FBI documents with a Scientology critic.[51] Furthermore, he explained how Scientology and Hubbard decided upon on various controversial courses of action.

Similar to the *St. Louis Dispatch*, Marshall avoided the use of sensational adjectives. Instead, he used personal narratives to demonstrate how Scientology's activities had negatively affected critics—especially author Paulette Cooper and such former Scientologists as the McLean family (whom I discuss later). The *Globe and Mail* series expanded newspaper reporting on Scientology in North America beyond the U.S. context and illustrated the growing need for careful and accurate coverage in Canada.

1990, *Los Angeles Times*

The *Los Angeles Times* series appeared three years before the IRS settled its dispute with Scientology. This series described the controversies that the earlier series had introduced, in addition to more recent events and activities. Particularly, this series reported how Hubbard went into hiding in 1980, how David Miscavige became Hubbard's representative for Scientology, and how Miscavige seized power when Hubbard passed away in 1986. The authors described Scientology's harassment of recent critics, reviewed various newer Scientology front organizations, and explained Scientology's internal punitive system (the Rehabilitation Project Force). As well, the series examined Scientology's efforts to recruit celebrities and discussed why Hubbard's book sales continued to top the charts.

Like the *St. Petersburg Times*, this series provided readers with a great deal of detail on Scientology and its activities. It also justified allegations against Scientology and its religious status by explaining the various means through which Scientology sought legitimacy. For instance, the newspaper demonstrated how Scientology strived to infiltrate businesses, scientific, and educational organizations with programs like Applied Scholastics. This program uses supportive teachers to restructure curricula and place Scientology materials in public schools.[52] In addition, the *Times* reported Hubbard's explanation of Christianity: "Heaven, he said, is a 'false dream' and a 'very painful lie' intended to direct thetans toward a non-existent goal and convince them they have only one life."[53] This comparison to Christianity reiterated previous series' normative statements about mainstream religions and the way in which they contrast Scientology to them.

2009, *Tampa Bay Times* (formerly *St. Petersburg Times*)

In 2012, the *St. Petersburg Times* became the *Tampa Bay Times*. I refer to this 2009 series as the *Tampa Bay Times* series in order to distinguish it from the earlier *St. Petersburg Times* series published in 1979.

This series was a three-part narrative that began and ended with the story of David Miscavige's now infamous game of musical chairs.[54] *Tampa Bay* authors appended the narratives of four high-ranking defectors to well-known accounts about Scientology. This series addressed a number of topics: First, it reported allegations that Scientology's current leader, David Miscavige, engaged in physical violence against his followers. Second, the paper described the group's use of confessions and punishments against Scientologists. Third, the author recounted the death of Lisa McPherson, who died under Scientology's care. The paper reported the details surrounding this case, and it explained the ways in which Scientology destroyed the evidence that implicated it in her death. Fourth, the paper detailed Scientology's battle with the IRS. Finally, this series explained the manner in which Scientology encourages followers to purchase its books in order to inflate sales figures. While detailing each of these topics, the authors acknowledged that Scientology spokespersons denied these events.

COMMON NARRATIVES AND EVENTS IN THE NEWS SERIES ON SCIENTOLOGY

As some scholars have argued, news media reaffirmed mainstream morals and heavily criticized Scientology for its deviance from them. Between the 1960s and 1970s, several scandals dominated media coverage of Scientology. Similar scandals continued appearing in the media between the 1980s and 2000s. In many cases, Scientology's controversial activities were cause for genuine public concern. The series that I analyzed addressed real and often very serious issues, some of which developed into major problems for non-Scientologists. Over the long term, such news coverage may have undermined Scientology's goals to influence or take over various facets of social life through political, religious, pseudomedical, and other initiatives.[55] Various themes recurred in the news series under consideration.

L. Ron Hubbard (1911–1986)

The *Clearwater Sun* and *The Globe and Mail* focused on events that transpired after 1975. Likewise, the *Tampa Bay Times* focused on events after 1987, which is when David Miscavige (b. 1960) took over leadership. The other three series each provided lengthier, unflattering, but factual renditions of L. Ron Hubbard's personal history and Scientology's origins. They recounted Hubbard's career writing science fiction, his ostentatious claims about himself and the potential of *Dianetics* (1950), and his founding of Scientology (1953).[56]

The *St. Louis Post-Dispatch* included Hubbard's scandalous comment from a lecture in 1949 in Newark, New Jersey: "Writing for a penny a word is ridiculous. If a man really wanted to make a million dollars, the best way to do it would be to start his own religion."[57] The *L.A. Times* began with the question, "What is Scientology?" then discussed how Scientology emerged. In the process, the paper examined Scientology's once secret teachings about engrams,[58] thetans,[59] and the intergalactic warlord, Xenu, all of which Hubbard claimed were responsible for many of the problems that people now experience.[60] During the course of their reports, these newspapers framed Scientology as illegitimate or fraudulent in a number of ways.

All three series unfavorably presented Hubbard's personality traits and the financial gains he made through Scientology. For instance, *St. Petersburg Times* author, Bill Cornwell (1979), evidenced Hubbard's personal struggles with mental health and accusations that he engaged in bigamy and spousal torture (from his second wife, Sara Northrup Hubbard).[61] Then, he demonstrated how Hubbard's personal problems influenced others' by sharing former Scientologists Dell and Ernest Hartwell's experiences.[62] The Hartwells explained that Hubbard ordered them to work over 12 hours per day under strict directives. They stated that failures to meet Hubbard's standards were met with anger.[63]

Authors untangled Hubbard's personal history from his grandiose claims, citing biographical inconsistencies that they found in evidence from the FBI raids.[64] Both Cornwell (1979) and Marshall (1980, *The Globe and Mail*) stated that Scientology supported Hubbard's fraudulent claims to authority in such areas as atomic physics.[65] Hubbard had boasted about his training in atomic and molecular phenomenon, despite having received an "F" in a course related to this topic, before dropping out of university.[66] (Hubbard claimed to be an expert in several disciplines.[67] For example, he wrote *All About Radiation* and signed off as a "medical doctor" and as a "nuclear physicist"; then he wrote, "C.E., Ph.D [sic]" following his name at the start of "Book Two."[68]) Cornwell demonstrated the lack of evidence to support Hubbard's claim to have earned a Doctorate of Divinity.[69] Moreover, the *L.A. Times* and *St. Petersburg Times* discussed how Hubbard's claims about his experiences and achievements conflicted with U.S. Navy and government records.[70]

In 1966, Hubbard publicly resigned from leadership, but the FBI found evidence that he continued giving orders for over a decade.[71] The *L.A. Times* reported that Scientology's current leader, David Miscavige, slowly gained power while Hubbard was in hiding with two Scientologists.[72] The news series suggested that Hubbard's hiding may have related to his continued influence upon Scientology's actions and illegal activities against the IRS.[73]

Clearly, these reports were critical. Some did discuss also Hubbard's charismatic qualities, citing them as one of the reasons that his followers were attracted to him and his teachings.

Costs, Commitment, and Training

Each series related to popular concerns about the validity of Scientology's training, associated costs, and expected commitment from members. For example, *Post-Dispatch* authors Adams and Viets (1974) contrasted what appeared to be "vocational training" in a Scientology church in Missouri to the practices of "normal" religions.[74] Adams and Viets (1974) discussed adherents as "zealous evangelists," and they detailed Scientology's intensive marketing, recruitment, and growth-oriented practices.[75] To reinforce readers' understanding of the nature of Scientologists' commitment, they explained by way of illustration that a Scientologist spouse might divorce her loved one if he strongly resists Scientology.[76] With this example, the journalists used former Scientologists' stories to encourage concern that commitment to Scientology could interrupt such established social institutions as the family.

Journalists expressed particular concern about the financial expenses associated with Scientology training. For example, the *St. Petersburg Times* stated that Scientology requested exorbitant "donations" for courses that started around $25, climbed to $1,000–$5,000, and reached $10,000–$12,000 for those who attained Scientology's state of "Clear."[77] By 1990, *L.A. Times* authors reported that some courses cost over $55,000, and then, in 2009, the *Tampa Bay Times* authors cited former members' statements that special auditing courses could cost $1,000 per hour.[78] These series reviewed also how Scientology's leaders benefited from adherents' investments in Scientology's courses and from aggressively pursuing tax-exempt status. One *St. Petersburg Times* author estimated Scientology's world headquarters (Saint Hill Manor) received over $100 million per year from its various activities, then cited church denials that Hubbard received 10 percent of that value annually.[79]

Likewise, these series reported on Scientology's zealous recruitment initiatives. The *L.A. Times* and *St. Louis Post-Dispatch* stated that Scientologists tirelessly recruited celebrities and utilized staff to promote their cause.[80] The *L.A. Times* explained, "the Church of Scientology is run like a lean, no-nonsense business in which potential members are called 'prospects,' 'raw meat,' and 'bodies in the shop.'"[81] The paper's authors explained that Scientology training supposedly created the potential for superpowers, good health, and an end to worldly problems.[82] They cited prominent former

Scientologist Larry Wollersheim's statement that people commit to Scientology because of "Fear and hope" and that they wrote "success stories" about their accomplishments in Scientology because of fears of being shunned or punished.[83] Scientology has used these stories, staff efforts, and celebrity membership to pursue greater growth and success.

Legal Battles with the FDA and the IRS (1960s)

In 1963, the Food and Drug Administration (FDA) seized "100 E-meters and about 20,000 pages of church literature" and initiated a notable legal battle with Scientology.[84] Scientology uses "E-Meters" (short for Electrometers)— machines that preceded modern polygraph technology, which register changes in the skin's conductivity to a small electrical current.[85] Hubbard (1963) argued that E-Meters demonstrated Scientology's strength over religions that presented Heaven as "a false dream." He stated, "New religions always overthrow the false gods of the old . . . We can improve man. We can show the old gods false."[86]

The *St. Louis Post-Dispatch* covered the FDA raid in more detail than the other series. This newspaper explained that the FDA seized the E-Meters on the grounds that Scientology's claims about them were "false and misleading," but the authors omitted Hubbard's claims that E-Meters could cure numerous diseases and ailments.[87] Omitting these claims understated some of the controversies involving E-Meters. Specifically, such claims can result in adherents to Scientology forgoing medical care in lieu of Dianetic auditing using an E-Meter.[88] Instead, they cited that the presiding Judge Gerhard A. Gesell denied government requests to destroy the E-Meters in 1971. The *St. Petersburg Times* further explained that the FDA's investigation into Scientology ended in 1973 with Gesell's ruling that "(1) the church could no longer advertise its services as a scientific cure for disease, (2) must label E-meters as ineffective in treating illnesses, and (3) could only use the E-meter in 'bona fide religious counseling.'"[89] Gesell deemed E-Meters acceptable as a "confessional aid" and unlike the IRS at the time, recognized Scientology as a religion that was protected by the First Amendment.[90]

Between 1957 and 1967, Scientology enjoyed tax-exempt status on its American profits because the IRS recognized it as a religion.[91] In 1967, the IRS revoked this status and Scientology initiated a 16-year battle with it—a crusade that epitomized many of Scientology's controversial activities. Each news series reviewed controversies involving the IRS. They overwhelmingly legitimized the IRS's actions, emphasized how Scientology attempted to model a religious institution, and detailed the implications for the IRS and associated individuals.

For example, the *Post-Dispatch* stated that Scientology had used religious terminology, such as "Divine Being" or "conventional liturgical rites or preaching" but omitted standardized dogmas about these concepts.[92] *Post-Dispatch* authors juxtaposed this information to Scientology's statements about student successes and their spokesperson's claims that Scientology was "a genuine—though different—religion."[93] Similarly, the *L.A. Times* contrasted Hubbard's early claims that Scientology was a "precision science" with "completely predictable results" to his later religious claims.[94] The *L.A. Times* series detailed how Scientology changed its language to reflect its religious status. This series informed its readers that "students" changed to "parishioners," "franchises" changed to "missions," and "courses" became "sacred scriptures."[95] Moreover, *St. Petersburg Times* author Stafford (1979) delved into Scientology's religious claims and tax disputes in incredible detail but employed rather sensational language (e.g., "Is Scientology a religion, or a pseudo-scientific con game involving amateur psychology?").[96]

Stafford (1979) emphasized the implications of Scientology facing over $8 million in back taxes due to the case with the IRS. But he critiqued how Scientology paid large tithes to the International Organization (the *L.A. Times* [1990] made a more conservative estimate of over $1 million for two years of back taxes).[97] Scientology responded aggressively to this financial burden. The *Clearwater Sun* covered Hubbard's attempt to create front organizations to make purchases that were separate from Scientology's tax debt and to retreat to if the IRS continued refusing to grant Scientology tax exemption.[98]

All but one series appeared before or during 1990. Consequently, only the *Tampa Bay Times* picked up the story again after Scientology regained religious status from the IRS in 1993. By this time, several high-ranking Scientologists had left the organization. Former Scientologists, including Marty Rathbun, told the *Times* that the tactic was to "overwhelm the IRS and force mistakes." Scientology's organizations filed 200 lawsuits, and about 2,300 Scientologists filed individual lawsuits against the IRS.[99] The newspaper contended that Scientology's efforts had upset the legal process and had resulted in Scientology gaining rights and privileges that prevented government intervention against some of its activities. Furthermore, the paper asserted that these changes had significant implications for Scientologists, former Scientologists, surrounding communities, and critics.

The Sea Organization (1967) and Flag Land Base (1975)

Each newspaper series incorporated former Scientologists' accounts about Scientology's Sea Organization (SO). Hubbard claimed that the SO's main purpose was to "explore ancient civilizations."[100] Scientology, however, created the SO the year it began its battles with the IRS as a means to keep Hubbard safe from various international legal battles by moving him around in international waters.[101] By 1971, the SO had six ships, and by 1975, it began establishing its Flagship land base in Clearwater Florida.[102] Since the 1970s, the SO expanded its land-based organizations worldwide but maintained the *Freewinds* as its only seafaring ship.[103] The *Clearwater Sun* emphasized Hubbard's goal for the Flag base in Clearwater to be SO's "headquarters," and the *St. Petersburg Times* explained it was partly intended as a location from which to battle the IRS.[104]

Eventually, Scientology claimed that the SO was a religious order, which garnered further media interest. The *St. Louis Post-Dispatch* called the SO Scientology's "aristocracy," then referred to its underpaid and poorly supported staff.[105] The *L.A. Times* cited SO staff's claims that "their lifestyle is no more unusual or harsh than that of a monk."[106] Then, the series reported that staff signed billion year contracts, worked long hours with "military cadence," wore "mock navy uniforms," and followed "authoritarian rules" for a small weekly allowance and housing.[107] The *L.A. Times* reported that when staff broke rules or fell behind their quotas, they were subjected to Scientology's internal punishment program—the Rehabilitation Project Force (RPF).[108] Those in the RPF are segregated from other Scientologists and their loved ones, fed only rice and beans, and are ordered to complete various menial tasks.[109] The *L.A. Times* authors suggested that leaving the RPF and SO resulted in several serious costs, including becoming one of Scientology's "enemies," being charged "freeloader debt" for courses they took before their contract expires, and fearing that loved ones within Scientology would shun them.[110] Finally, the paper suggested that although the SO was designed for the most dedicated Scientologists, its presence greatly affected local communities.

In 1975, 12 years into the SO's existence, the residents of Clearwater and Pinellas County witnessed the arrival of Scientology in the guise of a front group called the "United Churches of Florida."[111] The *Clearwater Sun* and the *St. Petersburg Times* emphasized their journalistic duty to inform residents of Scientology's arrival and plans to take over Clearwater (and the world), which were found in the documents that the FBI released. In hindsight, the *Clearwater Sun*'s quote from former mayor Charles LeCher foreshadowed what would follow: "Down the road, I hope when people think of Clearwater, they don't think of Scientology."[112] As of 2016, a Scientology website boasted: "The Church of Scientology in Clearwater (FSO) is a religious retreat which serves as the spiritual headquarters for Scientologists from all over the world." It continued by saying that the Flag Service Operation (FSO) "is the largest single church of Scientology in the world."[113] On this website, Scientology estimated that over 2,300 Scientology staff and more than 22 Scientology-owned buildings service 2,000 out-of-town visitors along with over 12,000 local Scientologists.[114]

Arguably, Scientology has lost much momentum in recent years, but it has maintained extensive influence in Clearwater. According to the *Tampa Bay Times*, Hubbard expected the Fort Harrison Hotel to become "the friendliest place in the world" because of Scientology's arrival.[115] In reality, Scientology's secretive, covert, and antagonistic operations in Clearwater have fostered a divisive climate in which local residents have experienced many problems because of the movement's overbearing presence. Reporting on these topics was no mere moral panic—the ramifications of Scientology's immense presence in the region were all too real.

FBI Raids (1977–1978)

With the exception of the 1974 publication of the *St. Louis Post-Dispatch*, all of the series recounted information that they had gathered from the 1977 FBI raids on Scientology buildings in Los Angeles, Hollywood, and Washington D.C. The three news series from between 1979 and 1980 made extensive use of these documents, especially when covering the indictment of Mary Sue Hubbard (L. Ron Hubbard's wife) and ten other members of Scientology's Guardian's Office (GO). (The GO was an organization within Scientology that managed public relations, pursued legal actions, and gathered intelligence. This organization conducted Scientology's highest surveillance operations, many of which now fall under the Office of Special Affairs [OSA].[116])

Before the convictions of the Scientologists following the FBI raid, the "U.S. Ministerial Conference of Scientology Ministers" published a book titled *The American Inquisition—U.S. Government Agency Harassment, Religious Persecution and Abuse of Power*.[117] *St. Petersburg Times* author Stafford (1979) demonstrated that this book positioned Scientology as a victimized religious minority that needed the GO to operate "a widespread, intercontinental espionage system" for protection from the government and other enemies.[118] He summarized such self-defense with the religious reference: "an eye for an eye."[119] These series evidenced the GO's involvement in various criminal activities.[120]

The GO implemented "Operation Snow White" in 1973. Snow White aimed to covertly reclaim "false and secret files on Scientology, LRH . . ." that Scientology was unable to acquire legally.[121] Journalists described Snow White as part of Scientology's drive to eliminate "negative publicity" and "false reports" about the group.[122] This operation involved espionage activities within various agencies and government institutions—including the IRS and FBI. Scientology intended these activities to interfere with the actions of perceived enemies. Moreover, Snow White monitored potential investigations against Scientology and attempted to maintain the secrecy of Scientology's internal documents.[123] *The Globe and Mail* reported that these attacks primarily aimed to enable Hubbard to "visit 'all western nations . . . without threat.'"[124]

Operation Snow White was central to the convictions of 11 of Scientology's Guardians. Most news series covered these sentences as evidence of Scientology's ongoing illicit activities. Stafford (1979) described them as Scientology's "downfall." He wrote in past tense as though the panic surrounding Scientology's actions culminated with the conviction of Scientology Guardians after the FBI raid. He then detailed Scientology's actions preceding the raid, beginning with a break-in using fake IRS identification cards by two Scientologists (Mike Meisner and Gerald Bennett Wolfe) who eventually got caught.[125] Stafford asserted that after Wolfe's arrest, Scientology harbored fugitive Meisner for 11 months until he surrendered to the FBI. By this time the FBI had enough evidence to undertake the raid that Stafford claimed ". . . was the end."[126]

As the *L.A. Times* and *Tampa Bay Times* news series demonstrated, however, Scientology's covert operations and controversial activities continued for decades. These series exposed some of Scientology's controversial policies, operations, and retaliations against enemies. The four earlier series (pre-1981) included detailed accounts of Scientology's operations against Clearwater residents and other outsiders, whereas the later series (1990 and 2009) extensively described how Scientology regulated its own membership as well.

Other Controversial Policies, Surveillance, and Covert Operations

Each series used evidence from the FBI raid and statements from former Scientologists to review how Scientology labels, targets, and attacks critics. They explained that Scientology labels enemies and then targets critics aggressively with controversial policies and operations. For example, the *Post-Dispatch* reported that Scientology labels many supposed enemies "Suppressive Persons" (SPs). The organization claims an SP "actively seeks to suppress or damage Scientology or a Scientologist by 'Suppressive Acts.'"[127] (Suppressive acts "include testifying in a court of law against Scientology, bringing forth a civil suit against Scientology or any of its members, and the resignation of a member from Scientology courses and sessions."[128]) Supposedly, reporting on Scientology constituted a suppressive act. Hubbard alleged that media representations of Scientology were created by SPs whose "lies and confusions are slanderous, choppy or destructive."[129]

Journalists reported on Scientology's notorious "Fair Game" policy. For example, the *St. Petersburg Times* quoted Hubbard's Fair Game policy, which designated that any SP "May be deprived of property or injured by any means by any Scientologist without any discipline of the Scientologist. May be tricked, sued or lied to or destroyed."[130] Hubbard allegedly canceled Fair Game in a 1968 policy letter. Despite this cancellation, he stated that he would leave "the treatment or handling" of Scientology's enemies unchanged.[131]

The *St. Louis Post-Dispatch* and the *Tampa Bay Times* reported that Scientologists retaliated against former Scientologists with confidential material from Scientology auditing sessions. This material included data from invasive "security check" questions that Scientology began using during the 1960s to uncover Scientologists who could be enemies.[132] (Security checks are involuntary auditing sessions in which a Scientology auditor "uses an E-Meter reputedly to detect infringements of the Scientology code of conduct."[133])

In the mid-1970s, Scientologists orchestrated numerous operations against perceived "enemies." Scientology's spokespersons portrayed these operations as "self-defense," stating also that they were secretive by necessity.[134] Furthermore, Scientology claimed that "self-defense" measures emerged from *individual* Scientologists. The *St. Louis Dispatch* authors explained Scientology ensured that if individuals undertook these activities, then they could not reflect poorly on Scientology or Hubbard.[135] Similarly, the *St. Petersburg Times* cited Scientology Reverend Whitman's statements that those who violated the law on Scientology's behalf acted alone.[136]

With these claims, it is unsurprising that secrecy and surveillance were central to the operations Scientologists undertook.[137] For instance, Scientology spokespersons asserted that Hubbard had retired before Snow White began. Marshall's piece for *The Globe and Mail* illustrated otherwise. Marshall (1980) cited Guardian Order 1206, which stated that Operation Snow White was "written by the Commodore."[138] Likewise, he explained that Scientology attempted to hide Hubbard's involvement with Scientology's covert activities through "Operation Bulldozer Leak" in 1976.[139] This operation sought to "spread the rumor that will lead Government, media, and individual SPs . . . to conclude that LRH [Hubbard] has no control of the C of S [Church of Scientology] and no legal liability for Church activity."[140] Furthermore, Scientology created numerous front groups to secretly advocate for its causes. For example, Scientology created groups such as the Clearwater-based "American Citizens for Honesty in Government" and the "Committee for the Protection of Mental Patients' Rights," which sought to investigate the State Department of Transportation, local IRS and FBI activities, and local hospitals.[141]

The *Clearwater Sun* and *St. Petersburg Times* paid particular attention to similar operations in their local community of Clearwater. The *Sun* outlined how Hubbard and Scientology initially sought support from political figures and opinion leaders through various operations. For example, they targeted those who they perceived to be the enemies of former Clearwater Mayor Gabriel Cazares (1920–2006, mayor from 1975 to 1978), but when Cazares refused to side with Scientology, he became subject to attacks. In other activities, Scientology pursued covert operations against various Clearwater residents (including Cazares, a banker named Wilby F. Anderson, the head of the police department, several city officials, and various journalists, including the *Sun*'s editor Ron Stuart).[142]

Similarly, in *The Globe and Mail* series, Marshall overviewed the FBI raid as well as Scientology's espionage activities in the United States, the United Kingdom, and Canada.[143] He explained that Scientology had planted spies in the offices of U.S. federal attorneys, the IRS, and the Better Business Bureau in their efforts to stay ahead of perceived "enemies."[144] His series reported also on operations against the American Medical Association and the American Cancer Society as defense against what Scientology perceived to be attacks.[145] Marshall (1980) found an order called "Shell Game," which directed Scientology officials to inform newspapers about a controversial psychiatrist in Canada named Dr. Brock Chisholm who, prior to his death, had directed the World Health Organization.[146] Marshall found evidence that Scientologists had "Penetrated Toronto mental hospital and established an agent as director of volunteers."[147] Furthermore, he explained that Scientology undertook operations against the Canadian Mental Health Association. Marshall (1980) suggested that some of these attacks orientated around promoting a drug-treatment program that Hubbard designed—an expansion of Narconon.[148]

Twelve years after Marshall's story, a court convicted the Church of Scientology, Toronto, on "two counts of criminal breach of trust and fined it $250,000 for spying on police and government office in the Canadian province of Ontario" in addition to other activities.[149] These activities involved infiltrating such Canadian government offices as "the Royal Canadian Mounted Police, the Ontario Provincial Police, Revenue Canada, and the Ontario Attorney-General's office."[150] By recounting these events, Marshall publicized important information about Scientology in Canada, but he also presented Scientology as a criminal conspiracy, or "cult" organization, that ran illicit operations internationally.[151] Likewise, the five U.S. news series each listed various organizations that Scientology had infiltrated and individuals who Scientology had acted against. Media accounts of Scientology's controversial activities both shared relevant information and fueled apparent moral panics, especially when Scientologists pursued further activities in response to the publication of that information. Once again, however, newspaper reporting fulfilled an important role by alerting its readership to the movement's actual criminal activities—many of which had occurred over a protracted period of time and in numerous geographical locations. These were not one-off actions that fueled unnecessary panic. Rather, they indicated Scientology's institutionalized approach to socially controlling its perceived enemies.

Former Members, Critics, and the Media

Every series used narratives from former Scientologists, critics, and journalists to personalize the implications of Scientology's operations. The first three series each mentioned the McLean family among other defectors. The *L.A. Times* cited another couple at length, and the *Tampa Bay Times* series quoted several high-ranking defectors who had recently left Scientology. Each series reported official Scientology spokespersons' counter-commentaries to defectors' claims. For example, Marshall at the *Globe and Mail* explained how Scientology spokespersons responded to an earlier 1974 article of his in which he reported on Scientology's harassment of defectors. They denied the claims of harassment and said that Marshall's account constituted "misrepresentation and distortion."[152]

Former Scientologists' narratives have often composed the only information about Scientology that differed from Scientology spokespersons' accounts. Journalist Dart (1997) identified the spokespersons as "stakeholders" or "spin-doctors."[153] Each former member's account is unique, although common motifs emerge. For instance, the McLean family's experiences appeared both in the *Clearwater Sun* and in *The Globe and Mail*.[154] They offered insiders' perspectives on the elusive organization that fostered Hubbard's extravagant lifestyle, operated tight security, and benefited greatly from its followers' financial investments.

The McLean family left Scientology in 1972 after spending over $9,000 on the church.[155] Nancy, her husband Eric, and their son John recounted how exiting the SO was stressful, scary, and costly.[156] Nancy and Eric provided Marshall (1980) with information about how Scientology used espionage tactics against critics and former Scientologists. They explained that Scientologists held a mock funeral for their family, picketed their home, likely reported fabricated criminal activities to their neighbors, and hired private detectives to follow their family.[157] Following these accusations, the family was involved in court cases with Scientology.[158]

Regarding critics, writer Paulette Cooper's experiences were most extensively reported. Cooper wrote a scathing book titled *The Scandal of Scientology* that hit bookstores in 1971. Journalistic accounts defended Cooper, who suspected Scientology was responsible for the intermittent events that she experienced in the years following 1971. These events included harassing telephone calls, threats on her life, and her neighbors receiving letters that alleged she was a prostitute.[159] FBI documents evidenced that Scientology implemented "Operation Freakout," which involved Fair Game attacks against her. The goal of Operation Freakout was to place Cooper in a mental institution or in prison.[160]

Marshall (1980) detailed his experience searching through files from the FBI raid on Cooper. He explained that Scientologists filed 14 lawsuits against her, had a covert Scientologist act as her confidant, and framed her for a bomb threat charge for which she was convicted—before evidence collected in the 1977 FBI raid proved her innocence.[161] Marshall concluded his series with a statement from the covert Scientologist who Cooper had confided in about her potential suicide: "Wouldn't this be a great thing for Scientology?"[162]

Scientology's efforts against critics and former members demonstrated how some NRMs employ "various instruments of social control" and often possess immense "financial and lobbying power."[163] The authors of the earlier news series quickly realized that these instruments could be used against journalists. As one journalist explained: "Scientology stands ready and able to unleash an assault on the journalist that can include private detectives and lawsuits, making it little wonder that publications have grown reluctant to write about the Hubbard empire."[164]

The authors of these series stated that they pursued stories about Scientology to fulfill journalistic duties despite risks of retaliation. For example, the *St. Petersburg Times* alluded to Scientology's "Black Propaganda" program, which sought to covertly destroy the reputations of perceived enemies.[165] As part of "Black Propaganda," Hubbard provided followers with directives as to how to "handle" the media. Scientology became known as litigious against perceived enemies with the goal to harass and discourage rather than to win lawsuits—or, as the *St. Petersburg Times* quoted Hubbard, "If possible, of course, ruin him [the enemy] utterly").[166] Rather than succumb to such tactics, Stafford (1979) emphasized that journalists from the *Clearwater Sun* and the *St. Petersburg Times* had publicized Scientology's secret activities. Consequently, "Black Propaganda" and Scientology's other initiatives illustrate the deviance amplification model. Journalists' response to initiatives amplified their self-presentation as professionals who informed the public despite any personal costs.

The *St. Petersburg Times* series began with author Eugene Patterson's (1979) assertion, "a newspaper has a particular duty to resist intimidation itself and inform citizens fully of what is going on."[167] Patterson (1979) stated that he intended the information in his series to "guide citizens in their judgments" so that "the community's uncertainty about the facts is forever

gone."[168] Then, he explained that the paper "toiled to answer the community's question."[169] That is, the *St. Petersburg Times* intended to fill an information void for a district that would eventually be overrun by the Church of
Scientology. Patterson (1979) explained that Scientology responded to the
St. Petersburg Times by placing the paper "at the top of the cult's 'enemies'
list." Notably, this statement used the derogatory label "cult."[170]

The *St. Petersburg Times* publicized its experiences with Scientology's litigation, which occurred frequently against "enemies," including newspapers,
reporters, former Scientologists, and critics.[171] In his account of the charges
that the *Times* filed against Scientology and eventually dropped, Patterson
(1979) explained that Scientology had engaged in "infiltration or burglary
or both" against the *St. Petersburg Times*, individual journalists, and their
attorneys.[172] Afterward, Scientology operatives stole from the law firm that
represented the paper, created a publication that alleged the newspaper's
president, Gene Patterson, was employed by the Central Intelligence Agency,
and implemented "Operation Bunny Bust" against journalist Bette Orsini.[173]
In response to Bunny Bust's threats against reporter Orsini, the *St. Petersburg
Times* stated that it dropped its charges against Scientology.[174]

Likewise, FBI documents evidenced Scientology's activities against the
Clearwater Sun. Stafford explained that a Scientologist, who went by the
name June Phillips (June Byrne), had stolen documents from the American Medical Association in 1974, then infiltrated the *Sun* in 1976 as part
of "Operation China Shop."[175] In reference to China Shop, one report from
Scientology stated, "Our target on this, very confidentially, is ownership and
control of the paper."[176] After infiltrating the *Sun* in 1976, Phillips eventually became a clerk in the newsroom. From there, she shared information
about reporters and news stories with Scientology.[177] Moreover, Scientology
threated legal action against the *Clearwater Sun* and then filed a $250,000
damage suit accusing the *Sun* of violating privacy and confidentiality of the
Church because a reporter had covertly joined Scientology.[178]

Globe and Mail author, Marshall (1980) discussed similar attacks against
American journalists, then both himself and a critical Canadian reporter
named Mark Bonokoski.[179] Marshall highlighted Scientology's activities that
involved using private detectives to find scandalous information about journalists (i.e., "any criminal or Communist background").[180]

Scientology's efforts to control critical representations changed over time.
For instance, following the *L.A. Times* series in 1990, Scientology bought
advertising space on over 120 billboards and 1,000 bus placards around Los
Angeles.[181] One *Times* journalist later explained, "The ads, which prominently included the newspaper's logo and our names, quoted from our series,
but they had edited the excerpts to create the impression that the Los Angeles

Times was endorsing Scientology."[182] Furthermore, Welkos (1991) explained that the people he interviewed for his series had strange visits from private investigators who posed as a documentary film crew making a film about Scientology.[183] He provided these details as cautions to those who were considering investigating Scientology.[184]

Scientology had lost much of its control over the media prior to the publication of the 2009 *Tampa Bay Times* series.[185] As Scientology's ability to control the media has stagnated, the organization has begun using other tactics, such as hiring journalists to write complimentary stories instead of directly attacking critical journalists.[186]

Ongoing Controversies Involving Scientology

Since the 1970s, "global changes in media technology and consumption" have occurred, influencing the content of the news coverage about Scientology.[187] Moreover, in the early 1980s, the number of stories about NRMs declined.[188] More recently, conflicts involving Internet groups including "hacktivist" group Anonymous have initiated worldwide protests through social media.[189] As such, the 1990 and 2009 series addressed different topics but demonstrated that the "moral panic" surrounding Scientology involved events that were anything but transient.

The 1990 *L.A. Times* series bridged these changes by expanding upon various issues including in previous newspaper series, such as Hubbard's claims, Operation Snow White, and the FBI raid. This series appeared when Scientology's battle against psychiatry and its various front organizations were gaining momentum. In 1969, one notable front group called the Citizens Commission on Human Rights (CCHR) emerged. Then, in 1987, CCHR launched an effective campaign against the pharmaceutical, Ritalin. CCHR worked with other critics of this drug to allege that children were fraudulently diagnosed with ADHD (Attention Deficit/Hyperactivity Disorder) by health professionals who complied with the financial interests of Ciba-Geigy (now the Novartis Pharmaceuticals Corporation), the makers of the drug.[190] CCHR provided parents with alarming but exaggerated statistics about the dangers of Ritalin and became a moral entrepreneur in the panic surrounding Ritalin, which Scientologists call "a 'chemical straitjacket.'"[191]

In addition, the *L.A. Times* explained that Hubbard hid with a Scientology couple (Pat and Anne Broeker) for the final six years of his life.[192] The Broekers and other Scientologists underwent great efforts to conceal Hubbard's influence over the church. While in hiding, David Miscavige relayed messages to Scientologists for the Broekers and Hubbard. Then, in 1986, Miscavige announced to Scientologists that Hubbard consciously decided to "sever all ties" to the physical world (meaning that he died).[193] By 1987, Miscavige displaced the Broekers and became the leader of Scientology.

Miscavige's rule in the church was the center of the *Tampa Bay Times*'s series. Authors Childs and Tobin (2009) reported the punishment and control that former executives stressed had occurred under Miscavige's leadership. This series explained how Scientology continued to brutally control its staff and membership to the extent that one Scientologist (Lisa McPherson) died after being isolated in Scientology's care for 17 days in 1995.[194] The investigation into McPherson's death ended in a settlement, but former Scientologist Marty Rathbun explained that prior to that settlement, Scientology had destroyed much of the evidence about her care.[195] Indeed, every topic covered in the *Tampa Bay* series, as well as many covered in other recent media, demonstrate that the journalistic outcry surrounding Scientology was grounded in concerns regarding tangible events with, at times, catastrophic implications.

CONCLUSION

One can understand media coverage of Scientology and other new religious movements (NRMs) as a "stream of controversies."[196] Many academics have stated that media often present NRMs as stereotypical representations that readers can easily understand because they provide "information by outsiders for outsiders."[197] For example, Wilson (1990) argued that NRMs need time to run their course and establish some semblance of routine before they can be presentable to the media: "The media quickly detect and exploit the divergence between the spiritual message and the practical organization of new religious movements, finding scandal in what, on reflection, must of necessity be brought into some relationship if the movement is to operate at all."[198] Wilson (1990) alleged that the media focuses on nonspiritual, harmful, and destructive phenomena that occur as NRMs work toward becoming sustainable mainstream religions. He explained also that traditional religious bodies often target these apparent discrepancies, which trigger media accusations against NRMs that fuel escalating moral panics.[199]

In addition, NRMs that avoid such controversial activities attract less legal and media attention. In fact, Zellner and Petrowsky (1998) asserted that the only groups that the public is aware of are those that experience legal difficulties, which the media reports.[200] Certainly, amplification of deviance is a tangible outcome of such news reporting. Although negative representations of NRMs may relay much needed information to the public regarding specific groups, these representations fail to demonstrate the *diversity* of NRMs that exist beyond those that attract the most controversy. In the case of Scientology, reporting on the group was at times sensational and focused on its more scandalous activities and characteristics. It is worth considering, however, that the sum of Scientology's controversial activities constitutes so much *more* than newspapers have reported. Indeed, rather than only newsprint, a fuller catalog of details has emerged online, in books, and journal articles.

Nonetheless, at times, journalists can uncover previously unknown information about various NRMs. Reporters' perspectives and knowledge about NRMs can offer immediate and necessary information to help communities deal with such phenomenon as Scientology's incursion in Clearwater. For example, since the 1979 series in the *Clearwater Sun* and *St. Petersburg Times*, Scientology's influence over Clearwater has grown. Scientology has "procured local off-duty police officers to act as a private Scientology police force," installed surveillance cameras on Scientology properties that are aimed at public spaces, and supervised Lisa McPherson during her controversial death.[201] Some of Scientology's controversies arose from the use of surveillance, secrecy, and punishments that are more common to NRMs than more established religions.[202] Due to its extensive surveillance system, however, Scientology is exceptionally active against threats to stability that emerge from journalists, critics, and its membership.[203]

Scientology's actions against critics have averted some academics from researching that organization.[204] These aggressive tactics could stagnate some news coverage even though Scientology has received ongoing media attention: "Dubbed the 'Cult of Greed' by *Time* magazine (1991), Scientology has long been singled out by the media and anticult groups as the most rapacious and dangerous new religious movement today."[205] Moreover, Scientology's attempts to block publications and interfere with journalists' lives have fueled some news stories, which resulted in Lewis's (2015) statement that "the Church of Scientology has proven to be its own worst enemy."[206]

Despite their value exposing relevant and timely controversies, the news series that I discussed reflected some of the trends that other academics have critiqued. Doherty (2014) asserted that "New religion reports almost always are framed with a strong dualism between good (victims) and evil (cultists)," and some claim that news reporters "risked it all" to tell the truth.[207] Many of the stories I reviewed reinforced this dichotomy, and the narrative methods that writers used drove that dichotomy home. Nevertheless, many of the topics covered in these series have had ongoing implications across many facets of society.

NOTES

1. Hugh B. Urban, "The Truth Rundown: Scientology Changes Strategy in War with Media," *Religion Dispatches* (March 18, 2010): 1, http://religiondispatches.org/the-rundown-truth-scientology-changes-strategy-in-war-with-media/.

2. Richard Leiby, "Tampa Jury May Get Sect Documents," *Clearwater Sun,* November 7, 1979, 1A-2A.

3. For example, Wilson wrote, "Sects and new religious movements make news only when there is supposed scandal or sensation to report; in the 'human stories' of apostates or the anguish of parents about children exposed to sectarian influence . . ." Bryan Wilson, *The Social Dimensions of Sectarianism: Sects and New Religious Movements in Contemporary Society* (Oxford: Clarendon Press, 1990), 66.

4. Roy Wallis, "Societal Reaction to Scientology: A Study in the Sociology of Deviant Religion," in *Sectarianism,* ed. Roy Wallis (London: Peter Own, 1975), 101–102.

5. Stanely Cohen quoted in James Lewis, "Scientology vs. the Media," *Alternative Spirituality and Religion Review* 6, no. 1 (2015): 73, doi:10.5840/asrr201572010; and Wallis, "Societal Reaction to Scientology," 86.

6. Lewis, "Scientology vs. the Media," 73; Wallis, "Societal Reaction to Scientology," 89.

7. Ibid. See also Joseph Laycock, "Where Do They Get These Ideas? Changing Ideas of Cults in the Mirror of Popular Culture," *Journal of the American Academy of Religion* 81, no. 1 (2013): 85, doi:10.1093/jaarel/lfs091.

8. Erich Goode and Nachman Ben-Yehuda, "Moral Panics: Culture, Politics, and Social Construction," *Annual Review of Sociology* 20 (1994): 155, doi:10.2307/3512179.

9. Wallis (1975) added Neil Smelser's impressions that a collective sense of "immediate, powerful, but ambiguous threat" accompanied moral panics and created a sense that you need immediate action to preserve norms and values. This threat may have been less ambiguous by the time Lewis's (2015) article emerged than it was when Wallis (1975) reviewed media coverage. Lewis, "Scientology vs. the Media"; Wallis, "Societal Reaction to Scientology," 86.

10. Urban, "Fair Game: Secrecy, Security, and the Church of Scientology in Cold War America," *Journal of the American Academy of Religion* 74 (2006): 363.

11. Barend van Driel and James T. Richardson, "Print Media Coverage of New Religious Movements: A Longitudinal Study," *Journal of Communication* 38, no. 3 (September 1988): 37, doi:10.1111/j.1460-2466.1988.tb02059.x.

12. Journalists have produced influential nonfiction written reports of Scientology in addition to televised and audio fiction and nonfiction narratives about that organization. For example, see Richard Behar, "The Thriving Cult of Greed and Power," *Time Magazine,* May 6, 1991, http://content.time.com/time/magazine/article /0,9171,972865,00.html; Janet Reitman, "Inside Scientology," *Rolling Stone Magazine,* February 8, 2011, http://www.rollingstone.com/culture/news/inside-scientology -20110208; Lawrence Wright, "The Apostate: Paul Haggis vs. the Church of Scientology," *The New Yorker,* February 14 and 21, 2011, http://www.newyorker.com /magazine/2011/02/14/the-apostate-lawrence-wright.

13. John Dart, "Covering Conventional and Unconventional Religion," *Review of Religious Research* 39, no. 2 (December 1997): 145, doi:10.2307/3512179.

14. Dart, "Covering Conventional and Unconventional Religion," 145.

15. Ibid., 145.

16. Ibid., 146.

17. Urban, "Fair Game," 365.

18. Jon Atack, *A Piece of Blue Sky* (New York: Carol Publishing Group, 1990), 113; Terra Manca, "L. Ron Hubbard's Alternative to the Bomb Shelter: Scientology's Emergence as a Pseudo-Science during the 1950s," *Journal of Religion and Popular Culture* 24, no. 1 (2012): 81, doi:10.3138/jrpc.24.1.80; Roy Wallis, *The Road to Total Freedom* (London: Heinemann, 1976), 24.

19. Charles E. Bures, "A Review of Dianetics," *Engineering and Science* 14, no. 2 (1950): 1–32; Yvette Gittleson, "Sacred Cows in Collision," *American Scientist* 38, no. 4 (1950): 603–609.

20. Hubbard Dianetic Research Foundation, "The Dianamic" (Elizabeth, NJ: Hubbard Dianetic Research Foundation, 1951), 8; Wallis, *The Road to Total Freedom*, 22.

21. Joseph Winter, "Introduction" in L. Ron Hubbard. *Dianetics: The Modern Science of Mental Health* (New York: Hermitage House 1950), xxiii.

22. For an overview of these book reviews, see Kent and Manca, "A War over Mental Health Professionalism," *Mental Health, Religion & Culture* 1 (January 2014): 6–7, doi:10.1080/13674676.2012.737552.

23. Van Driel and Richardson, "Print Media Coverage of New Religious Movements," 37.

24. See Terra Manca, "Alternative Therapy, Dianetics, and Scientology," *Marburg Journal of Religion* 15 (2010): 1–20, https://www.uni-marburg.de/fb03/ivk/mjr/pdfs/2010/articles/manca_2010.pdf; Roy Wallis, "Societal Reaction to Scientology," 101–102.

25. Urban, "The Truth Rundown."

26. L. Ron Hubbard, "The Scientologist: A Manual on the Dissemination of Material," *Ability* (1955, mid-March), in *The Technical Bulletins of Dianetics and Scientology*, 2 (Scientology Publications: Los Angeles, 1976): 155. Quotes such as this one have been widely cited in the media and academic works. See Doherty, "Sensational Scientology!," fnt. 8; Roy Wallis, "Religious Sects and the Fear of Publicity," *New Society* 24 (June 7, 1973): 546; Robert W. Welkos, "Shudder into Silence," *The Quill* 9, no. 9 (1991): para. 37.

27. Quoted in Urban, "The Truth Rundown"; L. Ron Hubbard, *Manual of Justice* (London: Hubbard Communications Office, 1959), 1.

28. Doherty, "Sensational Scientology!," 40.

29. Ibid., 39.

30. Bernard Doherty, "Sensational Scientology! The Church of Scientology and Australian Tabloid Television," *Nova Religio: The Journal of Alternative and Emergent Religion* 17, no. 3 (February 2014): 39, doi:10.1525/nr.2014.17.3.38.

31. Van Driel and Richardson, "Print Media Coverage of New Religious Movements," 53.

32. Ibid., 53.

33. Ibid., 53–54.

34. Ibid., 54; Laycock, "Where Do They Get These Ideas?," 86.

35. Urban, "The Truth Rundown," 1–3.

36. See Ann Brill and Ashley Packard, "Silencing Scientology's Critics on the Internet: A Mission Impossible?," *Communications and Law* (December 1997), http://www.heinonline.org; Michael Peckman, "New Dimensions of Social Movement/Countermovement Interaction: The Case of Scientology and Its Internet Critics," *Canadian Journal of Sociology* 24, no. 1 (1998), http://www.jstor.org/stable/3341804; Urban, "The Truth Rundown."

37. Urban, "The Truth Rundown."

38. James E. Adams and Elaine Viets, "Expensive Trip to Spirituality," *St. Louis Post-Dispatch*, March 3, 1974, 2E.

39. Ibid.

40. Ibid.

41. Richard Lieby, "Scientologists Plot City Takeover," *Clearwater Sun*, November 3, 1979, 1A–2A.

42. L. Ron Hubbard, *Modern Management Technology Defined* (Los Angeles: Bridge Publications, 1979), 535. This quote appeared frequently throughout the news series. For instance, it appeared four times between December 16 and 30 in the *St. Petersburg Times* series. See Charles Stafford, "Scientology Brings 4 Years of Discord," in *Special Report: Scientology: An In-Depth Profile of a New Force in Clearwater* (series), *St. Petersburg Times*, December 16–30, 1979, 3; Charles Stafford, "Individual Life Force Is Focus of Scientology," in *Special Report: Scientology: An In-Depth Profile of a New Force in Clearwater* (series), *St. Petersburg Times*, December 16–30, 1979, 4.

43. *Clearwater Sun*, "Opinion: Of Grudges and Lies," November 7, 1979, 8A.

44. Ron Stuart, "Opinion: Documents Remove Last Faint Doubts about Scientology," *Clearwater Sun*, November 4, 1979, 1F.

45. Ibid.

46. *Clearwater Sun*, "Opinion."

47. Stafford, "Scientology Brings 4 Years of Discord," 3.

48. Ibid., 3.

49. Ibid. Van Driel and Richardson (1988) problematized such uses of Christian rhetoric. Van Driel and Richardson, "Print Media Coverage of New Religious Movements," 53.

50. John Marshall, "Big FBI Raid Led to Conspiracy Trial of Cult Leaders," *The Globe and Mail*, January 22, 1980, 10; John Marshall, "Secret Ontario Documents Found in U.S. Cult's Files," *The Globe and Mail*, January 22, 1980, 1–2.

51. John Marshall, "Two Leaders in Britain Still to Face US Court in Conspiracy Case," *The Globe and Mail*, January 1, 1980.

52. Joel Sappell and Richard W. Welkos, "Church Seeks Influence in Schools, Business, and Science," in *The Scientology Series, Los Angeles Times*, June 27, 1990: A1, A18.

53. Joel Sappell and Richard W. Welkos, "Creating the Mystique: Hubbard's Image Was Crafted of Truth by Distorted Myth," in *The Scientology Series, Los Angeles Times*, June 24, 1990, A38–39.

54. Miscavige's game of musical chairs involved 70 high-ranking Scientologists fighting to stay in the game so that they wouldn't be "offloaded." The brutal game

raised fears among its players that they might be expelled from Scientology, sent to a Scientology "prison" known as Rehabilitation Project Force (RPF), or any number of other fear-inducing outcomes. At the end of the game, Miscavige, who had been in a rage, announced that he had changed his mind and would not offload anyone. Janet Reitman, "Inside Scientology: The Story of America's Most Secretive Religion," *Rolling Stone Magazine*, 2011, http://www.rollingstone.com/culture/news/inside-scientology-20110208.

55. For details regarding Scientology's attempts to influence these facets, see Stephen A. Kent, "Scientology—Is This a Religion?," *Marburg Journal of Religion* 4, no. 1 (1999): 1–23, https://www.uni-marburg.de/fb03/ivk/mjr/pdfs/1999/articles/kent1999.pdf.

56. James E. Adams and Elaine Viets, "The Reclusive Founder of Scientology," *St. Louis Dispatch*, March 4, 1974, 3D; Joel Sappell and Richard W. Welkos, "Creating the Mystique"; Stafford, "Individual Life Force is Focus of Scientology."

57. Adams and Viets, "The Reclusive Founder of Scientology."

58. Hubbard began his definition of engrams by describing engrams as "a mental image picture which is a recording of a time of physical pain or unconsciousness. It must by definition have impact or injury as part of its content." L. Ron Hubbard, *Dianetics and Scientology Technical Dictionary* (Los Angeles: Publications Organization, 1975), 141.

59. In another lengthy definition, Hubbard explained thetans are "the source of life and life itself," referred to the thetan as "spirit," and stated that "The **thetan** is immortal and is possessed of capability well in excess of those hitherto predicted for man" (bold in original). Hubbard, *Dianetics and Scientology Technical Dictionary*, 432.

60. Joel Sappell and Richard W. Welkos, "Defining the Theology," in *The Scientology Series, Los Angeles Times*, June 24, 1990, A36.

61. These events are detailed in Lawrence Wright, *Going Clear: Scientology, Hollywood, & the Prison of Belief* (New York: Alfred A. Knopf, 2013). Bill Cornwell, "The Mystery Man Behind Scientology," in *Special Report: Scientology: An In-Depth Profile of a New Force in Clearwater* (series), *St. Petersburg Times*, December 16–30, 1979, 18.

62. Cornwell, "The Mystery Man Behind Scientology," 17.

63. Ibid., 20.

64. Ibid., 17; Jodi M. Lane and Stephen A. Kent, "Politiques de rage et narcissisme malin," *Criminologie* 41 no. 2 (2008): 117–155, doi:10.7202/019435ar (English translation, pp. 1–52).

65. John Marshall, "Cult Harassment, Spying in Canada Documented," *The Globe and Mail*, January 23, 1980, 4.

66. Hubbard's inability to complete his education is well documented. Cornwell, "The Mystery Man Behind Scientology," 17; Marshall, "Cult Harassment"; Lane and Kent, "Politiques de rage et narcissisme malin."

67. See Bent Corydon, *L. Ron Hubbard: Messiah or Madman* (Fort Lee, NJ: Barricade Books, 1992), 227; Lane and Kent, "Politiques de rage et narcissisme malin," 10.

68. Medicus and L. Ron Hubbard, *All About Radiation (Man's Inhumanity to Man)* (London: The Hubbard Association for Scientologists International, 1957), 39. It is

highly likely that "Medicus" is one of Hubbard's pseudonyms. Atack, *A Piece of Blue Sky*, 142.

69. Cornwell, "The Mystery Man Behind Scientology," 17.

70. Stafford, "Individual Life Force Is Focus of Scientology"; Sappell and Welkos, "Creating the Mystique."

71. John Marshall, "Hubbard Still Gave Orders, Records Show," *The Globe and Mail*, January 24, 1980, 11.

72. Joel Sappell and Robert W. Welkos, "The Final Days: Deep in Hiding, Hubbard Kept Tight Grip on the Church," in *The Scientology Series*, *Los Angeles Times*, June 25, 1990, A40.

73. Richard Leiby, "Letter Indicates Hubbard Came to City to 'Save the Operation,'" *Clearwater Sun*, November 7, 1979, 9A.

74. James E. Adams and Elaine Viets, "A System of Engrams and Thetans," *St. Louis Post-Dispatch*, March 5, 1974, 3D.

75. James E. Adams and Elaine Viets, "A Hard Sell to Build a Faith," *St. Louis Post-Dispatch*, March 6, 1974, 3E.

76. Ibid.

77. Hubbard stated, "The completely **cleared** individual would have all his self-determinism in present time and would be completely self-determined" (emphasis in original). Hubbard, *Modern Management Technology Defined*, 84; Stafford, "Individual Life Force Is Focus of Scientology."

78. Joel Sappell and Robert W. Welkos, "Church Markets Its Gospel with High-Pressure Sales," in *The Scientology Series*, *Los Angeles Times*, June 25, 1990, A1; Thomas C. Tobin and Joe Childs, "Death in Slow Motion," in *The Truth Rundown* (series), *Tampa Bay Times*, June 21, 2009.

79. Cornwell, "The Mystery Man Behind Scientology."

80. Adams and Viets, "A Hard Sell to Build a Faith"; Joel Sappell and Robert W. Welkos, "The Courting of Celebrities," in *The Scientology Series*, *Los Angeles Times*, June 25, 1990, A18.

81. Sappell and Welkos, "Church Markets Its Gospel with High-Pressure Sales."

82. Ibid.

83. Wollersheim had won a court case against Scientology. Scientology had sued him because he owned Operating Thetan documents that they wanted to keep away from the public. Then, he joined another former Scientologist (Arnaldo Lerma) who had started F.A.C.T.Net ("Fight Against Coercive Tactics"), which was a nonprofit archive that countered groups that used mind control. Sappell and Welkos, "Church Markets Its Gospel with High-Pressure Sales." See also Brill and Packard, "Silencing Scientology's Critics on the Internet," 12.

84. Charles Stafford, "Dispute over Tax Status Goes to Court," in *Special Report: Scientology: An In-Depth Profile of a New Force in Clearwater* (series), *St. Petersburg Times*, December 16–30, 1979, 5.

85. Stephen Kent, "Scientology's Relationship with Eastern Religious Traditions," *Journal of Contemporary Religion* 11 (1996): 30, doi:10.1080/13537909608580753.

86. Urban, "Fair Game," 364; L. Ron Hubbard, "Routine 3: Heaven," *Hubbard Communications Office Bulletin* (May 11, 1963): 4.

87. Adams and Viets, "The Reclusive Founder of Scientology."

88. For example, Roxanne Friend believed Scientologists' claims that auditing would cure her yet-to-be diagnosed cancer symptoms. She passed away after leaving Scientology and lacking resources to access mainstream medical care. Friend spent over $80,000 on auditing, was nearly broke, and lacked medical insurance. ABCNews, "Scientology Leader Gave ABC First-Ever Interview" (transcribed from *Nightline* Television in 2006 broadcast 1992), *ABC News*, http://abcnews.go.com /print?id=2664713.

89. Stafford, "Dispute over Tax Status Goes to Court."

90. Although absent from the *St. Louis Dispatch*, Gesell required Scientology to relinquish E-Meter related-health claims. *United States of America v. Founding Church of Scientology et al.*, No. D.C. 1–63 (July 30, 1971), U.S. Dist. of Columbia, Federal Supplement, 33 1972 (357–369) (St. Paul, MN: West Publishing Co.), 357, 364.

91. Theresa A. Lyons, "Scientology or Censorship: You Decide," *Journal of Law and Religion* 2 (2000): 5, http://lawandreligion.com/volume-2.

92. Adams and Viets, "Expensive Trip to Spirituality."

93. Ibid. These authors cited United States District Judge Gerhard A. Gesell of the District of Columbia statement that Scientology was "quackery" and "pseudo-science." Then they cited two religious leaders (one Christian and one neo-pagan), who could arguably be defined as "moral entrepreneurs" in that they work to maintain dominant values (although the authors said that the neo-pagan "might be expected to be a natural ally of Scientology"). Adams and Viets, "A System of Engrams and Thetans."

94. Joel Sappell and Robert W. Welkos, "Shoring Up Its Religious Profile," in *The Scientology Series*, *Los Angeles Times*, June 25, 1990, A18.

95. Ibid.

96. Stafford, "Dispute over Tax Status Goes to Court."

97. Ibid.; Sappell and Welkos, "Shoring Up Its Religious Profile."

98. Richard Leiby, "Sect Front Started to Launder Cash," *Clearwater Sun*, November 7, 1979, 1A, 9A.

99. Joe Childs and Thomas C. Tobin, "Scientology: The Truth Rundown," in *The Truth Rundown* (series), *Tampa Bay Times*, June 21, 2009, http://www.tampabay.com /topics/specials/scientology.page.

100. Wallis, *The Road to Total Freedom*, 140.

101. Adams and Viets, "The Reclusive Founder of Scientology." See Wallis, *The Road to Total Freedom*, 140.

102. Wallis, *The Road to Total Freedom*, 140.

103. Susan Raine, "Surveillance in a New Religious Movement: Scientology as a Case Study," *Religious Studies and Theology* 28, no. 1 (2009): 85, doi:10.1558/rsth .v28i1.63.

104. Charles Stafford, "Church Entered Clearwater on Path of Deceit," in *Special Report: Scientology: An In-Depth Profile of a New Force in Clearwater* (series),

St. Petersburg Times, December 16–30, 1979, 7; Richard Leiby, "Sect Front Started to Launder Cash," 1A.

105. Adams and Viets, "The Reclusive Founder of Scientology."

106. Joel Sappell and Robert W. Welkos, "Defectors Recount Lives of Hard Work, Punishment," *Los Angeles Times*, June 26, 1990, A1, A16.

107. Ibid.

108. Ibid.

109. Ibid.

110. Ibid.

111. Stafford, "Scientology Brings 4 Years of Discord."

112. Debbie Winsor, "Shocked Officials Say They'll Fight," *Clearwater Sun*, November 3, 1979, 1A–2A.

113. The Church of Scientology International, "Scientology in Clearwater the Spiritual Headquarters of the Scientology Religion," *Church of Scientology in Clearwater, Florida*. (2000–2004), http://scientology.fso.org/

114. Ibid.

115. Childs and Tobin, "Scientology."

116. Raine, "Surveillance in a New Religious Movement," 83.

117. Charles Stafford, "Book Spells Out Rationale for Church's 'Spy System,'" in *Special Report: Scientology: An In-Depth Profile of a New Force in Clearwater* (series), *St. Petersburg Times*, December 16–30, 1979, 15.

118. Ibid.

119. Ibid.

120. Childs and Tobin, "Scientology"; Lieby, "Scientologists Plot City Takeover"; Joel Sappell and Richard W. Welkos, "Burglaries and Lies Paved a Path to Prison," in *The Scientology Series*, *Los Angeles Times*, June 24, 1990, A39; Marshall, "Two Leaders in Britain Still to Face U.S. Court in Conspiracy Case"; Charles Stafford, "Court Tangle Gave Scientology Its First 'Martyrs,'" in *Special Report: Scientology: An In-Depth Profile of a New Force in Clearwater* (series), *St. Petersburg Times*, December 16–30, 1979, 5.

121. Marshall, "Hubbard Still Gave Orders."

122. Lieby, "Scientologists Plot City Takeover."

123. Ibid.; Raine, "Surveillance in a New Religious Movement," 83.

124. Marshall, "Two Leaders in Britain Still to Face U.S. Court in Conspiracy Case."

125. Charles Stafford, "Scientologists' Downfall Began with Phony IDs," in *Special Report: Scientology: An In-Depth Profile of a New Force in Clearwater* (series), *St. Petersburg Times*, December 16–30, 1979, 14. Wolfe worked a secretarial position in the IRS in Washington. There, he provided the GO with copies of over 30,000 pages of documents regarding Scientology. Raine, "Surveillance in a New Religious Movement," 83.

126. Stafford, "Scientologists' Downfall Began with Phony IDs."

127. L. Ron Hubbard, "Ethics, Suppressive Acts, Suppression of Scientology and Scientologists, The Fair Game Law," *Hubbard Communications Office Policy Letter* 41

(December 23, 1965), in L. Ron Hubbard, *The Organization Executive* Course, vol. 1 (Copenhagen: Scientology Publications Organization, 1970), 552. Cited in Lane and Kent, "Politiques de rage et narcissisme malin"; Raine, "Surveillance in a New Religious Movement," 77.

128. Raine, "Surveillance in a New Religious Movement," 77.

129. Hubbard, *Dianetics and Scientology Technical Dictonary*, 144. In Raine, "Surveillance in a New Religious Movement," 77.

130. L. Ron Hubbard, "Penalties for Lower Conditions," *Hubbard Communications Office Policy Letter* (October 18, 1967): 1p. Cited in Lane and Kent, "Malignant Narcissism," 25; Urban, "The Rundown Truth," 4.

131. James E. Adams and Elaine Viets, "Counterattack: The Response to Criticism," *St. Louis Post-Dispatch*, March 7, 1974; Charles Stafford, "Church Moves to Defend Itself against 'Attackers,'" in *Special Report: Scientology: An In-Depth Profile of a New Force in Clearwater* (series), *St. Petersburg Times*, December 16–30, 1979, 6.

132. Adams and Viets, "Counterattack," *St. Louis Post-Dispatch*, March 7, 1974; Thomas C. Tobin and Joe Childs, "Scientology: Ecclesiastical Justice," in *The Truth Rundown* (series), *Tampa Bay Times*, June 22, 2009.

133. Raine, "Surveillance in a New Religious Movement," 73.

134. Adams and Viets, "Counterattack."

135. Ibid.

136. Charles Stafford, "Court Tangle Gave Scientology Its First 'Martyrs,'" 15.

137. Raine, "Surveillance in a New Religious Movement"; Urban, "Fair Game."

138. Mary Sue Hubbard's assistant Fred Hare wrote this order. Marshall, "Hubbard Still Gave Orders."

139. Ibid. Also in Stafford, "Church Moves to Defend Itself against 'Attackers.'"

140. Marshall, "Hubbard Still Gave Orders, Records Show."

141. Lieby, "Scientologists Plot City Takeover."

142. Richard Leiby, "Scientologists' Goal: World Takeover," *Clearwater Sun*, November 6, 1979, 1C; Richard Leiby, "Memo: Scientologists Aimed Attack at Local Man," *Clearwater Sun*, November 4, 1979, 9A. Adams and Viets (1974), Stafford (1979), and Marshall (1980) also discussed these topics. See Charles Stafford, "Church Tried to Infiltrate Pinellas Police Agencies," in *Special Report: Scientology: An In-Depth Profile of a New Force in Clearwater* (series), *St. Petersburg Times*, December 16–30, 1979, 13; Adams and Viets, "Counterattack"; Marshall, "Cult Harassment."

143. Marshall, "Two Leaders in Britain Still to Face U.S. Court in Conspiracy Case."

144. Ibid.

145. Ibid.

146. Ibid.

147. Ibid.

148. Marshall, "Hubbard Still Gave Orders."

149. Raine, "Surveillance in a New Religious Movement," 84.

150. Ibid., 84.

151. Marshall, "Two Leaders in Britain Still to Face U.S. Court in Conspiracy Case."

152. John Marshall, "Cult Harassment."

153. Dart, "Covering Conventional and Unconventional Religion," 145.

154. Adams and Viets, "The Reclusive Founder of Scientology"; Marshall, "Cult Harassment," *The Globe and Mail.* See Wallis, *The Road to Total Freedom* (1976), 140.

155. Adams and Viets, "Counterattack"; John Marshall, "Cult Harassment, Spying in Canada Documented."

156. Adams and Viets, "The Reclusive Founder of Scientology." See Wallis, *The Road to Total Freedom*, 140.

157. Adams and Viets, "Counterattack"; Marshall, "Cult Harassment."

158. Adams and Viets, "Counterattack."

159. This series missed the conviction of Cooper on fraudulent bomb threat charges, which was discussed in later series. Adams and Viets, "Counterattack."

160. Scientology's surveillance of Cooper included tapping her phone, following her, attempting to break into her apartment, and burglarizing her lawyer's office. Raine, "Surveillance in a New Religious Movement," 81–82.

161. Marshall, "Hubbard Still Gave Orders"; John Marshall, "Files Show Spy Reported Woman's Intimate Words," *The Globe and Mail*, January 25, 1980, 11.

162. Ibid.

163. Van Driel and Richardson, "Print Media Coverage of New Religious Movements," 40.

164. Robert Young, "Scientology from Inside Out: A Former Insider Reveals Strategies for Managing the News Media," *The Quill* 81, no. 9 (November–December, 1993): 39.

165. Charles Stafford, "Church Moves to Defend Itself against 'Attackers,'" in *Special Report: Scientology: An In-Depth Profile of a New Force in Clearwater* (series), *St. Petersburg Times*, December 16–30, 1979, 7.

166. Stafford, "Church Moves to Defend Itself against 'Attackers.'"

167. Eugene Patterson, "Shedding Light on Scientology's Dark Side," in *Special Report: Scientology: An In-Depth Profile of a New Force in Clearwater* (series), *St. Petersburg Times*, December 16–30, 1979, 2.

168. Ibid.

169. Ibid.

170. Ibid.

171. Lyons, "Scientology or Censorship," 12.

172. Patterson, "Shedding Light on Scientology's Dark Side."

173. Charles Stafford, "St. Petersburg Times Topped 'Enemies' List," in *Special Report: Scientology: An In-Depth Profile of a New Force in Clearwater* (series), *St. Petersburg Times*, December 16–30, 1979, 10; Charles Stafford, "Operation Bunny Bust," in *Special Report: Scientology: An In-Depth Profile of a New Force in Clearwater* (series), *St. Petersburg Times*, December 16–30, 1979, 11.

174. Charles Stafford, "St. Petersburg Times Topped 'Enemies' List."

175. Charles Stafford, "Church Infiltrated the Clearwater Sun," in *Special Report: Scientology: An In-Depth Profile of a New Force in Clearwater* (series), *St. Petersburg Times*, December 16–30, 1979, 12.

176. Stafford, "Church Infiltrated the Clearwater Sun."

177. Ibid.

178. Ibid.

179. Marshall, "Two Leaders in Britain Still to Face U.S. Court in Conspiracy Case."

180. Marshall, "Hubbard Still Gave Orders, Records Show."

181. Welkos, "Shudder into Silence," para. 18.

182. Ibid., para. 18.

183. Ibid., para. 16.

184. Ibid., para. 37.

185. Urban, "The Truth Rundown."

186. Ibid. See also Brill and Packard, "Silencing Scientology's Critics on the Internet"; Peckman, "New Dimensions of Social Movement/Countermovement Interaction."

187. Doherty, "Sensational Scientology!," 41.

188. Van Driel and Richardson, "Print Media Coverage of New Religious Movements," 55.

189. Doherty, "Sensational Scientology!," 41.

190. Kent and Manca, "A War over Mental Health Professions," 10–11. Fred Charatan, "US Parents Use Psychiatrists for Promoting Ritalin," *British Medical Journal* 321, no. 7263 (2000): 723; Sandra Thomas, "From the Editor—Combatting the Assault on Childhood Mental Disorders," *Issues in Mental Health Nursing* 23 (2002): 1–2.

191. Joel Sappell and Robert W. Welkos, "Suits, Protests Fuel a Campaign against Psychiatry," in *The Scientology Series*, *Los Angeles Times*, June 29, 1990, A48.

192. Sappell and Welkos, "The Final Days."

193. Ibid.

194. Ibid.

195. Tobin and Childs, "Death in Slow Motion."

196. Van Driel and Richardson, "Print Media Coverage of New Religious Movements," 57.

197. Ibid., 56.

198. Bryan Wilson, *The Social Dimensions of Sectarianism*.

199. Ibid., 64, 236, 242, 247.

200. William Zellner and Marc Petrowsky, "Freedom Park," in *Sects, Cults, and Spiritual Communities*, ed. William W. Zellner and Marc Petrowsky (Westport, CT: Praeger, 1998), 159.

201. Raine, "Surveillance in a New Religious Movement," 86.

202. Ibid., 67.

203. Ibid., 69.

204. Lewis, "Scientology vs. the Media," 63; Raine, "Surveillance in a New Religious Movement," 81–82; Wallis, "Societal Reaction to Scientology," 109–110.

205. Urban, "Fair Game," 357.

206. Lewis, "Scientology vs. the Media," 63.

207. Doherty, "Sensational Scientology!," 51.

BIBLIOGRAPHY

Atack, Jon. *A Piece of Blue Sky*. New York: Carol Publishing Group, 1990.

Brill, Ann, and Ashley Packard. "Silencing Scientology's Critics on the Internet: A Mission Impossible?" *Communications and Law* 4 (December 1997): 1–23. http://www.heinonline.org.

Bures, Charles E. "A Review of Dianetics." *Engineering and Science* 14, no. 2 (1950): 1–32.

Charatan, Fred. "US Parents Use Psychiatrists for Promoting Ritalin." *British Medical Journal* 321, no. 7263 (2000): 723.

Church of Scientology International, The. "Scientology in Clearwater the Spiritual Headquarters of the Scientology Religion." *Church of Scientology in Clearwater, Florida*, 2000–2004. Accessed April 14, 2016. http://scientology.fso.org/.

Corydon, Bent. *L. Ron Hubbard: Messiah or Madman?* Fort Lee, New Jersey: Barricade Books, 1992.

Dart, John. "Covering Conventional and Unconventional Religion: A Reporter's View." *Review of Religious Research* 39, no. 2 (December 1997): 144–152. doi:10.2307/3512179.

Doherty, Bernard. "Sensational Scientology! The Church of Scientology and Australian Tabloid Television." *Nova Religio: The Journal of Alternative and Emergent Religion* 17, no. 3 (February 2014): 38–63. doi:10.1525/nr.2014.17.3.38.

Gittleson, Yvette. "Sacred Cows in Collision." *American Scientist* 38, no. 4 (1950): 603–609.

Goode, Erich, and Nachman Ben-Yehuda. "Moral Panics: Culture, Politics, and Social Construction." *Annual Review of Sociology* 20 (1994): 149–171. doi:10.2307/3512179.

Hubbard, L. Ron. *All About Radiation (Man's Inhumanity to Man)*. London: The Hubbard Association for Scientologists International, 1957.

Hubbard, L. Ron. *Dianetics and Scientology Technical Dictionary*. Los Angeles: Publications Organization, 1975.

Hubbard, L. Ron. "Ethics. Suppressive Acts. Suppression of Scientology and Scientologists. The Fair Game Law." *Hubbard Communications Office Policy Letter* 41 (December 23, 1965); in L. Ron Hubbard, *The Organization Executive Course*, Vol. 1. Copenhagen: Scientology Publications Organization (1970): 552–557.

Hubbard, L. Ron. *Manual of Justice*. London: Hubbard Communications Office, 1959.

Hubbard, L. Ron. *Modern Management Technology Defined*. Los Angeles: Bridge Publications, 1979.

Hubbard, L. Ron. "Penalties for Lower Conditions." *Hubbard Communications Office Policy Letter* (October 18, 1967): 1p.

Hubbard, L. Ron. "Routine 3: Heaven." *Hubbard Communications Office Bulletin* (May 11, 1963).

Hubbard, L. Ron. "The Scientologist: A Manual on the Dissemination of Material." *Ability* (1955, mid-March). In *The Technical Bulletins of Dianetics and Scientology*, 2. Los Angeles: Scientology Publications, 1976: 151–171.

Hubbard Dianetic Research Foundation. "The Dianamic." Elizabeth, NJ: Hubbard Dianetic Research Foundation, 1951.

Kent, Stephen. "Scientology—Is This a Religion?" *Marburg Journal of Religion* 4, no. 1 (1999): 1–23. https://www.uni-marburg.de/fb03/ivk/mjr/pdfs/1999/articles/kent 1999.pdf.

Kent, Stephen. "Scientology's Relationship with Eastern Religious Traditions." *Journal of Contemporary Religion* 11 (1996): 21–36. doi:10.1080/13537909608580753.

Kent, Stephen A., and Terra A. Manca. "A War over Mental Health Professionalism: Scientology Versus Psychiatry." *Mental Health, Religion & Culture* 1 (January 2014): 1–23. doi:10.1080/13674676.2012.737552.

Lane, Jodi M., and Stephen A. Kent, "Politiques de Rage et Narcissisme Malin." *Criminologie* 41, no. 2 (2008): 117–155. doi:10.7202/019435ar. (English version, pp. 1–52).

Laycock, Joseph. "Where Do They Get These Ideas? Changing Ideas of Cults in the Mirror of Popular Culture." *Journal of the American Academy of Religion* 81, no. 1 (2013): 80–106. doi:10.1093/jaarel/lfs091.

Lewis, James R. "Scientology vs. the Media." *Alternative Spirituality and Religion Review* 6, no. 1 (2015): 61–78. doi:10.5840/asrr201572010.

Lyons, Theresa A. "Scientology or Censorship: You Decide." *Journal of Law and Religion* 2 (2000): 1–22. http://lawandreligion.com/volume-2.

Manca, Terra. "Alternative Therapy, Dianetics, and Scientology." *Marburg Journal of Religion* 15 (2010): 1–20. https://www.uni-marburg.de/fb03/ivk/mjr/pdfs/2010 /articles/manca_2010.pdf.

Manca, Terra. "L. Ron Hubbard's Alternative to the Bomb Shelter: Scientology's Emergence as a Pseudo-Science during the 1950s." *Journal of Religion and Popular Culture* 24, no. 1 (Spring 2012): 80–96. doi:10.3138/jrpc.24.1.80.

Peckman, Michael. "New Dimensions of Social Movement/Countermovement Interaction: The Case of Scientology and Its Internet Critics." *Canadian Journal of Sociology* 24, no. 1 (1998): 317–347. http://www.jstor.org/stable/3341804.

Rain, Susan. "Surveillance in a New Religious Movement: Scientology as a Case Study." *Religious Studies and Theology* 28, no. 1 (2009): 63–94. doi:10.1558/rsth .v28i1.63.

Thomas, Sandra P. "From the Editor—Combatting the Assault on Childhood Mental Disorders." *Issues in Mental Health Nursing* 23 (2002): 1–2. doi:10 .1080/01612840252825437.

United States of America v. Founding Church of Scientology et al. No. D.C. 1–63. July 30, 1971. U.S. Dist. of Columbia. Federal Supplement, 33 (1972): 357–369. St. Paul, MN: West Publishing Co.

Urban, Hugh B. "Fair Game: Secrecy, Security, and the Church of Scientology in Cold War America." *Journal of the American Academy of Religion* 74, no. 2 (June 2006): 356–389. doi:10.1093/jaarel/lfj084.

Urban, Hugh B. "The Truth Rundown: Scientology Changes Strategy in War with Media." *Religion Dispatches* (March 18, 2010): 1–4. http://religiondispatches .org/the-rundown-truth-scientology-changes-strategy-in-war-with-media/.

Van Driel, Barend, and James T. Richardson. "Print Media Coverage of New Religious Movements: A Longitudinal Study." *Journal of Communication* 38, no. 3 (September 1988): 37–61. doi:10.1111/j.1460-2466.1988.tb02059.x.

Wallis, Roy. "Religious Sects and the Fear of Publicity." *New Society* 24 (June 7, 1973): 545–547.

Wallis, Roy. *The Road to Total Freedom*. New York: Columbia University Press, 1976.

Wallis, Roy. "Societal Reaction to Scientology: A Study in the Sociology of Deviant Religion." In *Sectarianism*, edited by Roy Wallis, 86–116. London: Peter Own, 1975.

Welkos, Robert W. "Shudder into Silence." *The Quill* 9, no. 9 (November–December 1991): 36–38.

Wilson, Bryan. *The Social Dimensions of Sectarianism: Sects and New Religious Movements in Contemporary Society*. Oxford: Clarendon Press, 1990.

Winter, Joseph. "Introduction." In *Dianetics: The Modern Science of Mental Health*. Written by L. Ron Hubbard. New York: Hermitage House, 1950.

Wright, Lawrence. *Going Clear: Scientology, Hollywood, & the Prison of Belief*. New York: Alfred A. Knopf, 2013.

Young, Robert. "Scientology from Inside Out: A Former Insider Reveals Strategies for Managing the News Media." *The Quill* 81, no. 9 (November–December 1993): 38–41.

Zellner, William, and Marc Petrowsky. "Freedom Park." In *Sects, Cults, and Spiritual Communities*, edited by William W. Zellner and Marc Petrowsky, 157–177. Westport, CT: Praeger, 1998.

NEWS MEDIA

ABCNews. "Scientology Leader Gave ABC First-Ever Interview." Transcribed from *Nightline* Television November 18, 2006. Broadcast February 14, 1992. *ABC News*. http://abcnews.go.com/print?id=2664713.

Adams, James E., and Elaine Viets. "Counterattack: The Response to Criticism." *St. Louis Post-Dispatch*, March 7, 1974.

Adams, James E., and Elaine Viets. "Expensive Trip to Spirituality." *St. Louis Post-Dispatch*. March 3, 1974.

Adams, James E., and Elaine Viets. "A Hard Sell to Build a Faith." *St. Louis Post-Dispatch*. March 6, 1974.

Adams, James E., and Elaine Viets. "A System of Engrams and Thetans." *St. Louis Post-Dispatch*, March 5, 1974.

Adams, James E., and Elaine Viets. "The Reclusive Founder of Scientology." *St. Louis Dispatch*, March 4, 1974.

Behar, Richard. "The Thriving Cult of Greed and Power." *Time Magazine*, May 6, 1991. http://content.time.com/time/magazine/article/0,9171,972865,00.html.

Childs, Joe, and Thomas C. Tobin. "Scientology: The Truth Rundown." In *The Truth Rundown* (series). *Tampa Bay Times*, June 21, 2009. http://www.tampabay.com /topics/specials/scientology.page.

Clearwater Sun. "Opinion: Of Grudges and Lies." November 7, 1979.

Cornwell, Bill. "The Mystery Man Behind Scientology." In *Special Report: Scientology: An In-Depth Profile of a New Force in Clearwater* (series). *St. Petersburg Times*, December 16–30, 1979.

Lieby, Richard. "Letter Indicates Hubbard Came to City to 'Save the Operation.'" *Clearwater Sun*, November 7, 1979.

Lieby, Richard. "Memo: Scientologists Aimed Attack at Local Man." *Clearwater Sun*, November 4, 1979.

Lieby, Richard. "Scientologists' Goal: World Takeover." *Clearwater Sun*, November 6, 1979.

Lieby, Richard. "Scientologists Plot City Takeover." *Clearwater Sun*, November 3, 1979.

Lieby, Richard. "Sect Front Started to Launder Cash." *Clearwater Sun*, November 7, 1979.

Lieby, Richard. "Tampa Jury May Get Sect Documents." *Clearwater Sun*, November 7, 1979.

Marshall, John. "Big FBI Raid Led to Conspiracy Trial of Cult Leaders." *The Globe and Mail*, January 22, 1980.

Marshall, John. "Cult Harassment, Spying in Canada Documented." *The Globe and Mail*, January 23, 1980.

Marshall, John. "Files Show Spy Reported Woman's Intimate Words." *The Globe and Mail*, January 25, 1980.

Marshall, John. "Hubbard Still Gave Orders, Records Show." *The Globe and Mail*, January 24, 1980.

Marshall, John. "Secret Ontario Documents Found in U.S. Cult's Files." *The Globe and Mail*, January 22, 1980.

Marshall, John. "Two Leaders in Britain Still to Face U.S. Court in Conspiracy Case." *The Globe and Mail*, January 1, 1980.

Patterson, Eugene. "Shedding Light on Scientology's Dark Side." In *Special Report: Scientology: An In-Depth Profile of a New Force in Clearwater* (series). *St. Petersburg Times*, December 16–30, 1979, 2.

Reitman, Janet. "Inside Scientology." *Rolling Stone Magazine*, February 8, 2011. http://www.rollingstone.com/culture/news/inside-scientology-20110208.

Sappell, Joel, and Richard W. Welkos. "Burglaries and Lies Paved a Path to Prison." In *The Scientology Series. Los Angeles Times*, June 24, 1990. http://www.latimes.com.

Sappell, Joel, and Richard W. Welkos. "Church Markets Its Gospel with High-Pressure Sales." In *The Scientology Series. Los Angeles Times*, June 25, 1990. http://www.latimes.com.

Sappell, Joel, and Richard W. Welkos. "Church Seeks Influence in Schools, Business, and Science." In *The Scientology Series. Los Angeles Times*, June 27, 1990. http://www.latimes.com.

Sappell, Joel, and Richard W. Welkos. "The Courting of Celebrities." In *The Scientology Series. Los Angeles Times*, June 25, 1990. http://www.latimes.com.

Sappell, Joel, and Richard W. Welkos. "Creating the Mystique: Hubbard's Image Was Crafted of Truth by Distorted Myth." In *The Scientology Series. Los Angeles Times*, June 24, 1990. http://www.latimes.com.

Sappell, Joel, and Richard W. Welkos. "Defectors Recount Lives of Hard Work, Punishment." In *The Scientology Series. Los Angeles Times*, June 26, 1990. http://www.latimes.com.

Sappell, Joel, and Richard W. Welkos. "Defining the Theology." In *The Scientology Series. Los Angeles Times*, June 24, 1990. http://www.latimes.com.

Sappell, Joel, and Richard W. Welkos. "The Final Days: Deep in Hiding, Hubbard Kept Tight Grip on the Church." In *The Scientology Series. Los Angeles Times*, June 24, 1990. http://www.latimes.com.

Sappell, Joel, and Richard W. Welkos. "Shoring Up Its Religious Profile." In *The Scientology Series. Los Angeles Times*, June 25, 1990. http://www.latimes.com.

Sappell, Joel, and Richard W. Welkos. "Suits, Protests Fuel a Campaign against Psychiatry." In *The Scientology Series. Los Angeles Times*, June 29, 1990. http://www.latimes.com.

Stafford, Charles. "Book Spells Out Rationale for Church's 'Spy System.'" In *Special Report: Scientology: An In-Depth Profile of a New Force in Clearwater* (series). *St. Petersburg Times*, December 16–30, 1979.

Stafford, Charles. "Church Entered Clearwater on Path of Deceit." In *Special Report: Scientology: An In-Depth Profile of a New Force in Clearwater* (series). *St. Petersburg Times*, December 16–30, 1979.

Stafford, Charles. "Church Infiltrated the Clearwater Sun." In *Special Report: Scientology: An In-Depth Profile of a New Force in Clearwater* (series). *St. Petersburg Times*, December 16–30, 1979.

Stafford, Charles. "Church Moves to Defend Itself against 'Attackers.'" In *Special Report: Scientology: An In-Depth Profile of a New Force in Clearwater* (series). *St. Petersburg Times*, December 16–30, 1979.

Stafford, Charles. "Church Tried to Infiltrate Pinellas Police Agencies." In *Special Report: Scientology: An In-Depth Profile of a New Force in Clearwater* (series). *St. Petersburg Times*, December 16–30, 1979.

Stafford, Charles. "Court Tangle Gave Scientology Its First 'Martyrs.'" In *Special Report: Scientology: An In-Depth Profile of a New Force in Clearwater* (series). *St. Petersburg Times*, December 16–30, 1979.

Stafford, Charles. "Dispute over Tax Status Goes to Court." In *Special Report: Scientology: An In-Depth Profile of a New Force in Clearwater* (series). *St. Petersburg Times*, December 16–30, 1979.

Stafford, Charles. "Individual Life Force Is Focus of Scientology." In *Special Report: Scientology: An In-Depth Profile of a New Force in Clearwater* (series). *St. Petersburg Times*, December 16–30, 1979.

Stafford, Charles. "Operation Bunny Bust." In *Special Report: Scientology: An In-Depth Profile of a New Force in Clearwater* (series). *St. Petersburg Times*, December 16–30, 1979.

Stafford, Charles. "Scientologists' Downfall Began with Phony IDs." In *Special Report: Scientology: An In-Depth Profile of a New Force in Clearwater* (series). *St. Petersburg Times*, December 16–30, 1979.

Stafford, Charles. "Scientology Brings 4 Years of Discord." In *Special Report: Scientology: An In-Depth Profile of a New Force in Clearwater* (series). *St. Petersburg Times*, December 16–30, 1979.

Stafford, Charles. "St. Petersburg Times Topped 'Enemies' List." In *Special Report: Scientology: An In-Depth Profile of a New Force in Clearwater* (series). *St. Petersburg Times*, December 16–30, 1979.

Stuart, Ron. "Opinion: Documents Remove Last Faint Doubts about Scientology." *Clearwater Sun*, November 4, 1979.

Tobin, Thomas C., and Joe Childs. "Death in Slow Motion." In *The Truth Rundown* (series). *Tampa Bay Times*, June 21, 2009. http://www.tampabay.com/topics/specials/scientology.page.

Tobin, Thomas C., and Joe Childs. "Scientology: Ecclesiastical Justice." In *The Truth Rundown* (series). *Tampa Bay Times*, June 22, 2009. http://www.tampabay.com /topics/specials/scientology.page.

Winsor, Debbie. "Shocked Officials Say They'll Fight." *Clearwater Sun*, November 3, 1979.

Wright, Lawrence. "The Apostate: Paul Haggis vs. the Church of Scientology." *The New Yorker*, February 14 and 21, 2011. http://www.newyorker.com/magazine /2011/02/14/the-apostate-lawrence-wright.

10

Scientology's Relationship with the Internet: The Struggles of Contemporary Perception Management

Max Halupka

Since the early 1990s, the Church of Scientology has sought to control the flow of digital content pertaining to its operations and governing theology. From alt.religion.scientology to WikiLeaks and Google, the Church of Scientology has taken a firm approach to mitigating criticisms. While some authors[1] have interpreted such an approach as tied closely to Scientology's capacity to maintain its proclaimed profit-centric model in the face of an increasingly digitalized society, the Church itself contends that its aim is to protect copyrighted material. It has been primarily through litigation that the Church of Scientology has looked to control this material, issuing infringement letters to websites that house protected content and more serious legal challenges to those individuals who propagate it. In many ways, the Church's use of litigation in these cases is a direct evolution of similar tactics employed between 1967 and 1993 in its campaign to reacquire its tax-exempt status. Indeed, the use of litigation to control criticisms has been at the core of the Church of Scientology's approach to perception management.[2] However, although there are similarities here, the proliferation of Internet-capable technologies, together with the emergence of Web 2.0, has forced the Church of Scientology to alter its tactical approach.

This chapter has two purposes. First, it explores Scientology's approach to perception management in an era of postmodernity, where the fluidity of information distribution and the rise of the reflexive citizen have undermined conventional approaches. Here, the Church of Scientology has been forced to soften its tactics, utilizing strategies that limit the capacity for social criticism. Second, the chapter explores a number of recent examples where

Scientology has "gone into battle" with the Internet over access to information on the group. In this way, the chapter updates Lippard and Jacobsen's earlier work on Scientology's relationship with the Internet.[3]

This chapter begins by looking at several recent examples where the Church of Scientology has attempted to censor sensitive material online. In addition to briefly revisiting the Church's confrontation with alt.religion.scientology,[4] the chapter also covers its opposition to Wikipedia,[5] WikiLeaks,[6] and Google.[7] Drawing upon these cases, the chapter contrasts Scientology's contemporary approach to perception management to that employed during the reacquisition of its tax-exempt status. Finally, the article will consider how Scientology's use of censorship has contributed to the "Streisand effect," that is, the "inadvertent popularity of any material as a result of its suppression."[8] By contrasting the tactics used between 1967 and 1993 with those employed throughout these more recent cases, we gain a better understanding of how new religions process significant technological development.

A NEW RELIGION IN THE DIGITAL AGE

Scientology is, first and foremost, a new religion.[9] It is a fledgling faith struggling to establish a level of theological legitimacy against the rising tide that is a highly digitalized and, as some would argue,[10] more critical society. Other, more established, religions have had the benefit of centuries of propagation and indoctrination. Scientology however, finds its early years, those so crucial to establishing legitimacy and longevity, marked by the rise of the Internet and the proliferation of reflexive citizens.[11] The advent of the Internet has brought with it a change in society. It has forced media, politics, business, and religion to change the way in which they engage their "consumer" base. Traditional methods, specifically those tied to civic sociability, have been undermined by the popularization of the Internet throughout society and the flexibility it affords. The Internet, at a basic level, facilitates the gathering of like-minded individuals around a common concern or interest.[12] This social component was, at first, restricted by the limited nature of early digital infrastructure, specifically the linking practices of webmasters. The development of Web 2.0 sociotechnical environments saw this infrastructure both streamlined and expanded to improve the browsing experience for the user. With these changes came a greater focus on social experience and the capacity of a user to manage content and interaction across multiple platforms simultaneously.[13]

The early years of a religion are often problematic, as theological legitimacy hinges upon whether the religion can establish the validity of its gnostic soteriology or successfully capitalize upon a gap not covered by existing faiths. To successfully navigate this period, a religion needs to manage how its beliefs are interpreted and, in doing so, mitigate any criticisms that may arise from its rejection. A new religion must see that its governing doctrine is faithfully interpreted in the public domain so that its message and purpose is faithfully conveyed. Criticism, while inevitable, serves to undermine this legitimacy, as it leads to a questioning of the validity of claims and doctrinal rationality. Here, it is easier to soften criticism or guide theological interpretation if the group targeted are part of a thick, strong network. The communicative pathways of a thick social network are more easily mapped as they are highly centralized and often guided by principal ideology. This centrality allows a new faith to manage how it is perceived by responding quickly to denunciation and correcting misinterpretation. It stands to reason then that the Internet makes this process more difficult by facilitating the development of thin, loose, and highly decentralized networks.

As traditional social structures decline in popularity, we have witnessed a seemingly related thinning of civic sociability. With social interaction now largely located online, we find that individual's social networks are far larger than ever before. However, this greater level of connection has been accompanied by a decrease in familiarity. While traditional social structures promoted a certain level of interpersonal awareness—in large part due to physicality—contemporary social structures are much looser, tying individuals together based on similarity rather than familiarity. Simply put, individuals are now connected with more people, but they don't know them as well as they once may have. While this decline in traditional civic sociability has undermined the capacity for thick solidarity, it also excels as a mean of content distribution and consumption.[14] Information is now more easily distributed, consumed, and accessed, as the networks that deliver it are more diverse and far reaching. It has been argued that, as a result of this, the modern citizen is less ideological and, consequently, more reflexive.[15] As ideological driven action gives way to project oriented identities, we find that the layperson is more reflexive, empowered by both an increase in available information and new avenues for communication and participation. The contemporary citizen is now more critically aware about the world around them, and it is this increased reflexivity with which the Church of Scientology must contend.

Passas and Castillo[16] suggest that Scientology relies heavily on its religious title and recognition as a religious entity. The Church of Scientology must manage how it is perceived by the general public, as its label as a religion is paramount to its capacity to function effectively. Actions that strengthen Scientology's characterization as a legitimate religion reinforce the Church's longevity. Conversely, a lack of public legitimization decreases the intake of new members, which in itself affects the Church's ability to function and expand. As highlighted, new faiths benefit from thick social groups, as their communicative networks are easily influenced and co-opted. We can see an example of this through the Church of Scientology's use of litigation, entryism, and opposition research from 1955 to the mid-1990s. Looking to control the way in which the public perceived it, the Church of Scientology responded harshly to critics by either silencing them or discrediting their claims. Here, the Church of Scientology was successful in controlling the flow of information as it was able to manage the tight networks that distributed it. Drawing upon its profit-centric model, the Church was able to funnel vast resources into managing its public perception through the manipulation of social structures and, in this, capitalize upon what was a more easily influenced society. However, as already alluded to, the rise of the Internet was problematic, as it effectively broadened those social structures beyond the reach of the Church. Moreover, as these social structures widened, information began to flow more freely, and, as a final crushing blow to those traditional approaches, citizens started questioning long-held beliefs. In granular sociotechnical environments such as Twitter, where complexity is achieved through the aggregation of many smaller actions, networks of information are prone to collaborative filtering. Here, loose networks processes rumors differently than they do news. As Starbird et al.[17] find, social networks resist the spread of misinformation, with participants more thoroughly discussing and criticizing biased information. Given that the Church of Scientology is a young faith, these changes in society are detrimental to its capacity to ensure that its beliefs are interpreted correctly and critics managed.

For the first time since its inception, the Church of Scientology has found itself facing a spread of information that it cannot match. While its use of political tactics had steered it strongly through the reacquisition of its tax-exempt status, the proliferation of the Internet has effectively undermined its capacity to manage public perception.[18] However, this has not deterred the Church from attempting to do so. As the next section illustrates, the Church of Scientology has redirected its resources toward the censoring of online material—specifically official Church documents, content that paints the Church in a negative light—and criticism from ex-members. Yet, the battle that it wages online is of a different nature to that seen in its earlier years.

SCIENTOLOGY VS. THE INTERNET

Although much has been written on Scientology's battle with alt.religion.scientology during the 1990s, this case is slowly being forgotten, as new examples replace old. In many ways, alt.religion.scientology is a remnant of an "older" Internet, a digital landscape without the conveniences of embedded platforms and streamlined user interfaces. However, the tactics used by Scientology during this period are as relevant as ever. To ensure that the exchange is not forgotten as the literature moves forward, this chapter begins by recounting this conflict.

The newsgroup alt.religion.scientology (a.r.s) was created in 1991 by Scott Goehring, using a forged "newsgroup" message posted under the name "David Miscaviage" (a misspelling of the name of the church leader David Miscavige). During its early years, the forum served as a space in which ex-Scientologist's could promote and discuss Hubbard's ideas independent of the Church itself (here, the members were known as "Free Zoners"). However, in time, criticism of both the Church's doctrine and techniques came to dominate the discussion on a.r.s, and the Free Zoners left to create a separate newsgroup.

As the site grew, so too did its reputation as a home for those critical of Scientology and its practices. The group housed the usual type of Usenet debates (often descending into a series of insults) between Scientologists, Free Zoners, and critics, but, for the most part, it was left largely alone by the Church of Scientology itself. However, in 1994, an internal memo from Elaine Siegel of Scientology's Office of Special Affairs was brought to light on a.r.s detailing the Church's plan to mitigate the criticism stemming from the community. It suggested that the Church should flood the newsgroup with 40 to 50 posts promoting pro-Scientology material every few days. In this way, the Church hoped to limit the visibility of genuine posts and undermine the chance of critical posts gaining traction. This tactic continued throughout the following years, reaching a peak in 1995 when tens of thousands of junk articles flooded the newsgroup. Scientologist Russell Shaw was quoted as stating that this approach merely involved the Church "painting over the graffiti."[19]

On December 1994, an anonymous user employing a remailer in the Netherlands posted documents detailing specifics of the Church's Operating Thetan levels, specifically, OTI, OTII, OTIII, and "New OT" (NOTs) issues 34, 35, and 36. Prior to this, only OTIII of OTI–VIII had been made publically available as a result of a court case detailing the teachings. Save for OTIII, all other OT levels had been closely guarded by the Church of Scientology and made available only to those few who progressed through the teachings and achieved a level of "clear." Of significance here was L. Ron Hubbard's gnostic soteriology, understood generally as the story of "Xenu." Although this origin story had been written about previously in Kaufman's text *Inside Scientology*, it remained largely at the fringe of Scientology-centered debates, lacking acknowledgment by the Church or validation by ex-members. The significance of these leaked documents at this time was that their contents were validated by regular a.r.s contributor and former Scientologist, Dennis Erlich. As Lippard and Jacobsen state, "suddenly the material Scientology reveals only after investments of considerable time and money was accessible to a potential audience of 30 million Internet users."[20]

Due to his involvement, specifically his validation of the texts and the reposting of the original content, Erlich soon became the focus of the Church of Scientology's riposte. Given that the identity of the original poster was still clouded in anonymity, the Church's lawyers pursued legal action against Erlich, declaring that, in contributing to the board, he had republished copyrighted material. On the morning of February 13, 1995, Erlich was presented with a writ of seizure by federal marshals, accompanied by Scientology lawyers, allowing the Church to examine, confiscate, and delete any and all material that was in breach of copyright. In addition to the Erlich raid, several other individuals were also accused of spreading copyrighted material, specifically Arnaldo Lerma (a former Scientology member); Karin Spaink (journalist and critic); Robert Penny and Lawrence A. Wollershein (cofounders of FACT-Net and prolific Scientology critics); and Zenon Panoussis (content poster).[21] These people were similarly investigated, became the subjects of legal action, and were issued with temporary restraining orders prohibiting publication of Scientology-based material.

What followed was a series of actions on behalf of the Church of Scientology with the sole purpose of limiting the distribution, via a.r.s, of what it classified as copyrighted material. These actions included the Church contacting the Netherlands remailer to have the initial anonymous account disabled; attempting to have the newsgroup itself shut down on the grounds that it breached copyright and served no purpose other than to illegally promote trade secrets; and issuing numerous cancellation notices for copyright infringement.[22]

The Church of Scientology's use of the Digital Millennium Copyright Act (DMCA) was crucial here and in the following years. Established in 1998, DMCA has two core provisions. First, it has a "notice-and-takedown" provision, which contends that, if an Internet Service Provider (ISP) or content host obtains knowledge or awareness of its users' infringement, then it must look to remove, or disable, access to the material to avoid liability. Second, there is a "safe harbor" provision for content hosts, which makes the ISP or host not liable if it has no knowledge, or apparent knowledge, of the copyright infringement.[23] One of the first organizations to make use of the DMCA, the Church of Scientology issued countless takedown notices to ISP and hosts in an attempt to stem the diffusion of its more guarded religious teachings. Lyons argues that the Church primarily used the DMCA to assert its copyright privileges and, in doing so, "silence its critics and send a warning message to other disgruntled Church members."[24]

It is important to take note of Scientology's approach to perception management during this early digital period. Unlike the more surreptitious style employed in later years, as discussed in the next section, this early period of Web 1.0 involved the digitalization of existing practices. Much in the same way as political participation practices, such as petitions and advocacy groups, are streamlined by moving online, Scientology's political tactics took a logical evolutionary step by pursuing traditional approaches in a new space.[25] Simply put, at this stage, not enough was known about how the Internet functioned and the implications that it could have on socialization and information distribution. To this end, the Church of Scientology continued with "business as normal," using litigation, entryism, and opposition research to help control its public image. However, during this period, we also start to see a shift in both society and the Church itself, as the capacity for the Internet to effortlessly proliferate information becomes apparent. As such, Scientology's early years on the Internet are marked by a fevered attempt to plug a bursting damn with aging materials, inadvertently creating further issues as its practices became common knowledge.

Unlike the more aggressive tactics seen during the Church of Scientology's attack on a.r.s, the Church's use of, and conflict with, the online encyclopedia Wikipedia has been somewhat more restrained. Indeed, the Church's "battle" with Wikipedia is, in many ways, indicative of the religion's renewed approach to perception management in a Web 2.0 environment. Rather than attempting to outright silence critics through censorship and litigation, the Church of Scientology looked to make use of Wikipedia's open editing policy to further control its online image and the outside perception of the religion's theological content. What we saw in Scientology's conflict with a.r.s was "tactical teething," the evolution of traditional approaches to perception management updated for a new, digital landscape. In contrast, the Church of Scientology's relationship with Wikipedia marked a subtle shift in its tactical approach, spurred by the proliferation of Web 2.0 and Internet-capable technology. It would seem that, during this period, the Church became wise to the limiting, and ultimately damaging, nature of traditional approaches in a digital landscape and, in its place, looked to focus more on controlling narratives through utilizing the digital medium itself. This is not to say that Scientology abandoned its use of litigation and opposition research; rather, it diversified the political tactics employed and, consequently, its whole approach to perception management.

As already indicated, the Church of Scientology's battle with Wikipedia was primarily about perceptions and the capacity of a private entity to control and manipulate them. The single largest repository of information in human history, Wikipedia is an unrestricted collaborative online encyclopedia.[26] The content of Wikipedia is written and edited by the people who use it, allowing it to be rapidly improved, updated, and contributed to. It was this open-editing policy that the Church looked to take advantage of in managing perceptions in the digital age.[27] As I have argued elsewhere, the Church of Scientology places great emphasis on distancing itself from its "cult-like" status.[28] However, its characterization as a cult stemmed from its implementation of several contentious practices, including the following: forced labor, brainwashing, and the excommunication of ex-members.[29] A new faith's capacity to influence and propagate is strengthened significantly by how it is perceived by the general public. By distancing itself from its cult-like status, the Church of Scientology has looked to legitimize itself to the general public and, in this sense, establish itself as a credible religion. Given that Wikipedia is one of the world's most popular websites and often the first port of call for those looking to be informed on a new subject, how it is portrayed there is of paramount importance. Indeed, the tactics and steps taken to legitimate itself throughout the previous 50 years would mean little if the Church could not undermine its characterization as a cult on the world's largest information hub.

Scientology's conflict with Wikipedia began in 2005 when an ongoing dispute arose concerning whether the Church should be categorized as a cult or a religion.[30] Over the next several years, entries pertaining to Scientology (both the set of religious beliefs itself and the Church of Scientology as an organization) became the center of heavy edits and debate. For example, according to Wikipedia's own revision history logs, during December 2005 alone, the primary entry on Scientology's teachings and practices was edited over 663 times.[31] In comparison, during the same period of time, the entry on Christianity was edited only 313 times.[32] Here, Gerard[33] argues that the page dedicated to proposed edits was populated by both critics and proponents alike, exchanging ideology back and forth over a common ground. As such, the high level of edits resulted in one of the most balanced and informative accounts of Scientology to be found anywhere in the Web. Here, the merging of critics and advocates in a common space, bound by Wikipedia's enforcement that a "neutral point of view" be taken when creating entries, resulted in the creation of an informative, and relatively unbiased, entry.

While the entry pertaining to Scientology itself was held in balance by critics and proponents alike, the religion looked to cement its belief structure through changes to other, not obviously related, entries. It wasn't until the development of the searchable database WikiScanner that the full extent of Scientology's editing of content became known. Consisting of 34.4 million edits linked to 190,000 organizations, WikiScanner allows for edits to be cross-referenced against the IP addresses of organizations, showcasing the online content management practices of companies.[34] Drawing up this data, Lischka et al.[35] found that between 2003 to 2007, 170 edits were made by

IP addresses associated with the Church of Scientology. In many of these cases, changes were discrete—limited to adding links to official Scientology sites or affiliated organizations. Lischka et al.[36] suggest that "Many of these (changes) relate to the so-called antipsychiatry movement and Scientology's idiosyncratic ideas about drug abuse and withdrawal." Edits were made to add subtle support to this belief, including a link to the Scientology-funded, antipsychiatric-based organization "Citizens Commission on Human Rights" (CCHR) on the profile page of deceased Nirvana front man and legendary pop culture figure, Kurt Cobain.[37]

After years of editing by the Church, and counteredits by its critics, Scientology's use of Wikipedia in the pursuit of perception management reached unprecedented heights. In 2009, Wikipedia's Arbitration Committee ruled in favor of restricting editing from IP addresses originating from Scientology organizations. It was found that multiple users with Scientology IP addresses were openly editing entries relating to its beliefs, practices, structures, practices, and organization. Indeed, user accounts were created with the sole purpose of perception management, a practice counter to Wikipedia's pursuit of neutrality.[38] These changes were found to involve deleting negative references and criticism and replacing them with content and links that showed the Church in a positive light. These changes occurred so frequently, and at such high volume, that the Wikipedia administrators were unable to effectively monitor and manage them. While individuals had been banned from making edits previously, this marked the first time that an entire organization was restricted from contributing. Jay Walsh,[39] a spokesman for the Wikimedia Foundation, argued that the ban was, at its core, about enforcing a "neutral point of view." As if to support this, numerous anti-Scientology advocates, who countered the Church's editing with opposing material, were similarly banned from contributing to Scientology-specific topics. The arbitration committee established "the apparent presence of notable critics of Scientology, from several Internet organisations . . . editing under their own names and citing either their own or each other's self-published material."[40] In this way, both parties in this longstanding battle were found to be editing content not in the pursuit of neutrality but rather to establish the validity of their preferred ideological position.

Along with its battles with a.r.s and Anonymous, which we will cover next, the Church of Scientology's conflict with Wikipedia marked a significant development in its pursuit of perception management. Adjusting to the digitalization of society, Scientology's use of Wikipedia to help control its public image and theological interpretation highlights the evolution of religious-based political tactics. This evolution will be explored in greater depth later in this chapter. However, first I briefly explore a number of smaller examples of Scientology engaging digital targets. While these cases are narrower, they are no less important as they help paint a broader picture of tactical evolution and of perception management.

In 2008, the Church of Scientology's editing and censoring practices drew the attention of the decentralized virtual community Anonymous.[41] Known for broadly pursuing the notion of "freedom of information," Anonymous launched a campaign aimed at limiting the Church's capacity to manipulate its public perception. Dubbed "Project Chanology," the campaign grew as a direct response to the Church's attempt to remove a religious promotional video featuring actor (and prominent member) Tom Cruise from the Internet.[42] Although this campaign related thematically to the Church's conflict with Wikipedia, it was pursued as a wholly separate issue.

To the political participation literature, Anonymous speaks to the current arguments on the granular nature of sociotechnical environments.[43] Anonymous promotes collaborative action platforms, where differentiated modes of engagement are pursued alongside each other. Consequently, notions of identity are challenged as Anonymous employs a horizontal leadership structure by having all of its participants adopt a collective pseudonym. In this way, Anonymous is both a decentralized virtual community and an identity adopted by its agents, empowered to pursue differentiated political and social campaigns. This faceless mass of online collaboration saw the birth of the 2008–2009 anti-Scientology social movement, Project Chanology.

Following reports that the Church of Scientology harassed ex-members of the religion and those who openly opposed its operations, Anonymous saw an opportunity to pursue its own unique brand of entertainment. In its earlier years, specifically from 2005 to 2007, Anonymous was more concerned with the act of "trolling" than with moralistic crusades.[44] Trolling (or "griefing," in this context) is the act of purposefully causing anguish to members of an online community with the intended outcome the entertainment of the propagator.[45] With Scientology, Anonymous was presented with an adversary that would react if provoked, a temptation too strong to resist given its predilection for such conflict.[46] The first step was to construct a false public image, one that would serve as a decoy, hiding the true intention of the attacks. This would help frame the collective as an online activist group with a moralistic agenda, rather than one orchestrating hate crimes, an angle that the Church of Scientology could use to its advantage in retaliating. Underwood[47] argues that Anonymous portrayed itself as "an altruistic group fighting for human rights and freedom of speech." rather than an "online group that revelled in a dark sense of humour." Hoping that the attacks would draw the attention of the international media, Anonymous saw its constructed public image as an elaborate joke, one that only the insiders would ultimately "get."[48]

The Church's push for the removal of the leaked Tom Cruise video in 2008 served as the perfect masthead for the operation. According to the Church, the video was not meant for public distribution and that it had a right to recall what it considered a religious document. Anonymous framed the Church's push to take down the video as a violation of its pursuit for the freedom of information. Anonymous's participants created a press release, stating that the Church's enforcement of censorship went against the collective's "moralist principles" and that information should be freely accessible.[49]

On January 14, 2008, Anonymous initiated Project Chanology with a series of DDoS attacks against the Church of Scientology. While these attacks were successful in their intended purpose, Anonymous received negative criticism from existing anti-Scientology groups, suggesting that the aggressive nature of the tactics hurt its cause more than it helped. Following a plea from anti-Scientologist Mark Bunker, Anonymous ceased its DDoS attacks and began to work on orchestrating live protests.[50] On January 21 Anonymous uploaded the YouTube video *Message to Scientology* along with a press release entitled *War on Scientology*. It stated that the enforcement of copyright and trademark laws in the pursuit of Scientology's own agenda subverted the freedom speech and created an inability to speak out against the organization. Following this, Anonymous declared that it would "destroy" the Church of Scientology and its ability to function online. A video entitled *Call to Action* was posted on January 28, outlining dates and procedures in what would be Anonymous's first attempt to orchestrate mass participation outside of its virtual setting. Prior to the set date, "test runs" on January 26 and February 2 saw 150 Anonymous participants protest outside the Church of Scientology center in Orlando, with similar, yet smaller demonstrations held in Santa Barbara and Manchester.[51] Underwood describes these initial protests as "flash mobs." Flash mobs are understood as groups of people who converge on a designated area for a brief time, engage in an unusual act (e.g., pillow fight), and then quickly disperse. The purpose is often entertainment and or satire. The protests that soon followed, however, grew well beyond this, developing into a fully realized social movement.

On February 10, 7,000 people protested outside of Scientology centers in more than 93 cities worldwide. A subsequent demonstration was held on the March 15, with the number estimated to be between 7,000 and 8,000, similar in size to the first wave.[52] During early protests, specifically the initial demonstrations on January 26 and February 2, participants wore scarfs and gas masks to ensure that their identity remained anonymous. During the latter protests, various Anonymous communities adopted the "Guy Fawkes" mask as an unofficial symbol of the collective, inspired by the film (and the graphic novel to a lesser degree) *V for Vendetta*. Proliferated through subsequent protests, the symbol is now synonymous with Anonymous as a community. As

anticipated, the progression of Project Chanology resulted in media attention on an international scale. Latching onto the created persona, the media
framed Anonymous as a "loose knit community of cyber hackers" who fought
for freedom of information and anticensorship ideals. Following the February
10 demonstrations, the constructed public image was firmly ingrained within
the global perception.[53] Ironically, the manufactured identity worked too
well and Anonymous-inspired message boards were soon inundated with new
"members," all looking to contribute to the fight against Scientology.

Google. In 2002, the Church of Scientology, drawing upon provisions outlined in the DMCA, forced the Internet search engine Google to remove
links to the anti-Scientology website Xenu.net (also known as *Operation
Clambake*).[54] Claiming that the sites housed copyrighted material, and in this
way promoted copyright infringement, the Church of Scientology effectively
removed the websites from the Internet by making its content nearly inac-
cessible to the general public. This removal was later reversed after a public
outcry and complaints from freedom of speech activists.

More recently, the Church has used Google itself to help mitigate the
impact of the highly critical film, *Going Clear: Scientology and the Prison of
Belief.* Following the release of the film, the Church purchased ad space on
both Twitter and Google, with the link directing individuals to FreedomMag.
org, the Church of Scientology's in-house magazine.[55] Under the guise of an
impartial site, the hyperlink redirects the user to an article that refutes the
claims made in the documentary and attacks the credibility of those involved.

WikiLeaks. The Church of Scientology's brief interaction with the journalistic website, WikiLeaks, highlights the diminished efficacy of traditional
tactical approaches to perception management in the digital environment
and, consequently, the capacity of that environment to resist censorship.
On March 24, 2008, WikiLeaks posted what it termed "the collected secret
'bibles' of Scientology."[56] What it had released was the typed and handwrit-
ten pages of Church founder L. Ron Hubbard detailing Operating Thetan
levels I to VIII and related New Era Dianetics for OTs (NOTs). Provided
by breakaway Scientology "Freezoners," it represented the first time that full
details of OT levels had been released to the public. Citing U.S. Copyright
Act, 17 U.S.C. §106, the Church of Scientology threatened WikiLeaks with
legal action if the unpublished, copyrighted, Scientology documents were not
removed. WikiLeaks promptly refused, stating:

> Wikileaks will remain a place where people of the world may safely
> expose injustice and corruption. Indeed, in response to the attempted
> suppression, Wikileaks will release several thousand pages of additional
> Scientology materials next week.[57]

True to its word, WikiLeaks proceeded to release a plethora of additional information over the next several years. To date (mid-2015), WikiLeaks hosts 110 leaked Scientology documents, including: religious and business practices, legal files, and financial records. WikiLeaks continues to do so without fear of legal reprisal.

This case is significant as it clearly highlights the limitations of the Church of Scientology's traditional litigation-based approach in the face of a decentralized digital platform. As the Internet gives way to diffused engagement networks through the condensing of centrality and legal sovereignty, methods of information control and mitigation are undermined. It is this idea that the chapter now explores, as it considers the Church of Scientology's use of approach to perception management in an increasingly digital society.

THE EVOLUTION OF PERCEPTION MANAGEMENT

As has been established, the Church of Scientology needs to control how it is perceived by the public, both to further its characterization as a legitimate religion and, in this, to strengthen its profit-centric model that fuels its operations.[58] A negative public perception undermines these goals, weakening their operational capacity and significance in the public realm. Perception management has been a core component of the Church of Scientology's operational agenda since its inception and continues as Scientology looks to normalize its beliefs and practices to a point where emerging criticism is dulled or largely negated by public acceptance. This process involves a shift from cult to new faith to mainstream religion.[59] I argue that the Church of Scientology's approach to this process of perception management has changed significantly since the inception of the Internet, with the emergence of Web 2.0 applications and the streamlining of user-end processes. At its core, perception management involves the management of resource flows and the ability to moderate the interpretation of belief and practice.[60] The Internet has fundamentally altered resource flows and the way in which actors and structures distribute, aggregate, and consume them. This, in turn, has required the Church of Scientology to change the way in which it manages its public image.

We can effectively separate the Church of Scientology's approach to perception management into three periods: traditional (1967–1990), transitional (1990–2000), and contemporary (2000 to the present). As I have argued elsewhere,[61] in the "traditional" period the Church of Scientology was largely driven by a desire to reacquire its tax-exempt status in the United States of America. The transition from cult-like status to mainstream religion relies on both legal recognition and public legitimacy. Both public legitimacy and legal recognition are imbedded; each one strengthens the other. For the public, legal recognition achieved through satisfying §501(c)(3) of the Internal Revenue Service serves as a marker for religious authenticity. Similarly, in this process of legitimatization through legal recognition (read: tax exemption), a new faith's legal recognition is tied to its public perception. During this period, the Church of Scientology was able to alleviate much of the negative publicity surrounding its practices through the heavy use of litigation, entryism, and opposition research. In controlling this outward image, the Church was better able to promote itself as a genuine religion and distance itself from its lingering cult-like status. However, the Church's ability to do so relied on relatively limited channels of resource flows, bounded by limiting factors such as time, space, and identity. Here, the aggressive tactics employed were strengthened by the limited capacity of the layperson to resist them. However, by early 1990s and the popularization of digital environments, the layperson was empowered through broader communication networks and new avenues for the aggregation of marginalized opinion.

The Church of Scientology's approach to perception management during this period should be understood as transitional in so much as the tactics employed reflected a digitalization of traditional approaches, coupled with a desire to continue with "business as normal." The Church's battle with a.r.s is indicative of this approach. Still relying heavily on litigation, the Church attempted to censor the spread and distribution of information much in the same way as it had in during its traditional period. However, the Church of Scientology's heavy-handed approach to censorship during this period led to the inadvertent proliferation of the amended material. This process has since been referred to as the "Streisand Effect," referring to a similar situation where singer Barbra Streisand attempted to have aerial photos of her home removed from the Internet.[62] As Jansen and Martin[63] contend, "the Streisand case triggered awareness of analogous instances in which attempts to suppress information had the unintended consequence of stimulating greater demand for information than would have occurred if no action had been taken." Prior to this request, the photos in question had only been viewed a handful of times. However, the pursuit of censorship led to an increase in attention, with individuals purposefully seeking out and distributing the photos, purely because they were told that it was not allowed. Indeed, its subsequent proliferation resulted in it being downloaded over 420,000 times within a month. The Church of Scientology's attempt to limit the distribution of the OT documents resulted in a similar propagation—effectively increasing the public's interest in the content. Such was the level of distribution that they became a mainstay in popular culture; the pinnacle of which was the TV show *South Park*'s infamous sketch on the Xenu story. The presence of the

Streisand Effect in this case highlights the diminished efficacy of traditional censorship tactics in more fluid, sociotechnical environments.

During the transitional period, the Church of Scientology's diminished capacity to control the flow of information, coupled with an overreliance on more aggressive, traditional tactics for perception management, resulted in increased criticisms and erosion of public legitimacy.[64] The level of theological acceptance that the Church had worked so tirelessly to establish during its traditional period was effectively reset as its heavy-handed approach to censorship and perception management thrust them into the public eye in a negative and critical light. Interestingly though, we can observe a foreshadowing of the Church's tactical evolution in Elaine Siegel's introduction of astroturfing tactics in 1994.[65] Here, rather than countering public forum criticism via a direct, and ultimately, detrimental approach, the Church looked to control the emerging narrative by fragmenting the conversation with overwhelming alternative, positive content. While the effectiveness of this approach was lessened by the Church's own introduction of the Streisand Effect, it does highlight the willingness of the organization to widen the modes of engagement they employed to better suit the changing environment.

The Church of Scientology's "contemporary" period coincides with the advent of Web 2.0, and demonstrates an evolution in the organization's tactical repertoire. While the traditional and transitional periods saw the Church rely heavily on litigation and censorship claims in the pursuit of perception management, the Internet's effect on society, and the manner in which resource flows have developed, have seen an analogous development in both tactics and approach. Rather than attempting to control its public image through force or mitigate criticism through censorship, the Church of Scientology looked to "normalize" its beliefs and practices by rationalizing them and, consequently, bringing them closer in line with similar mainstream doctoral claims.[66] That is, the Church of Scientology looked to control the narrative that emerged rather than the person who was telling it. The Church's editing of Wikipedia is the most telling example here. As the Wikiscanner uncovered, the Church of Scientology made a concerted effort to insert elements of its belief structure and practices into seemingly unrelated articles. Here, theological legitimacy was pursued in much the same way as in the traditional period's use of entryism—normalizing contentious belief by introducing rationality into areas of, or near, significance.

We can draw similarities between the Church's approach to narrative control in the contemporary period and the use of "storytelling" as a political tactic by advocacy groups. To Vromen and Coleman,[67] storytelling is a tactic that looks to create shared experiences by persuading the target audience to move from a "story of self" to a "story of us." While Vromen and Coleman

speak about storytelling in a context unrelated to religious perception management, the intent behind the tactic itself is the same. Storytelling, as a
narrative device, influences debates by personalizing content through the
transformation of private narratives into public rationales.[68] Consider, for
example, Wikipedia's Arbitration Committee restriction of Scientology IP
addresses. The decision was ultimately reached in response to the Church's
evident abuse of the site's self-editing function. However, in the pursuit of
a "neutral point of view," the Committee also banned a number of prolific
anti-Scientology critics. The Church refocused this narrative as a win for
the religion and, ultimately, a positive. As such, Scientology spokeswoman
Karin Pouw stated, "Wikipedia finally banned those who were engaged in
unobjective and biased editing for the purposes of antagonism as opposed
to providing accurate information."[69] In this retold narrative, Scientology
is the victim of religious persecution, and any "wrongdoing" by the Church
was the pursuit of neutral and factual representation. By rationalizing it as
such, the laypersons can sympathize with the Church's struggle for equality,
shifting the narrative in the religion's favor.

The Church of Scientology's approach to narrative control and storytelling in the contemporary period can also be seen as drawing heavily upon
"half-truths" and propaganda organizations. The Church often establishes
organizations, websites, and content providers that to the layperson appear
impartial but are, in fact, agents of the Church itself. The Citizens Commission on Human Rights International (CCHR) is an excellent example.
The name itself implies a level of legitimacy, and, in its mission statement, it
claims to be "a non-profit, non-political, non-religious mental health watchdog."[70] The manner in which it presents itself is not unlike the Centre for
Human Rights and Humanitarian Law or the International Federation for
Human Rights. However, unlike these organizations, the CCHR is a supported by the Church of Scientology and granted tax exemption as part of the
Church's International and Religious Technology Center.[71] This is similar to
the Church's creation of FreedomMag.org, a seemingly independent magazine used to rebuke the critical film, *Going Clear*. Platforms such as CCHR
or FreedomMag are effective vehicles for storytelling and narrative control.
Their names and professed impartiality are intentional devices employed to
help establish an outward image of legitimacy independent from the Church
of Scientology itself. Here, contentious content can be streamlined and
remolded so that criticism (a story of self) can develop into public rationales
(a story of us).

The Church of Scientology has had a history of employing propaganda
organizations in the pursuit of narrative control. Most notable was its purchase of the Cult Awareness Network in 1996.[72] One of the religion's most

vocal critics, the Church forced the organization to close through the use of tactical litigation, specifically SLAPP-like behavior.[73] Following the network's closure, the Church of Scientology bought a number of its assets and staffed the organization with its own members.[74] However, the capacity of the Church of Scientology to use propaganda organizations has increased significantly with the Internet's conflation of identity. We now find that the visible face of both structures and agents alike is highly malleable, allowing for the creation of personas, false fronts, and, consequently, anonymity.[75] In this way, Web 2.0 platforms enable religious organizations such as the Church of Scientology to more easily influence opinion and perception through the manipulation of its own online identity. While paper trails always exist, it requires a high level of reflexivity and critical awareness to uncover them. Given the passive nature of the general Internet-browsing culture,[76] the Internet effectively expands the tactical repertoire available to new religions in the pursuit of perception management by allowing them to hide their influence, agenda, and intent.

CONCLUSION

As this chapter has highlighted, the introduction of the Internet initially limited the Church's capacity to mitigate disapproval and silence critics. Here, the combination of increased resource flows and the development of loose, decentralized, information networks weakened the Church's ability to control how its practices were perceived by the public. Continuing with heavy-handed, aggressive traditional approaches to perception management, the Church opened itself up to further ridicule. Its fevered quest for content censorship served to undermine its operations as it brought about the Streisand Effect. Yet, as the Internet developed, so too did the Church of Scientology's understanding of how it functioned and how best to capitalize upon it. Moving away from traditional approaches, the Church of Scientology employed more nuanced tactics, relying more heavily on controlling the narratives that emerged rather than silencing the messenger. In this way, the Church looks to repair the damage suffered during the transitional period through the use of storytelling devices, rationalizing both religious and organization practices to appeal to the layperson.

The Church of Scientology continues to be a source of great interest as it presents a unique opportunity to witness firsthand how new religions adapt to significant societal change. By following the Church of Scientology's approach to perception management from traditional to contemporary periods, we gain a better understanding about how new faiths strive for public legitimacy and the normalization of belief and practice. As society enters its next period of technological development, we must take note of how the Church of Scientology adapts to change and what practices it employs in the pursuit of public legitimization.

NOTES

1. Michael Peckham, "New Dimensions of Social Movement/Countermovement Interaction: The Case of Scientology and Its Internet Critics," *Canadian Journal of Sociology/Cahiers canadiens de sociologie* 23, no. 4 (1998): 317–147.

2. Max Halupka, "The Church of Scientology: Legitimacy through Perception Management," *Politics and Religion* 7, no. 3 (2014): 613–630.

3. Ibid.

4. Jim Lippard and Jeff Jacobsen, "Scientology v. the Internet: Free Speech & Copyright Infringement on the Information Super-Highway," *Skeptic* 3, no. 3 (1995): 35–41.

5. Wes Finley-Price, "Wikipedia Bans Church of Scientology," *SciTechBlog*, http://scitech.blogs.cnn.com/2009/05/29/wikipedia-bans-church-of-scientology/.

6. Cade Metz, "Scientology Threatens Wikileaks with Injunction," http://www.theregister.co.uk/2008/04/08/church_of_scientology_contacts_wikileaks/.

7. Dave Lee, "How Scientology Changed the Internet," http://www.bbc.com/news/technology-23273109.

8. Zubair Nabi, "Resistance Censorship Is Futile," *First Monday* 19, no. 11 (2014).

9. Stephen A. Kent, "The French and German versus American Debate over 'New Religions,' Scientology, and Human Rights," *Marburg Journal of Religion* 6, no. 1 (2001): 1–11.

10. Henrik P. Bang, "'Yes We Can': Identity Politics and Project Politics for a Late-Modern World," *Urban Research & Practice* 2, no. 2 (2009): 117–137.

11. J. Gordon Melton, "Birth of a Religion," in *Scientology* (2009): 17; Marsh, David, Paul 't Hart, and Karen Tindall, "Celebrity Politics: The Politics of the Late Modernity?" *Political Studies Review* 8, no. 3 (2010): 322–340; Bang, Henrik P., and Eva Sørensen, "The Everyday Maker: A New Challenge to Democratic Governance," *Administrative Theory & Praxis* (1999): 325–341.

12. Michael J. Jensen and Henrik P. Bang, "Occupy Wall Street: A New Political Form of Movement and Community?" *Journal of Information Technology & Politics* 10, no. 4 (2013): 444–461.

13. Andrew Chadwick, "Recent Shifts in the Relationship between the Internet and Democratic Engagement in Britain and the United States: Granularity, Informational Exuberance, and Political Learning," in *Digital Media and Political Engagement Worldwide: A Comparative Study* (2012): 39–55.

14. W. Lance Bennett and Alexandra Segerberg, *The Logic of Connective Action: Digital Media and the Personalization of Contentious Politics*, Cambridge: Cambridge University Press, 2013.

15. Henrik P. Bang, "The Politics of Threats: Late-Modern Politics in the Shadow of Neoliberalism," *Critical Policy Studies* 5, no. 4 (2011): 434–448.

16. Nikos Passas and Manuel Escamilla Castillo, "Scientology and Its 'Clear' Business," *Behavioral Sciences & the Law* 10, no. 1 (1992): 103–116.

17. Kate Starbird, Grace Muzny, and Leysia Palen, "Learning from the Crowd: Collaborative Filtering Techniques for Identifying on-the-Ground Twitterers during Mass Disruptions," *Proceedings of ISCRAM* (2012): 1–10.

18. Max Halupka, "The Church of Scientology."

19. Jim Lippard and Jeff Jacobsen, "Scientology v. the Internet."

20. Ibid.

21. Lam Nguyen, "Virginia Man's Computer Seized in Internet Lawsuit," *Washington Post*, August 13, 1995; Peckham, Michael, "New Dimensions of Social Movement/Countermovement Interaction."

22. Hugh B. Urban, "Fair Game: Secrecy, Security, and the Church of Scientology in Cold War America," *Journal of the American Academy of Religion* 74, no. 2 (2006): 356–389.

23. Theresa A. Lyons, "Scientology or Censorship: You Decide: An Examination of the Church of Scientology, Its Recent Battles with Individual Internet Users and Service Providers, the Digital Millennium Copyright Act, and the Implications for Free Speech on the Web," *Rutgers Journal of Law & Religion* 2 (2000): 1–6; and Doherty, Davis, "Downloading Infringement: Patent Law as a Roadblock to the 3d Printing Revolution," *Harvard Journal of Law & Technology* 26 (2012): 353.

24. Theresa A. Lyons, "Scientology or Censorship: You Decide."

25. Marc Hooghe, Bengü Hosch-Dayican, and Jan W. van Deth, "Conceptualizing Political Participation," *Acta Politica* 49, no. 3 (2014): 337–348.

26. Jaap Kamps and Marijn Koolen, "Is Wikipedia Link Structure Different?" Paper presented at the Second International ACM Conference on Web Search and Data Mining, 2009.

27. Ryan Singel, "Wikipedia Bans Church of Scientology," *Wired.com*, May 29, 2009.

28. Max Halupka, "The Church of Scientology."

29. Stephen A. Kent, "Scientology—Is This a Religion?" *Marburg Journal of Religion* 4, no. 1 (1999): 1–23.

30. Jonathan Zittrain, *The Future of the Internet—and How to Stop It*. Yale University Press, 2008.

31. Wikipedia, "Scientology: Revision History," *Wikipedia*, https://en.wikipedia.org/w/index.php?title=Scientology&offset=20060101000000&limit=500&action=history&tagfilter=.

32. Wikipedia, "Christianity: Revision History," *Wikipedia*, https://en.wikipedia.org/w/index.php?title=Christianity&offset=20060101000000&limit=500&action=history&tagfilter=.

33. Mick Brown, "Wiki's World," *Telegraph*, http://www.telegraph.co.uk/culture/3656157/Wikis-world.html.

34. Emily Biuso, "Wikiscanning," *New York Times Magazine*, December 9, 2007, http://www.nytimes.com/2007/12/09/magazine/09wikiscanning.html.

35. Konrad Lischka, Frank Patalong, and Christian Stocker, "Netz-Lexikon: Wiki-Scanner spürt Manipulationen auf," http://www.spiegel.de/netzwelt/web/netz-lexikon-wiki-scanner-spuert-manipulationen-auf-a-500163-5.html.

36. Ibid., 5.

37. Kurt Cobain, an American musician, is best known as the front man for the grunge band Nirvana. A hugely popular and influential figure in popular culture, Cobain died in 1994 of suicide. Having no affiliation with the Church of Scientology prior to his death, the placement of the CCHR in his profile page was the religion's attempt at drawing connections between his suicide and their beliefs about drug abuse and withdrawal.

38. Marisa Taylor, "Wikipedia Bans Scientology Church's Edits," *Wall Street Journal*, http://blogs.wsj.com/digits/2009/06/01/wikipedia-bans-scientology-churchs-edits/.

39. Wikipedia, "Wikipedia:Requests for Arbitration/Scientology," *Wikipedia*, https://en.wikipedia.org/wiki/Wikipedia:Requests_for_arbitration/Scientology.

40. Ibid.

41. Patrick Underwood and Howard T. Welser, "'The Internet Is Here': Emergent Coordination and Innovation of Protest Forms in Digital Culture," in *Proceedings of the 2011 iConference*, 2011.

42. Max Halupka, *The Evolution of Anonymous as a Political Actor*, Flinders University: South Australia, 2012.

43. Max Halupka, "What Anonymous Can Tell Us about the Relationship between Virtual Community Structure and Participatory Form," *Policy Studies* (2016).

44. Patrick Underwood and Howard T. Welser, "'The Internet Is Here.'"

45. Gabriella Coleman, "Hackers and Trollers as Tricksters," *Social Text*, 2010.

46. Patrick C. Underwood, "New Directions in Networked Activism and Online Social Movement Mobilization: The Case of Anonymous and Project Chanology," Ohio University, 2009.

47. Ibid., 156.

48. Gabriella Coleman, *Hacker, Hoaxer, Whistleblower, Spy: The Many Faces of Anonymous*, Verso Books, 2014.

49. Max Halupka and Cassandra Star, "The Utilisation of Direct Democracy and Meritocracy in the Decision Making Process of the Decentralised Virtual Community Anonymous," Paper presented at the Australian Political Studies Association Conference, Australian National University, Canberra, 2011.

50. Mark Bunker, "About Anonymous," *Xenu TV*, http://www.xenutv.com/blog/?page_id=3132.

51. Chris Landers, "Serious Business: Anonymous Takes on Scientology (and Doesn't Afraid of Anything)," *City Paper*, 2008, 8.

52. D. C. Elliott, "Anonymous Rising," in *Linq*, edited by Lindsay Simpson and Victoria Kuttainen, Townsville: Department of Humanities, School of Arts and Social Sciences James Cook University, 2009.

53. Max Halupka, *The Evolution of Anonymous*.

54. Evan Hansen, "Google Pulls Anti-Scientology Links," http://www.cnet.com/news/google-pulls-anti-scientology-links/.

55. Jacob Siegel, "Scientology's Sneaky Google Ads Slam HBO Documentary?" http://www.thedailybeast.com/articles/2015/03/23/scientology-s-sneaky-ads-slam-critics.html.

56. WikiLeaks, "Church of Scientology Collected Operating Thetan Documents," https://wikileaks.org/wiki/Church_of_Scientology_collected_Operating_Thetan_documents.

57. WikiLeaks, "Scientology Threatens Wikileaks over Secret Cult Bibles," *WikiLeaks*, https://wikileaks.org/wiki/Scientology_threatens_Wikileaks_over_secret_cult_bibles.

58. Nikos Passas and Manuel Escamilla Castillo, "Scientology and Its 'Clear' Business."

59. Anson Shupe, "The Nature of the New Religious Movements–Anticult 'Culture War' in Microcosm: The Church of Scientology versus the Cult Awareness Network," in *Scientology*, edited by James R. Lewis, 269–282, Oxford University Press, 2009.

60. C. Kopp, "Classical Deception Techniques and Perception Management vs. The Four Strategies of Information Warfare," in *Proceedings of the 6th Australian Information Warfare and Security Conference*, Monash University, 2005; Siegel, Pascale Combelles, "Perception Management: IO's Stepchild?" *Low Intensity Conflict & Law Enforcement* 13, no. 2 (2005): 117–134; Godlewski, R. J., "Practical Deception and Perception Management," *Tactical Extractions Counterterrorism Paper* (2010), http://www.rjgodlewski.com/PracticalDeceptionAndPerceptionManagementByRJGodlewskiTACTICALEXTRACTIONSSecurityPaper42010.pdf.

61. Max Halupka, "The Church of Scientology."

62. Zubair Nabi, "Resistance Censorship Is Futile."

63. Sue Curry Jansen and Brian Martin, "The Streisand Effect and Censorship Backfire," (2015): 657.

64. Derek H. Davis, "The Church of Scientology: In Pursuit of Legal Recognition," paper presented at the Cesnur 2004 International Conference, Baylor University, Waco, Texas, 2004; Kumar, J. P., "'Fair Game': Leveling the Playing Field in Scientology Litigation," *Review of Litigation* 16 (1997): 747–772.

65. Caroline W. Lee, "The Roots of Astroturfing," (2010); Cho, Charles H., Martin L. Martens, Hakkyun Kim, and Michelle Rodrigue, "Astroturfing Global Warming: It Isn't Always Greener on the Other Side of the Fence," *Journal of Business Ethics* 104, no. 4 (2011): 571–587.

66. This is not to say that the Church of Scientology has completely forgone the legal-based approach employed in earlier periods. Indeed, its pioneering of Digital Millennium Copyright Act, as outlined earlier, highlights its continued commitment to pursuit of copyright law across platforms.

67. Ariadne Vromen and William Coleman, "Online Campaigning Organizations and Storytelling Strategies: Getup! In Australia," *Policy & Internet* 5, no. 1 (2013): 76–100.

68. Ibid., 76.
69. Wikipedia, "Scientology: Revision History."
70. CCHR, " About Us," *CCHR*, http://www.cchrint.org/about-us/.
71. See §III.4-5, Service Determinations Regarding Scientology-Related Entities, CoS / IRS Closing Agreement.
72. Carol Giambalvo, Michael Kropveld, and Michael Langone, "Changes in the North American Cult Awareness Organizations," in *Revisionism and Diversification in New Religious Movements* (2013): 227–46.
73. SLAPP stands for "strategic lawsuit against public participation." SLAPPs, legally, masquerade as ordinary lawsuits. They act as counterattacks, draining the target's resources and diverting the original issue. Individuals or organizations coming up against a multimillion-dollar SLAPP suit are prone either to retreat or to commit finite resources to an uphill battle.
74. Stephen A. Kent, "The Globalization of Scientology: Influence, Control, and Opposition in Transnational Markets," *Religion* 29, no. 2 (1998): 147–169.
75. Michael D. Ayers, "Comparing Collective Identity in Online and Offline Feminist Activists," in *Cyberactivism: Online Activism in Theory and Practice*, edited by Martha McCaughey and Michael D. Ayers. Routledge, 2003.
76. Esharenana E. Adomi, "Overnight Internet Browsing Among Cyber Café Users in Abraka, Nigeria," *Journal of Community Informatics* 3, no. 2 (2007).

BIBLIOGRAPHY

Adomi, Esharenana E. "Overnight Internet Browsing Among Cyber Café Users in Abraka, Nigeria." *Journal of Community Informatics* 3, no. 2 (2007).
Ayers, Michael D. "Comparing Collective Identity in Online and Offline Feminist Activists." In *Cyberactivism: Online Activism in Theory and Practice*, edited by Martha McCaughey and Michael D. Ayers, Routledge, 2003.
Bang, Henrik P. "The Politics of Threats: Late-Modern Politics in the Shadow of Neoliberalism." *Critical Policy Studies* 5, no. 4 (2011): 434–448.
Bang, Henrik P. "'Yes We Can': Identity Politics and Project Politics for a Late-Modern World." *Urban Research & Practice* 2, no. 2 (2009): 117–137.
Bang, Henrik P., and Eva Sørensen. "The Everyday Maker: A New Challenge to Democratic Governance." *Administrative Theory & Praxis* (1999): 325–341.
Bennett, W. Lance, and Alexandra Segerberg. *The Logic of Connective Action: Digital Media and the Personalization of Contentious Politics*, Cambridge University Press, 2013.
Biuso, Emily. "Wikiscanning." *New York Times Magazine*. December 9, 2007. http://www.nytimes.com/2007/12/09/magazine/09wikiscanning.html.
Brown, Mick. "Wiki's World." *Telegraph*. http://www.telegraph.co.uk/culture/3656157/Wikis-world.html.
Bunker, Mark. "About Anonymous." *Xenu TV*. http://www.xenutv.com/blog/?page_id=3132.
CCHR. "About Us." *CCHR*. http://www.cchrint.org/about-us/.

Chadwick, Andrew. "Recent Shifts in the Relationship between the Internet and Democratic Engagement in Britain and the United States: Granularity, Informational Exuberance, and Political Learning." In *Digital Media and Political Engagement Worldwide: A Comparative Study.* 2012, 39–55.

Cho, Charles H., Martin L. Martens, Hakkyun Kim, and Michelle Rodrigue. "Astroturfing Global Warming: It Isn't Always Greener on the Other Side of the Fence." *Journal of Business Ethics* 104, no. 4 (2011): 571–587.

Coleman, Gabriella. *Hacker, Hoaxer, Whistleblower, Spy: The Many Faces of Anonymous.* Verso Books, 2014.

Coleman, Gabriella. "Hackers and Trollers as Trickster." *Social Text,* 2010.

Davis, Derek H. "The Church of Scientology: In Pursuit of Legal Recognition." Paper presented at the Cesnur 2004 International Conference. Baylor University, Waco, Texas, 2004.

Doherty, Davis. "Downloading Infringement: Patent Law as a Roadblock to the 3d Printing Revolution." *Harvard Journal of Law & Technology* 26 (2012): 353.

Elliott, D. C. "Anonymous Rising." In *Linq,* edited by Lindsay Simpson and Victoria Kuttainen. Townsville: Department of Humanities, School of Arts and Social Sciences James Cook University, 2009.

Finley-Price, Wes. "Wikipedia Bans Church of Scientology." *SciTechBlog.* http://scitech.blogs.cnn.com/2009/05/29/wikipedia-bans-church-of-scientology/.

Giambalvo, Carol, Michael Kropveld, and Michael Langone. "Changes in the North American Cult Awareness Organizations." In *Revisionism and Diversification in New Religious Movements.* 2013, 227–46.

Godlewski, R. J. "Practical Deception and Perception Management." *Tactical Extractions Counterterrorism Paper* (2010). http://www.rjgodlewski.com/PracticalDeceptionAndPerceptionManagementByRJGodlewskiTACTICALEXTRACTIONSSecurityPaper42010.pdf.

Halupka, Max. "The Church of Scientology: Legitimacy through Perception Management." *Politics and Religion* 7, no. 3 (2014): 613–630.

Halupka, Max. *The Evolution of Anonymous as a Political Actor.* Flinders University: South Australia, 2012.

Halupka, Max. "What Anonymous Can Tell Us about the Relationship between Virtual Community Structure and Participatory Form." *Policy Studies* (2016).

Halupka, Max, and Cassandra Star. "The Utilisation of Direct Democracy and Meritocracy in the Decision Making Process of the Decentralised Virtual Community Anonymous." Paper presented at the Australian Political Studies Association Conference. Australian National University, Canberra, 2011.

Hansen, Evan. "Google Pulls Anti-Scientology Links." http://www.cnet.com/news/google-pulls-anti-scientology-links/.

Hooghe, Marc, Bengü Hosch-Dayican, and Jan W. van Deth. "Conceptualizing Political Participation." *Acta Politica* 49, no. 3 (2014): 337–348.

Jansen, Sue Curry, and Brian Martin. "The Streisand Effect and Censorship Backfire." (2015).

Jensen, Michael J., and Henrik P. Bang. "Occupy Wall Street: A New Political Form of Movement and Community?" *Journal of Information Technology & Politics* 10, no. 4 (2013): 444–461.

Kamps, Jaap, and Marijn Koolen. "Is Wikipedia Link Structure Different?" Paper presented at the Second ACM International Conference on Web Search and Data Mining. 2009.

Kent, Stephen A. "The French and German versus American Debate Over 'New Religions,' Scientology, and Human Rights." *Marburg Journal of Religion* 6, no. 1 (Month 2001): 1–11.

Kent, Stephen A. "The Globalization of Scientology: Influence, Control, and Opposition in Transnational Markets." *Religion* 29, no. 2 (1998): 147–169.

Kent, Stephen A. "Scientology—Is This a Religion?" *Marburg Journal of Religion* 4, no. 1 (1999): 1–23.

Kopp, C. "Classical Deception Techniques and Perception Management vs. The Four Strategies of Information Warfare." In *Proceedings of the 6th Australian Information Warfare and Security Conference*, Monash University, 2005.

Kumar, J. P. "'Fair Game': Leveling the Playing Field in Scientology Litigation." *Review of Litigation* 16 (1997): 747–772.

Landers, Chris. "Serious Business: Anonymous Takes on Scientology (and Doesn't Afraid of Anything)." *City Paper*, 2008, 8.

Lee, Caroline W. "The Roots of Astroturfing." (2010).

Lee, Dave. "How Scientology Changed the Internet." http://www.bbc.com/news /technology-23273109.

Lippard, Jim, and Jeff Jacobsen. "Scientology v. the Internet: Free Speech & Copyright Infringement on the Information Super-Highway." *Skeptic* 3, no. 3 (1995): 35–41.

Lischka, Konrad, Frank Patalong, and Christian Stocker. "Netz-Lexikon: Wiki-Scanner spürt Manipulationen auf." http://www.spiegel.de/netzwelt/web/netz -lexikon-wiki-scanner-spuert-manipulationen-auf-a-500163-5.html.

Lyons, Theresa A. "Scientology or Censorship: You Decide: An Examination of the Church of Scientology, Its Recent Battles with Individual Internet Users and Service Providers, the Digital Millennium Copyright Act, and the Implications for Free Speech on the Web." *Rutgers Journal of Law & Religion* 2 (2000): 1–6.

Marsh, David, Paul 't Hart, and Karen Tindall. "Celebrity Politics: The Politics of the Late Modernity?" *Political Studies Review* 8, no. 3 (2010): 322–340.

Melton, J. Gordon. "Birth of a Religion." *Scientology* (2009): 17.

Metz, Cade. "Scientology Threatens Wikileaks with Injunction." http://www .theregister.co.uk/2008/04/08/church_of_scientology_contacts_wikileaks/.

Nabi, Zubair. "Resistance Censorship Is Futile." *First Monday* 19, no. 11 (2014).

Nguyen, Lam. "Virginia Man's Computer Seized in Internet Lawsuit." *Washington Post*, August 13, 1995.

Passas, Nikos, and Manuel Escamilla Castillo. "Scientology and Its 'Clear' Business." *Behavioral Science & the Law* 10, no. 1 (1992): 103–116.

Peckham, Michael. "New Dimensions of Social Movement/Countermovement Interaction: The Case of Scientology and Its Internet Critics." *Canadian Journal of Sociology/Cahiers canadiens de sociologie* 23, no. 4 (1998): 317–347.

Shupe, Anson. "The Nature of the New Religious Movements–Anticult 'Culture War' in Microcosm: The Church of Scientology versus the Cult Awareness

Network." In *Scientology*, edited by James R. Lewis, 269–282. Oxford University Press, 2009.

Siegel, Jacob. "Scientology's Sneaky Google Ads Slam HBO Documentary?" http://www.thedailybeast.com/articles/2015/03/23/scientology-s-sneaky-ads-slam-critics.html.

Siegel, Pascale Combelles. "Perception Management: IO's Stepchild?" *Low Intensity Conflict & Law Enforcement* 13, no. 2 (2005): 117–134.

Singel, Ryan. "Wikipedia Bans Church of Scientology." *Wired.com*, May 29, 2009.

Starbird, Kate, Grace Muzny, and Leysia Palen. "Learning from the Crowd: Collaborative Filtering Techniques for Identifying on-the-Ground Twitterers during Mass Disruptions." *Proceedings of ISCRAM* (2012): 1–10.

Taylor, Marisa. "Wikipedia Bans Scientology Church's Edits." *Wall Street Journal*, http://blogs.wsj.com/digits/2009/06/01/wikipedia-bans-scientology-churchs-edits/.

Underwood, Patrick C. "New Directions in Networked Activism and Online Social Movement Mobilization: The Case of Anonymous and Project Chanology." Ohio University, 2009.

Underwood, Patrick, and Howard T. Welser. "'The Internet Is Here': Emergent Coordination and Innovation of Protest Forms in Digital Culture." In *Proceedings of the 2011 iConference*. 2011.

Urban, Hugh B. "Fair Game: Secrecy, Security, and the Church of Scientology in Cold War America." *Journal of the American Academy of Religion* 74, no. 2 (2006): 356–389.

Vromen, Ariadne, and William Coleman. "Online Campaigning Organizations and Storytelling Strategies: Getup! In Australia." *Policy & Internet* 5, no. 1 (2013): 76–100.

WikiLeaks. "Church of Scientology Collected Operating Thetan Documents." https://wikileaks.org/wiki/Church_of_Scientology_collected_Operating_Thetan_documents.

WikiLeaks. "Scientology Threatens Wikileaks over Secret Cult Bibles." *WikiLeaks*. https://wikileaks.org/wiki/Scientology_threatens_Wikileaks_over_secret_cult_bibles.

Wikipedia. "Christianity: Revision History." *Wikipedia*. https://en.wikipedia.org/w/index.php?title=Christianity&offset=20060101000000&limit=500&action=history&tagfilter=.

Wikipedia. "Scientology: Revision History." *Wikipedia*. https://en.wikipedia.org/w/index.php?title=Scientology&offset=20060101000000&limit=500&action=history&tagfilter=.

Wikipedia. "Wikipedia:Requests for Arbitration/Scientology." *Wikipedia*. https://en.wikipedia.org/wiki/Wikipedia:Requests_for_arbitration/Scientology.

Zittrain, Jonathan. *The Future of the Internet—and How to Stop It*. Yale University Press, 2008.

11

Remember the Whole Track? The Hidden Persuaders in Scientology Art

George Shaw[1] and Susan Raine

INTRODUCTION

"I am not from this planet."[2]

L. Ron Hubbard uttered these words during a taped lecture before a group of Scientologists in November 1968. This special event, the playing of *Ron's Journal 1968*, occurred in every Scientology organization from New York in the United States to Sydney, Australia. A large life-size photograph of a standing L. Ron Hubbard mounted on a stiff backing sat beside a reel-to-reel tape recorder. The audience of 50 people applauded at various intervals. I (George Shaw) had been with Scientology for only a few months at this point and concepts such as "whole track," "past lives," and "incidents happening millions of years ago," were becoming quite common but still startling to me.

Just one month earlier I heard the tape, *Ron's Journal 1967*, where Hubbard had described a "wall of fire" incident—a catastrophe that allegedly had occurred on this planet 75 million years ago. The backdrop to this cataclysmic event was an immense galactic confederacy fraught with danger and evildoing.[3] Because of his "wall of fire" breakthrough and his claims to new knowledge, Hubbard ordered complete changes to over 20 Dianetics and Scientology book cover images. The new book cover designs would incorporate "whole track" and "space opera" imagery representing Hubbard's latest insights into the history of humanity—a history that he proposed only he had access to.

This chapter discusses the specific reasons for the cover changes and the artistic renderings presented on them. As we illustrate, in each case, Hubbard conceived of images that were meant to act as powerful symbolic reminders of past events. Consequently, the artworks that he commissioned were integral to his attempts at effecting particular responses in those who viewed them. Furthermore, Hubbard intended these responses to be favorable to Scientology's domestic and global progress.

Hubbard's use of visual art to communicate and even *stimulate* his ideological position is perhaps not surprising. Art, in a variety of forms, is important to many, if not all, religious and other ideological traditions, and the case is no different for Scientology. Indeed, religious art, has, historically, and in the contemporary era, been a vital part of representing important religious ideas and concepts.[4] Art is an integral component part of religious expression and one can appreciate it as a mediator between humans and the alleged supernatural realm. Indeed, it may well be that individuals' feel they cannot fully connect to the transcendent realm without the presence of some form of creative-artistic vehicle.[5] Broadly speaking, the academic literature on religion and art focuses mostly on mainstream religions, cross-cultural spiritual artistic expressions, and, in North America, indigenous or aboriginal art. Because art is central to human activity, however, art manifests within the context of alternative religious movements and cults too.[6]

Carefully devised to conjure great meaning and power, the symbols of Scientology's art—like symbols in art generally—must be analyzed in order to uncover their full meaning to the viewer. We do no not have the space in this chapter to examine and discuss all Dianetics and Scientology art or even all their pertinent book covers; instead, we limit our analyses to an overview and discussion of those book covers that were a part of the new "whole track" series. Moreover, we contextualize Hubbard's use of art by discussing some of his strategic motivations and influences. For example, Hubbard carefully observed advertising trends in the United States and stated that he believed in the efficacy of the "subliminal" advertising techniques that marketers allegedly used in the 1960s. His embrace of subliminal theories is significant: as we discuss, Hubbard proposed that the artwork depicted on the new whole track covers would have pronounced persuasive abilities in the public realm.

As well, Hubbard's use of Christian symbolism is a recurring theme and speaks to his intention to draw on such symbols not only in order to legitimize Scientology's public presence but also as a means to attract potential converts from Christian traditions. Finally, in terms of the overall artistic process, we discuss the fact that although not a visual artist himself, Hubbard maintained creative control of all artistic procedures. Accordingly, we look at some of the ways in which he ensured that his artistic visions were executed according to his plans.

Before proceeding with our discussion, however, it is important to note that we could not include any of Scientology's copyrighted visual art images in this chapter. Consequently, we do our best to describe the art works under consideration in detail so that the reader obtains a clear idea of the pertinent images and symbolism. We recommend, however, that readers refer to the relevant images via online sources or consult hardcopy version of the books where available. Certainly, not being able to include the images here is a limitation; but the art of Scientology is an important and fascinating topic that, nonetheless, deserves academic attention.

THE WHOLE TRACK BOOK COVER CAMPAIGN

"ART is a word which summarizes THE QUALITY OF COMMUNICATION."[7]

Just three months after the *Ron's Journal 1967* event, a series of proceedings took place. These events dealt with the concepts of "whole track" and "space opera" and of the planned artistic recreation of specific incidents from human galactic history.

The concept of the "whole track" is, in many ways, central to Scientology mythology, as it refers to Hubbard's version of history across the universe over trillions of years. Hubbard proposed that the whole track "is the moment to moment record of a person's existence in this universe in picture and impression form."[8] He claimed that he had been searching for the whole track for many years but only uncovered it and gained access to it when Volney Mathison presented him with the Electropsychometer (E-Meter). This instrument would become a central feature of Scientology's counselling strategy: auditing. Hubbard claimed that with it, he could chart the *entirety* of the whole track,[9] allowing him unprecedented access to human galactic history. Critically, he alleged that with this exceptional access to the whole track, he had uncovered the existence of multiple past lives.[10]

The other key concept here, "space opera," is a complex one. Primarily, it refers to a science fiction (SF) genre that has had several incarnations over the evolution of this literary field. Many scholars of SF, including prominent writers of SF, have used the label space opera as a derogatory term to describe much of the early to mid-20th-century pulp SF works—including works that Hubbard himself wrote. The term has evolved, however, and in the contemporary era, it refers to large sweeping SF narratives that garner both popular and critical acclaim.[11] For the purposes of this chapter, however, the most pertinent definition of space opera is Hubbard's own:

> **space opera:** of or relating to time periods on the whole track millions of years ago which concerned activities in this and other galaxies. Space opera has space travel, spaceships, spacemen, intergalactic travel, wars, conflicts, other beings, civilizations and societies, and other planets

and galaxies. *It is not fiction and concerns actual incidents and things that occurred on the track* [emphasis added].[12]

Clearly, Hubbard borrowed the literary tradition concept to explain reality. As he clearly identified, space opera refers to galactic events that are in integral part of the whole track (or simply, "the track" as he calls it here.)[13]

The first event to occur around the new whole track/space opera book covers was Hubbard's organization of a secret Scientology meeting at Saint Hill Manor in England. There, he gathered his top executives and aides along with the officers of The Publications Organization (the group in charge of publishing and printing all the Scientology books) in a clandestine meeting. This special talk[14] was not for public consumption nor was it for general Sea Organization members.[15] Rather, only a handful of trusted Sea Org members were privileged enough to attend and to get insight into the subject of the lecture. Hubbard recorded this unusual lecture and it remains in Scientology archives—it has never been revealed to the public.

In the talk, Hubbard discussed his claimed discovery of whole track and space opera material. He asserted that the wall of fire event opened a flood gate of material, incidents, and symbols that Scientology subsequently could use on its new book covers. According to Hubbard, the new book cover symbols contained a form of power that would affect the person viewing them.[16] Moreover, "Hubbard told his marketing staff that this imagery would make the books irresistible to purchasers by reactivating unconscious memories."[17]

The second event followed just weeks after the secret lecture. The Publications Organization at Saint Hill Manor in England released Issue Number 1 of *Expand* magazine. The cover page showed a bust of Hubbard surrounded by Scientology books. With the June 1968 issue, however, the entire reason for the creation of this new magazine became apparent. This issue was historic as it revealed the new worldwide book sales campaign. A total revamping of all the existing Scientology book covers had begun, and this book campaign was the largest worldwide promotional event in Scientology's history to date. Furthermore, this issue included the announcement that "The LRH programme to put new covers on Scientology books which are on sale to the public is well under way. Sales of the new books have so far exceeded all expectations in Org and public bookstores."[18]

The magazine explained that the new book covers were inspired by Hubbard's discovery of the whole track and the events therein. As well, *Expand* magazine stated that "The symbols on the books were discovered by ron after long research on the higher levels. Each cover is specially designed to sell the book it represents." *Expand* included several photos of the new book covers. Moreover, a slogan near the top of page eight read: *"symbols sell books."*[19]

Thus, Hubbard immediately put the newly discovered whole track and space opera symbols to use. As Bent Corydon, a former Scientology mission holder, recounted:

> A special "Book Mission" was sent out to promote these books, now empowered and made irresistible by the addition of these supposedly overwhelming symbols or images. Organization staff were assured that if they simply held up one of the books, revealing its cover, that any bookstore owner would immediately order crateloads of them. A customs officer, seeing any of the book covers in one's luggage, would immediately pass one on through.[20]

It appears, then, that Hubbard was quite certain that art could play a vital role in contributing to the expansion of Scientology and the range of its influence. Certainly, Hubbard had been pondering the purpose and nature of art since the 1940s.[21] Core to his understanding of art (whether fine art, photography, music, or film) was its ability to communicate. He surmised, "'Art for art's sake' is a complete paradox of a remark. 'Art for the sake of communication' . . . [is] the plus . . . of it all."[22] In terms of what constitutes "good art," Hubbard asserted that, regardless of artistic style, "TECHNICAL EXPERTISE" is critical. He claimed that artists who are technically proficient are able to produce the necessary "emotional impact."[23]

Hubbard was confident that the new whole track/space opera book covers communicated the appropriate message in each case. The artwork on each cover was quite clearly meant to communicate very effectively with the viewer and, of course, illicit the desired emotional—and then, behavioral—response.

THE INVENTOR AND THE ARTIST: THE COLLABORATION OF L. RON HUBBARD AND RICHARD GORMAN

Fortunately for Hubbard, he had, among his followers, a talented and technically proficient artist who could translate his ideas into fine art covers. While aboard the Flagship Apollo, Hubbard's floating Sea Org headquarters, I (Shaw) came across a reel-to-reel tape box in the study area, labeled, "CONFIDENTAL—SEA ORG MEMBERS ONLY—TAPE BY RICHARD GORMAN—LRH ARTIST." Gorman, a renowned Canadian artist from Toronto, had joined Scientology in England following the collapse of his marriage to model Anna Gorman.[24] After leaving Canada to join Scientology, he became a Sea Organization member and artist for L. Ron Hubbard.[25] The central focus of Gorman's 45-minute taped talk was the creation of the whole track/space opera book covers. The tape revealed the entire modus operandi of the book cover images—the progression from the creative mind of Hubbard to Gorman's painted canvases.

The talk revealed that Hubbard conceived of all of the covers himself. Thus, Hubbard scripted and designed all the characters, objects, and scenery. Gorman spoke very enthusiastically about the mysterious aura that the book cover symbols contained, saying, "the book covers are symbols of the bank, [reactive mind]." He continued:

> The book cover images and symbols have a power, a power to impinge and somehow transform the viewer. The person seeing the whole track book cover symbols is just not the same after the viewing. Marvelous results occur when you lay out the book covers on a table for a press conference. The book covers attract people as they are universal symbols everyone has in common.[26]

Gorman likened this experience to "blowing off charge." This phrase is Scientology parlance for "the sudden dissipation of mass in the mind with accompanying feeling of relief."[27] Gorman stated also that the book covers had a negative effect on Scientology's enemies when they view them. Gorman seemed satisfied then, that he had achieved the communicative outcomes that Hubbard desired.

Gorman's tape outlined also the *procedures* for producing the cover art. He explained that Hubbard would send him a written order for the painted book covers that he wanted, and then Gorman followed a standard step-by-step set of practices: First, Gorman received Hubbard's order for a particular book cover. Each order contained a written outline of all the design components, characters, objects, and actions that Gorman should portray. Second, Gorman would paint the image that Hubbard had scripted. Next, Gorman would send the completed painting to Hubbard for final approval in a "CSW" form, "CSW" being Scientology argot for "Completed Staff Work." Gorman then sent a cover sheet listing all the pertinent information to Hubbard, requiring only that he signed off on a line identifying the work as "approved" or "disapproved."[28]

Gorman marveled at Hubbard's memory and special abilities in recalling, in such excruciating, exact detail, the image of an event that he claimed had occurred millions of years ago. In his tape, Gorman cited *The Creation of Human Ability* (1968) book cover as an example of Hubbard's extraordinary recall. In this case, Gorman's freshly painted image contained a bizarre assemblage of figures and objects. The cover art is of a woman dressed in a costumed bear suit, face revealed, and sitting, cross-legged on a wooden, green chair, eating a chicken leg. The chair with the costumed woman sits on a barren, wooden stage floor. A red theater curtain forms the background. Gorman sent the faithfully rendered, completed painting with the attached CSW to Hubbard. Hubbard returned the CSW as "disapproved," the reason being that the woman in the bear suit had her leg crossed in the wrong direction. Gorman then repainted the woman's legs so that they were in the correct position; Hubbard then approved the project. Reflecting on this process, Gorman remarked, "That is how exact Hubbard's memory was of whole track incidents."[29]

When completed works met with Hubbard's approval, they were ready to be photographed by Pubs [Publications] World Wide and made into the finished book covers. This same process was repeated over and over again until Gorman painted the entire series of 24 book covers.[30] As the next section illustrates, Hubbard believed fully in the power of the subliminal nature of these new covers—and this alleged power is tested when Scientology experiences problems in the United Kingdom.

THE BRITISH GOVERNMENT AND SCIENTOLOGY: USING ART TO SUBVERT AUTHORITY

From 1966 through 1968, Scientology experienced turbulent times with the British government, often having to endure quite stringent attacks from it.[31] In 1966, many members of the British parliament sought an inquiry into Scientology and its practices. They questioned Hubbard's credentials as a "doctor" and the organization's use of what appeared to be psychological treatments. (Subsequently, Hubbard abandoned the title of "doctor.") On July 25, 1968, the British government banned entry into the United Kingdom to Scientology students headed for services at Scientology's head office at Saint Hill Manor in East Grinstead, Sussex. Henceforth, American students were not permitted to enter the country at the airport and had to take a return flight home.[32] Then, less than a month later, the British Home Secretary banned Hubbard from the United Kingdom also.[33]

These difficulties prompted Hubbard to write one of the most revealing policy letters regarding the whole track book covers. Titled, "IMMIGRATION TIP," the policy letter offered new entrees to the United Kingdom a method— a tip on how to pass through customs without difficulty. In order to achieve this end, however, one needed to purchase one or two new book editions with the new covers. Hubbard claimed that Scientologists could use these books as tools of persuasion at the country's entry points. Hubbard selected two specific new books for use with Immigration and Customs officials. One was *Have You Lived Before This Life?*, the cover of which depicts a hooded and robed man holding a torch inside a cave full of skeletons. The other was *Self*

Analysis. The new cover of this book showed a quiet, serene image of a boy looking out of a window. Hubbard claimed that these book covers "operate as a sort of open-the-gate at Immigration and Customs if placed in plain sight." The phrase "open-the-gate" implied that the book covers had some magical and mystical powers—powers that Richard Gorman alluded to and described in his talk. To this end, Hubbard advised that upon entry into the United Kingdom, Scientologists "hold up the book covers to them [Immigration & custom officials]." Allegedly, the whole track book covers would subliminally sway Immigration and Custom officials so that they would grant Scientologists free, untroubled passage into the United Kingdom.[34]

Whether the whole track book covers possessed these manipulative powers or not was irrelevant; Hubbard believed that they did, and he did not hesitate to use this covert method and request that his followers do the same. In this way, we can see that Hubbard proposed that even the art of Scientology had the ability to effect change in the world and accord Scientologists with a particular form of power over other individuals—including those in positions of authority such as government employees.

Britain's scrutiny represented a major crisis for Hubbard and for Scientology. In addition to the new whole track and space opera book covers, Hubbard issued a 29-page, paper cover, damage control booklet titled *Successes of Scientology* (1968). He designed this booklet to be distributed to the press, to government officials, and to the general public in the United Kingdom. The practice of issuing such a booklet had precedent in Scientology. In the 1960s, a similar government crisis occurred in the state of Victoria in Australia. The findings of that government's Board of Inquiry into Scientology was published in 1965, and the practice of Scientology was made illegal. In response, Hubbard wrote a handling procedure that incorporated the Scientology success stories.[35]

Successes of Scientology contained page after page of testimonials to the professed efficacy of Scientology training and auditing. People from all walks of life were photographed next to their success stories. For example, photographs of a concert pianist, an office worker, and a housewife, in addition to many others, filled the pages. Thus, the persuasive images in this case were photographs of seemingly everyday people thriving due to their engagement with Scientology. As one would expect, the content of this booklet presented Scientology in entirely positive terms.[36] Interestingly, the cover design of this booklet included an embedded Christian cross.

Hubbard published also *The Character of Scientology* as a companion damage control booklet to *Successes of Scientology*. Hubbard designed the cover of this publication that was specifically to be shown to the British press and the British government. In this case, Christian motifs are clearly present. A choir boy in long, white church vestments, holding a hymn book, with his mouth open, as if singing, dons the cover of the booklet.

Positive positioning of Scientology characterizes both booklets. The text and images illustrate the most admirable aspects of Scientology in the hopes of presenting Scientology in a new light to the British public and politicians. Whether attempting to generate subliminal responses or trying to illicit positive representations of the group, Hubbard undoubtedly trusted in the value of artistic expression through visual media in communicating his message to his target audience.

SUBLIMINAL MESSAGES: HUBBARD'S PURSUIT OF SUBCONSCIOUS INFLUENCE

As the previous segment illustrates, Hubbard proposed that the whole track/space opera images that he claimed to have recalled were full of persuasive power. But how exactly did he believe this power manifested? Hubbard's writings indicate that he believed in the ability of subliminal messages and that his interest in this claimed form of manipulation derived from his engagement with the literature on subliminal manipulation in advertising. Purportedly, advertising companies had found success with this strategy. This segment, therefore, reviews the concept of subliminal influence and Hubbard's belief in it.

Since the 1960s, several authors have periodically revived the concept of subliminal advertising. For an image to be considered subliminal it is meant to influence an individual without their knowledge (i.e., the person receives the images at a level below the threshold of conscious perception). The idea of subliminal influence emerged with the "experimental" work of psychologist James M. Vicary (1915–1977). Vicary claimed to have established the efficacy of subliminal messaging when he interspersed brief images urging viewers to "eat popcorn" and "drink Coca-Cola" while they watched a movie. He claimed that sales of the prompted snack and drink subsequently increased. He stated also that the advertising industry commonly used such tactics to increase sales.

The media immediately reported Vicary's findings, and the public became outraged at the advertising industry's apparent covert tactics. Although Vicary later confessed that he had fabricated the results of the study, the public became convinced that the industry did indeed use such manipulative strategies.[37] Since that time several publications have supported the idea of subliminal persuasion and manipulation despite an abundance of research to the contrary.[38]

Regardless of the *actual* efficacy of materials designed to be subliminal in nature, important to the present discussion is that *Hubbard* certainly believed in the persuasive power of them. In a taped lecture in 1964 Hubbard commented on the use of secret, manipulative, "push button" triggers in advertising. He spoke angrily against those in the advertising media who used manipulative techniques to unduly influence the unconscious minds of viewers in order to make them think or feel in certain ways.[39] To his followers, Hubbard recommended Vance Packard's (1957) book, *The Hidden Persuaders*, which claimed to expose the various underhanded, subliminal, advertising techniques used by New York advertising companies.[40] Hubbard stated that *The Hidden Persuaders* gave the public a thorough examination of all the nefarious advertising techniques being used by modern advertising agencies.

Hubbard continued by saying, "They're trying to restimulate something one way or the other in order to sell their soap." Hubbard found this practice in this context to be a problem: "Now, this material, of course—I mean this type of use—is a debased use of this information."[41] Referring to subliminal advertising and the role of psychologists in society, he claimed that "There's certain things that are supposed to happen here by stimulus response. In other words, you haven't got policy you have manipulation. And human beings in society grossly object to manipulation, particularly hidden manipulation."[42] It seems that although Hubbard found it distasteful and even abusive for product marketers to use subliminal advertising on the American public, he felt that it was entirely appropriate when promoting Scientology. As was often the case with Hubbard, he could be quite contrary about a practice, depending on who employed it, and how they did so. When advertising Scientology products, Hubbard positioned them next to allegedly subliminal images that he believed would attract customers. In many of his advertisement critiques, Hubbard recommended to his art designers the 1971 book, *History of the Poster*, by Josef Muller-Brockman. Specifically, he told them to focus on one line (from the 265-page book) that gives the essence of what the art poster is all about. The pertinent line stated, "It [the poster] *must create a subliminal desire on the part of the viewer.*"[43]

From a subliminal message perspective—one that Hubbard embraced—the use of whole track imagery allows one to tap into peoples' deep, instinctual thought processes. Basic and repressed desires and experiences are exploited and channeled in order to sell a product—in this case, Scientology. From this perspective, the image is the trigger—an unconscious entrance point to the mind. Hubbard employed this approach both with the whole track book covers and in his advertising techniques. Hubbard hoped that the art that Gorman produced would restimulate memories of past lives—memories from the whole track that would initiate favorable responses. He anticipated also that by using subliminal imagery in advertisements, he could sell more of these books and other Scientology products.

In the next section, we address Hubbard's use of Christian symbolism in his artwork, proposing that in doing so, he was able to use Christianity as a promotional device—one that he hoped would contribute to the legitimacy of Scientology in society. It seems likely that he considered the pairing of subliminal motifs with Christian imagery a potent combination that would elicit favorable public results.

CHRISTIAN SYMBOLS: THE SYMBIOTIC RELATIONSHIP BETWEEN SCIENTOLOGY AND CHRISTIANITY

From Scientology's inception in 1953, L. Ron Hubbard fostered a partnership with Christianity: certificates of incorporation for the Church of Scientology and certificates of incorporation for another of Hubbard's organizations, the Church of American Science, were issued on the same day (along with a third, the Church of Spiritual Engineering).[44] Hubbard designed the Church of American Science as a Christian religion; he did not sculpt Scientology in the same way. Revealing the nature of the relationship between the two entities, Hubbard stated that

> There is a difference between the Church of American Science and the Church of Scientology. The Church of American Science is a Christian Religion. It believes in the Holy Bible, Jesus is the Savior of man and everything that's necessary to be a Christian religion. People who belong to that church are expected to be Christians. These two churches fit together. We take somebody in as a Church of American Science. It doesn't disagree with his baptism or other things like that, and he could gradually slide over into some sort of better, wider activity such as the Church of Scientology and a little more wisdom and come a little more close to optimum. Then if he was good and one of the people that we would like to have around he would eventually slide into the HASI [Hubbard Association of Scientologists Int.]. So we have provided stepping stones to Scientology with these organizations.[45]

In his own words, Hubbard used a 2000-year tradition—namely, Christianity, its acceptability, respect, and social prominence—in order to recruit members to Scientology. Thus, a symbiotic relationship between Christianity and Scientology began, and it continues to this day. (Symbiotic relationships usually result in the smaller of the two entities being the beneficiary of the relationship.) This apparent alliance with Christian religions, is just that—an appearance. Privately, Hubbard disdained Christianity and considered it a fraudulent religion. Publicly, he positioned Scientology in terms of neutrality and friendship with it and extended a nondenominational welcome to all people of the Christian faith.

Hubbard revealed his thoughts on Christianity only to higher level Scientologists. He claimed, "the man on the cross, there was no Christ." According to Hubbard, Jesus was an implanted false memory—part of the R6 implant that produced the Christian tradition. Later, however, he seems to have abandoned the idea of Jesus as an implant, instead stating,

> For those of you whose Christian toes I may have stepped on, let me take the opportunity to disabuse you of some lovely myths. For instance, the historic Jesus was not nearly the sainted figure [he] has been made out to be. In addition to being a lover of young boys and men, he was given to uncontrollable bursts of temper and hatred. . . . You have only to look at the history his teachings inspired to see where it all inevitably leads. It is historic fact and yet man still clings to the ideal, so deep and insidious is the biologic implanting.[46]

Here, he implies that Jesus was, in fact, real but that implants *about* him obscure his true character.

So, despite his initial denial and subsequent criticisms of Christianity, Hubbard appreciated that this religious tradition could be beneficial to him. Therefore, as well as mimicking Christian motifs and imagery in practices such as Scientology services, he embraced also Christian symbols in his artwork, using them to further his goals. As the next section illustrates, Christian themes figured in the new whole track book covers quite frequently and prominently.

THE ART OF THE WHOLE TRACK: SELECT COVERS

In this segment we take a look at some of the new whole track covers. As we stated previously, we cannot analyze all of the whole track covers—we simply do not have the space to do so. Instead, we have attempted to include a cross section of images—from those books that seem to evidently embrace space opera/whole track themes to those that seem more subtle. Consequently, we provide a succinct description of each cover and offer analyses of them. Art analysis is, of course, a subjective process, so alternative readings may be possible. We do not, therefore, mean to imply that our analyses are definitive; rather, we hope to open up further discussion and debate around the art of Scientology by offering our own insights. Hubbard's Dianetics and Scientology writings inform our exploration of the art covers, though, so we are confident that we offer plausible explanations of the works under consideration.

It seems prudent to start with the book that has become known as "Book 1" among Scientologists, the foundational book that Hubbard wrote prior to Scientology's existence.[47] Hubbard proposed *Dianetics: The Modern Science of Mental Health* (*DMSH*) as a new, breakthrough approach to understanding the human mind, human behavior, human ability, illness, and other conditions.[48] He made many remarkable (and mostly unsubstantiated) claims in this work, but it remains critical to understanding Hubbard and Scientology.

The first edition of this book had a very plain cover: a dark green background with a foreground design of black-and-white ellipses. Conversely, the whole track cover for *DMSH* is very colorful and dynamic. It depicts a volcano erupting: flames, black smoke clouds, and debris explode skyward; and hot, molten lava spills over and runs down the mountain's sides. It is a simple, visually striking image that stands alone on the page, needing no further context or embellishment. According to Jeff Hawkins, ex–Sea Organization member and former head of marketing in Scientology, it was Hubbard's intention to "splash the volcano" at the general public. This idea came from Hubbard's belief that the image of a volcano has been embedded in people's minds from a particular shared experience in a former lifetime. The shared experience to which Hubbard alluded was "Incident II" also known as the "Wall of Fire."

When Hubbard stated in 1967 that in he had broken through the "the Wall of Fire" and survived, he claimed also that he had accessed overwhelming and devastating knowledge through this peculiar experience—the details of which he shared with other Scientologists only when they attained the level of OTIII. Upon completion of this level, Scientologists learn that 75 million years ago, a figure named Xenu—who was the ruler of a Galactic Confederacy of 178 billion people, 26 stars, and 76 planets including Earth (or "Teegeeack" as Hubbard claims it was then known)—conducted terrible atrocities in order to resolve the acute overpopulation issues that plagued the confederacy. Xenu transferred the excess population to Teegeeack in airplanes that looked like DC-8s. Then the confederacy placed the doomed individuals inside volcanoes and blasted them with hydrogen bombs. Hubbard's narrative goes on to explain how the remaining spirits of these individuals—or *thetans* as he identified them—then were exposed to intense religious and technological implants for 36 days (priests and psychiatrists supervised these implants, known as the R6 implants). Xenu then sent the thetans to either Los Palmas or Hawaii where they were clustered together. Hubbard claimed that clusters of *body thetans* then attach themselves to humans and are responsible for the majority of their problems, both somatic and emotional.[49]

Hawkins said that the process of "Splashing the volcano at them was supposed to hypnotize people back, or what they call 'key them in' to the whole

Xenu incident." He continued, "And then they would be somehow hypnotized to go and buy the book."[50] In this case, then, Hubbard used the image both on the book cover and in advertisements for the book. The artwork in this case symbolizes Incident II, a key space operatic myth.[51] Hubbard claimed that full knowledge of the details of this incident would be dangerous to Scientologists if they were exposed to it before they were ready.[52] It appears that *suggestion* of this pivotal incident through the cover art, however, would be subtle enough to ignite a sense of affinity with the movement without overtly foisting the full body of allegedly dangerous knowledge upon them.

It seems likely that of all the new whole track images, this one is the most important. The cover art of many Dianetics and Scientology books has changed throughout several editions since this time, although some have remained fairly constant, including this volcanic image for Dianetics. The exact rendering of the volcanic eruption varies in terms of color and style, but the symbol and meaning remain the same, indicating the central position that this narrative maintains in the more secret levels of Scientology ideology.

The space opera motif continues in *Dianetics: The Evolution of a Science.* Originally published in 1955, this book is Hubbard's expansion of his original article on Dianetics as published in the prominent pulp era SF magazine, *Astounding Science Fiction.* Hence, in this book, Hubbard revisited his original proposals and discussed how he defined concepts such as the "reactive mind" and how he established techniques to deal with the problems that it generates. According to Hubbard, the subconscious reactive mind comprises "engrams"—images of painful whole track experiences, which, as Scientologists discover are caused by body thetans.

The whole track artwork for the *Dianetics: The Evolution of a Science* cover is perhaps even more indicative of Incident II than *DMSMH*, since it portrays a spaceship being loaded up by three helmeted and uniformed space men. Each man carries a box, and it seems likely that the boxes shown contain the packaged thetans of alien populations frozen in alcohol and glycol.[53] Again, the image is simple, yet striking. The three men as well as the space ship are portrayed in white and set against a dark charcoal backdrop. The image is largely monochromatic with little other color present.

Hubbard did not reveal Incident II and the role of Xenu in creating thetans until 1967, and so it seems fitting that having encountered such groundbreaking and fundamental knowledge, he applied images of it to his foundational works. From a strategic standpoint, pairing these important visual stimuli with his introductory works could be beneficial: new converts to Scientology reading the early books would be, from Hubbard's perspective, exposed to highly suggestive subliminal work that would strengthen their commitment to their new belief system by triggering some long-repressed memory fragments. Hubbard may have hypothesized that this realization might in turn lead them to believe that Scientology was a good fit for them, thus leading to further commitment.

Another of Hubbard's recommended books, *Have You Lived Before This Life?*, has had several fascinating covers including the whole track one. This book details claims of past lives on the whole track—including those on other planets. The cover shows a black robed and hooded figure (Hubbard referred to this figure as the Inquisitor) holding a flaming torch, lighting the interior of a cave that is strewn with skeletons. The torch light is reflected on his arm, which is slanted downward toward a Christian cross on his chest area. The cross is wide, thick, and stark white against the black robe—magnifying the importance of it. It occupies a central position on the cover; thus, this cross focuses the viewer's attention because of the way it is presented. Moreover, there may be a number of other embedded Christian crosses on the wall of the cave—visual configurations that suggest Hubbard's attempted use of subliminal imagery (i.e., if one looks closely at the art work, one can discern other crosses embedded in the painting). In this case, we viewed the image from Hubbard's proposal that one can imbed imagery for subliminal use: thus, looking at the brushstrokes one can identify a number of crosses. Did Hubbard plan these crosses or can one find then purely through creative viewing? Obviously, it is difficult to determine retrospectively the extent of Hubbard's attempts to use subliminal imagery. Alternative explanations and analyses are possible also. Moreover, given that Hubbard's claimed access to the whole track was the inspiration for the new covers, a further question arises: *What event on the whole track does this scene represent?*

If Hubbard identified the figure as the Inquisitor, then, paradoxically, he drew on a very troubling period of Catholic history to use as a tool of persuasion. Historians debate the total number of trials and deaths resulting from the Inquisition, but certainly it was a period of violent intolerance. The skeletons piled on the floor are perhaps Hubbard's way of illustrating the outcome of the many forms that the Inquisition took, revealing yet again his disdain for all forms of Christianity. As noted earlier, Hubbard selected *Have You Lived Before This Life?* along with *Self Analysis* (see below) as influential books for use at U.K. customs. Clearly, he believed in their specific persuasive and subliminal powers.

Other covers have less obvious connections to whole track or space opera themes. The *Self Analysis* cover, for example, seems quite mundane compared to other covers. The cover image in this case is of a boy looking out of a window at a green landscape with a row trees. Focusing on the vertical and horizontal elements of the wooden slats that divide the four glass window panes reveals the image of a dominant cross on the cover. Is this embedded cross meant to represent a Christian cross, illustrating perhaps Hubbard's attempt to create a subliminal gesture to Christian readers? The cross is the tallest object on the cover, adding to its centrality. Finally, the light blue sky background—which takes up about large proportion of the cover—shows off the darker cross to great effect. Of interest also is that Hubbard used this particular cover image on other Scientology publications. For example, he used this artwork on the previously discussed booklet, *Successes of Scientology* (also designed to be shown to governments and the press), as well as on the cover of the first issue of the publication, *Scientology: Clear Procedure*.[54]

Beyond the immediate subliminal impact that Hubbard desired from this cover, one can read a deeper level of meaning. Because the boy is looking out of the window (and beyond the cross) to the landscape outside, perhaps Hubbard meant to suggest that only through contemplation and self-reflection can one move beyond the bounds of false reality (i.e., Christianity). Since *Self Analysis* is, in part, about improving one's memory and concentration perhaps the contemplative theme is meant to suggest the importance of thinking and remembering. Of course, according to Hubbard, only Scientology auditing can truly help one access the whole track and one's multiple incarnations. Again, the cover art raises further questions: *What event on the whole track does this image represent?* and *Who is the boy?* Perhaps the artwork is meant to represent a young Hubbard. If so, this conclusion might offer some further insight in to why this particular image is so important.

Notes on the Lectures of L. Ron Hubbard is a compilation of notes that students attending Hubbard's 1950s lecture had written. Hubbard requested that these notes be published until he could make copies of the audio recordings available for purchase.[55] The artwork for the cover portrays a Catholic priest, with white collar and black robe, walking in a barren forest of trees. A Catholic priest, is, of course, one of the more recognizable representatives of the Christian tradition. The trees on either side of the priest are stripped of all leaves. One of the most curious features of this book cover image is that one floating leaf is set against the naked forest of leafless trees. This appears to be a directional marker, enticing the viewer to look further in this area. Again, drawing on Hubbard's acceptance of subliminal theories, we looked further. To the right side of the leaf and touching it is a diagonal branch, which intersects with another to form a cross. At the bottom of the leaf is a branch forming another cross like the tail on a kite. Are these crosses by design?

In this case, the deeper underlying message here seems to be that the priest is wandering "lost in the woods," both literally and metaphorically. This image, therefore, may be representative of the confusion and purposelessness that Hubbard equated with the Christian tradition. Alternatively (or perhaps concurrently) the image might represent the crisis of faith that people may experience in their transition into upper levels of Scientology where they will receive new truths about the nature of reality, the nature of the cosmos, and the nature of their true identities. Most challenging, may be their new understanding of Christianity—its apparent falsehoods—and the role that Hubbard claimed that priests played in implanting thetans during the Wall of Fire/Incident II event.

The whole track cover for *Scientology 8-80* depicts a winged angel with long blond hair dressed in a long white gown standing off to the side and behind a winged soldier or warrior figure. The winged soldier wears a helmet, the style of which was commonly used by both American and British soldiers during World War I. The soldier's clothing, however, is not: he is wearing a tunic with a skirted bottom. He holds a sword, the design of which corresponds neither with the American bayonets nor with British swords from the World War I era. The sword stands on the ground, in the center of the cover, at a slight diagonal and balanced by the warrior's hand. The sword's handle, horizontal cross guard, and vertical blade make a Christian cross. The warrior's strange, chainmail armor tunic (which is more indicative of medieval armor) has rows of grids, that crisscross enveloping the entire upper body and arms. If looking for suggestive material, then, one can find many minute hidden crosses therein. Using this strategy, upon close examination, a total of 68 crosses can be discerned.

In terms of the figures themselves, a body of artwork and posters from the World War I era depicts fallen soldiers in battle being tended by guardian angels. In Hubbard's image the soldier has wings too—indicating that he is dead. These figures appear also on the whole track cover of *Scientology 8-8008* and as a design on some Scientology official writing paper for the Guardian's Office during the 1970s.[56] The wording on the stationary paper is "Church of Scientology WorldWide: Your Guardian Angel to Complete Success." The angel is on the left side of the paper, the winged soldier on the right. Some former Scientologists have suggested that the male soldier represents the Guardian's Office and that the angel represents the Sea Org (although debate exists on this issue).[57] In both cases, these organizations offer protection to Scientology.

Hubbard may have used the motif of the guardian angel due to his experimentation with the occult. In the 1930s, Hubbard had informed his friend Arthur Banks that a guardian angel watched over him while he flew gliders. During his time experimenting with the black magic of Aleister Crowley, Hubbard identified his guardian angel as "the Empress," also known as the Egyptian goddess, Hathor. Hathor not only symbolized "Love and Beauty," but also she represented a more troubling, devastating force as the "destroyer of man." It may well have been the case that through his attempts at ritual magic, Hubbard tried to control her more perturbing aspect, while enjoying her protective properties.[58]

Certainly, it is difficult to ascertain the exact reasoning behind Hubbard's use of these specific images, but clearly they imbue deep symbolic meanings that may draw on a number of different sources.

CONCLUSION

As this chapter demonstrates, one can understand Hubbard's use of specific images in terms of the social power that he hoped they would garner. Hubbard sought to establish social and political influence through the public divisions of Scientology—those branches that "specialize in human emotion and reaction"—by tapping into those emotions in order to capture the public.[59] Confident in the ability of subliminal effects, Hubbard anticipated that viewing the art work would elicit a deep response in all those who observed it.

Hubbard's use of Christian imagery and symbols illustrates the way in which he attempted to appeal to the public. The Christian tradition in a variety of forms dominated the British, American, and other religious landscapes. While many of the symbols were explicit: robed priests, obvious crosses, and so forth, the meanings required further consideration. Hubbard believed in the profound effects of such suggestive symbols. Given his recognition of the power and ubiquity of Christianity as well as his desire to associate Scientology with it, it is understandable that he would attempt to sway people in this way.

Hubbard's overt use of space opera and whole track imagery, however, speaks more to his reliance on claimed subliminal effects. Anticipating that they would elicit a stimulus response in those viewing the images, Hubbard employed a variety of richly symbolic pieces of art that portrayed pivotal space opera scenes. Given his proposal that all people on Earth are inhabited by a multitude of body thetans derived from Incident II, he expected that these artworks would rouse in people a latent response—a response favorable to Scientology.

So much more could be said about Hubbard, Scientology, and art. Given the enormous output of Scientology publications and services, including books, magazines, films, DVDs, CDs, and pamphlets, art is an important visual signifier of what Scientology is and does. For example, just a cursory look at the artwork (both on the cover and within) of a Scientology publication such as *Advance!* magazine illustrates the abundance of analysis opportunities. This magazine and others contain a wide variety of artistic images, but many of them are indicative of the whole track and of space opera narratives.

Likewise, the art and design of other Scientology merchandise and organizations are explicitly science fiction themed and styled, illustrating the importance of Hubbard's retelling of cosmic history to Scientology beliefs and practices. One of the most important symbols of Scientology is the emblematic laurel wreath and star of the Sea Org. According to Hubbard, the wreath represents "victory" and the star represents the "spirit." Combined, they "signify the victory of the spirit which is rising upward towards the point of origin or source." Critically, he identified that the symbol of the Sea Org had been "adopted and used as the **symbol** of a Galactic Confederacy far back in the history of this sector" and that it "derives much of its power and authority from that association."[60] Historically, laurel wreaths were indeed used to signify victory, although depending on the context, they could symbolize "peace, eternity . . . unrequited love and the supreme ruler."[61] Laurel wreaths are found on a number of military wreaths and insignia as well as coats of arms and so on. For example, the British Royal Marines use the laurel wreath in some of their emblems. Given that the Sea Org adopted many formal naval characteristics, Hubbard's use of it is not surprising.

Elsewhere, the art of *advertising* Scientology offers up research opportunities. Rather than hire advertising agencies to design specific advertisements for Scientology books, E-Meters, courses and processing, and so forth, Hubbard trained in-house Scientology artists, designers, and copywriters (as well as the rest of the advertisement team), to do the jobs. Once again, Hubbard retained total control of all the art work images that were produced. From 1970 up through the early 1980s Hubbard wrote hundreds of orders, advisories, and critiques on the subject of artwork and advertisements. Specific policy and advice issues were devoted to layout, mocks, directional lines, color wheels, and centers of interest. As such, Hubbard addressed every aspect of the creation of an advertisement.[62] Furthermore, he crafted a compliance list of ingredients in advertising art work to ensure a high standard of execution.[63]

In closing, as this chapter contends, Hubbard took the art of Dianetics and Scientology very seriously. Hubbard believed that the art that he commissioned would have a transformative capacity, contributing further to the reach of his belief system around the globe. Key Scientology ideas—whole track and space opera—permeated the art that we have discussed here. Likely, they are pivotal to other art and design components in Scientology. Furthermore, the discovery of a number of overt and embedded Christian crosses in several of the book covers opens the door to further investigation of Hubbard's use of explicit and allegedly subliminal Christian images in his attempt to gain wider acceptance of Scientology. We hope that other academics take on the challenge to further analyze and discuss this as yet understudied area of Scientology.

NOTES

1. "George Shaw" is a pseudonym. The author is a former Scientologist who wishes to remain anonymous.

2. L. Ron Hubbard, *Ron's Journal 1968*, Taped lecture, Golden Era Studios, 1983. Scientology banned public distribution of this tape, but it appeared online in 2011. The quote "I am not from this planet" is approximately 22 minutes in.

3. L. Ron Hubbard, *Ron's Journal 1967*, Taped lecture, Golden Era Studios, 1983. In this lecture, Hubbard revealed his Los Palmas "Wall of Fire Discovery." In it he states, "It is very true that a great catastrophe occurred on this planet and in the other seventy-five planets which form this confederacy seventy-five million years ago."

4. Earl J. Coleman, *Creativity and Spirituality: Bonds Between Art and Religion* (New York: State University of New York, 1998), xvi.

5. Ibid., xvi–xvii.

6. Hubbard devised Dianetics as a therapeutic *science*. He crafted Scientology in a number of different ways: as a therapeutic system, as a philosophical system *and* as a religion. Scholars have discussed the variety of ways that one might categorize Scientology including as the aforementioned and as a business practice. For example, see the following works: Benjamin Beit-Hallahmi, Benjamin, "Scientology: Religion or Racket?," *Marburg Journal of Religion* 8 (2003), ahttp://www.uni-marburg.de/religion wissenschaft/journal/mjr/kent3.html; David G. Bromley and Mitchell Bracey Jr., "The Church of Scientology: A Quasi Religion," in *Sects, Cults and Spiritual Communities: A Sociological Analysis*, ed. William W. Zellner and Marc Petrowsky (Praeger, 1998), 141–156; Stephen A. Kent, "Scientology—Is This a Religion?," *Marburg Journal of Religion* 4 (1999): 1–23, http://www.uni-marburg.de/religionwissenschaft/journal/mjr /kent3.html; Nikos Passas and Manuel Escamilla Castillo, "Scientology and Its 'Clear' Business," *Behavioral Sciences and the Law* 10 (1992): 103–116.

We take the approach that to *Scientologists*, Scientology is *all* of these entities and more—it is a complete lifestyle system that offers a range of philosophies, practices, goods, and services, including those pertaining to the supernatural realm. Hubbard's specific reasons for labelling Scientology as a religion at all, are well documented. See, for example, Hugh Urban, *The Church of Scientology: A History of a New Religion* (Princeton: Princeton University Press, 2011), 19, 58.

The complexity lies in trying to disentangle the elements of Scientology that Hubbard *believed* and the ones that he created for convenience or with some other goal in mind. The further complexity lies in Hubbard as an individual: his likely substance abuse and mental health issues means that way may never fully understand what Hubbard believed to be true; indeed, his "truth" may have changed over time as he moved through different periods of his life.

7. L. Ron Hubbard, "Art Series 1," HCO Bulletin of 30 August AD15R Revised December 30, 1979, in L. Ron Hubbard, *Art Series* (Los Angeles: Bridge Publications, 1984), 1. Many of Hubbard's HCO Bulletins on art are part of a book that Scientology published later, called *Art*. See L. Ron Hubbard, *Art* (Los Angeles: Bridge Publications, 1991).

8. L. Ron Hubbard, "Whole Track," *Dianetics and Scientology Technical Dictionary*, Original Publication date 1975 (Los Angeles: Publications Organization, 1978), 468.

9. L. Ron Hubbard, A *History of Man*, originally published 1952 (Denmark: Scientology Publications Organization, 1980), 6.

10. Ibid., 7.

11. David G. Hartwell and Kathryn Cramer, eds. *The Space Opera Renaissance* (New York: Tor Books, 2006), 17–18.

12. Since writing "Astounding History," I (Raine) discovered another definition of space opera from Hubbard's A *Mission into Time*. It reads: "**space opera** a novel, motion picture, radio, T.V. play or comic strip featuring interplanetary and interstellar travel and highly developed galactic societies. As uncovered by L. Ron Hubbard in his investigation into the whole track, space opera is a reality and not just a creation of the imagination." See L. Ron Hubbard, A *Mission into Time* (Los Angeles: The American Saint Hill Organization, 1973), 103. See Susan Raine, "Astounding History: L. Ron Hubbard's Scientology Space Opera," *Religion* 45 (2015): 66–88 for a full discussion of space opera in the SF genre and as Hubbard employed it in Scientology.

13. See Susan Raine, "Astounding History: L. Ron Hubbard's Scientology Space Opera," *Religion* 45 (2015): 66–88 for a full discussion of Scientology space opera.

14. L. Ron Hubbard, "Ron's Talk to Pubs WW & Execs re: Symbols and Their Use," December 10, 1967, in *Sea Organization Flag Information Letter 148*, April 18, 1978, LRH Tape lectures from circa 1950 to 1972.

15. The Sea Org is Scientology's most elite organization. Its members are the movement's most dedicated—they sign a billion year contract to illustrate their commitment to reincarnating over and over again with the sole purpose of "return[ing] life after life to fulfill 'Ron's purpose.'" See Jon Atack, A *Piece of Blue Sky: Scientology, Dianetics and L. Ron Hubbard Exposed* (New York: Lyle Stuart, 1990), 20.

16. L. Ron Hubbard, "Ron's Talk to Pubs WW & Execs re: Symbols and Their Use," December 10, 1967, in *Sea Organization Flag Information Letter 148*, April 18, 1978, LRH Tape lectures from circa 1950 to 1972.

17. Matt Davis, "Selling Scientology," *Portland Mercury News*, August 7, 2008.

18. Scientology, *EXPAND!* 1 (1968).

19. Ibid., 8.

20. Bent Corydon, *L. Ron Hubbard: Messiah or Madman?* (Fort Lee: Barricade Books, 1987), 361.

21. L. Ron Hubbard Library, *Ron The Artist: Art and Philosophy of Art* (L. Ron Hubbard Library, 1998), 41.

22. L. Ron Hubbard, "Art Series 1," HCO Bulletin of July 29, 1973, in L. Ron Hubbard, *Art Series* (Los Angeles: Bridge Publications, 1984), 3.

23. L. Ron Hubbard, "Art, More About," HCO Bulletin of 30 August AD15R Revised December 30, 1979, in L. Ron Hubbard, *Art Series* (Los Angeles: Bridge Publications, 1984), 3.

24. Betty Ann Jordon, "The Wise Man of Canadian Abstract Painting Made His Mark Right to the End of a Bravura Career," *The Globe and Mail*, September 8, 2010. Jordon's article on Gorman states that "Disillusioned but silent on the subject

of those missing years, Gorman returned to Canada in 1971, to live and work in a garage-studio in Ottawa. There he painted very large abstract paintings implying the regional landscape."

25. The Editorial Staff of the Auditor, *Successes of Scientology* (East Grinstead: Publications Organization Worldwide, 1968), 8.

26. Richard Gorman, "CONFIDENTAL—SEA ORG MEMBERS ONLY— TAPE BY RICHARD GORMAN—LRH ARTIST," Tape recording.

27. L. Ron Hubbard, *Dianetics and Scientology Technical Dictionary* (Los Angeles: Publications Organization, 1975), 49.

28. L. Ron Hubbard, *Modern Management Technology Defined* (Los Angeles: Publications Organization, 1978), 98.

29. Richard Gorman, "CONFIDENTAL—SEA ORG MEMBERS ONLY— TAPE BY RICHARD GORMAN—LRH ARTIST," Tape recording.

30. L. Ron Hubbard, *The Creation of Human Ability* (Los Angeles: The Publications Organization World Wide, 1968).

31. The British parliamentary inquiries into Scientology were damning. On December 5, 1966, MP Kenneth Robinson stated: "I do not think any further inquiry is necessary to establish that the activities of this organization are potentially harmful. I have no doubt that Scientology is totally valueless in promoting health and, in particular, that people seeking help with problems of mental health can gain nothing from the attentions of this organization." These and other conclusions are part of a report on Scientology by British MP Sir John Foster. See John Foster, "Enquiry into the Practice and Effects of Scientology" (Her Majesty's Stationery Office, 1971), vii.

32. On July 25, 1968, British MP Kenneth Robinson, announced to the House of Commons: "The Government have concluded that [Scientology] is so objectionable that it would be right to take all steps within their power to curb its growth." The government ruled that all U.K. Scientology establishments would no longer have educational status and that foreigners may neither work in nor study Scientology in the United Kingdom. Anthony Lewis, "Britain Curbs Activities of Cult of Scientologists," *New York Times*, August 1, 1968.

33. The *Scottish Daily Mail* reported that "Mr. Hubbard, who claims to have relinquished control of his movement, has now been banned by the Home Secretary from entering the country." Furthermore, "A number of Scientology students have been refused entry to Britain since the Government decided to take action to curb the growth of the movement in Britain." Daily Mail Reporter, "'Let's Talk' Appeal by Scientology's Hubbard," *Scottish Daily Mail*, August 5, 1968.

34. L. Ron Hubbard, "IMMIGRATION TIP," Hubbard Communications Office Policy Letter, May 24, 1968. Note that this policy letter is not included in any of the HCO Executive Volumes. A copy of it resides in the Stephen A. Kent Collection on Alternative Religions housed at the University of Alberta in Edmonton, Canada. In it, Hubbard stated, "The new books covers, particularly the one with the Inquisitor (Have You Lived Before This Life?) and the boy looking out the window (Self Analysis) operate as a sort of open-the gate at Immigration and Customs if placed in plain sight in baggage or carried and shown."

35. The Editorial Staff of the Auditor, *Successes of Scientology* (East Grinstead: Publications Organization Worldwide, 1968).

36. Ibid.

37. Sheri J. Broyles, "Subliminal Advertising and the Perpetual Popularity of Playing to People's Paranoia," *Journal of Consumer Affairs* 40 (2006): 392–393. Broyles's article offers and excellent overview of the history of the concept of subliminal advertising.

38. Ibid., 393.

39. L. Ron Hubbard, "Study: Evaluation of Information," The Study Tape Lecture Transcripts, August 11, 1964 (Los Angeles: Bridge Publications, 1982), 54.

40. In *The Hidden Persuaders*, first published in 1957, Packard explores the use of consumer motivational research and other psychological techniques, including depth psychology and subliminal tactics by advertisers to manipulate expectations and induce desire for products, particularly in the American postwar era. The book questions the morality of using these techniques.

41. L. Ron Hubbard, "Study: Evaluation of Information," The Study Tape Lecture Transcripts, August 11, 1964 (Los Angeles: Bridge Publications 1982), 54.

42. L. Ron Hubbard, "Scientology and Tradition," Taped lecture, September 15, 1964, Tape number 2765 SB SPEC – 40.

43. L. Ron Hubbard, "Art Off I/T RE: Passport to Freedom Poster and Flyer," January 11, 1980.

44. Jon Atack, *A Piece of Blue Sky: Scientology, Dianetics and L. Ron Hubbard Exposed* (New York: Lyle Stuart, 1990), 137–138.

45. L. Ron Hubbard, "Organizations of Scientology 1B," Taped lecture, October 4, 1954.

46. L. Ron Hubbard, "OT VIII, Series 1: Student Briefing," HCO Bulletin, Hubbard Communication Office, May 1980.

47. Hubbard initially published *Dianetics: The Modern Science of Mental Health* in May 1950, although he revealed his Dianetic ideas first in the popular pulp magazine, *Astounding Science Fiction*, in March 1950.

48. For an overview of the many claims that Hubbard made about Dianetics, see Terra Manca, "Alternative Therapy, Dianetics and Scientology," *Marburg Journal of Religion* 15 (2010).

49. As cited, for example, in Jon Atack, *A Piece of Blue Sky: Scientology, Dianetics and L. Ron Hubbard Exposed*, 31–32; Stephen A. Kent, "The Creation of 'Religious' Scientology," *Religious Studies and Theology* 18 (1999): 103–104; and Mikael Rothstein, "'His Name was Xenu. He used renegades . . .': Aspects of Scientology's Founding Myth," in *Scientology*, ed. James Lewis (Oxford University Press, 2009), 365–388.

50. Matt Davis, "Selling Scientology," *Portland Mercury News Paper*, August 7, 2008.

51. See Susan Raine, "Astounding History: L. Ron Hubbard's Scientology Space Opera."

52. Hugh Urban, *The Church of Scientology: A History of a New Religion*, 39.

53. As per Hubbard's space opera narrative, Incident II.

54. L. Ron Hubbard, Clear Procedure, Issue One 1957 (The Department of Publications World Wide, 1968). Another booklet with the same title and cover image was reprinted by Bridge Publication, Los Angeles, California, in October 1982.

55. http://www.bridgepub.com/store/catalog/dianetics-professional-course-lectures.html.

56. http://ocmb.xenu.net/ocmb/viewtopic.php?t=32018.

57. Ibid.

58. Atack, A *Piece of Blue Sky: Scientology, Dianetics and L. Ron Hubbard Exposed,* 100–101.

59. L. Ron Hubbard, "Populations Surveys," Hubbard Communications Office Policy Letter. January 25, 1972. Also published in L. Ron Hubbard, *Management Series* (Los Angeles: Church of Scientology of California Publications Organization, 1974).

60. L. Ron Hubbard, "SEA ORG SYMBOL," In *Modern Management Technology Defined: Hubbard Dictionary of Administration and Management* (Los Angeles: Publications Organization United States, 1976), 467.

61. Dragana Rogic, Jelena Andelkovic Grasar, and Emilija Nicolic, "Wreath: Its Use and Meaning in Ancient Visual Culture," *Religion and Tolerance: The Journal for the Center for Empirical Research on Religion* X, no. 18 (2012): 343.

62. For example, see the following items: L. Ron Hubbard. "Re: THE FORMAL RULES OF COMPOSITION," April 7, 1980; L. Ron Hubbard. "ART SUBMISSIONS or HOW TO GET AN OK FROM DEPT 21," October 24, 1978; and L. Ron Hubbard. "RE: TECH DICTIONARY FLIER," August 7, 1979.

63. Hubbard developed a thorough compliance list that incorporated the following elements: First, Hubbard required the use of a color harmony wheel so that his artists achieved full color coordination in their works. Second, he mandated *impingement.* This term means that one must reach some subliminal urge. Hubbard proposed that the first step in this regard is to get into the mind first, so that one can achieve influence at a subliminal glance. Third, *positioning* became an ingredient in Scientology images. Positioning Scientology products with other items ensures positive associations. Fourth, Hubbard directed *typographical design.* For example, he ordered that in each issue the logo on *Advance!* magazine must be different. Fifth, the *message* is extremely important, as it determines how the art work is to be composed. Sixth, Hubbard emphasized achieving depth and a three-dimensional effect in the artwork by paying particular attention to *color depth.* Finally, the *eight depth perceptions* refers to additional techniques used—for example, perspective, shadow, depth, and so forth to further ensure a three-dimensional effect.

All Scientology art work had to pass this checklist or one similar to it before Hubbard it considered camera ready. Because of Hubbard's attention to detail, Scientology art work is slick, glossy, and very polished and professional (and it remains so). Today, the art production takes place in Hemet, California, in a separate building called Golden Era Studios, where many Sea Organization personnel work.

Interestingly, in 1979, Hubbard's entire approach to book cover imagery and advertisements changed once again. The new approach this time was called *positioning*—a process where you compare or position your product in relation to another. The art of Scientology advertising then focused on product positioning. Important to the process of positioning is that the product being sold is placed next to or incorporated with an object that triggers an *emotional* connection and response. Placing the product, in this case an image of a book cover, next to a suggestive image that complements or attracts the viewer to the book's content is an effective way to generate positive associations. Hubbard was so enthusiastic about this advertising concept that in 1979 he wrote a policy letter about it. In this letter, Hubbard applauds the work of the positioning method creators, Jack Trout and Al Ries, and recommends their article, *The Positioning Era* (1972). See L. Ron Hubbard, "POSITIONING, PHILO-SOPHIC THEORY," HCO Policy Letter of January 30, 1979, Hubbard Communications Office. As was often the case when he discussed specific ideas and concepts, Hubbard proposed that he was the authority on understanding positioning. Trout and Ries first published *The Positioning Era* as part of a series on marketing in the publication, *Advertising Age*. Trout and Ries went on to write many articles on positioning in advertising, culminating in their book, *Positioning: The Battle for Your Mind* (1981). The book is considered a classic in the world of advertising and marketing.

BIBLIOGRAPHY

Atack, Jon. *A Piece of Blue Sky: Scientology, Dianetics and L. Ron Hubbard Exposed.* New York: Lyle Stuart, 1990.

Beit-Hallahmi, Benjamin. "Scientology: Religion or Racket?" *Marburg Journal of Religion* 8 (2003). http://www.unimarburg.de/religionwissenschaft/journal/mjr/kent3.html.

Bromley, David G., and Mitchell Bracey Jr. "The Church of Scientology: A Quasi Religion." In William W. Zellner and Marc Petrowsky, eds., *Sects, Cults and Spiritual Communities: A Sociological Analysis*, 141–156. Praeger, 1998.

Broyles, Sheri J. "Subliminal Advertising and the Perpetual Popularity of Playing to People's Paranoia." *Journal of Consumer Affairs* 40 (2006).

Coleman, Earle J. *Creativity and Spirituality: Bonds Between Art and Religion.* New York: State University of New York, 1998.

Corydon, Bent. *L. Ron Hubbard, Messiah or Madman?* 1996 edition. New Jersey: Barricade Books, 1987.

Daily Mail Reporter. "'Let's Talk' Appeal by Scientology's Hubbard." *Scottish Daily Mail.* August 5, 1968.

Davis, Matt. "Selling Scientology." *Portland Mercury News.* August 7, 2008.

Editorial Staff of the Auditor, The. *Successes of Scientology.* East Grinstead: Publications Organization Worldwide, 1968.

Foster, Sir John. "Enquiry into the Practice and Effects of Scientology." London: Her Majesty's Stationery Office, 1971.

Gorman, Richard. "CONFIDENTAL—SEA ORG MEMBERS ONLY—TAPE BY RICHARD GORMAN—LRH ARTIST." Tape recording. Private Collection.

Hartwell, David G., and Kathryn Cramer, eds. *The Space Opera Renaissance.* New York: Tor Books, 2006.

Hubbard, L. Ron. *Art.* Los Angeles: Bridge Publications, 1991.

Hubbard, L. Ron. "Art, More About." HCO Bulletin of 30 August AD15R Revised December 30, 1979. In L. Ron Hubbard, *Art Series*. Los Angeles: Bridge Publications, 1984.

Hubbard, L. Ron. "Art Off I/T RE: Passport to Freedom Poster and Flyer." January 11, 1980.

Hubbard, L. Ron. "Art Series 1." HCO Bulletin of August 30. Revised December 30, 1979. In L. Ron Hubbard, *Art Series*. Los Angeles: Bridge Publications, 1984.

Hubbard, L. Ron. "ART SUBMISSIONS or HOW TO GET AN OK FROM DEPT 21." October 24, 1978.

Hubbard, L. Ron. *The Creation of Human Ability*. Los Angeles: The Publications Organization World Wide, 1968.

Hubbard, L. Ron. *Dianetics and Scientology Technical Dictionary*. Los Angeles: Publications Organization, 1975.

Hubbard, L. Ron. *A History of Man*. Originally published 1952. Denmark: Scientology Publications Organization, 1980.

Hubbard, L. Ron. "IMMIGRATION TIP." Hubbard Communication Office Policy Letter. May 24, 1968.

Hubbard, L. Ron. *A Mission into Time*. Los Angeles: The American Saint Hill Organization, 1973.

Hubbard, L. Ron. *Modern Management Technology Defined: Hubbard Dictionary of Administration and Management*. Los Angeles: Publications Organization, 1976.

Hubbard, L. Ron. "Organizations of Scientology 1B." Taped lecture. October 4, 1954.

Hubbard, L. Ron. "OT VIII, Series 1: Student Briefing." HCO Bulletin. Hubbard Communication Office. May 1980.

Hubbard, L. Ron. "Populations Surveys." Hubbard Communications Office Policy Letter. January 25, 1972. Also published in L. Ron Hubbard. *Management Series*. Church of Scientology of California Publications Organization, 1974.

Hubbard, L. Ron. "RE: TECH DICTIONARY FLIER." August 7, 1979.

Hubbard, L. Ron. "Re: THE FORMAL RULES OF COMPOSITION." April 7, 1980.

Hubbard, L. Ron. *Ron's Journal 1967*. Taped lecture. Golden Era Studios, 1983.

Hubbard, L. Ron. *Ron's Journal 1968*. Taped lecture. Golden Era Studios, 1983.

Hubbard, L. Ron. "Ron's Talk to Pubs WW & Execs re: Symbols and Their Use." December 10, 1967, in *Sea Organization Flag Information Letter 148*. April 18, 1978. LRH tape lectures from circa 1950 to 1972.

Hubbard, L. Ron. "Scientology and Tradition." Taped lecture. Tape number 2765 SB SPEC – 40. September 15, 1964.

Hubbard, L. Ron. *Scientology 8-8008*. Originally published 1953. Los Angeles: The American Saint Hill Organization, 1967.

Hubbard, L. Ron. "Study: Evaluation of Information." The Study Tape Lecture Transcripts. August 11, 1964. Los Angeles: Bridge Publications, 1982.

Hubbard, L. Ron. "Whole Track." *Dianetics and Scientology Technical Dictionary*. Originally published 1975. Los Angeles: Scientology Publications Organization, 1978.

Jordon, Betty Ann. "The Wise Man of Canadian Abstract Painting Made His Mark Right to the End of a Bravura Career." *The Globe and Mail*. September 8, 2010.

Kent, Stephen A. "Scientology—Is This a Religion?" *Marburg Journal of Religion* 4 (1999): 1–23. http://www.unimarburg.de/religionwissenschaft/journal/mjr/kent3 .html.

Lewis, Anthony. "Britain Curbs Activities of Cult of Scientologists." *New York Times.* August 1, 1968.

L. Ron Hubbard Library. *Ron The Artist: Art and Philosophy of Art.* L. Ron Hubbard Library, 1998.

Manca, Terra. "Alternative Therapy, Dianetics and Scientology." *Marburg Journal of Religion* 15 (2010).

Passas, Nikos, and Manuel Escamilla Castillo. "Scientology and its 'Clear' Business." *Behavioral Sciences and the Law* 10 (1992): 103–116.

Raine, Susan. "Astounding History: L. Ron Hubbard's Scientology Space Opera." *Religion* 45 (2015): 66–88.

Rogic, Dragana, Jelena Andelkovic Grasar, and Emilija Nikolic. "Wreath: Its Use and Meaning in Ancient Visual Culture." *Religion and Tolerance: The Journal for the Center for Empirical Research on Religion* X, no. 18 (2012): 341–356.

Rothstein, Mikael. "'His Name was Xenu. He used renegades . . .': Aspects of Scientology's Founding Myth." In James Lewis, ed., *Scientology*, 365–388. Oxford: Oxford University Press, 2009.

Scientology. *EXPAND!* 1, 1968.

Scientology. http://www.bridgepub.com/store/catalog/dianetics-professional-course -lectures.html.

Urban, Hugh. *The Church of Scientology: A History of a New Religion.* Princeton: Princeton University Press, 2011.

12

L. Ron Hubbard's Foray into the World of Music

Mark Evans

INTRODUCTION

In the second verse of the song, "Thank You for Listening," from the album *The Road to Freedom* (1986), the voice of L. Ron Hubbard sings, "I do not sing what I believe." However, Hubbard most certainly did sing about his beliefs and how they pertained particularly to Scientology. The song goes on to assert that, regardless of the listeners' personal beliefs, Hubbard's lyrics will "have impact." This leads to a more important question: what *was* the "impact" of his musical endeavors? He was involved in producing music in several genres, worked with some fantastic musicians, and certainly saw himself as a musician. But his musical legacy is not strong. The Church of Scientology has not become known for its musical contributions; Hubbard's outputs in soundtrack or other genres have not been universally recognized. If anything, there is a disparaging note to most accounts of Hubbard's work. This chapter aims to look critically at several of Hubbard's (and Scientology's) musical projects and analyze them both for their musical quality, as well as for the "impact" Hubbard's baritone voice—a rare occurrence of Hubbard's own performativity—assures us will arrive.

HUBBARD AND MUSIC

One of the most instructive, albeit biased, accounts of Hubbard's musical heritage comes from Book 12 of the *L. Ron Hubbard Series, Music Maker: Composer & Performer*, a Scientology-published volume extolling Hubbard's achievements and philosophies across a range of cultural forms. As with much of the information surrounding Hubbard's credentials and experience, it tends to be circumstantial. Nonetheless, we read that

> His formal entrance into the [musical] field began in the early 1930s as a balladeer on Washington, DC's radio WOL. Although no recordings were preserved, he was said to have performed his own works in an admirable baritone while accompanying himself on ukulele.[1]

His "official" music biography then skips forward, via a brief stint with Alaskan radio, to his work with the Apollo Stars in the mid-1970s (see below).

In Lawrence Wright's (2013) book, *Going Clear: Scientology, Hollywood and the Prison of Belief* (later made into the documentary, *Going Clear*[2]), about Scientology and Hubbard and his early life, we get more insight into Hubbard's everyday engagement with music:

> The house echoed with his [Hubbard's] booming laugh, he taught the children how to play "Chopsticks" on the piano and showed them card tricks with his quick hands and perfectly manicured fingernails. He would play records and dance with the children to Beethoven or Ravel or Edward Grieg's Peer Gynt Suite—bold, soaring music. He liked to sing and he would bust into "Farewell and Adieu to you Fair Spanish Ladies" and "Be Kind to your Web-Footed friends." A children's song that is sung to the tune of "Stars and Stripes Forever."[3]

Here we see a vision of Hubbard involved in normal vernacular musical practices mixed with high art (classical music) engagements. What we can read into this description is a love for music, and even a lightheartedness, and certainly Hubbard's willingness to involve himself as an active performer. While the active performance would gradually wane over his musical outputs, one can trace the lighthearted aspect throughout his musical repertoire. If a lightheartedness is there in musicality, in aim, in experimentation, then it is certainly not present in Hubbard's philosophies, writing, and musings about music generally. Nor is it a feature of his devotees and their discussions of his musical outputs. For example, in the "Friends of L. Ron Hubbard" liner notes to *The Road to Freedom* (1986) album, it states: "Whether writing or composing music, a common theme ran through all of his work. Mr. Hubbard concentrated on the human condition, and on raising the awareness of his readers and listeners about themselves."[4]

More objectively, this is not a theme that runs throughout Hubbard's musical output. There is no doubt that some works seek to elevate the cause of Scientology—which could be construed as listeners raising awareness about themselves. But, more often, this output is designed to extoll the teachings of Scientology.

His musical works did try to push boundaries. Unlike his pulp fiction works, designed to appeal to genre formulas, his musical works are often bounded in genre-pushing agendas. For instance, he was the first person to write the soundtrack for a *book*. In reality he wrote a soundtrack for a film that had not yet been made, but nonetheless the philosophy was there. His jazz exploits, whether part of "Space Jazz" or "Mission Earth," sought to fuse new musical combinations and, in particular, with the use of new technology.[5] To that end, his embrace of the Fairlight Computer Musical Instrument was—as was the case with its other early adopters—groundbreaking. Whether the results of that exploration produced the most compelling texts is another question. Nonetheless, what is curious about his musical exploits is that they all sought to push boundaries, often within distinct cultural contexts. For example, he formed a jazz-fusion group that attempted to operate at the highest levels of musical expression, yet it served as an attractional cultural force for a church that had recently become nomadic and was barely welcome globally. He wrote a soundtrack for a book, in light of no funds foreseeable to make a film, and he participated in producing "religious" musical texts for a church founded from his science-fiction-based writings, with no historical liturgy or musical tradition to contain it. Thus, while the claims of *Music Maker* may be hard to agree with in totality, his musical outputs should be critiqued within this context. Certainly, early on, Hubbard appeared to display an enthusiasm for the longevity and "purity" of music. Jeff Berkwits quotes Hubbard from a lecture given in 1952: "A song can racket down the ages . . . It doesn't corrode. It doesn't have to be polished, maintained, oiled, shelved or put in a vault. It happens that a song is far more powerful than any blaster ever invented."[6] However, as with all of Hubbard's cultural outputs, this is shifting sand; his unpredictability, egocentrism, delusion, and greed could easily shift the underlying rationale for any of his work.

Perhaps the most concerning report of Hubbard's musical philosophy comes from his claims that he actually invented music.[7] One widely reported story notes that during a Scientology event just months after his death, Annie Broeker—making her first appearance since the 1970s—told the assembled fans that

> Hubbard had once told her that "after the first tick of time" that one "Arp Cola" had invented music. There was a strong implication that Hubbard had been Cola. He had supposedly borrowed some of these early tunes and refashioned them into the modern style. The result was an album called "The Road to Freedom," which was released that night.[8]

Annie Broeker, whose real name was Ann Tidman,[9] had effectively been one of Hubbard's maidservants—known in the Church as "messengers"—serving him on the *Apollo* from the age of 12.[10] More importantly, it was Tidman (along with her husband Pat Broeker) who had cared for Hubbard when he went into seclusion in 1980. Reportedly, it was Tidman who was with Hubbard when he died on January 24, 1986. Either way, she had many years in isolation with Hubbard to hear his self-proclaimed projections of greatness.

What is significant is that the launch of the album, *The Road to Freedom*, took place in March 1986 and was timed to celebrate his death (which, for Scientologists, was merely Hubbard casting off his earthly body and moving to the next level). Hubbard's "teachings" and autobiographical musings were no doubt still fresh in Tidman's mind. Apart from the ridiculousness of the sentiment—before Arp Cola there was no music in the universe—the name Arp Cola has been disparaged by critics and ridiculed for its lack of imagination. Several commentators, often from blog sites devoted to critiquing Scientology, note the simplicity of "Arp" being short for arpeggio—or arpeggiator on a synthesizer. Indeed, Arp was the name of a company that produced synthesizers. The whole name, "Arp Cola," is an anagram of "crapola," and at the very least, it is hard to move away from the possible "cola" references.[11] Yet when one former devotee was questioned about his response to hearing this news—he was there at the launch event for *The Road to Freedom*—he wrote: "I believed it, hook, line and sinker. As always at events, grandiose pronunciations about the Dear Leader were met with wild applause."[12] So Hubbard created music within this context. Within that context he was able also to promote his critical views on musical practices in contemporary society; as well, he made textbook-like proclamations about how music works. In some musically themed missives from the Hubbard Communications Office we gain more insight into his self-proclaimed understanding of music.

In a communication dated April 25, 1974, entitled "Art Series 4," Hubbard pays particular attention to the machinations of rhythm. Here, Hubbard defines rhythm and rhythmic terms. He delineates six types of rhythm—delineations that one could find already in basic musicological texts. He does go on, however, to nominate rhythm as the fundamental musical element that speaks to the human condition:

All life is a repeating pulse and ebb and surge of motion.

Life becomes difficult when rhythmic prediction cannot occur. Anxiety sets in. It is a relief to participate in predictable rhythm in an art form. It is safe and reassuring. If the rhythm is exciting it is also exciting. Therefore participation in predictable rhythm is pleasure and even joy.[13]

As has been documented elsewhere in relation to sound in horror cinema, often it is the disruption or cessation of predictable rhythm that most unsettles the viewer/listener.[14] Likewise, a complete absence of sound is to all intents and purposes unnatural. In this sense, Hubbard's assertions about the pleasure to be gained from stable, predictable rhythm are well founded. Hubbard takes this notion to the extreme, noting that "Rhythm and its expression is the basic key to all art forms."[15]

The Scientology-sanctioned coffee table book *Music Maker, Composer & Performer*, part of the *L. Ron Hubbard Series*, contains various contributions from Hubbard about music alongside glowing accounts of his musical achievements. It includes essays on "Proportionate Sound"—a concept largely derided by audio engineers worldwide as overclaiming, "Music and Theater," Music Form and Music Type," and "An Analysis of Rock Music." From the latter essay we learn that Hubbard, who claimed to have analyzed several thousand popular recordings while aboard the *Apollo* in 1974 (although none of these analyses are documented nor are Hubbard's analytical schema revealed), can write authoritatively that

> it became fairly visible, at least to me, that the sophisticated world was rolling back into the past and reaching for its tribal roots. The savage breast was stirred by rhythms mostly because they had very little in the way of instruments. But it seems the savage breast is with us again.[16]

The telling factor behind each of these essays is Hubbard's lack of critical engagement and absence of a methodologically proven analysis and objective presentation. Moreover, the essays are a part of a very biased Scientology account of Hubbard's musical endeavors.

Perhaps most revealing of all Hubbard's communications in terms of his own productions comes from "Art Series 2," dated July 29, 1973. Entitled "Art, More About," the document addresses the question: "How good does a professional work of art have to be?"[17] Insinuating that the reader may find the question imponderable, Hubbard goes on to proclaim: "I have a surprise for you. There IS an answer."[18] Over several pages, Hubbard then goes on to describe techniques used by painters, Chinese poets, musicians, and even magicians to bring about a "work of art." His summary of what then creates art is encapsulated in the following statement: "TECHNICAL EXPERTISE ITSELF ADEQUATE TO PRODUCE AN EMOTIONAL IMPACT." [19] After discussing technical expertise in detail and even proffering the quizzical statement, "Some people are themselves a work of art because they have mastered the small practical techniques of living,"[20] Hubbard seeks to conclude his discussion on quality art: "That is how good a work of art has to be. Once one is capable of executing that technical expertise for that art form he can pour on the message. Unless the professional form is there first, the message will not transmit."[21]

In this short treatise we gain an insight into some of Hubbard's musical practices. On the whole, his musical outputs do contain a level of technical expertise. Whether it be mastery over new technological capabilities (*Space Jazz*), the technical mastery of jazz musicians working with him (*Power of Source, Space Jazz*), or high production values delivered through state-of-art facilities (*The Road to Freedom*), Hubbard's music can claim technical expertise adequate to illicit emotional impact. Ironically, where the music fails is on the message layered on top. As will be seen, expertise may be one thing but delivering an overall artistic product is more important.

THE APOLLO STARS

Undoubtedly one of Hubbard's greatest strengths was his ability to surround himself with talented musicians. Often these musicians included converts to Scientology, yet they remained esteemed musicians in their own right. There is nothing distinctive about this practice—many religions and political groups have long sought to gain publicity and credibility via the musicians and popular culture figures who identify with their respective beliefs and ideologies. Every four years the two dominant American political parties, the Democrats and the Republicans, gain additional exposure through the musicians (and other popular figures) supporting them. In contemporary religious terms, Hillsong Church in Australia received much media attention for the VIP presence of pop singer Justin Bieber at their huge annual conference in 2015,[22] despite many reports of his decidedly less than Pentecostal behaviors.

Hubbard's embrace of gifted musicians with whom to share the stage probably began with the formation of the Apollo Stars in 1973. The Apollo Stars was the "house" band that Hubbard put together on his vessel *Apollo* during the period 1967–1975, where he and his most dedicated followers sailed the world in three vessels, collectively known as the Sea Organization (or Sea Org). The reasons for Hubbard's nautical retreat are documented elsewhere (including in this volume) and need not be reiterated. What is important here is the birth of the Apollo Stars and the musical legacy Hubbard would leave through them. Essentially a jazz band, the Apollo Stars' musicians were drawn from Sea Org members, either crew or other followers of Hubbard. As Don Jolly notes:

"The Apollo Stars" were first assembled in 1973 for an impromptu performance at a Portuguese winter festival on the island of Maderia. Hubbard, their "musical director," ran the group through a series of

intense drills and daily practice routines, many of which were designed
to increase the musician's ability to capture various emotional tones . . .
From 1973 to 1975, as the *Apollo* moved from port to port, the Stars
came with it, giving goodwill performances in Spain and Portugal and
winning some degree of local radio play.[23]

The "intense drills and daily practice routines" in order to convey emotional
impact speak to Hubbard's writings about technical expertise. Notably, his
official communication on the subject occurred in the same year. Clearly the
Apollo Stars was one attempt by Hubbard to bring his philosophical notions
into reality and, by association, to further the cause of Scientology. To assist in
this realization, Hubbard composed original songs for the band to play, although
only two titles, "We're Moving In" and "My Dear Portugal," from the Apollo
Stars' only album release, *Power of Source*, are credited to him. *Music Maker*
claims that Hubbard was attempting to create a style of "savage" performance,
the technique for which was "gregarious, heavily syncopated [with] a strong
reliance on percussion."[24] The goodwill or free performances of the band were
often public relations exercises—important at a time when Scientology and
Hubbard's flotilla were struggling to find port—or were simply not welcome.

Power of Source was released in 1974 by the Scientology-run record label
Source Music. Don Jolly poetically sets the context for the album when he
writes:

It was a time of music and madness, violence and espionage — when
everything was tried, nothing discarded, and the narrative of Scientology as both a movement and a cosmography was tantalizingly fluid.
"Power of Source," in its dark, wax grooves, captures some measure of
that chaos.[25]

The back cover of the album itself unsurprisingly sees none of this chaos, boldly
proclaiming, "In 1973 L. Ron Hubbard developed an incredible new sound in
music."[26] And, as if that is not convincing enough, "Radio, TV and stage people
have uniformly decreed that the Apollo Stars ARE a new and exciting sound in
music. It is often repeated that the STARS are playing the music of the future."[27]
While maybe not the music of the future, the album has attracted more positive
or, at least begrudgingly favorable, critiques than any other Hubbard release.
Comments to a YouTube posting of the album include the following:

It's really good jazz. You guys should be proud for sure. (Spencer Thayer)
I dig it! (crallspace)
You guys sound really awesome! I love the album. (Happy Lion)

Not a Scientologist but this is really good! (brian phillip)
One good thing Scientology produced. (richard dietl)
I despise this religion, but this album is bonkers. 100% badass music. (King
    Green)
This album is decent. Scientology licks balls. (Lyle Farris)[28]

The album was uploaded to YouTube by Tom Rodriguez, the bongo player in
the band and featured in the recording. In announcing the post, Rodriguez
comments:

> [T]ruth is we recorded this album too prematurely having only been a
> band for a few weeks. As with ANY band, vocal group, dance team,
> actor etc. . . . it requires a lot of practice, time and effort to become
> really good. What is unfortunate is that you haven't heard how good
> we became unless you saw and heard us months and years later and at
> sessions that were recorded in studios later on were never released.[29]

In the context of Hubbard's aims for the album and for the band, this is an important revelation. Hubbard's mission was to expose technical mastery in order
to illicit emotional responses. The frenetic style of playing on the album and
upbeat tempos throughout, partly reminiscent of earlier bebop styles, requires
enormous technical proficiency. Hubbard's rush to release his "incredible new
sound" probably diminished its effectiveness in communicating his message.

Citing an ex-Scientologist messageboard, *Buzzfeed* reporter Katie Notopoulos notes that "several former members posted about how they were forced
to listen to *Power of Source* at Scientology events and how they loathed it."[30]
Once again, bongo player Rodriguez jumps in, this time to defend the band
more earnestly:

> None of you ever got to hear any of the other incredible albums we
> recorded—that's right! We recorded others. To this day I don't know
> why they never got mixed and put onto vinyl . . . and I so wish I had
> copies of those tapes for personal reasons. I wonder if they still exist and
> may one day surface as "The Lost Apoolo [sic] Stars tapes"
>   One cassette tape I recorded during a kick ass band rehearsal, which
> contained 15 of our later songs . . . I sent to my mom back in 1974 . . . I
> got it back, but then I lost it sometime in the recent 2000's.
>   I hate myself for this.[31]

Ultimately, *Power of Source* does not live up to the lofty claims of its album
cover. Even if the Apollo Stars musicians were "thunderously welcomed

wherever they have appeared in the world . . ." (as stated on the album cover), *Power of Source* was not thunderously received by the music world, the jazz scene of the time, or by the wider public. As Jolly surmises, the album "partic-ipates well in no wider discourse, either traditional or avant-garde. Instead, it chooses to operate primarily as an adolescent exercise in trying things on."[32]

SCIENTOLOGY AND MUSIC

The early years of Scientology had not focused on music as a proselytizing tool. Rather, the musical exploits of Hubbard had been read into his oeuvre as a great communicator, or as the liner notes to *The Road to Freedom* (penned by "Friends of L. Ron Hubbard") put it: "L. Ron Hubbard's tremendous con-tributions to virtually all walks of life have made him the greatest humani-tarian in history." They go on to speak of *The Road to Freedom* as "Hubbard's musical statement of what Scientology is really all about."

Before *The Road to Freedom*, Scientology, and by implication Hubbard, had not released any musical text specifically associated with the Church. Prior to 1986, Hubbard had released various musical compositions with sci-ence fiction influences (and others that were equally in line with Scientology values) but nothing explicitly detailing the beliefs and perceived benefits of Scientology. In that sense, *The Road to Freedom* is a landmark release, a "con-gregational" offering that extolls the values of Scientology and gives us more insight into the musical sensibilities of Hubbard himself.

According to the record's liner notes, "ALL SELECTIONS [ARE] WRIT-TEN AND COMPOSED BY L. RON HUBBARD."[33] The album was released in the year of Hubbard's death, so his actual contribution to the finished album is probably more fluid. Jon Atack reports: "The record was made by Scientologist musicians, with Hubbard supervising at long distance through taped messages."[34] Certainly, each track on the album is credited with an arranger, including some impressive names in the music industry: Chick Corea, Misha Segal, and Peter Schless. The richness and complexity of arrangement throughout the album speak less to Hubbard's abilities than to the abilities of those who supported and worked with him. Nonetheless, the compositions are credited to him and reveal more about his musical processes and proselytizing intentions.

Scientology and devotees of Hubbard are keen to point to *The Road to Freedom* as a musical reference text for the Church:

Essentially religious music Scientology style, *The Road to Freedom* rep-resents the culmination of all Ron pioneered as a Maker of Music. The album offers ten L. Ron Hubbard compositions to convey essential

Scientology truths for what he described as "wide public acquaintance with what Scientology is all about." If the result does not immediately match preconceived ideas of devotional music, it is because Scientology does not require blind devotion. Its truths are self-evident and not a matter of faith. *The Road to Freedom*, then, does not preach; it informs.[35]

Several aspects of this observation are worth noting. First, the author(s) (while unknown but clearly sanctioned by Scientology) acknowledge(s) this to be a "religious" style of music, in that it was to hold some liturgical, missional, and/or pastoral benefit. The clearest purpose of the music is identified as education— informing people of Scientology beliefs and Hubbard's knowledge. In this sense there is clearly a missional quality invoked, and, as will be shown below, unlike contemporary congregational music, the music on Hubbard's album could be construed as "performative." In contemporary settings, performative music is music sung *over* a group or congregation rather than music they *participate* in. There are deviations from this though, with the rallying cry of the title track, "Get on the road to freedom/Help us free all mankind," which is not dissimilar to any "call to worship"[36] song in contemporary Christian settings. Returning to the quoted observation above, its purpose as missional music designed to "inform" the public accounts for the often forced, nonpoetic lyric structures present. Not surprisingly, they often resemble a Scientology manual or a Hubbard science-fiction book set to music.

Between March and June 1986, more than 600 residents in the city of Clearwater[37] in Florida received cassette copies of *The Road to Freedom* in the mail. A front-page article published in the local *St. Petersburg Times* noting the mailout quotes Scientology spokesman Ludwig Alpers saying that the cassettes were paid for by Scientologists who "thought others might enjoy learning more about Scientology . . . It's got some good words."[38] The article then provides pointed but relatively objective examples of lyrics from the album; for example, the lyrics of "Why Worship Death," sung by opera singer Julia Migenes-Johnson and featuring jazz artist Chick Corea, talk of the deception perpetrated by "psychs and priests."[39]

The extremity of the lyrics and the rawness of their Scientology doctrine are often invoked negatively in public critiques of the album. Perhaps the most scathing and widely disseminated is Nathan Rabin's critique, published in *Slate*:

The tone is painfully earnest, the jargon thick. No one can accuse *The Road to Freedom* of being off-message: "Take the route of auditing and once again be free," the title track admonishes. "Give them the cans

and audit it out!" implore "The Evil Purposes" . . . The Road to Freedom still feels like it was recorded in another language and them only
intermittently translated into English.[40]

Rather fascinatingly, in the research for this chapter, it was impossible to
find a full lyric listing for the album online. To that end, the album did not
achieve the intended proselytization goals. A former devotee of Scientology
has written that

> "The Road To Freedom" was supposed to be the cure-all for getting new
> people into the orgs. The rationale was, wogs[41] would hear Ron's won-
> drous music and profound lyrics, and go rushing into the nearest org or
> mission to find out more.
>   The album was supposed to get massive radio airplay, but that never
> happened because the ignorant wogs in the music business just didn't
> appreciate, Ron's genius. Ron invented music, how could wogs not like
> Ron's theta masterpieces?[42]

So the missional aspect of the album was clearly promoted within Scientology. "OTBT" facetiously refers above to Hubbard's claim to have once been
the first being to invent music and questions why the inventor could not
produce a finer musical product. While critical success (see below) was certainly not forthcoming, even the aspiration to commercial success seems to
have evaded Hubbard and the Church. In *Music Maker* we read a caption to a
photo of gold albums exclaiming: "Ron Hubbard wrote the music for the gold
album *The Road to Freedom* which is performed by many of his friends including: John Travolta, Karen Black and Chick Corea. The album is available
in eight languages and has been released in countries around the world."[43]
It is impossible to verify this claim of gold-record status. Of course, this may
have been instituted upon the album via the studio producing the album
(a Scientology-owned label).[44] There is nothing in the *Billboard* archives to
indicate *The Road to Freedom* achieved the kind of sales required to gain gold
status, or even to register in the top 100 releases for 1986, 1987, or following
years. In fact, there is no mention of the album at all.

There was much happening in the mid-1980s that would have attracted
Scientology to the benefits of a populdist music product. At the time Christian artist Amy Grant was in her ascendancy, managing to bridge the gap
between the gospel *Billboard* charts and the general pop charts. Grant,
who would have 16 number-one albums on the Christian *Billboard* charts
and reach the general U.S. top 10 on three occasions, proved that religious
content could traverse the mainstream music charts.[45] Aside from material

success and doctrinal exposure, Grant's success paved the way for popular culture celebrity among religious artists. This would have been readily apparent and, no doubt, attractive to Hubbard and his Scientology leaders. At the same time, Pentecostal churches in North America were firmly entrenched in utilizing popular music within their services, with labels like Integrity—via their Hosanna! music series—establishing themselves as key music producers. In popular music at the time, bands like Bon Jovi continued to produce their chart-topping guitar-driven anthemic rock; Bruce Springsteen maintained his dominance with lyrically driven rock songs; and the synthesizer pop of Prince, Madonna, and Wham! filled the airwaves. Hubbard had at his disposal some great musical talent with which to speak to this music climate: *The Road to Freedom* was the result.

THE ROAD TO FREEDOM

The following analysis seeks to uncover exactly how the title track "The Road to Freedom" operates and its connection with other contemporary religious songs of the time. As noted above, the title track—like the rest of the album—displays Scientology doctrine in full light. Lyrics in the chorus (which begins the song) encourage us to "Get on the road to freedom / help us free all mankind." Later in the final verse and outro we get more specific information about our possibilities as humans capable of "auditing."[46]

To help deliver the message the song employs a basic verse/chorus structure, omitting a bridge section and adding an eight-bar solo played over the chorus chord progression.[47] The verse/chorus structure was well established by the mid-1980s and had largely superseded the previous AABA form (32-bar form). Popular congregational songs from Christian churches at the time were still tending toward strophic form or else were moving through the AABA structure that had been prominent in popular music in the 1960s and early 1970s. That Hubbard should choose the verse/chorus structure shows that he was aligning with the popular music forms of the time. As O'Regan observes:

> Overall, it is clear that the song was written by someone with a general understanding of pop song construction, though structurally there are some inconsistences—a double chorus before the last verse, a one-off 4-bar re-intro section that only appears once, and so forth.[48]

The two main sections of the song are quite different in their construction but not unlike popular congregational song. The verse, in the somber A minor key, is melodically far more disjunctive than the chorus. The melody is fairly inconsistent, with some higher leaps that make singing it more difficult. The informational lyrics of the verses are served well by the contemplation created by the emotional rising and falling of the melody.

In contrast, and in keeping with much congregational song, the chorus lifts to the key of c minor and is anthemic in construction. To achieve its catchy, singable hook the chorus utilizes a pentatonic blues scale (without sounding bluesy at all). The chorus is entirely conjunctive, often revolving around only two notes, and thus is extremely easy to sing even for untrained singers. This accords well with call of the lyrics to "Get on," and the inclusionary ("help us") tone. Such simple, repetitive, consistent but powerful, anthemic choruses are features of congregational song[49] but also of stadium rock acts popular in the 1980s (see U2 and Bon Jovi for examples). The emotional intensity of the chorus is furthered after the instrumental solo by a "truck-driver" key change for the last two choruses. This common modulation of a half step (as here) or full step gives the final chorus a tangible "lift" and often adds a further victorious element to the song's conclusion.[50]

The harmonic and melodic differences in the song are not replicated in the textual construction: "The overall texture of the song is quite repetitive, and often awash in the 'roomy' reverb and triggered drums that defined much pop music from the mid-1980s."[51] The verses contain some soft guitar and synthesized strings to help bring out the emotional impact, while the chorus uses stabbing synthesized horn parts to add to the bombast created there. In all textual elements though, aside from vocals, synthesized sounds and computer-generated instruments dominate. This effect ties in well to the synthesized pop music of the early 1980s and Hubbard's thirst for technology. There seems no doubt, from an analysis of "The Road to Freedom," that Hubbard was trying to tap into the sounds of the day and create a culturally relevant expression of Scientology. Albeit with a different doctrine, the Pentecostal/Charismatic churches of the West were trying to do exactly the same thing. Musically, Hubbard has achieved many of his aims with this album, and certainly there was enough celebrity and exposure to launch it. Despite that, the album remains largely derided in popular opinion and a blip on Scientology's cultural output. Ultimately, one must question whether the bold lyrics, with their raw doctrine and terminology,[52] was the reason the music failed to achieve its purpose.

The only other dedicated Scientology music release came in 2001, 15 years after Hubbard's death. The *Joy of Creating* pulls together lyrics from Hubbard's writing and from the tenets of Scientology. Once again a stellar cast of Scientologists, including Isaac Hayes, Chick Corea, and Edgar Winter, contribute to the musical oeuvre, and once again the results fall flat. The title track appears six times, in different genre guises and arrangements but unfortunately the lyrics remain unaltered. Rabin's critique of the album best surmises those found elsewhere in Internet reviews:

> *The Joy of Creating* is an album of surreal blandness and empty polish: Remove the jarring strangeness of Hubbard's words and you have an album begging to accompany massages or afternoons at the spa. *The Joy of Creating* was seemingly designed as a proselytizing tool; the album puts a friendly face on the tenets of Scientology, but an awful lot of creepiness seeps through . . . The Friends of L. Ron Hubbard nursed an earnest, sincere desire to share their hero's words and ideas with the world, with music as their medium. Yet *The Joy of Creating*, and Hubbard's entire strange output as a songwriter in the 1980s, suggests that his "music" was the worst possible advertisement for his ideas (at least until the release of the film version of *Battlefield Earth*).[53]

HUBBARD AS MUSICIAN

As has been shown, Hubbard had a strong belief in his own musical abilities and particularly in his ability to understand how music could affect an audience. Partly he was motivated by a desire to further the cause and reach of Scientology; partly he was motivated by his own desire to be recognized in the artform. Most glaringly, Hubbard himself wrote:

> What really separates the flubbers and amateurs from the professional are these two skills. One has to be able to view or hear anything he is working on at any time in a brand-new unit of time. And one has to be able to see or hear his production from the viewpoint of the eventual audience.[54]

While the former point Hubbard was clearly skilled at, the latter he lacked genuinely sincere devotion to. Hubbard's musical outputs are fairly universally panned. Whether regarding new jazz idioms, soundtracks, or religious albums, it is hard to find critical support. To be fair, part of this lack of support is due to reading Scientology over the top of the texts themselves, with people quick to take issue with the art due to the association with the Church. Hubbard was not able to read musical texts from the "viewpoint of the eventual audience." If he had he might have tempered the lyrical prose of *The Road to Freedom*, he might have delayed the release of *Power of Source*, and he might have waited until a film existed before writing the score to it. What Hubbard did not foresee in 1974 or even in 1986 was the public's ability to document their approval or otherwise of a cultural text in a split second. As it stands, the Internet is full of derision for Hubbard's musical endeavors, whether the critiques are fair, objective, considered, or not. Aside from the positive comments about *Power of Source* identified earlier in the chapter, most are extremely negative, unless we look at those written by Scientology itself. And the negativity is across the board. In terms of *Space Jazz* one criticism reads:

> What does *Space Jazz* sound like? Well, it sounds a lot like *Star Trek* incidental music if you strip out all the lush chords and play it on a $19 monophonic toy keyboard, or maybe your touchtone keypad. It's bad. Real Bad. The Real Bad only pompous jerks with too much money and delusions of godhood can ever hope to attain.[55]

Of *The Road to Freedom*, a reviewer at leading British music magazine *Melody Maker* surmised, "You're supposed to eat vegetables, not listen to them."[56]

And taking Hubbard's musical outputs as a whole, after his analysis of several albums, Rabin writes:

> Collectively, these albums offer a fascinating glimpse into both Hubbard's psyche and rampant egomania. (To describe these albums as music at all represents runaway narcissism on Hubbard's part.) Though designed as proselytizing tools, these albums instead function as fascinating sociological and anthropological artifacts chronicling the secretive and insular world of Scientology at a strange, uncertain time.[57]

And Rabin concludes his oft-cited, multialbum review thus:

> These albums constitute one of the strangest and least explored crannies of Hubbard's bizarre and fascinating career. Hubbard set out to uplift all mankind; he saw his music, like his books and teachings and ideas, as gifts to a humanity whose true potential only he could unlock. But these albums live on only as gifts to lovers of camp the world over. Splurge on it!

In none of these accounts, of which there are hundreds more, is there a sense in which the "eventual audience" was held in high regard. Here we have music speaking to—preaching *at*—its audience, in the hope that some of the messages will sink in. They didn't. Hubbard's successes in other creative fields were not to be replicated in music. And despite the voice of Scientology extolling his musical virtues, the voice of the collective people has spoken, both critically and commercially.

CONCLUSION

As with most areas of his endeavor, Hubbard claimed a lot in the musical realm. Unfortunately the texts that survive him do not speak to the same universal acclaim. There is no doubt he managed to surround himself with some very accomplished artists who improved his output immensely. Despite that, the critical response to his musical work is largely disparaging. There are some decent jazz-influenced works among his catalog, again, seriously enhanced by those he worked with. But unlike his pulp fiction and science fiction writing, there is little in his body of musical works to commend. Even breakthrough notions, like the creation of a soundtrack for a book, ultimately fall flat due to the lack of musicality present. Hubbard did make use of the latest technology and advanced sonic construction as a result. His embrace of the Fairlight CMI system was very public and proficient and no doubt led many others to explore the possibilities it offered.

What is most striking about his musical output is his failure in a "religious" context to produce music that would enhance and further the cause of Scientology. For one so apparently immersed in an understanding of popular music (and its failings), he failed to offer a musical text that would have value, let alone lasting value, to the movement he founded. Scientology involved itself in "congregational" music production at a curious time. While Pentecostal and other movements were beginning to use popular music as a vehicle to engage souls, Scientology (and Hubbard) chose to use popular music to preach a message and speak *over* the public, rather than draw them in. Part of this might have been the timing of Hubbard's death in relation to production and release of Scientology's first "church" offering, or more likely, it is symptomatic of Hubbard's self-belief in his musical understanding and abilities. The "impact" he was sure his music would have is sadly not the kind of impact he was hoping for.

NOTES

1. L. Ron Hubbard, "Music Maker, Composer & Performer." *The L. Ron Hubbard Series, The Complete Biographical Encyclopedia, Book 12* (Los Angeles: Bridge Publications, Inc. 2012), 34.

2. Alex Gibney, *Scientology: Going Clear and the Prison of Belief*, Jigsaw Productions, HBO Documentary Films, 2015.

3. Lawrence Wright, *Going Clear: Scientology, Hollywood and the Prison of Belief* (New York: Alfred A. Knopf, 2013), 105.

4. Hubbard, *The Road to Freedom*, Revenimus Music Publishing, Golden Era Studios, 1986.

5. For a more detailed account of *Space Jazz* and the *Battlefield Earth* soundtrack, see Mark Evans, "Straining the Future: *Battlefield Earth*, *Space Jazz* and the sounds of Scientology," *Science Fiction Film and Television* 3, no. 2 (2010): 201–216.

6. While Berkwits does not attribute the quote, it comes from a transcript of a speech Hubbard gave called "How to Talk to Friends about Scientology," December 18, 1952, as part of the *Philadelphia Doctorate Course*.

7. See http://www.postindependent.com/news/grandjunction/8099807-113/hubbard -album-craven-music for one among numerous references to this claim.

8. Jon Atack, *A Piece of Blue Sky: Scientology, Dianetics and L. Ron Hubbard Exposed* (New York: Lyle Stuart, 1990), 355.

9. Tidman is the woman to the far left of the cover of the Apollo Stars album, *Power of Source*.

10. Ann Tidman's story is ultimately quite a tragic one. She died alone, basically imprisoned in a Scientology compound and unable to be with the man she loved. She died of lung cancer, with her death barely acknowledged by Scientology. See Tony Ortega, "Death of a Scientologist: Why Annie Broeker, Famous in the Church, Had to Die in Secret," *Village Voice*, January 30, 2012.

11. See https://whyweprotest.net/threads/an-analysis-of-rock-music-by-l-ron-hubbard .60163/ for one example of many of bloggers riffing on "Arp Cola."

12. Quoted by "OTBT," June 19, 2010, at https://whyweprotest.net/threads /an-analysis-of-rock-music-by-l-ron-hubbard.60163/.

13. L. Ron Hubbard, "Art Series 4: Rhythm," *Hubbard Communication Office Bulletin*, April 25, 1974.

14. See Mark Evans, "Rhythms of Evil: Exorcizing Sound from *The Exorcist*," in *Terror Tracks: Music, Sound and Horror Cinema*, ed. Philip Hayward (London: Equinox Publishing, 2009), 112–115.

15. Hubbard, "Rhythm."

16. Don Jolly, "The Last Twentieth Century Book Club: Power of Source," *The Revealer: A Review of Religion and Media*. April 8, 2014.

17. L. Ron Hubbard, "Art Series 2: Art, More About," *Hubbard Communication Office Bulletin*, April 29, 1973.

18. Ibid., 1. Emphasis in the original.

19. Ibid., 3. Emphasis in the original.

20. Ibid., 5.

21. Ibid.

22. "Justin Bieber Arrives in Sydney for Hillsong Conference with Hailey Baldwin," *Sydney Morning Herald*, June 29, 2015, http://www.smh.com.au/entertainment /music/justin-bieber-arrives-in-sydney-for-hillsong-conference-with-hailey-baldwin -20150629-gi09t7.html#ixzz3yomwgKol, accessed January 23, 2016.

23. Jolly, "The Last Twentieth Century Book Club."

24. Hubbard, *Music Maker*, 35.

25. Jolly, "The Last Twentieth Century Book Club."

26. The Apollo Stars, *The Power of Source*. Source Music, 1974.

27. Ibid.

28. All quotes taken from https://www.youtube.com/watch?v=Wka6ZKUd8WQ, accessed January 27, 2016. All original spelling and punctuation has been maintained.

29. Ibid.

30. Katie Notopoulos, "L. Ron Hubbard's Weird Music Career," *Buzzfeed*, 2012 http://www.buzzfeed.com/katienotopoulos/l-ron-hubbardss-weird-music-career#.njYXNe62gx, accessed September 10, 2015.

31. Ibid.

32. Jolly, "The Last Twentieth Century Book Club."

33. Emphasis in the original.

34. Atack, *A Piece of Blue Sky*, 355.

35. Hubbard, *Music Maker*, 38–39.

36. "An invitation to the congregation to join in corporate worship (based on OT models, found particularly in the psalms." Mark Evans, *Open Up the Doors: Music in the Modern Church* (London: Equinox Publishing, 1996), 114.

37. The international headquarters of Scientology since 1975.

38. Wilma Norton, "Followers Singing the Praises of Scientology," *St. Petersburg Times: Clearwater Times Edition*, June 7, 1986, 1.

39. Ibid., 14.

40. Nathan Rabin, "L. Rock Hubbard: Revisiting the Curious Career of the Ultimate Cult Musician," *Slate*, May 1 (New York: The Slate Group, 2014), http://www.slate.com/articles/arts/culturebox/2014/05/the_music_of_l_ron_hubbard_space_jazz_and_other_scientology_albums.2.html,_accessed September 10, 2015.

41. "Wog" is a disdainful term for a non-Scientologist. It was originally used in this sense by Hubbard and is present in many of his communications to the Church. For more, see https://caliwog.wordpress.com/2011/06/20/scientologists-and-wogs-what-did-lrh-have-to-say/.

42. Posted by "OTBT," June 19, 2010, https://whyweprotest.net/threads/an-analysis-of-rock-music-by-l-ron-hubbard.60163/, accessed January 27, 2016.

43. L. Ron Hubbard, *Music Maker*, 39.

44. For more on Golden Era Productions and the studio facilities used to record the album, see http://www.scientologynews.org/node/842 and https://orgsaroundtheworld.wordpress.com/2010/08/01/video-tour-of-the-golden-era-productions-facility/.

45. Grant's *Heart in Motion* rose to number 10 in the *Billboard* general charts and achieved sales in excess of 5 million copies. It would pave the way for a slew of cross-over Christian artists, including Michael W. Smith, and DC Talk.

46. Hubbard, *The Road to Freedom*.

47. My sincere thanks to musicologist Jadey O'Regan for her observations and analysis of this track.

48. Jadey O'Regan, personal communication with the author, January 19, 2016.

49. See Mark Evans, *Open Up the Doors: Music in the Modern Church* (London: Equinox Publishing, 1996).

50. See Bon Jovi's "Living on a Prayer" (released in the same year as *The Road to Freedom*) for a very clear example of this.

51. O'Regan, personal communication with the author, January 19, 2016.

52. The album liner notes even included a glossary of Scientology terms to help decode the songs' meaning.

53. Rabin, "L. Rock Hubbard."

54. L. Ron Hubbard, "How to View Art," *L. Ron Hubbard Presents Writers of the Future Volume 27* (Hollywood: Galaxy Press, 2011), 129.

55. Karl Mamer, "Space Jazz," 2003, http://www.yrad.com/essays/spacejazz.html, accessed September 10, 2015.

56. Atack, *A Piece of Blue Sky*, 355.

57. Rabin, "L. Rock Hubbard."

BIBLIOGRAPHY

Apollo Stars, The. *The Power of Source*. Source Music, 1974.

Atack, Jon. *A Piece of Blue Sky: Scientology, Dianetics and L. Ron Hubbard Exposed*. New York: Lyle Stuart, 1990.

Berkwits, Jeff. "Singing the Body Electric: Science Fiction Writers and Their Music." *Locus Online*. 2003. http://www.locusmag.com/2003/Reviews/Berkwits09_Song writers.html.

Evans, Mark. *Open Up the Doors: Music in the Modern Church*. London: Equinox Publishing, 2006.

Evans, Mark. "Rhythms of Evil: Exorcizing Sound from *The Exorcist*." In *Terror Tracks: Music, Sound and Horror Cinema*, edited by Philip Hayward, 112–124. London: Equinox Publishing, 2009.

Evans, Mark. "Straining the Future: *Battlefield Earth*, *Space Jazz* and the Sounds of Scientology." *Science Fiction Film and Television* 3, no. 2 (2010): 201–216.

Hubbard, L. Ron. "Art Series 2: Art, More About." *Hubbard Communication Office Bulletin*. April 29, 1973.

Hubbard, L. Ron. "Art Series 4: Rhythm." *Hubbard Communication Office Bulletin*. April 25, 1974.

Hubbard, L. Ron. "How to Talk to your Friends about Scientology." December 18. Recorded Lecture. *The Philadelphia Doctorate Course*, 1952.

Hubbard, L. Ron. "How to View Art." In *L. Ron Hubbard Presents Writers of the Future Volume 27*, 123–130. Hollywood: Galaxy Press, 2001.

Hubbard, L. Ron. *Music Maker, Composer & Performer: The L. Ron Hubbard Series, The Complete Biographical Encyclopedia, Book 12*. Los Angeles: Bridge Publications, Inc. 2012.

Hubbard, L. Ron. *The Road to Freedom*. Revenimus Music Publishing. Golden Era Studios, 1986.

Jolly, Don. "The Last Twentieth Century Book Club: Power of Source." *The Revealer: A Review of Religion and Media*, April 8, 2014. http://therevealer.org/archives/19207.

Loftus, Jamie. "'Space Jazz': A Look Back on L. Ron Hubbard's Music Career." *BCD-wire*. Boston: The Boston Globe, 2015.

Mamer, Karl. "Space Jazz." 2003. http://www.yrad.com/essays/spacejazz.html.

Norton, Wilma. "Followers Singing the Praises of Scientology." *St. Petersburg Times: Clearwater Times Edition*. June 7, 1986.

Notopoulos, Katie. "L. Ron Hubbard's Weird Music Career." *Buzzfeed*. 2012. http://www.buzzfeed.com/katienotopoulos/l-on-hubbardss-weird-music-career#.njYXNe62gx.

Ortega, Tony. "Death of a Scientologist: Why Annie Broeker, Famous in the Church, Had to Die in Secret." *Village Voice*. January 30, 2012. http://www.villagevoice.com/news/death-of-a-scientologist-why-annie-broeker-famous-in-the-church-had-to-die-in-secret-6666642.

Rabin, Nathan. "L. Rock Hubbard: Revisiting the Curious Career of the Ultimate Cult Musician." *Slate*. May 1. New York: The Slate Group, 2014.

Wright, Lawrence. *Going Clear: Scientology, Hollywood and the Prison of Belief*. New York: Alfred A. Knopf, 2013.

About the Editors and Contributors

EDITORS

Stephen A. Kent, PhD, is a Professor of Sociology and Adjunct Professor in the Interdisciplinary Program in Religious Studies at the University of Alberta. He teaches undergraduate and graduate courses on deviance, the sociology of religion, and the sociology of sectarian groups. He has published articles in numerous sociology, history, and religious studies journals. His 2001 book, *From Slogans to Mantras: Social Protest and Religious Conversion in the Late Vietnam War Era*, was selected by Choice: Current Reviews for Academic Libraries as an "Outstanding Academic Title for 2002." Many of his publications can be downloaded from his website at http://skent.ualberta.ca/.

Susan Raine (PhD, University of Alberta) is an Associate Professor in the department of sociology at MacEwan University in Canada. She has published articles on a variety of alternative religious movements including the Children of God, Heaven's Gate, and Scientology. Her research interests include identity formation in alternative religions, UFO religions, and the intersections between science fiction and religion. She teaches courses on sociology of religion; deviance, conformity, and social control; and the paranormal and conspiracy theories.

CONTRIBUTORS

Tami M. Bereska (PhD, University of Alberta) is a Sociology Professor at MacEwan University in Edmonton. She teaches courses and publishes on the topics of deviance, media, and popular culture. She is author of the book *Deviance, Conformity, and Social Control in Canada* and coauthor of the book *Sociology in Action: A Canadian Perspective*. Her work has appeared in the *Encyclopedia of Social Deviance*, *Qualitative Research Journal*, *Journal of Men and Masculinities*, and *Canadian Journal of Human Sexuality*.

Stefano Bigliardi has a PhD in Philosophy from the University of Bologna. He has been working as a researcher and a teacher at various institutions in Germany, Sweden, Mexico, and Switzerland. His research encompasses the relationship of both Abrahamic religions and NRMs with contemporary science. He has published numerous articles in peer-reviewed journals such as *Zygon*, *Nova Religio*, and *Temenos*. He is the author of *Islam and the Quest for Modern Science* (SRII, 2014).

Mark Evans is Professor and Head of the School of Communication at the University of Technology Sydney. His recent books include *Sounding Funny: Sound and Comedy Cinema* (Equinox Publishing); *Movies, Moves and Music: The Sonic World of Dance Films* (Equinox Publishing); and *The New Music Industries* (Palgrave). He is also Executive Editor of the forthcoming *Encyclopedia of Film Music and Sound*.

Max Halupka is an expert on contemporary forms of political participation, where he specializes in the relationship between technology and politics. A Research Fellow at the Institute for Governance and Policy Analysis, University of Canberra, Max has published work on political communication, new forms of political participation, internet activism, and The Church of Scientology. Max teaches public policy for the Institute's Graduate Certificate and MPA programs.

Terra Manca is a PhD candidate in Sociology at the University of Alberta under the supervision of Professor Stephen Kent. She has published articles that discuss various topics involving Scientology and health, Christian Scientists' healthcare practices, family life in strict religions, and the Lord's Resistance Army. Manca's current research addresses health professionals' experiences with vaccine uncertainties.

George Shaw is an independent writer and former Scientologist. Since leaving Scientology a number of years ago he has developed an interest in art and design.

Hugh B. Urban (PhD, University of Chicago) is a professor of Religious Studies in the Department of Comparative Studies at Ohio State University. He is primarily interested in the study of religion and secrecy, particularly in relation to questions of knowledge and power. He is author of nine books, including *Tantra: Sex, Secrecy, Politics and Power in the Study of Religion* (2003); *The Church of Scientology: A History of a New Religion* (2011); and *Zorba the Buddha: Sex, Spirituality and Capitalism in the Global Osho Movement* (2016).

Index

Delirious (movie), satire about
  Scientology cut from final version
  after harassment, 197
DeMille, Ricard, 85, 96n15
Democracy, ridiculed, 69
Deviance amplification, 240
De Vocht, Tom, 165
Dianetics, 39, 239, 241–242; as a best-
  seller, 242; as a therapeutic science,
  324n6; opposition from the American
  medical profession, xii; medical
  practice and, 242; Scientology and, xii
Dianetics: The Evolution of a Science,
  meaning of book cover, 317
*Dianetics: The Modern Science of Mental
  Health,* ix, xi, 16, 37, 38, 164;
  meaning of book cover, 317
Digital Lightwave, 129–130
Digital Millennium Copyright ACT
  (DMCA), 284
Dincalci, Jim, 46
Disconnection 165, 174, 177, 184n88
Doherty, Bernard, 218, 220, 262
"Don't ever defend; always attack," 221
Drug Free Heroes, 116
Dynamics, third, 83, 85

Earthlink, 166
Electropsychometer. *See* E-meter
Elfman, Bodhi, 160
Elfman, Jenna, 108, 109, 225; financial
  wealth, 122; praises Scientology
  courses, 125; threw a D.C. party with
  Scientology lobbyist Greg Mitchell,
  122; took classes from Milton
  Katselas, 109
Eli Lilly, 224
E-meter, xii, 9, 24n64, 154, 198, 206,
  250, 255, 307, 323; restricting claims
  about, 250
Emmy Award, 225
Empire-building, 2, 3, 13, 18, 19
English Romantic literature, 34, 44
Engrams, xi, 248; defined, 266n58
"Enquiry into the Practice and Effects of
  Scientology," 326n31

Entertainment media, xxi–xxii
Entheta, 121
Erlich, Dennis, 283, 284
Estates Project Force (EPF), 89, 167
Evans, Robert, 116
Expand (Scientology magazine), 308
The Explorers Journal, 20
Ex-Scientologists. *See* Apostasy;
  Apostates; and specific individuals
Ex-Scientology Kids, 165
Extended Elaboration Likelihood
  Model, 193
Exteriorization, 42

F.A.C.T.Net (Fight Against Coercive
  Tactics Network), 267n83, 284
Fair game, 137, 173, 203, 242, 255, 258
Fairman, Michael, 107, 109
False Purpose Rundown, 161
FBI (Federal Bureau of Investigation),
  xii. 19, 101, 196, 200, 202, 207,
  234n32, 244, 246, 252, 253–254, 255,
  259, 260; raid(s), 248, 250, 253–254,
  256, 258, 260
FDA (Food and Drug Administration),
  244, 250
Fear, 35
Federal Legislative Associates, 120
Feltmate, David, 193, 202
Ferguson, Craig, 197, 205
Ferrigno, Lou, 116
Feshbach, Jessica, 171
Finance, Scientology's goal of taking
  over international, 19
Find or manufacture evidence against
  critics, 158
Flag Land Base, xxiii, 16, 19, 199, 206,
  221, 252
Flag Service Organization, 173, 252–253
Florida House Education Council, 119
Florida Senate Education Committee,
  119
Florida State Department of Education,
  255
Forge, 1, 130
Fort Harrison Hotel, 19, 118, 253

Lightning Source UK Ltd.
Milton Keynes UK
UKHW020635071222
413510UK00005B/59

9 781440 832499